WEBSTER'S NEW WORLD™ POCKET DICTIONARY

Second Edition

Compiled by
the staff of

**Webster's
New World Dictionary®**
of American English

Third College Edition

Jonathan L. Goldman
Senior Editor

MACMILLAN • USA

Macmillan General Reference
A Simon & Schuster Macmillan Company
1633 Broadway
New York, NY 10019

This book is based on and includes material from
Webster's New World Dictionary®, Third College Edition,
copyright © 1991.

A Webster's New World™ Book

MACMILLAN is a registered trademark of Macmillan, Inc.
WEBSTER'S NEW WORLD DICTIONARY is a registered trademark
of Simon & Schuster, Inc.

Dictionary Editorial Offices:
New World Dictionaries,
850 Euclid Avenue, Cleveland, Ohio, 44114

Database and principal typesetting by Lexi-Comp, Inc.,
Hudson, Ohio.

Library of Congress Cataloging-in-Publication Data

Webster's new world dictionary / compiled by the staff of
    Webster's new world dictionary of American English, third
    college edition; Jonathan L. Goldman, senior editor.—2nd ed.
        p. cm
    ISBN 0-671-86613-3
        1. English language—Dictionaries. I. Goldman, Jonathan L.,
1944- . II. Webster's new world dictionary of American English.
PE1628. W56373 1993
    423—dc20   92-39176
                                                CIP

Manufactured in the United States of America
10 9 8 7 6 5 4

KEY TO PRONUNCIATION

	as in		*as in*
a	cat	u̵	fur
ā	ape	ə	a *in* ago
ä	cot		o *in* atom
e	ten	'	fertile (furt''l)
ē	me	ch	chin
i	fit	ŋ	ring
ī	ice	sh	she
ō	go	th	thin
ô	fall	*th*	then
oi	oil	zh	measure
oo	look	n	Indicates nasal quality
oo	tool		of preceding vowel
ou	out	ë	Pronounce e with
u	up		mouth rounded as for ō

ABBREVIATIONS USED

a.	adjective	Naut.	nautical
abbrev.	abbreviated	Obs.	obsolete
adv.	adverb	orig.	originally
alt.	alternate	pl.	plural
Ar.	archaic	Poet.	poetic
Biol.	biology	pp.	past participle
Br.	British	ppr.	present participle
Chem.	chemistry	pref.	prefix
Col.	colloquial	prep.	preposition
con.	conjunction	pres.	present
Dial.	dialectal	pron.	pronoun
esp.	especially	pt.	past tense
etc.	et cetera	R.C.Ch.	Roman Catholic
fem.	feminine		Church
Fr.	French	Rom.	Roman
Gr.	Greek	sing.	singular
Gram.	grammar	Sl.	slang
int.	interjection	Sp.	Spanish
L.	Latin	sp.	spelling; spelled
Math.	mathematics	spec.	specifically
Mil.	military	suf.	suffix
Mus.	music	t.	tense
myth.	mythology	Theol.	theology
n.	noun	v.	verb

Other abbreviations will be found on pages 338-341.

EDITORIAL STAFF

Executive Editor: Michael Agnes
Project Editor: Jonathan L. Goldman
Editor and Database Administrator: Donald Stewart
Editors: Laura J. Borovac, Andra I. Kalnins, James E.
Naso, Katherine Goidich Soltis, Stephen P. Teresi
Assistants: Alisa Murray, Betty Dziedzic Thompson

RULES FOR SPELLING

Words that end in a silent -e usually drop the *-e* when a suffix beginning with a vowel is added [*file—filing*]. However, before the suffixes *-able* and *-ous*, the *-e* is usually kept if it follows a soft *c* or *g* [*outrage—outrageous*]. The *-e* is usually kept when a suffix beginning with a consonant is added [*time—timely*].

Words that end in a single consonant preceded by a single vowel usually double that consonant when a suffix beginning with a vowel is added, if: a) the word is a monosyllable [*sin—sinning*], or b) the word has more than one syllable but is stressed on the last syllable [*refer—referring*]. If the final consonant is *not* preceded by a single vowel or, in American usage, if the last syllable is not stressed, the final consonant is usually *not* doubled [*hurl—hurling; travel—traveling*].

Words that end in a double letter usually drop one letter when a suffix beginning with the same letter is added [*free—freest*].

Words that end in -y preceded by a consonant usually change the *-y* to an *i* when a suffix that does not begin with *i* is added [*marry—married*]. If it follows a vowel, the *-y* is usually kept [*play—played*].

Words that end in -ie change the *-ie* to a *y* when the suffix *-ing* is added [*lie—lying*].

Words that end in -c usually take on a *k* when a suffix beginning with *i* or *e* is added [*picnic—picnicker*].

Words containing ie or ei: The combination *ei* is usually used following the letter *c* and is always used to represent the sound (ā). In most other native English words the combination *ie* is used.

Note that the suffix -ful, unlike the adjective *full*, has only one *l* [*cupful*].

Verbs ending in -cede and -ceed: Three common words (*exceed*, *proceed,* and *succeed*) end in *-ceed.* Most other verbs end in *-cede.*

RULES FOR FORMING PLURALS

Most nouns in English form the plural by adding *-s* or *-es.* When the singular noun ends in a sound that allows *-s* to be added and pronounced without the formation of a new syllable, *-s* is used [*book—books*]. When the singular noun ends in a sound such that *-s* cannot be joined to it and pronounced without the formation of an additional syllable, *-es* is used [*kiss—kisses; torch—torches*].

The chief exceptions to this basic rule are listed below.

Words that end in -o usually form the plural by adding *-es* [*hero—heroes*]; however, some of them do so by adding *-s* [*solo—solos*]. There is no rule that deals with the distinction.

Some words that end in -f form the plural by changing the *-f* to *v* and adding *-es* [*wolf—wolves*].

Words that end in -y preceded by a consonant usually form the plural by changing the *-y* to *i* and adding *-es* [*lady—ladies*]. If the *-y* is preceded by a vowel, they form the plural regularly, by adding *-s* [*day—days*].

Some words form the plural by a vowel change. Among the commonest examples are: *foot—feet; man—men; tooth—teeth; woman—women.*

Some words have special plurals to which none of the above general statements apply. Among them are words such as: *alumna—alumnae; child—children; phenomenon—phenomena; radius—radii; sheep—sheep.*

A

a *a.*, *indefinite article* **1** one **2** each; any one

a- *pref.* not

aard'vark' (ärd'-) *n.* African mammal that eats ants

ab- *pref.* away; from; down

a·back' *adv.*, *a.* [Ar.] back —**taken aback** surprised

ab'a·cus *n.* frame with beads for doing arithmetic

a·ba'lo·ne *n.* sea mollusk

a·ban'don *v.* **1** give up entirely **2** to desert —*n.* lack of restraint

a·base' *v.* to humble

a·bash' *v.* embarrass

a·bate' *v.* lessen —**a·bate'ment** *n.*

ab·bé (a'bā) *n.* priest's title in France

ab'bess *n.* woman who is head of a nunnery

ab'bey *n.*, *pl.* **-beys** monastery or nunnery

ab'bot *n.* man who is head of a monastery

ab·bre'vi·ate' *v.* shorten, as a word —**ab·bre'vi·a'tion** *n.*

ABC *n.*, *pl.* **ABC's 1** pl. the alphabet **2** basics; rudiments

ab'di·cate' *v.* give up, as a throne —**ab'di·ca'tion** *n.*

ab'do·men (*or* ab dō'-) *n.* part of the body between chest and pelvis —**ab·dom'i·nal** (-däm'-) *a.*

ab·duct' *v.* kidnap —**ab·duc'tion** *n.* —**ab·duc'tor** *n.*

a·bed' *adv.* in bed

ab'er·ra'tion *n.* deviation from normal, right, etc.

a·bet' *v.* **a·bet'ted**, **a·bet'ting** to help, esp. in crime —**a·bet'tor**, **a·bet'ter** *n.*

a·bey'ance (-bā'-) *n.* temporary suspension

ab·hor' *v.* **-horred'**, **-hor'ring** shun in disgust, hatred, etc. —**ab·hor'rence** *n.*

ab·hor'rent *a.* detestable

a·bide' *v.* **a·bode'** or **a·bid'ed**, **a·bid'ing 1** remain **2** [Ar.] reside **3** await **4** endure —**abide by** keep (a promise) or obey (rules)

a·bil'i·ty *n.*, *pl.* **-ties 1** a being able **2** talent

ab'ject *a.* miserable

ab·jure' *v.* renounce on oath

a·blaze' *adv.*, *a.* on fire

a'ble *a.* **1** having power (*to do*) **2** talented; skilled —**a'bly** *adv.*

-able *suf.* **1** that can or should**be 2** tending to

a'ble-bod'ied *a.* healthy

ab·lu'tion *n.* a washing of the body, esp. a rite

ab'ne·gate' *v.* renounce; give up —**ab'ne·ga'tion** *n.*

ab·nor'mal *a.* not normal —**ab'nor·mal'i·ty** *n.*, *pl.* **-ties** —**ab·nor'mal·ly** *adv.*

a·board' *adv.*, *prep.* on or in (a train, ship. etc.)

a·bode' *n.* home

a·bol'ish *v.* do away with

ab'o·li'tion *n.* an abolishing, spec. [A-] of slavery in the U.S. —**ab'o·li'tion·ist** *n.*

A'-bomb' *n.* atomic bomb

a·bom'i·na·ble *a.* **1** disgusting **2** very bad —**a·bom'i·na·bly** *adv.*

a·bom'i·nate' *v.* loathe —**a·bom'i·na'tion** *n.*

ab'o·rig'i·ne' (-rij'ə nē') *n.* first known inhabitant —**ab'o·rig'i·nal** *a.*, *n.*

a·bort' *v.* **1** have or cause to have a miscarriage **2** cut short (a flight, etc.), as because of equipment failure

a·bor'tion *n.* miscarriage, esp. one induced —**a·bor'tive** *a.*

a·bound' *v.* be plentiful

a·bout' *adv.* **1** around **2** near **3** in an opposite direction **4** nearly —*a.* astir —*prep.* **1** around **2** near to **3** just starting **4** concerning

a·bout'-face' *n.* a reversal

a·bove' *adv.* **1** higher **2** earlier on a page —*prep.* **1** over **2** higher than —*a.* mentioned above

a·bove'board' *a.*, *adv.* in plain view; honest(ly)

a·brade' *v.* scrape away —**a·bra'sive** *a.*, *n.*

a·bra'sion *n.* **1** an abrading **2** abraded spot

a·breast' *adv.*, *a.* **1** side by side **2** informed (*of*)

a·bridge' *v.* shorten, as in wording; lessen —**a·bridg'ment**, **a·bridge'ment** *n.*

a·broad' *adv.* **1** far and wide **2** outdoors **3** to or in foreign lands

ab'ro·gate' *v.* abolish; repeal —**ab'ro·ga'tion** *n.*

a·brupt' *a.* **1** sudden **2** brusque; curt **3** steep

ab'scess' (-ses) *n.* inflamed, pus-filled area in body

ab·scond' (-skänd') *v.* flee and hide to escape the law

ab'sent (*v.*: ab sent') *a.* **1** not present; away **2** lacking —*v.*

keep (oneself) away —**ab'sence** n.

ab'sen·tee' n. absent person —a. of, by, or from one who is absent —**ab'sen·tee'ism** n.

ab'sent-mind'ed a. 1 not attentive 2 forgetful

ab'so·lute' a. 1 perfect 2 complete 3 not mixed; pure 4 certain; positive 5 real —**ab'so·lute'ly** adv.

ab'so·lu'tion n. 1 forgiveness 2 remission (of sin)

ab·solve' v. to free from guilt, a duty, etc.

ab·sorb' v. 1 suck up 2 engulf wholly 3 interest greatly —**ab·sorp'tion** n. —**ab·sorp'tive** a.

ab·sorb'ent a. able to absorb moisture, etc.

ab·stain' v. do without; refrain —**ab·sten'tion** n.

ab·ste'mi·ous a. not eating or drinking too much

ab'sti·nence n. an abstaining from food, liquor, etc.

ab·stract' (a. also, n. always: ab' strakt') a. 1 apart from material objects; not concrete 2 theoretical —v. summarize —n. summary —**ab·strac'tion** n.

ab·stract'ed a. preoccupied

ab·struse' a. hard to understand

ab·surd' a. ridiculous —**ab·surd' i·ty** n., pl. **-ties**

a·bun'dance n. more than is needed —**a·bun'dant** a.

a·buse' (-byōōz'; n.: -byōōs') v. 1 use wrongly 2 mistreat 3 berate —n. 1 wrong use 2 mistreatment 3 vile language —**a·bu'sive** a.

a·but' v. **a·but'ted, a·but'ting** to border (on or upon)

a·but'ment n. part supporting an arch, strut, etc.

a·bys'mal (-biz'-) a. too deep to be measured

a·byss' (-bis') n. deep or bottomless gulf

a·ca'cia (-kā'shə) n. tree with yellow or white flowers

ac'a·dem'ic a. 1 of schools or colleges 2 of liberal arts 3 theoretical —**ac'a·dem'i·cal·ly** adv.

a·cad'e·my n., pl. **-mies** 1 private high school 2 school for special study 3 society of scholars, etc.

a·can'thus n. plant with large, graceful leaves

ac·cede' (ak sēd') v. 1 agree (to) 2 enter upon the duties (of an office)

ac·cel'er·ate' v. 1 increase in speed 2 make happen sooner —**ac·cel'er·a'tion** n. —**ac·cel'er·a' tor** n.

ac'cent n. 1 stress on a syllable in speaking 2 mark showing this 3 distinctive way of pronouncing 4 rhythmic stress —v. emphasize

ac·cen'tu·ate' (-chōō-) v. to accent; emphasize; stress

ac·cept' v. 1 receive willingly 2 approve 3 agree to 4 believe in —**ac·cept'ance** n.

ac·cept'a·ble a. satisfactory —**ac·cept'a·bly** adv.

ac·cess' n. 1 right to enter, use, etc. 2 means of approach

ac·ces'si·ble a. 1 easy to enter, etc. 2 obtainable

ac·ces'sion n. 1 an attaining (the throne, etc.) 2 an addition or increase

ac·ces'so·ry n., pl. **-ries** 1 thing added for decoration 2 helper in a crime

ac'ci·dent n. 1 unexpected happening 2 mishap 3 chance —**ac'ci·den'tal** a.

ac'ci·dent-prone' a. likely or tending to be in or have accidents

ac·claim' v. greet with applause —n. great approval

ac'cla·ma'tion n. 1 strong approval or loud applause 2 spoken vote of "yes" by many

ac·cli'mate (ak'lə māt') v. get used to a new climate or situation: also **ac·cli'ma·tize'**

ac'co·lade' n. high praise

ac·com'mo·date' v. 1 adjust 2 do a favor for 3 have room for; lodge —**ac·com'mo·da'tion** n.

ac·com'mo·dat'ing a. obliging

ac·com'pa·ny v. **-nied, -ny·ing** 1 add to 2 go with 3 play music supporting a soloist —**ac·com' pa·ni·ment** n. —**ac·com'pa·nist** n.

ac·com'plice (-plis) n. partner in crime

ac·com'plish v. do; complete —**ac·com'plish·ment** n.

ac·com'plished a. skilled

ac·cord' v. 1 agree 2 grant —n. agreement —**according to** 1 consistent with 2 as stated by —**of one's own accord** voluntarily —**ac·cord'ance** n.

ac·cord'ing·ly adv. 1 in a fitting way 2 therefore

ac·cor'di·on n. musical instrument with a bellows

ac·cost' v. approach and speak to

ac·count' v. 1 give reasons (for)

2 judge to be —**n. 1** pl. business records **2** worth **3** explanation **4** report —**on account** as part payment —**on account of** because of —**on no account** never —**take into account** consider

ac·count'a·ble a. **1** responsible **2** explainable

ac·count'ing n. the keeping of business records —**ac·count'ant** n.

ac·cou'ter·ments (or -kōō'trə-) n.pl. personal outfit; clothes

ac·cred'it v. **1** authorize; certify **2** believe in

ac·cre'tion n. **1** growth in size **2** accumulated matter

ac·crue' v. be added, as interest on money

ac·cu'mu·late' v. pile up; collect —**ac·cu'mu·la'tion** n.

ac'cu·rate (-yar at) a. exactly correct —**ac'cu·ra·cy** n. —**ac'cu·rate·ly** adv.

ac·curs'ed a. damnable

ac·cuse' (-kyōōz') v. **1** to blame **2** charge with doing wrong —**ac'cu·sa'tion** n.

ac·cus'tom v. make familiar by habit or use

ac·cus'tomed a. **1** usual; customary **2** used (to)

ace n. **1** playing card with one spot **2** expert —a. [Col.] first-rate

a·cer'bi·ty (-sur'-) n. sourness; sharpness —**a·cer'bic** a.

a·cet·a·min·o·phen (ə sēt'ə min' ə fən) n. drug used to lessen fever or pain

ac'e·tate' (as'-) n. **1** salt or ester of an acid (a·ce'tic acid) found in vinegar **2** fabric made of an acetate of cellulose

ac'e·tone' n. liquid solvent for certain oils, etc.

a·cet·y·lene (ə set'l ēn') n. gas used in a blowtorch

ache (āk) n. dull, steady pain —v. have such pain

a·chieve' v. **1** do; accomplish **2** get by effort —**a·chieve'ment** n.

ac'id (as'-) n. **1** sour substance **2** chemical that reacts with a base to form a salt —a. **1** sour; sharp **2** of an acid —**a·cid'ic** a. —**a·cid'i·ty** n.

a·cid'u·lous (-sij'ōō-) a. somewhat acid or sour

ac·knowl'edge v. **1** admit or recognize **2** to answer (a greeting, etc.) **3** express thanks for —**ac·knowl'edg·ment, ac·knowl'edge·ment** n.

ac'me (-mē) n. highest point

ac'ne (-nē) n. pimply skin

ac'o·lyte' n. altar boy

a'corn' n. nut of the oak

a·cous'tics (-kōōs'-) n.pl. qualities of a room that affect sound —n. science of sound —**a·cous'tic, a·cous'ti·cal** a. —**a·cous'ti·cal·ly** adv.

ac·quaint' v. **1** make familiar (with) **2** inform

ac·quaint'ance n. **1** personal knowledge **2** person one knows slightly

ac·qui·esce (ak'wē es') v. consent without protest —**ac'qui·es'cence** n. —**ac'qui·es'cent** a.

ac·quire' v. get as one's own —**ac·quire'ment** n.

ac·qui·si·tion (ak'wə zish'ən) n. **1** an acquiring **2** something or someone acquired —**ac·quis'i·tive** (-kwiz'-) a.

ac·quit' v. -**quit'ted, -quit'ting 1** declare not guilty **2** conduct (oneself) —**ac·quit'tal** n.

a·cre (ā'kər) n. measure of land, 43,560 sq. ft. —**a'cre·age'** n.

ac'rid a. sharp or bitter

ac'ri·mo'ny n. bitterness, as of manner or speech —**ac'ri·mo'ni·ous** a.

ac'ro·bat' n. performer on the trapeze, tightrope, etc. —**ac'ro·bat'ic** a.

ac'ro·bat'ics n.pl. acrobat's tricks

ac'ro·nym' (-nim') n. a word formed from the first letters of several words

a·cross' adv. from one side to the other —prep. **1** from one side to the other of **2** on the other side of **3** into contact with

a·cryl'ic (-kril'-) a. of certain synthetic fibers or resins used to make fibers, paints, etc.

act n. **1** thing done **2** a doing **3** a law **4** division of a play or opera —v. **1** perform in a play, etc. **2** behave **3** function **4** have an effect (on)

act'ing a. substitute

ac·tin'ic a. designating rays causing chemical change

ac'tion n. **1** a doing of something **2** thing done **3** pl. behavior **4** way of working **5** lawsuit **6** combat

ac'ti·vate' v. make active —**ac'ti·va'tion** n.

ac'tive a. **1** acting; working **2** busy; lively; agile —**ac·tiv'i·ty** n., pl. -**ties**

ac'tor n. one who acts in plays —

ac'tress n.fem.

ac'tu·al (-chōō-) a. existing; real —**ac'tu·al'i·ty** n.

ac'tu·al·ly adv. really

ac'tu·ar·y n., pl. **-ies** insurance statistician —**ac·tu·ar'i·al** a.

ac'tu·ate v. 1 put into action 2 impel to action

a·cu'i·ty (-kyōō-) n. keenness of thought or vision

a·cu'men (ə kyōō'-, ak'yə-) n. keenness of mind

ac'u·punc'ture (ak'yōō-) n. the practice of piercing the body with needles to treat disease or pain

a·cute' a. 1 sharp-pointed 2 shrewd 3 keen 4 severe 5 critical 6 less than 90°: said of angles

ad n. [Col.] advertisement

A.D. of the Christian era

ad'age (-ij) n. proverb

a·da'gio (-dä'jō) a., adv. Mus. slow(ly)

ad'a·mant a. unyielding

Ad'am's apple n. bulge in the front of a man's throat

a·dapt' v. fit or adjust as needed —**a·dapt'a·ble** a. —**ad'ap·ta'tion** n. —**a·dapt'er, a·dap'tor** n.

add v. 1 join (to) so as to increase 2 increase 3 find the sum of 4 say further —**add up** seem reasonable —**add up to** signify

ad·den'dum n., pl. **-da** thing added, as an appendix

ad'der n. small snake, sometimes poisonous

ad·dict (ə dikt'; n.: ad'ikt) v. give (oneself) up (to a habit) —n. one addicted, as to a drug —**ad·dic'tion** n. —**ad·dic'tive** a.

ad·di'tion n. 1 an adding 2 part added —**ad·di'tion·al** a.

ad'di·tive n. something added

ad'dle v. make or become confused —**ad'dled** a.

ad·dress' (ə dres'; n.: also a' dres') v. 1 speak or write to 2 write the destination on (mail, etc.) 3 apply (oneself to) —n. 1 a speech 2 place where one lives —**ad·dress·ee'** n.

ad·duce' v. give as proof

ad'e·noids' n.pl. growths in the throat behind the nose

a·dept' (n.: ad'ept') a. highly skilled —n. an expert

ad'e·quate (-kwət) a. enough or good enough —**ad'e·qua·cy** n.

ad·here' v. 1 stick fast 2 give support (to) —**ad·her'ence** n. —**ad·her'ent** n.

ad·he'sive a. sticking —n. sticky substance, as glue —**ad·he'sion** n.

ad hoc' a., adv. for a specific purpose

a·dieu (ə dyōō') int. goodbye

ad in'fi·ni'tum (-nīt'əm) n. [L.] endlessly

a·diós (ä'dē ōs') int. goodbye

ad'i·pose' (-pōs') a. fatty

ad·ja'cent (ə jā'sənt) a. near or next

ad·jec'tive (aj'ik tiv) n. word that qualifies a noun —**ad'jec·ti'val** (-tī'-) a.

ad·join' v. be next to

ad·journ' (-jurn') v. suspend (a meeting, etc.) for a time —**ad·journ'ment** n.

ad·judge' v. judge, declare, or award

ad·ju'di·cate' v. act as judge (in or on)

ad'junct n. a nonessential addition

ad·jure' n. 1 order solemnly 2 ask earnestly

ad·just' v. 1 alter to make fit 2 regulate 3 settle rightly —**ad·just'a·ble** a. —**ad·just'ment** n.

ad·ju·tant (aj'ə tənt) n. assistant, esp. to a commanding officer

ad'-lib' [Col.] v. **-libbed', -lib'**bing improvise (words, etc.) —n. ad-libbed remark: also **ad lib**

ad·min'is·ter v. 1 manage; direct: also **ad·min'is·trate'** 2 give; attend (to) —**ad·min'is·tra'tor** n.

ad·min'is·tra'tion n. 1 an administering 2 executive officials; management —**ad·min'is·tra'tive** a.

ad'mi·ra·ble a. worth admiring —**ad'mi·ra·bly** adv.

ad'mi·ral n. high-ranking naval officer

ad'mi·ral·ty n. department of naval affairs

ad·mire' v. have high regard for —**ad'mi·ra'tion** n.

ad·mis'si·ble a. acceptable

ad·mis'sion n. 1 an admitting 2 entrance fee 3 confession or concession

ad·mit' v. **-mit'ted, -mit'ting** 1 let enter 2 concede or confess —**ad·mit'tance** n. —**ad·mit'ted·ly** adv.

ad·mix'ture n. mixture

ad·mon'ish v. 1 warn or advise 2 reprove mildly —**ad·mo·ni'tion** v. —**ad·mon'i·to'ry** a.

ad nau'se·am (-nô'zē-) adv. to

the point of disgust

a·do' n. fuss; trouble

a·do·be' (-dō'bē) n. unburnt, sun-dried brick

ad·o·les'cence n. time between childhood and adulthood; youth —**ad·o·les'cent** a., n.

a·dopt' v. 1 take legally as one's child 2 take as one's own —**a·dop'tion** n. —**a·dop'tive** a.

a·dore' v. 1 worship 2 love greatly —**a·dor'a·ble** a. —**ad·o·ra'tion** n.

a·dorn' v. decorate; ornament —**a·dorn'ment** n.

a·dre'nal glands (ə drē'-) n.pl. two ductless glands on the kidneys

A·dren'a·lin' (ə dren'-) trademark synthetic hormone —n. [a—] this hormone when secreted by the adrenal glands, which increases strength, etc.

a·drift' adv., a. floating aimlessly

a·droit' a. skillful and clever —**a·droit'ly** adv.

ad·u·la'tion (aj'ə-) n. too high praise

a·dult' a. grown-up; mature —n. mature person, animal, or plant —**a·dult'hood** n.

a·dul'ter·ate' v. make impure by adding things —**a·dul'ter·ant** n., a. —**a·dul'ter·a'tion** n.

a·dul'ter·y n. sexual unfaithfulness in marriage —**a·dul'ter·er** n. —**a·dul'ter·ess** n.fem. —**a·dul'ter·ous** a.

ad·vance' v. 1 bring or go forward 2 pay before due 3 rise or raise in rank —n. 1 a move forward 2 pl. approaches to get favor —**in advance** ahead of time —**ad·vance'ment** n.

ad·van'tage n. 1 superiority 2 gain; benefit —**take advantage of** use for one's own benefit —**ad·van·ta'geous** a.

ad·ven·ti'tious (-tish'əs) a. not inherent; accidental

ad·ven'ture n. 1 dangerous undertaking 2 exciting experience —**ad·ven'tur·er** n. —**ad·ven'ture·some** a. —**ad·ven'tur·ous** a.

ad'verb' n. word that modifies a verb, adjective, or other adverb —**ad·ver'bi·al** a.

ad'ver·sar·y n., pl. **-ies** foe; opponent

ad·verse' (or ad'vʉrs) a. 1 opposed 2 harmful

ad·ver'si·ty n., pl. **-ties** misfortune

ad'ver·tise' v. tell about publicly to promote sales, etc. —**ad'ver·tis'ing** n.

ad'ver·tise'ment (or -vʉr'tiz-) n. public notice, usually paid for

ad·vice' n. opinion on what to do

ad·vis'a·ble (-vīz'-) a. being good advice; wise —**ad·vis·a·bil'i·ty** n.

ad·vise' v. 1 give advice (to) 2 offer as advice 3 inform —**ad·vis'or, ad·vis'er** n. —**ad·vi'so·ry** a.

ad·vis'ed·ly adv. with due consideration

ad·vise'ment n. careful consideration

ad·vi'so·ry a. advising or empowered to advise —n., pl. **-ries** a report, esp. about weather conditions

ad'vo·cate' (-kāt'; n.: -kət) v. support or urge —n. one who supports another or a cause —**ad'vo·ca·cy** n.

adz, adze n. axlike tool

ae·gis (ē'jis) n. sponsorship

ae·on (ē'ən) n. eon

aer·ate' (er'-) v. expose to air —**aer·a'tion** n.

aer'i·al a. 1 of or like air 2 of flying —n. radio or TV antenna

aero- pref. 1 air; of air 2 of aircraft

aer·o'bic a. of exercise that conditions heart and lungs —n.pl. [sing. or pl. v.] aerobic exercises

aer'o·nau'tics n. aviation —**aer'o·nau'ti·cal** a.

aer'o·sol' (-sôl', -säl') a. using gas under pressure to dispense liquid or foam

aer'o·space' n. earth's atmosphere and outer space

aes·thet'ic (es thet'-) a. 1 of beauty or aesthetics 2 sensitive to art and beauty —**aes·thete'** (-thēt') n.

aes·thet'ics n. study or philosophy of beauty

a·far' adv. far away

af·fa·ble a. pleasant; sociable —**af·fa·bil'i·ty** n.

af·fair' n. 1 matter; event 2 pl. business matters 3 amorous relationship of two people not married to each other

af·fect' v. 1 act on; influence 2 stir emotionally 3 like to wear, use, etc. 4 pretend to be or feel

af'fec·ta'tion n. 1 pretense 2 artificial behavior

af·fect'ed a. 1 artificial 2 diseased 3 influenced 4 emotionally moved

af·fec'tion n. 1 fond feeling 2 disease

af·fec'tion·ate a. tender and loving

af·fi·da·vit n. sworn statement in writing

af·fil'i·ate' (-āt'; n.: -ət) v. join as a member; associate —n. affiliated member —**af·fil'i·a'tion** n.

af·fin'i·ty n., pl. **-ties** 1 close relationship or kinship 2 attraction

af·firm' v. assert or confirm —**af'fir·ma'tion** n.

af·firm'a·tive a. affirming; positive —n. assent

af·fix' (ə fiks'; n.: af'iks) v. attach —n. thing affixed, as a prefix

af·flict' v. cause pain to; distress —**af·flic'tion** n.

af'flu·ence n. 1 plenty 2 riches —**af'flu·ent** a.

af·ford' v. 1 have money enough for 2 provide

af·front' v., n. insult

af'ghan (-gan') n. crocheted or knitted wool blanket

a·field' adv. away; astray

a·fire' adv., a. on fire

a·flame' adv., a. in flames

a·float' a. 1 floating 2 at sea 3 current

a·foot' adv., a. 1 on foot 2 in motion; astir

a·fore'men'tioned a. mentioned before

a·fore'said' a. said before

a·foul' adv., a. in a tangle

a·fraid' a. 1 frightened 2 regretful

a·fresh' adv. anew; again

Af'ri·can a. of Africa —n. native of Africa

Af'ri·can-A·mer'i·can a., n. (of) a black American of African ancestry

aft adv. near the stern

af'ter adv. 1 behind 2 later — prep. 1 behind 2 in search of 3 later than 4 because of 5 in spite of 6 in imitation of 7 for —con. later than —a. later

af'ter·birth' n. placenta, etc. expelled after childbirth

af'ter·ef·fect' n. an effect coming later, or as a secondary result

af'ter·math' n. (bad) result

af'ter·noon' n. time from noon to evening

af'ter·thought' n. thought coming later or too late

af'ter·ward adv. later: also **af'ter·wards**

a·gain' adv. 1 once more 2 besides

a·gainst' prep. 1 opposed to 2 so as to hit 3 next to 4 in preparation for

a·gape' adv., a. with mouth wide open

ag'ate (-ət) n. hard semiprecious stone, often striped

age n. 1 length of time of existence 2 time of getting full legal rights 3 stage of life 4 old age 5 historical period —v. grow old or make old

-age suf. act or state of; amount of; place of or for

a·ged (ā'jəd; 2: ājd) a. 1 old 2 of the age of

age'less a. 1 seemingly not older 2 eternal

a'gen·cy n., pl. **-cies** 1 action or means 2 firm acting for another

a·gen'da n. list of things to be dealt with

a'gent n. 1 force, or cause of an effect 2 one that acts for another

age'-old' a. ancient

ag·gran'dize' (ə gran'-) v. to increase in power, riches, etc. —**ag·gran'dize·ment** n.

ag'gra·vate' v. 1 make worse 2 [Col.] vex; annoy —**ag'gra·va'tion** n.

ag'gre·gate (-gət; v.: -gāt') a., n., v. total; mass —**ag'gre·ga'tion** n.

ag·gres'sion n. unprovoked attack —**ag·gres'sor** n.

ag·gres'sive a. 1 quarrelsome 2 bold and active —**ag·gres'sive·ly** adv.

ag·grieve' v. offend

a·ghast' (-gast') a. horrified

ag·ile (aj'əl) a. quick; nimble —**a·gil'i·ty** (-jil'-) n.

ag'i·tate' (aj'-) v. 1 stir up 2 disturb 3 talk to arouse support (for) —**ag'i·ta'tion** n. —**ag'i·ta'tor** n.

a·glow' adv., a. in a glow

ag·nos'tic (-näs'-) n. one who doubts the existence of God —**ag·nos'ti·cism'** n.

a·go' a., adv. (in the) past

a·gog' a. eager; excited

ag'o·nize' v. cause agony

ag'o·ny n. great suffering

a·grar'i·an (-grer'-) a. of land and farming

a·gree' v. 1 to consent 2 be in harmony or accord —**a·gree'ment** n.

a·gree'a·ble a. 1 pleasing 2 willing to consent

ag'ri·cul'ture n. farming —**ag'ri·cul'tur·al** a.

a·gron'o·my n. science, etc. of

crop production —**a·gron'o·mist** *n.*

a·ground' *adv., a.* on or onto the shore, a reef, etc.

ah *int.* cry of pain, delight, etc.

a·head' *adv., a.* in front; forward; in advance

a·hoy' *int. Naut.* hailing call

aid *v., n.* help

aide *n.* **1** assistant **2** military officer assisting a superior: also **aide'-de-camp'**, *pl.* **aides'-**

AIDS *n.* viral condition resulting in infections, cancer, etc.: usually fatal

ail *v.* **1** to pain **2** be ill

ai·le·ron (ā'lə rän') *n.* hinged flap of an airplane wing

ail'ment *n.* chronic illness

aim *v.* **1** direct (a gun, blow, etc.) **2** intend —*n.* **1** an aiming **2** direction of aiming **3** intention; goal —**aim'less** *a.*

ain't 1 [Col.] am not **2** [Dial.] is not; are not; has not; have not

air *n.* **1** mixture of gases around the earth **2** appearance **3** *pl.* haughty manners **4** tune — *v.* **1** let air into **2** publicize —*a.* of aviation —**on the air** broadcasting on TV or radio

air'borne' *a.* **1** carried in the air **2** aloft

air conditioning *n.* controlling of humidity and temperature of air in a room, etc. —**air'-con·di'tion** *v.* —**air conditioner** *n.*

air'craft' *n., pl.* **-craft'** machine or machines for flying

air'field' *n.* field where aircraft can take off and land

air force *n.* aviation branch of a country's armed forces

air'head' *n.* [Sl.] silly, ignorant person

air'line' *n.* air transport system or company: also **air line**

air'lin'er *n.* large, passenger aircraft of an airline

air'mail' *n.* mail transported by air

air'man *n., pl.* **-men** **1** aviator **2** enlisted person in U.S. Air Force

air'plane' *n.* motor-driven or jet-propelled aircraft

air'port' *n.* airfield with facilities for repair, etc.

air raid *n.* attack by aircraft

air'ship' *n.* steerable aircraft that is lighter than air

air'sick' *a.* nauseated because of air travel

air'tight' *a.* too tight for air to enter or escape

air'y *a.* **-i·er, -i·est 1** open to the air **2** flimsy as air **3** light; graceful **4** lighthearted —**air'i·ly** *adv.*

aisle (il) *n.* passageway between rows of seats

a·jar' *adv., a.* slightly open

a·kim'bo *adv., a.* with hands on hips

a·kin' *a.* similar; alike

-al *suf.* **1** of; like; fit for **2** act or process of

a'la·bas'ter *n.* whitish, translucent gypsum

a' la carte' *adv., a.* with a separate price for each dish

a·lac'ri·ty *n.* quick willingness; readiness

a' la mode' *adv., a.* **1** in fashion **2** served with ice cream

a·larm' *n.* **1** signal or device to warn or waken **2** fear —*v.* to frighten

alarm clock *n.* clock with device to sound at set time

a·larm'ist *n.* one who expresses needless alarm

a·las' *int.* cry of sorrow, etc.

al'ba·core *n.* kind of tuna

al'ba·tross' *n.* large, web-footed seabird

al·be'it (ôl-) *con.* although

al·bi'no (-bī'-) *n., pl.* **-nos** individual lacking normal coloration

al'bum *n.* blank book for photographs, stamps, etc.

al·bu'men (-byoō'-) *n.* white of an egg

al·bu'min *n.* protein in egg, milk, muscle, etc.

al'che·my (-kə-) *n.* chemistry of the Middle Ages —**al'che·mist** *n.*

al'co·hol' *n.* colorless, intoxicating liquid obtained from fermented grain, fruit, etc.

al'co·hol'ic *a.* of alcohol —*n.* one addicted to alcohol

al'co·hol·ism' *n.* addiction to alcohol

al'cove' *n.* recess; nook

al'der (ôl'-) *n.* small tree of the birch family

al'der·man *n., pl.* **-men** member of a city council

ale *n.* kind of beer

a·lert' *a.* watchful; ready —*n.* an alarm —*v.* warn to be ready —**a·lert'ness** *n.*

al·fal'fa *n.* plant used for fodder, pasture, etc.

al'gae (-jē) *n.pl.* primitive water plants

al'ge·bra *n.* mathematics using letters and numbers in equations —**al'ge·bra'ic** a.

a·li·as (ā'lē əs) n. assumed name —adv. otherwise named

al'i·bi' (-bī') n., pl. -**bis'** 1 plea that the accused was not at the scene of the crime 2 [Col.] any excuse —v. give an excuse

al'ien (āl'yən, ā'lē ən) a. foreign —n. foreigner

al'ien·ate' v. make unfriendly —**al'ien·a'tion** n.

a·light' v. 1 dismount 2 land after flight —a. lighted up

a·lign' (-līn') v. 1 line up 2 make agree —**a·lign'ment** n.

a·like' a. similar —adv. 1 similarly 2 equally

al'i·men'ta·ry canal n. the passage in the body that food goes through

al'i·mo'ny n. money paid to support one's former wife

a·live' a. 1 living; in existence 2 lively —**alive with** teeming with

al'ka·li' (-lī') n., pl. -**lies'** or -**lis'** substance that neutralizes acids —**al'ka·line'** a. —**al'ka·lize'** v.

al'ka·loid' n. alkaline drug from plants, as cocaine

all a. 1 the whole of 2 every one of 3 complete —pron. 1 [pl. v.] everyone 2 everything 3 every bit —n. a whole —adv. entirely —**after all** nevertheless —**at all** in any way

Al·lah (ä'lə) God: Muslim name

all'-a·round' a. having many abilities, uses, etc.

al·lay' v. to calm; quiet

all'-clear' n. siren or signal that an air raid is over

al·lege' v. declare, esp. without proof —**al·le·ga'tion** n. —**al·leg'ed·ly** adv.

al·le'giance (-lē'jəns) n. loyalty, as to one's country

al'le·go'ry n., pl. -**ries** story in which things, actions, etc. are symbolic

al·le'gro (-le'-) a., adv. Mus. fast

al'ler·gen n. allergy-causing substance —**al'ler·gen'ic** a.

al'ler·gy n., pl. -**gies** sensitive reaction to certain food, pollen, etc. —**al·ler'gic** a.

al·le'vi·ate' v. relieve; ease —**al·le'vi·a'tion** n.

al'ley n., pl. -**leys** 1 narrow street 2 bowling lane

al·li'ance (-lī'-) n. 1 an allying 2 association; league

al·lied' a. 1 united by treaty, etc. 2 related

al'li·ga'tor n. large lizard like a crocodile

al·lit'er·a'tion n. use of the same initial sound in a series of words

al'lo·cate' v. allot —**al'lo·ca'tion** n.

al·lot' v. -**lot'ted**, -**lot'ting** 1 distribute in shares 2 assign —**al·lot'ment** n.

all'-out' a. thorough

al·low' v. 1 to permit 2 let have 3 grant —**allow for** leave room, time, etc. for —**al·low'a·ble** a.

al·low'ance n. 1 thing allowed 2 amount given regularly

al'loy (v.: ə loi') n. metal mixture —v. mix (metals)

all right 1 satisfactory 2 unhurt 3 correct —adv. yes

all'spice' n. pungent spice from a berry

all'-star' a. made up of star performers —n. member of an all-star team

all'-time' a. unsurpassed up to the present time

al·lude' v. refer; mention

al·lure' v. tempt; attract —**al·lur'ing** a.

al·lu'sion n. indirect or casual mention —**al·lu'sive** a.

al·ly' (n.: al'ī) v. -**lied'**, -**ly'ing** unite; join —n., pl. -**lies** country or person joined with another

al'ma ma'ter (mät'ər) n. college or school that one attended

al'ma·nac' n. calendar with miscellaneous data

al·might'y a. all-powerful —**the Almighty** God

al'mond (ä'mənd, ôl'-) n. edible, nutlike, oval seed of a tree of the peach family

al'most' adv. very nearly

alms (ämz) n. money, food, etc. given to the poor

al'oe' (-ō') n. African plant whose juice is used in ointments, etc.

a·loft' adv. high up

a·lo·ha (ä lō'hä) n., int. love: Hawaiian "hello" or "goodbye"

a·lone' a., adv. with no other —**let alone** not to mention

a·long' prep. on or beside the length of —adv. 1 onward 2 together (with) 3 with one —**all along** from the beginning —**get along** manage

a·long'side' adv. at the side —prep. beside

a·loof' (-lōōf') adv. apart —a. cool and reserved

a·loud' adv. loudly

al·pac'a n. 1 kind of llama 2 cloth from its long, silky wool

al'pha n. first letter of the Greek alphabet

al'pha·bet' n. letters of a language, in the regular order —**al'pha·bet'i·cal** a.

al'pha·bet·ize' v. arrange in alphabetical order

al·read'y adv. by or before the given time; previously

al'so adv. in addition; too

al'tar (-tər) n. table, etc. for sacred rites, as in a church

al'ter n. change; modify —**al'ter·a'tion** n.

al'ter·ca'tion n. a quarrel

al'ter·nate (-nət; v.: -nāt') a. 1 succeeding each other 2 every other —n. a substitute —v. do, use, act, etc. by turns —**al'ter·na'tion** n.

alternating current n. electric current that reverses its direction

al·ter'na·tive n. choice between two or more —a. giving such a choice

al·though' con. in spite of the fact that

al·tim'e·ter (al-) n. instrument for measuring altitude

al'ti·tude' n. height, esp. above sea level

al'to n., pl. **-tos** lowest female voice

al·to·geth'er adv. wholly

al'tru·ism' (al'-) n. unselfish concern for others —**al'tru·ist** n. —**al'tru·is'tic** a.

al'um n. astringent salt

a·lu'mi·num n. silvery, lightweight metal, a chemical element: also [Br.] **al'u·min'i·um**

a·lum'nus n., pl. **-ni'** (-nī') former student of a certain school or college —**a·lum'na** n.fem., pl. **-nae** (-nē)

al'ways adv. 1 at all times 2 continually

Alz'hei·mer's disease (älts'hī'mərz) n. disease causing degeneration of brain cells

am v. pres. t. of BE: used with I

AM before noon: also **a.m.**, **A.M.**

a·mal'gam (-gəm) n. alloy of mercury and another metal

a·mal'ga·mate' v. unite —**a·mal'ga·ma'tion** n.

am'a·ranth' n. plant with showy flowers

am'a·ryl'lis (-ril'-) n. bulb plant with lilylike flowers

a·mass' v. pile up; collect

am'a·teur (-chər) n. 1 one who does something for pleasure, not pay 2 unskillful person —**am'a·**

teur'ish a.

am'a·to'ry a. of love

a·maze' v. astonish; surprise —**a·maze'ment** n.

am'a·zon' n. strong woman

am·bas'sa·dor n. top-ranking diplomatic official —**am·bas'sa·dor·ship'** n.

am'ber n. 1 yellowish fossil resin 2 its color

am'ber·gris' (-grēs') n. waxy secretion of certain whales, used in perfumes

am·bi·dex'trous a. using both hands with equal ease

am'bi·ence n. milieu; environment: also **am'bi·ance**

am'bi·ent a. surrounding

am·big'u·ous a. having two or more meanings; vague —**am·bi·gu'i·ty** n., pl. **-ties**

am·bi'tion n. 1 desire to succeed 2 success desired —**am·bi'tious** a.

am·biv'a·lence n. simultaneous conflicting feelings —**am·biv'a·lent** a.

am'ble v. move in an easy gait —n. easy gait

am·bro'si·a (-zhə) n. Gr. & Rom. myth. food of the gods

am'bu·lance (-byōō-) n. car to carry sick or wounded

am'bu·la·to'ry a. 1 of walking 2 able to walk

am'bus·cade' (-,) v. ambush

am'bush' n. 1 a hiding for a surprise attack 2 the hiding place or group —v. to attack from hiding

a·me'ba n. amoeba

a·mel'io·rate' (-mēl'yə-) v. improve —**a·mel'io·ra'tion** n.

a·men' int. may it be so!

a·me'na·ble (-men'ə-, -mēn'ə-) a. willing to obey or heed advice; responsive —**a·me'na·bly** adv.

a·mend' v. 1 to correct 2 improve 3 revise, as a law —**a·mend'ment** n.

a·mends' n.pl. a making up for injury, loss, etc.

a·men'i·ty n., pl. **-ties** 1 pleasantness 2 pl. courtesies 3 convenience: often used in pl.

A·mer'i·can a. 1 of America 2 of the U.S. —n. 1 native of America 2 U.S. citizen

A·mer'i·can·ize' v. make or become American

am'e·thyst (-thist) n. purple quartz for jewelry

a'mi·a·ble a. good-natured; friendly

am'i·ca·ble a. friendly; peaceable

—**a·mi′ca·bly** adv.

a·mid′, a·midst′ prep. among

a·mid′ships′ adv. in or toward the middle of a ship

a·mi′go n., pl. **-gos** friend

a·mi′no acid (-mē-) n. any of several basic building blocks of protein

a·miss′ adv., a. wrong

am′i·ty n. friendship

am·me′ter n. instrument for measuring amperes

am′mo n. [Sl.] ammunition

am·mo′ni·a n. 1 acrid gas 2 water solution of it

am·mu·ni′tion n. bullets, gunpowder, bombs, etc.

am·ne′si·a (-zha) n. loss of memory

am′nes·ty n. general pardon for political offenses

am·ni·o·cen·te′sis n. extracting fluid (am′ni·ot′ic fluid) from a pregnant woman

a·moe′ba (-mē-) n., pl. **-bas** or **-bae** (-bē) one-celled animal —**a·moe′bic** a.

a·mok′ (-muk′) a., adv. used chiefly in **run amok**, lose control and behave violently

a·mong′, a·mongst′ prep. 1 surrounded by 2 in the group of 3 to or for each of

a·mor′al (ā-) a. with no moral sense or standards

am′o·rous a. fond of making love 2 full of love

a·mor′phous a. 1 shapeless 2 of no definite type

am′or·tize′ v. provide for gradual payment of —**am′or·ti·za′tion** n.

a·mount′ v. 1 add up (to) 2 be equal (to) —n. 1 sum 2 quantity

a·mour′ (-moor′) n. love affair

am·per·age n. strength of an electric current in amperes

am·pere′ (-pir′) n. unit of electric current

am′per·sand′ n. sign (&) meaning and

am·phet′a·mine (-mēn′) n. drug used as a stimulant and to lessen appetite

am·phib′i·an n. 1 land-and-water animal, as the frog 2 land-and-water vehicle —a. amphibious

am·phib′i·ous a. adapted to both land and water

am′phi·the′a·ter, am′phi·the′a·tre n. open theater with central space circled by tiers of seats

am′ple a. 1 large 2 adequate;

plenty —**am′ply** adv.

am′pli·fy′ v. **-fied′, -fy′ing** make stronger, louder, or fuller —**am′pli·fi·ca′tion** n. —**am′pli·fi′er** n.

am′pli·tude′ n. 1 extent or breadth 2 abundance

am′pul′ n. small container for a dose of medicine to be injected: also **am′pule′**

am′pu·tate′ (-pyoo-) v. to cut off, esp. by surgery —**am′pu·ta′tion** n.

am′pu·tee′ n. one who has had a limb amputated

a·muck′ n. amok

am′u·let (-yoo-) n. charm worn against evil

a·muse′ v. 1 entertain 2 make laugh —**a·mus′ing** a. —**a·muse′ment** n.

amusement park n. entertainment area with rides, food, etc.

an a., indefinite article 1 one 2 each; any one

-an suf. 1 of 2 born in; living in 3 believing in

a·nach′ro·nism (-nak′-) n. thing out of proper historical time —**a·nach′ro·nis′tic** a.

an′a·con′da n. large South American boa snake

an′a·gram′ n. word made by rearranging the letters of another word

a′nal a. of the anus

an′al·ge′sic (-jē′zik) n., a. (drug) that eases pain

an′a·log′ a. 1 of electronic equipment, recordings, etc. in which the signal corresponds to physical change 2 using hands, dials, etc. to show number amounts

an′a·logue′ n. something analogous

a·nal′o·gy (-jē) n., pl. **-gies** similarity in some ways —**a·nal′o·gous** (-gəs) a.

a·nal′y·sis (-ə sis) n., pl. **-ses′** (-sēz′) 1 separation of a whole into its parts to find out their nature, etc. 2 psychoanalysis —**an′a·lyst** (-list) n. —**an′a·lyt′ic, an′a·lyt′i·cal** a. —**an′a·lyze′** (-līz′) v.

an′ar·chism′ (-ər kiz′əm) n. opposition to all government —**an′ar·chist′** n.

an′ar·chy n. 1 absence of government and law 2 great disorder —**an·ar′chic** a.

a·nath′e·ma n. 1 person or thing accursed or detested 2 ritual curse —**a·nath′e·ma·tize′** v.

a·nat′o·my n. 1 science of plant

or animal structure **2** structure of an organism —**an'a·tom'i·cal** a.

-ance suf. **1** action or state of **2** a thing that (is)

an'ces·tor n. person from whom one is descended

an'ces'try n. **1** family descent **2** all one's ancestors —**an·ces'tral** a.

an'chor (-kər) n. **1** metal weight lowered from a ship to prevent drifting **2** one who anchors a newscast: also **an'chor·man'**, pl. **-men**, or **an'chor·wom'an**, pl. **-wom'en**, or **an'chor·per'son** v. **1** hold secure **2** coordinate and report (a newscast) —at anchor anchored —**an'chor·age** n.

an'cho·vy (-chō'-) n., pl. **-vies** tiny herring

an·cient (ān'chənt, -shənt) a. **1** of times long past **2** very old —the ancients people of ancient times

an'cil·lar·y a. auxiliary

and con. **1** also **2** plus **3** as a result

an·dan·te (än dän'tā) a., adv. Mus. moderately slow

and'i'ron n. either of a pair of metal stands for logs in a fireplace

an'dro·gen n. male sex hormone

an'droid' n. fictional, human-looking robot

an'ec·dote' n. brief story

a·ne'mi·a (-zhə) n. loss of the sense of pain, touch, etc.

a·ne'mom·e·ter n. gauge measuring wind velocity

a·nem'o·ne' (-nē') n. plant with cup-shaped flowers

a·nent' prep. [Now Rare] concerning

an·es·the'si·a (-zhə) n. loss of the sense of pain, touch, etc.

an·es·thet'ic n., a. (drug, gas, etc.) that produces anesthesia —**an·es'the·tist** n. —**an·es'the·tize'** v.

an'eu·rysm', an'eu·rism' (-yōo riz'əm) n. sac formed by swelling in an artery wall

a·new' adv. **1** once more **2** in a new way

an·gel (ān'jəl) n. messenger of God, pictured with wings and halo —**an·gel'ic** (an-) a.

angel food cake n. light, spongy, white cake: also **angel cake**

an'ger n. hostile feeling; wrath —v. make angry

an·gi·na pec'to·ris (-ji'-) n. heart disease with chest pains

an'gle n. **1** space formed by two lines or surfaces that meet **2** point of view —v. **1** bend at an angle **2** fish with hook and line **3** use tricks to get something —**an'gler** n.

an'gle·worm' n. earthworm

Anglo- pref. English (and)

An·glo-Sax'on n. **1** native of England before 12th c. **2** person of English descent **3** Old English

An·go'ra n. wool from longhaired goat or rabbit

an'gry a. **-gri·er, -gri·est 1** feeling anger; enraged **2** stormy —**an'gri·ly** adv.

ang·strom (aŋ'strəm) n. unit for measuring length of light waves: also **angstrom unit**

an'guish n. great pain, worry, or grief

an'gu·lar (-gyōo-) a. having angles —**an'gu·lar'i·ty** n.

an'i·line (-lin) n. oily liquid made from benzene, used in dyes, etc.

an'i·mad·ver'sion n. criticism

an'i·mal n. **1** living organism able to move about **2** any four-footed creature —a. **1** of an animal **2** bestial

an'i·mate' (-māt'; a.: -mət) v. **1** give life to **2** make lively —a. **1** living **2** lively —**an'i·mat'ed** a. —**an'i·ma'tion** n. —**an'i·ma'tor** n.

an'i·mos'i·ty n. strong hatred; ill will

an'i·mus n. ill will

an·ise (-is) n. plant whose seed is used as flavoring

an'kle n. joint connecting foot and leg

an'klet n. short sock

an'nals n.pl. historical records, year by year

an·neal' v. toughen (glass or metal) by heating and then cooling slowly

an·nex (ə neks'; n.: an'eks) v. attach or join to a larger unit —n. something annexed —**an'nex·a'tion** n.

an·ni'hi·late' (-ni'ə-) v. destroy —**an·ni'hi·la'tion** n.

an'ni·ver'sa·ry n., pl. **-ries** yearly return of the date of some event

an'no·tate' v. provide explanatory notes for —**an'no·ta'tion** n.

an·nounce' v. make known; tell about —**an·nounc'er** n. —**an·nounce'ment** n.

an·noy' v. to bother or anger —**an·noy'ance** n.

an·nu·al *a.* yearly —*n.* 1 plant living one year 2 yearbook —**an·nu·al·ly** *adv.*

an·nu·i·ty *n., pl.* -**ties** investment yielding fixed annual payments

an·nul *v.* -**nulled'**, -**nul'ling** make null and void —**an·nul'ment** *n.*

an'ode *n.* positive electrode

an'o·dyne' (-dīn) *n.* anything that relieves pain

a·noint' *v.* put oil on, as in consecrating

a·nom'a·ly *n., pl.* -**lies** unusual or irregular thing —**a·nom'a·lous** *a.*

a·non' *adv.* 1 soon 2 at another time

a·non'y·mous (-ə məs) *a.* with name unknown or withheld; unidentified —**an'o·nym'i·ty** (-nim'-) *n.*

an'o·rex'i·a *n.* ailment characterized by lack of appetite for food —**an'o·rex'ic** *a.*

an·oth'er *a., pron.* 1 one more 2 a different (one)

an'swer (-sər) *n.* 1 thing said or done in return; reply 2 solution to a problem —*v.* 1 reply (to) 2 serve or suit 3 be responsible —**an'swer·a·ble** *a.*

ant *n.* small insect living in colonies

-ant *suf.* 1 that has, shows, or does 2 one that

ant·ac'id *n., a.* (substance) counteracting acids

an·tag'o·nism' *n.* hostility —**an·tag'o·nis'tic** *a.*

an·tag'o·nist *n.* opponent

an·tag'o·nize' *v.* incur the dislike of

ant·arc'tic *a.* of or near the South Pole —*n.* antarctic region

an'te (-tē) *n.* player's stake in poker —*v.* -**ted** or -**teed**, -**te·ing** put in one's stake

ante- *pref.* before

ant'eat'er *n.* long-snouted mammal that feeds on ants

an'te·ced'ent (-sēd'-) *a.* prior —*n.* 1 thing prior to another 2 word or phrase to which a pronoun refers

an'te·cham'ber *n.* room leading to larger room

an'te·date' *v.* occur before

an'te·di·lu'vi·an *a.* 1 before the Biblical Flood 2 outmoded

an'te·lope' *n.* horned animal like the deer

an·ten'na *n., pl.* -**nae** (-ē) or -**nas** 1 feeler on the head of an insect, etc. 2 *pl.* -**nas** wire(s) for sending and receiving radio waves

an·te'ri·or *a.* 1 toward the front 2 earlier

an'te·room' *n.* room leading to another room

an'them *n.* religious or patriotic choral song

an'ther *n.* pollen-bearing part of a stamen

an·thol'o·gy *n., pl.* -**gies** collection of poems, stories, etc. —**an·thol'o·gist** *n.*

an'thra·cite' *n.* hard coal

an'thrax' *n.* disease of cattle

an'thro·poid' *a.* manlike —*n.* an anthropoid ape

an'thro·pol'o·gy *n.* study of the races, customs, etc. of mankind —**an'thro·pol'o·gist** *n.*

an'thro·po·mor'phism' *n.* an attributing of human qualities to animals or things —**an'thro·po·mor'phic** *a.*

anti- *pref.* 1 against 2 that acts against

an'ti·bi·ot'ic (-bī-) *n.* substance produced by some microorganisms, able to kill or weaken bacteria

an'ti·bod'y *n., pl.* -**ies** substance produced in body to act against toxins, etc.

an'tic *n.* silly act; prank

an·tic'i·pate' (-tis'-) *v.* 1 expect 2 act on before —**an·tic'i·pa'tion** *n.*

an'ti·cli'max' *n.* sudden drop from the important to the trivial —**an'ti·cli·mac'tic** *a.*

an'ti·de·pres'sant *n.* drug that lessens medical depression

an'ti·dote' *n.* remedy to counteract a poison or evil

an'ti·freeze' *n.* substance used to prevent freezing

an'ti·gen *n.* substance to which the body reacts by producing antibodies

an'ti·his'ta·mine' (-mēn) *n.* drug used to treat allergies

an'ti·mo'ny *n.* silvery metal in alloys, a chemical element

an'ti·pas'to (-päs'-) *n.* appetizer of spicy meat, fish, etc.

an·tip'a·thy *n., pl.* -**thies** strong dislike

an'ti·per'spi·rant (-pur'spə-) *n.* skin lotion, cream, etc. for reducing perspiration

an·tip'o·des' (-dēz') *n.pl.* opposite places on the globe

an'ti·quar'i·an (-kwer'-) *a.* of antiques or antiquaries —*n.* antiquary

an·ti·quar·y *n.*, *pl.* **-ies** collector or student of antiquities

an·ti·quate' *v.* make obsolete —**an·ti·quat'ed** *a.*

an·tique' (-tēk') *a.* 1 of a former period 2 out-of-date —*n.* piece of furniture, etc. from earlier times

an·tiq·ui·ty (-tik'wə-) *n.*, *pl.* **-ties** 1 ancient times 2 great age 3 ancient relic, etc.

an·ti·sem'i·tism' *n.* prejudice against Jews —**an·ti·sem'ite'** *n.* —**an·ti·se·mit'ic** *a.*

an·ti·sep'tic *a.* preventing infection by killing germs —*n.* antiseptic substance

an·ti·so'cial *a.* 1 not sociable 2 harmful to society

an·tith·e·sis *n.*, *pl.* **-ses'** (-sēz') exact opposite —**an·ti·thet'i·cal** *a.*

an·ti·tox'in *n.* serum that counteracts a disease

an·ti·trust' *a.* regulating business trusts

ant'ler *n.* branched horn of a deer, elk, etc.

an'to·nym' (-nim') *n.* word opposite in meaning

a'nus (ā'-) *n.* opening at rear end of the alimentary canal

an'vil *n.* block on which to hammer metal objects

anx·i·e·ty (aŋ zī'-) *n.*, *pl.* **-ties** worry about what may happen

anx·ious (aŋk'shəs) *a.* 1 worried 2 eagerly wishing —**anx'ious·ly** *adv.*

an'y *a.* 1 one of more than two 2 some 3 every —*pron.* [*sing.* or *pl. v.*] any person(s) or amount —*adv.* at all

an'y·bod'y *pron.* anyone

an'y·how' *adv.* 1 in any way 2 in any case

an'y·one' *pron.* any person

an'y·thing' *pron.* any thing —**anything** but not at all

an'y·way' *adv.* anyhow

an'y·where' *adv.* in, at, or to any place

A–OK *a.* [Col.] excellent, fine, etc.: also **A'–O·kay'**

A one *a.* [Col.] superior; first-class: also **A1, A number 1**

a·or'ta (ā-) *n.* main artery leading from the heart

a·pace' *adv.* swiftly

a·part' *adv.* 1 aside 2 away from (one) another 3 into pieces —*a.* separated

a·part'heid' (-pär'tāt', -tīd') *n.* strict racial segregation as practiced in South Africa

a·part'ment *n.* room or set of rooms to live in

ap'a·thy *n.* lack of feeling or interest —**ap'a·thet'ic** *a.*

ape *n.* large, tailless monkey —*v.* imitate

a·pe·ri·tif (ə per'ə tēf') *n.* alcoholic drink before meals

ap'er·ture (-chər) *n.* opening

a'pex' *n.* highest point

a·pha·si·a (-zhə) *n.* loss of power to use or understand words

a'phid (ā'fid, af'id) *n.* insect that sucks the juices of plants

aph'o·rism' *n.* wise saying

aph'ro·dis'i·ac' (-diz'-) *n.*, *a.* (drug, etc.) arousing sexual desire

a'pi·ar'y *n.*, *pl.* **-ies** collection of beehives

a·piece' *adv.* to or for each one

a·plomb' (ə pläm') *n.* poise

a·poc'a·lypse' (-lips') *n.* total devastation, as doomsday —**a·poc'a·lyp'tic** *a.*

a·poc'ry·phal (-rə fəl) *a.* of doubtful authenticity

ap'o·gee' *n.* point farthest from earth in a satellite's orbit

a·pol'o·gist *n.* defender of a doctrine, action, etc.

a·pol'o·gy *n.*, *pl.* **-gies** 1 expression of regret for a fault, etc. 2 defense of an idea, etc. —**a·pol'o·get'ic** *a.* —**a·pol'o·gize'** *v.*

ap'o·plex'y *n.* paralysis caused by a broken blood vessel in the brain —**ap'o·plec'tic** *a.*

a·pos'tate' *n.* one who abandons faith, principles, etc. —**a·pos'ta·sy** *n.*

A·pos·tle (-päs'əl) *n.* 1 any of the disciples of Jesus 2 [a-] leader of a new movement —**ap'os·tol'ic** *a.*

a·pos'tro·phe (-fē) *n.* sign (') indicating: *a*) omission of letter(s) from a word *b*) possessive case

a·poth'e·car'y *n.*, *pl.* **-ies** druggist

ap·pall', ap·pal' *v.* to dismay —**ap·pall'ing** *a.*

ap'pa·ra·tus (-rat'əs; -rāt'-) *n.* 1 tools, etc. for a specific use 2 complex device

ap·par'el *n.* clothes —*v.* clothe; dress

ap·par'ent *a.* 1 obvious; plain 2 seeming —**ap·par'ent·ly** *adv.*

ap'pa·ri'tion *n.* ghost

ap·peal' *n.* 1 request for help 2 attraction 3 request for rehearing by a higher court —*v.* 1 make an appeal 2 be attractive

ap·pear (-pir') v. **1** come into sight **2** seem **3** come before the public —**ap·pear'ance** n.

ap·pease' (-pēz') v. to quiet by satisfying —**ap·pease'ment** n.

ap·pel'lant n. one who appeals to a higher court

ap·pel'late court (-pel'ət) n. court handling appeals

ap·pel·la'tion n. a name

ap·pend' v. add or attach

ap·pend'age (-pen'dij) n. an attached part, as a tail

ap·pen·dec'to·my n., pl. **-mies** surgical removal of the appendix

ap·pen·di·ci'tis (-sī'-) n. inflammation of the appendix

ap·pen'dix n., pl. **-dix·es** or **-di·ces'** (-də sēz') **1** extra material at the end of a book **2** small, closed tube attached to large intestine

ap·per·tain' v. pertain

ap'pe·tite' n. desire, esp. for food

ap'pe·tiz·ing a. stimulating the appetite; savory —**ap'pe·tiz·er** n.

ap·plaud' v. show approval, esp. by clapping the hands; praise

ap·plause' n. approval, esp. by clapping

ap'ple n. round, fleshy fruit —**ap'ple·sauce'** n.

ap'ple·jack n. brandy distilled from apple cider

ap·pli'ance n. device or machine, esp. for home use

ap'pli·cant n. one who applies, as for a job

ap·pli·ca'tion n. **1** an applying **2** thing applied **3** formal request

ap·pli·ca'tor n. device for applying medicine, etc.

ap'pli·qué' (-kā') n. decoration of one fabric on another

ap·ply' v. **-plied', -ply'ing 1** to put on **2** put into use **3** devote (oneself) diligently **4** ask formally **5** be relevant —**ap'pli·ca·ble** a.

ap·point' v. **1** set (a time, etc.) **2** name to an office **3** furnish —**ap·point·ee'** n. —**ap·point'ive** a. —**ap·point'ment** n.

ap·por'tion v. portion out —**ap·por'tion·ment** n.

ap'po·site (-zit) a. fitting

ap'po·si'tion n. placing of a word or phrase beside another in explanation —**ap·pos'i·tive** a., n.

ap·praise' v. estimate the value of —**ap·prais'al** n. —**ap·prais'er** n.

ap·pre'ci·a·ble (-shə bəl) a.

enough to be noticed —**ap·pre'ci·a·bly** adv.

ap·pre'ci·ate (-shē-) v. **1** value; enjoy **2** recognize rightly or gratefully —**ap·pre'ci·a'tion** n. —**ap·pre'ci·a·tive** a.

ap·pre·hend' v. **1** arrest **2** understand —**ap·pre·hen'sion** n.

ap·pre·hen'sive a. anxious

ap·pren'tice n. helper who is being taught a trade —v. to place as apprentice —**ap·pren'tice·ship** n.

ap·prise', ap·prize' (-prīz') v. inform; notify

ap·proach' v. **1** come nearer (to) **2** speak to —n. **1** a coming near **2** way of beginning **3** access

ap·pro·ba'tion n. approval

ap·pro'pri·ate' (-āt'; a.: -ət) v. **1** take for one's own use **2** set (money) aside for some use —a. suitable —**ap·pro'pri·ate·ly** adv. —**ap·pro'pri·a'tion** n.

ap·prove' v. **1** consent to **2** have a favorable opinion (of) —**ap·prov'al** n.

ap·prox'i·mate' (-māt'; a.: -mət) v. be about the same as —a. nearly exact or correct —**ap·prox'i·ma'tion** n.

ap·pur'te·nance (-pur'-) n. **1** adjunct **2** additional right

ap·pur'te·nant a. pertaining

a'pri·cot' (ap'rə-, ā'prə-) n. small peachlike fruit

A'pril n. fourth month

a'pron n. to protect the front of one's clothing

ap'ro·pos' (-pō') a. appropriate —**apropos of** regarding

apt a. **1** fitting; suitable **2** likely (to) **3** quick to learn

ap'ti·tude' n. **1** ability **2** quickness to learn

aq·ua·ma·rine' (ak'wə-, äk'-) n., a. bluish green: also **aq'ua**

a·quar'i·um (-kwer'-) n. tank, etc. for keeping fish or other water animals

A·quar'i·us 11th sign of the zodiac; Water Bearer

a·quat'ic (-kwät'-, -kwat'-) a. **1** living in water **2** taking place in water

aq'ue·duct' (ak'wə-) n. large pipe or channel bringing water from a distance

a'que·ous (ā'kwē-) a. of or like water

aq'ui·line' (ak'wə lin') a. curved like an eagle's beak

Ar'ab n., a. **1** (native) of Arabia **2** (one) of a people now scat-

tered through lands around Arabia

A·ra'bi·an *a.* of Arabia or the Arabs —*n.* ARAB (n. 1)

Ar'a·bic *a.* of the people or language of Arabia, etc. —*n.* this language

Arabic numerals *n.* figures 1, 2, 3, 4, 5, 6, 7, 8, 9, and 0

ar'a·ble *a.* fit for plowing

a·rach'nid (-rak'-) *n.* small, eight-legged animal, as the spider or mite

ar'bi·ter *n.* judge; umpire

ar'bi·trar'y *a.* using only one's own wishes or whim —**ar'bi·trar'i·ly** *adv.*

ar'bi·trate' *v.* settle (a dispute) by using or being an arbiter —**ar'bi·tra'tion** *n.* —**ar'bi·tra'tor** *n.*

ar'bor *n.* place shaded by trees, shrubs, or vines

ar·bo're·al (-bôr'ē-) *a.* of, like, or living in trees

ar'bo·re'tum *n.*, *pl.* **-tums** or **-ta** place where many kinds of trees are grown

ar'bor·vi'tae (-vī'tē) *n.* evergreen tree or shrub

ar·bu'tus (-byōō'-) *n.* evergreen trailing plant

arc *n.* 1 curved line, as part of a circle 2 band of light made by electricity leaping a gap

ar·cade' *n.* 1 covered passage, esp. one lined with shops 2 row of arches on columns

ar·cane' *a.* secret or esoteric

arch *n.* curved support over an opening —*v.* form (as) an arch —*a.* 1 chief 2 mischievous; coy

arch- *pref.* chief; main

ar'chae·ol'o·gy (-kē-) *n.* study of ancient peoples, as by excavation of ruins: also sp. **ar'che·ol'o·gy** —**ar'chae·o·log'i·cal** *a.*

ar·cha'ic (-kā'-) *a.* 1 out-of-date 2 now seldom used

arch'an'gel (ärk'-) *n.* angel of the highest rank

arch'bish'op (ärch'-) *n.* bishop of the highest rank

arch'di'o·cese *n.* diocese headed by an archbishop

arch'duke' *n.* ruling prince

arch'en'e·my *n.* chief enemy

arch'er·y *n.* practice or sport of shooting with bow and arrow —**arch'er** *n.*

ar'che·type' (-kə-) *n.* original model —**ar'che·typ'al, ar'che·typ'i·cal** *a.*

ar'chi·pel'a·go (-kə-) *n.*, *pl.* **-goes'** or **-gos'** chain of islands in a sea

ar'chi·tect' *n.* one who designs buildings

ar'chi·tec'ture *n.* science of designing and constructing buildings —**ar'chi·tec'tur·al** *a.*

ar'chives' (-kīvz') *n.pl.* public records or place to store them —**ar'chi·vist** *n.*

arch'way' *n.* passage under an arch

arc'tic *a.* of or near the North Pole —*n.* arctic region

ar'dent *a.* passionate; eager —**ar'dent·ly** *adv.*

ar'dor *n.* passion; zeal

ar'du·ous (-jōō-) *a.* laborious or strenuous

are *v.* pres. t. of BE: used with *you, we,* or *they*

ar'e·a (er'ē-) *n.* 1 region 2 total surface, measured in square units 3 scope

a·re'na *n.* 1 center of amphitheater, for contests, etc. 2 area of struggle

aren't are not

ar'gon *n.* chemical element, gas used in light bulbs, etc.

ar'go·sy *n.* [Poet.] large merchant ship or fleet

ar'got (-gō, -gət) *n.* special vocabulary, as of thieves

ar'gu·a·ble *a.* supportable by argument —**ar'gu·a·bly** *adv.*

ar'gue *v.* 1 give reasons (*for* or *against*) 2 dispute; debate —**ar'gu·ment** *n.* —**ar'gu·men·ta'tion** *n.* —**ar'gu·men'ta·tive** *a.*

ar'gyle' (-gīl') *a.* knitted or woven in a diamond-shaped pattern, as socks

a'ri·a (ä'rē-) *n.* solo in an opera, etc.

-arian *suf.* of one specified age, belief, work, etc.

ar'id (er'-) *a.* 1 dry 2 dull —**a·rid'i·ty** *n.*

Ar·ies (er'ēz) first sign of the zodiac; Ram

a·right' *adv.* correctly

a·rise' *v.* **a·rose', a·ris'en, a·ris'ing** 1 get up; rise 2 come into being

ar'is·toc'ra·cy *n.* 1 government by an upper class minority 2 upper class —**a·ris'to·crat'** *n.* —**a·ris'to·crat'ic** *a.*

a·rith'me·tic (*a.:* er'ith met'ik) *n.* science of computing by numbers —*a.* of arithmetic: also **ar'ith·met'i·cal** *a.*

ark *Bible* boat in which Noah, etc. survived the Flood

arm *n.* 1 one of two upper limbs of the human body 2 anything like this **3** weapon **4** military branch **5** pl. coat of arms —v. provide with weapons —**arm in arm** with arms interlocked —**up in arms** indignant —**with open arms** cordially

ar·ma·da (-mä'-) n. fleet of warships

ar·ma·dil·lo n., pl. **-los** tropical mammal covered with bony plates

ar·ma·ments n.pl. military forces and equipment

ar·ma·ture n. revolving coil in an electric motor or dynamo

arm'chair' n. chair with supports for one's arms

arm'ful n., pl. **-fuls** as much as the arms can hold

ar'mi·stice n. truce

ar'mor n. protective covering —**ar'mored** a.

ar'mor·y n., pl. **-ies 1** arsenal **2** military drill hall

arm'pit' n. the hollow under the arm at the shoulder

ar'my n., pl. **-mies 1** large body of soldiers **2** any very large group

a·ro'ma n. pleasant odor —**ar'o·mat'ic** a.

a·rose' v. pt. of ARISE

a·round' adv., prep. **1** in a circle (about) **2** on all sides (of) **3** to the opposite direction **4** [Col.] nearby

a·rouse' v. wake; stir up

ar·peg'gi·o (-pej'ō) n., pl. **-os** chord with notes played in quick succession

ar·raign' (-rān') v. **1** bring to court for trial **2** accuse —**ar·raign'ment** n.

ar·range' v. **1** put in a certain order **2** plan **3** adjust; adapt —**ar·range'ment** n.

ar'rant (er'-) a. out-and-out

ar·ray' v. **1** place in order **2** dress finely —n. **1** an orderly grouping **2** impressive display **3** finery

ar·rears' n.pl. overdue debts —**in arrears** behind in payment

ar·rest' v. **1** stop or check **2** seize **3** seize and hold by law —n. an arresting

ar·rest'ing n. interesting

ar·rive' v. **1** reach one's destination **2** come —**ar·riv'al** n.

ar'ro·gant a. haughty; overbearing —**ar'ro·gance** n.

ar'ro·gate v. seize arrogantly

ar'row n. **1** pointed shaft shot from a bow **2** sign (→) to show direction

ar'row·head' n. pointed tip of an arrow

ar'row·root' n. starch from a tropical plant root

ar·roy'o n., pl. **-os 1** dry gully **2** stream

ar'se·nal n. place for making or storing weapons

ar'se·nic' n. silvery-white, poisonous chemical element

ar'son n. crime of purposely setting fire to property —**ar'son·ist** n.

art n. **1** skill; craft **2** aesthetic work, as painting, sculpture, music, etc. **3** pl. academic studies **4** cunning; wile —v. [Ar.] form of ARE: used with *thou*

art dec·o' n. decorative style of the 1920's and 1930's

ar·te'ri·o·scle·ro'sis (-tir'ē-) n. hardening of the arteries

ar'ter·y n., pl. **-ies 1** tube carrying blood from the heart **2** a main road —**ar·te'ri·al** (-tir'ē-) a.

ar·te'sian well (-tē'zhən) n. deep well with water forced up by underground water pressure

art'ful a. **1** skillful; clever **2** crafty; cunning

ar·thri'tis n. inflammation of joints —**ar·thrit'ic** a.

ar'thro·pod' n. invertebrate animal with jointed legs and segmented body

ar'thro·scope' n. surgical device for use inside a joint —**ar'thro·scop'ic** a.

ar'ti·choke' n. **1** thistlelike plant **2** its flower head, cooked as a vegetable

ar'ti·cle n. **1** single item **2** separate piece of writing, as in a magazine **3** section of a document **4** any of the words *a*, *an*, or *the*

ar·tic'u·late (-lāt'; a.: -lət) v. **1** speak clearly **2** join —a. **1** clear in speech **2** jointed: usually **ar·tic'u·lat'ed** —**ar·tic'u·la'tion** n.

ar'ti·fact' n. any object made by human work

ar'ti·fice (-fis) n. **1** trick or trickery **2** clever skill

ar'ti·fi'cial a. **1** made by man; not natural **2** not genuine; affected —**ar'ti·fi'ci·al'i·ty** n.

ar·til'ler·y n. **1** mounted guns, as cannon **2** military branch using these

ar'ti·san (-zən) n. skilled craftsman

art'ist n. person with skill, esp. in any of the fine arts

ar·tis'tic *a.* 1 of art or artists 2 skillful —**art'ist·ry** *n.*

art'less *a.* 1 unskillful 2 simple; natural

art'y *a.* **-i·er, -i·est** [Col.] affectedly artistic: also **art'sy, -si·er, -si·est**

as *adv.* 1 equally 2 for instance —*con.* 1 in the way that 2 while 3 because 4 though —*pron. that* —*prep.* in the role of —**as for** (or **to**) concerning —**as is** [Col.] just as it is, as damaged merchandise —**as of** on or up to (a certain time)

as·bes'tos *n.* fibrous mineral used in fireproofing

as·cend' (-send') *v.* go up; climb —**as·cen'sion** *n.*

as·cend'an·cy, as·cend'en·cy *n.* domination —**as·cend'ant, as·cend'ent** *a.*

as·cent' *n.* 1 an ascending 2 upward slope

as·cer'tain' *v.* find out with certainty

as·cet'ic (-set'-) *a.* self-denying —*n.* one who denies pleasures to himself or herself —**as·cet'i·cism'** *n.*

a·scor'bic acid *n.* vitamin C

as'cot *n.* scarflike necktie

as·cribe' *v.* assign or attribute —**as·crip'tion** *n.*

a·sep'tic (ā-) *a.* free from disease germs

a·sex'u·al (ā-) *a.* sexless

ash *n.* 1 often *pl.* grayish powder left from something burned 2 shade tree —**ash'en** *a.* —**ash'y** *a.*

a·shamed' *a.* feeling shame

a·shore' *adv.,a.* to or on shore

ash'tray' *n.* container for smokers' tobacco ashes: also **ash tray**

A'sian (zhən) *n.,a.* (native) of the continent of Asia: also, now less preferred, **A'si·at'ic** (-zhē·at'-)

a·side' *adv.* 1 on or to one side 2 away 3 apart —*n.* an actor's words spoken aside —**aside from** except for

as'i·nine' (-nīn') *a.* stupid; silly —**as'i·nin'i·ty** (-nin'-) *n.*

ask *v.* 1 call for an answer to 2 inquire of or about 3 request 4 invite

a·skance' *adv.* 1 sideways 2 with suspicion

a·skew' (-skyōō') *adv.,a.* awry

a·slant' *adv.,a.* on a slant —*prep.* slantingly across

a·sleep' *a.* 1 sleeping 2 numb —*adv.* into sleep

a·so'cial (ā-) *a.* not social; avoiding others

asp *n.* poisonous snake

as·par'a·gus *n.* plant with edible green shoots

as'par·tame' *n.* an artificial, low-calorie sweetener

as'pect' *n.* 1 look or appearance 2 side or facet

as'pen *n.* poplar tree with fluttering leaves

as·per'i·ty *n., pl.* **-ties** harshness; sharpness

as·per'sion *n.* a slur; slander

as'phalt' *n.* tarlike substance used for paving, etc.

as'pho·del' *n.* plant like a lily, with white or yellow flowers

as·phyx'i·ate' (-fik'sē-) *v.* overcome by cutting down oxygen in the blood —**as·phyx'i·a'tion** *n.*

as'pic' *n.* jelly of meat juice, tomato juice, etc.

as'pi·ra'tion *n.* ambition

as'pi·ra'tor *n.* apparatus using suction to remove air, fluids, etc.

as·pire' *v.* be ambitious (*to*) —**as'pi·rant** *n.* —**as·pir'ing** *a.*

as'pi·rin' *n.* drug that relieves pain or fever

ass *n.* 1 donkey 2 fool

as·sail' *v.* attack

as·sail'ant *n.* attacker

as·sas'sin *n.* murderer

as·sas'si·nate' *v.* murder, esp. for political reasons —**as·sas'si·na'tion** *n.*

as·sault' (-sôlt') *n., v.* attack

assault and battery *n. Law* the carrying out of threatened physical harm

as'say' *n., v.* test; attempt

as·sem'ble *v.* 1 gather in a group 2 put together —**as·sem'blage** (-blij') *n.*

as·sem'bly *n., pl.* **-blies** 1 an assembling 2 group 3 [A-] legislative body

as·sem'bly·man *n., pl.* **-men** member of a legislative assembly

as·sent' *v., n.* consent

as·sert' *v.* 1 declare 2 defend, as rights —**as·ser'tion** *n.* —**as·ser'tive** *a.*

as·sess' *v.* 1 set a value on for taxes 2 impose a fine, tax, etc. —**as·sess'ment** *n.* —**as·ses'sor** *n.*

as'set *n.* 1 valuable thing 2 *pl.* property, cash, etc.

as·sev'er·ate' *v.* declare

as·sid'u·ous (-sij'ŏō-) *a.* diligent

as·sign' *v.* 1 designate 2 appoint 3 allot; give —**as·sign'ment** *n.*

as'sig·na'tion n. lovers' secret meeting

as·sim'i·late' v. merge; absorb —**as·sim'i·la'tion** n.

as·sist' v. 1 help; aid —**as·sist'ance** n. —**as·sist'ant** a., n.

as·so'ci·ate' (-āt'; n., a.: -ət) v. 1 join 2 connect in the mind 3 join (with) as a partner, etc. — n. partner, colleague, etc. —a. associated —**as·so'ci·a'tion** n.

as'so·nance n. likeness of sound

as·sort'ed a. 1 miscellaneous 2 sorted

as·sort'ment n. variety

as·suage' (-swāj') v. ease (pain, hunger, etc.)

as·sume' v. 1 take on (a role, look, etc.) 2 undertake 3 take for granted 4 pretend to have —**as·sump'tion** n.

as·sure' v. 1 make sure; convince 2 give confidence to 3 promise 4 guarantee —**as·sur'ance** n. —**as·sured'** a.

as'ter n. daisylike flower

as'ter·isk' n. sign (*) used to mark footnotes, etc.

a·stern' adv. at or toward the rear of a ship

as'ter·oid' n. any of the small planets between Mars and Jupiter

asth'ma (az'-) n. chronic disorder characterized by coughing, hard breathing, etc. —**asth·mat'ic** a.

a·stig'ma·tism' n. eye defect that keeps light rays from focusing to one point

a·stir' adv., a. in motion

as·ton'ish v. fill with sudden surprise —**as·ton'ish·ing** a. —**as·ton'ish·ment** n.

as·tound' v. astonish greatly —**as·tound'ing** a.

a·strad'dle adv. in a straddling position

as'tra·khan (-kən) n. curled fur from young lamb pelts

as'tral a. of, from, or like the stars

a·stray' adv., a. off the right path

a·stride' adv., prep. with a leg on either side (of)

as·trin'gent n., a. (substance) contracting body tissue and blood vessels

as·trol'o·gy n. pseudo science of effect of stars, etc. on human affairs —**as·trol'o·ger** n. —**as'tro·log'i·cal** a.

as'tro·naut' n. traveler in outer space

as'tro·nau'tics n. science of spacecraft and space travel —**as'tro·nau'ti·cal** a.

as·tron'o·mi·cal a. 1 of or in astronomy 2 huge, as numbers Also **as'tro·nom'ic**

as·tron'o·my n. science of the stars, planets, etc. —**as·tron'o·mer** n.

as·tute' a. shrewd; keen

a·sun'der adv. 1 into parts or pieces 2 apart or separate

a·sy'lum n. 1 place of safety 2 institution for the mentally ill, aged, etc.

a·sym'me·try (ā sim'-) n. lack of symmetry —**a·sym·met'ri·cal** a.

at prep. 1 on; in; near 2 to or toward 3 busy with 4 in the state of 5 because of

at'a·vism' n. a throwback

ate v. pt. of EAT

-ate suf. 1 make, become, or form 2 to treat with 3 of or like

a'the·ism' n. belief that there is no God —**a'the·ist** n. —**a'the·is'tic** a.

a·thirst' a. eager

ath'lete' n. one skilled at sports requiring strength, speed, etc. —**ath·let'ic** a. —**ath·let'ics** n.pl.

athlete's foot n. ringworm of the feet

a·thwart' prep., adv. 1 across 2 against

a·tin'gle a. tingling

at'las n. book of maps

at'mos·phere' (-fir') n. 1 the air surrounding the earth 2 general feeling or spirit 3 [Col.] interesting effect produced by decoration, etc. —**at'mos·pher'ic** a.

at·oll' (a'tôl') n. coral island surrounding a lagoon

at'om n. smallest particle of a chemical element, made up of electrons, protons, etc. —**a·tom'ic** a.

atomic (or atom) bomb n. bomb whose immense power derives from nuclear fission

atomic energy n. energy released from an atom in nuclear reactions

at'om·iz'er n. device for spraying liquid in a mist

a·to·nal'i·ty (ā'-) n. Mus. organization of tones without relation to a key —**a·ton'al** a.

a·tone' v. make amends (for) —**a·tone'ment** n.

a·top' adv., prep. on the top (of)

a'tri·um n. hall or lobby rising up through several stories

a·tro'cious (-shəs) a. 1 cruel or evil 2 very bad —**a·troc'i·ty**

(-träs'-) n., pl. -ties

at'ro·phy (-fē; v.: also -fī') v. -phied, -phy·ing waste away or shrink up —n. an atrophying

at'ro·pine' (-pēn) n. alkaloid used to relieve spasms

at·tach' v. 1 fasten; join 2 tie by devotion 3 seize by legal order —at·tach'ment n.

at·ta·ché' (-shā') n. member of a diplomatic staff

at·tack' v. 1 to fight or work against 2 undertake vigorously —n. 1 an attacking 2 fit of illness

at·tain' v. 1 to gain; achieve 2 arrive at —at·tain'a·ble a. —at·tain'ment n.

at'tar (-ər) n. perfume made from flower petals

at·tempt' v., n. try

at·tend' v. 1 be present at 2 pay attention 3 go with —attend to take care of —at·tend'ant n.

at·tend'ance n. 1 at attending 2 number present

at·ten'tion n. 1 a giving heed 2 heed; notice 3 pl. kind acts —at·ten'tive a.

at·ten'u·ate' v. thin out; weaken —at·ten'u·a'tion n.

at·test' v. 1 declare to be true 2 be proof of

at'tic n. space just below the roof; garret

at·tire' v. clothe; dress up —n. clothes

at'ti·tude' n. 1 bodily posture 2 way of looking at things, or manner

at·tor'ney (-tur'-) n., pl. -neys lawyer: also attorney at law

attorney general n. chief law officer of a government

at·tract' v. 1 draw to itself 2 make notice or like one —at·trac'tion n. —at·trac'tive a.

at·trib'ute (ə trib'yoot; n.: a'trə byoot') v. think of as belonging or owing (to) —n. characteristic —at·trib'ut·a·ble a. —at'tri·bu'tion n.

at·tri'tion (-trish'ən) n. a wearing down bit by bit

at·tune' v. bring into harmony or agreement

a·typ'i·cal (ā-) a. not typical

au'burn n. red-brown

auc'tion n. public sale in which items go to the highest bidder —v. sell at auction —auc'tion·eer' n., v.

au·da'cious (-shəs) a. 1 bold; reckless 2 insolent —au·dac'i·ty (-das'-) n.

au'di·ble a. loud enough to be heard —au'di·bly adv.

au'di·ence n. 1 group seeing or hearing a play, concert, radio or TV show, etc. 2 formal interview

au'di·o' a. of the sound portion of a TV broadcast

au'di·o·phile' n. devotee of hi-fi sound reproduction

au'di·o·vis'u·al a. involving both hearing and sight

au'dit v. examine and check (accounts) —n. an auditing —au'di·tor n.

au·di'tion n. a hearing to try out a singer, actor, etc. —v. try out in an audition

au'di·to'ri·um n. a hall for speeches, concerts, etc.

au'di·to'ry a. of hearing

au'ger (-gər) n. tool for boring holes in wood

aught (ôt) n. 1 anything 2 zero

aug·ment' v. increase —aug'men·ta'tion n.

au gra·tin (ō grät'n) a. with browned cheese crust

au'gur (-gər) v. foretell —augur ill (or well) be a bad (or good) omen —au'gu·ry (-gyə rē) n.

Au'gust n. eighth month

au·gust' a. imposing

au jus (ō zhoo') a. in its natural gravy

auk n. diving seabird

aunt (ant, änt) n. 1 sister of one's parent 2 uncle's wife

au'ra n. radiance or air about a person or thing

au'ral a. of hearing

au're·ole' n. halo

au re·voir (ō'rə vwär') n. good-bye

au'ri·cle n. outer part of the ear

au·ro'ra n. dawn

aurora bo·re·al'is (bôr'ē-) n. luminous bands in the northern night sky

aus'pi·ces (-pə siz) n.pl. patronage

aus·pi'cious (-pish'əs) a. favorable; of good omen —aus·pi'cious·ly adv.

aus·tere' (ô stir') a. 1 strict 2 very plain; severe —aus·ter'i·ty (ô ster'-) n., pl. -ties

Aus·tral'i·an n., a. (native) of the continent or country of Australia

au·then'tic a. true, real, genuine, etc. —au·then·tic'i·ty (-tis'-) n.

au·then'ti·cate' v. 1 make valid 2 verify 3 prove to be genuine —au·then'ti·ca'tion n.

au·thor *n.* writer or originator —**au'thor·ship'** *n.*

au·thor·i·tar·i·an *a.* enforcing or favoring strict obedience to authority

au·thor·i·ta·tive *a.* having or showing authority

au·thor·i·ty *n., pl.* **-ties** 1 power to command 2 *pl.* persons with such power 3 expert; reliable source

au·thor·ize' *v.* 1 give official approval to 2 empower —**au'thor·i·za'tion** *n.*

au·tism' *n.* mental state marked by disregard of external reality —**au·tis'tic** *a.*

au·to *n., pl.* **-tos** automobile

auto- *pref.* self

au·to·bi·og·ra·phy *n., pl.* **-phies** one's own life story written by oneself —**au'to·bi'o·graph'i·cal** *a.*

au·to·crat' *n.* ruler with unlimited power —**au·toc'ra·cy** *n.* —**au'to·crat'ic** *a.*

au·to·di'dact *n.* person who is self-taught

au'to·graph' *n.* signature —*v.* write one's signature on

au·to·mat' *n.* restaurant dispensing food from coin-operated compartments

au'to·mate' *v.* convert to automation

au·to·mat'ic *a.* 1 done without conscious effort 2 operating by itself —**au'to·mat'i·cal·ly** *adv.*

automatic pilot *n.* gyroscopic instrument for piloting an aircraft, missile, etc.: also **au'to·pi'lot**

au·to·ma'tion *n.* automatic system of manufacture, as by electronic devices

au·tom'a·ton' *n.* robot

au·to·mo·bile' *n.* passenger vehicle propelled by an engine, for use on streets and roads —**au'to·mo'tive** *a.*

au·to·nom'ic *a.* of the nervous system regulating the heart, lungs, etc.

au·ton'o·my *n.* self-government —**au·ton'o·mous** *a.*

au'top·sy *n., pl.* **-sies** examination of a corpse to find cause of death

au·tumn (ôt'əm) *n.* season after summer, when leaves fall —**au·tum'nal** (ô tum'nəl) *a.*

aux·il·ia·ry (ôg zil'yə rē) *a.* 1 helping 2 subsidiary —*n., pl.* **-ries** auxiliary group, etc.

auxiliary verb *v.* verb used to help form tenses, etc., as *will, shall, have, do, be,* etc.

a·vail' *v.* be of use or help (to) —*n.* use or help —**avail oneself of** make use of

a·vail'a·ble *a.* that can be got or had —**a·vail'a·bil'i·ty** *n.*

av'a·lanche' *n.* great fall of rock, snow, etc. down a hill

a·vant-garde' (ä'vänt-gärd') *n.* vanguard

av'a·rice' *n.* greed for money —**av'a·ri'cious** (-rish'əs) *a.*

a·venge' *v.* get revenge for —**a·veng'er** *n.*

av'e·nue' *n.* 1 street 2 way to something; approach

a·ver' (-vur') *v.* **a·verred', a·ver'-ring** declare to be true

av'er·age *n.* 1 sum divided by the number of quantities added 2 usual kind, amount, etc. —*a.* being the average —*v.* 1 figure the average of 2 do on the average —**on the average** as an average amount, rate, etc.

a·verse' *a.* unwilling

a·ver'sion *n.* dislike

a·vert' *v.* 1 turn away 2 prevent

a'vi·ar·y (ä'vē-) *n., pl.* **-ies** large cage for many birds

a'vi·a'tion *n.* science or work of flying airplanes —**a'vi·a'tor** *n.*

av'id *a.* eager or greedy

av·o·ca'do (-kä'-) *n., pl.* **-dos** thick-skinned tropical fruit with buttery flesh

av·o·ca'tion (-kā'-) *n.* hobby

a·void' *v.* keep away from; shun —**a·void'a·ble** *a.* —**a·void'ance** *n.*

av·oir·du·pois (av'ər də poiz') *n.* weight system in which 16 oz. = 1 lb.

a·vow' *v.* declare openly; admit —**a·vow'al** *n.*

a·wait' *v.* wait for

a·wake' *v.* **a·woke'** or **a·waked', a·waked'** or **a·wok'en, a·wak'ing** rouse from sleep —*a.* 1 not asleep 2 alert

a·wak'en *v.* rouse; awake —**a·wak'en·ing** *n., a.*

a·ward' *v.* give after judging —*n.* 1 decision, as by judges 2 prize

a·ware' *a.* conscious; knowing —**a·ware'ness** *n.*

a·way' *adv.* 1 to another place 2 aside 3 from one's keeping —*a.* 1 absent 2 at a distance —**do away with** 1 get rid of 2 kill

awe *n.* reverent fear and wonder —*v.* inspire awe in —**awe'struck'** or, **awe'strick'en** *a.*

awe'some *a.* causing awe

aw'ful *a.* 1 terrifying; dreadful 2 bad —*adv.* [Col.] very —**aw'ful·ly** *adv.*

a·while' *adv.* for a short time

awk'ward *a.* 1 clumsy 2 uncomfortable 3 embarrassing —**awk'ward·ly** *adv.*

awl *n.* pointed tool for making holes in wood, etc.

awn *n.* bristly fibers on a head of barley, oats, etc.

awn'ing *n.* overhanging shade of canvas, metal, etc.

a·wry (ə rī') *adv., a.* 1 with a twist to a side 2 amiss

ax, axe *n., pl.* **ax'es** tool for chopping wood, etc.

ax'i·om *n.* an evident truth — **ax'i·o·mat'ic** *a.*

ax'is *n., pl.* **ax'es** (-ēz) straight line around which a thing rotates —**ax'i·al** *a.*

ax'le *n.* rod on which a wheel revolves

aye (ā) *adv.* [Ar.] always

aye, ay (ī) *adv.* 1 yes

a·za'lea (-zāl'yə) *n.* shrub with brightly colored flowers

az'ure (azh'-) *a., n.* sky blue

B

baa (bä) *v., n.* bleat

bab'ble *v.* 1 talk in a foolish or jumbled way 2 murmur —*n.* babbling talk or sound —**bab'bler** *n.*

babe *n.* baby

ba·boon' *n.* ape with doglike snout

ba·bush'ka *n.* scarf worn on the head

ba'by *n., pl.* **-bies** very young child; infant —*a.* 1 of, for, or like a baby 2 small or young — *v.* **-bied, -by·ing** pamper —**ba'by·hood'** *n.* —**ba'by·ish** *a.*

ba'by-sit' *v.* **-sat', -sit'ting** take care of children when parents are away —**baby sitter** *n.*

bac·ca·lau're·ate (-lôr'ē ət) *n.* 1 bachelor's degree 2 a talk to graduating class

bac·cha·nal (bak'ə nal') *n.* drunken orgy —**bac·cha·na'li·an** (-nā'-) *a.*

bach'e·lor *n.* unmarried man — **bach'e·lor·hood'** *n.*

Bachelor of Arts (or **Science,** etc.) *n.* four-year college degree

ba·cil'lus (-sil'-) *n., pl.* **-li** (-ī) kind of bacteria

back *n.* 1 rear or hind part 2

backbone 3 the reverse 4 football player behind the line —*a.* 1 at the rear 2 of the past 3 backward —*adv.* 1 at or to the rear 2 to a former time, place, etc. 3 in return —*v.* 1 move backward 2 support 3 provide a back for —**back down** retract an opinion, etc. —**back'er** *n.* —**back'ing** *n.*

back'bite' *v.* to slander

back'board' *n.* Basketball board behind the basket

back'bone' *n.* 1 spinal column 2 courage; firmness

back'break'ing *a.* very tiring

back'drop' *n.* curtain at the back of a stage

back'field' *n.* Football players behind the line

back'fire' *n.* faulty ignition in an engine —*v.* 1 have a backfire 2 go awry, as plans

back·gam'mon *n.* game played on a special board

back'ground' *n.* 1 the part behind, more distant, etc. 2 past events, causes, etc.

back'hand' *n.* a backhanded stroke, as in tennis

back'hand'ed *a.* 1 with the back of the hand forward 2 insincere

back'lash' *n.* sharp reaction

back'log' *n.* piling up, as of work to be done

back'pack' *n.* knapsack —*v.* hike wearing a backpack

back'side' *n.* 1 back part 2 rump

back'slide' *v.* to fall back in morals, religious faith, etc.

back'stage' *adv.* in theater dressing rooms, etc.

back'stroke' *n.* swimming stroke made while lying face upward

back talk *n.* [Col.] insolence

back'track' *v.* to retreat

back'ward *adv.* 1 toward the back 2 with the back foremost 3 into the past Also **back'wards** —*a.* 1 turned to the rear or away 2 shy 3 retarded — **back'ward·ness** *n.*

back'woods' *n.pl.* remote, wooded areas —**back'woods'man** *n., pl.* **-men**

ba'con *n.* cured meat from hog's back or sides

bac·te'ri·a *n.pl., sing.* **-ri·um** microorganisms causing diseases, fermentation, etc. —**bac·te'ri·al** *a.*

bac·te'ri·ol'o·gy *n.* study of bacteria

bad *a.* **worse, worst** 1 not good

2 spoiled 3 incorrect 4 wicked 5 severe —*adv.* [Col.] badly —*n.* anything bad —**bad'ly** *adv.* — **bad'ness** *n.*

bade (bad) *v.* pt. of BID (*v.* 1 & 2)

badge *n.* pin or emblem worn to show rank, membership, etc.

badg'er *n.* burrowing animal — *v.* to nag; pester

bad'min·ton *n.* game using rackets and a feathered cork

bad'-tem'pered *a.* irritable

baf'fle *v.* puzzle; bewilder —*n.* deflecting screen —**baf'fling** *a.*

bag *n.* 1 container made of fabric, paper, etc. 2 suitcase 3 purse —*v.* **bagged', bag'ging** 1 hang loosely 2 kill or capture 3 put into a bag —**in the bag** [Sl.] certain —**bag'gy** *a.*

bag·a·telle' *n.* a trifle

ba'gel (-gal) *n.* hard bread roll like a small doughnut

bag'gage *n.* luggage

bag'pipe' *n.* musical instrument with a bag from which air is forced into pipes: also **bag'pipes'** *n.pl.*

bah (bä) *int.* shout of scorn

bail *n.* money left as security to free a prisoner until trial —*v.* 1 get freed by giving bail 2 dip out (water) from (a boat) —**bail out** to parachute

bail'iff *n.* 1 court officer guarding prisoners and jurors 2 sheriff's assistant

bail'i·wick (bal'ē-) *n.* one's field of interest or authority

bait *v.* 1 torment, as by insults 2 put food on (a hook, etc.) as a lure —*n.* anything used as a lure

bake *v.* 1 cook by dry heat in an oven 2 harden by heat —**bak'er** *n.*

bak'er·y *n., pl.* **-ies** place where bread, etc. is baked

baking powder *n.* leavening powder

baking soda *n.* sodium bicarbonate, powder used as leavening and as an antacid

bal'ance *n.* 1 instrument for weighing, with two pans 2 equilibrium 3 harmonious proportion 4 equality of or difference between credits and debits 5 remainder —*v.* 1 compare 2 offset; counteract 3 put, keep, or be in equilibrium 4 be equal 5 sum up or equalize the debits and credits of (an account) —**in the balance** not yet settled

bal'co·ny *n., pl.* **-nies** 1 platform projecting from an upper story 2 tier of theater seats above main floor

bald *a.* 1 lacking hair on the head 2 plain and frank —**bald'ness** *n.*

bal'der·dash' (bôl'-) *n.* nonsense

bald'faced' *a.* shameless

bale *n.* large bundle, as of raw cotton —*v.* make into bales

bale'ful *a.* harmful; evil

balk *v.* 1 stop and refuse to move 2 obstruct —*n.* 1 hindrance; obstruction 2 *Baseball* illegal motion by pitcher — **balk'y** *a.*, **-i·er, -i·est**

ball *n.* 1 round object; sphere 2 round or oval object used in games 3 formal social dance 4 *Baseball* pitched baseball that is not a strike 5 [Sl.] good time — *v.* form into a ball —**be on the ball** [Sl.] be alert

bal'lad *n.* 1 popular love song 2 folk song or poem telling a story

bal'last (-ast) *n.* heavy matter put in a ship, etc. to keep it steady —*v.* to furnish with ballast

ball bearing *n.* 1 bearing in which the parts turn on rolling metal balls 2 one of these balls

bal'le·ri'na *n.* woman ballet dancer

bal·let (ba lā') *n.* intricate, formalized group dance

bal·lis'tics *n.* science of the motion of projectiles

bal·loon' *n.* bag that rises when filled with light gas —*v.* swell; expand

bal'lot *n.* 1 paper marked in voting 2 voting —*v.* to vote

ball'park' *n.* baseball stadium

ball'play'er *n.* baseball player

ball'point' (pen) *n.* pen with ink cartridge and small ball bearing for a point

ball'room' *n.* large room for social dances

bal'ly·hoo' *n.* exaggerated or sensational advertising or propaganda

balm (bäm) *n.* fragrant healing ointment or oil

balm'y *a.*, **-i·er, -i·est** soothing, mild, etc.

ba·lo'ney *n.* 1 bologna 2 [Sl.] nonsense

bal'sa (bôl'-) *n.* lightweight wood of a tropical tree

bal'sam (bôl'-) *n.* 1 aromatic resin 2 tree yielding it

bal'us·ter (bal'-) *n.* railing post

bal'us·trade' *n.* row of balusters supporting a rail

bam·boo' n. tropical grass with hollow, treelike stems

bam·boo'zle v. 1 trick 2 confuse

ban v. **banned**, **ban'ning** forbid —n. formal forbidding by authorities

ba·nal (bā'nal, bə nal')' a. trite —**ba·nal'i·ty** n., pl. **-ties**

ba·nan'a n. long tropical fruit with creamy flesh

band n. 1 strip of cloth, etc. as for binding 2 stripe 3 range of radio wave lengths 4 group of people 5 group of performing musicians —v. 1 mark or tie with a band 2 join

band'age n. cloth strip to bind an injury —v. bind with a bandage

Band'-Aid' trademark bandage of gauze and adhesive tape —n. [b- a-] such a bandage: also **band'aid'**

ban·dan'na, ban·dan'a n. large, colored handkerchief

ban'dit n. robber; brigand —**ban'dit·ry** n.

band'stand' n. (outdoor) platform for an orchestra

band'wag'on n. winning or popular side

ban'dy v. **-died**, **-dy·ing** toss or pass back and forth —a. curved outward —**ban'dy-leg'ged** a.

bane n. cause of harm or ruin —**bane'ful** a.

bang v., n. (make, or hit with a) loud noise

ban'gle n. bracelet

bangs n.pl. short hair worn across the forehead

ban'ish v. 1 to exile 2 dismiss —**ban'ish·ment** n.

ban'is·ter n. a handrail, held up by balusters, along a staircase

ban'jo n., pl. **-jos** or **-joes** stringed musical instrument with a circular body

bank n. 1 mound; heap 2 steep slope, as beside a river 3 row; tier 4 business handling savings, loans, etc. —v. 1 form a bank 2 put (money) in a bank 3 cover (a fire) to make last —**bank on** [Col.] rely on —**bank'er** n.

bank'roll' n. supply of money —v. [Col.] supply with money

bank'rupt' a. 1 legally declared unable to pay one's debts 2 lacking —n. bankrupt person —v. make bankrupt —**bank'rupt·cy** n.

ban'ner n. 1 flag 2 long strip of

cloth with writing, etc. —a. foremost; leading

banns n.pl. church notice of an upcoming marriage

ban'quet n. formal dinner

ban'shee n. Folklore wailing female spirit

ban'tam (-tam) n. breed of small chickens —a. small

ban'ter v. tease playfully —n. genial teasing

ban'yan (-yan) n. Asian fig tree with many trunks

bap'tism' n. rite of admission into a Christian church by dipping in or sprinkling with water —**bap·tis'mal** (-tiz'məl) a. —**bap'tize'** v.

bar n. 1 long, narrow piece of wood, metal, etc. 2 oblong piece, as of soap 3 obstruction 4 band or strip 5 law court 6 legal profession 7 counter or place for serving liquor 8 Mus. a measure or vertical line marking it off —v. **barred**, **bar'ring** 1 obstruct; close 2 oppose 3 exclude —prep. excluding

barb n. sharp, back-curving point —**barbed** a.

bar·bar'i·an (-ber'-) n. uncivilized person; savage —a. uncivilized —**bar·bar'ic** a.

bar'ba·rous a. 1 uncivilized 2 crude; coarse 3 brutal —**bar'ba·rism'** n.

bar'be·cue' n. 1 animal roasted whole over open fire 2 picnic at which such meat is served —v. 1 roast whole 2 broil in spicy sauce (**barbecue sauce**)

bar'ber n. one who cuts hair, shaves beards, etc.

bar·bi'tu·rate (-bich'ōō ət) n. drug used as a sedative

bard n. poet

bare a. 1 naked 2 exposed 3 empty 4 mere —v. uncover —**bare'foot', bare'foot'ed** a., adv. —**bare'head'ed** a., adv.

bare'back' adv., a. on a horse with no saddle

bare'-bones' a. simple; basic

bare'faced' a. shameless

bare'ly adv. only just

bar'gain (-gən) n. 1 agreement or contract 2 item bought at a favorable price —v. haggle —**bargain for** (or **on**) expect —**into** (or **in**) **the bargain** besides

barge n. flat-bottomed freight boar —v. enter abruptly (into)

bar'i·tone' (ber'ə-) n. male voice, or instrument, between tenor and bass

bar'i·um (ber'ē-) *n.* silver-white metallic element

bark *n.* 1 outside covering of trees 2 sharp cry of a dog 3 sailing vessel —*v.* 1 utter a bark 2 scrape off the skin of

bark'er *n.* announcer at a carnival sideshow

bar'ley *n.* cereal grain

bar'maid *n.* waitress in a bar

bar mitz'vah (-və) *n.* religious ceremony for a Jewish boy when he becomes thirteen years old

barn *n.* farm building for livestock, storage, etc. —**barn'yard'** *n.*

bar'na·cle *n.* shellfish that clings to ships, etc.

barn'storm' *v.* tour small towns, acting plays, etc.

ba·rom'e·ter *n.* instrument to measure atmospheric pressure —**bar'o·met'ric** *a.*

bar'on *n.* nobleman of lowest rank —**bar'on·ess** *n.fem.* —**ba·ro'ni·al** (-rō'-) *a.*

bar'on·et' *n.* Br. man with hereditary rank of honor

ba·roque' (-rōk') *a.* having elaborate decoration

bar'racks *n.pl.* building(s) for housing soldiers

bar'ra·cu'da (-kōō'-) *n., pl.* **-da** or **-das** fierce tropical fish

bar'rage (bə räzh') *n.* curtain of artillery fire

barred *a.* 1 having bars or stripes 2 closed off with bars 3 not allowed

bar'rel *n.* 1 round, wooden container with bulging sides 2 tube of a gun

bar'ren *a.* 1 sterile 2 unproductive

bar·rette' (bə ret') *n.* clasp for a girl's hair

bar'ri·cade' *n.* barrier for defense —*v.* block with a barricade

bar'ri·er *n.* fence, wall, or other obstruction

bar'ring *prep.* excepting

bar'ris·ter *n.* in England, courtroom lawyer

bar'room' *n.* room with a BAR (*n.* 7)

bar'row *n.* traylike frame for carrying loads

bar'tend'er *n.* person serving drinks at a BAR (*n.* 7)

bar'ter *v.* exchange (goods) —*n.* a bartering

ba·sal (bā'səl) *a.* basic

ba·salt (bə sôlt') *n.* dark volcanic rock

base *n.* 1 part that a thing rests on 2 basis 3 goal in some games 4 headquarters or a source of supply 5 substance reacting with an acid to form a salt —*v.* put on a base —*a.* 1 morally low 2 inferior —**base'ly** *adv.*

base'ball' *n.* 1 team game played with a bat and ball 2 the ball used

base'board' *n.* molding along the bottom of a wall

base'less *a.* unfounded

base'man *n., pl.* **-men** Baseball infielder at first, second, or third base

base'ment *n.* story just below the main floor

base on balls *n.* Baseball walk

base runner *n.* Baseball player at or trying to reach a base

bash *n.* [Col.] hit or attack hard

bash'ful *a.* socially timid; shy —**bash'ful·ly** *adv.*

ba'sic *a.* of or at the base; fundamental —**bas'i·cal·ly** *adv.*

bas'il (baz'-, bāz'-) *n.* an herb

ba·sil'i·ca *n.* ancient kind of church building

ba'sin *n.* 1 wide, shallow container for liquid 2 a sink 3 bay, cove, etc. 4 area drained by a river

ba'sis *n., pl.* **-ses'** (-sēz') 1 base or foundation 2 main constituent

bask *v.* warm oneself

bas'ket *n.* 1 container made of interwoven strips 2 goal in basketball

bas'ket·ball' *n.* 1 team game with raised open nets through which a large ball must be tossed 2 this ball

bas'-re·lief' (bä'-, bas'-) *n.* sculpture with figures projecting a little from the background

bass (bās) *n.* 1 lowest male singing voice 2 singer or instrument with low range

bass (bas) *n.* perchlike fish

bas'set *n.* short-legged hound

bas'si·net' *n.* baby's bed like a large basket

bas·soon' *n.* double-reed, bass woodwind instrument

bass vi·ol (vī'əl) *n.* double bass

bast *n.* plant fiber used for ropes, mats, etc.

bas'tard *n.* illegitimate child —*a.* 1 illegitimate 2 sham, not standard, etc. —**bas'tard·ize'** *v.*

baste *v.* 1 sew with loose, temporary stitches 2 moisten (a roast) with drippings, etc. —

bast'ing (-chən) n. 1 part of a fort that juts out 2 any strong defense

bas'tion (-chən) n. 1 part of a fort that juts out 2 any strong defense

bat n. 1 a club to hit a ball, as in baseball 2 nocturnal, mouse-like, flying mammal —v. **bat'ted**, **bat'ting** 1 hit as with a bat 2 [Col.] blink

batch n. quantity taken, made, etc. in one lot

bat'ed a. held in, as the breath in fear

bath n. 1 a washing of the body 2 water, etc. for bathing or soaking something 3 bathtub 4 bathroom

bathe (bāth) v. 1 give a bath to, or take a bath 2 put into a liquid 3 cover as with liquid — **bath'er** n.

bath'ing suit n. swimsuit

ba'thos' (bā'-) n. a shift from noble to trivial

bath'robe' n. loose robe worn to and from the bath

bath'room' n. room with a bath-tub, toilet, etc.

bath'tub' n. tub to bathe in

ba·tik' (-tēk') n. cloth with design dyed only on parts not coated with wax

ba·tiste' (-tēst') n. fine, thin cotton fabric

bat mitz'vah (bät-) n. religious ceremony for a Jewish girl similar to bar mitzvah: also **bas mitz'vah** (bäs-)

ba·ton' n. 1 stick used in leading an orchestra, etc. 2 staff serving as a symbol of office

bat·tal'ion n. subdivision of a regiment

bat'ten n. strip of wood —v. 1 fasten with battens 2 fatten; thrive

bat'ter v. 1 strike repeatedly 2 injure by hard use —n. 1 player at bat in baseball 2 mixture of flour, milk, etc. for making cakes

bat'ter·ing ram n. heavy beam, etc. to batter down gates, etc.

bat'ter·y n., pl. **-ies** 1 cell or cells providing electric current 2 set of artillery guns 3 pitcher and catcher in baseball 4 illegal beating of a person

bat'ting n. wadded fiber

bat'tle n., v. fight, esp. between armies —**bat'tler** n.

bat'tle-ax', bat'tle-axe' n. heavy ax formerly used as a weapon

bat'tle·field' n. place of battle: also **bat'tle·ground'**

bat'tle·ment n. low wall on a tower with open spaces for shooting

bat'tle·ship' n. large warship with big guns

bat'ty a. **-ti·er, -ti·est** [Sl.] crazy, odd, queer, etc.

bau'ble n. trinket

baud (bôd) n. the number of bits per second transmitted in a computer system

baux·ite (bôk'sīt') n. claylike aluminum ore

bawd'y a. **-i·er, -i·est** obscene — **bawd'i·ness** n.

bawl v. 1 to shout 2 to weep noisily —**bawl out** [Sl.] scold angrily

bay n. 1 wide inlet of a sea or lake 2 alcove 3 recess in a wall, as for a window (**bay window**) 4 laurel tree 5 a) reddish brown b) horse of this color —v. bark or howl in long, deep tones —**at bay** 1 with escape cut off 2 held off —**bring to bay** cut off escape of

bay'ber·ry n., pl. **-ries** 1 wax myrtle 2 its berry

bay'o·net' n. blade attached to a rifle barrel —v. to stab with a bayonet

bay·ou (bī'ōō') n. marshy inlet or outlet, as a lake

ba·zaar' (-zär') n. 1 Oriental market place 2 benefit sale for a club, etc.

ba·zoo'ka n. portable tubelike weapon for firing rockets

BB (shot) n. tiny metal shot for an air rifle (**BB gun**)

B.C. before Christ

be v. **was** or **were, been, be'ing** 1 exist; live 2 occur 3 remain; continue **Be** is also an important auxiliary verb

be- pref. 1 around 2 completely 3 away 4 about

beach n. stretch of sandy shore —v. ground (a boat)

beach'comb'er n. hobo living on a beach

beach'head' n. shore area taken by invading troops

bea'con n. guiding light

bead n. 1 small ball of glass, etc., pierced for stringing 2 pl. string of beads 3 drop or bubble —**draw a bead on** take careful aim at —**bead'ed** a. —**bead'y** a.

bea'gle n. small, short-legged hound

beak n. 1 bird's bill 2 any beak-like mouth part

beak'er n. broad glass container

beam n. 1 long, thick piece of timber, etc. 2 ship's greatest breadth 3 shaft of light 4 radiant look or smile 5 guiding radio signal —v. 1 radiate in a beam 2 smile warmly

bean n. 1 edible seed of some plants 2 pod of these

bear n. 1 large, heavy mammal with shaggy fur 2 rough, rude person —v. **bore, borne** or **born, bear'ing** 1 carry 2 have or show 3 give birth to 4 produce 5 permit 6 endure —**bear down** exert pressure —**bear on** relate to —**bear out** confirm —**bear up** endure —**bear with** tolerate —**bear'a-ble** a. —**bear'er** n.

beard n. 1 hair on a man's face 2 awn —**beard'ed** a.

bear'ing n. 1 way one carries oneself 2 relative position or direction 3 relation 4 ball, roller, etc. on which something turns or slides

bear'ish a. 1 bearlike 2 causing a drop in stock exchange prices

beast n. 1 any large four-footed animal 2 brutal, gross person —**beast'ly** a.

beat v. **beat, beat'en, beat'ing** 1 strike repeatedly 2 punish by striking 3 mix by stirring 4 defeat 5 throb 6 flap (wings) 7 make (a path) by tramping —n. 1 a throbbing 2 habitual route 3 unit of musical rhythm —a. [Col.] tired —**beat back** (or **off**) drive back —**beat it!** [Sl.] go away! —**beat up** (on) [Sl.] thrash —**beat'er** n.

be·a·tif'ic a. blissful

be·at'i·fy' v. **-fied', -fy'ing** R.C.Ch. declare one who has died to be among the blessed in heaven

be·at'i·tude' n. bliss

beau n. pl. **beaus** or **beaux** (bōz) woman's lover

beau·ti·cian (-tish'ən) n. one who works styling hair, etc.

beau'ti·ful (byōo'-) a. having beauty: also **beau'te·ous** —**beau'ti·ful·ly** adv.

beau'ti·fy' v. **-fied', -fy'ing** make beautiful

beau'ty n. pl. **-ties** 1 pleasing quality as in looks, sound, etc. 2 person or thing of beauty

bea'ver n. 1 amphibious animal with webbed hind feet 2 its brown fur

be·cause' con. for the reason that —**because of** on account of

beck'on v. call by gesture

be·cloud' v. to obscure

be·come' v. **-came', -come', -com'ing** 1 come to be 2 suit —**become of** happen to

be·com'ing a. right or suitable; attractive

bed n. 1 piece of furniture to sleep on 2 plot of soil for plants 3 flat bottom or foundation 4 layer —v. **bed'ded, bed'ding** put or go to bed

bed'bug' n. small, wingless, biting insect

bed'clothes' n.pl. bedsheets, blankets, etc.

bed'ding n. mattresses and bedclothes

be·deck' v. adorn

be·dev'il v. to torment or worry —**be·dev'il·ment** n.

bed'fel'low n. 1 person who shares one's bed 2 any associate

bed'lam (-ləm) n. noisy confusion

Bed·ou·in' (-ŌŌ-) n. Arab nomad

bed'pan' n. shallow pan used as a toilet by one bedridden

be·drag'gled a. wet and dirty; messy

bed'rid'den a. confined to bed, as by long illness

bed'rock' n. 1 solid rock under soil 2 base or bottom

bed'room' n. sleeping room

bed'sore' n. sore on a bedridden person

bed'spread' n. ornamental cover for a bed

bed'spring' n. framework of springs under a mattress

bed'stead' n. frame of a bed

bee n. 1 winged insect that makes honey 2 meeting of group, as to work together

beech n. tree with gray bark and beechnuts

beech'nut' n. small, edible, three-cornered nut of the beech

beef n. pl. **beeves** or **beefs** 1 cow, bull, or steer 2 its meat —v. [Sl.] complain

beef'y a. **-i·er, -i·est** brawny

bee'hive' n. hive for bees

bee'line' n. straight course

been v. pp. of BE

beep n. brief, shrill sound of a horn or electronic signal —v. make this sound

beep'er n. portable electronic device for contacting people

beer n. mildly alcoholic drink brewed from malt, hops, etc.

bees'wax' n. wax from bees,

used in their honeycomb

beet *n.* plant with edible red or white root

bee′tle *n.* insect with hard front wings —*v.* jut out

be·fall′ *v.* -**fell′**, -**fall′en**, -**fall′ing** happen (to)

be·fit′ *v.* -**fit′ted**, -**fit′ting** be fitting for

be·fore′ *adv.* 1 in front 2 till now 3 earlier —*prep.* 1 ahead of 2 in sight of 3 earlier than 4 rather than —*con.* earlier or sooner than

be·fore′hand *adv., a.* ahead of time

be·friend′ *v.* be a friend to

be·fud′dle *v.* confuse

beg *v.* **begged**, **beg′ging** 1 ask for (alms) 2 entreat —**go begging** be unwanted

be·gat′ *v.* [Ar.] pt. of BEGET

be·get′ *v.* -**got′**, -**got′ten** or -**got′**, -**get′ting** 1 to father 2 to cause

beg′gar *n.* 1 one who lives by begging 2 very poor person —*v.* 1 make a beggar of 2 make seem useless

beg′gar·ly *a.* poor; mean

be·gin′ *v.* -**gan′**, -**gun′**, -**gin′ning** 1 start 2 originate —**be·gin′ner** *n.*

be·gin′ning *n.* 1 start 2 origin 3 first part

be·gone′ *int., v.* go away

be·gon′ia *n.* plant with showy flowers

be·grudge′ *v.* 1 envy the possession of 2 give reluctantly —**be·grudg′ing·ly** *adv.*

be·guile′ (-gīl′) *v.* 1 deceive or trick 2 charm 3 pass (time) pleasantly

be·half′ *n.* support, side, etc. —**in (or on) behalf of** in the interest of

be·have′ *v.* 1 conduct (oneself), esp. properly 2 act

be·hav′ior *n.* conduct —**be·hav′ior·al** *a.*

be·head′ *v.* cut off the head of

be·he′moth (bē hē′-) *n.* huge animal

be·hest′ *n.* a command

be·hind′ *adv.* 1 in the rear 2 slow; late 3 to the back —*prep.* 1 in back of 2 later or slower than 3 supporting —*a.* 1 that follows 2 in arrears

be·hold′ *v.* -**held′**, -**hold′ing** see; look at —*int.* look! see!

be·hold′en *a.* indebted

be·hoove′ *v.* be necessary or fitting (for)

beige (bāzh) *n.* grayish tan

be′ing *n.* 1 existence; life 2 one that lives

be·la′bor *v.* spend too much time on

be·lat′ed *a.* too late

belch *v.* 1 expel stomach gas orally 2 eject with force —*n.* a belching

be·lea′guer (-lē′gər) *v.* 1 besiege 2 beset

bel′fry (-frē) *n., pl.* -**fries** bell tower

be·lie′ *v.* -**lied′**, -**ly′ing** 1 misrepresent 2 prove false

be·lief′ *n.* 1 conviction; faith 2 trust 3 opinion

be·lieve′ *v.* 1 take as true 2 have faith (in) 3 suppose; guess —**be·liev′a·ble** *a.* —**be·liev′er** *n.*

be·lit′tle *v.* make seem little or unimportant

bell *n.* 1 hollow metal object that rings when struck 2 sound of a bell

bel′la·don′na *n.* 1 poisonous plant yielding a drug that relieves spasms 2 the drug

belle (bel) *n.* pretty girl

bell′hop′ *n.* one who does errands at a hotel: also **bell′boy**

bel′li·cose′ *a.* quarrelsome —**bel′li·cos′i·ty** (-käs′-) *n.*

bel·lig′er·ent (bə lij′-) *a.* warlike —*n.* nation or person at war —**bel·lig′er·ence** *n.*

bel′low *v., n.* roar or shout

bel′lows *n., pl.* -**lows** collapsible device for producing a stream of air

bell pepper *n.* large, sweet red pepper

bell′weth′er *n.* 1 male sheep that leads a flock 2 indicator of a trend, style, etc.

bel′ly *n., pl.* -**lies** 1 abdomen 2 stomach —*v.* -**lied**, -**ly·ing** to bulge

bel′ly·ache′ *n.* pain in the belly —*v.* [Sl.] complain

be·long′ *v.* have a proper place —**belong to** 1 be a part of 2 be owned by 3 be a member of

be·long′ings *n.pl.* possessions

be·lov′ed (-luv′əd, -luvd′) *a., n.* dearly loved (person)

be·low′ *adv.* 1 in or to a lower place; beneath —*prep.* lower than; beneath

belt *n.* 1 encircling band, as around the waist 2 distinct area —*v.* strike as with a belt —**below the belt** unfair(ly)

be·moan′ *v.* lament

be·mused' a. preoccupied

bench n. 1 long seat 2 work-table 3 seat for judges 4 status of a judge —v. remove (a player) from a game

bench mark n. standard or model: also **bench'mark'**

bend v. bent, bend'ing 1 to curve, as by pressure 2 (make) yield 3 stoop —n. 1 a bending 2 bent part

be·neath' adv., a. below; underneath —prep. 1 below; under 2 unworthy of

ben'e·dic'tion n. blessing

ben'e·fac'tor n. one who has given money or aid —**ben'e·fac'tion** n. —**ben'e·fac'tress** n.fem.

ben'e·fice (-fis) n. endowed church position

be·nef'i·cence n. 1 kindness 2 kindly act or gift —**be·nef'i·cent** a.

ben'e·fi'cial (-fish'əl) a. producing benefits

ben'e·fi'ci·ar'y (-fish'ər ē) n., pl. -ies one receiving benefits, as from insurance

ben'e·fit n. 1 help or advantage 2 a show, etc. to raise money for a cause —v. 1 to help 2 profit

be·nev'o·lence n. the wish to do good; kindness; generosity —**be·nev'o·lent** a.

be·night'ed a. ignorant

be·nign' (-nīn') a. 1 kindly 2 favorable 3 not malignant

be·nig'nant a. benign

bent a. 1 curved 2 determined (on) —n. inclination

be·numb' v. make numb

ben'zene n. coal-tar derivative used as a solvent

ben'zo·ate' n. chemical used to preserve food

be·queath' (-kwēth', -kwēth') v. 1 leave (property) to another by one's will 2 hand down —**be·quest'** n.

be·rate' v. scold severely

be·reave' v. -reaved' or -reft', -reav'ing 1 deprive 2 leave forlorn, as by death —**be·reave'ment** n. —**be·reft'** a.

be·ret' (-rā') n. flat, round, soft cap

beri·beri n. disease caused by lack of vitamin B₁

berm n. ledge along the edge of a paved road

ber'ry n., pl. -ries small, fleshy fruit with seeds

ber·serk' (-surk', -zurk) a., adv. in(to) a violent rage

berth (burth) n. 1 ship's place of

anchorage 2 built-in bed 3 position or job

ber'yl (-əl) n. hard, bright mineral, as the emerald

be·seech' v. -sought' or -seeched', -seech'ing ask (for) earnestly; entreat —**be·seech'ing·ly** adv.

be·set' v. -set', -set'ting 1 attack from all sides 2 surround

be·side' prep. 1 at the side of; near 2 as compared with 3 besides aside from —adv. besides —**beside oneself** wild, as with fear or anger

be·sides' adv. 1 in addition 2 else 3 moreover —prep. in addition to

be·siege' v. 1 lay siege to; hem in 2 overwhelm, harass, etc. 3 close in on

be·smirch' v. to soil; sully

be·sot'ted a. stupefied, as with liquor

be·speak' v. 1 speak for; reserve 2 indicate

best a. 1 most excellent 2 most suitable —adv. 1 in the best way 2 most —n. 1 best person, thing, etc. 2 the utmost —v. outdo; beat —**all for the best** turning out to be good —**at best** under the most favorable conditions —**get (or have) the best** of defeat or outwit —**had best** should —**make the best of** adjust to

bes'tial (-chəl) a. like a beast; brutal

be·stir' v. stir up; busy

best man n. main attendant of a bridegroom

be·stow' v. present as a gift (on or upon)

bet n. 1 agreement that the one proved wrong will pay something 2 thing so staked —v. bet or bet'ted, bet'ting 1 make a bet 2 stake in a bet —**bet'tor, bet'ter** n.

be·ta (bā'tə) n. second letter of the Greek alphabet

be·take' v. take (oneself); go

be·tel nut (bēt'l) n. fruit of a tree (betel palm), chewed with leaves of a plant (betel pepper) by some Asian peoples

be·tide' v. happen (to)

be·to'ken v. be a sign of

be·tray' v. 1 be disloyal to 2 deceive 3 seduce 4 reveal —**be·tray'al** n.

be·troth' (-trōth', -trôth') v. promise in marriage —**be·troth'al** (-trōth'-) n. —**be·**

trothed' (-trōthd') a., n.

bet'ter a. 1 more excellent 2 more suitable 3 improved —adv. 1 in a better way 2 more —n. 1 a superior 2 a better thing, etc. —v. to surpass or improve —**better off** in better circumstances —**get** (or **have**) **the better of** defeat or outwit —**had better** should

bet'ter·ment n. improvement

be·tween' prep. 1 in the space or time separating 2 involving 3 joining 4 in the common possession of 5 one of —adv. in the middle

be·twixt' prep., adv. [Ar.] between

bev'el n. 1 angled part or surface 2 tool for marking angles —v. cut or slope at an angle

bev'er·age n. drink

bev'y n., pl. **-ies** 1 group, as of girls or women 2 flock of quail

be·wail' v. wail over

be·ware' v. guard against

be·wil'der v. confuse —**be·wil'der·ment** n.

be·witch' v. to enchant —**be·witch'ing** a.

be·yond' prep. 1 farther or later than; past 2 more than —adv. farther away —**the (great) beyond** whatever follows death

bez'el n. slanting faces of a cut jewel

bi- pref. two or twice

bi·an'nu·al a. twice a year

bi'as (bī'əs) n. 1 diagonal or slanting line 2 prejudice —v. to prejudice —**on the bias** diagonally

bib n. cloth tied under a child's chin at meals

Bi'ble sacred book of Christians or of Jews —**Bib'li·cal, bib'li·cal** a.

bib'li·og'ra·phy n., pl. **-phies** list of writings on one subject or by one author

bi·cam'er·al a. having two legislative branches

bi·car'bon·ate of soda (-ət) n. baking soda

bi'cen·ten'ni·al n. 200th anniversary

bi'ceps' n., pl. **-ceps'** large front muscle of the upper arm

bick'er v., n. quarrel

bi·cus'pid n. tooth with two-pointed crown

bi'cy·cle (-si kəl) n. two-wheeled vehicle —v. ride a bicycle —**bi'cy·clist** n.

bid v. **bade** (bad) or **bid, bid'den**

or **bid, bid'ding** 1 command or ask 2 tell 3 bid, **bid'ding** offer as a price —n. 1 amount bid 2 attempt —**bid'der** n.

bide v. **bode** or **bid'ed, bid'ed, bid'ing** 1 stay 2 dwell 3 wait —**bide one's time** wait patiently for a chance

bi·en'ni·al a. 1 every two years 2 lasting two years —n. plant living two years

bier (bir) n. frame on which a coffin is put

bi'fo'cals n.pl. eyeglasses with lenses having two parts, for close and far focus

big a. **big'ger, big'gest** 1 of great size 2 loud 3 important 4 noble —adv. [Col.] 1 boastfully 2 impressively —**big'ness** n.

big'a·my n. crime of marrying again while still married —**big'a·mist** —**big'a·mous** a.

big'heart'ed a. generous

big'horn' n. horned, wild sheep of Rocky Mountains

bight (bīt) n. 1 loop in a rope 2 curve in a coastline 3 a bay formed by such a curve

big'ot n. narrow-minded, intolerant person —**big'ot·ed** a. —**big'ot·ry** n.

bike n., v. [Col.] 1 bicycle 2 motorcycle

bi·ki'ni n., pl. **-nis** 1 women's very brief, two-piece swimsuit 2 very brief underpants or trunks

bi·lat'er·al a. on, by, or having two sides

bile n. 1 bitter liver secretion 2 bad temper

bilge (bilj) n. 1 lower part of a ship's hold 2 stale water that gathers there 3 [Sl.] nonsense

bi·lin'gual a. of, in, or speaking two languages

bil'ious (-yəs) a. 1 having a disorder of the bile or liver 2 bad-tempered

bilk v. to swindle

bill n. 1 statement of charges, as for goods 2 list of things offered 3 proposed law 4 piece of paper money 5 bird's beak —v. present a bill of charges to

bill'board' n. signboard

bil'let n. lodging, as for soldiers —v. assign to lodging

bill'fold' n. wallet

bil'liards (-yərdz) n. game played with cue and three balls on a table with raised edges

bil'lion n. thousand millions —**bil'lionth** a., n.

bil'lion·aire' n. one having at

least a billion dollars

bill of fare n. menu

bill of sale n. paper transferring ownership by sale

bil'low n. 1 large wave 2 swelling mass, as of smoke —v. surge or swell —**bil'low·y** a., **-i·er**, **-i·est**

bil'ly goat n. [Col.] male goat

bi·month'ly a., adv. once every two months

bin n. box or enclosed space for storage

bi·na·ry (bī'nə rē) a. 1 twofold 2 of a number system with only two digits

bind v. **bound, bind'ing** 1 tie together 2 to hold; restrain 3 encircle with (a belt, etc.) 4 bandage 5 put together (a book) with a cover 6 to obligate —**bind'er** n.

bind'er·y n., pl. **-ies** place where books are bound

bind'ing n. 1 anything that binds 2 covers and backing of a book

binge (binj) n. [Col.] spree

bin'go n. game played on cards with numbered squares

bin·oc'u·lars (bī näk'-, bin äk'-) n.pl. field glasses

bi'o·chem'is·try n. chemistry of living organisms

bi'o·de·grad'a·ble (-grād'-) a. readily decomposed by bacteria

bi'o·feed'back n. technique for controlling emotions

bi·og'ra·phy n., pl. **-phies** one's life story written by another —**bi·og'ra·pher** n. —**bi'o·graph'i·cal** a.

bi·ol'o·gy n. science of plants and animals —**bi'o·log'i·cal** a. —**bi·ol'o·gist** n.

bi·par'ti·san (-zan) a. representing two parties

bi'ped n. two-footed animal

birch n. 1 tree with smooth bark 2 its hard wood

bird n. warmblooded vertebrate with feathers and wings

bird'ie n. Golf score of one under par for a hole

bird's'-eye' view a. 1 view from above or at a distance 2 general view

birth n. 1 a being born 2 descent or origin 3 beginning —**give birth to** bring into being —**birth'place'** n.

birth'day' n. day of birth or its anniversary

birth'mark' n. skin blemish present at birth

birth'rate' n. number of births per year in an area

birth'right' n. rights a person has by birth

bis'cuit (-kit) n. 1 small bread roll 2 [Br.] cracker

bi·sect' v. divide into two equal parts —**bi·sec'tor** n.

bi·sex'u·al a. sexually attracted to both sexes —n. bisexual person

bish'op n. 1 clergyman heading a diocese 2 chessman moving diagonally

bish'op·ric n. diocese, rank, etc. of a bishop

bis'muth (biz'-) n. metallic chemical element whose salts are used in medicine

bi'son n., pl. **bi'son** shaggy, oxlike animal of North America

bisque (bisk) n. thick, creamy soup made from shellfish, etc. or strained vegetables

bis'tro (bēs'-) n., pl. **-tros** small cafe

bit n. 1 mouthpiece on a bridle, for control 2 cutting part of a drill 3 small piece or amount 4 single digit in a binary number system 5 [Col.] short time —**bit by bit** gradually —**do one's bit** do one's share

bitch n. female dog, fox, etc. —v. [Sl.] complain

bite v. **bit, bit'ten** or **bit, bit'ing** 1 seize or cut as with the teeth 2 sting, as a bee 3 cause to smart 4 swallow a bait —n. 1 a biting 2 biting quality; sting 3 wound from biting 4 mouthful 5 [Col.] light meal

bit'ing a. 1 cutting; sharp 2 sarcastic

bit'ter a. 1 sharp to the taste 2 sorrowful, painful, resentful, etc. 3 harsh —**bit'ter·ly** adv.

bit'tern n. heronlike bird

bit'ter·sweet' a. both bitter and sweet

bi·tu'men n. natural asphalt or similar substance made from coal, etc.

bi·tu'mi·nous coal n. soft coal, easy to burn but smoky

bi'valve n. mollusk with two shells, as a clam

biv'ou·ac' (-wak', -ōō ak') n. temporary camp (of soldiers) —v. **-ou·acked', -ou·ack'ing** make such a camp

bi·week'ly a., adv. once every two weeks

bi·zarre (bi zär') a. odd; fantastic

blab v. **blabbed, blab'bing** to tattle, gossip, etc.

black a. 1 of the color of coal; opposite to white 2 having dark skin 3 without light; dark 4 dirty 5 evil 6 sad —n. 1 black pigment 2 member of a dark-skinned people, or person having African ancestry —v. to blacken —**black out** lose consciousness —**black'ness** n.

black'-and-blue' a. discolored by a bruise

black'ball' n., v. (a) vote against

black'ber'ry v., pl. **-ries** 1 small, edible, dark fruit 2 bramble it grows on

black'bird' n. bird the male of which is all black

black'board' n. smooth surface for writing with chalk

black'en v. 1 make or become black 2 slander

black'guard (blag'ərd) n. scoundrel; villain

black'head' n. plug of dirt in a pore of the skin

black'jack' n. 1 small bludgeon 2 a card game

black'list' n. list of those to be punished, refused jobs, etc.

black'mail' n. money extorted on threat of disclosing something disgracing —v. (try to) get blackmail from —**black'mail'er** n.

black market n. system for selling goods illegally during rationing, etc.

black'out' n. 1 concealing of light, facts, etc. 2 a faint 3 loss of electricity in an area

black sheep n. disgraceful member of a family, etc.

black'smith' n. one who forges iron and shoes horses

black'top' n. asphalt mixture used to surface roads, etc.

black widow n. small, poisonous spider

blad'der n. sac that collects urine from the kidneys

blade n. 1 leaf of grass 2 cutting part of a knife, tool, etc. 3 flat surface, as of an oar

blame v. 1 accuse of being at fault 2 put the responsibility of (on) —n. 1 a blaming 2 responsibility for a fault —**be to blame** deserve blame —**blame'less** a. —**blame'wor'thy** a.

blanch v. 1 bleach 2 make or turn pale

bland a. mild; soothing

blan'dish v. flatter; coax —**blan'-**dish'ment n.

blank a. 1 not written on 2 empty 3 utter —n. 1 (printed form with) space to be filled in 2 cartridge without a bullet —**draw a blank** [Col.] be unable to remember something

blan'ket n. 1 wool spread used as bed cover, etc. 2 a covering, as of snow —a. all-inclusive —v. to cover

blare v. sound loudly —n. loud, trumpetlike sound

blar'ney (blär'-) n. flattery

bla·sé (blä zā') a. bored

blas'phe·my (-fə mē) n., pl. **-mies** profane abuse of God —**blas·pheme'** (-fēm') v. —**blas'-**phe·mous a.

blast n. 1 strong rush of air 2 loud sound of horn, etc. 3 explosion —v. 1 explode 2 to blight; wither

blast furnace n. furnace for smelting iron ore

blast'off', blast'-off' n. launching of a rocket, etc.

bla'tant a. loud and vulgar —**bla'-**tan·cy n.

blaze n. 1 burst of flame 2 bright light 3 vivid display 4 outburst 5 white spot on an animal's face —v. 1 burn or shine brightly 2 mark (a trail)

blaz'er n. lightweight sports jacket in a solid color

bla'zon (-zən) n. coat of arms —v. proclaim

bleach v. whiten —n. chemical that bleaches

bleach'ers n.pl. roofless stand where spectators sit

bleak a. 1 unsheltered; bare 2 cheerless; gloomy

blear (blir) v. to dim or blur, as with tears —**blear'y** a.

bleat n. cry of a sheep or goat —v. make this cry

bleed v. **bled, bleed'ing** 1 lose blood 2 draw blood, air, etc. from 3 [Col.] extort from

blem'ish v. mar; injure —n. defect; fault

blend v. 1 mix 2 shade into each other —n. 1 a blending 2 mixture

blend'er n. kitchen appliance for chopping, mixing, etc.

bless v. **blessed** or **blest, bless'-**ing 1 make holy 2 ask divine favor for 3 make happy —**bless·ed** (bles'əd, blest) a. —**bless'ing** n.

blew v. pt. of BLOW

blight (blīt) n. 1 insect, disease,

etc. that destroys plants 2 anything that destroys —v. destroy; ruin

blimp n. small airship like a dirigible

blind a. 1 without sight 2 lacking insight 3 having no outlet 4 not controlled by reason —n. 1 window shade 2 a decoy 3 make sightless —**blind'ly** adv. —**blind'ness** n.

blind'fold' v. cover the eyes of —n. cloth used for this

blind'side' v. hit someone who is unprepared or looking away

blink v. 1 wink rapidly 2 flash on and off —n. 1 a blinking 2 glimmer —**blink at** ignore —**on the blink** [Sl.] out of order

blink'er n. flashing light

blip n. image on radar

bliss n. great happiness —**bliss'ful** a.

blis'ter n. fluid-filled skin swelling caused by a burn, etc. —v. form blisters

blithe (blīth, blith) a. carefree; cheerful

blitz n. sudden, overwhelming attack

bliz'zard n. severe snowstorm with high wind

bloat v. swell up

blob n. small drop or mass

bloc n. group united for a common purpose

block n. 1 solid piece 2 auction platform 3 obstruction 4 city square or street section 5 pulley in a frame 6 part taken as a unit —v. 1 obstruct 2 shape —**block out** sketch roughly —**on the block** for sale

block·ade' n. shutting off of a place by warships, etc. —v. subject to a blockade

block'bust'er n. an expensive movie, etc. intended to have wide appeal

block'head' n. stupid person

block'house' n. wooden fort

blond a. 1 having light-colored hair and skin 2 light-colored Also **blonde** —n. blond man or boy —**blonde** n.fem.

blood n. 1 red fluid in the arteries and veins 2 lineage 3 kinship —**bad blood** hatred —**in cold blood** deliberately —**blood'less** a.

blood'cur'dling (-kurd'liŋ) a. very frightening; terrifying

blood'hound' n. large, keen-scented tracking dog

blood'shed' n. killing

blood'shot' a. tinged with blood: said of the eyes

blood'thirst'y a. murderous

blood'y a. -i·er, -i·est 1 of or covered with blood 2 involving bloodshed 3 bloodthirsty —v. -ied, -y·ing stain with blood

bloom n. 1 a flower 2 time of flowering 3 healthy glow —v. be in bloom

bloom'ers n.pl. women's baggy underpants

bloop'er n. [Sl.] stupid mistake

blos'som n., a. flower

blot n. spot or stain —v. **blot'ted, blot'ting** 1 spot, as with ink 2 erase or cancel (out) 3 to dry with soft paper, etc. —**blot'ter** n.

blotch n. discolored spot —v. mark with blotches —**blotch'y** a., -i·er, -i·est

blouse (blous) n. shirtlike garment for girls

blow v. **blew, blown, blow'ing** 1 move, as (by) wind 2 force air out, as with the mouth 3 sound by blowing —n. 1 a blowing 2 gale 3 a hit 4 shock —**blow out** 1 extinguish 2 burst —**blow up** 1 inflate 2 explode —**blow'er** n.

blow'gun' n. tubular weapon through which darts, etc. are blown

blow'out' n. bursting of a tire

blow'torch' n. small, hot-flamed torch for welding

blow'up' n. 1 an explosion 2 enlarged photograph

blub'ber n. whale fat —v. weep loudly

bludg·eon (bluj'ən) n. short, heavy club —v. to club

blue a. 1 of the color of the clear sky 2 gloomy —n. color of the clear sky —v. use bluing on —**the blues** 1 [Col.] depressed feeling 2 slow, sad jazz song

blue'bell' n. plant with blue, bell-shaped flowers

blue'ber'ry n., pl. -ries small, edible, bluish berry

blue'bird' n. small bird with blue back and wings

blue'-col'lar a. of industrial workers

blue'fish' n. silvery-blue Atlantic food fish

blue'jay' n. crested bird with blue head

blue'jeans' n.pl. jeans of blue denim

blue'print' n. 1 photographic copy, white on blue, of architectural plans, etc. **2** any detailed plan —v. make a blueprint for

bluff v. mislead by a fake, bold front —a. rough and frank —n. **1** a buffing **2** one who bluffs **3** steep bank

blu'ing n. blue rinse for white fabrics

blu'ish a. somewhat blue: also sp. **blue'ish**

blun'der n. foolish mistake —v. **1** make a blunder **2** move clumsily

blun'der·buss' n. obsolete gun with a broad muzzle

blunt a. **1** dull-edged **2** plain-spoken —v. make dull

blur v. **blurred, blur'ring 1** to smudge **2** make or become indistinct —n. indistinct thing —**blur'ry** a., **-ri·er**, **-ri·est**

blurb n. [Col.] exaggerated advertisement

blurt v. say impulsively

blush v. redden, as from shame —n. a blushing

blus'ter v. **1** blow stormily **2** speak noisily or boastfully —n. swaggering talk —**blus'ter·y** a.

bo·a (bō′ə) n. **1** large snake that crushes its prey in its coils **2** scarf of feathers

boar n. wild hog

board n. **1** broad, flat piece of wood, etc. **2** meals provided regularly for pay **3** council —v. **1** cover (up) with boards **2** get on (a ship, train, etc.) **3** get meals regularly for pay —**on board** on a ship, etc. —**board'er** n.

board'ing·house' n. house where one can pay for a room and meals

board'walk' n. wooden walk along a beach

boast v. **1** talk with too much pride **2** take pride in —n. thing boasted of —**boast'er** n. —**boast'ful** a.

boat n. water craft, esp. a small one —**rock the boat** [Col.] disturb the status quo —**boat'man** n., pl. **-men**

boat'ing n. rowing, sailing, etc.

boat'swain (bō′sən) n. petty officer directing deck work

bob n. **1** small hanging weight **2** float on a fishing line —v. **bobbed, bob'bing 1** move jerkily **2** cut short, as hair

bob'bin n. spool for thread

bobby pin n. tight hairpin

bobby socks (or **sox**) n. [Col.] girls' short socks

bob'cat' n. American lynx

bob'o·link' n. songbird with a call like its name

bob'sled' n. racing sled

bob'white' n. small quail

bock (beer) n. a dark beer

bode v. **1** be an omen of **2** pt. of **BIDE**

bod·ice (bäd′is) n. snug upper part of a dress

bod'y n., pl. **-ies 1** whole physical structure **2** trunk of a man or animal **3** main part **4** distinct mass or group **5** [Col.] person —**bod'i·ly** a., adv.

bod'y·guard' n. guard to protect a person

body stocking n. one-piece, tight-fitting garment

bog n. a small swamp —v. **bogged, bog'ging** sink (down) as in a bog —**bog'gy** a.

bog'gle v. **1** be startled or hesitate (at) **2** confuse

bo'gus a. not genuine

bo·gy (bō′gē) n., pl. **-gies** imaginary evil spirit; goblin: also sp. **bo'gey** or **bo'gie**

Bo·he'mi·an n. one who lives unconventionally

boil v. **1** bubble up into vapor by heating **2** be agitated **3** cook by boiling —n. **1** boiling state **2** pus-filled pimple —**boil down** condense

boil'er n. tank for making steam or storing hot water

bois'ter·ous a. rough, noisy, lively, etc.

bold a. **1** daring; fearless **2** impudent **3** sharp and clear —**bold'ly** adv.

bo·le'ro (-ler′ō) n., pl. **-ros 1** Spanish dance **2** short, open vest

boll weevil n. beetle that harms cotton pods (**bolls**)

bo·lo'gna (-lō′nē) n. type of smoked sausage

bol'ster (bōl′-) n. long pillow —v. prop (up)

bolt n. **1** flash of lightning **2** sliding bar that locks **3** threaded metal rod used with a nut **4** roll of cloth —v. **1** gulp (food) **2** rush out **3** fasten with a bolt **4** sift —**bolt upright** straight upright

bomb (bäm) n. **1** explosive device or missile **2** [Col.] complete failure —v. **1** attack with bombs **2** [Col.] be a failure

bom·bard' v. attack with artillery or bombs —**bom'bar·dier'** (-bər dir′) n. —**bom·bard'**

ment *n.*

bom'bast' *n.* pompous speech —**bom·bas'tic** *a.*

bomb'er *n.* airplane designed for dropping bombs

bomb'shell' *n.* 1 bomb 2 shocking surprise

bo·na fi·de (bō'nə fīd', bä'-) *n.* in good faith; sincere

bo·nan'za *n.* 1 rich vein of ore 2 any rich source

bon'bon' *n.* piece of candy

bond *n.* 1 thing that binds or unites 2 binding agreement 3 interest-bearing certificate 4 surety against theft, etc. —*v.* 1 bind 2 furnish a **bond** (*n.* 4) for

bond'age *n.* slavery —**bond'man** *n., pl.* **-men** —**bond'wom·an** *n.fem., pl.* **-wom·en**

bonds'man *n., pl.* **-men** one furnishing **BOND** (*n.* 4)

bone *n.* material of the skeleton or piece of this —*v.* 1 remove the bones from 2 [Sl.] study hard: with *up* —**make no bones about** admit freely —**bone'less** *a.*

bon'er (bōn'-) *n.* [Sl.] a blunder

bon'fire *n.* outdoor fire

bon'go *n., pl.* **-gos** either of a pair of small drums struck with the hands

bo·ni'to (-nē'tō) *n., pl.* **-tos** or **-toes** kind of tuna

bon·jour (bōn zhoor') *int., n.* ‖ Fr.‖ good day; hello

bon'net *n.* hat

bon'ny *a.* **-ni·er** or **-ni·est** handsome; pretty

bon·sai (-sī) *n., pl.* **-sai** dwarfed tree or shrub

bo'nus *n.* payment over the usual or required amount

bon'y *a.* **-i·er, -i·est** 1 full of bones 2 lean; thin —**bon'i·ness** *n.*

boo *int., n., pl.* **boos** sound made to show disapproval or to startle —*v.* shout "boo" at

boo'-boo', boo'boo' *n., pl.* **-boos** [Sl.] stupid mistake

boo'by *n., pl.* **-bies** a fool

book *n.* 1 a bound, printed work 2 a division of a long literary work 3 ledger —*v.* 1 to list in a book 2 to reserve, as rooms

book'case' *n.* set of shelves for holding books

book'end' *n.* end piece to hold a row of books upright

book'ie *n.* [Sl.] bookmaker

book'ish *a.* 1 inclined to read or study 2 pedantic

book'keep'ing *n.* work of recording business transactions —**book'keep'er** *n.*

book'let *n.* small book

book'mak'er *n.* one who takes bets, esp. on horses

book'mark' *n.* slip, etc. for marking a place in a book

book'worm' *n.* one who reads or studies much

boom *v.* 1 make a deep, hollow sound 2 grow rapidly 3 promote —*n.* 1 deep sound 2 long beam on a derrick 3 spar at the foot of a sail 4 period of prosperity

boom'er·ang' *n.* 1 Australian curved stick that returns to the thrower 2 scheme that backfires

boon *n.* benefit

boon'docks' *n.pl.* [Col.] remote rural region

boon'dog'gle *n.* pointless work financed with public funds

boor *n.* rude person

boost *v., n.* [Col.] 1 to push upward; raise 2 to support —**boost'er** *n.*

boot *n.* outer covering for the foot and leg —*v.* 1 to kick 2 [Col.] dismiss

booth *n.* small stall or enclosure

boot'leg' *n.* **-legged', -leg'ging** sell (liquor) illegally —*a.* sold illegally —**boot'leg'ger** *n.*

boot'less *a.* useless

boo'ty *n.* plunder; spoils

booze *n.* [Col.] liquor

bo·rax (bôr'aks') *n.* a white salt used in glass, soaps, etc.

bor'der *n.* 1 edge; margin 2 boundary —*v.* put or be a border on —*a.* near a border —**border on** (or **upon**) be next to —**bor'der·land'** *n.*

bor'der·line' *n.* boundary —*a.* 1 on a boundary 2 indefinite

bore *v.* 1 drill a hole (in) 2 weary by being dull —*n.* 1 inside or diameter of a tube 2 dull person or thing —**bore'dom** *n.*

bore *v.* pt. of BEAR

bo·ric acid (bôr'ik) *n.* powder used in solution as an antiseptic

born *v.* pp. of BEAR (*v.* 3) —*a.* 1 brought into life 2 by nature

borne *v.* pp. of BEAR (*v.* 1)

bo'ron' *n.* nonmetallic chemical element

bor·ough (bur'ō) *n.* 1 in some States, self-governing town 2 division of New York City

bor'row *v.* 1 take on loan 2 adopt (an idea)

bos'om (booz'-) n. breast —a. intimate, as a friend

boss n. 1 employer or supervisor 2 head politician —v. 1 supervise 2 [Col.] order about — **boss'y** a., -i-er, -i-est

bo'sun n. boatswain

bot'a-ny n. science of plants — **bo-tan'i-cal** a. —**bot'a-nist** n.

botch v. spoil; bungle —n. bungled work

both a., pron. the two —con., adv. equally

both'er (bäth'-) v. 1 annoy; worry 2 trouble (oneself) —n. trouble —**both'er-some** a.

bot'tle n. glass container for liquids —v. put into a bottle — **bottle up** hold in or suppress

bot'tle-neck' n. 1 narrow passage 2 any hindrance

bot'tom n. 1 lowest part; base; underside 2 basis or cause

bot'u-lism' (bäch'ə-) n. poisoning caused by bacteria in foods improperly preserved

bou-doir' (boo dwär') n. woman's private room

bouf-fant (boo fänt') a. puffed out; full

bough (bou) n. tree branch

bought (bôt) v. pt. & pp. of BUY

bouil-lon (bool'yän) n. clear broth

boul'der (bōl'-) n. large rock

bou'le-vard' (bool'-) n. broad, tree-lined street

bounce (bouns) v. 1 spring back on impact 2 make bounce 3 leap —n. a bouncing —**bounc'y** a., -i-er, -i-est

bounc'ing a. healthy

bound v. 1 pt. & pp. of BIND 2 leap or bounce 3 be a limit or boundary to —a. 1 tied 2 certain (to) 3 obliged 4 with a binding 5 headed (for) 6 [Col.] determined —n. 1 a leap or bounce 2 boundary —**out of bounds** prohibited —**bound'less** a.

bound'a-ry n., pl. -ries anything marking a limit

boun'te-ous a. 1 generous 2 abundant

boun'ti-ful a. bounteous

boun'ty n., pl. -ties 1 generosity 2 gift or reward

bou-quet (bō kā', bōō-) n. 1 bunch of flowers 2 aroma

bour'bon (bur'bən) n. corn whiskey

bour-geoi-sie (boor'zhwä zē') n. social middle class —**bourgeois'** (-zhwä') a., n.

bout (bout) n. 1 struggle; contest 2 spell or term

bou-tique' (boo tēk', bō-) n. small shop selling costly articles

bo'vine' (-vīn) a. cowlike

bow (bou) v. 1 bend down in respect 2 to submit 3 weigh (down) —n. 1 bending of the head or body 2 front part of a ship —**take a bow** acknowledge applause

bow (bō) n. 1 curved stick strung with cord for shooting arrows 2 stick strung with horsehairs, for playing a violin, etc. 3 knot with broad loops — a. curved —v. play (a violin) with a bow

bow'els (bou'-) n.pl. 1 intestines 2 depths

bow'er (bou'-) n. arbor

bowl (bōl) n. 1 hollow, rounded dish or part 2 amphitheater 3 ball for bowling —v. 1 roll (a ball) in bowling 2 move fast — **bowl over** knock over

bow'leg'ged (bō'-) a. with the legs curved out

bowl'ing n. game in which a ball is rolled along a wooden lane (**bowling alley**) at ten wooden pins

bow'man (bō'-) n., pl. -men archer

box n. 1 container made of wood, cardboard, etc. 2 an enclosed group of seats 3 blow with the hand 4 evergreen shrub: also **box'wood'** —v. 1 put (in) or shut (up) in a box 2 fight with the fists —**box'er** n. —**box'ing** n.

box'car' n. enclosed railroad freight car

box office n. place in a theater to buy tickets

boy n. male child —**boy'hood'** n. —**boy'ish** a.

boy'cott' v. refuse to deal with — n. a boycotting

boy'friend' n. [Col.] 1 sweetheart of a girl or woman 2 boy who is one's friend

boy'sen-ber'ry n., pl. -ries berry crossed from raspberry, loganberry, and blackberry

bra n. brassiere

brace v. 1 strengthen with supports 2 prepare for a shock 3 stimulate —n. 1 pair 2 clamp 3 supporting device 4 handle of a drilling tool (**brace and bit**) 5 either of the signs { }, for connecting lines, etc.

brace'let n. decorative band for

the arm

brack′et n. 1 projecting support 2 either of the signs [ ], for enclosing words 3 classification —v. 1 support with brackets 2 enclose in brackets 3 classify together

brack′ish a. salty or rank

brad n. thin wire nail

brag n., v. **bragged, brag′ging** boast

brag′gart (-ərt) n. boaster

braid v. 1 interweave strands of 2 trim with braid —n. braided strip

Braille, braille (brāl) n. system of printing for the blind, using raised dots

brain n. 1 mass of nerve tissue in the head 2 pl. intelligence —v. smash the brains of —[Col.]

brain′y a., -i-er, -i-est

brain′storm′ n. [Col.] sudden idea

brain′wash′ v. [Col.] indoctrinate thoroughly

braise (brāz) v. brown (meat), then simmer it

brake n. 1 thicket 2 device to stop or slow a machine, etc. —v. stop or slow as with a brake

brake′man n., pl. **-men** train conductor's assistant

bram′ble n. prickly shrub

bran n. husks separated from grains of wheat, etc.

branch n. 1 limb of a tree 2 off-shoot or division 3 tributary stream 4 local unit of an organization —v. put forth branches —**branch off** diverge —**branch out** broaden one's interest —**branch′like′** a.

brand n. 1 burning stick 2 owner's mark burned on cattle 3 iron used to brand 4 stigma 5 trademark 6 make or kind —v. mark with a brand

bran′dish v. wave about

brand′-new′ a. fully new

bran′dy n., pl. **-dies** liquor distilled from wine or fruit juice

brash a. rash or insolent

brass n. 1 alloy of copper and zinc 2 [often with pl. v.] coiled musical instruments, as the trumpet, tuba, etc. 3 [Col.] rude boldness 4 [Sl.] military officer —**brass′y** a., -i-er, -i-est

bras·siere (bra zir′) n. woman's undergarment for supporting the breasts

brat n. unruly child

brat·wurst (brät′wurst′) n. sausage of veal and pork

bra·va′do (-vä′-) n. pretended courage

brave a. full of courage —n. a North American Indian warrior —v. 1 defy 2 meet with courage —**brav′er·y** n.

bra′vo (brä′-) int., n., pl. **-vos** shout of approval

brawl v. quarrel or fight noisily —n. noisy fight

brawn n. muscular strength —**brawn′y** a., -i-er, -i-est

bray n. sound a donkey makes —v. make this sound

bra′zen (brä′-) a. 1 of or like brass 2 shameless —**brazen it out** act unashamed of

bra·zier (brā′zhar) n. pan for holding burning coals

Bra·zil′ nut n. edible, three-sided, tropical nut

breach n. 1 break in something; gap 2 violation of a promise, friendship, etc. —v. make a breach in

bread n. 1 baked food of flour dough 2 livelihood —v. cover with bread crumbs

breadth n. width or scope

bread′win′ner n. one who supports dependents by earning money

break v. **broke, bro′ken, break′-ing** 1 split apart; smash 2 make or become unusable 3 tame by force 4 make penniless 5 surpass (a record) 6 violate (a law) 7 interrupt 8 stop 9 make or become known —n. 1 a breaking 2 broken place 3 interruption 4 beginning (of day) 5 sudden change 6 a chance —**break off** stop abruptly —**break out** develop pimples —**break up** 1 to separate 2 to stop 3 [Col.] (make) laugh —**break′a·ble** a.

break′age′ n. 1 a breaking 2 loss due to breaking

break′down′ n. 1 mechanical failure 2 physical or mental collapse 3 analysis

break′er n. breaking wave

break·fast (brek′fast′) n. first meal of the day —v. eat breakfast

break′-in′ n. forcible entering of a building, to rob it

break′through′ n. 1 act, place, etc. of breaking through resistance 2 important discovery

break′up′ n. a going apart

break′wa′ter n. barrier to break the impact of waves

breast (brest) n. 1 milk-secreting gland on a woman's body 2 upper front of the body 3 the emotions —v. to face bravely — **make a clean breast of** confess

breast'bone' n. sternum

breast'work' n. low barrier to protect gunners

breath (breth) n. 1 air taken into and let out of the lungs 2 easy breathing 3 life 4 slight breeze

breathe (brēth) v. 1 inhale and exhale 2 live 3 whisper 4 rest

breath-er (brē'thər) n. [Col.] pause for rest

breath'less a. panting

breath'tak'ing a. exciting

breech n. 1 back part 2 gun part behind the barrel

breech'es (brich'-) n.pl. knickers or trousers

breed v. bred, breed'ing 1 bring forth (offspring) 2 produce 3 raise (animals) —n. 1 race; stock 2 type

breeze n. gentle wind —v. [Col.] move briskly —breez'y a., -i-er, -i-est

breth'ren n.pl. [Ar.] brothers

bre'vi-ar'y (brē'-) n. R.C.Ch. book of daily prayers

brev'i-ty n. briefness

brew v. 1 make (beer, etc.) 2 steep (tea, etc.) 3 form —n. beverage brewed —brew'er n.

brew'er-y n., pl. -ies place where beer is brewed

bri-ar (brī'ar) n. tobacco pipe

bribe n. thing given or promised as an inducement, esp. to wrongdoing —v. offer or give a bribe to —brib'er-y n.

bric'-a-brac' n. figurines, curios, etc.

brick n. 1 building block of baked clay 2 any oblong piece —a. built of brick —v. to cover with bricks

brick'lay'ing n. work of building with bricks

bride n. woman just married or about to be married —brid'al a.

bride'groom' n. man just married or being married

brides'maid n. any of the bride's wedding attendants

bridge n. 1 structure for crossing a river, etc. 2 thing like a bridge in shape, etc. 3 mounting for false teeth 4 card game for two pairs of players —v. build or be a bridge over

bridge'work' n. dental bridge(s)

bri'dle n. 1 head harness for a horse 2 thing that restrains —v. 1 put a bridle on 2 curb

bridle path n. path for horseback riding

brief a. short; concise —n. summary, as of a law case —v. summarize the facts for

brief'case' n. small case for carrying papers, books, etc.

bri'er (brī'-) n. 1 thorny bush 2 its root, used for making tobacco pipes

brig n. 1 two-masted ship with square sails 2 ship's prison

bri-gade' n. 1 military unit of several regiments 2 group organized for a task

brig'a-dier' general (-dir') n. officer just above a colonel

brig'and n. roving bandit

bright a. 1 shining; full of light 2 vivid 3 cheerful 4 mentally quick —bright'en v. —bright'ly adv. —bright'ness n.

bril'liant (-yant) a. 1 shining brightly 2 splendid 3 keenly intelligent —bril'liance n. —bril'liant-ly adv.

brim n. 1 top edge of a cup, etc. 2 projecting rim of a hat —v. brimmed, brim'ming fill or be full to the brim —brim'ful' a.

brim'stone' n. sulfur

brin'dled a. having dark streaks, as a cow: also sp. **brin'dle**

brine n. 1 water full of salt 2 ocean —brin'y a., -i-er, -i-est

bring v. brought, bring'ing cause to come or happen; fetch, get, lead to, etc. —bring about to cause —bring forth give birth to; produce —bring off accomplish —bring out reveal —bring to revive —bring up 1 rear (children) 2 mention

brink n. edge, as of a cliff

bri-quette', bri-quet' (-ket') n. small block of charcoal

brisk a. 1 quick; energetic 2 invigorating

bris'ket n. breast meat

bris-tle (bris'al) n. short, stiff hair —v. 1 stiffen like bristles 2 stiffen with anger —bris'tly a.

britch'es n.pl. [Col.] breeches

Brit'ish a. of Great Britain or its people

British thermal unit n. unit of heat, equal to about 252 calories

brit'tle a. hard but easily broken —brit'tle-ness n.

broach n. tapered bit for reaming out holes —v. 1 make a hole in 2 start a discussion of

broad a. 1 wide 2 obvious 3

tolerant 4 extensive; general —
broad'en v.

broad'cast' v. **-cast'** or **-cast'ed,
-cast'ing 1** spread widely **2**
send by radio, TV, etc. —n.
radio, TV, etc. program —adv.
far and wide —**broad'cast'er** n.

broad'cloth' n. a fine cloth

broad jump n. long jump

broad'loom' a. woven on a wide
loom, as a carpet

broad'-mind'ed a. liberal

broad'side' n. **1** firing of all
guns on a ship's side **2** large
sheet with advertising —adv.
with the side facing

bro-cade' n. cloth of a richly pat-
terned weave —v. weave a
raised design in

broc'co-li n. green-headed cauli-
flower

bro-chure' (-shoor') n. pamphlet

brogue (brōg) n. Irish accent

broil v. cook by direct heat

broil'er n. **1** pan or stove section
for broiling **2** chicken fit for
broiling

broke v. pt. of BREAK —a. [Sl.]
without money

bro'ken v. pp. of BREAK —a. **1**
fractured **2** not in working
order **3** violated, as a vow **4**
ruined **5** interrupted **6** imper-
fectly spoken **7** tamed

bro'ken-down' a. **1** sick or
worn out **2** out of order

bro'ken-heart'ed a. crushed by
grief

bro'ker n. agent hired to buy and
sell —**bro'ker-age** n.

bro'mide' (-mīd) n. **1** sedative **2**
trite saying

bro'mine' (-mēn') n. fuming
liquid, a chemical element

bron'chi-al (-kē-) a. of the
branches of the windpipe

bron-chi'tis (-kī'-) n. inflammation of the bronchial tubes

bron'co n., pl. **-cos** small, wild
horse of the West

bron'to-saur' (-sôr') n. large
plant-eating dinosaur: also **bron'
to-saur'us**

bronze n. **1** alloy of copper and
tin **2** reddish brown —v. make
bronze in color

brooch (brōch, brōōch) n. large
ornamental pin with a clasp

brood n. **1** birds hatched at one
time **2** offspring —v. dwell on
moodily

brook n. a small stream —v.
endure or tolerate

broom n. **1** long-handled brush
for sweeping **2** kind of shrub

broom'stick' n. broom handle

broth n. clear soup

broth'el n. house of prostitution

broth'er n. **1** male related to one
by having the same parents **2**
fellow member —**broth'er-
hood'** n. —**broth'er-ly** a.

broth'er-in-law' n., pl.
broth'ers- **1** brother of one's
spouse **2** sister's husband

brought v. pt. & pp. of BRING

brou'ha-ha' (brōō'-) n. uproar

brow n. **1** eyebrow **2** forehead
3 edge of a cliff

brow'beat' v. **-beat, -beat-en,
-beat-ing** to bully

brown a. **1** chocolate-colored **2**
tanned; dark-skinned —n.
brown color —v. to make or
become brown

brown'-bag' v. carry (one's)
lunch) to work, etc.

brown'ie n. square of flat chocolate cake

brown'out' n. dimming of lights
during a power shortage

brown'stone' n. reddish-brown
sandstone, used for building

browse v. **1** feed on grass, etc. **2**
to glance through books —
brows'er n.

bru'in n. a bear

bruise (brōōz) v. injure and discolor (the skin) without breaking it —n. discolored injury of
the skin

bruis'er n. pugnacious man

bruit (brōōt) n., v. rumor

brunch n. [Col.] combined
breakfast and lunch

bru-net' a. having dark hair and
complexion —n. brunet person

bru-nette' (-net') a. brunet —n.
brunette woman or girl

brunt n. main impact

brush n. **1** device with bristles,
wires, etc. for cleaning, painting,
etc. **2** a brushing **3** skirmish **4**
underbrush **5** sparsely settled
land —v. **1** use a brush on **2**
touch lightly **3** remove as with a
brush —**brush off** dismiss —
brush up refresh one's memory

brush'off' n. [Sl.] rude dismissal

brusque (brusk) a. abrupt in
manner —**brusque'ly** adv.

bru'tal a. savage, cruel, etc. —
bru-tal'i-ty n., pl. **-ties** —**bru'
tal-ly** adv.

bru'tal-ize' v. **1** make brutal **2**
treat brutally

brute a. of or like an animal;
cruel, stupid, etc. —n. **1** animal
2 brutal person —**brut'ish** a.

bub'ble n. globule of air or gas in

a liquid —v. **1** rise in bubbles **2** gurgle —**bub′bly** a.

bu·bon·ic plague (byōō bän′ik) n. deadly contagious disease

buc′ca·neer′ n. pirate

buck n. **1** male deer, goat, etc. **2** a bucking **3** [Sl.] dollar —v. **1** rear up, as to throw off (a rider) **2** [Col.] resist —**pass the buck** [Col.] shift the blame

buck′et n. container with a handle, for water, etc.; pail —**buck′et·ful′** n.

buck′le n. clasp for fastening a belt, etc. —v. **1** fasten with a buckle **2** bend or crumple —**buckle down** apply oneself

buck′ler n. round shield

buck′ram (-rəm) n. stiff cloth

buck′shot′ n. large lead shot for a gun

buck′skin′ n. leather from skins of deer or sheep

buck′tooth′ n., pl. -**teeth′** projecting tooth —**buck′toothed′** a.

buck′wheat′ n. plant with seeds ground into dark flour

bu·col·ic (byōō käl′ik) a. rustic

bud n. small swelling on a plant, start of a leaf, shoot, or flower —v. **bud′ded, bud′ding 1** put forth buds **2** begin to develop

Bud·dhism (bood′iz′əm, bood′-) n. a religion of Asia —**Bud′dhist** n., a.

bud′dy n., pl. -**dies** [Col.] comrade

budge v. move slightly

budg′et n. **1** plan adjusting expenses to income **2** estimated cost of operating, etc. —v. **1** put on a budget **2** schedule

buff v. polish, as with soft leather —**buff′er** n.

buf′fa·lo′ n., pl. -**loes** or -**los 1** wild ox **2** American bison —v. [Sl.] to bluff

buff′er n. anything that lessens shock

buf′fet′ (-ət) n., v. blow; slap

buf·fet′ (-fā′) n. **1** cabinet for dishes, silver, etc. **2** food which guests serve themselves as from a buffet

buf·foon′ (-fōōn′) n. a clown —**buf·foon′er·y** n.

bug n. **1** crawling insect, esp. when a pest **2** [Col.] germ **3** [Sl.] defect **4** [Sl.] tiny microphone

bug′bear′ n. imaginary terror: also **bug′a·boo′**, pl. -**boos′**

bug′gy n., pl. -**gies 1** light, one-horse carriage **2** baby carriage

bu′gle (byōō′-) n. small, valueless trumpet —**bu′gler** n.

build v. built, build′ing **1** make by putting together parts **2** create, develop, etc. —n. form or structure —**build up** to make more attractive —**build′er** n.

build′ing n. structure

build′up′, build′-up′ n. [Col.] **1** praise **2** gradual increase

built′-in′ a. **1** made as part of the structure **2** inherent

built′-up′ a. **1** made higher, etc. with added parts **2** with many buildings on it

bulb n. **1** underground bud, as the onion **2** bulblike electric lamp —**bul′bous** a.

bulge n. outward swelling —v. swell out —**bulg′y** a.

bu·lim′i·a (byōō lē′-) n. an eating disorder —**bu·lim′ic** a.

bulk n. **1** size or mass, esp. if great **2** main part —v. have, or gain in, size or importance —a. not packaged —**bulk′y** a., -i·er, -i·est

bulk′head′ n. vertical partition, as in a ship

bull n. **1** male bovine animal, or male seal, elephant, etc. **2** edict of the Pope —a. male

bull′dog′ n. heavily built dog with a stubborn grip

bull′doz′er n. tractor with a large shovellike blade

bul′let n. shaped metal piece to be shot from a gun

bul′le·tin n. **1** brief news item **2** regular publication of a group

bull′fight′ n. spectacle in which a bull is goaded to fury, then killed —**bull′fight′er** n.

bull′finch′ n. small European songbird

bull′frog′ n. large frog

bull′head′ed a. stubborn

bul·lion (bool′yən) n. gold or silver ingots

bull′ish a. **1** like a bull **2** causing a rise in stock exchange prices

bull′ock n. castrated bull

bull′s-eye′ n. target center

bul′ly n., pl. -**lies** one who hurts or threatens weaker people —v. -**lied, -ly·ing** act the bully (toward)

bul′rush′ n. tall grasslike plant, in marshes, etc.

bul′wark n. rampart; defense

bum n. [Col.] a vagrant —v. bummed, bum′ming **1** [Sl.] beg **2** [Col.] loaf —a. [Sl.] **1** poor in quality **2** false **3** lame

bum′ble v. blunder or stumble —**bum′bler** n.

bum′ble-bee n. large bee

bum′mer n. [Sl.] unpleasant experience

bump v. collide (with) —n. 1 light collision 2 swelling —**bump′y** a., -i-er, -i-est

bump′er n. device, as on a car, for easing collisions —a. unusually abundant

bump′kin n. awkward or simple person from the country

bun n. small bread roll

bunch n. cluster of similar things —v. gather; group

bun′dle n. 1 number of things bound together 2 package —v. 1 make into a bundle 2 hustle (off) —**bundle up** dress warmly

bun′ga·low′ n. small house

bun′gle v. do clumsily; spoil —**bun′gler** n.

bun′ion n. swelling at the base of the big toe

bunk n. 1 built-in bed 2 [Col.] any narrow bed 3 [Sl.] empty talk —v. sleep in a bunk

bunk′er n. 1 large bin 2 obstacle on a golf course

bun′ny n., pl. -nies [Col.] rabbit

bunt Baseball v. to bat (a pitch) so it does not go beyond the infield —n. a bunted ball

bun′ting n. 1 thin cloth for flags, etc. 2 baby's hooded blanket 3 small finch

buoy (boi, boo′ē) n. floating marker —v. 1 keep afloat 2 lift up in spirits

buoy′an·cy (boi′-) n. 1 ability to float 2 cheerfulness —**buoy′ant** a.

bur n. prickly seedcase

bur′den n. 1 load carried 2 thing hard to bear —v. weigh down —**bur′den·some** a.

bur′dock n. plant with prickly burs

bu·reau (byoor′ō) n., pl. -reaus or -reaux (-rōz) 1 chest of drawers 2 government department 3 office

bu·reauc·ra·cy (byoo rä′krə sē) n., pl. -cies (government by) officials following rigid rules —**bu′reau·crat** (byoor′ə-) n. —**bu′reau·crat′ic** a.

burg n. [Col.] city or town

bur′geon (-jən) v. sprout

bur′ger n. [Col.] hamburger or cheeseburger

bur′glar n. one who breaks into a building to steal —**bur′gla·ry** n., pl. -ries

bur′glar·ize′ v. commit burglary in

Bur′gun·dy n. 1 kind of wine 2 purplish red

bur′i·al (ber′-) n. burying of a dead body

bur′lap′ n. coarse cloth of hemp, etc., used for bags

bur·lesque′ (-lesk′) n. 1 broadly comic satire 2 type of vaudeville —v. imitate comically

bur′ly a. -li·er, -li·est big and strong

burn v. burned or burnt, burn′ing 1 be or set on fire 2 destroy or be destroyed by fire 3 hurt or be hurt by acid, friction, etc. 4 feel or make feel hot 5 be excited 6 [Sl.] cheat or trick —n. injury from fire, acid, etc.

burn′er n. part of a stove, etc. producing the flame

bur′nish v., n. polish

burn′out′ n. state of emotional exhaustion from stress, etc.

burp v., n. [Sl.] belch

burr n. 1 rough edge left on metal 2 trilling of r 3 bur

bur′ro n., pl. -ros donkey

bur′row n. hole dug by an animal —v. make a burrow

bur·sar (-sər) n. college treasurer

bur·si′tis n. inflammation of a sac between bone joints

burst v. burst, burst′ing 1 come apart suddenly; explode 2 appear, enter, etc. suddenly 3 be too full —n. a bursting

bur·y (ber′ē) v. -ied, -y·ing 1 put in a grave, tomb, etc. 2 cover; hide

bus n., pl. bus′es or bus′ses large motor coach

bus′boy′ n. assistant to waiter or waitress

bush n. 1 low, woody plant 2 uncleared land —**bush′y** a., -i-er, -i-est

bushed a. [Col.] exhausted

bush′el n. a dry measure equal to 4 pecks

bush′ing n. removable metal lining to reduce friction

bush′whack′ v. ambush

busi·ness (biz′nəs) n. 1 commerce 2 commercial or industrial establishment; store, factory, etc. 3 occupation 4 rightful concern 5 matter; affair —**busi′ness·man′** n., pl. -men′

busi′ness·like′ a. efficient

bus′ing, bus′sing n. a taking children by bus to a school out of their neighborhood so as to achieve racial balance

bust n. 1 sculpture of head and shoulders 2 woman's bosom — v. [Sl.] break

bus·tle (bus'al) v. hurry busily — n. 1 a bustling 2 padding for the back of a skirt

bus·y (biz'-) a. **-i·er, -i·est** 1 active; at work 2 full of activity — v. **-ied, -y·ing** make busy

bus·i·ly adv. —**bus'y·ness** n.

bus·y·bod·y n., pl. **-ies** meddler

but prep. except —con. 1 yet 2 on the contrary 3 unless —adv. 1 only 2 merely —**all but** almost —**but for** if it were not for

bu·tane (byōō'-) n. organic compound used as fuel

butch a. [Col.] designating a man's close-cropped haircut

butch·er n. 1 one who kills and dresses animals for meat 2 one who sells meat 3 killer — v. 1 slaughter 2 botch —**butch·er·y** n.

but·ler n. head manservant

butt n. 1 thick end 2 stub 3 object of ridicule 4 large cask — v. 1 join end to end 2 ram with the head —**butt in(to)** [Sl.] meddle (in)

butte (byōōt) n. small mesa

but·ter n. yellow fat churned from cream — v. spread with butter —**but'ter·y** a.

but·ter·cup n. a small, bright-yellow flower

but·ter·fat n. fatty part of milk

but·ter·fly n., pl. **-flies** insect with four broad, colorful wings

but·ter·milk n. sour milk left after churning butter

but·ter·nut n. white walnut tree or its edible nut

but·ter·scotch n. hard candy made with butter

but·tocks n.pl. fleshy, rounded parts of the hips

but·ton n. 1 small disk for fastening a garment, etc. 2 button-like part — v. to fasten with buttons —**on the button** [Sl.] precisely

but·ton·hole n. slit for a button — v. detain in talk

but·tress n. 1 outer structure supporting a wall 2 a prop — v. prop up

bux·om a. shapely, with a full bosom

buy v. **bought, buy·ing** 1 get by paying money, etc. 2 to bribe — n. [Col.] something worth its price —**buy'er** n.

buy·out n. the purchase of a

business by employees, etc.

buzz v. hum like a bee — n. buzzing sound

buz·zard n. 1 kind of large hawk 2 kind of vulture

buzz·er n. electrical device signaling with a buzz

buzz·word n. jargon word having little meaning, but sounding impressive

by prep. 1 near; beside 2 during 3 not later than 4 through 5 past 6 for 7 according to — adv. 1 near 2 past —**by and by** after a while —**by and large** in most respects —**by the by** incidentally

bye n. advancement to next round of tournament without having to compete

bye'-bye' n., int. goodbye

by·gone a. past — n. anything past

by·law n. local law or rule

by·line n. writer's name heading a newspaper article

by·pass n. 1 road, pipe, etc. that gets around the main way 2 surgery or passage to route blood around a diseased part — v. 1 to detour around 2 ignore

by·path n. side path

by·prod·uct, by'-prod·uct n. secondary product or result

by·stand·er n. one standing near but not taking part

byte (bīt) n. string of bits: basic unit in computing

by·way n. side road

by·word n. 1 proverb 2 thing well-known for some quality

C

cab n. 1 taxicab 2 place in a truck, etc. where the operator sits

ca·bal (ka bal') n. 1 group of conspirators 2 plot

ca·ba·na n. 1 cabin 2 small shelter for swimmers, etc. to change clothes

cab·a·ret (-rā') n. cafe with entertainment

cab·bage n. vegetable with round head of thick leaves

ca·ber·net (-nā') n. dry red wine

cab·in n. 1 hut 2 a room on a ship, etc.

cab·i·net n. 1 case with drawers or shelves 2 [C-] body of official advisers

ca·ble n. 1 thick rope, often of wire 2 cablegram 3 cable TV —

v. send a cablegram (to)

ca'ble·gram' *n.* telegram sent overseas by wire

cable TV *n.* TV system transmitting via cables to subscribers

ca·boose' *n.* crew's car on a freight train

ca·ca·o (bean) (kə kā'ō) *n.* seed of tropical American tree: source of chocolate

cache (kash) *n.* **1** place for hiding food, supplies, etc. **2** anything so hidden —*v.* to place in a cache

ca·chet' (-shā') *n.* sign of official approval or of quality

cack'le *v., n.* (make) the shrill sound of a hen

ca·coph'o·ny (kə käf'-) *n., pl.* -nies harsh, jarring sound(s) — **ca·coph'o·nous** *a.*

cac'tus *n., pl.* -tus·es or -ti (-tī') spiny desert plant

cad *n.* ungentlemanly man

ca·dav'er (kə dav'-) *n.* corpse — **ca·dav'er·ous** *a.*

cad'die, cad'dy *n., pl.* -ies attendant to a golfer —*v.* -died, -dy·ing be a caddy

cad'dy *n., pl.* -dies small container, as for tea

ca'dence *n.* **1** fall of the voice in speaking **2** rhythm; measured movement

ca·det' *n.* student at a military or naval school

cadge *v.* beg —**cadg'er** *n.*

cad'mi·um *n.* metallic chemical element used in alloys, etc.

ca·dre (ka'drē, kä'drā) *n.* nucleus of a larger organization

Cae·sar'e·an (section) *n.* surgery to deliver a baby

ca·fe (ka fā') *n.* **1** restaurant **2** barroom

caf·e·te'ri·a (-tir'ē ə) *n.* self-service restaurant

caf·fe·ine, caf·fe·in (kaf'ēn') *n.* stimulant in coffee, tea, etc.

caf'tan *n.* long-sleeved robe, worn in eastern Mediterranean lands

cage *n.* openwork structure, esp. for confining animals —*v.* put in a cage

cag'er *n.* [Sl.] basketball player

ca'gey, ca'gy *a.* -gi·er, -gi·est [Col.] sly; cunning —**ca'gi·ly** *adv.*

cais'son (kā'-) *n.* **1** ammunition wagon **2** watertight box for underwater construction work

ca·jole' *v.* coax or wheedle —**ca·jol'er·y** *n.*

Ca'jun, Ca'jan *n.* Canadian

French native of Louisiana

cake *n.* **1** baked dough or batter of flour, eggs, sugar, etc. **2** solid, formed, usually flat mass —*v.* form into a hard mass

cal'a·bash' *n.* gourdlike fruit of a tropical tree

ca·la·ma'ri *n.* squid cooked as food

cal'a·mine' *n.* zinc compound used in lotions, etc.

ca·lam'i·ty *n., pl.* -ties disaster —**ca·lam'i·tous** *a.*

cal'ci·fy' (-sə fī') *v.* -fied', -fy'ing change into stony matter —**cal'ci·fi·ca'tion** *n.*

cal'ci·mine' *n.* thin, watery paint for covering plaster —*v.* to cover with calcimine

cal'ci·um *n.* chemical element in bone, limestone, etc.

cal'cu·late' (-kyōo-) *v.* **1** figure by arithmetic **2** estimate —**cal'cu·la·ble** *a.* —**cal'cu·la'tion** *n.* —**cal'cu·la'tor** *n.*

cal'cu·lat'ing *a.* **1** scheming **2** shrewd; cautious

cal'cu·lus *n.* branch of higher mathematics

cal·dron (kôl'drən) *n.* large kettle or boiler

cal'en·dar *n.* **1** table showing the days, weeks, and months of a year **2** schedule

calf *n., pl.* **calves 1** young cow or bull **2** young elephant, seal, etc. **3** fleshy part of leg below the knee

calf'skin' *n.* leather made from the skin of a calf

cal'i·ber, cal'i·bre *n.* **1** diameter of a bullet, bore of a gun, etc. **2** quality

cal'i·brate' *v.* mark or fix the graduations of (a measuring device) —**cal'i·bra'tion** *n.* —**cal'i·bra'tor** *n.*

cal'i·co' *n.* cotton cloth, usually printed

cal'i·pers *n.pl.* instrument for measuring diameter

ca'liph, ca'lif (kā'-) *n.* old title of Muslim rulers

cal·is·then'ics *n.pl.* simple athletic exercises

calk (kôk) *v., n.* caulk

call *v.* **1** say loudly; shout **2** summon **3** name **4** telephone **5** stop (a game) —*n.* **1** shout or cry **2** summons **3** demand **4** need **5** short visit —**call for 1** demand **2** come and get —**call off** cancel —**call on 1** visit briefly **2** ask (one) to speak — **on call** available when called —

call'er n.

cal·lig'ra·phy n. artistic handwriting —**cal·lig'ra·pher** n.

call'ing n. vocation; trade

cal·li'o·pe (-lī'ə pē') n. organlike musical instrument with steam whistles

cal'lous a. 1 hardened 2 unfeeling —**cal'lous·ly** adv.

cal'low a. inexperienced

cal'lus n. hard, thickened place on the skin

calm n. stillness —a. still; tranquil —v. make or become calm —**calm'ly** adv. —**calm'ness** n.

ca·lor'ic a. of heat

cal'o·ry, cal'o·rie (-rē) n., pl. **-ries** unit of heat or of the energy gotten from food

ca·lum'ni·ate (kə lum'-) v. to slander —**ca·lum'ni·a'tion** n.

cal'um·ny n., pl. **-nies** slander

calve (kav) v. give birth to (a calf)

ca·lyp'so (-lip'-) n., pl. **-sos** improvised ballad sung in the West Indies

ca·lyx (kā'liks) n., pl. **-lyx'es** or **-ly·ces** (-lə sēz') sepals of a flower

cam n. projection on a wheel to give irregular motion, as to a shaft (**cam'shaft**)

ca·ma·ra·de·rie (kä'mə räd'ər ē) n. comradeship

cam'ber n. slight convexity

cam'bi·um n. cell layer under bark of plants from which new wood and bark grow

cam'bric (kām'-) n. fine linen or cotton cloth

cam'cord'er n. portable videotape recorder and TV camera

came v. pt. of COME

cam'el n. beast of burden with a humped back

ca·mel'li·a (-mēl'yə) n. large, roselike flower

cam'e·o n., pl. **-os'** 1 gem, etc. with figure carved on it 2 small role for notable actor

cam'er·a n. 1 device for taking photographs 2 TV device that first receives the images for transmission

cam'i·sole' n. short negligee

cam'o·mile n. chamomile

cam'ou·flage' (-ə fläzh') n. a disguising of potential targets in wartime —v. conceal by disguising

camp n. 1 place with tents, huts, etc., as for vacationers or soldiers 2 supporters of a cause —v. set up a camp —**camp'er** n.

cam·paign' (-pān') n. series of planned actions, as in war, an election, etc. —v. wage a campaign

cam'phor (-fər) n. strong-smelling crystalline substance used in mothballs, medicine, etc.

camp'site' n. place for camping

cam'pus n. school or college grounds —a. of students

camp'y a. [Sl.] so artificial or trite as to amuse

can v. pt. **could** auxiliary verb showing: 1 ability 2 likelihood 3 [Col.] permission

can n. metal container, as for foods —v. **canned, can'ning** preserve (food) in cans or jars —**can'ner** n.

Ca·na'di·an n., a. (native) of Canada

ca·nal' n. 1 artificial waterway 2 body duct

ca'na·pé' (-pā') n. appetizer on a cracker, etc.

ca·nard' n. false rumor

ca·nar'y n., pl. **-ies** yellow songbird kept in a cage

can'can' n. lively dance with much high kicking

can'cel v. 1 cross out 2 make invalid 3 abolish —**can'cel·la'tion** n.

can'cer n. 1 malignant tumor 2 a spreading evil —[C-] fourth sign of the zodiac; Crab —**can'cer·ous** a.

can·de·la'brum (-lä'-, -lā'-) n., pl. **-bra** or **-brums** large, branched candlestick: also **can·de·la'bra**, pl. **-bras**

can'did a. frank; honest

can'di·date' n. one seeking office, etc. —**can'di·da·cy** n.

can'dle n. wax taper with a wick, burned for light

can'dle·pow'er n. unit for measuring light

can'dle·stick' n. holder for a candle or candles

can'dor n. frankness

can'dy n., pl. **-dies** confection of sugar or syrup —v. **-died, -dy·ing** cook or preserve in sugar

cane n. 1 hollow, jointed stem, as of bamboo 2 walking stick 3 split rattan —v. to beat with a cane

ca'nine a. of or like a dog —n. dog

canine tooth n. any of the four sharp-pointed teeth

can'is·ter n. box or can for coffee, tea, etc.

can'ker n. a sore, esp. in the

mouth —can·ker·ous a.

can·na·bis n. 1 hemp 2 marijuana, etc. from the flowering tops of hemp

can·ner·y n., pl. -ies factory for canning foods

can·ni·bal n. person who eats human flesh —can·ni·bal·ism n. —can·ni·bal·is·tic a.

can·non n., pl. -nons or -non large mounted gun

can·non·ade' n. continuous firing of artillery

can·not cannot

can·ny a. -ni·er, -ni·est 1 cautious 2 shrewd —can·ni·ly adv.

ca·noe' (-nōō') n. narrow, light boat moved with paddles —v. paddle or go in a canoe

ca·no·la (oil) n. cooking oil, from the seed of the rape plant

can·on n. 1 body of church laws 2 any law 3 official list 4 clergyman serving in a cathedral 5 musical round —ca·non·i·cal, ca·non·ic a.

can·on·ize' v. name as a saint —can·on·i·za'tion n.

can·o·py n., pl. -pies covering hung over a bed, throne, etc. —can·o·pied a.

cant n. 1 special vocabulary of a class; jargon 2 hypocritical talk —v. use cant

cant n., v. tilt; slant

can't cannot

can·ta·loupe', can·ta·loup' (-ə lōp') n. sweet, juicy melon

can·tan·ker·ous a. bad-tempered; quarrelsome

can·ta·ta (kən tät'ə) n. dramatic choral composition

can·teen' n. 1 general store at an army post 2 soldier's water flask

can·ter n. easy gallop —v. go at this pace

can·ti·cle n. hymn

can·ti·le'ver n. structure that is anchored at only one end

can·to n., pl. -tos division of a long poem

can·ton n. a state in the Swiss Republic

can·tor n. liturgical singer in a synagogue

can·vas n. coarse cloth used for tents, sails, oil paintings, etc.

can·vas·back' n. wild duck with a grayish back

can·vass (-vəs) v. seek votes, opinions, etc. from —n. a canvassing —can'vass·er n.

can·yon n. a narrow valley between high cliffs

cap n. 1 brimless hat, often with a visor 2 caplike cover —v. capped, cap'ping 1 put a cap on 2 surpass

ca'pa·ble a. able; skilled —capable of able or likely to —ca'pa·bil'i·ty n., pl. -ties —ca'pa·bly adv.

ca·pa'cious a. roomy; wide

ca·pac'i·tor n. device for storing an electrical charge

ca·pac'i·ty n. 1 ability to contain or hold 2 volume 3 ability 4 position

cape n. 1 sleeveless coat fastened about the neck 2 land jutting into water

ca'per v. skip about playfully —n. 1 wild, foolish act 2 [Sl.] criminal act, esp. a robbery

ca'pers n.pl. tiny pickled buds used as seasoning

cap'il·lar'y a. having a tiny bore, as a tube —n., pl. -ies tiny blood vessel

cap'i·tal a. 1 bringing or punishable by death 2 chief; main 3 excellent —n. 1 capital letter 2 city from which a state is governed 3 money or property owned or used in business 4 capitalists collectively 5 top of a column

cap'i·tal·ism' n. economic system in which the means of production and distribution are privately owned

cap'i·tal·ist n. owner of wealth used in business —cap'i·tal·is'tic a.

cap'i·tal·ize' v. 1 convert into capital 2 use to advantage: with on 3 supply capital for 4 write with a capital letter —cap'i·tal·i·za'tion n.

capital letter n. large letter used to begin a sentence, name, etc.

Cap'i·tol n. building where a legislature meets

ca·pit'u·late' (-pich'ə-) v. surrender —ca·pit'u·la'tion n.

cap'let n. medicinal tablet with a protective coating

ca'pon' n. castrated rooster

cap·puc·ci·no (kä'pə chē'nō, kap'ə-) n. steamed coffee mixed with steamed milk

ca·price' (-prēs') n. whim

ca·pri·cious (-prish'əs, -prē'shəs) a. unpredictable

Cap'ri·corn' tenth sign of the zodiac; Goat

cap'size' v. 1 upset; overturn

cap'stan n. device around which cables are wound

cap'sule n. small case, as for a dose of medicine

cap'tain n. 1 leader 2 army officer above lieutenant 3 navy officer above commander 4 master of a ship —v. to head —**cap'tain·cy** n.

cap'tion n. 1 title, as under a newspaper picture 2 TV or film subtitle

cap'tious (-shəs) a. 1 made for the sake of argument 2 quick to find fault

cap'ti·vate v. fascinate

cap'tive a., n. (held) prisoner —**cap·tiv'i·ty** n.

cap'tor n. one who captures

cap'ture v. take by force, by surprise, etc. —n. a capturing or the thing captured

car n. 1 wheeled vehicle; esp., an automobile 2 elevator

ca·rafe' (-raf') n. bottle for water, coffee, etc.

car'a·mel (or kär'məl) n. 1 burnt sugar used to flavor 2 chewy candy

car'at n. 1 unit of weight for jewels 2 karat

car'a·van' n. group traveling together, as through a desert

car'a·way' n. spicy seeds used as flavoring

car·bine' (-bīn', -bēn') n. light, short-barreled rifle

car'bo·hy'drate n. compound of carbon, hydrogen, and oxygen, as sugar or starch

car·bol'ic acid n. an acid used as an antiseptic, etc.

car'bon n. nonmetallic chemical element in all organic compounds: diamond and graphite are pure carbon

car'bon·ate' v. charge with carbon dioxide —**car'bo·na'tion** n.

carbon dioxide n. odorless gas given off in breathing

car'bon·if'er·ous a. containing carbon or coal

carbon monoxide n. colorless, odorless, poisonous gas

carbon paper n. paper coated with a carbon preparation, used to make copies (**carbon copies**) of letters, etc.

carbon tet'ra·chlo'ride (-klôr'īd) n. cleaning fluid

car'bun'cle n. painful inflammation below the skin

car'bu·ret'or (-bə rāt'ər) n. device in an engine for mixing air with gasoline

car'cass (-kəs) n. dead body of an animal

car·cin'o·gen n. substance causing cancer —**car'ci·no·gen'ic** a.

car·ci·no'ma n. cancer of certain tissues, esp. the epidermis

card n. 1 flat piece of stiff paper 2 postcard 3 playing card 4 pl. game played with cards 5 metal comb for wool, etc. —v. comb with a card

card'board' n. stiff paper

car'di·ac' a. of the heart

car'di·gan n. knitted jacketlike sweater

car'di·nal a. 1 chief; main 2 bright-red —n. 1 high R.C. Church official 2 red American songbird

cardinal number n. number used in counting, as 7, 42, etc.

cardio- pref. of the heart

car'di·o·gram' n. electrocardiogram

car'di·o·graph' n. an electrocardiograph

car'di·ol'o·gy n. branch of medicine dealing with the heart —**car'di·ol'o·gist** n.

car'di·o·vas'cu·lar a. of the heart and blood vessels

care n. 1 worry 2 watchfulness 3 charge; keeping —v. 1 be concerned 2 wish (to do) —**cared for** 1 love or like 2 look after —**(in) care of** at the address of —**take care of** 1 look after 2 protect —**care'free'** a. —**care'ful** a. —**care'less** a.

ca·reen' v. tilt; lurch

ca·reer' n. 1 full speed 2 progress through life 3 profession or occupation

ca·ress' v. touch lovingly —n. affectionate touch

car'et n. mark (∧) to show where addition is to be made in a printed line

care'tak'er n. one who takes care of a building, etc.

care'worn' a. weary with care

car'fare' n. price of a ride on a bus, etc.

car'go n., pl. **-goes** or **-gos** load carried by a ship, etc.

car'i·bou' (-bōō') n. North American reindeer

car·i·ca·ture (kar'i kə chər) n. distorted imitation or picture for satire —v. do a caricature of

car·i·es (ker'ēz') n. decay of teeth, bones, etc.

car'mine (-min, -mīn') n. red or purplish red

car'nage n. slaughter

car'nal a. bodily; sensual

car·na'tion n. 1 variety of the

pink 2 its flower

car·ni·val n. **1** festivity **2** kind of fair, with rides, etc.

car·niv·o·rous a. flesh-eating — **car·ni·vore** n.

car·ob n. tree with sweet pods used in candy, etc.

car·ol n. (Christmas) song of joy —v. **sing** —**car·ol·er, car·ol·ler** n.

car·om n., v. hit and rebound

ca·rot·id (-rouz′) v., n. (join in a drinking party

ca·rouse (-rouz′) v., n. (join in a drinking party

car·ou·sel, car·rou·sel n. merry-go-round

carp n. freshwater fish —v. find fault pettily

car·pen·ter n. construction worker who makes wooden parts —**car·pen·try** n.

car·pet n. heavy fabric for covering a floor —v. to cover as with a carpet

car·pet·ing n. carpets or carpet fabric

car pool n. group plan to rotate cars, going to and from work

car·port n. roofed shelter for an automobile

car·rel, car·rell n. small enclosure for study in a library

car·riage n. **1** horsedrawn vehicle **2** posture **3** moving part that holds and shifts something

car·ri·er n. one that carries

car·ri·on n. decaying flesh of a dead body

car·rot n. plant with an edible, orange-red root

car·ry v. **-ried, -ry·ing 1** take to another place **2** lead, transmit, etc. **3** win (an election, etc.) **4** hold; support **5** bear (oneself) **6** keep in stock **7** cover a range — **be** (or **get**) **carried away to** become very emotional or enthusiastic —**carry on 1** do or continue **2** [Col.] behave wildly —**carry out** (or **through**) to accomplish

car·ry-out a. of prepared food sold to be eaten elsewhere

car·sick a. nauseated from riding in a car, etc.

cart n. small wagon or vehicle with wheels, pushed or pulled by hand —v. carry in a vehicle

cart·age n. **1** a carting **2** charge for this

carte blanche (blänsh′) n. full authority

car·tel n. national or international monopoly

car·ti·lage n. tough, elastic skeletal tissue

car·tog·ra·phy n. map-making — **car·tog·ra·pher** n.

car·ton n. cardboard box

car·toon n. **1** drawing that is a caricature **2** comic strip **3** film of drawn figures that seem to move —**car·toon·ist** n.

car·tridge n. **1** cylinder holding the charge and bullet or shot for a firearm **2** small container for film, etc.

cart·wheel n. a sideways turning, heels over head, with the legs extended

carve v. **1** make or shape by cutting **2** slice —**carv·er** n. —**carv·ing** n.

car·wash n. business at which cars are washed

ca·sa·ba n. melon with a yellow rind

cas·cade n. **1** waterfall **2** a shower —v. fall in a cascade

case n. **1** example or instance **2** situation **3** lawsuit **4** form of a noun, etc. showing its relation to neighboring words **5** container **6** protective cover —v. **1** put in a case **2** [Sl.] examine carefully —**in case** if —**in case of** in the event of

ca·se·in (-sē-) n. protein constituent of milk

case·ment n. hinged window that opens outward

cash n. money on hand —v. give or get cash for

cash·ew n. kidney-shaped, edible nut

cash·ier n. one in charge of cash transactions —v. dismiss in disgrace

cash·mere (kash′-, kazh′-) n. soft, fine goat's wool, or a cloth of this

cas·ing n. **1** outer covering **2** door frame

ca·si·no n., pl. **-nos** hall for dancing, gambling, etc.

cask n. barrel for liquid

cas·ket n. coffin

cas·sa·va (-sä′-) n. tropical plant with starchy roots

cas·se·role n. covered dish for baking and serving

cas·sette n. case with film or tape for a camera, tape recorder, VCR, etc.

cas·sock n. long vestment worn by clergymen

cast v. cast, cast·ing **1** throw **2** deposit (a vote) **3** mold **4** select (an actor) —n. **1** a throw **2**

plaster form for broken limb 3 the actors in a play 4 type or quality 5 tinge —**cast about** search —**cast aside** (or **away** or **off**) discard

cas'ta·nets' n.pl. two hollow pieces clicked together in one hand in rhythm

cast'a·way' n. shipwrecked person

caste (kast) n. class distinction based on birth, etc.

cast'er n. small swiveled wheel as on a table leg

cas'ti·gate' v. criticize severely —**cas'ti·ga'tion** n. —**cas'ti·ga'tor** n.

casting n. metal cast in a mold

cast iron n. hard, brittle pig iron —**cast'-i'ron** a.

cas'tle (-'əl) n. 1 large, fortified dwelling 2 ROOK (n. 2)

cast'off' a. discarded —n. person or thing abandoned

cas'tor oil n. oil used as a laxative

cas'trate' v. remove the testicles of —**cas·tra'tion** n.

cas'u·al (kazh'ōō-) a. 1 by chance 2 careless 3 nonchalant 4 informal

cas'u·al·ty n., pl. **-ties** one hurt or killed in an accident or in war

cas'u·ist·ry n. subtle but false reasoning

cat n. 1 small, soft-furred animal kept as a pet 2 any related mammal, as the lion

cat'a·clysm' (-kliz'əm) n. sudden, violent change —**cat'a·clys'mic** a.

cat'a·comb' (-kōm') n. tunnel-like burial place

cat'a·lep'sy n. loss of consciousness, with body rigidity —**cat'a·lep'tic** a., n.

cat'a·log', cat'a·logue' n. complete list, as of library books —v. to list

ca·tal'pa (-tal'-) n. tree with heart-shaped leaves

cat'a·lyst' (-list') n. substance that affects a chemical reaction but itself remains unchanged —**cat'a·lyt'ic** a.

cat'a·pult' n. device for throwing or launching —v. shoot as from a catapult

cat'a·ract' n. 1 large waterfall 2 opaque condition of eye lens

ca·tarrh' (ka tär') n. inflammation of the respiratory passages

ca·tas'tro·phe (-tra fē) n. sudden great disaster —**cat'a·stroph'ic** a.

cat'a·ton'ic a. being in a stupor in which the muscles are rigid

cat'bird' n. songbird with a call like a cat's

cat'call' n. derisive call

catch v. **caught, catch'ing** 1 capture 2 deceive 3 surprise 4 get 5 grab 6 understand 7 take or keep hold —n. 1 a catching or is caught 2 thing that catches or is caught —**catch on** 1 understand 2 become popular —**catch up** to overtake —**catch'er** n.

catch'ing a. 1 contagious 2 attractive

catch'up n. ketchup

catch'y a. **-i·er, -i·est** 1 easily remembered 2 tricky

cat'e·chism' (-kiz'əm) n. list of questions and answers to teach religious beliefs

cat'e·gor'i·cal a. 1 of or in a category 2 positive

cat'e·go·ry n., pl. **-ries** any of a system of classes —**cat'e·go·rize'** v.

ca'ter v. provide food, etc. for a party —**ca'ter·er** n.

cat'er-cor'nered (kat'ə-) a. diagonal —adv. diagonally Also **cat'er-cor'ner**

cat'er·pil'lar n. larva of a butterfly, moth, etc.

cat'er·waul' (-wôl') v., n. wail

cat'fish' n. fish with long feelers about the mouth

cat'gut' n. tough thread made from animal intestines

ca·thar'sis n. a relieving of the emotions

ca·thar'tic a. purging —n. a laxative

ca·the'dral n. large church

cath'e·ter n. tube put in the bladder to remove urine

cath'ode' n. 1 a negatively charged electrode 2 positive terminal of a battery

cathode rays n.pl. streams of electrons producing X-rays when striking solids

cath'o·lic a. 1 universal 2 liberal 3 [C-] Roman Catholic —n. [C-] member of the R.C. Church —**Ca·thol'i·cism'** n. —**cath'o·lic'i·ty** n.

cat'kin n. spike of clustered small flowers

cat'nap' n. short sleep; doze —v. take a catnap

cat'nip' n. plant like mint

cat'-o'-nine'-tails' n., pl. **-tails'** whip of nine knotted cords attached to a handle

CAT scan (kat) n. computerized

photographic technique using X-rays

cat's'-paw' n. a dupe

cat'sup (or kech'əp) n. ketchup

cat'tail' n. marsh plant with long, brown spikes

cat'tle n. 1 livestock 2 cows, bulls, steers, or oxen —**cat'tle-man** n., pl. **-men**

cat'ty a. **-ti-er, -ti-est** spiteful or mean

cat'ty-cor'nered a., adv. cater-cornered: also **cat'ty-cor'ner**

cat'walk' n. high, narrow walk

Cau-ca-soid (kô'kə soid') n., a. (member) of one of the major groups of human beings, loosely called the *white race*: also **Cau-ca-sian** (kô kā'zhən)

cau'cus n. political meeting to choose party candidates, etc. — v. hold a caucus

caught v. pt. & pp. of CATCH

caul'dron n. caldron

cau'li-flow'er n. hard, white head of a cabbagelike plant

caulk (kôk) v. make watertight or airtight by filling cracks with a puttylike sealant —n. this sealant

caus'al a. of a cause or causes — **cau-sal'i-ty** n.

cause n. 1 thing bringing a result 2 motive 3 group movement with an aim 4 lawsuit —v. bring about

cause'way' n. raised road, as across a marsh

caus'tic a. 1 corrosive 2 sarcastic —n. caustic substance

cau'ter-ize' v. burn dead tissue off, as with a hot iron

cau'tion n. 1 warning 2 prudence —v. warn —**cau'tious** a.

cav'al-cade' n. procession

cav-a-lier' (-lir') n. 1 knight 2 gallant gentleman —a. 1 casual 2 arrogant —**cav-a-lier'ly** adv.

cav'al-ry n., pl. **-ries** army troops on horses or in motorized vehicles —**cav'al-ry-man** n., pl. **-men**

cave n. hollow place in the earth —v. collapse (in)

cav'ern n. large cave —**cav'ern-ous** a.

cav'i-ar', cav'i-are' (-är') n. fish eggs eaten as a relish

cav'il v. quibble

cav'i-ty n., pl. **-ties** hole or hollow place

ca-vort' v. prance; caper

caw n. crow's harsh cry —v. make this sound

cay-enne' (kī-, kā-) n. ground

hot red pepper

CD n. compact disc

cease (sēs) v. to end; stop

cease'-fire' n. truce

cease'less a. unceasing

ce'dar n. evergreen tree with fragrant wood

cede (sēd) v. give up; transfer

ceil'ing n. 1 inner roof of a room 2 upper limit

cel'e-brate' v. 1 to perform (a ritual) 2 commemorate with festivity 3 honor; praise —**cel'e-bra'tion** n.

cel'e-brat'ed a. famous

ce-leb'ri-ty n. 1 fame 2 pl. **-ties** famous person

ce-ler'i-ty n. speed

cel'er-y n. plant with edible crisp stalks

ce-les'tial (-chəl) a. 1 of the heavens 2 divine

cel'i-ba-cy n. unmarried state — **cel'i-bate** (-bat) a., n.

cell n. 1 small room as in a prison 2 small unit of protoplasm 3 device for generating electricity chemically 4 unit of an organization —**cel'lu-lar** a.

cel'lar n. room(s) below ground under a building

cel·lo (chel'ō) n., pl. **-los** instrument like a large violin, held between the knees in playing — **cel'list** n.

cel'lo-phane' (sel'ə-) n. thin transparent cellulose material, used as a wrapping

cel'lu-lite' n. fatty deposits on the hips and thighs

cel'lu-loid' n. flammable plastic substance of cellulose

cel'lu-lose' (-yōō lōs') n. substance in plant cell walls, used in making paper, etc.

Cel'si-us a. of a thermometer on which 0° is the freezing point and 100° is the boiling point of water

ce-ment' n. 1 mixture of lime, clay, and water, used for paving, in mortar, etc. 2 any adhesive —v. join as with cement

cem'e-ter'y n., pl. **-ies** place for burying the dead

cen'ser n. container in which incense is burned

cen'sor n. one who examines books, mail, etc. to remove things considered unsuitable — v. act as a censor of —**cen'sor-ship'** n.

cen-so'ri-ous (-sôr'ē-) a. critical

cen'sure n., v. blame

cen'sus n. official count of population

cent *n.* 100th part of a dollar; penny

cen·taur' (-tôr') *n. Gr. myth.* monster with a man's head and trunk and a horse's body

cen·ta·vo (-tä'-) *n., pl.* **-vos** 100th part of a peso

cen·ten'ni·al *n.* 100th anniversary —*a.* of a centennial Also **cen'te·nar'y** (*or* sen ten'ər ē)

cen'ter *n.* 1 middle point, esp. of a circle or sphere 2 any central place, thing, or person —*v.* 1 put or be at the center 2 gather

cen'ter·fold' *n.* center facing pages of a magazine

cen'ter·piece' *n.* ornament for the center of a table

cen'ti·grade' *a.* Celsius

cen'ti·gram' *n.* 1⁄100 gram

cen·time (sän'tēm') *n.* 100th part of a franc

cen'ti·me·ter *n.* 1⁄100 meter

cen'ti·pede' *n.* wormlike animal with many pairs of legs

cen'tral *a.* 1 in or near the center 2 main; chief —**cen'tral·ly** *adv.*

cen'tral·ize' *v.* 1 bring to a center 2 organize under one control —**cen'tral·i·za'tion** *n.*

cen'tre *n., v.,* chiefly Br. sp. of CENTER

cen·trif'u·gal force *n.* force that makes rotating bodies move away from the center

cen'tri·fuge' (-fyōōj') *n.* machine using centrifugal force to separate particles

cen·trip'e·tal force *n.* force that makes rotating bodies move toward the center

cen'trist *n.* person with moderate political opinions

cen·tu'ri·on *n.* military commander in ancient Rome

cen'tu·ry (-chə-) *n., pl.* **-ries** period of 100 years

ce·ram'ics *n.* the making of pottery, porcelain, etc. —*n.pl.* pottery, etc. —**ce·ram'ic** *a.*

ce're·al (sir'ē-) *n.* 1 grain used for food, as wheat, oats, etc. 2 food made from grain

cer·e·bel'lum (ser'ə-) *n.* lower rear part of the brain

cer'e·bral (*or* sə rē'-) *a.* of the brain

cerebral palsy *n.* paralysis due to a lesion of the brain

cer·e·brum (*or* sə rē'-) *n.* upper, main part of the brain

cer·e·mo'ni·al *a.* ritual; formal —*n.* system of rites

cer'e·mo·ny *n., pl.* **-nies** 1 set of formal acts; rite 2 rigid etiquette; formality —**cer·e·mo'ni·ous** *a.*

ce·rise' (-rēz', rēs') *a.* clear red

cer'tain *a.* 1 fixed; settled 2 sure; positive 3 specific, but unnamed 4 some —**for certain** surely —**cer'tain·ly** *adv.* —**cer'tain·ty** *n.*

cer·tif'i·cate (-kət) *n.* written statement testifying to a fact, promise, etc.

cer'ti·fy' *v.* **-fied'**, **-fy'ing** 1 formally declare to be true, etc. 2 guarantee —**cer·ti·fi·ca'tion** *n.*

cer'ti·tude' *n.* assurance

cer'vix *n.* necklike part —**cer'vi·cal** *a.*

ces·sa'tion *n.* stop; pause

ces'sion *n.* a ceding

cess'pool' *n.* deep hole in the ground for sewage, etc.

Cha·blis (sha blē') *n.* dry white wine

chafe *v.* 1 make warm or sore by rubbing 2 be angry

chaff *n.* 1 threshed husks of grain 2 worthless stuff —*v.* to tease; banter

cha·grin' (shə-) *n.* disappointment, humiliation, etc. —*v.* to make feel chagrin

chain *n.* 1 flexible series of joined links 2 fetters 3 connected series —*v.* restrain as with chains

chain reaction *n.* a series of (nuclear) reactions whose products cause new reactions

chain saw *n.* portable power saw with an endless chain of cutting teeth

chain store *n.* any of a group of retail stores owned by one company

chair *n.* 1 seat with a back 2 office of authority

chair'lift' *n.* seats on a cable for carrying skiers uphill

chair'man *n., pl.* **-men** one who presides at a meeting —**chair'man·ship'** *n.* —**chair'per·son** *n.* —**chair'wom·an** *n.fem., pl.* **-wom·en**

chaise longue (shāz' lôŋ') *n., pl.* **chaise longues** couchlike chair with a long seat

cha·let (sha lā') *n.* cottage with overhanging eaves

chal·ice (chal'is) *n.* cup

chalk (chôk) *n.* soft limestone for writing on a blackboard —**chalk up** to record —**chalk'y** *a.*, **-i·er**, **-i·est**

chalk′board n. blackboard

chal′lenge n. 1 demand for identification 2 a calling into question 3 call to a contest, etc. 4 anything calling for special effort —v. put a challenge to —**chal′leng·er** n.

cham′ber (chām′-) n. 1 room 2 pl. judge's office 3 assembly or council 4 part of a gun for the cartridge

cham′ber·maid n. maid who keeps bedrooms neat

cham′bray (sham′-) n. smooth cotton fabric

cha·me′le·on (kə mē′-) n. lizard able to change its color

cham·ois (sham′ē) n., pl. **cham′ois** 1 small antelope 2 soft kind of leather

cham′o·mile (kam′-) n. flower used in medicinal tea

champ v. chew or bite noisily —n. [Sl.] champion

cham·pagne (sham pān′) n. effervescent white wine

cham′pi·on n. 1 one who fights for a cause 2 winner of first place —a. best —v. defend; support —**cham′pi·on·ship** n.

chance n. 1 luck; fortune 2 risk 3 opportunity 4 possibility —a. accidental —v. 1 happen 2 risk

chan′cel n. place around an altar for clergy and choir

chan′cel·lor n. 1 high state or church official 2 university head —**chan′cel·ler·y** n., pl. **-ies**

chan·cre (shaŋ′kər) n. sore or ulcer of syphilis

chanc′y a. **-i·er, -i·est** risky

chan·de·lier (shan′də lir′) n. hanging lighting fixture

chan′dler n. 1 candle maker 2 retailer of supplies, as for ships

change v. 1 to substitute 2 exchange 3 alter; vary —n. 1 alteration or variation 2 variety 3 money returned as overpayment 4 small coins —**change′a·ble** a. —**change′less** a.

change of life menopause

change′o′ver n. a complete change

chan′nel n. 1 bed of a river, etc. 2 wide strait joining two seas 3 any passage 4 official course of action 5 assigned frequency band, esp. in TV —v. make, or send through, a channel

chant n. song with several words to each tone —v. to utter in a chant

chan·tey (shan′tē, chan′-) n.

sailors' work song

Cha·nu·kah (khä′noo kä′) n. Hanuka

cha·os (kā′äs′) n. complete disorder —**cha·ot′ic** a.

chap n. [Col.] a fellow —v. chapped, chap′ping become rough and red as from the cold

chap′el n. small church

chap·er·on, chap·er·one (shap′ə rōn′) n. older person in charge of unmarried people at social affairs —v. be a chaperon to

chap′lain (-lən) n. clergyman in the armed forces

chap′let n. garland

chaps n.pl. leather trousers worn by cowboys

chap′ter n. 1 main division of a book 2 branch of an organization

char v. **charred, char′ring** scorch

char′ac·ter (ker′-) n. 1 letter or symbol 2 trait 3 kind or sort 4 personality 5 moral strength 6 person in a play, novel, etc. 7 [Col.] eccentric person

char·ac·ter·is′tic a. typical; distinctive —n. distinguishing quality

char′ac·ter·ize′ v. 1 describe 2 be a quality of —**char′ac·ter·i·za′tion** n.

cha·rade′ (shə-) n. word game in pantomime

char′broil′, char′-broil′ v. broil over a charcoal fire

char′coal′ n. pieces of incompletely burned wood

char·don·nay′ (shär′-) n. dry white wine

charge v. 1 fill (with) 2 add electricity to 3 command 4 accuse 5 ask as a price 6 ask payment (for) 7 put as a debt 8 attack —n. 1 load 2 responsibility or care (of) 3 chemical energy in a battery 4 someone in one's care 5 command 6 accusation 7 a cost 8 debt or charge 9 attack —**in charge (of)** in control (of)

charg′er n. war horse

char′i·ot n. ancient, horse-drawn, two-wheeled cart —**char′i·ot·eer′** n.

cha·ris′ma (kə riz′-) n. charming or inspiring quality —**char·is·mat′ic** a.

char′i·ty n., pl. **-ties** 1 leniency in judging others 2 a helping those in need 3 institution for so helping —**char′i·ta·ble** a.

char·la·tan (shär′lə tən) n. quack; impostor

char·ley horse n. [Col.] muscle cramp in the thigh

charm n. 1 words or thing supposed to have magic power 2 trinket on a bracelet, etc. 3 fascination; allure —v. 1 to use a magical charm on 2 fascinate; delight —**charm′ing** a.

char′nel (house) n. place for corpses

chart n. 1 map, esp. for navigation 2 graph, table, etc. —v. make a chart of

char·ter n. official paper licensing a new company, society, chapter, etc. —v. 1 grant a charter to 2 hire

char·treuse (shär trōōz′) n., a. pale, yellowish green

char′wom·an n., pl. -wom′en cleaning woman

char·y (cher′ē) a. -i·er, -i·est careful; cautious —**char′i·ly** adv.

chase v. 1 follow in order to catch 2 drive away 3 decorate (metal) as by engraving —n. a chasing —**give chase** pursue

chas′er n. [Col.] water, etc. taken after liquor

chasm (kaz′əm) n. deep crack in the earth's surface

chas·sis (chas′ē, shas′-) n., pl. -sis (-ēz) 1 frame, wheels, and motor of a car 2 frame, tubes, etc. of a radio or TV

chaste a. 1 sexually virtuous 2 decent; modest 3 simple in style —**chas′ti·ty** n.

chas·ten (chās′ən) v. 1 punish so as to correct 2 subdue

chas·tise′ (-tīz′) v. 1 punish as by beating 2 scold sharply —**chas·tise′ment** n.

chat v. **chat′ted, chat′ting;** n. talk in a light, informal way —**chat′ty** a., -ti·er, -ti·est

châ·teau (sha tō′) n., pl. -teaux′ (-tōz) mansion

chat′tel n. piece of movable property

chat·ter v. 1 talk much and foolishly 2 click together rapidly —n. a chattering

chauf·feur (shō′fər) n. man hired to drive one's car —v. act as chauffeur to

chau·vin·ism (shō′-) n. 1 fanatical patriotism 2 unreasoning devotion to one's race, sex, etc. —**chau·vin·ist** a., n.

cheap a. 1 low in price 2 of little value —adv. at a low cost —**cheap′ly** adv.

cheap′en v. make cheaper

cheat n. 1 fraud 2 swindler —v. 1 deceive or practice fraud 2 escape

check n. 1 sudden stop 2 restraint or restrainer 3 test of accuracy, etc. 4 mark (√) used to verify 5 token to show ownership 6 bill, as at a restaurant 7 written order to a bank to pay money 8 pattern of squares 9 Chess threat to the king —int. [Col.] right! —v. 1 stop or restrain 2 test, verify, etc. 3 mark with a check 4 deposit temporarily —**check in** register at a hotel, etc. —**check out** 1 officially leave a hotel, etc. 2 collect amount owed in a supermarket, etc. —**check′er** n.

check′book′ n. booklet of checks

check′er n. flat, round piece used in checkers

check′er·board′ n. board for checkers, with 64 squares

check′ered a. 1 having a pattern of squares 2 varied

check′ers n. game like chess, for two players

check′list′ n. list to be referred to: also **check list**

check′mate′ n. Chess position from which king cannot escape, ending the game —v. to put in checkmate

check′out′ n. place or time for checking out

check′room′ n. room for leaving hats, coats, etc.

check′up′ n. medical examination

Ched′dar (cheese) n. a hard, smooth cheese

cheek n. 1 side of face below eye 2 [Col.] impudence —**tongue in cheek** jestingly

cheer n. 1 joy; gladness 2 shout of excitement, welcome, etc. —v. 1 fill with cheer 2 urge on, praise, etc. with cheers —**cheer up** make or become glad

cheer′ful a. 1 joyful 2 bright and attractive Also **cheer′y**, -i·er, -i·est —**cheer′ful·ly** adv.

cheer′lead′er n. person who leads cheers for a team

cheer′less a. not cheerful

cheers int. [Chiefly Br.] good health!: used as a toast

cheese n. solid food made from milk curds

cheese′burg′er n. hamburger with melted cheese

cheese′cloth′ n. cotton cloth with a loose weave

chee′tah n. animal like the leopard

chef (shef) *n.* head cook

chem'i·cal (kem'-) *a.* of, in, or by chemistry —*n.* substance used in or obtained by chemistry —**chem'i·cal·ly** *adv.*

che·mise (shə mēz') *n.* woman's undergarment

chem'is·try *n.* science dealing with the composition, reactions, etc. of substances —**chem'ist** *n.*

che·mo·ther·a·py (kē'mō-) *n.* use of drugs in treating disease

che·nille (shə nēl') *n.* fabric woven with tufted cord

cheque (chek) *n.* Br. sp. of CHECK (*n.* 7)

cher'ish *v.* 1 hold or treat tenderly 2 keep in mind

cher'ry *n., pl.* **-ries** tree with small, red fruit

cher'ub *n., pl.* **-ubs** or **-u·bim'** angel, pictured as a chubby child with wings —**che·ru'bic** (-rōō'-) *a.*

chess *n.* checkerboard game for two players using various pieces (**chess'men**)

chest *n.* 1 box with a lid 2 piece of furniture with drawers 3 front part of the body above the abdomen

chest'nut *n.* 1 edible nut of a kind of beech 2 [Col.] trite joke —*a.* reddish-brown

chev'ron (shev'-) *n.* V-shaped sleeve insignia of rank

chew *v.* grind with the teeth —*n.* something for chewing —**chew'y** *a.,* **-i·er, -i·est**

chew'ing gum *n.* flavored chicle, etc. for chewing

chic (shēk) *a.* smartly stylish

chi·can·er·y (shi kān'-) *n., pl.* **-ies** 1 trickery 2 trick

Chi·ca·no (chi kä'nō) *n., pl.* **-nos** Mexican-American

chick *n.* young chicken

chick'a·dee' *n.* small bird of the titmouse family

chick'en *n.* hen or rooster, or its edible flesh

chick'en·pox' *n.* infectious disease with skin eruptions

chick'pea' *n.* pealike plant with edible seeds

chic'le *n.* gummy substance from a tropical tree

chic'o·ry *n.* plant with leaf used in salads and root used as a coffee substitute

chide *v.* scold; rebuke

chief *n.* leader —*a.* main; most important —**chief'ly** *adv.*

chief'tain (-tən) *n.* chief of a clan

or tribe

chif·fon (shi fän') *n.* sheer silk cloth

chig'ger *n.* a mite larva that causes itching

chil'blain' *n.* inflamed sore caused by exposure to cold

child *n., pl.* **chil'dren** 1 infant 2 boy or girl before puberty 3 son or daughter —**with child** pregnant —**child'hood'** *n.* —**child'like'** *a.*

child'birth' *n.* a giving birth to a child

child'ish *a.* silly; immature

chil'i *n., pl.* **-ies** 1 hot, dried pod of red pepper 2 spicy dish of beef, chilies, beans, etc.

chill *n.* 1 moderate coldness 2 body coldness with shivering 3 sudden fear —*a.* uncomfortably cool —*v.* make or become cold —**chill'y** *a.,* **-i·er, -i·est**

chime *n. usually pl.* set of tuned bells —*v.* to sound as a chime

chim'ney *n.* passage for smoke from a furnace, etc.

chim·pan·zee' *n.* medium-sized African ape

chin *n.* face below the lips —*v.* chinned, chin'ning pull (oneself) up until the chin is above a bar being grasped

chi'na *n.* dishes, etc. of fine porcelain

chin·chil'la *n.* 1 small South American rodent 2 its costly fur

Chi·nese' *n., pl.* **-nese'; *a.*** (native or language) of China

chink *n.* 1 crack 2 clinking sound —*v.* to clink

chintz *n.* glazed, printed cotton cloth

chintz'y *a.* **-i·er, -i'est** [Col.] cheap, stingy, etc.

chip *v.* chipped, chip'ping break or cut off bits from —*n.* 1 fragment 2 place where bit is chipped off 3 small disk used in gambling 4 thin slice of food 5 microchip —**chip in** [Col.] contribute

chip'munk *n.* small, striped squirrel

chip'per *a.* [Col.] lively

chi·rop'o·dist (ki räp'-) *n.* podiatrist

chi·ro·prac'tic (ki'rə-) *n.* treatment by manipulation of body joints, etc. —**chi'ro·prac'tor** *n.*

chirp *v.* make short, shrill sounds —*n.* such a sound

chir'rup *v., n.* chirp

chis'el (chiz'-) *n.* tool for chipping wood, stone, etc. —*v.* 1

chip with a chisel 2 [Col.] swindle —**chis'el·er, chis'el·ler**

chit'chat' n. small talk

chi'tin (kī'-) n. horny covering of insects, etc.

chit·ter·lings (chit'linz) n.pl. pig intestines, used for food: also **chit'lins** or **chit'lings**

chiv·al·ry (shiv'-) n. 1 medieval system of knighthood 2 courtesy, fairness, etc. —**chiv'al·rous** a.

chives n.pl. herb with slender leaves with mild onion odor

chlo·ride (klôr'īd') n. compound of chlorine

chlo'ri·nate' v. purify (water) with chlorine

chlo·rine (klôr'ēn') n. greenish gas, a chemical element

chlo·ro·form' n. colorless liquid anesthetic —v. anesthetize or kill with this

chlo'ro·phyll', chlo'ro·phyl' (-fil') n. green coloring in plants

chock n., v. block; wedge —adv. completely

choc'o·late (-lət) n. 1 ground cacao seeds 2 drink or candy made with this 3 reddish brown

choice n. 1 selection 2 right to choose 3 the one chosen —a. excellent

choir (kwīr) n. group of singers, esp. in a church

choke v. 1 stop the breathing of; suffocate 2 obstruct; clog —n. a choking

chol·er·a n. infectious, often fatal, intestinal disease

chol·er·ic (or kə ler'-) a. having a quick temper

cho·les'ter·ol' (kə-) n. substance in animal fats, etc.

chomp v. to champ

choose v. **chose, cho'sen, choos'ing** 1 take; select 2 prefer; decide

choos'y, choos'ey a. **-i·er, -i·est** [Col.] fussy in choosing

chop v. **chopped, chop'ping** 1 cut by blows of sharp tool 2 cut in bits —n. 1 sharp blow 2 a slice from the rib or loin

chop'per n. 1 pl. [Sl.] teeth 2 [Col.] helicopter

chop'py a. with rough, abrupt waves or motions

chops n.pl. 1 jaws 2 flesh about the mouth

chop'sticks' n.pl. two sticks used as eating utensils in some Asian countries

chop su·ey (sōō'ē) n. American-Chinese stew served with rice

cho·ral (kôr'əl) a. of or for a choir or chorus

cho·rale, cho·ral (kə ral') n. simple hymn tune

chord (kôrd) n. 1 straight line joining two points on an arc 2 three or more tones sounded together in harmony

chore n. daily task

chor'e·og'ra·phy (kôr'-) n. the devising of ballets —**chor'e·og'ra·pher** n.

chor·is·ter (kôr'-) n. choir member

chor·tle (chôrt'l) v., n. chuckle or snort

cho·rus (kôr'əs) n. 1 group of singers or of singers and dancers 2 music for group singing 3 refrain of a song —v. sing or recite in unison

chose v. pt. of CHOOSE

cho'sen v. pp. of CHOOSE —a. selected; choice

chow n. 1 medium-sized Chinese dog 2 [Sl.] food

chow'der n. fish or clam soup with vegetables

chow mein (mān) n. American-Chinese stew served on fried noodles

Christ Jesus as the Messiah

chris·ten (kris'ən) v. 1 baptize 2 name —**chris'ten·ing** n.

Chris'ten·dom (kris'ən-) Christians collectively

Chris'ti·an'i·ty n. religion based on teachings of Jesus —**Chris'tian** a., n.

Christ'mas n. celebration of Jesus' birth; Dec. 25

chro·mat'ic (krō-) a. 1 of color 2 Mus. in semitones

chrome n. chromium

chro'mi·um n. hard metal in alloys, a chemical element

chro'mo·some' n. any of the microscopic bodies carrying the genes of heredity

chron'ic a. long-lasting or recurring —**chron'i·cal·ly** adv.

chron'i·cle n. historical record —v. to tell the history of —**chron'i·cler** n.

chron'o·log'i·cal a. in order of occurrence —**chron'o·log'i·cal·ly** adv. —**chro·nol'o·gy** n.

chro·nom'e·ter n. very accurate clock or watch

chrys'a·lis (kris'-) n. pupa or its cocoon

chrys·an'the·mum n. plant with ball-shaped flowers

chub'by a. plump

chuck v. 1 tap playfully 2 toss

—n. 1 tap 2 toss 3 shoulder cut of beef 4 clamplike device as on a lathe

chuck'hole' n. rough hole in pavement

chuck'le v. laugh softly —n. soft laugh

chug n. explosive sound, as of an engine —v. **chugged, chug'ging** make this sound

chum [Col.] n. close friend —v. **chummed, chum'ming** be chums —**chum'my** a.

chump n. [Col.] fool

chunk n. thick piece

chunk'y a. **-i-er, -i-est** [Col.] short and thickset

church n. 1 building for public worship 2 religion or religious sect

church'go'er n. one who attends church regularly —**church'-go'ing** a.

church'yard' n. yard beside a church, often a cemetery

churl'ish a. rude; surly

churn n. device for making butter —v. 1 shake (cream) in a churn to make butter 2 stir about vigorously

chute (shōōt) n. inclined passage for sliding things

chutz'pah, chutz'pa (hōōts'-) n. [Col.] impudence; audacity

ci-ca'da (si kā'-) n. large flying insect making a shrill sound

ci'der n. juice from apples

ci-gar' n. roll of tobacco leaves for smoking

cig'a-rette', cig'a-ret' n. tobacco cut fine and rolled in paper for smoking

cil'i-a n.pl. small hairlike growths

cinch n. 1 saddle girth 2 [Sl.] thing easy to do

cin-cho'na (sin kō'-) n. tree whose bark yields quinine

cinc'ture (sink'-) n. belt or girdle —v. gird

cin'der n. 1 tiny charred piece of wood, etc. 2 pl. ashes

cin'e-ma n. used in the cinema, films collectively; the movies —**cin'e-mat'ic** a.

cin'e-ma-tog'ra-phy n. art of photography in making movies —**cin'e-ma-tog'ra-pher** n.

cin'na-mon n. brown spice from East Indian tree bark

ci'pher (si'fər) n. 1 zero; 0 2 code 3 key to a code

cir'ca prep. about; approximately

cir-ca'di-an a. of the body cycles associated with the earth's daily rotation

cir'cle n. 1 closed, curved line always equidistant from the center 2 cycle 3 group with interests in common 4 extent; scope —v. form or go in a circle around

cir'cuit (-kət) n. 1 boundary 2 regular, routine journey 3 theater chain 4 path for electric current

cir-cu'i-tous (-kyōō'-) a. roundabout; indirect

cir'cuit-ry n. electric circuit(s)

cir'cu-lar a. 1 round 2 roundabout —n. advertisement sent to many people

cir'cu-late' v. move or spread about —**cir'cu-la-to'ry** a.

cir'cu-la'tion n. 1 movement, as of blood through the body 2 distribution

cir'cum-cise' (-siz') v. cut off the foreskin of —**cir'cum-ci'sion** (-sizh'ən) n.

cir-cum'fer-ence n. distance around a circle, etc.

cir'cum-flex' v. pronunciation mark (^)

cir'cum-lo-cu'tion n. roundabout way of talking

cir'cum-nav'i-gate' v. sail around (the earth, etc.)

cir'cum-scribe' v. 1 encircle 2 limit; confine

cir'cum-spect a. cautious; discreet —**cir'cum-spec'tion** n.

cir'cum-stance' n. 1 connected fact or event 2 pl. financial condition 3 ceremony —**under no circumstances** never —**cir'cum-stan'tial** (-shəl) a.

cir'cum-vent' v. outwit or prevent by cleverness

cir'cus n. a show with acrobats, animals, clowns, etc.

cir-rho'sis (sə rō'-) n. disease, esp. of the liver

cir'rus (sir'əs) n. fleecy, white cloud formation

cis'tern n. large storage tank, esp. for rain water

cit'a-del' n. fortress

cite v. 1 summon by law 2 quote 3 mention as example 4 mention in praise —**ci-ta'tion** n.

cit'i-zen n. member of a nation by birth or naturalization —**cit'i-zen-ry** a. —**cit'i-zen-ship'** n.

cit'ric acid n. weak acid in citrus fruits

cit'ron n. lemonlike fruit

cit'ron-el'la n. pungent oil that repels insects

cit'rus n. orange, lemon, etc. —a.

of these trees or fruits

cit'y n., pl. **-ies** large town

civ'et n. fatty secretion of an animal (**civet cat**): used in perfume

civ'ic a. of a city or citizens

civ'ics n. study of civic affairs and duties

civ'il a. 1 of citizens 2 polite 3 not military or religious —**civ'il-ly** adv.

ci-vil'ian a., n. (of a) person not in armed forces

ci-vil'i-ty n. 1 courtesy 2 pl. **-ties** polite act

civ'i-li-za'tion n. 1 high social and cultural development 2 culture of a certain time or place

civ'i-lize' v. bring out of savagery or barbarism

civil liberties n.pl. rights of free speech, assembly, etc.

civil rights n.pl. rights of all people to equal treatment

civil service n. government employees except soldiers, legislators, and judges

civil war n. war between factions of the same nation

clack v. make an abrupt sharp sound —n. this sound

clad v. alt. pt. & pp. of CLOTHE

claim v. 1 demand as rightfully one's own 2 assert —n. 1 a claiming 2 right to something 3 thing claimed —**claim'ant** n.

clair-voy'ance n. supposed ability to perceive things not in sight —**clair-voy'ant** a., n.

clam n. hard-shelled, often edible, bivalve mollusk

clam'bake' n. picnic at which clams are served

clam'ber v. climb clumsily

clam'my a. **-mi-er, -mi-est** moist, cold, and sticky

clam'or n. 1 uproar 2 noisy demand —v. make a clamor —**clam'or-ous** a.

clamp n. device for clasping things together —v. fasten with a clamp

clan n. 1 group of related families 2 group with interests in common

clan-des'tine (-tin) a. secret

clang v. make a loud ringing sound —n. this sound

clang'or n. series of clangs

clank v. make a sharp metallic sound —n. this sound

clap v. **clapped, clap'ping** 1 make the sound of flat surfaces struck together 2 to strike together, as the hands in

applauding —n. sound or act of clapping —**clap'per** n.

clap-board (klab'ərd) n. tapered board for siding

clap'trap' n. insincere, empty talk, meant to get applause

clar'et (klar'-) n. dry red wine

clar'i-fy' v. **-fied', -fy'ing** make or become clear —**clar'i-fi-ca'tion** n.

clar'i-net' n. single-reed, woodwind instrument —**clar'i-net'ist, clar'i-net'tist** n.

clar'i-on a. clear and shrill

clar'i-ty n. clearness

clash v. 1 collide noisily 2 disagree —n. a clashing

clasp n. 1 device to fasten things 2 an embrace 3 grip of the hand —v. 1 fasten 2 hold tightly

class n. 1 group of like people or things; sort 2 social rank 3 group of students in school 4 grade or quality 5 [Sl.] excellence —v. classify —**class'mate'** n. —**class'room'** n.

clas'sic a. 1 most excellent 2 in the style of ancient Greece or Rome —n. a book, work of art, etc. of highest excellence —**the classics** writings of ancient Greece and Rome

clas'si-cal a. 1 CLASSIC (a. 2) 2 of such music as symphonies, concertos, etc.

clas'si-fy' v. **-fied', -fy'ing** 1 arrange in classes 2 designate as secret —**clas'si-fi-ca'tion** n.

class'y a. **-i-er, -i-est** [Sl.] first-class; elegant

clat'ter n. series of sharp noises —v. make a clatter

clause n. 1 part of a sentence, with a subject and verb 2 provision in a document

claus-tro-pho'bi-a n. fear of enclosed places

clav'i-chord' n. early kind of piano

clav'i-cle n. bone connecting the breastbone and shoulder

claw n. 1 sharp nail of an animal's or bird's foot 2 pincers of a lobster, crab, etc. —v. scratch as with claws

clay n. firm, plastic earth, used for pottery, etc.

clean a. 1 free from dirt 2 sinless 3 free from flaws 4 complete —adv. completely —v. make clean —**clean'er** n. —**clean'ly** (klēn'-) adv.

clean'-cut' a. trim, neat, etc.

clean'ly (klen'-) a. **-li-er, -li-est**

1 having clean habits 2 always kept clean —**clean'li·ness** n.

cleanse (klenz) v. make clean or pure —**cleans'er** n.

clear a. 1 free from clouds 2 transparent 3 distinct 4 obvious 5 free from charges, guilt, obstruction, debt, etc. —adv. 1 in a clear way 2 completely —v. 1 make or become clear 2 pass or leap over 3 make as profit 4 to empty or unload 5 rid (the throat) of phlegm —**clear away** (or **off**) remove —**in the clear** in the open —**clear'ly** adv. —**clear'ness** n.

clear'ance n. clear space between two objects

clear'ing n. plot of land cleared of trees

cleat n. piece used to give firmness or secure footing

cleav'age n. a split, crack, division, etc.

cleave v. cleft or cleaved, cleav'ing split; sever

cleave v. adhere; cling

cleav'er n. butcher's tool

clef n. musical symbol to indicate pitch

cleft a., n. split

clem'ent a. 1 lenient 2 mild —**clem'en·cy** n.

clench v. close tightly

cler'gy n., pl. -gies ministers, priests, etc. collectively

cler'gy·man n., pl. -men minister, priest, etc. —**cler'gy·wom'an** n.fem., pl. -wom·en

cler'ic n. member of the clergy

cler'i·cal a. 1 of the clergy 2 of office clerks

clerk n. 1 office worker who keeps records, etc. 2 salesperson in a store —v. work as a clerk

clev'er a. 1 skillful 2 intelligent —**clev'er·ness** n.

cli·ché' (klē shā') n. trite expression or idea —**cli·chéd'** a.

click n. slight, sharp sound —v. make a click

cli'ent n. 1 person or company for whom a lawyer, etc. acts 2 customer

cli'en·tele' (-tel') n. clients

cliff n. high, steep rock

cliff'hang'er, cliff'-hang'er n. highly suspenseful story, etc.

cli'mate n. average weather conditions —**cli·mat'ic** a.

cli'max n. highest point, as of interest or excitement; culmination —v. bring to a climax —**cli·mac'tic** a.

climb v. go up; ascend —n. a climbing —**climb down** to descend —**climb'er** n.

clinch v. 1 fasten (a nail) by bending the end 2 settle (an argument, etc.) 3 Boxing grip with the arms —n. a clinching in boxing

cling v. clung, cling'ing 1 hold fast 2 stay near

clin'ic n. 1 place where medical specialists practice as a group 2 outpatient department —**cli·ni'cian** (-nish'ən) n.

clin'i·cal a. 1 of medical treatment, as in clinics 2 dispassionate

clink n. short, tinkling sound —v. make this sound

clink'er n. fused mass left in burning coal

clip v. clipped, clip'ping 1 cut short 2 cut the hair of 3 [Col.] hit sharply 4 fasten together —n. 1 a clipping 2 [Col.] rapid pace 3 fastening device

clip'per n. 1 clipping tool 2 fast sailing ship

clique (klik, klēk) n. small, exclusive circle of people

clit'o·ris n. small, sensitive organ of the vulva

cloak n. 1 loose, sleeveless outer garment 2 thing that conceals —v. conceal; hide

clock n. device for measuring and showing time

clock'wise' adv., a. in the direction in which the hands of a clock rotate

clod n. 1 lump of earth 2 dull, stupid person

clog n. 1 thing that hinders 2 heavy shoe —v. clogged, clog'ging 1 hinder 2 block up

clois'ter n. 1 monastery or convent 2 covered walk along a wall —v. seclude

clomp v. walk heavily or noisily

clone n. exact genetic duplicate of an organism —v. produce as a clone

close (klōs) a. 1 confined 2 secretive 3 stingy 4 humid; stuffy 5 near together 6 intimate 7 thorough 8 nearly alike; nearly equal —adv. in a close way or position —n. enclosed place —**close'ly** adv.

close (klōz) v. 1 shut or stop up 2 end 3 come close, as to attack —n. end —**close down** (or **up**) stop entirely —**close in** surround

close'-knit' a. closely united

clos'et (kläz'-) *n.* small room for clothes, etc. —*v.* shut in a room for private talk

close'-up *n.* photograph, etc. taken at very close range

clo'sure (-zhər) *n.* a closing, finish, etc.

clot *n.* coagulated mass, as of blood —*v.* **clot'ted, clot'ting** coagulate

cloth *n.* 1 fabric of cotton, wool, synthetics, etc. 2 tablecloth, dustcloth, etc.

clothe (klōth) *v.* **clothed** or **clad, cloth'ing** 1 to put clothes on 2 provide with clothes

clothes (klōthz) *n.pl.* 1 clothing 2 bedclothes

cloth·ier (klōth'yər) *n.* dealer in clothes or cloth

cloth·ing (klōth'iŋ) *n.* wearing apparel; garments

cloud *n.* 1 mass of vapor in the sky 2 mass of smoke, dust, etc. 3 thing that darkens, etc. —*v.* darken as with clouds, gloom, etc. —**cloud'y** *a.*, **-i·er, -i·est**

cloud'burst' *n.* sudden heavy rain

clout *n.* [Col.] 1 a hard hit 2 political power

clove *n.* 1 pungent spice 2 segment of a bulb

clo'ven *a.* split

clo'ver *n.* small forage plant with triple leaves

clo'ver·leaf' *n.* highway intersection with curving ramps to ease traffic

clown *n.* comic entertainer as in a circus —*v.* act like a clown

cloy *v.* surfeit by excess

club *n.* 1 stick used as a weapon, or in games 2 social group or its meeting place 3 playing card marked with a ♣ —*v.* **clubbed, club'bing** strike with a club

cluck *n.* low, clicking sound made by a hen —*v.* make this sound

clue *n.* hint or fact that helps solve a mystery

clump *n.* 1 lump 2 cluster —*v.* tramp heavily

clum'sy (-zē) *a.* **-si·er, -si·est** awkward —**clum'si·ly** *adv.*

clung *v.* pt. & pp. of CLING

clunk'er *n.* [Sl.] old, noisy car

clus·ter *n., v.* group; bunch

clutch *v.* 1 snatch (*at*) 2 hold tightly —*n.* 1 pl. control 2 grip 3 device for engaging and disengaging an engine

clut·ter *n., v.* disorder

co- *pref.* 1 together 2 joint 3 equally

coach *n.* 1 big, four-wheeled carriage 2 railroad passenger car 3 bus 4 trainer of athletes, singers, etc. —*v.* be a coach (for)

co·ag'u·late' *v.* thicken; clot —**co·ag'u·la'tion** *n.*

coal *n.* 1 black mineral used as fuel 2 ember

co'a·lesce' (-les') *v.* unite into a single body —**co'a·les'cence** *n.*

co'a·li'tion *n.* union

coarse *a.* 1 made up of large particles 2 rough 3 vulgar —**coars'en** *v.*

coast *n.* seashore —*v.* 1 slide down an incline 2 continue moving on momentum —**coast'al** *a.*

coast'er *n.* small tray put under a glass

coast guard *n.* group defending a nation's coasts, aiding ships in distress, etc.

coast'line' *n.* contour of a coast

coat *n.* 1 sleeved outer garment 2 natural covering 3 layer, as of paint —*v.* cover with a layer

coat'ing *n.* surface layer

coat of arms *n.* heraldic symbols, as on a family escutcheon

coax *v.* urge or get by soothing words, etc.

co·ax'i·al cable *n.* cable for sending telephone, telegraph, or television impulses

cob *n.* corncob

co'balt (-bôlt) *n.* gray metallic chemical element

cob'bler *n.* 1 shoemaker 2 fruit pie

cob'ble·stone' *n.* rounded stone once used for paving

co'bra *n.* poisonous snake of Asia and Africa

cob'web' *n.* spider web

co·caine', co·cain' *n.* drug used as a narcotic or anesthetic

coc·cyx (käk'siks) *n., pl.* **coc·cy'ges'** (-si'jēz') bone at base of spine

coch·i·neal (käch'ə nēl') *n.* red dye from tropical insect

coch·le·a (käk'lē ə) *n.* spiral part of the inner ear

cock *n.* 1 rooster 2 any male bird 3 faucet —*v.* 1 tilt 2 set hammer of (a gun) to fire

cock·ade' *n.* badge on a hat

cock'a·too' *n.* crested Australian parrot

cock'er (spaniel) *n.* small spaniel with drooping ears

cock'eyed' *a.* 1 cross-eyed 2 [Sl.] *a)* awry *b)* absurd

cock'le n. edible shellfish —**cockles of one's heart** one's deepest feelings

cock'pit' n. space for pilot in an airplane

cock'roach' n. flat-bodied, dark insect, a kitchen pest

cocks'comb' n. red, fleshy growth on a rooster's head

cock'sure' a. self-confident

cock'tail' n. 1 mixed alcoholic drink 2 appetizer

cock'y a. [Col.] conceited

co'co n., pl. **-cos** coconut palm or coconut

co'coa' (-kō') n. 1 powder made from roasted cacao seeds 2 drink made of this

cocoa butter n. fat from cacao seeds

co'co·nut', co'coa·nut' n. hard-shelled fruit of a palm tree, with edible white meat

co·coon' n. silky case of certain insect larvae

cod n. N Atlantic food fish: also **cod'fish'**

co'da n. Mus. end passage

cod'dle v. pamper

code n. 1 body of laws 2 set of principles 3 set of signals or symbols for messages —v. put or write in code

co'deine' (-dēn') n. sedative drug derived from opium

codg'er n. [Col.] elderly man

cod'i·cil n. addition to a will

cod'i·fy' (or kō'də-) v. **-fied', -fy'ing** arrange (laws) in a code

co·ed', co'-ed' n. [Col.] young woman at a coeducational college

co'ed·u·ca'tion n. education of both sexes in the same classes —**co'ed·u·ca'tion·al** a.

co·erce' (-urs') v. force; compel —**co·er'cion** n. —**co·er'cive** a.

co·ex·ist' v. exist together —**co'ex·ist'ence** n.

cof'fee n. 1 drink made from roasted seeds of a tropical shrub 2 the seeds

cof'fee-cake' n. cake or roll to be eaten with coffee, etc.

cof'fee-pot' n. pot with a spout, for brewing or serving coffee

cof'fer n. 1 chest for money, etc. 2 pl. treasury

cof'fin n. case in which to bury a dead person

cog n. tooth on a cogwheel

co'gent (-jənt) a. convincing —**co'gen·cy** n.

cog'i·tate' (käj'-) v. think (about) —**cog'i·ta'tion** n.

co·gnac (kōn'yak') n. brandy

cog'nate' a. related; kindred

cog·ni'tion n. knowledge

cog'ni·zance n. awareness; notice —**cog'ni·zant** a.

cog·no'men n. surname

cog'wheel' n. wheel rimmed with teeth, as in a gear

co·hab'it v. live together, esp. as if legally married

co·here' (-hir') v. 1 to stick together 2 be connected logically

co·her'ent (-hir'-, -her'-) a. clear and intelligible —**co·her'ence** n.

co·he'sion n. a sticking together —**co·he'sive** a.

co'hort' n. 1 group, esp. of soldiers 2 an associate

coif·fure' (kwä fyoor') n. 1 headdress 2 hairstyle

coil v. to wind in a spiral —n. anything coiled

coin n. stamped metal piece, issued as money —v. 1 make into coins 2 make up (new word) —**coin'age** n.

co'in·cide' v. 1 occur at the same time 2 agree; match

co·in'ci·dence n. 1 a coinciding 2 accidental occurrence together of events —**co·in'ci·den'tal** a. —**co·in'ci·den'tal·ly** adv.

co·i'tus (kō'it əs) n. sexual intercourse: also **co·i'tion** (-ish'ən)

coke n. 1 fuel made by removing gases from coal 2 [Sl.] cocaine

co'la n. carbonated soft drink with flavoring from the nut of an African tree

col'an·der (kul'-, käl'-) n. perforated bowl used as a strainer

cold a. 1 low in temperature 2 feeling chilled 3 without feeling 4 unfriendly 5 [Col.] unprepared 6 [Col.] perfectly memorized 7 [Col.] unconscious —n. 1 absence of heat 2 common virus infection with sneezing, coughing, etc. —**catch cold** become ill with a cold

cold'blood'ed a. 1 having a body temperature that varies with the surroundings 2 cruel; callous

cold cream n. creamy cleanser for the skin

cold war n. conflict between nations without actual war

cole'slaw' n. salad made of shredded raw cabbage

col'ic n. sharp abdominal pain from the bowels —**col'ick·y** a.

Col·i·se'um n. large stadium

co·li'tis n. inflammation of the large intestine

col·lab'o·rate' v. 1 to work together 2 help the enemy — **col·lab·o·ra'tion** n. — **col·lab'o·ra'tor** n.

col·lage' (-läzh') n. bits of objects pasted onto a surface to make a work of art

col·lapse' v. 1 fall in or shrink 2 break down; fail 3 fold together —n. a collapsing — **col·laps'i·ble** a.

col'lar n. a band, or the part of a garment, around the neck —v. 1 put a collar on 2 seize by the collar

col'lar·bone' n. clavicle

col'lard n. kind of kale

col·late' (kä'lāt', kō'lāt') v. compare or sort (texts)

col·lat'er·al a. 1 of the same descent but in a different line 2 secondary —n. thing pledged as security for a loan

col'league' (käl'ēg) n. fellow worker; associate

col·lect' v. 1 gather together 2 get payment for 3 regain control of (oneself) —a., adv. with the receiver paying — **col·lect'i·ble, col·lect'a·ble** a. — **col·lec'tion** n. — **col·lec'tor** n.

col·lec'tive a. 1 of or as a group 2 singular in form, but referring to a group —n. 1 a collective enterprise 2 collective noun

col'lege n. 1 school of higher learning or special instruction 2 group with certain powers — **col·le'gi·an** (-jən) n. — **col·le'gi·ate** (-jət) a.

col·lide' v. 1 come into violent contact 2 to conflict; clash

col'lie n. large, long-haired sheep dog

col·li'sion (-lizh'ən) n. 1 a colliding 2 conflict

col'loid' n. substance of insoluble particles suspended in a fluid — **col·loi'dal** a.

col·lo'qui·al (-kwē-) a. used in informal talk and writing — **col·lo'qui·al·ism'** n.

col·lu'sion n. secret agreement for a wrong purpose

co·logne' (-lōn') n. scented liquid like perfume

co'lon n. 1 mark of punctuation (:) 2 lower part of the large intestine

colo·nel (kur'nəl) n. officer above lieutenant colonel

co·lo'ni·al·ism' n. economic exploitation of colonies

col'on·nade' n. row of evenly spaced columns

col'o·ny n., pl. -nies 1 group of settlers from a distant land 2 land ruled by a distant country 3 community with common interests — **co·lo'ni·al** a. — **col'o·nist** n. — **col'o·nize'** v.

col'or n. 1 effect on the eyes of light waves of different wavelengths 2 pigment 3 complexion 4 pl. a flag 5 outward appearance 6 picturesque quality —v. 1 paint or dye 2 alter or distort 3 blush — **of color** not Caucasoid; spec., black — **with flying colors** with great success — **col'or·a'tion** n. — **col'or·ful** a. — **col'or·ing** n. — **col'or·less** a.

col'or·blind' a. unable to distinguish (certain) colors

col'ored a. not Caucasoid; spec., black

col'or·fast' a. with color that will not fade or run

co·los'sal a. huge; immense

co·los'sus n. huge or important person or thing

col'our n., v. Br. sp. of COLOR

colt n. young male horse

col'um·bine' (-bīn') n. plant with showy, spurred flowers

col'umn (-əm) n. 1 slender upright structure 2 vertical section of printed matter 3 line of troops, etc. — **col'um·nist'** n.

co'ma n. deep unconsciousness, as from injury — **co'ma·tose'** (-tōs') a.

comb (kōm) n. 1 flat, toothed object for grooming the hair 2 cockscomb 3 honeycomb —v. 1 groom with a comb 2 search

com'bat' (v.: also kəm bat') v., n. fight; struggle — **com·bat'ant** n. — **com·bat'ive** a. ready or eager to fight

com'bi·na'tion n. 1 a combining 2 combined things, groups, etc. 3 series of numbers dialed to open a lock

com·bine' (n.: käm'bīn') v. join; unite —n. 1 machine for harvesting and threshing grain 2 commercial or political alliance

com'bo' n., pl. -bos' 1 [Col.] combination 2 a small jazz ensemble

com·bus'ti·ble n., a. flammable (thing)

com·bus'tion n. a burning

come v. came, come, com'ing 1

move from "there" to "here" 2
arrive or appear 3 happen 4
result 5 become 6 amount (to)
7 extend —**come by** get —
come to regain consciousness
—**come up** arise in discussion

come'back' n. 1 a return, as to
power 2 witty answer

co·me'di·an n. actor who plays
comic parts —**co·me'di·enne'**
(-en') n.fem.

com'e·dy n., pl. -**dies** a humorous play, TV show, etc.

come'ly (kum'-) a. -**li·er**, -**li·est**
attractive —**come'li·ness** n.

com'et n. mass of dust and gas
in space, with a luminous tail

com'fort v. soothe in distress;
console —n. 1 relief from distress 2 one that comforts 3
ease —**com'fort·a·ble** a.

com'fort·er n. 1 one that comforts 2 a quilt

com'ic a. 1 of comedy 2 funny:
also **com'i·cal** —n. 1 comedian
2 pl. comic strips

comic book n. booklet of comic
strips

comic strip n. cartoon series, as
in a newspaper

com'ma n. punctuation mark (,)

com·mand' v. 1 to order 2 to
control 3 deserve and get —n.
1 an order 2 control 3 military
force, etc. under someone's control

com'man·dant' (-dant', -dänt')
n. commanding officer

com·man·deer' v. seize for military or government use

com·mand'er n. 1 leader; officer
2 naval officer below a captain

commander in chief n. top commander of a nation's armed
forces

com·mand'ment n. command;
law

com·man'do n., pl. -**dos** or
-**does** member of a small force
for raiding enemy territory

com·mem'o·rate' v. honor the
memory of —**com·mem'o·ra'
tion** n.

com·mence' v. begin

com·mence'ment n. 1 beginning 2 graduation ceremony of
a school, etc.

com·mend' v. 1 entrust 2 recommend 3 to praise —**com·
mend'a·ble** a. —**com·men·da'
tion** n.

com·men'su·rate (-sə rət) a.
equal or proportionate

com'ment n. 1 explanatory
note 2 remark 3 talk —v. make

comments

com'men·tar'y n., pl. -**ies** series
of explanatory notes or remarks

com'men·ta'tor n. radio or TV
news analyst

com'merce n. trade on a large
scale

com·mer'cial (-shal) a. 1 connected with commerce 2 done
for profit —n. Radio & TV paid
advertisement

com·min'gle v. mix; blend

com·mis'er·ate' (-miz'-) v. sympathize (with)

com'mis·sar' n. government official in the U.S.S.R.

com·mis'sar·y (-ser'-) n. store in
an army camp for the sale of
food, etc.

com·mis'sion n. 1 authority to
act 2 group chosen to do something 3 percentage of a sale
allotted to the agent 4 military
officer's certificate of rank —v.
1 give a commission to 2
authorize —**in** (or **out of**) **commission** (not) usable

com·mis'sion·er n. governmental department head

com·mit' v. -**mit'ted**, -**mit'ting** 1
put in custody 2 do 3 pledge;
bind —**com·mit'ment** n.

com·mit'tee n. group chosen to
do something

com·mode' n. 1 a chest of
drawers 2 toilet

com·mo'di·ous a. spacious

com·mod'i·ty n., pl. -**ties** anything bought and sold

com'mo·dore' n. former naval
rank

com'mon a. 1 shared by all 2
general 3 usual; ordinary 4 vulgar 5 designating a noun that
refers to any of a group —n. also
pl. town's public land —**in common** shared by all

com'mon·er n. person not of the
nobility

common law n. unwritten law
based on custom, usage, etc.

com'mon·place' n. 1 trite or
obvious remark 2 anything
ordinary —a. ordinary

com'mon·weal' n. public welfare

com'mon·wealth' n. 1 people of
a state 2 democracy or republic

com·mo'tion n. turmoil

com·mu'nal (or kə myōō'-) a. of
a community; public

com·mune' n. small group living
communally

com·mune' v. talk intimately

com·mu'ni·cate' v. 1 transmit 2
give or exchange (information)

3 be connected —**com·mu·ni·ca·ble** a. —**com·mu·ni·ca·tive** a. —**com·mu·ni·ca·tor** n.

com·mu·ni·ca·tion n. 1 a communicating or means of doing this 2 message, etc.

com·mun·ion n. 1 a sharing or being close 2 group of the same religious faith 3 [C-] Holy Communion

com·mu·ni·qué (-kā') n. official communication

com·mu·nism n. theory or system of ownership of the means of production by the community —**com'mu·nist** n.

com·mu·ni·ty n., pl. **-ties** 1 body of people living in the same place 2 a sharing in common

com·mute' v. 1 lessen (a punishment, etc.) 2 travel by train, etc. to and from work —**com·mut'er** n.

com·pact' (or käm'pakt; n.: käm'pakt) a. 1 firmly packed 2 terse —n. 1 small case for face powder, etc. 2 agreement

compact disc (or **disk**) n. digital disc for recording music, etc.

com·pac'tor n. device that compresses trash

com·pan'ion n. 1 comrade; associate 2 thing that matches or goes with another —**com·pan'ion·a·ble** a. —**com·pan'ion·ship** n.

com·pa·ny n., pl. **-nies** 1 group of people associated for some purpose 2 [Col.] guest(s) 3 military unit

com·par'a·tive a. by comparison —n. the second degree of comparison of adverbs and adjectives

com·pare' v. 1 liken (to) 2 examine for similarities or differences 3 to form the positive, comparative, and superlative degrees of (adjective or adverb) —**beyond compare** without equal —**com·par'a·ble** a. —**com·par'i·son** n.

com·part'ment n. section partitioned off

com·pass (kum'pəs) n. 1 instrument for drawing circles, etc. 2 range; extent 3 instrument for showing direction

com·pas'sion n. pity —**com·pas'sion·ate** (-ət) a.

com·pat'i·ble a. in agreement

com·pa'tri·ot n. fellow countryman

com·pel' v. **-pelled'**, **-pel'ling** to force

com·pen'di·um n., pl. **-ums** or **-a** comprehensive summary

com'pen·sate' v. make up for; pay —**com·pen·sa'tion** n.

com·pete' v. 1 vie; rival 2 take part (in a contest)

com'pe·tent a. 1 capable; able 2 adequate —**com'pe·tence**, **com'pe·ten·cy** n.

com·pe·ti'tion (-tish'ən) n. 1 a competing; rivalry 2 contest —**com·pet'i·tive** a. —**com·pet'i·tor** n.

com·pile' v. compose by collecting from various sources —**com'pi·la'tion** n.

com·pla'cen·cy, **com·pla'cence** n. 1 contentment 2 smugness —**com·pla'cent** a.

com·plain' v. 1 express pain, dissatisfaction, etc. 2 make an accusation —**com·plaint'** n.

com·plain'ant n. plaintiff

com'ple·ment (-mənt; v.: -ment') n. 1 that which completes 2 entirety —v. to make complete —**com·ple·men'ta·ry** a.

com·plete' a. 1 lacking no parts 2 finished 3 thorough; perfect —v. make complete —**com·ple'tion** n.

com·plex' (or käm'pleks; n.: käm'pleks) a. 1 having two or more parts 2 complicated —n. 1 complex whole 2 mixed-up feeling about a thing —**com·plex'i·ty** n., pl. **-ties**

com·plex'ion (-plek'shən) n. 1 color or texture of the skin 2 nature; aspect

com'pli·cate' v. make difficult or involved —**com'pli·cat'ed** a. —**com'pli·ca'tion** n.

com·plic'i·ty (-plis'-) n. partnership in wrongdoing

com'pli·ment (-mənt; v.: -ment') n. 1 something said in praise 2 pl. respects —v. pay a compliment to

com'pli·men'ta·ry a. 1 giving praise 2 given free

com·ply' v., pl. **-plied'** or **-ply'ing** conform (with rules) —**com·pli'ance** n. —**com·pli'ant** a.

com·po'nent a., n. (being) part of a whole

com·port' v. 1 conduct (oneself) 2 accord (with) —**com·port'ment** n.

com·pose' v. 1 make by combining 2 put in proper form 3 write (a song, poem, etc.) 4 make calm —**com·posed'** a. —

com·pos·er n. —**com·po·si·tion** (-zish'ən) n.

com·pos·ite (-päz'it) n., a. (thing) formed of distinct parts

com'post n. rotting vegetation used as fertilizer

com·po'sure (-zhər) n. calmness; self-possession

com·pound (käm'pound'; v.: also kəm pound') v. combine —n. 1 substance with combined elements 2 enclosed place —a. with two or more parts

com'pre·hend' v. 1 understand 2 include —**com'pre·hen'si·ble** a. —**com'pre·hen'sion** n. —**com'pre·hen'sive** a.

com·press (kəm pres'; n.: käm' pres') v. press tight —n. wet pad —**com·pres'sion** n. —**com·pres'sor** n.

com·prise' v. consist of

com'pro·mise' n. settlement made with concessions —v. 1 settle by compromise 2 make suspect

comp·trol'ler (kən-) n. one who regulates finances

com·pul'sion n. a forcing or being forced —**com·pul'sive** a. —**com·pul'so·ry** a.

com·punc'tion n. slight regret for wrongdoing

com·pute' v. calculate; figure —**com'pu·ta'tion** n.

com·put'er n. an electronic machine that rapidly calculates or correlates data —**com·put'er·i·za'tion** n. —**com·put'er·ize'** v.

com'rade' (-rad') n. 1 a close friend 2 associate —**com'rade·ship'** n.

con adv. against —v. conned, con'ning 1 study carefully 2 [Sl.] swindle

con·cave' (or kän'kāv') a. curved like the inside of a sphere

con·ceal' v. hide —**con·ceal'ment** n.

con·cede' v. 1 admit as true 2 grant as a right

con·ceit' (-sēt') n. 1 vanity; pride 2 fanciful notion —**con·ceit'ed** a.

con·ceive' v. 1 become pregnant 2 think of 3 understand —**con·ceiv'a·ble** a.

con'cen·trate' v. 1 fix one's attention, etc. (on) 2 increase, as in density 3 concentrated substance —**con'cen·tra'tion** n.

con·cen'tric a. having a common center, as circles

con·cep'tion n. 1 a conceiving

2 concept

con·cep'tu·al·ize' v. form a concept of

con·cern' v. be related to; involve —n. 1 business 2 regard 3 worry

con·cerned' a. 1 involved or interested 2 anxious

con·cern'ing prep. relating to

con'cert n. 1 agreement 2 musical performance

con·cert'ed a. combined

con'cer·ti'na (-tē'-) n. small accordion

con·cer'to (-cher'-) n., pl. –tos composition for solo instrument(s) and orchestra

con·ces'sion n. 1 a conceding 2 thing conceded 3 franchise, as for selling food

con·ces'sion·aire' n. holder of a CONCESSION (n. 3)

conch (käŋk, känch) n. large, spiral seashell

con·cil'i·ate' v. make friendly —**con·cil'i·a'tion** n. —**con·cil'i·a'tor** n. —**con·cil'i·a·to'ry** a.

con·cise' (-sīs') a. short and clear; terse —**con·cise'ly** adv.

con'clave' n. private meeting

con·clude' v. 1 finish 2 decide 3 arrange —**con·clu'sion** n.

con·clu'sive a. decisive

con·coct' v. prepare or plan —**con·coc'tion** n.

con·com'i·tant a. accompanying —n. concomitant thing

con'cord' n. 1 agreement 2 peaceful relations

con·cord'ance n. 1 agreement 2 complete list of words used in a book —**con·cord'ant** a.

con'course' n. 1 a crowd 2 open space for crowds

con·crete' a. 1 real; actual 2 specific —n. hard material made of sand, gravel and cement —**con·crete'ly** adv. —**con·cre'tion** n.

con'cu·bine' (-kyōo-) n. wife of lesser status

con·cu'pis·cence (-kyōop'ə-) n. lust —**con·cu'pis·cent** a.

con·cur' v. -curred', -cur'ring 1 occur together 2 agree —**con·cur'rence** n. —**con·cur'rent** a.

con·cus'sion n. 1 jarring shock 2 brain injury from a blow

con·demn' (-dem') v. 1 disapprove of 2 declare guilty 3 doom 4 take for public use 5 declare unfit —**con·dem·na'tion** n.

con·dense' v. 1 make or become denser 2 express concisely —

con·den·sa·tion n. —**con·dens'er** n.

con·de·scend' (-send') v. stoop; deign —**con·de·scen'sion** n.

con·di·ment n. seasoning

con·di·tion n. 1 prerequisite 2 state of being 3 healthy state 4 rank —v. 1 to make healthy 2 make accustomed (to) —**on condition that** provided that —**con·di'tion·er** n.

con·di'tion·al a. qualified —**con·di'tion·al·ly** adv.

con·dole' v. show sympathy —**con·do'lence** n.

con'dom n. covering for the penis, generally of rubber, worn during sexual intercourse

con·do·min'i·um n. separately owned unit in a multiple-unit dwelling: also **con'do'**

con·done' (-dōn') v. forgive or overlook

con'dor (-dər, -dôr') n. large vulture

con·duce' v. tend; lead (to) —**con·du'cive** a.

con·duct' (v.: kən dukt') n. 1 management 2 behavior —v. 1 to lead 2 manage 3 to direct 4 behave (oneself) 5 transmit, as electricity —**con·duc'tion** n. —**con·duc·tiv'i·ty** n.

con·duc'tive a. —**con·duc·tiv'i·ty** n.

con·duc'tor n. 1 an orchestra leader 2 one in charge of passengers, etc. 3 thing that conducts heat, etc.

con'duit (-dōō it) n. pipe, tube, etc. for fluids or wires

cone n. 1 pointed, tapered figure with circular base 2 woody fruit of evergreens

con·fec'tion n. candy, ice cream, etc. —**con·fec'tion·er** n.

con·fec'tion·er·y n., pl. **-ies** confectioner's shop

con·fed'er·a·cy n., pl. **-cies** league —[C-] South in the Civil War

con·fed'er·ate (-ət; v.: -āt') a. united; allied —n. 1 an ally 2 accomplice —v. unite; ally —**con·fed'er·a·tion** n.

con·fer' v. **-ferred', -fer'ring** 1 give 2 meet to discuss —**con'fer·ence** n.

con·fess' v. 1 admit (a crime) 2 affirm (a faith) 3 tell (one's sins) —**con·fes'sion** n.

con·fes'sion·al n. box where a priest hears confessions

con·fes'sor n. priest who hears confessions

con·fet'ti n. bits of colored paper thrown as at carnivals

con'fi·dant' (-dant', -dänt') n. trusted friend —**con'fi·dante'** n.fem.

con·fide' v. 1 trust (in) 2 share as a secret

con'fi·dence n. 1 trust 2 assurance 3 self-reliance 4 a sharing of a secret —**con'fi·dent** a.

confidence game n. swindle done by one (**confidence man**) who gains the victim's trust

con'fi·den'tial (-shal) a. 1 secret 2 entrusted with private matters —**con'fi·den'tial·ly** adv.

con·fig'u·ra'tion n. form

con·fine' (v.: kən fīn') n. limit: used in pl. —v. 1 restrict 2 to shut up, as in prison —**con·fine'ment** n.

con·firm' v. 1 to strengthen 2 approve formally 3 prove to be true 4 admit to membership in a church —**con·fir·ma'tion** n.

con·firmed' a. firmly established; habitual

con'fis·cate' v. seize legally —**con'fis·ca'tion** n.

con'fla·gra'tion n. big, destructive fire

con·flict' (n.: kän'flikt') v. be in opposition —n. 1 a fight 2 sharp disagreement

con'flu·ence n. 1 a flowing together of streams 2 crowd

con·form' v. 1 be in accord 2 act according to rules, customs, etc. —**con·form'ist** n. —**con·form'i·ty** n.

con·found' v. confuse

con·found'ed a. 1 confused 2 damned

con·front' v. 1 face boldly 2 bring face to face —**con·fron·ta'tion** n. —**con·fron·ta'tion·al** a.

con·fuse' v. 1 mix up 2 bewilder —**con·fu'sion** n.

con·fute' v. prove wrong

con·geal' (-jēl') v. 1 freeze 2 thicken; jell

con·gen'ial (-jēn'yəl) a. friendly; agreeable —**con·ge'ni·al'i·ty** n.

con·gen'i·tal (-jen'-) a. existing from birth —**con·gen'i·tal·ly** adv.

con'ger (eel) (-gər) n. large, edible saltwater eel

con·gest' (-jest') v. fill too full, as with blood —**con·ges'tion** n. —**con·ges'tive** a.

con·glom'er·ate (-ət) n. large corporation formed by merging many companies

con·glom·er·a'tion n. mass

con·grat'u·late' (-grach'ə-) v. rejoice with (a fortunate person)

—**con·grat'u·la·to'ry** a.

con·grat'u·la'tions n.pl. expressions of pleasure over another's good luck, etc.

con'gre·gate v. gather into a crowd

con'gre·ga'tion n. assembly of people, esp. for worship

con'gress n. **1** assembly **2** legislature, esp. [C-] of the U.S. —**con·gres'sion·al** a. —**con'gress·man** n., pl. **-men** —**con'gress·per'son** n. —**con'gress·wom'an** n.fem., pl. **-wom'en**

con·gru'ent a. agreeing; corresponding

con'gru·ous a. suitable —**con·gru'i·ty** n.

con'i·cal (kän'-) a. of or like a cone: also **con'ic**

con'i·fer (kän'ə-, kō'nə-) n. cone-bearing tree

con·jec'ture (-chər) n., v. guess —**con·jec'tur·al** a.

con·join' v. join together

con·ju'gal a. of marriage

con'ju·gate v. give the inflectional forms of (a verb) —**con'ju·ga'tion** n.

con·junc'tion n. **1** a joining together; union **2** an occurring together **3** word used to join words, clauses, etc. —**con·junc'tive** a.

con·junc'ti·vi'tis n. inflammation of the mucous membrane covering the eye

con'jure v. **1** practice magic **2** entreat **3** cause to appear, etc. as by magic —**con'jur·er, con'jur·or** n.

conk [Sl.] n., v. hit on the head —**conk out 1** fail suddenly **2** fall asleep from fatigue

con man [Sl.] confidence man: also **con artist**

con·nect' v. **1** join; link **2** show or think of as related —**con·nec'tive** a.

con·nec'tion n. **1** a connecting or being connected **2** thing that connects **3** relation

con·nive' v. **1** pretend not to look (at crime, etc.) **2** cooperate secretly in wrongdoing —**con·niv'ance** n.

con·nois·seur (kän'ə sur') n. expert, esp. in the fine arts

con·note' v. **1** to suggest in addition to the explicit meaning —**con'no·ta'tion** n.

con·nu'bi·al a. of marriage

con'quer (-kər) v. defeat; overcome —**con'quer·or** n. —**con'quest** n.

con·quis'ta·dor (-kwis'-, -kēs'-) n., pl. **-dors** or **-do'res** (-dôr'ēz') 16th-c. Spanish conqueror of Mexico, Peru, etc.

con'science (-shəns) n. sense of right and wrong

con'sci·en'tious (-shē-) a. scrupulous; honest

con'scious (-shəs) a. **1** aware (of or that) **2** able to feel and think; awake **3** intentional —**con'scious·ness** n.

con·script' v. to draft (into the armed forces) —**con·scrip'tion** n.

con'se·crate v. **1** set apart as holy **2** devote —**con'se·cra'tion** n.

con·sec'u·tive a. following in order without a break —**con·sec'u·tive·ly** adv.

con·sen'sus n. general opinion

con·sent' v. agree —n. agreement or approval

con'se·quence n. **1** a result **2** importance

con'se·quent a. resulting

con'se·quen'tial (-shəl) a. **1** consequent **2** self-important

con'se·quent·ly adv. as a result; therefore

con·ser'va·tive a. **1** opposed to change **2** cautious —n. conservative person

con·serv'a·to'ry n. school of music, art, etc.

con·serve' v. keep from being damaged, lost, etc. —**con'ser·va'tion** n.

con·sid'er v. **1** think over **2** keep in mind **3** have regard for **4** believe to be —**con·sid'er·ate** (-ət) a. —**con·sid'er·a'tion** n.

con·sid'er·a·ble a. large or important —**con·sid'er·a·bly** adv.

con·sid'er·ing prep. taking into account

con·sign' v. **1** entrust **2** assign **3** deliver (goods) —**con·sign'ment** n.

con·sist' v. be make up (of)

con·sis'ten·cy n., pl. **-cies 1** thickness, as of a liquid **2** agreement **3** uniformity of action —**con·sis'tent** a.

con·sole' v. comfort; cheer up —**con·so·la'tion** n.

con'sole' n. floor cabinet of an organ, radio, TV, etc.

con·sol'i·date' v. unite —**con·sol'i·da'tion** n.

con'som·mé' (-sə mā') n. clear meat soup

con'so·nant n. letter for a

breath-blocked sound, as *p, t, l,* etc. —*a.* in harmony —**con'so·nance** *n.*

con'sort' (*v.:* kən sôrt') *n.* spouse, esp. of a monarch —*v.* to associate

con·sor'ti·um (or -sôr'shəm) *n.,* pl. **-ti·a** international alliance, as of banks

con·spic'u·ous *a.* 1 easy to see 2 outstanding —**con·spic'u·ous·ly** *adv.*

con·spire' *v.* join in a plot —**con·spir'a·cy** (-spir'-) *n.* —**con·spir'a·tor** *n.*

con'sta·ble *n.* policeman

con'stant *a.* 1 not changing; fixed 2 faithful 3 continual —*n.* unchanging thing —**con'stan·cy** *n.* —**con'stant·ly** *adv.*

con'stel·la'tion *n.* group of fixed stars

con'ster·na'tion *n.* great alarm or dismay

con'sti·pate' *v.* make it difficult to move the bowels —**con'sti·pa'tion** *n.*

con·stit'u·en·cy (-stich'ōō-) *n.,* voters in a district

con·stit'u·ent *n.* 1 necessary part 2 voter —*a.* needed to form a whole

con'sti·tute' *v.* form; set up

con'sti·tu'tion *n.* 1 structure; make up 2 basic laws of a government, etc., esp. [C—] of the U.S. —**con'sti·tu'tion·al** *a.*

con·strain' *v.* force or restrain —**con·straint'** *n.*

con·strict' *v.* make smaller by squeezing, etc.; contract —**con·stric'tion** *n.*

con·struct' *v.* build; devise

con·struc'tion *n.* 1 a constructing 2 structure 3 explanation 4 arrangement of words —**con·struc'tive** *a.*

con·strue' *v.* interpret

con'sul *n.* government official in a foreign city looking after his country's business there —**con'sul·ar** *a.* —**con'sul·ate** (-ət) *n.*

con·sult' *v.* 1 confer 2 ask the advice of 3 consider —**con·sult'ant** *n.* —**con'sul·ta'tion** *n.*

con·sume' *v.* 1 destroy 2 use up 3 eat or drink up —**con·sum'er** *n.*

con·sum·mate' (*a.:* kən sum'it) *v.* complete —*a.* complete —**con'sum·ma'tion** *n.*

con·sump'tion *n.* 1 a consuming 2 using up of goods 3 amount used up 4 tuberculosis of the lungs

con·sump'tive *n., a.* (one) having tuberculosis of the lungs

con'tact *n.* 1 a touching 2 being in touch (*with*) 3 connection —*v.* 1 place in contact 2 get in touch with

contact lens *n.* tiny, thin lens worn on the eye to improve vision

con·ta'gion (-tā'jən) *n.* a spreading of disease, an idea, etc. —**con·ta'gious** (-jəs) *a.*

con·tain' *v.* 1 have in it 2 be able to hold 3 restrain —**con·tain'er** *n.*

con·tam'i·nate' *v.* make impure; pollute —**con·tam'i·nant** *n.* —**con·tam'i·na'tion** *n.*

con'tem·plate' *v.* 1 to watch intently 2 meditate 3 intend —**con'tem·pla'tion** *n.* —**con·tem'pla·tive'** *a.*

con·tem'po·rar'y *n., a., pl.* **-ries** (one) living in the same period —**con·tem'po·ra'ne·ous** *a.*

con·tempt' *n.* 1 scorn 2 disgrace 3 disrespect shown for a judge, etc.

con·tempt'i·ble *a.* deserving contempt

con·temp'tu·ous (-chōō əs) *a.* scornful; disdainful

con·tend' *v.* 1 struggle 2 compete 3 assert

con·tent' *a.* satisfied: also **con·tent'ed** —*n.* satisfaction —**con·tent'ment** *n.*

con'tent' *n.* 1 *pl.* all that is contained 2 meaning 3 capacity

con·ten'tion *n.* argument or struggle —**con·ten'tious** *a.*

con·test' (*n.:* kän'test) *v.* 1 to dispute; question 2 fight for —*n.* 1 struggle 2 race, game, etc. —**con·test'ant** *n.*

con'text' *n.* words surrounding a word or phrase that fix their meaning

con·tig'u·ous *a.* in contact

con'ti·nence *n.* self-restraint, esp. sexually —**con'ti·nent** *a.*

con'ti·nent *n.* large landmass —**the Continent** Europe —**con'ti·nen'tal** *a.*

con·tin'gen·cy (-jən-) *n., pl.* **-cies** uncertain event

con·tin'gent *a.* dependent (*on*); conditional —*n.* quota, as of troops

con·tin'u·al *a.* 1 repeated often 2 continuous

con·tin'ue *v.* 1 keep on; go on 2 endure; last 3 resume 4 extend 5 postpone —**con·tin'u·ance** *n.,* **con·tin'u·a'tion** *n.*

con·ti·nu·i·ty *n., pl.* **-ties** 1 continuous state or thing 2 radio script, etc.

con·tin·u·ous *a.* without interruption; unbroken

con·tin·u·um *n., pl.* **-u·a** or **-u·ums** continuous whole, quantity, or series

con·tort' *v.* twist out of shape —**con·tor'tion** *n.*

con·tor'tion·ist *n.* one who can twist his or her body strangely

con'tour' *n.* outline of a figure, land, etc. —*v.* shape to contour —*a.* made to fit the contour of something

contra- *pref.* against

con'tra·band' *n.* smuggled goods —*a.* prohibited

con'tra·cep'tion *n.* prevention of human conception —**con'tra·cep'tive** *a., n.*

con·tract' (*n.* 2, 3: kän trakt') *v.* 1 undertake by contract 2 get; incur 3 shrink —**con'tract·or** *n.* —**con·trac'tu·al** (-choo əl) *a.*

con·trac'tion *n.* 1 a contracting 2 shortened form

con'tra·dict' *v.* say or be the opposite of —**con'tra·dic'tion** *n.* —**con'tra·dic'to·ry** *a.*

con·tral'to *n., pl.* **-tos** lowest female voice

con·trap'tion *n.* contrivance; gadget

con'tra·pun'tal *a.* of counterpoint

con'tra·ry *a.* 1 opposed; different 2 perverse —*n.* the opposite —**on the contrary** as opposed to what has been said —**con'trar·i·ly** *adv.*

con·trast' (*n.:* kän'trast') *v.* 1 compare 2 show difference —*n.* striking difference when compared

con'tra·vene' *v.* go against

con·trib'ute *v.* give, esp. to a common fund 2 furnish (an idea, article, etc.) —**contribute to** help bring about —**con'tri·bu'tion** *n.* —**con·trib'u·tor** *n.*

con·trite' *a.* remorseful —**con·tri'tion** (-trish'ən) *n.*

con·trive' *v.* 1 devise; invent 2 manage; bring about —**con·triv'ance** *n.*

con·trol' *v.* **-trolled', -trol'ling** 1 regulate (finances) 2 direct 3 restrain *n.* 1 authority 2 means of restraint 3 *pl.* regulating mechanism —**con·trol'ler** *n.*

con'tro·ver'sy *n.* debate or dispute —**con'tro·ver'sial** (-shəl) *a.*

con'tro·vert' *v.* to dispute —**con'tro·vert'i·ble** *a.*

con·tu'sion *n.* a bruise

co·nun'drum *n.* a puzzle

con'va·les'cence *n.* (period of) recovery after illness —**con'va·lesce'** *v.* —**con'va·les'cent** *a., n.*

con·vec'tion *n.* transmission of heat in currents

con·vene' *v.* assemble; meet

con·ven'ience *n.* 1 a being convenient 2 comfort 3 thing that saves work, etc.

con·ven'ient *a.* easy to do, use, or get to; handy

con'vent *n.* community of nuns or their living place

con·ven'tion *n.* 1 an assembly 2 custom; usage

con·ven'tion·al *a.* 1 customary 2 conforming

con·verge' *v.* come together —**con·ver'gence** *n.* —**con·ver'gent** *a.*

con·ver'sant *a.* familiar (*with*)

con'ver·sa'tion *n.* informal talk —**con'ver·sa'tion·al** *a.*

con·verse' (*n.:* kän'vers) *v.* to talk —*a.* opposite —*n.* 1 conversation 2 the opposite —**con·verse'ly** *adv.*

con·vert' (*n.:* kän'vert') *v.* change in form, use, etc. or in religion —*n.* person who has converted —**con·ver'sion** *n.* —**con·vert'er, con·ver'tor** *n.*

con·vert'i·ble *a.* that can be converted —*n.* automobile with a folding or removable top

con·vex' *a.* curved outward like the outside of a sphere —**con·vex'i·ty** *n.*

con·vey' *v.* 1 carry 2 transmit —**con·vey'or, con·vey'er** *n.*

con·vey'ance *n.* 1 a conveying 2 vehicle

con·vict' (*n.:* kän'vikt') *v.* prove or find guilty —*n.* prisoner serving a sentence

con·vic'tion *n.* 1 a being convicted 2 strong belief

con·vince' *v.* make feel sure —**con·vinc'ing** *a.*

con·viv'i·al *a.* sociable; jovial —**con·viv'i·al'i·ty** *n.*

con·voke' *v.* call together —**con'vo·ca'tion** *n.*

con'vo·lu'tion *n.* a twist or twisting —**con'vo·lut'ed** *a.*

con'voy *v.* escort —*n.* ships, etc. being escorted

con·vulse' *v.* shake as with violent spasms —**con·vul'sion** *n.* —**con·vul'sive** *a.*

coo *v.* make the soft sound of a

pigeon or dove —n. this sound

cook v. boil, bake, fry, etc. —n. one who cooks —**cook'er•y** n.

cook'book' n. book of recipes

cook'ie, cook'y n., pl. **-ies** small, sweet, flat cake

cook'out' n. meal cooked and eaten outdoors

cool a. 1 moderately cold 2 not excited 3 unfriendly 4 [Sl.] very good —n. cool place, time, etc. —v. make or become cool —**cool'ly** adv. —**cool'ness** n.

cool'ant n. fluid for cooling engines, etc.

cool'er n. refrigerator

coo'lie n., pl. **-lies** Oriental laborer

co-op n. [Col.] a cooperative

coop n. pen for poultry —v. confine as in a coop

co•op'er•ate', co-op'er•ate v. to work together: also co•öp'er•ate' —**co•op'er•a'tion, co•op'er•a'tion** n.

co•op'er•a•tive, co-op'er•a•tive a. cooperating —n. collective, profit-sharing enterprise Also co•öp'er•a•tive

co-opt' v. (get an opponent) to join one's side

co•or'di•nate, co-or'di•nate (-nət; v.: -nāt') a. equally important —v. to harmonize; adjust Also co•ör'di•nate —**co•or'di•na'tion, co-or'di•na'tion, co•ör'di•na'tion** n.

coot (kōōt) n. water bird

cop n. [Sl.] policeman

cope v. deal (with) successfully —n. priest's vestment

cop'i•er n. person who copies or machine that makes copies

co'pi•lot n. assistant pilot of an aircraft

cop•ing (kō'piŋ) n. top of masonry wall

co'pi•ous a. abundant

cop'per n. reddish-brown metal, a chemical element

cop'per•head' n. a poisonous snake

copse n. thicket

cop'u•late' v. have sexual intercourse —**cop•u•la'tion** n.

cop'y n., pl. **-ies** 1 thing made just like another 2 one of many books, etc. all alike —v. **-ied, -y•ing** 1 make a copy of 2 imitate

cop'y•cat' n. imitator: chiefly child's term —a. imitating a recent event

cop'y•right' n. exclusive rights over a book, song, etc. —v. protect by copyright

co•quette' (-ket') v. **-quet'ted, -quet'ting;** n. flirt —**co•quet'tish** a.

cor'al n. 1 hard mass of sea animal skeletons 2 yellowish red

cord n. 1 thick string 2 wood pile of 128 cu. ft. 3 insulated electric wire —**cord'less** a.

cor'dial (-jəl) a. friendly —n. syrupy alcoholic drink —**cor•di•al'i•ty** (-jē al'-) n. —**cor'dial•ly** adv.

cor'don n. a guarding group in a line

cor'do•van n. soft leather

cor'du•roy' n. ribbed cotton fabric

core n. 1 central part, as of an apple 2 most important part —v. remove the core of

co'ri•an'der n. an herb used for flavoring

cork n. 1 light, thick bark of a certain oak 2 stopper —v. stop with a cork

cork'screw' n. spiral device for uncorking bottles

corm n. bulblike underground stem of certain plants

cor'mo•rant n. seabird

corn n. 1 grain 2 grain that grows on large ears with a hard core (**corn'cob'**); maize 3 [Col.] trite humor 4 horny thickening of the skin —v. to pickle (meat, etc.)

cor'ne•a n. clear, outer layer of the eyeball —**cor'ne•al** a.

cor'ner n. 1 place where lines or surfaces meet 2 a region 3 monopoly —v. 1 put into a difficult position 2 get a monopoly in —**cut corners** cut down expenses, etc.

cor'ner•stone' n. stone at a corner of a building

cor'net n. brass instrument like a trumpet

corn'flow'er n. plant with showy disk flowers

cor'nice (-nis) n. molding along the top of a wall, etc.

corn'starch' n. starchy flour used in cooking

cor•nu•co'pi•a n. horn-shaped container overflowing with fruits, flowers, etc.

corn'y a. **-i•er, -i•est** [Col.] trite or sentimental

co•rol'la (-rōl'-, -räl'-) n. petals of a flower

cor'ol•lar'y n., pl. **-ies** proposition following from one already proved

co•ro'na n. ring of light around

the sun or moon

cor·o·nar·y *a.* of the arteries supplying the heart —*n.*, *pl.* **-ies** thrombosis in a coronary artery: in full **coronary thrombosis**

cor·o·na·tion *n.* crowning of a sovereign

cor·o·ner *n.* official who investigates unnatural deaths

cor·po·ral *n.* lowest ranking noncommissioned officer —*a.* of the body

cor·po·ra·tion *n.* group given legal status of an individual —**cor·po·rate** *a.*

cor·po·re·al (-pôr′ē-) *a.* 1 of the body 2 material

corps (kôr) *n.* 1 organized group 2 large military unit

corpse *n.* dead body

cor·pu·lent *a.* fat; fleshy —**cor′pu·lence** *n.*

cor·pus *n.* body, as of laws

cor·pus·cle (-əl) *n.* cell in the blood, lymph, etc.

cor·ral *n.* pen for horses, etc. —*v.* **-ralled′, -ral′ling** confine in a corral

cor·rect′ *v.* 1 make right 2 mark errors of 3 punish —*a.* right, true, etc. —**cor·rec′tion** *n.*

cor·rec′tion·al *a.* —**cor·rec′tive** *a.*, *n.* —**cor·rect′ly** *adv.*

cor·re·late *v.* bring into mutual relation —**cor·re·la′tion** *n.*

cor·rel′a·tive *n.*, *a.* (conjunction) showing mutual relation, as *either … or*

cor·re·spond′ *v.* 1 be similar or equal to 2 communicate as by letters —**cor·re·spond′ence** *n.*

cor·re·spond′ent *n.* 1 person exchanging letters with another 2 journalist sending in news to a home office

cor·ri·dor (-dər, -dôr′) *n.* long hall

cor·rob′o·rate *v.* confirm —**cor·rob′o·ra′tion** *n.* —**cor·rob′o·ra′tive** *a.*

cor·rode′ *v.* wear away; rust —**cor·ro′sion** *n.* —**cor·ro′sive** *a.*, *n.*

cor·ru·gate *v.* make fold or wrinkles in

cor·rupt′ *a.* 1 rotten 2 evil 3 taking bribes —*v.* to make or become corrupt —**cor·rupt′i·ble** *a.* —**cor·rup′tion** *n.*

cor·sage′ (-säzh′) *n.* small bouquet worn by a woman

cor·set *n.* tight undergarment to support the torso

cor·tege′ (-tezh′) *n.* ceremonial procession

cor·tex *n.*, *pl.* **-ti·ces′** (-tə sēz′) etc. —**cor′ti·cal** *a.*

cor′ti·sone′ (*or* -zōn′) *n.* hormone used to treat allergies, inflammations, etc.

co·run′dum *n.* mineral used for grinding wheels, etc.

cor·us·cate *v.* to glitter; sparkle —**cor·us·ca′tion** *n.*

co′sign′ *v.* sign jointly —**co′sign′er** *n.*

cos·met′ic (käz-) *n.*, *a.* (preparation) for enhancing beauty —**cos′me·tol′o·gist** *n.* —**cos′me·tol′o·gy** *n.*

cos′mic *a.* 1 of the cosmos; orderly 2 vast; huge

cos′mo·pol′i·tan *a.* at home all over the world; worldly —*n.* a worldly person

cos′mos (-məs, -mōs′) *n.* the universe seen as an orderly system

co′spon′sor *v.*, *n.* (be a) joint sponsor

cost *v.* cost, cost′ing require the payment, etc. of —*n.* 1 price 2 loss; sacrifice —**at all costs** by any means whatever

cost′ly *a.* **-li·er, -li·est** expensive —**cost′li·ness** *n.*

cos′tume′ *n.* 1 the dress of a people, period, etc. 2 set of outer clothes for some purpose

co′sy (-zē) *a.* **-si·er, -si·est** cozy —**co′si·ly** *adv.*

cot *n.* folding bed

cote *n.* small shelter for birds, sheep, etc.

co·te·rie (kōt′ər ē) *n.* social set; clique

co·til′lion (-yən) *n.* formal dance

cot′tage *n.* small house

cot′ter pin *n.* pin with two stems that can be spread apart

cot′ton *n.* 1 plant with head of soft, white fibers 2 thread or cloth from this —**cot′ton·y** *a.*

cot′ton·mouth′ *n.* water moccasin

cot′ton·seed *n.* 1 seed of the cotton plant 2 its oil (**cottonseed oil**) used in margarine, soap, etc.

cot′ton·wood′ *n.* poplar having seeds covered with cottony fibers

cot·y·le·don (kät′ə lēd′n) *n.* first leaf produced by a plant embryo

couch *n.* piece of furniture to lie on —*v.* put in words

cou′gar (-gər) *n.* large American wild cat

cough (kôf) *v.* expel lung air in a loud burst —*n.* 1 a coughing 2 condition of frequent coughing

cough drop n. small tablet for relief of coughs

could v. pt. of CAN: *could* is also used to show slightly more doubt than *can*

could'n't could not

coun'cil n. an advisory, administrative, or legislative body —**coun'cil-man** n., pl. **-men** — **coun'cil-wom'an** n.fem., pl. **-wom'en**

coun'ci-lor n. member of a council: also, Br. sp., **coun'cil-lor**

coun'sel n. 1 advice 2 lawyer(s) —v. to advise —**coun'se-lor, coun'sel-lor** n.

count v. 1 add up to get a total 2 name numbers in order 3 include or be included 4 consider 5 be important —n. 1 a counting 2 total number 3 each charge in an indictment 4 a nobleman —**count on** rely on

count'down' n. counting off of time units, in reverse order

coun'te-nance n. 1 a facial expression 2 face —v. to sanction

count'er n. long table for displaying goods, serving food, etc. —adv., a. contrary —v. oppose

counter- pref. 1 opposite 2 against 3 in return

coun'ter-act' v. act against; undo

coun'ter-at-tack' n., v. attack in return

coun'ter-bal'ance v. to offset

coun'ter-clock'wise' adv., a. like the hands of a clock moving in reverse

coun'ter-feit' (-fit') a. made in imitation with intent to defraud —n. fraudulent imitation —v. 1 make counterfeits 2 pretend

coun'ter-mand' v. cancel (a command)

coun'ter-part' n. matching or corresponding thing

coun'ter-point' n. harmonic interweaving of melodies

coun'ter-pro-duc'tive a. producing the opposite of what is intended

coun'ter-sign' n. password —v. confirm another's signature by signing

coun'ter-sink' v. sink a bolt or screw into a hole large enough to receive its head

count'ess n. wife or widow of a count or earl

count'less a. too many to count

coun'try (kun'-) n., pl. **-tries** 1 region 2 nation 3 rural area —

a. rural —**coun'try-man** n., pl. **-men** —**coun'try-side'** n.

coun'ty n., pl. **-ties** subdivision of a State

coup (kōō) n., pl. **coups** 1 bold, successful stroke 2 coup d'état

coup d'é-tat (kōō'dā tä') n. sudden overthrow of a ruler

cou-ple (kup'əl) n. 1 a pair 2 engaged, married, etc. man and woman 3 [Col.] a few —v. join together

cou'plet n. two successive rhyming lines of poetry

cou'pling n. device for joining things together

cou'pon (kōō'-, kyōō'-) n. certificate, ticket, etc. redeemable for cash or gifts

cour'age n. fearless or brave quality —**cou-ra'geous** a.

cou'ri-er (koor'ē-, kur'ē-) n. messenger

course n. 1 path or channel 2 direction taken 3 regular mode of action 4 series 5 separate part of a meal 6 a study or series of studies —v. run —**in the course of** during —**of course** 1 naturally 2 certainly

court n. 1 an open space surrounded by buildings or walls: also **court'yard'** 2 playing area 3 royal palace 4 family, advisers, etc. of a sovereign 5 courtship 6 *Law* a) judge(s) b) place where trials are held (also **court'room'**) —v. woo

cour'te-san (-zən) n. nobleman's mistress

cour'te-sy (kurt'ə-) n., pl. **-sies** polite behavior or act —**cour'te-ous** a.

court'house' n. building housing the offices and courtrooms of a county

cour'ti-er n. attendant at a royal court

court'ly a. dignified

court'-mar'tial n., pl. **courts'-mar'tial** or **court'-mar'tials** trial by a military or naval court —v. try by such a court

court'ship' n. period or act of courting a woman

cous'in (kuz'-) n. child of one's uncle or aunt

cove n. small bay

cov'en (kuv'-) n. witches' meeting

cov'e-nant (kuv'ə-) n. agreement; compact

cov'er v. 1 place something over 2 extend over 3 conceal 4 protect 5 include; deal with —n.

thing that covers —**take cover**
seek shelter —**cov'er·ing** n.

cov'er·age n. amount covered by
something

cov'er·alls' n.pl. one-piece work
garment with legs

cov'er·let n. bedspread

cov'ert (kuv'ərt, kō'vərt) n. hidden

cov'er-up' n. an attempt to keep
blunders, crimes, etc. undisclosed

cov'et v. desire ardently (what
belongs to another)

cov'et·ous a. greedy

cov'ey (kuv'ē) n. small flock of
birds, esp. quail

cow n. mature female of the ox,
or of the elephant, seal, etc. —v.
make timid

cow'ard n. one lacking courage
—**cow'ard·ice'** (-ər dis') n. —
cow'ard·ly a., adv.

cow'boy' n. worker who herds
cattle: also **cow'hand'**

cow'er v. cringe in fear

cow'hide' n. leather made from
the hide of a cow

cowl n. monk's hood

cow'lick' n. tuft of hair difficult
to comb flat

cowl'ing n. metal covering for an
airplane engine

cow'slip' n. 1 swamp plant with
yellow flowers 2 English primrose

cox'swain (käk'sən, -swān') n.
one who steers a boat

coy a. shy or pretending to be
shy —**coy'ly** adv.

coy·o·te (kī ōt'ē, kī'ōt') n. small
prairie wolf

coz'en (kuz'-) v. cheat

co'zy a. -zi·er, -zi·est warm and
comfortable; snug

CPU n. central processing unit

crab n. 1 shellfish with eight
legs and two pincers 2 complainer

crab apple n. small, sour apple

crab'by a. -bi·er, -bi·est peevish
—**crab'bi·ness** n.

crack v. 1 make a sudden, sharp
breaking noise 2 break without
separation of parts 3 [Sl.] make
(a joke) 4 solve —n. 1 sudden,
sharp noise 2 incomplete break
3 sharp blow 4 [Col.] try 5 [Sl.]
gibe 6 [Sl.] form of cocaine —a.
[Col.] first-rate —**crack down
(on)** become more strict (with)

crack'down' n. a resorting to
strict discipline or rules

crack'er n. thin, crisp wafer

crack'le v., n. (make) a series of

slight, sharp sounds

crack'pot' n. [Col.] fanatic

cra'dle n. baby's bed on rockers
—v. put as in a cradle

craft n. 1 skill; art 2 slyness 3
pl. **craft** boat or aircraft

crafts'man n., pl. -**men** skilled
workman —**crafts'man·ship'** n.

craft'y a. -i·er, -i·est sly; cunning
—**craft'i·ly** adv.

crag n. steep, projecting rock —
crag'gy a.

cram v. **crammed, cram'ming** 1
to stuff 2 study hurriedly for a
test

cramp n. 1 painful contraction
of a muscle 2 pl. intestinal pain
—v. hamper

cran'ber'ry n., pl. -**ries** sour,
edible, red berry

crane n. 1 long-legged wading
bird 2 machine for lifting heavy
weights —v. stretch (the neck)

cra'ni·um n. the skull —**cra'ni·al**
a.

crank n. 1 handle for turning a
shaft 2 [Col.] an eccentric —v.
start or work by a crank

crank'y a. -i·er, -i·est irritable;
cross

cran'ny n., pl. -**nies** chink

crap n. [Sl.] 1 nonsense 2 junk

crape n. crepe

craps n.pl. dice game

crash v. 1 fall, break, drop, etc.
with a loud noise 2 fail 3 [Col.]
get into uninvited —n. 1 loud
noise 2 a crashing failure, as
of business 4 coarse linen

crass a. grossly dull

crate n. wooden packing case —
v. pack in a crate

cra'ter n. bowl-shaped cavity or
pit, as of a volcano

cra·vat' n. necktie

crave v. ask or long for

cra'ven a. cowardly —n. coward

crav'ing n. intense desire

craw n. bird's crop

crawl v. 1 move slowly while flat
on the ground 2 creep 3 swarm
with crawling things —n. 1 a
crawling 2 swimming stroke

cray'fish', craw'fish' n. shellfish
like a small lobster

cray'on n. small stick of chalk,
wax, etc. for drawing

craze v. make or become insane
—n. fad

cra'zy a. -zi·er, -zi·est insane,
mad, etc. —**cra'zi·ly** adv. —**cra'**
zi·ness n.

creak v., n. squeak

cream n. 1 oily part of milk 2
creamy cosmetic 3 best part —

v. beat till smooth as cream —
cream of purée of —**cream'y** *a.*,
-i·er, -i·est
cream'er *n.* cream pitcher
cream'er·y *n., pl.* **-ies** place
where dairy products are made
or sold
crease *n.* line made by folding —
v. make a crease in
cre·ate' *v.* make; bring about —
cre·a'tion *n.* —**cre·a'tive** *a.* —
cre·a'tor *n.*
crea'ture *n.* living being, animal
or human
cre'dence *n.* belief; trust
cre·den'tials (-shalz) *n.pl.* papers
showing one's right to a certain
position, etc.
cre·den'za *n.* buffet or sideboard
cred'i·ble *a.* believable —**cred·i-
bil'i·ty** *n.*
cred'it *n.* **1** belief; trust **2** reputation **3** praise or source of
praise **4** trust that one will pay
later **5** completed unit of study
—*v.* **1** believe; trust **2** give
credit for —**cred'it·a·ble** *a.* —
cred'it·a·bly *adv.*
cred'i·tor *n.* one to whom
another owes a debt
cre'do (krē'-, krä'-) *n., pl.* **-dos**
creed
cred·u·lous (krej'ə ləs) *a.* believing too readily —**cre·du'li·ty**
(krə dōō'-) *n.*
creed *n.* statement of belief
creek *n.* small stream
creel *n.* basket for fish
creep *v.* **crept, creep'ing** **1** go on
hands and knees **2** go slowly or
stealthily **3** grow along the
ground, etc. —*n.* **1** [Sl.] disgusting
person —**the creeps** [Col.] feeling of fear, disgust, etc.
creep'y *a.* **-i·er, -i·est** causing
fear, disgust, etc.
cre'mate' *v.* burn (a dead body)
—**cre·ma'tion** *n.*
cre'ma·to'ry *n., pl.* **-ries** furnace
for cremating: also **cre'ma·to'ri-
um,** *pl.* **-ums** or **-a**
cre'o·sote' *n.* oily preservative
distilled from tar
crepe, crêpe (krāp; *n.* 2: *also*
krep) *n.* **1** thin, crinkled silk,
rayon, etc. **2** a thin pancake,
rolled and filled
crept *v.* pt. & pp. of CREEP
cre·scen'do' (-shən'-) *n., pl.*
-dos *Mus.* a growing louder
cres'cent *n.* shape of a quarter
moon
crest *n.* **1** tuft on an animal's
head **2** heraldic device **3** top;
summit

crest'fall'en *a.* dejected
cre'tin *n.* idiot
cre·vasse' (-vas') *n.* deep crack,
as in a glacier
crev'ice *n.* narrow crack
crew *n.* group of workers, as the
seamen on a ship
crew *v.* alt. pt. of CROW
crib *n.* **1** box for fodder **2** baby's
small bed **3** wood shed for grain
—*v.* **cribbed, crib'bing** **1** confine **2** [Col.] plagiarize
crib'bage *n.* card game
crick *n.* painful cramp
crick'et *n.* **1** leaping insect **2**
ball game played with bats and
wickets
cried *v.* pt. & pp. of CRY
cri'er *n.* one who cries, shouts
announcements, etc.
crime *n.* **1** an act in violation of
a law **2** sin
crim'i·nal *a.* of crime —*n.* person
guilty of crime
crim'i·nol'o·gy *n.* study of crime
and criminals
crimp *v.,* *n.* pleat or curl
crim'son (-zən, -sən) *n.* deep red
—*v.* make or become crimson
cringe (krinj) *v.* **1** shrink back
as in fear **2** to fawn
crin'kle *v.* to wrinkle or rustle —
crin'kly *a.*
crin'o·line' (-lin') *n.* **1** stiff cloth
2 hoop skirt
crip'ple *n.* disabled person —*v.*
disable
cri'sis *n., pl.* **-ses'** (-sēz') **1** turning point **2** crucial situation
crisp *a.* **1** brittle **2** clear **3** fresh;
bracing
criss'cross' *n.* crossed lines —*v.*
1 mark with crisscross **2** move
crosswise —*adv.* crosswise
cri·te·ri·on (krī tir'ē ən) *n., pl.*
-ri·a or **-ri·ons** standard; rule
crit'ic *n.* **1** judge of books, art,
etc. **2** faultfinder
crit'i·cal *a.* **1** finding fault **2** of
critics or their work **3** being a
crisis —**crit'i·cal·ly** *adv.*
crit'i·cize' *v.* **1** judge as a critic **2**
find fault (with) —**crit'i·cism'** *n.*
cri·tique' (-tēk') *n.* critical analysis or review
crit'ter *n.* [Dial.] creature
croak *v.,* *n.* (to make) a deep,
hoarse sound
cro·chet' (-shā') *v.* knit with one
hooked needle
crock *n.* earthenware jar
crock'er·y *n.* earthenware
croc'o·dile' *n.* large reptile of
tropical streams
cro'cus *n.* small plant of the iris

family

crois·sant (krə sänt′) *n.* a crescent-shaped bread roll

crone *n.* old hag

cro·ny *n., pl.* **-nies** close friend

crook *n.* 1 a bend or curve 2 [Col.] swindler

crook·ed *a.* 1 not straight 2 dishonest

croon *v.* sing in a soft tone —**croon′er** *n.*

crop *n.* 1 saclike part of a bird's gullet 2 farm product, growing or harvested 3 group 4 riding whip —*v.* **cropped, crop′ping** cut or bite off the ends of —

crop out (or **up**) appear suddenly —**crop′per** *n.*

crop′-dust′ing *n.* spraying of crops with pesticides from an airplane

cro·quet′ (-kā′) *n.* game with hoops in the ground through which balls are hit

cro·quette′ (-ket′) *n.* small mass of meat, fish, etc. deep-fried

cross *n.* 1 upright post with another across it 2 figure of this, symbolic of Christianity 3 any affliction 4 mark made by intersecting lines, bars, etc. 5 hybrid —*v.* 1 place, go, or lie across 2 go (*over*) to the other side 3 intersect 4 draw a line across 5 thwart 6 interbreed —*a.* 1 lying or passing across 2 irritable —**cross off** (or **out**) cancel as by drawing lines across —**cross′ing** *n.* —**cross′ness** *n.*

cross′bones′ *n.* picture of two crossed bones under a skull, symbolizing death

cross′bow′ *n.* medieval bow on a wooden frame for shooting arrows

cross′breed′ *n.* hybrid —*v.* to breed as a hybrid

cross′-coun′try *a.* across open country, as a race

cross′-ex·am′ine *v. Law* question (an opposition witness) —**cross′-ex·am′i·na′tion** *n.*

cross′-eyed′ *a.* having the eyes turned toward the nose

cross′hatch′ *v.* darken (a drawing) with crossing parallel lines

cross′-ref′er·ence *n.* reference from one part to another

cross′road′ *n.* 1 a road that crosses another 2 *pl.* road intersection

cross section 1 part cut straight across 2 broad sample

cross′walk′ *n.* pedestrians' lane across a street

cross′wise′ *adv.* across: also **cross′ways′**

crotch *n.* place where branches or legs fork

crotch′et·y *a.* cantankerous

crouch *v., n.* stoop with legs bent low

croup (krōōp) *n.* disease with cough and hard breathing

crou·pi·er (krōō′pē ā′) *n.* one controlling a gambling table

crou′ton (krōō′-) *n.* bit of toast served in soup

crow *n.* 1 large, black bird with a harsh call 2 rooster's cry —*v.* 1 make a rooster's cry 2 exult

crow′bar′ *n.* long, metal bar for prying, etc.

crowd *v.* to throng, press, cram, etc. —*n.* a mass of people —**crowd′ed** *a.*

crown *n.* 1 head covering of a monarch 2 power of a monarch 3 top part, position, quality, etc. —*v.* 1 make a monarch of 2 honor 3 be atop 4 climax

crow′s′-feet′ *n.pl.* wrinkles at outer corners of eyes

crow′s′-nest′ *n.* lookout platform on a ship's mast

CRT *n.* cathode-ray tube

cru·cial (-shəl) *a.* 1 decisive 2 trying

cru·ci·ble *n.* container for melting metals

cru·ci·fix *n.* representation of Jesus on the cross

cru·ci·fix′ion (-fik′shən) *n.*

cru·ci·fy *v.* **-fied′, -fy′ing** execute by suspending from a cross —**cru·ci·fix′ion** (-fik′shən) *n.*

crude *a.* 1 raw; unprocessed 2 rough or clumsy —**cru′di·ty, crude′ness** *n.*

cru′el *a.* causing suffering; pitiless —**cru′el·ty** *n.*

cru′et *n.* small bottle for vinegar, oil, etc.

cruise *v.* travel about, as by ship —*n.* voyage

cruis′er *n.* 1 police car 2 large, fast warship

crumb (krum) *n.* small piece, as of bread; bit —**crum′by** *a.*, **-bi·er, -bi·est**

crum′ble *v.* break into crumbs —**crum′bly** *a.*, **-bli·er, -bli·est**

crum′my *a.* **-mi·er, -mi·est** [Sl.] shabby, inferior, etc.

crum′ple *v.* to crush into wrinkles

crunch *v.* chew or crush with a crackling sound —**crunch′y** *a.*, **-i·er, -i·est**

cru·sade′ *v., n.* (to engage in) united action for some idea or cause —**cru·sad'er** n.

crush v. 1 press out of shape 2 pound into bits 3 subdue —n. 1 a crushing 2 crowded mass 3 [Col.] infatuation

crust n. 1 hard outer part of bread, earth, etc. 2 dry piece of bread

crus·ta'cean (-shən) n. hard-shelled invertebrate, as a shrimp, lobster, etc.

crust'y a. bad-tempered

crutch n. support held under the arm to aid in walking

crux n. essential point

cry v. **cried, cry'ing** 1 utter loudly 2 sob; weep —n., pl. **cries** 1 a shout 2 entreaty 3 call of a bird, etc. —**a far cry** great difference

cry·o·gen'ics n. science dealing with very low temperatures

crypt (kript) n. underground (burial) vault

cryp'tic a. secret; mysterious —**cryp'ti·cal·ly** adv.

cryp·tog'ra·phy n. secret-code writing or deciphering —**cryp·tog'ra·pher** n.

crys'tal n. 1 clear quartz 2 clear, brilliant glass 3 solidified substance with its molecules arranged symmetrically —**crys'tal·line** (-in) a.

crys'tal·lize' v. 1 form crystals 2 take on or give definite form —**crys'tal·li·za'tion** n.

cub n. young bear, lion, etc.

cub'by·hole' n. small, enclosed space

cube n. 1 a solid with six equal, square sides 2 product obtained by multiplying a number by its square —v. 1 get the CUBE (n. 2) of 2 cut into cubes —**cu'bic, cu'bi·cal** a.

cu'bi·cle n. small room

cuck'old n. man whose wife is unfaithful

cuck·oo (kōō'kōō') n. brown, slender bird —a. [Sl.] crazy

cu'cum·ber n. long, green-skinned, fleshy vegetable

cud n. food regurgitated by cattle and chewed again

cud'dle v. hold or lie close and snug —**cud'dle·some, cud'dly** a.

cudg'el (kuj'-) v., n. (beat with a) short club

cue n. 1 signal to begin 2 hint 3 rod for striking a billiard ball —v. to signal

cuff n. 1 band or fold at the wrist of a sleeve or the bottom

of a trouser leg 2 a slap —v. to slap

cui·sine (kwi zēn') n. 1 style of cooking 2 food cooked

cul'-de-sac' n. road, etc. with only one outlet

cu'li·nar·y (kyōō'-) a. of cookery

cull v. pick over; select

cul'mi·nate' v. reach its highest point —**cul·mi·na'tion** n.

cu·lottes' (-läts') n.pl. women's trousers resembling a skirt

cul'pa·ble a. deserving blame —**cul·pa·bil'i·ty** n.

cul'prit n. one accused, or found guilty, of a crime

cult n. system of worship or group of worshipers

cul'ti·vate' v. 1 prepare (land) for crops 2 grow (plants) 3 develop, as the mind —**cul·ti·va'tion** n.

cul'ture n. 1 animal or plant breeding 2 training of the mind, taste, etc. 3 civilization of a people or period —**cul'tur·al** a.

cul'vert n. drain or waterway under a road, etc.

cum (kum, koom) prep. with

cum'ber·some a. unwieldy

cum'mer·bund n. sash worn around the waist by men

cu'mu·la·tive (kyōō'myə-) a. increasing by additions

cu'mu·lus n. a cloud having rounded masses piled up

cu·ne'i·form' (kyōō nē'ə-) n. ancient wedge-shaped writing

cun'ning a. 1 sly; crafty 2 pretty —n. craft

cup n. small bowl with handle, for beverages —v. cupped, cup'ping shape like a cup —**cup'ful** n., pl. **-fuls'**

cup'board (kub'ərd) n. cabinet for dishes, food, etc.

cup'cake' n. small cake

cu·pid'i·ty (kyōō-) n. greed

cu'po·la (kyōō'-) n. small dome

cur n. 1 mongrel dog 2 contemptible person

cu·rate (kyoor'ət) n. clergyman helping a vicar or rector

cu'ra·tive a. having the power to cure —n. a remedy

cu·ra'tor n. one in charge, as of a museum

curb n. 1 chain or strap on a horse's bit for checking the horse 2 thing that restrains 3 edging along a street —v. to restrain

curd n. coagulated part of soured milk

cur'dle v. form curd

cure n. 1 a healing 2 remedy —v. 1 make well; heal 2 remedy 3 preserve (meat) —**cur'a·ble** a.

cur'few' n. evening deadline for being off the streets

cu'ri·o' n., pl. -os' odd art object

cu'ri·os'i·ty n. 1 desire to know 2 pl. -ties oddity

cu'ri·ous a. 1 eager to know; inquisitive 2 strange

curl v. 1 twist (hair, etc.) into ringlets 2 curve around; coil —n. 1 ringlet of hair 2 any curling —**curl'er** n. —**curl'y** a., -i·er, -i·est

cur'lew' n. wading bird

curl'i·cue' n. fancy curve

curl'ing n. game played on ice by sliding a flat stone

cur·mudg'eon (-muj'ən) n. cantankerous person

cur'rant n. 1 small, seedless raisin 2 sour berry

cur'ren·cy n., pl. -cies 1 money circulated in a country 2 general use; prevalence

cur'rent a. 1 of this day, week, etc. 2 commonly accepted or known —n. flow of air, water, electricity, etc.

cur·ric'u·lum n., pl. -lums or -la course of study

cur'ry n. spicy powder or sauce —v. -ried, -ry·ing brush the coat of (a horse, etc.) —**curry favor** try to win favor, as by flattery

curse v. cursed or curst, curs'ing 1 call or bring evil down on 2 swear (at) —n. 1 a cursing 2 evil or injury —**be cursed with** suffer from —**curs'ed** a.

cur'sive (-siv) a. of writing with joined letters

cur'sor n. movable indicator light on a computer screen

cur'so·ry a. hastily done —**cur'so·ri·ly** adv.

curt a. so brief as to be rude —**curt'ness** n.

cur·tail' v. cut short —**cur·tail'ment** n.

cur'tain n. piece of cloth hung, as at a window, to decorate or conceal —v. furnish with a curtain

curt'sy n., pl. -sies graceful bow that women make by bending the knees —v. -sied, -sy·ing make a curtsy

curve n. line, surface, etc. having no straight part —v. form or move in a curve —**cur'va·ture** n.

cush'ion n. 1 pillow or pad 2 something absorbing shock —v.

provide with a cushion

cusp n. arched, pointed end

cuss n., v. [Col.] curse

cus'tard n. pudding made with eggs, milk, and sugar

cus·to'di·an n. 1 one having custody 2 janitor

cus'to·dy n. 1 guarding; care 2 imprisonment —**cus·to'di·al** a.

cus'tom n. 1 usual or traditional practice; usage 2 pl. duties on imported goods —a. made to order; also **cus'tom-built'** or **cus'tom-made'**

cus'tom·ar·y a. usual —**cus'tom·ar·i·ly** adv.

cus'tom·er n. one who buys

cus'tom·ize' v. make according to personal specifications

cut v. cut, cut'ting 1 gash 2 pierce 3 sever 4 hew 5 reap 6 trim 7 pass across 8 reduce 9 [Col.] snub —n. 1 a cutting 2 part cut open or off 3 reduction 4 style 5 plate engraved for printing 6 insult 7 [Col.] share, as of profits —**cut and dried** dull; boring —**cut down (on)** reduce —**cut out for** suited for

cut'back' n. reduction or discontinuing of production, etc.

cute a. [Col.] 1 clever 2 pretty or pleasing

cu'ti·cle (kyōōt'-) n. hardened skin, as at the base and sides of a fingernail

cut'lass, cut'las n. short, thick, curved sword

cut'ler·y n. cutting tools, as knives, scissors, etc.

cut'let n. small slice of meat from the ribs or leg

cut'off' n. 1 short cut road, etc. 2 device for shutting off flow of a fluid, etc.

cut'-rate' a. selling or on sale at a lower price

cut'ter n. small, swift ship

cut'throat' n. murderer —a. merciless

cut'tle·fish' n. mollusk with ten arms

-cy suf. 1 quality or state of being 2 position, rank, or office of

cy'a·nide' (sī'-) n. poisonous white compound

cy'cla·mate' n. artificial sweetener

cy'cle n. 1 complete round of regular events, or period for this 2 bicycle, tricycle, etc. —v. ride a bicycle, etc. —**cy'clic, cy·cli'cal** a. —**cy'clist** n.

cy'clone' n. storm with heavy

rain and whirling winds

cy'clo·tron' *n.* apparatus that speeds up particles, as to split atomic nuclei

cyg'net (sig'-) *n.* young swan

cyl'in·der *n.* round figure with two flat ends that are parallel circles —**cy·lin'dri·cal** *a.*

cym'bals *n.pl.* pair of round brass plates struck together for a ringing sound

cyn'ic *n.* one inclined to question goodness, sincerity, etc. —**cyn'i·cal** *n.* —**cyn'i·cism'** *n.*

cy'press *n.* evergreen tree

cyst (sist) *n.* sac containing fluid or hard matter —**cyst'ic** *a.*

cystic fibrosis children's disease of the pancreas

czar (zär) *n.* 1 Russian emperor 2 an autocrat

D

dab *v.* **dabbed, dab'bing** put on with light, quick strokes —*n.* soft or moist bit —**dab'ber** *n.*

dab'ble *v.* 1 splash in water 2 do something superficially: (with *in* or *at*) —**dab'bler** *n.*

dachs'hund (däks'and) *n.* small dog with a long body

Da·cron (dä'krän', dak'rän') *trademark* synthetic fabric or fiber —*n.* [d-] this fabric or fiber

dad *n.* [Col.] father: also **dad'dy,** *pl.* **-dies**

daddy long'legs' *n., pl.* **-legs'** long-legged arachnid

da'do (dä'-) *n., pl.* **-does** lower part of a wall decorated differently

daf'fo·dil' *n.* yellow flower

daf'fy *a.* **-fi·er, -fi·est** [Col.] crazy; silly

daft *a.* 1 silly 2 insane

dag'ger *n.* 1 a short, sharppointed weapon 2 printed reference mark (†)

dahl'ia (dal'yə) *n.* plant with large, showy flowers

dai'ly *a., adv.* (done or happening) every day —*n.* daily newspaper

dain'ty *a.* **-ti·er, -ti·est** 1 delicately pretty 2 fastidious —*n.,* *pl.* **-ties** a delicacy —**dain'ti·ly** *adv.* —**dain'ti·ness** *n.*

dai·qui·ri (dak'ər ē) *n.* cocktail made with rum, lemon juice, etc.

dair'y *n., pl.* **-ies** place where milk, butter, etc. are made or sold —**dair'y·man** *n., pl.* **-men**

da·is (dā'is, dī'-) *n.* platform

dai'sy *n., pl.* **-sies** flower with white rays around a yellow disk

dale *n.* small valley

dal'ly *v.* **-lied, -ly·ing** 1 to toy or flirt 2 loiter

Dal·ma·tian (-shən) *n.* large, black-and-white dog

dam *n.* 1 barrier to hold back flowing water 2 female parent of a horse, cow, etc. —*v.* **dammed, dam'ming** keep back; confine

dam'age *n.* 1 injury; harm 2 *pl.* money paid for harm done —*v.* do damage to

dam'ask *n.* fabric with figured weave —*a.* deep-pink

dame *n.* 1 lady 2 [D-] woman's title of honor in Britain 3 [Sl.] any woman

damn (dam) *v.* **damned, damn'ing** condemn; declare bad, doomed, etc. —*a., adv.* [Col.] damned —**dam'na·ble** *a.*

dam·na'tion *n.*

damned *a.* 1 condemned 2 [Col.] outrageous —*adv.* [Col.] very

damp *n.* 1 moisture 2 mine gas —*a.* slightly wet; moist —*v.* 1 moisten 2 check or deaden Also **damp'en**

damp'er *n.* 1 one that depresses 2 valve in a flue to control the draft

dam'sel (-zəl) *n.* [Ar.] girl

dance *v.* move in rhythm to music —*n.* 1 rhythmic movement to music 2 party or music for dancing —**danc'er** *n.*

D and C medical procedure in which tissue is scraped from uterus

dan'de·li·on *n.* common weed with yellow flowers

dan'der *n.* [Col.] anger

dan'dle *v.* dance (a child) up and down on the knee

dan'druff *n.* little scales of dead skin on the scalp

dan'dy *n., pl.* **-dies** vain man —*a.* **-di·er, -di·est** [Col.] very good; first-rate

dan'ger *n.* 1 liability to injury, loss, etc.; peril 2 thing that may cause injury, etc. —**dan'ger·ous** *a.*

dan'gle *v.* hang loosely

Dan'ish (dān'-) *a.* of the people or language of Denmark —*n.* 1 language of Denmark 2 [*also* d-] pastry with a filling

dank *a.* disagreeably damp —**dank'ness** *n.*

dap′per a. trim; spruce

dap′ple a. spotted; mottled: also **dap′pled** —v. mottle

dare v. 1 have the courage (to) 2 challenge —n. a challenge —**dare say** think probable —**dar′ing** a., n.

dare′dev′il n., a. (one who is) bold and reckless

dark a. 1 with little or no light 2 not light in color 3 gloomy 4 ignorant —n. a being dark —**dark′en** v. —**dark′ness** n.

dark horse n. [Col.] one who wins or may win unexpectedly

dark′room′ n. dark room for developing photographs

dar′ling n., a. beloved

darn v. mend by sewing

dart n. 1 small pointed weapon for throwing 2 sudden movement —v. to throw or move quickly

dash v. 1 smash 2 strike violently against 3 do hastily: (with off) 4 rush —n. 1 bit of something 2 short race 3 vigor 4 mark of punctuation (—)

dash′board′ n. instrument panel in an automobile

dash′ing a. lively

das′tard·ly a. cowardly

da′ta (dāt′ə, dat′-) n. facts; information

da·ta·base n. large mass of organized data in a computer: also **data base**

date n. 1 time of an event 2 day of the month 3 social engagement 4 fruit of a tall palm —v. 1 mark with a date 2 belong to a particular time —**out of date** old-fashioned —**up to date** modern

daub v. 1 smear with sticky stuff 2 paint badly

daugh′ter n. female as she is related to her parents

daugh′ter-in-law′ n., pl. **daugh′ters-** wife of one's son

daunt v. 1 frighten 2 dishearten —**daunt′less** a.

dav′en·port′ n. large sofa

daw′dle v. waste time; loiter

dawn v. 1 begin to be day 2 begin to be understood —n. 1 daybreak 2 beginning

day n. 1 period from sunrise to sunset 2 period of 24 hours, esp. from midnight to midnight 3 a period; era —**day′light′** n. —**day′time′** n.

day′break′ n. time of the first light in the morning

day care n. daytime care for chil-

dren or adults —**day′-care′** a.

day′dream′ n. pleasant, dreamy thinking or wishing —v. have daydreams

daylight saving(s) time n. time one hour later than standard

day′time′ n. time between dawn and sunset

day′-to-day′ a. daily; routine

daze v. 1 stun 2 dazzle —n. dazed condition

daz′zle v. overpower with light or brilliance

DDT n. powerful insecticide

de- pref. 1 away from; off 2 reverse the action of

dea·con (dē′kən) n. one who assists a minister

de·ac′ti·vate′ v. 1 make (an explosive, etc.) inactive 2 disband (troops)

dead (ded) a. 1 not living 2 dull; inactive 3 complete —n. time of most cold, darkness, etc. —adv. completely

dead′beat′ n. [Sl.] one who avoids paying for things

dead′bolt′ n. door lock with a long, square bolt worked by a key

dead′en v. to dull

dead end n. street closed at one end —**dead′-end′** a.

dead heat n. a tie in a race

dead′line′ n. time limit

dead′lock′ n. standstill with equal forces opposed

dead′ly a. -li·er, -li·est 1 fatal 2 as or until death —adv. extremely

dead′pan′ a., adv. without expression

dead′wood′ n. useless thing

deaf (def) a. 1 unable to hear 2 unwilling to respond —**deaf′en** v.

deaf′-mute′ n. deaf person who has not learned speech

deal v. dealt (delt), deal′ing 1 distribute 2 have to do (with) 3 do business —n. transaction or agreement —**a good (or great) deal** 1 large amount 2 very much —**deal′er** n. —**deal′ing** n.

dean n. 1 church or college official 2 senior member of a group

dear a. 1 much loved 2 esteemed 3 costly 4 earnest —n. darling

dearth (durth) n. scarcity

death n. 1 a dying or being dead 2 cause of death

death′ly a. characteristic of death —adv. extremely

de·ba·cle (də bäk′əl) n. sudden

disaster

de·bar' v. -barred', -bar'ring exclude (from)

de·bark' v. leave a ship or aircraft —**de·bar·ka'tion** n.

de·base' v. to lower in quality, etc. —**de·base'ment** n.

de·bate' v. argue in a formal way —n. formal argument —**de·bat'a·ble** a. —**de·bat'er** n.

de·bauch' v. to corrupt —n. orgy —**de·bauch'er·y** n., pl. -ies

de·ben'ture (-chər) n. bond issued by a corporation, etc.

de·bil'i·tate' v. make weak —**de·bil'i·ta'tion** n.

de·bil'i·ty n. weakness

deb'it n. entry in an account of money owed —v. enter as a debt

deb'o·nair', deb'o·naire' (-ner') a. elegant and gracious; urbane

de·brief' v. receive information from about a recent mission

de·bris (də brē') n. broken, scattered remains; rubbish

debt (det) n. 1 something owed 2 state of owing

debt'or n. one owing a debt

de·bunk' v. to expose the false claims, etc. of

de·but (dā byōō', də-) n. 1 first public appearance, as of an actor 2 a formal introduction into society

deb'u·tante' (-tänt') n. girl making a social debut

dec'ade n. ten-year period

dec'a·dence n. a declining, as in morals or art —**dec'a·dent** a., n.

de·caf'fein·at'ed (-kaf'ə nāt'-) a. having its caffeine removed

de'cal' n. picture for transfer from prepared paper

de·camp' v. leave secretly

de·cant' v. pour off gently

de·cant'er n. decorative bottle for serving wine

de·cap'i·tate' v. behead —**de·cap'i·ta'tion** n.

dec·ath'lon' n. contest of ten track and field events

de·cay' v. 1 fall into ruin 2 rot —n. a decaying; rot

de·cease' n. death

de·ceased' a. dead —**the deceased** dead person(s)

de·ceit' (-sēt') n. 1 act of deceiving 2 deceitful quality —**de·ceit'ful** a.

de·ceive' v. make believe what is not true; mislead

de·cel'er·ate' (-sel'-) v. to slow down —**de·cel'er·a'tion** n.

De·cem'ber n. 12th month

de'cent a. 1 proper 2 respect-

able 3 adequate —**de'cen·cy** n.

de·cen'tral·ize' v. shift power from main to local units

de·cep'tion n. 1 a deceiving 2 illusion or fraud —**de·cep'tive** a.

dec'i·bel' (des'-) n. unit for measuring loudness of sound

de·cide' v. 1 settle by passing judgment 2 make up one's mind

de·cid'ed a. definite —**de·cid'ed·ly** adv.

de·cid'u·ous (-sij'ōō-) a. shedding leaves annually

dec'i·mal a. based on the number ten —n. a fraction with a denominator of ten or a power of ten, shown by a point (**decimal point**) before the numerator

dec'i·mate' v. destroy or kill a large part of

de·ci'pher (-sī'-) v. translate from code or illegibility

de·ci'sion (-sizh'ən) n. 1 a deciding 2 judgment 3 determination

de·ci'sive (-sī'siv) a. 1 conclusive 2 showing decision

deck n. 1 floor of a ship 2 pack of playing cards —v. adorn; trim

de·claim' v. speak in a loud, rhetorical way —**dec'la·ma'tion** n.

de·clare' v. 1 announce formally 2 say emphatically —**dec'la·ra'tion** n. —**de·clar'a·tive** a.

de·clas'si·fy v. make (secret documents) public and available

de·clen'sion n. grammatical inflection of nouns, etc.

de·cline' v. 1 slope downward 2 lessen, as in force 3 refuse politely 4 Gram. give inflected forms of —n. 1 a failing, decay, etc. 2 downward slope

de·cliv'i·ty n. downward slope

de·code' v. translate (a coded message) into plain language

de'com·pose' v. 1 break up into basic parts 2 rot —**de'com·po·si'tion** n.

de'com·press' v. free from air pressure —**de'com·pres'sion** n.

de'con·gest'ant n. medicinal relief for congestion, as of nasal passages

de'con·tam'i·nate' v. to rid of harmful substance

dé·cor, de·cor (dā kôr') n. decorative scheme

dec'o·rate' v. 1 adorn; ornament 2 give a medal to —**dec'o·ra'tive** a. —**dec'o·ra'tor** n. —**dec'o·ra'tion** n.

de·co'rum n. proper behavior, speech, etc. —**dec'o·rous** a. —

dec'o·rous·ly adv.

de'coy n. artificial bird, etc. used as a lure —v. lure

de·crease' (or dē'krēs) v. grow or make less or smaller —n. a decreasing

de·cree' n. official order; edict —v. **-creed', -cree'ing** order by decree

de·crep'it a. old and worn out —**de·crep'i·tude'** n.

de·crim'i·nal·ize' v. eliminate or reduce the penalties for

de·cry' v. **-cried', -cry'ing** to denounce; censure

ded'i·cate' v. 1 set apart formally 2 devote 3 inscribe —**ded'i·ca'tion** n.

de·duce' v. conclude by reasoning; infer

de·duct' v. subtract or take away —**de·duct'i·ble** a.

de·duc'tion n. 1 a deducing or deducting 2 amount deducted 3 conclusion

deed n. 1 act 2 feat of courage, etc. 3 legal document transferring property —v. to transfer by deed

deem v. think; believe

de·em'pha·size' v. make less important

deep a. 1 extending far down, in, or back 2 hard to understand 3 involved (in) 4 of low pitch 5 intense —n. deep place or part —adv. far down, etc. —**deep'en** v.

deep'freeze' v. freeze (food) suddenly so as to preserve

deep'-fry' v. fry in deep pan of boiling fat or oil

deep'-seat'ed a. firmly fixed: also **deep'-root'ed**

deer n., pl. **deer** hoofed, cud-chewing animal, the male of which bears antlers

de-es'ca·late' v. reduce in scope

de·face' v. mar

de fac'to a., adv. existing but not officially approved

de·fame' v. slander —**def'a·ma'tion** n.

de·fault' v., n. fail(ure) to do or pay as required

de·feat' v. 1 win victory over 2 frustrate —n. a defeating or being defeated

de·feat'ist n., a. (one) too readily accepting defeat

def'e·cate' v. excrete waste matter from bowels

de'fect (v.: dē fekt') n. imperfection; fault —v. to desert —**de·fec'tion** n. —**de·fec'tive** a.

de·fend' v. 1 protect 2 support by speech or act 3 Law act for (an accused) —**de·fend'er** n.

de·fend'ant n. Law person sued or accused

de·fense' n. 1 a defending against attack 2 something that defends 3 defendant and his counsel —**de·fense'less** a. —**de·fen'sive** a., n.

de·fer' (-fur') v. **-ferred', -fer'ring** 1 postpone 2 to yield in opinion, etc.

def'er·ence n. 1 a yielding in opinion, etc. 2 respect

de·fi'ance n. open resistance to authority —**de·fi'ant** a.

de·fi'cien·cy (-fish'ən-) n., pl. **-cies** shortage; lack —**de·fi'cient** a.

def'i·cit (-sit) n. amount by which a sum of money is less than expected, etc.

de·file' v. dirty; sully —n. narrow pass

de·fine' v. 1 mark the limits of 2 state the meaning of —**def'i·ni'tion** n.

def'i·nite (-nit) a. 1 having exact limits 2 explicit 3 certain

de·fin'i·tive (-tiv) a. 1 conclusive 2 most nearly complete

de·flate' v. 1 collapse by letting out air 2 lessen in amount, importance, etc. —**de·fla'tion** n.

de·flect' v. turn to one side

de·fog'ger n. device for clearing moisture from a window in a car, etc.

de·fo'li·ant n. chemical that strips plants of leaves

de·fo'li·ate' v. remove leaves from (trees, etc.)

de·for'est v. clear (land) of trees or forest —**de·for·est·a'tion** n.

de·form' v. mar the form of —**de·form'i·ty** n., pl. **-ties**

de·fraud' v. cheat

de·fray' v. pay (the cost)

de·frost' v. rid or become rid of frost or ice

deft a. quick and skillful

de·funct' a. no longer existing

de·fuse' v. 1 remove a fuse from 2 make less tense, etc.

de·fy' v. **-fied', -fy'ing** 1 resist openly 2 dare

de·gen'er·ate' (-āt'; a., n.: -at) v. lose normal or good qualities —a. deteriorated —n. a degenerate person —**de·gen'er·a·cy** n. —**de·gen'er·a'tion** n.

de·grade' v. lower in rank, value, etc. —**deg'ra·da'tion** n.

de·gree' n. 1 successive step in a

series 2 intensity, extent, etc. 3 rank given to a college graduate 4 unit of measure, as for angles, temperature, etc.

de·hu'man·ize' v. deprive of human qualities —**de·hu'man·i·za'tion** n.

de·hu·mid'i·fy' v. -**fied'**, -**fy'ing** remove moisture from (air, etc.) —**de·hu·mid'i·fi·er** n.

de·hy'drate' v. remove water from —**de'hy·dra'tion** n.

de·ice' v. to melt ice from (something) —**de·ic'er** n.

de'i·fy' v. -**fied'**, -**fy'ing** make a god of —**de'i·fi·ca'tion** (-fi-) n.

deign (dān) v. condescend

de'i·ty n., pl. -**ties** god or goddess

dé·jà vu' (dā'zhä vōō') n. [Fr.] feeling that one has been in a place or has had an experience before

de·ject'ed a. sad; depressed

de·jec'tion n. depression; sadness

de·lay' v. 1 put off; postpone 2 make late; detain —n. a delaying

de·lec'ta·ble a. delightful

del'e·gate (-gat; v.: -gāt') n. representative —v. 1 appoint as delegate 2 entrust to another

del'e·ga'tion n. group of delegates

de·lete' (-lēt') v. take out (a word, etc.) —**de·le'tion** n.

del'e·te'ri·ous (-tirē-) a. harmful to health, etc.

del'i n. [Col.] delicatessen

de·lib'er·ate' (-āt'; a.: -at) v. consider carefully —a. 1 done on purpose 2 not rash or hasty 3 unhurried —**de·lib'er·a'tion** n.

del'i·ca·cy n. 1 delicate quality 2 pl. -**cies** a choice food; dainty

del'i·cate a. 1 fine and lovely 2 fragile or frail 3 needing care 4 sensitive 5 considerate and tactful —**del'i·cate·ly** adv.

del'i·ca·tes'sen n. shop selling meats, fish, cheeses, etc.

de·li'cious (-lish'əs) a. very pleasing, esp. to taste or smell

de·light' v. please greatly —n. great pleasure —**de·light'ful** a.

de·lin'e·ate' v. 1 draw; sketch 2 describe

de·lin'quent a. 1 not obeying duty or law 2 overdue —n. one guilty of minor crimes —**de·lin'quen·cy** n.

de·lir'i·um n. 1 temporary mental illness 2 wild excitement —**de·lir'i·ous** a.

de·liv'er v. 1 set free; rescue 2

assist in birth 3 utter 4 hand over 5 distribute 6 strike or throw —**de·liv'er·ance** n.

de·liv'er·y n., pl. -**ies** a delivering of something delivered

dell n. small valley

del·phin'i·um n. tall plant with flower spikes

del'ta n. 1 letter of Greek alphabet 2 soil deposit at a river mouth

de·lude' v. mislead

del'uge' (-yooj') n. 1 great flood 2 heavy rainfall —v. 1 to flood 2 overwhelm

de·lu'sion n. false, esp. psychotic, belief —**de·lu'sive** a.

de·luxe' a. very good; elegant

delve v. investigate

dem'a·gogue, **dem·a·gog** (dem'ə gäg') n. one who appeals to prejudices, etc. to win power —**dem'a·gog'y** (-gä'jē), **dem'a·gogu'er·y** (-gäg'ər ē) n.

de·mand' v. 1 ask for boldly 2 require —n. 1 strong request 2 requirement —**on demand** when presented for payment

de'mar·ca'tion, de'mar·ka'tion n. boundary line

de·mean' v. degrade

de·mean'or n. behavior

de·ment'ed a. mentally ill

de·men'tia (-shə) n. loss of mental powers

de·mer'it n. 1 fault 2 mark for poor work, etc.

demi- pref. half

dem'i·god' n. minor deity

dem'i·john' n. large, wicker-covered bottle

de·mil'i·ta·rize' v. to free from military control

de·mise' (-mīz') n. death

dem'i·tasse' (-tas') n. small cup of coffee

dem'o n., pl. -**mos** recording made to demonstrate a song, performer's talent, etc.

de·mo'bi·lize' v. to disband (troops)

de·moc'ra·cy n., pl. -**cies** 1 government in which the power is vested in all the people 2 equality of rights, etc. —**dem'o·crat'** n. —**dem'o·crat'ic** a. —**dem'o·crat'i·cal·ly** adv.

de·mog'ra·phy n. statistical study of populations —**dem'o·graph'ic** a.

de·mol'ish v. destroy; ruin —**dem'o·li'tion** n.

de'mon n. devil; evil spirit

de·mon'ic a. 1 of a demon 2 fiendish; frenzied

dem'on·strate' v. 1 prove 2 explain with examples 3 show the working of 4 show feelings publicly —**de·mon'stra·ble** a. —**dem'on·stra'tion** n. —**dem'on·stra'tor** n.

de·mon'stra·tive a. 1 showing clearly 2 giving proof (of) 3 showing feelings openly

de·mor'al·ize' v. to lower in morale —**de·mor'al·i·za'tion** n.

de·mote' v. reduce in rank —**de·mo'tion** n.

de·mur' (-mur') v. **-murred'**, **-mur'ring** to scruple (at) —n. objection

de·mure' (-myoor') a. coy

den n. 1 animal's lair 2 haunt of thieves, etc. 3 small, cozy room

de·na'ture v. to make (alcohol) unfit to drink

de·ni'al n. 1 a denying 2 contradiction

den'i·grate' v. belittle —**den'i·gra'tion** n.

den'im n. coarse, twilled cotton cloth

den'i·zen n. inhabitant

de·nom'i·nate' v. to name

de·nom'i·na'tion n. 1 a name 2 specific class or kind 3 religious sect —**de·nom'i·na'tion·al** a.

de·nom'i·na'tor n. term below the line in a fraction

de·note' v. 1 indicate 2 mean explicitly —**de·no'ta'tion** n.

de·noue·ment, dé·noue·ment (dā'nōō män') n. unraveling of a plot

de·nounce' v. 1 accuse publicly 2 condemn strongly

dense a. 1 packed tightly 2 thick 3 stupid —**dense'ly** adv.

den'si·ty n. 1 number per unit 2 ratio of the mass of an object to its volume

dent n. slight hollow made in a surface by a blow —v. make a dent in

den'tal a. of the teeth

dental floss n. thread for removing food from the teeth

den'ti·frice (-fris) n. substance for cleaning teeth

den'tin (-tin) n. tissue under the enamel of teeth: also **den'tine** (-tēn', -tin)

den'tist n. one who cares for and repairs teeth —**den'tist·ry** n.

den'ture n. often pl. set of artificial teeth

de·nun'ci·a'tion n. a denouncing

de·ny' v. 1 declare untrue 2 refuse to give, accept, etc. —

deny oneself do without

de·o'dor·ize' v. counteract the odor of —**de·o'dor·ant** a., n. —**de·o'dor·iz'er** n.

de·part' v. 1 leave 2 die 3 deviate (from) —**de·par'ture** n.

de·part'ment n. 1 division 2 field of activity —**de·part'men'tal** a.

de·pend' v. 1 be determined by something else 2 rely, as for support —**de·pend'ence** n. —**de·pend'en·cy** n., pl. **-cies** —**de·pend'ent** a., n.

de·pend'a·ble a. reliable —**de·pend'a·bil'i·ty** n.

de·pict' v. 1 represent by drawing, etc. 2 describe

de·pil'a·to'ry n., pl. **-ries**; a. (substance or device for) removing unwanted hair

de·plete' v. 1 empty (wholly) 2 exhaust —**de·ple'tion** n.

de·plore' v. be sorry about —**de·plor'a·ble** a.

de·ploy' v. Mil. spread out

de·pop'u·late' v. to reduce the population of

de·port' v. 1 behave (oneself) 2 expel (an alien) —**de·por'ta'tion** n.

de·port'ment n. behavior

de·pose' v. 1 remove from office 2 testify —**de·po·si'tion** n.

de·pos'it v. 1 place for safekeeping 2 give as partial payment 3 set down —n. something deposited —**de·pos'i·tor** n.

de·pos'i·to'ry n., pl. **-ries** place to put things for safekeeping

de·pot (-pō) n. 1 warehouse 2 train or bus station

de·prave' v. make morally bad —**de·praved'** a. —**de·prav'i·ty** n.

dep're·cate' v. express disapproval of —**dep're·ca'tion** n. —**dep're·ca·to'ry** a.

de·pre'ci·ate' (-shē-) v. 1 lessen in value 2 belittle —**de·pre'ci·a'tion** n.

dep're·da'tion n. a looting

de·press' v. 1 press down 2 sadden 3 lower in value, etc. —**de·pres'sant** a., n. —**de·pressed'** a.

de·pres'sion n. 1 a depressing 2 hollow place 3 dejection 4 period of reduced business and prosperity

de·prive' v. take away or withhold from —**dep'ri·va'tion** n.

depth n. 1 distance from the top or back 2 deepness 3 profundity 4 pl. deepest part —**in depth** comprehensively

dep'u·ta'tion n. delegation

de·pute' v. 1 authorize as a deputy 2 appoint in one's place

dep'u·tize' v. make a deputy

dep'u·ty n., pl. **-ties** substitute or agent

de·rail' v. run off the rails —**de·rail'ment** n.

de·range' v. 1 upset or disturb 2 make insane

der'by n., pl. **-bies** stiff felt hat with a round crown

de·reg'u·late' v. remove regulations governing —**de·reg'u·la'tion** n.

der'e·lict' a. 1 abandoned 2 negligent —n. thing or person abandoned as worthless —**der'e·lic'tion** n.

de·ride' v. to ridicule —**de·ri'sion** (-rizh'ən) n. —**de·ri'sive** (-ri'siv) a.

de·rive' v. 1 take or get (from) 2 deduce 3 originate 4 trace to a source —**der'i·va'tion** n. —**de·riv'a·tive** a.

der'ma·ti'tis n. inflammation of the skin

der'ma·tol'o·gy n. study of the skin and its diseases —**der'ma·tol'o·gist** n.

der'o·gate' v. detract; disparage —**der'o·ga'tion** n.

de·rog'a·to'ry a. detracting; disparaging

der'rick n. 1 machine for moving heavy objects 2 framework for drilling, as over an oil well

der·ri·ère' (-ē er') n. the buttocks

de·scend' (-send') v. 1 move down 2 come from earlier times 3 derive 4 to make a sudden attack (on) —**de·scent'** n.

de·scend'ant n. offspring of a certain ancestor

de·scribe' v. 1 picture in words; tell about 2 trace the outline of —**de·scrip'tion** n. —**de·scrip'tive** a.

de·scry' v. **-scried', -scry'ing** catch sight of

des'e·crate' v. violate the sacredness of; profane —**des'e·cra'tion** n.

de·seg're·gate' v. end racial segregation (in) —**de·seg're·ga'tion** n.

de·sen'si·tize' v. make less sensitive —**de·sen'si·ti·za'tion** n.

de·sert' (-zurt') v. abandon —n. often pl. reward or punishment —**de·ser'tion** n.

des'ert n. arid, sandy region

de·serve' v. be worthy (of) —**de·**

serv'ing a.

des'ic·cate' v. dry up

de·sign' v. 1 to plan 2 contrive —n. 1 plan; scheme 2 purpose 3 a pattern —**by design** purposely —**de·sign'er** n. —**de·sign'ing** a., n.

des'ig·nate' v. 1 to point out; specify 2 appoint —**des'ig·na'tion** n.

de·sire' v. wish or long for; want —n. 1 a wish 2 thing wished for 3 sexual appetite —**de·sir'a·ble** a. —**de·sir'ous** a.

de·sist' v. stop; cease

desk n. writing table

des'o·late (-lət; v.: -lāt') a. 1 lonely; forlorn 2 uninhabited 3 laid waste —v. make desolate —**des'o·la'tion** n.

de·spair' v. lose hope —n. loss of hope

des'per·a'do (-pə rä') n., pl. **-does** or **-dos** reckless outlaw

des'per·ate (-ət) a. 1 reckless from despair 2 serious —**des'per·a'tion** n.

des·pi'ca·ble a. deserving scorn; contemptible

de·spise' v. 1 to scorn 2 loathe

de·spite' prep. in spite of

de·spoil' v. rob; plunder

de·spond'en·cy n. loss of hope; dejection: also **de·spond'ence** —**de·spond'ent** a.

des'pot n. tyrant —**des·pot'ic** a. —**des'pot·ism'** n.

des·sert' n. sweet dish ending a meal

des'ti·na'tion n. place to which one is going

des'tine (-tin) v. head for, as by fate —**destined for** bound or intended for

des'ti·ny n., pl. **-nies** (one's) fate

des'ti·tute' a. needy —**des'ti·tu'tion** n.

de·stroy' v. 1 tear down; demolish 2 ruin 3 kill

de·stroy'er n. fast warship

de·struct' n. deliberate destruction of a rocket, etc. —v. be automatically destroyed

de·struc'tion n. ruin —**de·struc'tive** a.

des'ul·to'ry a. 1 not methodical 2 random

de·tach' v. unfasten and remove —**de·tach'a·ble** a.

de·tached' a. aloof; impartial

de·tach'ment n. 1 separation 2 troops on special task 3 impartiality or aloofness

de·tail' (or dē'tāl) v. 1 tell minutely 2 Mil. choose for a special task —*n.* 1 minute account 2 small part 3 *Mil.* special task —**in detail** item by item

de·tain' *v.* 1 keep in custody 2 delay —**de·ten'tion** *n.*

de·tect' *v.* discover (thing hidden, etc.) —**de·tec'tion** *n.* —**de·tec'tor** *n.*

de·tec'tive *n.* one who investigates crimes, etc.

dé·tente, de·tente (dā tänt') *n.* lessening of tension between nations

de·ter' *v.* **-terred', -ter'ring** keep someone from an action —**de·ter'ment** *n.* —**de·ter'rent** *a., n.*

de·ter'gent *a., n.* cleansing (substance)

de·te'ri·o·rate' (-tir'ē-) *v.* make or become worse —**de·te'ri·o·ra'tion** *n.*

de·ter'mi·na'tion *n.* 1 firm intention 2 firmness of purpose

de·ter'mine *v.* 1 set limits to 2 decide; resolve 3 to find out exactly —**de·ter'mined** *a.*

de·test' *v.* hate —**de·test'a·ble** *a.* —**de·tes·ta'tion** *n.*

de·throne' *v.* to depose (a monarch)

det'o·nate' *v.* explode —**det'o·na'tor** *n.*

de·tour' *v., n.* (use) an indirect or alternate road

de·tox' [Col.] *v.* detoxify —**de·tox'i·ca'tion** *n.*

de·tox'i·fy' *v.* **-fied', -fy'ing** remove a poison or poisonous effect from —**de·tox'i·fi·ca'tion** *n.*

de·tract' *v.* take something desirable (*from*) —**de·trac'tor** *n.*

det'ri·ment *n.* damage; harm —**det'ri·men'tal** *a.*

deuce (dōōs, dyōōs) *n.* 1 playing card with two spots 2 in tennis, tie score after which one side must score twice in a row to win

de·val'ue *v.* lessen the value of: also **de·val'u·ate'**

dev'as·tate' *v.* destroy; ravage —**dev'as·ta'tion** *n.*

de·vel'op *v.* 1 grow, improve, expand, etc. 2 work out by degrees 3 treat (film) to make the picture visible —**de·vel'op·ment** *n.* —**de·vel'op·men'tal** *a.*

de'vi·ant *n., a.* (person) deviating from social norms

de'vi·ate' *v.* turn aside; diverge —**de'vi·a'tion** *n.*

de·vice' *n.* 1 a plan or scheme 2 mechanical contrivance 3 a design

dev'il *n.* 1 evil spirit; esp., [*often* D-] Satan 2 wicked or reckless person —*v.* 1 to season (food) highly 2 tease —**dev'il·try** *n., pl.* **-tries** —**dev'il·ish** *a.*

dev'il-may-care' *a.* reckless; careless

dev'il's-food' cake *n.* rich chocolate cake

de'vi·ous *a.* roundabout

de·vise' (-vīz') *v.* 1 to plan 2 bequeath by will

de·void' *a.* empty (*of*)

de·volve' *v.* pass (*on*) to another, as a duty

de·vote' *v.* 1 dedicate 2 apply to a purpose

de·vot'ed *a.* 1 dedicated 2 loyal —**de·vot'ed·ly** *adv.*

dev'o·tee' (-tē', -tā') *n.* one devoted to something

de·vo'tion *n.* 1 a devoting 2 *pl.* prayers 3 loyalty

de·vour' *v.* 1 eat up hungrily 2 take in eagerly

de·vout' *a.* pious or sincere

dew *n.* atmospheric moisture condensing on cool surfaces at night —**dew'y** *a.*, **-i·er, -i·est**

dex·ter'ous (-tər əs, -trəs) *a.* skillful in using one's hands, mind, etc.: also **dex'trous** (-trəs) —**dex·ter'i·ty** *n.*

dex'trose (-trōs) *n.* sugar found in plants and animals

di- *pref.* twice; double

di·a·be·tes (dī'ə bēt'ēz, -bēt'is) *n.* disease marked by excess sugar in the blood and urine —**di·a·bet'ic** *a., n.*

di·a·bol'ic *a.* devilish: also **di·a·bol'i·cal**

di·a·crit'ic *n.* a mark to show pronunciation —**di·a·crit'i·cal** *a.*

di'a·dem' *n.* a crown

di·ag·no'sis *n.* identifying of a disease —**di·ag·nose'** *v.* —**di·ag·nos'tic** *a.*

di·ag'o·nal *a.* slanting between opposite corners —*n.* a diagonal line

di'a·gram' *n., v.* sketch, plan, etc. to help explain

di'al *n.* 1 face of a clock, meter, etc. for indicating some variable 2 rotating disk, or numbered buttons, on a telephone —*v.* 1 tune in on a radio dial 2 call by using a telephone dial

di'a·lect' *n.* form of speech peculiar to a region, group, etc. —**di'a·lec'tal** *a.*

di'a·lec'tic *n. often pl.* logical examination of ideas

di'a·logue', di'a·log' *n.* conversation

di·al'y·sis (-al'ə-) n. separation of impurities in the blood by diffusion through a membrane

di·am'e·ter n. 1 straight line through the center of a circle, etc. 2 its length —**di·a·met'ri·cal** a.

di·a·mond (dī'mənd, dī'ə-) n. 1 precious gem of great brilliance 2 figure shaped like ◊ 3 baseball field

di·a·mond·back' n. large, poisonous rattlesnake

di·a·per (dī'pər, dī'ə-) n. cloth worn about a baby's crotch —v. to put a diaper on

di·aph'a·nous a. gauzy

di·a·phragm' (-fram') n. 1 wall of muscle between chest and abdomen 2 vibrating disk producing sound waves 3 vaginal contraceptive

di·ar·rhe'a (-rē'ə) n. very loose bowel movements

di'a·ry n., pl. **-ries** daily record of personal notes

di·a·ton'ic a. of any standard musical scale of eight tones

di'a·tribe' n. denunciation

dice n.pl., sing. **die** small, spotted cubes, used in gambling —v. cut into cubes

di·chot'o·my (-kät'-) n., pl. **-mies** division into two parts

dick'er v. barter; haggle

dick'ey n. detachable collar or shirt front

dic'tate' v. 1 speak (something) for another to write down 2 command —n. an order —**dic·ta'tion** n.

dic·ta'tor n. an absolute ruler; tyrant —**dic·ta·to'ri·al** a. —**dic·ta'tor·ship'** n.

dic'tion n. 1 choice of words 2 enunciation

dic'tion·ar'y n., pl. **-ies** book of words alphabetically listed and defined

dic'tum n. formal opinion

did v. pt. of DO

di·dac'tic a. meant to teach

did'n't did not

die v. **died, dy'ing** 1 stop living 2 to end 3 [Col.] wish very much —n. 1 sing. of DICE 2 device for molding, stamping, etc. —**die away** (or **down**) cease gradually —**die off** one by one until all are gone —**die out** go out of existence

die'-hard', **die'hard'** n. stubborn, resistant person

die·sel (dē'zəl, -səl) n. [often D-]

---

internal-combustion engine that burns fuel oil

di'et n. 1 one's usual food 2 special food taken as for health —v. follow a diet, as to lose weight —**di'e·tar'y** a.

di'e·ti'tian (-tish'ən) n. planner of diets —**di'e·tet'ic** a.

dif'fer v. 1 to be different or unlike 2 disagree

dif'fer·ence n. 1 a being unlike 2 distinguishing characteristic 3 disagreement 4 amount by which two quantities differ —**dif'fer·en'tial** a., n.

dif'fer·ent a. 1 not alike 2 distinct 3 unusual

differential gear (or **gear'ing**) n. arrangement allowing one axle to turn faster than another

dif'fer·en'ti·ate' (-shē-) v. 1 be or make different 2 distinguish

dif'fi·cult' a. hard to do, learn, deal with, etc. —**dif'fi·cul'ty** n., pl. **-ties**

dif'fi·dent a. shy —**dif'fi·dence** n.

dif·frac'tion n. a breaking up of light as into the colors of the spectrum

dif·fuse' (-fyōōs'; v.: fyōōz') a. 1 spread out 2 wordy —v. spread widely —**dif·fu'sion** n.

dig v. **dug, dig'ging** 1 turn up (soil), as with a spade 2 make or get by digging —n. [Col.] sarcastic remark

di·gest' (v.: di jest') n. summary —v. 1 to change (food) in the stomach, etc. so that it can be absorbed 2 absorb mentally —**di·gest'i·ble** a. —**di·ges'tion** n. —**di·ges'tive** a.

dig'it (dij'-) n. 1 any number from 0 to 9 2 a finger or toe

dig'i·tal a. 1 of a digit 2 showing time, temperature, etc. in a row of digits 3 designating a recording method in which sounds or images are converted into electronic bits 4 of a computer processing data by electronic means

dig'i·tal'is n. 1 plant with long spikes of flowers 2 heart medicine made from its leaves

dig'ni·fy' v. **-fied', -fy'ing** give dignity to

dig'ni·tar'y n., pl. **-ies** person of high position

dig'ni·ty n. 1 worthiness 2 high repute; honor 3 calm stateliness

di·gress' v. wander from the subject, as in talking —**di·gres'sion**

n. —**di·gres'sive** a.

dike n. embankment to hold back the sea, etc.

di·lap'i·dat·ed (-dāt'-) a. falling to pieces

di·late' (or dī lāt') v. make or become wider —**di·la'tion** n.

dil'a·to·ry a. 1 causing delay 2 slow

di·lem'ma n. perplexing situation

dil'et·tante' (-tänt', tant') n. dabbler in the arts

dil'i·gent a. careful and industrious —**dil'i·gence** n.

dill n. plant with aromatic seeds

dil'ly·dal'ly v. -lied, -ly·ing waste time

di·lute' v. weaken as by mixing with water —a. diluted —**di·lu'tion** n.

dim a. **dim'mer, dim'mest** not bright or clear —v. **dimmed, dim'ming** make or grow dim

dime n. silver coin equal to ten cents

di·men'sion n. 1 any measurable extent 2 pl. measurement in length, breadth, and, often, height

di·min'ish v. lessen

di·min'u·tive a. tiny

dim'ple n. small, natural hollow, as on the cheek

dim'wit' n. [Sl.] stupid person —**dim'wit'ted** a.

din n. confused clamor —v. **dinned, din'ning** 1 make a din 2 keep repeating

dine v. 1 eat dinner 2 give dinner to

din'er n. 1 railroad car for serving meals 2 restaurant built like this

di·nette' (-net') n. small dining room or alcove

ding n. sound of a bell: also **ding'-dong** (diŋ'gē) n., pl. **-ghies** small boat

din·ghy (diŋ'gē) n., pl. **-ghies** small boat

din'gy (-jē) a. **-gi·er, -gi·est** dirty; shabby

dink'y a. **-i·er, -i·est** [Col.] small

din'ner n. chief daily meal

din'ner·ware n. dishes

di'no·saur' (-sôr') n. huge extinct reptile

dint n. force: now chiefly in by dint of

di'o·cese (-sis, -sēz') n. district headed by a bishop —**di·oc'e·san** (-äs'ə sən) a.

di'ode' n. device used esp. as a rectifier

di·ox'ide' n. oxide with two oxy-

gen atoms per molecule

dip v. **dipped, dip'ping** 1 plunge into liquid for a moment 2 scoop up 3 sink or slope down —n. 1 a dipping 2 sauce into which food may be dipped 3 downward slope

diph·the·ri·a (dif thir'ē ə) n. acute infectious disease of the throat

diph'thong (dif'-, dip'-) n. sound made by gliding from one vowel to another in one syllable

di·plo'ma n. certificate of graduation from a school

di·plo'ma·cy n. 1 the conducting of relations between nations 2 tact —**dip'lo·mat'** n. —**dip'lo·mat'ic** a.

dip'per n. long-handled cup, etc. for dipping

dip'stick' n. graduated rod for measuring depth

dire a. 1 dreadful; terrible 2 urgent

di·rect' a. 1 straight 2 frank 3 immediate 4 exact —v. 1 manage; guide 2 order 3 aim —adv. directly —**di·rect'ly** adv. —**di·rec'tor** n.

direct current n. electric current moving in one direction

di·rec'tion n. 1 management; guidance 2 pl. instructions 3 an order 4 the point one faces or moves toward —**di·rec'tion·al** a.

di·rec'tive (-tiv) n. an order

di·rec'to·ry n., pl. **-ries** book of names and addresses of a specific group

dirge (durj) n. song of mourning

dir'i·gi·ble (-ij'ə-) n. airship

dirk n. long dagger

dirt n. 1 dust, filth, etc. 2 earth; soil

dirt'y a. **-i·er, -i·est** 1 soiled 2 obscene 3 mean 4 unfair 5 rough —v. **-ied, -y·ing** to soil —**dirt'i·ness** n.

dis- pref. 1 the opposite of 2 reverse the action of

dis·a'ble v. make unable or unfit; cripple —**dis·a·bil'i·ty** n., pl. **-ties**

dis·a·buse' v. rid of false ideas

dis'ad·van'tage n. drawback; handicap; detriment —**dis·ad'van·ta'geous** a.

dis'ad·van'taged a. poor

dis'af·fect' v. make hostile —**dis'af·fec'tion** n.

dis'a·gree' v. 1 differ 2 quarrel 3 give distress: with with —**dis'a·gree'ment** n.

dis·a·gree·a·ble *a.* 1 unpleasant 2 quarrelsome

dis·al·low' *v.* reject

dis·ap·pear' *v.* 1 go out of sight 2 cease being —**dis·ap·pear'ance** *n.*

dis·ap·point' *v.* spoil the hopes of —**dis·ap·point'ment** *n.*

dis·ap·prove' *v.* 1 have an unfavorable opinion 2 reject —**dis·ap·prov'al** *n.*

dis·arm' *v.* 1 remove weapons from 2 make friendly —**dis·ar'ma·ment** *n.*

dis·ar·range' *v.* disorder

dis·ar·ray' *n., v.* disorder

dis·as·sem'ble *v.* take apart

dis·as·so'ci·ate *v.* sever association with

dis·as'ter *n.* sudden misfortune; calamity —**dis·as'trous** *a.*

dis·a·vow' *v.* deny knowing or approving —**dis·a·vow'al** *n.*

dis·band' *v.* break up

dis·bar' *v.* —**barred', -bar'ring** deprive of the right to practice law

dis·be·lieve' *v.* fail to believe (*in*) —**dis·be·lief'** *n.*

dis·burse' *v.* pay out

disc *n.* 1 disk 2 phonograph record, etc.

dis·card' (*n.:* dis'kärd') *v.* throw away —*n.* thing discarded

dis·cern' (di surn', -zurn') *v.* perceive —**dis·cern'i·ble** *a.*

dis·cern'ing *a.* astute

dis·charge' (*n.:* dis'chärj') *v.* 1 dismiss 2 unload 3 shoot 4 emit 5 do (a duty) —*n.* a discharging or thing discharged

dis·ci'ple *n.* follower; pupil

dis·ci·pli·nar'i·an *n.* enforcer of discipline

dis'ci·pline (-plin) *n.* 1 orderly training or conduct 2 punishment —*v.* 1 train; control 2 punish —**dis'ci·pli·nar'y** *a.*

disc jockey *n.* one who plays recordings on the radio, in a nightclub, etc.

dis·claim' *v.* disown; deny

dis·close' *v.* to reveal —**dis·clo'sure** *n.*

dis·co *n., pl.* **-cos** nightclub for dancing to recorded music

dis·col'or *v.* to stain; tarnish —**dis·col·or·a'tion** *n.*

dis·com'fit *v.* upset; embarrass —**dis·com'fi·ture** *n.*

dis·com'fort *n.* lack of comfort or cause of this

dis'com·mode' *v.* to inconvenience

dis'con·cert' *v.* confuse

dis'con·nect' *v.* to separate

dis·co·thèque (-tek') *a.* disco very unhappy

dis'con·tent' *n.* dissatisfaction: also **dis·con·tent'ment** *n.*

dis'con·tent'ed *a.* not contented

dis'con·tin'ue *v.* to stop —**dis'con·tin'u·ous** *a.*

dis'cord *n.* 1 disagreement 2 dissonance; harsh sound —**dis·cord'ant** *a.*

dis'co·thèque (-tek') *n.* disco

dis'count' (*v.:* also dis kount') *v.* 1 deduct, as from a price 2 disregard in part or entirely —*n.* deduction

dis·cour'age *v.* 1 deprive of hope or confidence 2 dissuade 3 work against —**dis·cour'age·ment** *n.*

dis'course' *n.* talk or formal lecture —*v.* to talk

dis·cour'te·ous *a.* impolite —**dis·cour'te·sy** *n.*

dis·cov'er *v.* 1 be the first to find, see, etc. 2 find out —**dis·cov'er·y** *n., pl.* **-ies**

dis·cred'it *v.* 1 disbelieve 2 cast doubt on 3 disgrace —*n.* 1 doubt 2 disgrace

dis·creet' *a.* careful; prudent —**dis·creet'ly** *adv.*

dis·crep'an·cy *n., pl.* **-cies** inconsistency

dis·crete (di skrēt') *a.* separate; distinct

dis·cre'tion (di skresh'ən) *n.* 1 freedom to decide 2 prudence —**dis·cre'tion·ar'y** *a.*

dis·crim'i·nate *v.* 1 distinguish 2 show partiality —**dis·crim'i·na'tion** *n.* —**dis·crim'i·na·to'ry** *a.*

dis·cur'sive (-siv) *a.* rambling

dis'cus *n.* heavy disk thrown in a contest

dis·cuss' *v.* talk or write about —**dis·cus'sion** *n.*

dis·dain' *v., n.* scorn —**dis·dain'ful** *a.*

dis·ease' *n.* (an) illness —**dis·eased'** *a.*

dis'em·bark' *v.* go ashore

dis'em·bod'y *v.* **-bod'ied, -bod'y·ing** to free from bodily existence

dis'en·chant' *v.* disillusion —**dis'en·chant'ment** *n.*

dis'en·gage' *v.* disconnect

dis'en·tan'gle *v.* extricate

dis·fa'vor *n.* 1 dislike 2 a being disliked

dis·fig'ure *v.* spoil the looks of; mar —**dis·fig'ure·ment** *n.*

dis·gorge' *v.* to vomit

dis·grace' n. shame; dishonor —v. to bring shame upon —**dis·grace'ful** a.

dis·grun'tle v. make sulky

dis·guise' (-gīz') v. make unrecognizable —n. thing, as clothing or makeup, used for disguising

dis·gust' n. sickening dislike; loathing —v. cause disgust in —**dis·gust'ed** a. —**dis·gust'ing** a.

dish n. 1 plate, etc. for food 2 kind of food

dish'cloth' n. cloth for washing dishes

dis·heart'en v. discourage

di·shev'el v. muss up (hair, etc.); rumple

dis·hon'est a. not honest —**dis·hon'es·ty** n.

dis·hon'or n., v. shame; disgrace —**dis·hon'or·a·ble** a.

dish'wash'er n. a person or machine that washes dishes

dis·il·lu'sion v. 1 free from illusion 2 make disappointed

dis·in·clined' a. unwilling

dis·in·fect' v. kill bacteria in —**dis·in·fect'ant** n.

dis·in·her'it v. to deprive of an inheritance

dis·in'te·grate' v. separate into parts; break up —**dis·in'te·gra'tion** n.

dis·in'ter·est·ed a. 1 impartial 2 indifferent

dis·joint' v. 1 put out of joint 2 dismember

dis·joint'ed a. without unity or coherence

disk n. 1 thin, flat, circular thing 2 thin plate for storing computer data 3 disc

disk·ette (di sket') n. floppy disk

disk jockey n. disc jockey

dis·like' v., n. (have) a feeling of not liking

dis·lo·cate' v. 1 put out of joint 2 disarrange —**dis·lo·ca'tion** n.

dis·lodge' v. force from its place

dis·loy'al a. not loyal —**dis·loy'al·ty** n.

dis'mal (diz'-) a. dreary

dis·man'tle v. take apart

dis·may' v. make afraid; daunt —n. loss of courage

dis·mem'ber v. tear apart —**dis·mem'ber·ment** n.

dis·miss' v. 1 request or allow to leave 2 discharge 3 set aside —**dis·miss'al** n.

dis·mount' v. 1 get off 2 take from its mounting

dis'o·bey' v. refuse or fail to obey —**dis'o·be'di·ence** n. —**dis'o·be'di·ent** a.

dis·or'der n. 1 confusion 2 commotion 3 ailment —v. to cause disorder in —**dis·or'der·ly** a.

dis·or'gan·ize' v. throw into confusion —**dis·or'gan·i·za'tion** n.

dis·o'ri·ent' v. confuse mentally

dis·own' v. refuse to acknowledge as one's own

dis·par'age v. belittle —**dis·par'age·ment** n.

dis·par'i·ty n., pl. -ties difference; unlikeness

dis·pas'sion·ate a. free from emotion or bias

dis·patch' (n. 2, 3: also dis'pach') v. 1 send 2 finish quickly 3 kill —n. 1 speed 2 message 3 news story —**dis·patch'er** n.

dis·pel' v. -pelled', -pel'ling drive away

dis·pen'sa·ry n., pl. -ries place in a school, etc. for getting medicines or first aid

dis·pense' v. 1 deal out 2 prepare and give out —**dispense with** do without —**dis·pen·sa'tion** n. —**dis·pens'er** n.

dis·perse' v. scatter —**dis·per'sal** n. —**dis·per'sion** n.

dis·pir'it·ed a. dejected

dis·place' v. 1 move from its usual place 2 replace —**dis·place'ment** n.

dis·play' v. to show; exhibit —n. exhibition

dis·please' v. annoy; offend —**dis·pleas'ure** n.

dis·port' v. 1 to play 2 amuse (oneself)

dis·pose' v. 1 arrange 2 incline mentally —**dispose of** 1 settle 2 get rid of —**dis·pos'a·ble** a. —**dis·pos'al** n. —**dis'po·si'tion** n.

dis'pos·sess' v. to force to give up property; oust

dis'pro·por'tion n. lack of proportion —**dis'pro·por'tion·ate** a.

dis·prove' v. prove false

dis·pute' v., n. 1 debate 2 quarrel —**in dispute** not settled —**dis·put'a·ble** a. —**dis·pu·ta'tion** n.

dis·qual'i·fy' v. -fied', -fy'ing make ineligible —**dis·qual'i·fi·ca'tion** n.

dis·qui'et v. make uneasy

dis·re·gard' v. ignore —n. lack of attention

dis're·pair' n. worn state

dis're·pute' n. bad reputation —**dis·rep'u·ta·ble** a.

dis're·spect' n. lack of respect —**dis're·spect'ful** a.

dis·robe' v. undress

dis·rupt' v. break up; disorder —**dis·rup'tion** n. —**dis·rup'tive** a.

dis·sat·is·fy' v. **-fied', -fy'ing** make discontented —**dis·sat·is·fac'tion** n.

dis·sect' (or dī'sekt') v. **1** cut apart so as to examine **2** analyze closely —**dis·sec'tion** n.

dis·sem'ble v. feign; conceal

dis·sem'i·nate v. spread widely —**dis·sem'i·na'tion** n.

dis·sen'sion n. strife

dis·sent' v. disagree —n. difference of opinion

dis·ser·ta'tion n. formal essay

dis·ser'vice n. harm

dis·si·dence n. disagreement —**dis'si·dent** a., n.

dis·sim'i·lar a. not alike

dis·si·pate' v. **1** vanish or dispel **2** squander **3** indulge in wild, harmful pleasure —**dis·si·pa'tion** n.

dis·so'ci·ate' v. sever association (with)

dis'so·lute' a. dissipated and immoral

dis'so·lu'tion n. a dissolving or breaking up

dis·solve' v. **1** melt **2** pass or make pass into solution **3** break up **4** end **5** disappear or make disappear

dis'so·nance n. lack of harmony, esp. in sound; discord —**dis'so·nant** a.

dis·suade' (-swād') v. cause to turn from a purpose

dis'taff' n. staff for holding flax, wool, etc. in spinning —a. female

dis'tance n. **1** length between two points **2** aloofness **3** faraway place

dis'tant a. **1** far apart; remote **2** away **3** aloof

dis·taste' n. dislike —**dis·taste'ful** a.

dis·tem'per n. infectious disease of dogs, etc.

dis·tend' v. swell —**dis·ten'tion, dis·ten'sion** n.

dis·till' v. subject to or obtain by distillation

dis'til·la'tion n. process of purifying a mixture by heating it and condensing the vapor

dis·till'er·y n., pl. **-ies** place for distilling liquor —**dis·till'er** n.

dis·tinct' a. **1** not alike **2** separate **3** definite

dis·tinc'tion n. **1** a keeping distinct **2** quality that differentiates **3** fame; eminence

dis·tinc'tive a. making distinct

dis·tin'guish v. **1** perceive or show a difference **2** classify **3** make famous —**dis·tin'guish·a·ble** a. —**dis·tin'guished** a.

dis·tort' v. **1** twist out of shape **2** misrepresent —**dis·tor'tion** n.

dis·tract' v. **1** divert (the mind, etc.) **2** confuse **3** derange —**dis·trac'tion** n.

dis·traught' a. **1** harassed **2** crazed

dis·tress' v., n. pain, trouble, worry, etc.

dis·trib'ute v. **1** deal out **2** spread out **3** arrange —**dis'tri·bu'tion** n.

dis·trib'u·tor n. **1** one who distributes, deals in a product, etc. **2** device distributing electricity to spark plugs in a gasoline engine

dis'trict n. **1** division of a state, etc. **2** region

district attorney n. prosecuting attorney of a district

dis·trust' n. lack of trust —v. to mistrust —**dis·trust'ful** a.

dis·turb' v. **1** break up the quiet or settled order of **2** make uneasy **3** interrupt —**dis·turb'ance** n.

dis·u·nite' v. divide; separate

dis·use' n. lack of use

ditch n. channel dug out for drainage, etc. —v. **1** [Sl.] get rid of —v. **2**

dith'er n. excited state

ditto mark n. mark (") in lists showing the item above is to be repeated: also **dit'to,** pl. **-tos**

dit'ty n., pl. **-ties** short, simple song

di·u·ret'ic (-yoo-) n., a. (substance) increasing urine discharge

di·ur'nal (-ʉr'-) a. daily

di'va (dē'-) n. prima donna

dive v. **dived** or **dove, dived, div'ing** **1** plunge into water **2** plunge suddenly or deeply —n. **1** sudden plunge **2** [Col.] cheap saloon

di·verge' v. **1** branch off **2** deviate

di'vers (-vʉrz) a. various

di·verse' (-vʉrs') a. **1** different **2** varied

di·ver'si·fy' v. **-fied', -fy'ing** vary

di·ver'sion n. **1** a diverting **2** pastime; amusement

di·ver'si·ty n. variety

di·vert' v. **1** turn aside (from) **2** amuse

di·vest' v. strip or deprive (of)

di·vide' v. **1** separate into parts

2 apportion 3 *Math.* separate into equal parts by a divisor — *n.* ridge —**di·vis'i·ble** (-viz'-) *a.*

div'i·dend *n.* 1 number to be divided 2 sum divided among stockholders, etc.

di·vine' *a.* 1 of God or a god 2 supremely good —*n.* clergyman —*v.* 1 prophesy 2 guess

di·vin'i·ty *n.* 1 a being divine 2 *pl.* **-ties** a god

di·vi'sion *n.* 1 a dividing 2 thing that divides 3 segment, group, etc. 4 section of an army corps

di·vi'sive *a.* causing disagreement

di·vi'sor *n.* number by which the dividend is divided

di·vorce' *n.* 1 legal dissolution of a marriage 2 separation —*v.* separate from, as by divorce

di·vor·cée' (-sā') *n.* divorced woman —**di·vor·cé'** (-sā') *n.masc.*

div'ot *n.* turf dislodged by a golf club

di·vulge' *v.* make known

diz'zy *a.* **-zi·er, -zi·est** 1 giddy; confused 2 causing dizziness — **diz'zi·ly** *adv.* —**diz'zi·ness** *n.*

DJ *n.* disc jockey

DNA *n.* basic material of chromosomes that transmits hereditary pattern

do *v.* **did, done, do'ing** 1 perform (an action) 2 finish 3 cause 4 deal with as required 5 have as one's work 6 get along 7 be adequate *Do* is also an important auxiliary verb —**do in** [Sl.] kill —**do's (or dos) and don'ts** [Col.] things permitted and things forbidden —**do without** get along without —**have to do** with relate to —**do'er** *n.*

doc'ile (däs'əl) *a.* easy to train — **do·cil'i·ty** *n.*

dock *n.* 1 landing pier; wharf 2 water between piers 3 place for the accused in a courtroom —*v.* 1 bring or come to a dock 2 cut short 3 deduct from

dock'et *n.* list of cases to be tried by a law court

dock'yard *n.* shipyard

doc'tor *n.* 1 person with the highest degree from a university 2 physician or surgeon —*v.* [Col.] 1 try to heal 2 tamper with

doc'tri·naire' (-ner') *a.* adhering strictly to a doctrine

doc'trine (-trin) *n.* something taught, as a religious tenet

doc'u·ment *n.* written record relied on as evidence —*v.* to support by documents

doc'u·men'ta·ry *a.* 1 of or supported by documents 2 recording news events dramatically — *n., pl.* **-ries** documentary film

dod'der *v.* shake as from old age

dodge *v.* 1 move quickly aside 2 avoid; evade —*n.* 1 a dodging 2 a trick

do'do *n.* 1 large extinct bird 2 [Sl.] stupid person

doe *n.* female deer, rabbit, etc.

does (duz) *v.* pres. t. of DO: used with *he, she,* or *it*

doe'skin' *n.* leather from the skin of a female deer

does'n't does not

doff *v.* take off; remove

dog *n.* 1 domesticated animal of the wolf family 2 mean fellow —*v.* **dogged, dog'ging** follow like a dog

dog'ear' *n.* turned-down corner of a page —**dog'eared'** *a.*

dog'ged *a.* stubborn

dog'ger·el *n.* trivial, monotonous verse

do·gie (dō'gē) *n.* stray calf

dog'ma *n.* strict doctrine

dog·mat'ic *a.* 1 of a dogma 2 positive in stating opinion; arrogant —**dog·mat'i·cal·ly** *adv.* — **dog'ma·tism'** *n.*

dog'wood' *n.* tree with pink or white flowers

doi'ly *n., pl.* **-lies** small mat to protect a table, etc.

do'ings *n.pl.* actions

dol'drums (dōl'-) *n.pl.* low spirits

dole *n.* money paid to the unemployed by the government: with *the* —*v.* give (out) sparingly

dole'ful *a.* sad; sorrowful

doll *n.* child's toy made to resemble a person

dol'lar *n.* U.S. monetary unit, equal to 100 cents

dol'lop *n.* small quantity of something soft

dol'ly *n., pl.* **-lies** 1 [Col.] doll 2 low, wheeled frame for moving heavy objects

do'lor·ous (dō'lər-, däl'ər-) *a.* sorrowful

dol'phin *n.* sea mammal with a beaklike snout

dolt *n.* stupid person —**dolt'ish** *a.*

-dom *suf.* 1 rank or domain of 2 state of being

do·main' *n.* 1 territory under one ruler 2 field of activity

dome *n.* large, round roof

do·mes'tic a. 1 of home or family 2 of one's country 3 tame —n. a maid, cook, etc. —**do·mes'ti·cal·ly** adv. —**do·mes'tic'i·ty** n.

do·mes'ti·cate' v. to tame —**do·mes'ti·ca'tion** n.

dom'i·cile' (-sīl') n. home

dom'i·nate' v. 1 rule or control 2 to rise high above —**dom'i·nance** n. —**dom'i·nant** a. —**dom'i·na'tion** n.

dom'i·neer' v. rule harshly

do·min'ion n. 1 rule; power 2 governed territory

dom'i·noes', dom'i·nos' n. game with tiles marked with dots

don v. donned, don'ning put on (clothes)

do'nate' v. give; contribute —**do·na'tion** n.

done (dun) v. pp. of DO

don'key n., pl. -keys horse-like animal with long ears

do'nor n. one who donates

don't do not

doo'dle v., n. scribble

doom n. 1 a judgment 2 fate 3 ruin —v. 1 condemn 2 destine to a tragic fate

dooms'day' n. the end of the world

door n. 1 movable panel for closing an entrance 2 entrance, with or without a door: also **door'way** —**out of doors** outdoors

door'man' n., pl. -men' one whose work is opening doors, hailing taxicabs, etc.

dope n. 1 [Col.] narcotic 2 [Sl.] information 3 [Col.] stupid person —v. to drug

dor'mant a. 1 sleeping 2 quiet; inactive

dor'mer n. an upright window structure in a sloping roof

dor'mi·to'ry n., pl. -ries 1 room with many beds 2 building with many bedrooms Also **dorm**

dor'mouse' n., pl. -mice' small, squirrel-like rodent

dor'sal a. of the back

do'ry n., pl. -ries small, flat-bottomed fishing boat

dose n. amount of medicine taken at one time —v. to give doses to —**dos'age** n.

dos·si·er' (-sē ā') n. documents about a person

dost (dust) v. [Ar.] do: used with *thou*

dot n. tiny mark or round spot —v. **dot'ted, dot'ting** mark with dots

dot'age (dōt'-) n. feebleness of old age

dote v. be too fond

doth (duth) v. [Ar.] does

dot'-ma'trix a. of computer printing in which characters are formed of tiny dots

dou'ble a. 1 of or for two 2 twice as much or as many —adv. twofold or twice —n. 1 twice as much or as many 2 a duplicate 3 *Baseball* hit putting the batter on second —v. 1 make or become double 2 fold 3 duplicate 4 turn backward 5 serve two purposes, etc. —**on the double** [Col.] quickly

double bass (bās) n. largest, deepest-toned instrument of violin family

dou'ble-cross' v. [Col.] to betray —**dou'ble-cross'er** n.

double date [Col.] n. social engagement shared by two couples —**dou'ble-date'** v.

dou'ble-deck'er n. 1 vehicle, etc. with upper deck 2 [Col.] two-layer sandwich

dou'ble-head'er n. two games played in succession

dou'ble-park' v. to park next to another vehicle parked at a curb

double standard n. rules applied unequally

dou'blet n. formerly, man's tight jacket

dou'bly adv. twice

doubt (dout) v. 1 be uncertain about 2 to disbelieve —n. 1 wavering of belief 2 uncertainty —**no doubt** certainly —**doubt'ful** a.

doubt'less adv. certainly

douche (dōōsh) n. liquid jet for cleaning a body part —v. use a douche (on)

dough (dō) n. 1 thick mixture of flour, liquid, etc. for baking 2 [Sl.] money

dough'nut n. small, fried cake, usually ring-shaped

dour (door, dour) a. gloomy

douse (dous) v. 1 thrust into liquid 2 drench 3 [Col.] extinguish (a light)

dove (dōv) v. alt. pt. of DIVE

dove (duv) n. kind of pigeon

dove'tail' (duv'-) n. joint formed by fitting together wedge-shaped parts —v. join closely, as with dovetails

dow'a·ger n. wealthy widow

dow'dy a. -di·er, -di·est not neat or not stylish

dow'el n. peg fitted into holes to

join two pieces

dow'er n. widow's inheritance

down adv. 1 to or in a lower place, state, etc. 2 to a later time 3 in cash 4 in writing —a. 1 descending 2 in a lower place 3 gone, paid, etc. down 4 discouraged —prep. down toward, into, along, etc. —v. put down —n. 1 descent 2 misfortune 3 soft feathers or hair 4 pl. high, grassy land —**down with!** overthrow!

down'cast' a. 1 directed downward 2 sad

down'er n. [Sl.] any sedative

down'fall' n. sudden fall, as from power

down'grade' n. downward slope —adv., a. downward —v. to demote

down'heart'ed a. sad

down'hill' adv., a. down a slope; downward

down'-home' a. of rural folk or rural life

down'play' v. minimize

down'pour' n. a heavy rain

down'right' adv. thoroughly —a. 1 utter 2 plain

down'scale' a. for people who are not affluent or stylish

down'spout' n. pipe for carrying rainwater from roof gutter

down'stairs' adv., a. to or on a lower floor —n. lower floor or floors

down'-to-earth' a. sensible

down'town' n. city's business district

down'trod'den a. oppressed

down'turn' n. downward trend

down'ward adv., a. toward a lower place, etc.: also **down'wards** adv.

down'y a. soft and fluffy

dow'ry n. property a bride brings to her husband at marriage

doze v., n. sleep; nap

doz'en n. set of twelve

drab a. **drab'ber, drab'best** dull —**drab'ness** n.

draft n. 1 drink 2 rough sketch of a writing 3 plan 4 current of air 5 written order for money 6 selection for compulsory military service 7 depth of water a ship displaces —v. 1 select to serve 2 make a plan, outline, etc. for —a. drawn from a cask —**on draft** ready to be drawn from a cask

draft'ee' n. one drafted for military service

drafts'man n., pl. **-men** one who

draws plans of structures or machinery

draft'y a. **-i·er, -i·est** open to drafts of air

drag v. **dragged, drag'ging** 1 pull or be pulled with effort, esp. along the ground 2 search (a river bottom, etc.) as with a net 3 pass slowly —n. 1 hindrance 2 [Sl.] puff of a cigarette, etc.

drag'net' n. 1 net dragged along water bottom 2 a system for catching criminals

drag'on n. large, mythical reptile breathing out fire

drag'on·fly' n., pl. **-flies'** long insect with four wings

dra·goon' n. armed cavalryman —v. force to do something

drag race n. race between cars accelerating from a standstill on a short, straight course

drain v. 1 draw off (liquid, etc.) gradually 2 empty 3 exhaust, as energy 4 flow off —n. channel; pipe

drain'age n. 1 a draining or system for draining 2 that which is drained off

drain'pipe' n. large pipe carrying off water, etc.

drake n. male duck

dram n. 1 apothecaries' weight, ⅛ oz. 2 small drink of alcoholic liquor

dra'ma n. 1 a play 2 art of writing and staging plays

dra·mat'ic n. 1 of drama 2 vivid, exciting, etc.

dra·mat'ics n. performing or producing of plays

dram'a·tist n. playwright

dram'a·tize' v. 1 make into a drama 2 regard or show in a dramatic manner —**dram'a·ti·za'tion** n.

drank v. pt. of DRINK

drape v. cover or hang as with cloth in loose folds —n. curtain: usually used in pl.

drap'er·y n., pl. **-ies** curtain

dras'tic a. severe; harsh —**dras'ti·cal·ly** adv.

draught (draft) n., v., a. draft

draw v. **drew, drawn, draw'ing** 1 pull 2 attract 3 inhale 4 take out; get 5 come; move 6 write (a check) 7 deduce 8 stretch 9 make (lines, pictures, etc.) as with a pencil —n. 1 stalemate 2 thing that attracts

draw'back' n. disadvantage

draw'bridge' n. bridge that can be raised

drawer (drôr) n. 1 sliding box in

a table, etc. **2** pl. underpants

draw'ing n. **1** art of sketching **2** picture sketched

drawing room n. parlor

drawl n. slow, prolonged manner of speech —v. to speak with a drawl

drawn a. haggard

dread (dred) v. await with fear or distaste —n. fear —a. inspiring fear —**dread'ful** a.

dream n. **1** images, etc. seen during sleep **2** reverie **3** fond hope —v. **dreamed** or **dreamt** (dremt) **dream'ing** have dreams —**dream'y** a.

drear'y a. -i·er, -i·est dismal —**drear'i·ness** n.

dredge n. apparatus for scooping up mud, etc. as in deepening channels —v. **1** enlarge with a dredge **2** gather (up) as with a dredge **3** sprinkle with flour

dregs n.pl. **1** particles at the bottom in a liquid **2** most worthless part

drench v. soak

dress v. **1** clothe **2** adorn **3** treat (a wound, etc.) **4** prepare (a fowl, etc.) by skinning, etc. — n. **1** clothes **2** woman's garment —**dress up** improve the look of, as by decorating —**dress'mak'er** n.

dress'er n. chest of drawers with a mirror

dress'ing n. **1** bandages, etc. **2** salad sauce **3** stuffing for roast fowl

dress'y a. -i·er, -i·est elegant

drew v. pt. of DRAW

drib'ble v. **1** flow in drops **2** drool —n. dribbling flow

dried v. pt. & pp. of DRY

dri'er n. device or substance that dries

drift v. be carried along, as by a current —n. **1** snow, etc. driven into a heap **2** trend **3** meaning —**drift'er** n.

drift'wood' n. wood that has drifted ashore

drill n. **1** tool for boring **2** systematic training **3** seeding machine **4** coarse, twilled cloth —v. **1** bore with a drill **2** train systematically —**drill'er** n.

drink v. **drank, drunk, drink'ing** swallow (liquid) —n. **1** liquid for drinking **2** alcoholic liquor

drip v. **dripped, drip'ping** fall or let fall in drops —n. a dripping

drip'-dry' a. of clothing that needs little or no ironing

drive v. **drove, driv'en** (driv'-),

driv'ing 1 force to go, do, pierce, etc. **2** operate, or go in, a vehicle —n. **1** trip in a vehicle **2** paved road **3** energy **4** urge **5** campaign —**drive at** to mean —**driv'er** n.

drive'-in' n. place for eating, etc. in one's car

driv'el n. silly talk

drive'way' n. path for cars

driz'zle v., n. rain in fine, mistlike drops

droll a. quaintly amusing

drom'e·dar'y n., pl. -ies onehumped camel

drone n. **1** male honeybee **2** constant hum —v. **1** to hum **2** talk monotonously

drool v. drip saliva

droop v. **1** sink or bend down **2** lose vitality —n. a drooping —**droop'y** a., -i·er, -i·est —**droop'i·ly** adv.

drop n. **1** small, round mass, as of falling liquid **2** tiny amount **3** sudden fall **4** distance down —v. **dropped, drop'ping 1** fall or let fall **2** to send **3** utter (a hint, etc.) —**drop in** visit —**drop out** stop taking part —**drop'per** n.

drop'cloth' n. large cloth, etc. used as cover when painting

drop'let n. very small drop

drop'-off' n. a steep drop or decline

drop'out' n. student who leaves school before graduating

drop'sy n. abnormal amount of fluid in the body

dross n. rubbish; refuse

drought (drout) n. spell of dry weather

drove v. pt. of DRIVE —n. herd of cattle, etc.

drown v. **1** die or kill by suffocation in water **2** muffle (sound, etc.): with out

drowse v. be sleepy; doze —**drows'y** a., -i·er, -i·est

drub v. **drubbed, drub'bing 1** thrash **2** defeat —**drub'bing** n.

drudge n. one who does hard or dull work —v. do such work —**drudg'er·y** n.

drug n. **1** medicinal substance **2** narcotic —v. **drugged, drug'ging** add or give a drug to —**drug'gist** n. pharmacist —**drug'store'** n.

drum n. **1** hollow form covered with a membrane and used as a percussion instrument **2** container, as for oil **3** eardrum —v. **drummed, drum'ming** beat as on a drum —**drum up** solicit (business) —**drum'mer** n.

drum major n. one who leads a marching band —**drum ma'jor·ette'** (-et') n.fem.

drum'stick' n. 1 stick for beating a drum 2 lower leg of a cooked fowl

drunk v. pp. of DRINK —a. overcome by alcohol —n. [Sl.] drunken person —**drunk'ard** n.

drunk'en a. intoxicated —**drunk'en·ness** n.

dry a. **dri'er, dri'est** 1 not wet 2 lacking rain 3 thirsty 4 not sweet 5 matter-of-fact 6 dull —v. **dried, dry'ing** to make or become dry —**dry'ly** adv.

dry'-clean' v. to clean (garments) with a solvent, as naphtha —**dry cleaner** n.

dry'er n. a drier

dry goods n. cloth (products)

dry ice n. carbon dioxide in a solid state

dry run n. [Col.] rehearsal

dry'wall' n. plaster board used for interior walls of a house, etc.

du'al a. 1 of two 2 double

dub v. **dubbed, dub'bing** 1 confer a title upon 2 insert (dialogue, etc.) in film soundtrack

du'bi·ous a. doubtful

du'cal a. of a duke

duch'ess n. duke's wife

duch'y n., pl. **-ies** land ruled by a duke

duck n. 1 flat-billed, webfooted swimming bird 2 cloth like canvas but lighter —v. 1 dip under water briefly 2 bend suddenly, as to avoid a blow 3 [Col.] avoid

duck'bill' n. small, egg-laying water mammal

duck'ling n. young duck

duct n. tube or channel for fluid —**duct'less** a.

duc'tile (-tal) a. that can be drawn thin 2 easily led

dud n. [Col.] 1 bomb, etc. that fails to explode 2 failure

dude n. 1 dandy; fop 2 [Sl.] man or boy

due a. 1 owed 2 suitable 3 expected to arrive —adv. exactly —n. anything due —**due to** 1 caused by 2 [Col.] because of

due bill n. receipt for money paid, exchangeable for goods, etc. only

du'el n. planned formal fight between two armed persons —v. fight a duel —**du'el·ist** n.

dues n.pl. 1 fee or tax 2 money

paid for membership

du·et' n. musical composition for two performers

duf'fel bag n. large canvas bag for clothes, etc.: also **duf'fle bag**

dug v. pt. & pp. of DIG

dug'out' n. 1 boat hollowed out of a log 2 Baseball shelter for players when not in the field

duke n. nobleman next in rank to a prince —**duke'dom** n.

dul'cet (-sat) a. pleasant to hear

dul'ci·mer (-sa-) n. stringed musical instrument

dull a. 1 stupid 2 sluggish 3 boring 4 not sharp 5 not bright —v. make or become dull —**dul'ly** adv.

dull'ard n. stupid person

du'ly adv. properly

dumb a. 1 unable to talk 2 silent 3 [Col.] stupid

dumb'bell' n. short bar joining two weights, used in exercising

dumb'wait'er n. small elevator for food, etc.

dum'found', dumb'found' v. make speechless; amaze

dum'my n., pl. **-mies** 1 humanlike figure for displaying clothes 2 imitation 3 [Sl.] stupid person —a. sham

dump v. 1 unload in a heap 2 throw away —n. a place for dumping rubbish —**(down) in the dumps** dejected

dump'ling n. 1 piece of boiled dough 2 crust filled with fruit

Dump'ster trademark large, metal trash bin —n. [d-] such a trash bin

dump truck n. truck with tilting container for unloading

dump'y a. **-i·er, -i·est** 1 squat; stumpy 2 [Col.] ugly; run-down

dun a. dull grayish-brown —v. **dunned, dun'ning** to demand money owed

dunce n. stupid person

dune n. hill of drifted sand

dung n. animal excrement

dun'ga·rees' n.pl. work clothes of coarse cotton

dun'geon (-jan) n. dark underground prison

dunk v. 1 dip (food) into coffee, etc. 2 Basketball thrust (the ball) into the basket

du'o n., pl. **-os** performers of a duet

du'o·de'num n. first section of small intestine

dupe n. person easily tricked —v. deceive

du'plex' n. house with two separate family units

du'pli·cate (-kət; v.: -kāt') a. 1 double 2 exactly alike —n. exact copy —v. 1 make a copy 2 make happen again —**du'pli·ca'tion** n. —**du'pli·ca'tor** n.

du·plic'i·ty (-plis'-) n., pl. **-ties** cunning deception

du'ra·ble a. lasting a long time —**du'ra·bil'i·ty** n.

du·ra'tion n. time that a thing continues or lasts

du·ress' n. coercion

dur'ing prep. 1 throughout 2 in the course of

du'rum (door'əm) n. hard wheat used for pasta, etc.

dusk n. evening twilight

dust n. finely powdered matter, esp. earth —v. 1 sprinkle with powder 2 wipe dust from —**dust'y** a., **-i·er**, **-i·est**

dust'pan' n. pan into which floor dust is swept

Dutch n., a. (of) the people or language of the Netherlands — **go Dutch** [Col.] have each pay own expenses

du'ti·ful a. showing respect; obedient: also **du'te·ous** —**du'ti·ful·ly** adv.

du'ty n., pl. **-ties** 1 respect owed, as to parents 2 sense of obligation, justice, etc. 3 thing one must do 4 tax, as on imports

dwarf n. unusually small being or thing —v. 1 stunt in growth 2 make seem small —a. stunted

dwell v. **dwelt** or **dwelled**, **dwell'ing** make one's home —**dwell on** (or **upon**) talk or think about at length

dwelling (place) n. residence

dwin'dle v. decrease

dye n. coloring matter in solution —v. **dyed**, **dye'ing** to color with a dye —**dy'er** n.

dyed'-in-the-wool' a. not changing, as in beliefs

dy'ing v. ppr. of DIE

dy·nam'ic a. 1 of energy 2 energetic; forceful —**dy·nam'i·cal·ly** adv.

dy'na·mism' n. energetic quality

dy'na·mite' n. powerful explosive —v. blow up with dynamite

dy'na·mo' n., pl. **-mos'** 1 generator: earlier term 2 dynamic person

dy'nas·ty n., pl. **-ties** family line of rulers

dys'en·ter'y (dis'-) n. disease characterized by bloody diarrhea

dys·func'tion n. abnormal func-

tioning —**dys·func'tion·al** a.

dys·lex'i·a n. impairment of reading ability —**dys·lec'tic**, **dys·lex'ic** a., n.

dys·pep'si·a n. indigestion

E

each a., pron. every one of two or more —adv. apiece

ea'ger a. keenly desiring

ea'gle n. large bird of prey with sharp vision

ea'gle-eyed' a. having keen vision

ear n. 1 organ of hearing 2 sense of hearing 3 attention 4 grain-bearing spike of a cereal plant

ear'drum' n. thin membrane inside the ear

earl n. Br. nobleman

ear'ly adv., a. **-li·er**, **-li·est** 1 near the beginning 2 before the expected or usual time

ear'mark' v. reserve for a special purpose

ear'muffs' n.pl. warm covering for the ears

earn v. 1 receive for one's work 2 get as deserved 3 gain as profit

ear'nest a. serious or sincere — **in earnest** 1 serious 2 with determination

earn'ings n.pl. 1 wages 2 profits, interest, etc.

ear'phone' n. receiver as for a telephone, held to the ear

ear'ring' n. ear ornament

ear'shot' n. distance within which a sound can be heard

earth n. 1 the planet we live on 2 land 3 soil

earth'en·ware' n. dishes, etc. made of baked clay

earth'ly a. 1 terrestrial 2 worldly 3 conceivable

earth'quake' n. a shaking of the crust of the earth

earth'work' n. embankment; fortification

earth'worm' n. common worm in soil

earth'y a. **-i·er**, **-i·est** 1 of or like earth 2 coarse

ease n. 1 comfort 2 poise 3 facility —v. 1 to comfort 2 relieve 3 facilitate 4 shift carefully

ea·sel (ē'zəl) n. a stand to hold an artist's canvas

eas'i·ly adv. 1 with ease 2 without a doubt

east *n.* **1** direction in which sunrise occurs **2** region in this direction —[E-] the Orient —*a.*, *adv.* in, toward, or from the east —**east′er·ly** *a., adv.* —**east′ern** *a.* —**east′ern·er** *n.* —**east′ward** *a., adv.* —**east′wards** *adv.*

Eas′ter *n.* spring Christian festival

eas′y *a.* **-i·er, -i·est 1** not difficult **2** without worry, pain, etc. **3** comfortable **4** not stiff **5** not strict **6** unhurried —*adv.* [Col.] easily —**take it easy** [Col.] refrain from anger, etc. **2** relax

eas′y·go·ing *a.* not worried, rushed, or strict

eat *vt.* **ate, eat′en, eat′ing 1** chew and swallow (food) **2** wear away, corrode, etc. **3** make by eating

eaves *n.pl.* projecting edge of a roof

eaves′drop′ *v.* **-dropped′, -drop′ping** listen secretly

ebb *n., v.* **1** flow back toward the sea: said of the tide **2** decline

eb′on·y *n., pl.* **-ies** hard, dark, tropical wood —*a.* black

e·bul′lient (e bool′yənt) *a.* bubbling with joy —**e·bul′lience** *n.*

ec·cen′tric (ek sen′-) *a.* **1** having its axis off center **2** odd in conduct —*n.* eccentric person —**ec′cen·tric′i·ty** (-tris′-) *n., pl.* **-ties**

ec·cle′si·as′tic *n.* clergyman —*a.* ecclesiastical

ec·cle′si·as′ti·cal *a.* of the church or clergy

ech′e·lon′ (esh′-) *n.* **1** steplike formation of troops, ships, or planes **2** level of command

ech′o (ek′ō) *n., pl.* **-oes** repetition of a sound by reflection of sound waves —*v.* **1** resound **2** repeat

é·clair′ (ā kler′) *n.* oblong pastry filled with custard, etc.

ec·lec′tic *a.* using various sources

e·clipse′ *n.* the obscuring of the sun by the moon, or of the moon by the earth's shadow —*v.* surpass

e·clip′tic *n.* sun's apparent annual path

e·col′o·gy *n.* science dealing with organisms in their environment —**ec′o·log′i·cal** *a.* —**e·col′o·gist** *n.*

ec′o·nom′ic (or ē′kə-) *a.* **1** of the management of income, expenditures, etc. **2** of economics

ec′o·nom′i·cal *a.* thrifty —**ec′o-**

nom′i·cal·ly *adv.*

ec′o·nom′ics *n.* science that deals with the production, distribution, and use of wealth —**e·con′o·mist** *n.*

e·con′o·mize′ *v.* be thrifty

e·con′o·my *n., pl.* **-mies 1** management of finances **2** thrift **3** system of producing and consuming wealth

ec′o·sys′tem (or ē′kō-) *n.* community of animals, plants, etc.

ec′ru′ (-rōō′) *a., n.* light tan

ec′sta·sy *n., pl.* **-sies** overpowering joy —**ec·stat′ic** *a.*

ec·u·men′i·cal *a.* of the Christian Church as a whole

ec′u·men·ism′ *n.* movement to unify Christian churches

ec·ze′ma (or eg′-) *n.* itchy, scaly skin disease

-ed *suf.* **1** having or being **2** pt. and pp. ending of many verbs

ed′dy (-ē) *n., pl.* **-dies** little whirlpool or whirlwind —*v.* **-died, -dy·ing** to whirl

e·de′ma *n.* dropsy

E′den *Bible* garden where Adam and Eve first lived

edge *n.* **1** blade's cutting side **2** brink **3** border **4** [Col.] advantage —*v.* **1** put an edge on **2** move sideways —**on edge** tense

edg′ing *n.* trimming on an edge

edg′y *a.* **-i·er, -i·est** tense

ed′i·ble *a.* fit to be eaten

e′dict *n.* public order

ed′i·fice (-fis) *n.* large, imposing building

ed′i·fy *v.* **-fied′, -fy′ing** instruct or improve morally —**ed′i·fi·ca′tion** *n.*

ed′it *v.* **1** revise, select, etc. (writing) for publication **2** be in charge of (a newspaper, etc.) **3** prepare (film, etc.) by cutting, etc. —**ed′i·tor** *n.*

e·di′tion *n.* **1** form in which a book is published **2** total copies of a book, etc. published at one time

ed′i·to′ri·al *n.* article in a newspaper, etc. stating the opinions of the editor or publisher —*a.* of an editor —**ed′i·to′ri·al·ize′** *v.*

ed′u·cate′ *v.* develop the knowledge, skill, etc. of by schooling —**ed′u·ca′tion** *n.* —**ed′u·ca′tor** *n.*

eel *n.* snakelike fish

e′er (er) *adv.* [Poet.] ever

ee·rie, ee′ry (ir′ē) *a.* **-ri·er, -ri·est** weird; uncanny —**ee′ri·ly** *adv.*

ef·face′ *v.* erase; wipe out

ef·fect n. 1 a result 2 influence 3 meaning 4 pl. belongings —v. bring about —**in effect** 1 actually 2 in operation —**take effect** begin to act

ef·fec·tive a. 1 producing a desired result 2 in operation —**ef·fec·tive·ly** adv.

ef·fec·tu·al (-chōō əl) a. EFFECTIVE (a. 1) —**ef·fec·tu·al·ly** adv.

ef·fem·i·nate (-nət) a. showing womanly traits; unmanly

ef·fer·vesce (-ves´) v. to bubble —**ef·fer·ves·cent** a.

ef·fete (-fēt´) a. spent and sterile

ef·fi·ca·cious a. effective

ef·fi·cient (-fish´ənt) a. effective with a minimum of effort, expense, etc. —**ef·fi·cien·cy** n. —**ef·fi·cient·ly** adv.

ef·fi·gy n., pl. **-gies** statue or image; esp., a crude figure as for mock hanging

ef·flu·ent n. outflow of a sewer, etc.

ef·fort n. 1 use of energy to do something 2 attempt

ef·fron·ter·y n. impudence

ef·fu·sive (-fyo͞o´-) a. gushing

e.g. for example

e·gal·i·tar·i·an a. advocating full equality for all

egg n. 1 oval body from which young of birds, fish, etc. are hatched 2 ovum —v. to urge on

egg·head´ n. [Sl.] intellectual

egg´nog´ n. drink made of eggs, milk, sugar, etc.

egg´plant´ n. large, purple, pear-shaped vegetable

eg·lan·tine (-tīn´, -tēn´) n. kind of pink rose

e·go n. 1 the self 2 conceit

e·go·cen·tric a. self-centered

e·go·ism n. 1 selfishness 2 conceit —**e·go·ist** n. —**e·go·is´tic** a.

e·go·tism n. 1 excessive reference to oneself 2 self-conceit —**e·go·tist** n. —**e·go·tis´tic, e·go·tis´ti·cal** a.

e·gre·gious (-jəs) a. flagrant

e·gress´ n. an exit

e·gret´ n. heron having long, white plumes

E·gyp·tian (ē jip´shən) n., a. (native) of Egypt

eh (ā, e) int. sound expressing surprise, doubt, etc.

ei·der (ī´-) n. large sea duck with soft, fine down (**ei´der·down´**)

eight a., n. one more than seven —**eighth´** a., n.

eight·een´ a., n. eight more than ten —**eight´eenth´** a., n.

eight´y a., n., pl. **-ies** eight times

ten —**eight´i·eth** a., n.

ei·ther (ē´thər, ī´-) a., pron. one or the other (of two) —con. correlative used with or —adv. any more than the other

e·jac·u·late v. 1 eject (esp. semen) 2 exclaim suddenly —**e·jac·u·la´tion** n.

e·ject´ v. throw out; expel

eke (ēk) v. barely manage to make (a living): with out

e·lab·o·rate (-rət´; a.: -rət) v. add details —a. in great detail

é·lan (ā län´) n. spirited self-assurance; dash

e·lapse´ v. pass, as time

e·las·tic a. 1 springing back to shape —n. band, etc. with rubber in it —**e·las·tic´i·ty** (-tis´-) n.

e·late´ v. make proud, happy, etc. —**e·la´tion** n.

el´bow´ n. joint between the upper and lower arm —v. shove as with the elbows

elbow grease n. [Col.] hard work

el´bow·room´ n. ample space

eld´er a. older —n. 1 older person 2 church official 3 shrub with dark berries

el·der·ber·ry n., pl. **-ries** 1 the elder 2 its berry

eld·er·ly a. somewhat old

eld·est a. oldest

e·lect´ v. select, esp. by voting —a. specially chosen —**e·lec´tion** n.

e·lec·tion·eer´ v. canvass votes in an election

e·lec·tive a. 1 filled by election 2 optional —n. optional subject in school

e·lec·tor n. 1 qualified voter 2 member of the electoral college

e·lec·tor·al college n. assembly that formally elects the U.S. president

e·lec·tor·ate (-ət) n. the body of qualified voters

e·lec·tric, e·lec·tri·cal a. of, charged with, or worked by electricity

e·lec·tri·cian (-trish´ən) n. one who installs and repairs electrical apparatus

e·lec·tric´i·ty (-tris´-) n. 1 form of energy with magnetic, chemical, and radiant effects 2 electric current

e·lec·tri·fy v. **-fied´, -fy´ing** 1 equip for the use of electricity 2 thrill

e·lec·tro·car´di·o·gram´ n. tracing showing electrical changes in the heart

e·lec·tro·car·di·o·graph' *n.* an instrument for making electrocardiograms

e·lec·tro·cute' *v.* kill by electricity —**e·lec·tro·cu'tion** *n.*

e·lec'trode' *n.* terminal of an electric source

e·lec·tro·en·ceph·a·lo·gram' (-sef'-) *n.* tracing showing electrical activity in brain

e·lec·tro·en·ceph·a·lo·graph' *n.* instrument for making electroencephalograms

e·lec·trol'y·sis (-träl'ə-) *n.* breakdown into ions of a chemical compound in solution by electrical current

e·lec'tro·lyte' (-līt') *n.* substance which in solution conducts electric current —**e·lec·tro·lyt'ic** (-lit'-) *a.*

e·lec·tro·mag'net *n.* soft iron core made magnetic by an electric current —**e·lec·tro·mag·net'ic** *a.* —**e·lec·tro·mag'net·ism'** *n.*

e·lec·tro·mo'tive *a.* producing an electric current

e·lec'tron' *n.* negatively charged particle in an atom —**e·lec'tron'ic** *a.*

electronic mail *n.* messages sent to and from computer terminals, as by telephone lines

e·lec·tron'ics *n.* science of electronic action

electron microscope *n.* instrument using electrons to enlarge the image of an object

electron tube *n.* electronic device used in radio, etc.

e·lec'tro·plate' *v.* coat with metal by electrolysis

el'e·gant *a.* tastefully luxurious —**el'e·gance** *n.*

el'e·gy (-jē) *n., pl.* **-gies** poem lamenting a dead person —**e·le·gi'ac** (-jī'-) *a.*

el'e·ment' *n.* 1 natural environment 2 basic part or feature 3 *Chem.* substance that cannot be separated into different substances except by nuclear disintegration —**the elements** wind, rain, etc. —**el'e·men'tal** *a.*

el·e·men'ta·ry *a.* of fundamentals; introductory

elementary school *n.* school of the first six (or eight) grades

el'e·phant *n.* huge, thick-skinned mammal with a long trunk and ivory tusks

el·e·phan'tine' (-tin', -tēn') *a.* huge, clumsy, etc.

el'e·vate' *v.* 1 raise 2 raise in rank 3 elate

el·e·va'tion *n.* 1 high place 2 height, as above sea level

el'e·va'tor *n.* 1 suspended cage for hoisting or lowering goods or people 2 warehouse for grain

e·lev'en *a., n.* one more than ten —**e·lev'enth** *a., n.*

elf *n., pl.* **elves** small fairy —**elf'in** *a.*

e·lic'it (-lis'-) *v.* draw forth

e·lide' *v.* slur over

el'i·gi·ble *a.* qualified —*n.* eligible person —**el'i·gi·bil'i·ty** *n.*

e·lim'i·nate' *v.* 1 remove 2 excrete —**e·lim'i·na'tion** *n.*

e·lite' (ā lēt') *n.* best or most powerful part of a group

e·lit'ism' *n.* government or control by an elite —**e·lit'ist** *a., n.*

e·lix'ir (-ər) *n.* drug in alcoholic solution

elk *n.* large deer

el·lipse' *n.* closed curve that is a symmetrical oval —**el·lip'ti·cal** *a.*

el·lip'sis *n.* 1 omission of a word or words 2 mark (...) showing this

elm *n.* tall shade tree

el·o·cu'tion *n.* art of public speaking

e·lon'gate' *v.* lengthen —**e·lon·ga'tion** *n.*

e·lope' *v.* run away to marry —**e·lope'ment** *n.*

el'o·quent *a.* vivid or forceful in expression —**el'o·quence** *n.*

else *a.* 1 different; other 2 in addition —*adv.* 1 otherwise 2 if not

else'where' *adv.* in or to some other place

e·lu'ci·date' *v.* explain

e·lude' *v.* escape; evade

e·lu'sive *a.* hard to grasp; baffling

elves *n.* pl. of ELF

e·ma'ci·ate' (-shē-, -sē-) *v.* make too thin —**e·ma'ci·a'tion** *n.*

e-'mail' *n.* electronic mail

em'a·nate' *v.* come or issue —**em'a·na'tion** *n.*

e·man'ci·pate' *v.* set free —**e·man'ci·pa'tion** *n.* —**e·man'ci·pa'tor** *n.*

e·mas'cu·late' *v.* castrate

em·balm' (-bäm') *v.* preserve (a dead body)

em·bank'ment *n.* bank of earth, etc. as to keep back water

em·bar'go *n., pl.* **-goes** legal restriction of commerce or shipping

em·bark' *v.* 1 go aboard a ship

2 begin; start **—em'bar·ka'tion** n.

em·bar'rass v. cause to feel self-conscious **—em·bar'rass·ment** n.

em'bas·sy n., pl. **-sies** staff or headquarters of an ambassador

em·bed' v. **-bed'ded, -bed'ding** set firmly (in)

em·bel'lish v. 1 decorate 2 add details, often untrue **—em·bel'lish·ment** n.

em'ber n. glowing piece of coal or wood

em·bez'zle v. steal (money entrusted) **—em·bez'zle·ment** n. **—em·bez'zler** n.

em·bit'ter v. make bitter

em·bla'zon v. 1 decorate 2 display openly

em'blem n. visible symbol; sign **—em·blem·at'ic** a.

em·bod'y v. **-ied, -y·ing** 1 give form to 2 include **—em·bod'i·ment** n.

em·bold'en v. make bold

em'bo·lism' n. obstruction of a blood vessel

em·boss' v. decorate with raised designs

em·brace' v. 1 hug lovingly 2 adopt, as an idea 3 include **—n.** an embracing

em·broi'der v. ornament with needlework **—em·broi'der·y** n., pl. **-ies**

em·broil' v. get involved

em'bry·o' (-brē-) n., pl. **-os'** animal or plant in earliest stages of development **—em'bry·on'ic** a.

em·cee' v. **-ceed', -cee'ing** n. [Col.] (act as) master of ceremonies

e·mend' v. correct, as a text **—e'men·da'tion** n.

em'er·ald n. green jewel

e·merge' v. come out; appear **—e·mer'gence** n.

e·mer'gen·cy n., pl. **-cies** sudden occurrence demanding quick action

e·mer'i·tus a. retired, but keeping one's title

em'er·y n. hard corundum used for grinding, etc.

e·met'ic n., a. (substance) causing vomiting

em'i·grate' v. leave one country to settle in another **—em'i·grant** a., n. **—em'i·gra'tion** n.

é·mi·gré, é·mi·gré (em'i grā') n. one forced to flee for political reasons

em'i·nent a. prominent or high **—em'i·nence** n.

em'is·sar'y n., pl. **-ies** one sent on a mission

e·mit' v. **e·mit'ted, e·mit'ting** 1 send out; discharge 2 utter **—e·mis'sion** n. **—e·mit'ter** n.

e·mol'li·ent n., a. (medicine) for soothing the skin

e·mol'u·ment (-yōō-) n. salary

e·mote' v. [Col.] show emotion dramatically

e·mo'tion n. strong feeling, as of love, fear, anger, etc. **—e·mo'tion·al** a.

em·pa·thet'ic a. showing empathy

em'pa·thize' v. have empathy (with)

em'pa·thy n. ability to share another's feelings

em'per·or n. ruler of an empire **—em'press** n.fem.

em'pha·sis n., pl. **-ses'** (-sēz') 1 stress; importance 2 stress on a syllable

em'pha·size' v. to stress

em·phat'ic a. 1 using emphasis 2 forcible **—em·phat'i·cal·ly** adv.

em'phy·se'ma (-fə-) n. disease of the lungs

em'pire n. group of countries under one sovereign

em·pir'i·cal (-pir'-) a. based on experiment or experience

em·place'ment n. prepared position for a large gun

em·ploy' v. 1 use 2 keep busy 3 hire or have as workers **—n.** employment

em·ploy·ee', em·ploy'e (-ē) n. person working for another for pay

em·ploy'er n. one who employs others for pay

em·ploy'ment n. 1 an employing or being employed 2 work; occupation

em·pow'er v. 1 authorize 2 enable

emp'ty a. **-ti·er, -ti·est** 1 with nothing or no one in it 2 worthless **—v.** **-tied, -ty·ing** 1 make or become empty 2 pour out **—n., pl.** **-ties** empty bottle, etc. **—emp'ti·ness** n.

e'mu' n. ostrichlike bird

em'u·late' v. try to equal or surpass **—em'u·la'tion** n.

e·mul'si·fy' v. **-fied', -fy'ing** form into an emulsion

e·mul'sion n. oil suspended in watery liquid

en- pref. 1 to put on 2 to make 3 in or into

-en suf. 1 make or become 2 get

or give 3 made of

en·a'ble v. make able

en·act' v. 1 pass, as a law 2 act out

en·am'el n. 1 glassy coating fused to metal 2 white coating of teeth 3 hard, glossy paint — v. coat with enamel —en·am'el·ware' n.

en·am'or v. fill with love; charm

en·cap'su·late' v. 1 enclose in a capsule 2 condense

en·case' v. enclose

-ence suf. act, state, or result: also -ency

en·ceph·a·li'tis n. inflammation of the brain

en·chant' v. charm; delight

en·chi·la·da (-lä'-) n. tortilla rolled with meat inside

en·cir'cle v. surround

en·clave' n. foreign land inside another country

en·close' v. 1 surround; shut in 2 insert in an envelope —en·clo'sure n.

en·code' v. put (a message) into code

en·co'mi·um n. high praise

en·com'pass v. 1 surround 2 contain

en·core' (än'-) int. again! —n. song, etc. added by request

en·coun'ter v. 1 meet unexpectedly 2 fight —n. 1 unexpected meeting 2 fight

en·cour'age v. 1 give courage or hope to 2 help —en·cour'age·ment n.

en·croach' v. intrude (on) —en·croach'ment n.

en·crust' v. incrust —en·crus·ta'tion n.

en·cum'ber v. 1 hinder 2 burden —en·cum'brance n.

en·cyc'li·cal (-sik'-) n. papal letter to bishops

en·cy·clo·pe'di·a n. book or set of books on one or all branches of knowledge —en·cy·clo·pe'dic a.

end n. 1 last part; finish 2 destruction 3 tip 4 purpose — v. finish; stop —a. final —end'ing n.

en·dan'ger v. put in danger

en·dear' v. make beloved

en·dear'ment n. affection

en·deav'or (-dev'-) v. try hard —n. earnest attempt

en·dem'ic a. prevalent in a place, as a disease

en'dive n. salad plant

end'less a. 1 eternal; infinite 2 lasting too long 3 with the ends

joined to form a ring

en'do·crine' (gland) (-krin'-) n. any of the ductless glands that regulate bodily functions

en·dorse' v. 1 sign on the back of (a check) 2 approve —en·dorse'ment n.

en·dow' v. 1 provide with some quality 2 give money to —en·dow'ment n.

en·dur'ance n. ability to last, stand pain, etc.

en·dure' v. 1 stand (pain, etc.) 2 tolerate 3 last

end'ways' adv. 1 lengthwise 2 end to end Also end'wise'

en'e·ma n. therapeutic flushing of the rectum

en'e·my n., pl. -mies person or nation hostile to another; foe

en'er·gize' v. give energy to

en'er·gy n., pl. -gies 1 vigor; power 2 capacity to do work — en·er·get'ic a.

en·er'vate' v. weaken

en·fee'ble v. weaken

en·fold' v. 1 wrap up 2 embrace

en·force' v. 1 impose by force 2 make people obey (a law) —en·force'ment n. —en·forc'er n.

en·fran'chise' v. 1 free from slavery 2 give the right to vote

en·gage' v. 1 bind by a promise of marriage 2 involve oneself 3 hire 4 attract and hold 5 enter into conflict with 6 interlock; mesh —en·gaged' a. —en·gage'ment n.

en·gag'ing a. charming

en·gen'der v. cause

en'gine n. 1 a machine using energy to develop mechanical power 2 locomotive

en·gi·neer' n. 1 one trained in engineering 2 locomotive driver —v. manage skillfully

en·gi·neer'ing n. practical use of sciences in industry, building, etc.

Eng'lish a., n. (of) the people or language of England

en·grave' v. cut (designs) on (a metal plate, etc.), as for printing —en·grav'er n. —en·grav'ing n.

en·gross' (-grōs') v. take the full attention of

en·gulf' v. swallow up

en·hance' v. make greater

e·nig'ma n. baffling matter, person, etc. —en·ig·mat'ic, e·nig·mat'i·cal a.

en·join' v. 1 to command 2 prohibit by law

en·joy' v. 1 get pleasure from 2 have the use of —enjoy oneself have a good time —**en·joy'a·ble** *a.* —**en·joy'ment** *n.*

en·large' *v.* make larger — **enlarge on (or upon)** discuss fully —**en·large'ment** *n.*

en·light'en *v.* free from ignorance, prejudice, etc.

en·list' *v.* 1 enroll in an army, etc. 2 engage in a cause —**en·list'ment** *n.*

en·liv'en *v.* liven up

en masse' *adv.* all together

en·mesh' *v.* entangle

en·mi·ty *n.* ill will

en·no·ble *v.* dignify

en·nui (än'wē) *n.* boredom

e·nor·mi·ty *n., pl.* **-ties** 1 great wickedness 2 outrageous act

e·nor·mous *a.* huge; vast

e·nough' *a., adv.* as much as is needed —*n.* amount needed —*int.* no more!

en·plane' *v.* board an airplane

en·quire' *v.* inquire —**en·quir'y** *n., pl.* **-ies**

en·rage' *v.* put into a rage

en·rap·ture *v.* fill with delight

en·rich' *v.* make rich(er) —**en·rich'ment** *n.*

en·roll' *v.* put or be put in a list, as a member, etc. —**en·roll'ment** *n.*

en route (en rōōt', än-) *adv., a.* [Fr.] on the way

en·sconce' *v.* place snugly

en·sem·ble (än säm'-) *n.* 1 total effect 2 costume of matching parts 3 group of musicians playing together

en·shrine' *v.* hold as sacred

en·shroud' *v.* hide

en·sign' (-sin; *n. 2:* -sən) *n.* 1 flag 2 lowest-ranking navy officer

en·slave' *v.* make a slave of

en·snare' *v.* catch as in a snare

en·sue' *v.* follow; result

en·tail' *v.* make necessary

en·tan·gle *v.* trap; confuse

en·ter *v.* 1 come or go in 2 put in a list, etc. 3 join 4 begin — **enter into** 1 take part in 2 form a part of — **enter on (or upon)** begin

en·ter·i'tis *n.* inflammation of the intestine

en·ter·prise' *n.* 1 important undertaking 2 energy and boldness

en·ter·pris'ing *a.* full of energy and boldness

en·ter·tain' *v.* 1 amuse 2 act as host to 3 consider, as an idea — **en·ter·tain'er** *n.* —**en·ter·tain'ment** *n.*

en·thrall' *v.* fascinate

en·thuse' (-thōōz') *v.* [Col.] act or make enthusiastic

en·thu·si·asm' *n.* eager interest —**en·thu·si·ast'** *n.* —**en·thu·si·as'tic** *a.*

en·tice' *v.* tempt

en·tire' *a.* complete; whole —**en·tire'ly** *adv.* —**en·tire'ty** *n.*

en·ti·tle' *v.* 1 give a title to 2 give a right to

en·ti·ty *n., pl.* **-ties** thing having real existence

en·to·mol·o·gy *n.* study of insects

en·tou·rage (än'tōō räzh') *n.* retinue; attendants

en·trails *n.pl.* inner organs; spec., intestines

en·trance (*v.:* en trans') *n.* 1 act of entering 2 door, gate, etc. 3 permission to enter —*v.* to delight

en·trant *n.* one who enters a contest

en·trap' *v.* catch in a trap

en·treat' *v.* ask earnestly

en·treat'y *n., pl.* **-ies** earnest request; prayer

en·tree, en·trée (än'trā) *n.* main dish

en·trench' *v.* set securely —**en·trench'ment** *n.*

en·tre·pre·neur (än'trə prə noor') *n.* one who organizes and operates a business

en·tro·py *n.* tendency of energy system to run down

en·trust' *v.* assign the care of (to)

en·try *n., pl.* **-tries** 1 entrance 2 item in a list, etc. 3 contestant

en·twine' *v.* twist together or around

e·nu·mer·ate' *v.* name one by one —**e·nu·mer·a'tion** *n.*

e·nun·ci·ate' *v.* 1 to state 2 pronounce (words) clearly —**e·nun'ci·a'tion** *n.*

en·vel·op *v.* 1 wrap up 2 surround —**en·vel·op·ment** *n.*

en·ve·lope *n.* covering, esp. for a letter

en·vi·ron·ment *n.* surroundings —**en·vi·ron·men'tal** *a.*

en·vi·ron·men'tal·ist *n.* person working to solve environmental problems

en·vi·rons *n.pl.* suburbs

en·vis·age (-viz'-) *v.* imagine

en·vi·sion *v.* imagine

en·voy' (än'-, en'-) *n.* 1 messenger 2 diplomatic official

en·vy *n.* 1 discontent and ill will over another's advantages, etc. 2 object of such feeling —*v.* feel envy toward —**en'vi·a·ble** *a.* —**en'vi·ous** *a.*

en'zyme' (-zīm') *n.* a catalyst formed in body cells

e'on *n.* very long time

ep'au·let' (ep'ə-) *n.* shoulder ornament on a uniform

e·phem'er·al *a.* short-lived

ep'ic *n.* long poem about a hero's deeds —*a.* heroic

ep'i·cen'ter *n.* focal point, as of an earthquake

ep'i·cure' *n.* one with a fine taste for foods and liquors —**ep'i·cu·re'an** *a.*

ep'i·dem'ic *n., a.* (disease) that spreads rapidly

ep'i·der'mis *n.* outermost layer of the skin

ep'i·glot'tis *n.* thin lid of cartilage covering windpipe during swallowing

ep'i·gram' *n.* witty saying

ep'i·lep'sy *n.* disease marked by convulsive fits, etc. —**ep'i·lep'tic** *a., n.*

ep'i·logue', ep'i·log' (-lôg') *n.* part added at the end of a novel, play, etc.

e·pis'co·pal *a.* of or governed by bishops

ep'i·sode' *n.* incident —**ep'i·sod'ic** *a.*

e·pis'tle (-pis'əl) *n.* 1 letter 2 [E-] *Bible* letter of an Apostle

ep'i·taph' *n.* inscription on a tomb

ep'i·thet' *n.* word or phrase characterizing a person, etc.

e·pit'o·me' (-mē') *n.* 1 typical part or thing 2 summary —**e·pit'o·mize'** *v.*

ep'och (-ək) *n.* period marked by certain events —**ep'och·al** *a.*

ep·ox'y *n.* resin used in strong glues, enamels, etc.

Ep'som salts (or **salt**) *n.* salt used as a cathartic

eq'ua·ble (ek'wə-) *a.* even; calm —**eq'ua·bly** *adv.*

e'qual *a.* of the same quantity, value, rank, etc. —*n.* person or thing that is equal —*v.* be, or do something, equal to —**equal to** capable of —**e·qual'i·ty** *n.* —**e'qual·ize'** *v.* —**e'qual·ly** *adv.*

equal mark (or **sign**) *n.* sign (=) indicating equality

e'qua·nim'i·ty (ek'wə-, ē'kwə-) *n.* composure

e·quate' *v.* treat, regard, or express as equal

e·qua'tion *n.* 1 an equating 2 equality of two quantities as shown by the equal mark

e·qua'tor *n.* imaginary circle around the earth, equidistant from the North and South Poles —**e'qua·to'ri·al** *a.*

e·ques'tri·an *a.* of horses or horsemanship —*n.* a rider or acrobat on horseback

equi– *pref.* equal, equally

e'qui·dis'tant *a.* equally distant

e'qui·lat'er·al *a.* having all sides equal

e'qui·lib'ri·um *n.* state of balance

e'quine *a.* of a horse

e'qui·nox' *n.* time when the sun crosses the equator, making night and day of equal length everywhere

e·quip' *v.* **-quipped', -quip'ping** fit out, as for an undertaking —**e·quip'ment** *n.*

eq'ui·ta·ble *a.* fair; just

eq'ui·ty *n.* 1 fairness 2 value of property beyond amount owed on it

e·quiv'a·lent *a.* equal in quantity, meaning, etc. —*n.* equivalent thing

e·quiv'o·cal *a.* 1 purposely ambiguous 2 doubtful —**e·quiv'o·cate'** *v.*

-er *suf.* one that

e'ra *n.* period of time

e·rad'i·cate' *v.* wipe out —**e·rad'i·ca'tion** *n.*

e·rase' *v.* rub out, as writing —**e·ras'er** *n.* —**e·ras'a·ble** *a.*

e·ra'sure (-shər) *n.* place where something was erased

ere (er) *con., prep.* [Ar. or Poet.] before

e·rect' *a.* upright —*v.* 1 construct; build 2 set upright —**e·rec'tion** *n.*

e·rec'tile (-təl, -til') *a.* that becomes rigid when filled with blood

erg *n.* unit of work

er·mine (ur'min) *n.* weasel with white fur in winter

e·rode' *v.* wear away —**e·ro'sion** *n.*

e·rog'e·nous (-räj'-) *a.* sensitive to sexual stimulation

e·rot'ic *a.* causing sexual feelings or desires

e·rot'i·ca *n.pl.* [*sing.* or *pl. v.*] erotic books, etc.

err (ur, er) *v.* 1 be wrong 2 violate a moral code

er'rand *n.* short trip to do a thing

er'rant *a.* wandering

er·ra'ta (-rät'ə) *n.pl., sing.* **-tum** printing errors

er·rat·ic *a.* irregular; odd

er·ro·ne·ous *a.* wrong

er·ror *n.* **1** mistake; blunder **2** mistaken belief

er·satz' (-zäts') *a.* being an inferior substitute

erst'while *a.* former

er·u·dite' *a.* learned; scholarly — **er·u·di'tion** *n.*

e·rupt' *v.* **1** burst forth **2** break out in a rash —**e·rup'tion** *n.*

-ery *suf.* **1** a place to or for **2** act or product of **3** condition of

e·ryth·ro·cyte (e rith'rō sit') *n.* mature red blood cell

es·ca·late' *v.* rise, expand, or increase —**es·ca·la'tion** *n.*

es·ca·la·tor *n.* moving stairway on an endless belt

es·cal·lop, es·ca·lop (e skäl'əp, -skal'-) *n., v.* scallop

es·ca·pade' *n.* reckless adventure or prank

es·cape' *v.* **1** get free **2** slip away from —*n.* act or means of escape

es·cap·ee' *n.* one who has escaped

es·cape'ment *n.* notched wheel regulating movement in a clock

es·cap'ism' *n.* tendency to escape reality by fantasy

es'ca·role' *n.* plant with leaves used in salads

es·carp'ment *n.* cliff

es·chew' *v.* shun

es'cort' (*v.:* es kôrt') *n.* person(s) accompanying another to protect, honor, etc. —*v.* go with as an escort

es'crow' *n.* state of a deed held by a third party until conditions are fulfilled

es·cutch'eon (-ən) *n.* shield bearing a coat of arms

Es'ki·mo' *n., a.* (member) of a people living in Greenland, arctic N. America, etc.

e·soph·a·gus *n., pl.* **-gi** (-jī') passage between the pharynx and stomach

es·o·ter'ic *a.* known by few

es·pe'cial *a.* special; chief —**es·pe'cial·ly** *adv.*

es'pi·o·nage' (-näzh') *n.* a spying

es·pouse (e spouz') *v.* **1** marry **2** support (an idea or cause) — **es·pous'al** *n.*

es·pres'so *n.* coffee made by forcing steam through ground coffee beans

es·py (e spī') *v.* **-pied', -py'ing** catch sight of; spy

Es'quire' *n.* title of courtesy put after a man's surname, or, in U.S., after a lawyer's name: abbrev. Esq.

es·say' (*n.:* es'ā) *v.* to try —*n.* **1** a try **2** short personal writing on one subject —**es'say·ist** *n.*

es'sence *n.* **1** basic nature **2** substance in concentrated form **3** perfume

es·sen'tial (-shəl) *n., a.* (something) necessary

es·tab'lish *v.* **1** set up; fix **2** to found **3** prove —**es·tab'lish·ment** *n.*

es·tate' *n.* **1** one's possessions **2** piece of land with a residence

es·teem' *v.* value highly —*n.* high regard

es'ter *n.* organic salt

es'thete *n.* aesthete —**es·thet'ic** *a.*

es'ti·ma·ble *a.* worthy of esteem

es'ti·mate' (-māt'; *n.:* -mət) *v.* figure roughly, as size or cost —*n.* **1** rough calculation **2** opinion —**es'ti·ma'tion** *n.*

es·trange' *v.* make unfriendly

es'tro·gen *n.* female sex hormone

es·tu·ar·y (-tyoo-, -choo-) *n., pl.* **-ies** wide mouth of a river

et cet'er·a and so forth: abbrev. etc.

etch *v.* put a design on metal plates or glass with acid, often for making prints —**etch'ing** *n.*

e·ter'nal *a.* **1** everlasting **2** forever the same

e·ter'ni·ty *n.* **1** a being eternal **2** endless time

eth'ane' *n.* gaseous hydrocarbon used as fuel

e'ther *n.* an anesthetic

e·the're·al (-thir'ē-) *a.* **1** light; delicate **2** heavenly

eth'ic *n.* **1** ethics **2** particular moral standard or value

eth'i·cal *a.* **1** of ethics **2** proper; right

eth'ics *n.pl.* moral standards; system of morals

eth'nic *a.* of any of the many peoples of mankind —*n.* member of a nationality group in a larger community

eth·nic'i·ty (-nis'-) *n.* ethnic affiliation

eth·nol'o·gy *n.* study of the world's peoples and cultures — **eth'no·log'i·cal** *a.*

e'thos' (-thäs') *n.* characteristic attitudes, beliefs, etc.

eth'yl (-əl) *n.* carbon-hydrogen radical of common alcohol, etc.

e'ti·ol'o·gy (ēt'ē-) *n., pl.* **-gies** cause of a disease, etc.

et'i·quette (-kat) *n.* social forms; good manners

é'tude' (ā'-) *n. Mus.* instrumental piece stressing a technique

et'y·mol'o·gy *n., pl.* **-gies** 1 origin of a word 2 study of word origins

eu'ca·lyp'tus (yōō'kə lip'-) *n.* a subtropical evergreen

Eu'cha·rist (-kə-) *n.* Holy Communion

eu·gen'ics *n.* science of improving the human race by heredity control **—eu·gen'ic** *a.*

eu'lo·gy *n., pl.* **-gies** praise **—eu'lo·gize'** *v.*

eu'nuch (-nək) *n.* castrated man

eu'phe·mism' *n.* mild word replacing an offensive one **—eu'phe·mis'tic** *a.*

eu·pho'ni·ous *a.* pleasant sounding **—eu·pho'ny** *n.*

eu·pho'ri·a *n.* feeling of wellbeing **—eu·phor'ic** *a.*

Eu'ro·pe'an *a.* (native) of Europe

eu·sta'chi·an tube (-stā'kē ən, -stā'shən) *n.* tube between middle ear and pharynx

eu'tha·na'si·a (-nā'zhə) *n.* painless death to end suffering

e·vac'u·ate' *v.* 1 make empty 2 to discharge (excrement) 3 remove 4 withdraw (from) **—e·vac'u·a'tion** *n.*

e·vac'u·ee' *n.* person evacuated from area of danger

e·vade' *v.* avoid by deceit, indirect answer, etc. **—e·va'sion** *n.* **—e·va'sive** *a.*

e·val'u·ate' *v.* find the value of **—e·val'u·a'tion** *n.*

ev'a·nes'cent *a.* fleeting

e·van·gel'i·cal *a.* of the Gospels or New Testament

e·van'ge·list *n.* 1 [E-] Gospel writer 2 revivalist preacher **—e·van'ge·lism'** *n.* **—e·van'ge·lize'** *v.*

e·vap'o·rate' *v.* 1 change into vapor 2 condense by heating 3 vanish **—e·vap'o·ra'tion** *n.*

eve *n.* 1 [Poet.] evening 2 evening before a holiday 3 time just before

e'ven *a.* 1 flat; level 2 constant; uniform 3 calm 4 equal 5 divisible by two 6 exact **—adv.** 1 indeed 2 exactly 3 still **—v.** make or become even **—even if** though **—e'ven·ly** *adv.*

e'ven·hand'ed *a.* fair; just

eve'ning *n.* end of day and beginning of night

e·vent' *n.* 1 an occurrence 2 sports contest in a series **—in any event** no matter what happens **—in the event of** in case of

e·ven·tem'pered *a.* not quickly angered or excited

e·vent'ful *a.* full of events; important

e·ven'tu·al (-chōō-) *a.* final **—e·ven'tu·al·ly** *adv.*

e·ven·tu·al'i·ty *n., pl.* **-ties** possible outcome

ev'er *adv.* 1 always 2 at any time 3 at all

ev'er·glade *n.* swampy land

ev'er·green' *a.* (tree or plant) having green leaves all year

ev'er·last'ing *a.* eternal

ev'er·y *a.* 1 each of a group 2 all possible **—every now and then** occasionally **—every other** each alternate **—ev'er·y·bod'y, ev'er·y·one'** *pron.* **—ev'er·y·thing'** *pron.* **—ev'er·y·where'** *adv.*

ev'er·y·day' *a.* 1 daily 2 usual; common

e·vict' *v.* put (a tenant) out by law **—e·vic'tion** *n.*

ev'i·dence *n.* 1 sign; indication 2 proof **—v.** make evident

ev'i·dent *a.* easy to see; clear **—ev'i·dent·ly** *adv.*

e'vil *a.* 1 morally bad 2 harmful **—n.** wickedness **—e'vil·do'er** *n.* **—e'vil·ly** *adv.*

e·vince' *v.* show plainly (a quality, feeling, etc.)

e·vis'cer·ate' (-vis'ər-) *v.* remove the entrails from

e·voke' *v.* call forth; produce **—ev'o·ca'tion** *n.*

ev'o·lu'tion *n.* 1 an evolving 2 theory that all species developed from earlier forms **—ev'o·lu'tion·ar'y** *a.*

e·volve' *v.* develop gradually; unfold

ewe (yōō) *n.* female sheep

ew'er *n.* large, wide-mouthed water pitcher

ex- *pref.* former

ex·ac'er·bate' (eg zas'-) *v.* aggravate **—ex·ac'er·ba'tion** *n.*

ex·act' *a.* strictly correct; precise **—v.** demand and get **—ex·ac'ti·tude'** *n.* **—ex·act'ly** *adv.*

ex·act'ing *a.* strict; hard

ex·ag'ger·ate' *v.* make seem greater than it really is; overstate **—ex·ag'ger·a'tion** *n.*

ex·alt' *v.* 1 raise in dignity 2 praise 3 fill with joy **—ex'al·ta'tion** *n.*

ex·am' *n.* examination

ex·am'ine *v.* 1 inspect 2 test by

example 103 **exile**

questioning —ex·am'i·na'tion n.

ex·am'ple n. 1 sample 2 a warning 3 illustration 4 model

ex·as'per·ate' v. annoy; vex —ex·as'per·a'tion n.

ex'ca·vate' v. 1 make a hole in 2 unearth 3 dig out —ex'ca·va'tion n. —ex'ca·va'tor n.

ex·ceed' v. 1 go beyond (a limit) 2 surpass

ex·ceed'ing a. extreme —ex·ceed'ing·ly adv.

ex·cel' v. -celled', -cel'ling be better than

Ex'cel·len·cy n., pl. -cies title of honor

ex'cel·lent a. unusually good —ex'cel·lence n.

ex·cel'si·or' n. wood shavings used for packing

ex·cept' prep. leaving out; but —v. exclude —except for if it were not for

ex·cept'ing prep. except

ex·cep'tion n. 1 person or thing excluded 2 case to which a rule does not apply 3 objection —take exception to object

ex·cep'tion·al a. 1 unusual 2 gifted or handicapped

ex'cerpt' (v.: ek surpt') n. passage selected from a book, etc. —v. select; extract

ex·cess' (a.: ek'ses') n. 1 more than is needed 2 surplus —a. extra —ex·ces'sive a.

ex·change' v. 1 to trade; barter 2 to interchange —n. 1 an exchanging 2 thing exchanged 3 place for exchanging —ex·change'a·ble a.

ex·cheq'uer (-chek'ər) n. 1 treasury 2 funds

ex·cise' (v.: ek siz') n. tax on certain goods within a country: also excise tax —v. cut out —ex·ci'sion (-sizh'ən) n.

ex·cite' v. 1 make active 2 arouse; stir the feelings of —ex·cit'a·ble a. —ex·cite'ment n.

ex·claim' v. utter sharply —ex'cla·ma'tion n.

ex·clude' v. keep out or shut out —ex·clu'sion n.

ex·clu'sive a. 1 not shared 2 snobbish —exclusive of not including —ex·clu'sive·ly adv.

ex·com·mu'ni·cate' v. expel from communion with a church —ex·com·mu'ni·ca'tion n.

ex·co'ri·ate' (-kôr'ē-) v. denounce

ex·cre'ment n. waste material from the bowels

ex·crete' v. eliminate (waste) from the body —ex·cre'tion n. —ex'cre·to'ry a.

ex·cru'ci·at'ing (-shē āt'-) a. very painful; agonizing

ex·cur'sion n. short trip, esp. for pleasure

ex·cuse' (ek skyōōz'; n.: ek skyōōs') v. 1 apologize for 2 overlook (an offense or fault) 3 release from a duty, etc. 4 let leave 5 justify —n. 1 apology 2 something that excuses 3 pretext —ex·cus'a·ble a.

ex'e·cra·ble a. detestable

ex'e·cute' v. 1 carry out; do 2 put to death legally 3 make valid (a will, etc.) —ex'e·cu'tion n.

ex'e·cu'tion·er n. official who puts to death legally

ex·ec'u·tive a. 1 having to do with managing 2 administering laws, etc. —n. one who administers affairs

ex·ec'u·tor n. one who carries out the provisions of a legal will

ex·em'plar (-plər, -plär') n. model; pattern

ex·em'pla·ry a. serving as a model or example

ex·em'pli·fy' v. -fied', -fy'ing show by example

ex·empt' v., a. free(d) from a rule or obligation —ex·emp'tion n.

ex'er·cise' n. 1 active use 2 activity to develop the body, a skill, etc. 3 pl. program, as at a graduation ceremony —v. 1 use 2 do or give exercises

ex·ert' v. put into action

ex·er'tion n. 1 act of exerting 2 effort

ex·hale' v. breathe forth —ex'ha·la'tion n.

ex·haust' v. 1 use up 2 drain 3 tire out —n. discharge from an engine —ex·haust'i·ble a. —ex·haus'tion n.

ex·haus'tive a. thorough

ex·hib'it (eg zib'-) v., n. show; display —ex·hib'i·tor n.

ex'hi·bi'tion (eks'ə-) n. 1 a (public) showing 2 that which is shown

ex·hi·bi'tion·ist n. one who likes to show off —ex·hi·bi'tion·ism' n.

ex·hil'a·rate' (eg zil'-) v. stimulate —ex·hil'a·ra'tion n.

ex·hort' (eg zôrt') v. urge earnestly —ex'hor·ta'tion n.

ex·hume' v. dig out of the earth

ex'i·gen·cy n., pl. -cies urgency

ex'ile' n. 1 a prolonged, often

---

en·forced, living away from one's country **2** person in exile —v. send into exile

ex·ist' v. **1** be **2** occur **3** live —**ex·ist'ence** n.

ex·is·ten'tial a. of existence

ex'it n. a (way of) leaving

ex'o·dus n. departure

ex of·fi·ci·o (ə fish'ē ō') adv. by virtue of one's position

ex·on'er·ate v. to free from blame

ex·or'bi·tant a. excessive —**ex·or'bi·tance** n.

ex'or·cise', ex'or·cize' v. drive out (an evil spirit), as by magic —**ex'or·cism'** n.

ex·ot'ic a. **1** foreign **2** strangely beautiful, etc.

ex·pand' v. **1** spread out **2** enlarge —**ex·pan'sion** n.

ex·panse' n. wide extent

ex·pan'sive a. **1** broad **2** warm and open in talk, etc.

ex·pa'ti·ate (-pā'shē-) v. speak or write at length

ex·pa'tri·ate' (-āt'; n., a.: -ət) v., n., a. exile(d)

ex·pect' v. **1** look for as likely or due **2** [Col.] suppose —**be expecting** [Col.] be pregnant —**ex·pect'an·cy** n. —**ex·pect'ant** a. —**ex·pec·ta'tion** n.

ex·pec'to·rant n. medicine to bring up phlegm

ex·pec'to·rate' v. to spit

ex·pe'di·ent a. **1** useful for the purpose **2** based on self-interest —n. a means to an end —**ex·pe'di·en·cy** n.

ex·pe·dite' v. speed up; facilitate —**ex'pe·dit'er** n.

ex·pe·di'tion n. **1** a journey, as for exploration **2** those on such a journey

ex·pe·di'tious (-dish'əs) a. prompt

ex·pel' v. **-pelled', -pel'ling 1** force out **2** dismiss by authority

ex·pend' v. spend; use up —**ex·pend'a·ble** a.

ex·pend'i·ture n. **1** spending of money, time, etc. **2** amount spent

ex·pense' n. **1** cost **2** pl. the charges met with in one's work, etc.

ex·pen'sive a. high-priced

ex·pe'ri·ence n. **1** a living through an event **2** thing one has done or lived through **3** skill gotten by training, work, etc. —v. have experience of

ex·per'i·ment n., v. test to discover or prove something —**ex·**

---

per'i·men'tal a. —**ex·per'i·men·ta'tion** n.

ex'pert a. very skillful —n. one with great skill or knowledge in a field

ex'per·tise' (-tēz', -tēs') n. skill or knowledge of an expert

ex'pi·ate v. atone for —**ex'pi·a'tion** n.

ex·pire' v. **1** die **2** end **3** exhale —**ex'pi·ra'tion** n.

ex·plain' v. **1** make plain or understandable **2** account for —**ex'pla·na'tion** n. —**ex·plan'a·to'ry** a.

ex'ple·tive n. oath or exclamation

ex'pli·cate' v. explain fully

ex·plic'it a. clearly stated; definite

ex·plode' v. **1** burst noisily **2** discredit —**ex·plo'sion** n.

ex'ploit' (v.: ek sploit') n. bold deed —v. use to advantage —**ex'ploi·ta'tion** n.

ex·plore' v. **1** investigate **2** travel in (a region) for discovery —**ex'plo·ra'tion** n. —**ex·plor'a·to'ry** a.

ex·plo'sive a. of or like an explosion —n. substance that can explode

ex·po'nent n. **1** interpreter **2** example or symbol **3** Math. symbol at upper right showing times as a factor

ex·port' (n.: eks'pôrt') v. send (goods) to another country for sale —n. something exported —**ex'por·ta'tion** n.

ex·pose' v. **1** lay open, as to danger **2** reveal **3** to subject photographic film to light —**ex·po'sure** n.

ex·po·sé' (-zā') n. disclosure of a scandal

ex'po·si'tion n. **1** explanation **2** public exhibition

ex·pos'i·to'ry a. explaining

ex·pos'tu·late' (-päs'chə-) v. reason with a person in protest

ex·pound' v. explain fully

ex·press' v. **1** put into words **2** reveal; show **3** symbolize —a. **1** explicit **2** exact **3** fast and direct —adv. by express —n. an express train, bus, delivery service, etc.

ex·pres'sion n. **1** an expressing or way of expressing **2** certain word or phrase **3** look, etc. that shows how one feels —**ex·pres'sion·less** a. —**ex·pres'sive** a.

ex·press'way' n. divided highway for high-speed traffic

ex·pro'pri·ate' v. take (land, etc.) for public use —**ex·pro'pri·a'tion** n.

ex·pul'sion n. an expelling or being expelled

ex·punge' v. erase

ex'pur·gate' v. delete (from) as a censor

ex'qui·site a. 1 beautiful, delicate, etc. 2 very keen

ex'tant a. still existing

ex·tem·po·re (-rē) adv., a. without preparation: also **ex·tem'po·ra'ne·ous** a.

ex·tem'po·rize' v. speak, do, etc. extempore

ex·tend' v. 1 prolong 2 expand 3 stretch forth 4 offer

ex·ten'sion n. 1 an extending 2 an addition

ex·ten'sive a. vast; far-reaching

ex·tent' n. 1 size 2 scope 3 vast area

ex·ten'u·ate' v. lessen the seriousness of (an offense)

ex·te'ri·or a. on or from the outside —n. the outside

ex·ter'mi·nate' v. to destroy entirely —**ex·ter'mi·na'tion** n. —**ex·ter'mi·na'tor** n.

ex·ter'nal a. 1 on or from the outside 2 superficial

ex·tinct' a. no longer existing or active

ex·tinc'tion n. a dying out; annihilation

ex·tin'guish v. 1 put out (a fire) 2 destroy

ex'tir·pate' v. root out

ex·tol', ex·toll' v. -tolled', -tol'ling praise highly

ex·tort' v. get (money) by threats, etc. —**ex·tor'tion** n.

ex'tra a. more than expected; additional —n. extra person or thing —adv. especially

extra- pref. outside, besides

ex·tract' v. (n.: eks'trakt') v. 1 pull out 2 get by pressing, distilling, etc. 3 select —n. something extracted —**ex·trac'tion** n.

ex'tra·cur·ric'u·lar a. not part of required curriculum

ex'tra·dite' v. return (a fugitive) —**ex'tra·di'tion** n.

ex'tra·ne'ous a. 1 from outside 2 not pertinent

ex'tra·or'di·nar'y (ek strôr'-) a. very unusual

ex·trap'o·late' v. to estimate on basis of known facts —**ex·trap'o·la'tion** n.

ex'tra·sen'so·ry a. apart from normal sense perception

ex·trav'a·gant a. 1 excessive 2 wasteful —**ex·trav'a·gance** n.

ex·trav·a·gan'za n. spectacular show

ex·treme' a. 1 utmost 2 final 3 excessive or drastic 4 radical —n. extreme degree, state, etc. —**ex·treme'ly** adv.

ex·trem'i·ty (ek strem'-) n., pl. -ties 1 end 2 extreme need, danger, etc. 3 pl. hands and feet

ex'tri·cate' v. set free

ex·trin'sic (-sik, -zik) a. 1 not essential 2 external

ex'tro·vert' n. one not given to introspection —**ex'tro·ver'sion** n. —**ex'tro·vert'ed** a.

ex·trude' v. 1 force through a small opening 2 project —**ex·tru'sion** n.

ex·u'ber·ant a. 1 very healthy and lively 2 luxuriant —**ex·u'ber·ance** n.

ex·ude' v. 1 discharge 2 radiate

ex·ult' v. rejoice greatly —**ex·ult'ant** a. —**ex·ul·ta'tion** n.

eye n. 1 organ of sight 2 vision 3 a look 4 attention —v. eyed, **eye'ing** or **ey'ing** look at

eye'ball' n. ball-shaped part of the eye

eye'brow' n. bony arch over the eye, or the hair on this

eye'ful' n. [Sl.] striking person or thing

eye'glass'es n.pl. pair of lenses to help faulty vision

eye'lash' n. hair on the edge of the eyelid

eye'let n. small hole, as for a hook, cord, etc.

eye'lid' n. either of two folds of flesh that cover and uncover the eyeball

eye'-o'pen·er n. surprising news, sudden realization, etc.

eye'sight' n. power of seeing

eye'sore' n. ugly sight

eye'tooth' n., pl. -teeth' upper canine tooth

eye'wit'ness n. one who has seen something happen

F

fa'ble n. 1 brief tale having a moral 2 untrue story

fab'ric n. cloth

fab'ri·cate' v. 1 make 2 make up (a reason, etc.)

fab'u·lous a. 1 fictitious 2 incredible 3 [Col.] wonderful

fa·cade', fa·çade' (fə säd') n. main face of a building

face n. 1 front of the head 2

(main) surface 3 appearance 4
dignity —v. 1 turn, or have the
face turned, toward 2 confront
—**make a face** to grimace —**on
the face of it** apparently —**fa'
cial** (-shəl) a.

face'less a. anonymous

face lifting n. 1 plastic surgery
to remove wrinkles from the
face 2 altering of an exterior
Also **face lift**

face'-saving a. preserving one's
self-respect

fac'et (fas'-) n. 1 a surface of a
cut gem 2 aspect

fa·ce·tious (fə sē'shəs) a. joking,
esp. at the wrong time

facial tissue n. soft tissue paper
used as a handkerchief, etc.

fac·ile (fas'əl) a. 1 easy 2 superficial

fa·cil'i·tate' v. make easier

fa·cil'i·ty n., pl. **-ties** 1 ease or
skill 2 pl. things that help do
something 3 building, etc. for
some activity

fac·sim'i·le (-lē) n. exact copy

fact n. 1 actual happening 2
truth —**in fact** really

fac'tion n. 1 clique 2 dissension
—**fac'tion·al** a. —**fac'tious** a.

fac'tor n. 1 causal element 2
Math. any of the quantities
multiplied together

fac'to·ry n., pl. **-ries** building in
which things are manufactured

fac'tu·al (-chōō-) a. of facts; real

fac'ul·ty n., pl. **-ties** 1 natural
power or aptitude 2 staff of
teachers

fad n. passing fashion —**fad'dish**
a.

fade v. 1 (make) lose color or
strength 2 die out

fag v. **fagged**, **fag'ging** make
tired

fag'ot, fag'got n. bundle of sticks
or twigs

Fahr·en·heit (fer'ən hīt') a. of a
thermometer on which the boiling point of water is 212°, the
freezing point 32°

fail v. 1 fall short 2 weaken 3
become bankrupt 4 not succeed
5 neglect 6 not pass a test or
course

fail'ing n. 1 failure 2 fault —
prep. lacking

fail'ure n. 1 act of failing 2 one
that fails

faint a. 1 weak, dim, etc. 2 weak
and dizzy —n. state of temporary unconsciousness —v. fall
into a faint —**faint'ness** n.

fair a. 1 beautiful 2 blond 3

clear and sunny 4 just 5
according to the rules 6 average
—adv. in a fair way —n. exposi-
tion with exhibits, amusements,
etc. —**fairly** adv. —**fair'ness** n.

fair'y n., pl. **-ies** tiny imaginary
being in human form, with
magic powers

faith n. 1 unquestioning belief,
esp. in religion 2 particular religion 3 loyalty

faith'ful a. 1 loyal 2 exact —
faith'ful·ly adv.

faith'less a. disloyal

fake v., n., a. sham

fa·kir (fə kir')' n. Muslim or
Hindu religious mendicant

fa·la'fel (-lä'-) n. deep-fried patty
of ground chickpeas

fal'con (fal'-, fôl'-) n. hawk
trained to hunt —**fal'con·ry** n.

fall v. **fell**, **fall'en**, **fall'ing** 1 to
drop or descend 2 tumble 3
occur —n. 1 a falling 2 autumn
3 overthrow or ruin 4 amount
of what has fallen 5 pl. a waterfall —**fall back** retreat —**fall off**
lessen or worsen —**fall on** (or
upon) to attack —**fall out** quarrel —**fall through** fail —**fall to**
begin

fal'la·cy n., pl. **-cies** 1 false idea;
error 2 false reasoning —**fal·la'-
cious** a.

fal'li·ble a. liable to error —**fal·li-
bil'i·ty** n.

fal·lo'pi·an tube n. [also F- t-]
either of two tubes carrying ova
to the uterus

fall'out' n. 1 descent of radioactive particles after a nuclear
explosion 2 these particles

fal·low (fal'ō) a. 1 plowed but
unplanted 2 inactive

false a. 1 not true 2 lying 3
unfaithful 4 not real —**fal'si·fy'**
v., **-fied'**, **-fy'ing** —**fal'si·ty** n.

false'hood' n. a lie or lying

fal·set'to n. artificial, high-
pitched singing

fal'ter v. 1 stumble 2 stammer
3 waver

fame n. great reputation

fa·mil'iar a. 1 friendly; intimate
2 too intimate; presumptuous 3
closely acquainted (with) 4
well-known —**fa·mil'i·ar'i·ty** n.
—**fa·mil'iar·ize'** v.

fam'i·ly n., pl. **-lies** 1 parents
and their children 2 relatives 3
lineage 4 group of related
things

fam'ine (-in) n. 1 widespread
food shortage 2 starvation

fam'ished a. very hungry

fa'mous _a._ having fame

fan _n._ 1 device to move air for cooling, etc. 2 [Col.] enthusiastic supporter —_v._ **fanned, fan'ning** 1 blow air toward 2 stir up 3 spread (_out_)

fa·nat'ic _a._ too enthusiastic or zealous: also **fa·nat'i·cal** —_n._ fanatic person —**fa·nat'i·cism'** _n._

fan'ci·er _n._ person with a special interest, esp. plant or animal breeding

fan'cy _n., pl._ **-cies** 1 playful imagination 2 notion, whim, etc. 3 a liking —_a._ **-ci·er, -ci·est** 1 extravagant 2 elaborate 3 of superior quality —_v._ **-cied, -cy·ing** 1 imagine 2 be fond of 3 suppose —**fan'ci·ful** _a._ —**fan'ci·ness** _n._

fan'cy-free' _a._ carefree

fan'fare' _n._ 1 blast of trumpets 2 showy display

fang _n._ long, pointed tooth

fan'ta·size' _v._ have fantasies (about)

fan·tas'tic _a._ 1 unreal 2 grotesque 3 extravagant —**fan·tas'ti·cal·ly** _adv._

fan'ta·sy _n., pl._ **-sies** 1 fancy 2 illusion; reverie 3 fantastic poem, play, etc.

far _a._ **far'ther, far'thest** distant —_adv._ 1 very distant 2 very much —**by far** very much —(**in**) **so far as** to the extent that

far'a·way' _a._ distant

farce _n._ 1 exaggerated comedy 2 absurd thing —**far'ci·cal** _a._

fare _v._ get along —_n._ 1 transportation charge 2 paying passenger 3 food

fare·well' (_a._: fer'wel') _int._ good-bye —_a., n._ parting (wishes)

far'-fetched' _a._ not reasonable; strained

far'-flung' _a._ extensive

fa·ri'na _n._ flour or meal eaten as cooked cereal

farm _n._ land used to raise crops or animals —_v._ 1 cultivate (land) 2 let out (work or workers) on contract —**farm'er** _n._ —**farm'house'** _n._ —**farm'ing** _n._

far'-off' _a._ distant

far'-reach'ing _a._ having wide range, influence, etc.

far'sight'ed _a._ 1 planning ahead 2 seeing far objects best

far'ther _a._ 1 more distant 2 additional —_adv._ 1 at or to a greater distance or extent 2 in addition

far'thest _a._ most distant —_adv._

at or to the greatest distance

fas'ci·nate' _v._ hold spellbound; captivate —**fas·ci·na'tion** _n._

fas·cism (fash'iz'əm) _n._ militaristic dictatorship —**fas'cist** _n., a._

fash'ion _n._ 1 kind; sort 2 manner 3 current style —_v._ make; form

fash'ion·a·ble _a._ stylish

fast _a._ 1 firm 2 loyal 3 unfading 4 rapid; quick 5 of loose morals —_adv._ 1 firmly 2 rapidly —_v._ abstain from food —_n._ period of fasting

fas·ten (fas'ən) _v._ 1 attach 2 make secure; fix —**fas'ten·er** _n._

fas'ten·ing _n._ thing used to fasten

fast'-food' _a._ of a business serving quickly prepared food

fas·tid'i·ous _a._ not easy to please; particular

fat _a._ **fat'ter, fat'test** plump —_n._ oily animal substance —**fat'ty** _a._, **-ti·er, -ti·est**

fa'tal _a._ causing death

fa'tal·ism' _n._ belief that all events are destined by fate —**fa'tal·ist** _n._ —**fa'tal·is'tic** _a._

fa·tal'i·ty _n., pl._ **-ties** death caused by disaster

fate _n._ 1 power supposedly making events inevitable 2 one's lot in life 3 outcome 4 death; ruin —**fate'ful** _a._

fat'ed _a._ destined

fa'ther _n._ 1 male parent 2 founder; creator 3 Christian priest —_v._ beget, found, etc. —[**F-**] God —**fa'ther·hood'** _n._ —**fa'ther·ly** _a._

fa'ther-in-law' _n., pl._ **fa'thers-in-law'** father of one's wife or husband

fa'ther·land' _n._ one's native land

fath·om (fath'əm) _n. Naut._ six feet —_v._ understand

fa·tigue' (-tēg') _n._ weariness —_v._ to weary

fat'ten _v._ make or get fat

fat'u·ous (fach'-) _a._ foolish

fau'cet _n._ device with valve to draw liquid from a pipe

fault _n._ 1 flaw 2 error 3 blame —**find fault (with)** criticize —**fault'less** _a._

fault'y _a._ **-i·er, -i·est** defective

faun _n._ Roman deity, half man and half goat

fau'na _n._ the animals of a certain region

faux pas (fō pä') _n., pl._ **faux pas'** (-päz') social blunder

fa'vor _n._ 1 approval 2 partiality 3 kind act 4 small gift —_v._ 1

show favor toward 2 resemble Also, Br. sp., **fa'vour** —**in favor of** approving —**fa'vor·a·ble** a.

fa'vor·ite a., n. preferred (one) —**fa'vor·it·ism'** n.

fawn v. 1 show affection as by licking 2 flatter servilely —n. baby deer

fax n. 1 electronic sending of pictures, print, etc., as over telephone lines 2 device for such sending —v. send by fax

faze v. [Col.] disturb

fear n. 1 anxious anticipation of danger, pain, etc. 2 awe —v. 1 be afraid (of) 2 be in awe (of) —**fear'ful** a. —**fear'less** a.

fea'si·ble (fē'zə-) a. 1 possible 2 probable 3 suitable —**fea'si·bil'i·ty** n.

feast n. 1 religious festival 2 banquet —v. 1 have a feast (for) 2 delight

feat n. bold and daring deed

feath'er n. 1 one of the outgrowths covering a bird 2 kind —**feath'er·y** a.

fea'ture n. 1 pl. form of the face or its parts 2 special part, article, etc. 3 main attraction —v. make a feature of

Feb'ru·ar'y (-rōō-, -yōō-) n. second month

fe'ces' (-sēz') n.pl. excrement —**fe'cal** (-kəl) a.

fe'cund a. fertile

fed'er·al a. of a union of states under a central government 2 of the central government, esp. [F-] of the U.S.

fed'er·ate' v. unite in a federation

fed'er·a'tion n. union of states or groups; league

fe·do'ra n. man's felt hat

fee n. charge for some service or right

fee'ble a. weak; not strong —**fee'bly** adv.

feed v. fed, feed'ing 1 give food to 2 supply as fuel, material, etc. 3 gratify 4 eat —n. fodder

feed'back' n. 1 transfer of part of the output back to the input, as of electricity or information 2 a response

feel v. felt, feel'ing 1 touch 2 have a feeling (of) 3 be aware of 4 believe 5 be or seem to be 6 grope —n. 1 sense of touch 2 way a thing feels —**feel like** [Col.] have a desire for

feel'er n. 1 antenna or other organ of touch 2 remark or offer made to elicit opinions

feel'ing n. 1 sense of touch 2 sensation 3 an emotion 4 pl. sensitiveness 5 sympathy 6 opinion

feet n. pl. of FOOT

feign (fān) v. 1 make up (an excuse) 2 pretend

feint (fānt) n. pretended attack, as in boxing —v. make a feint

feist·y (fīs'tē) a. -i·er, -i·est [Col.] 1 lively 2 quarrelsome, belligerent, etc.

feld'spar' n. hard, crystalline mineral

fe·lic'i·tate' (-lis'-) v. congratulate —**fe·lic'i·ta'tion** n.

fe·lic'i·tous a. appropriate

fe·lic'i·ty n. 1 happiness 2 pl. -ties apt and pleasant expression

fe'line a. of or like a cat —n. a cat

fell v. 1 pt. of FALL 2 knock down 3 cut down

fel'low n. 1 an associate 2 an equal 3 a mate 4 man or boy —a. associated —**fel'low·ship'** n.

fel'on n. criminal

fel'o·ny n. major crime —**fe·lo'ni·ous** a.

felt n. fabric made of fibers pressed together

fe'male a. 1 designating or of the sex that bears offspring 2 feminine —n. female person or animal

fem'i·nine (-nin) a. of or like women or girls; female —**fem'i·nin'i·ty** n.

fem'i·nism' n. movement to win equal rights for women —**fem'i·nist** n., a.

fe'mur n. thighbone

fen n. swamp; bog

fence n. 1 barrier of posts, wire, etc. 2 dealer in stolen goods —v. 1 enclose with a fence 2 engage in fencing —**fenc'er** n.

fenc'ing n. sport of fighting with foils or swords

fend v. ward (off) —**fend for oneself** manage by oneself

fend'er n. a guard over an automobile wheel

fen'nel n. an herb used to flavor

fer·ment' (v.: fər ment') n. 1 thing causing fermentation 2 agitation —v. undergo or cause fermentation (in)

fer'men·ta'tion n. chemical change caused by yeast, bacteria, etc.

fern n. nonflowering plant with fronds

fe·ro'cious (-shəs) a. savage;

fierce —**fe·roc'i·ty** n.

fer'ret n. kind of weasel —v. search (out)

fer'ric, fer'rous a. of iron

Fer'ris wheel n. large, revolving wheel with hanging seats, as in amusement park

fer'ry v. **-ried, -ry·ing** take across a river, etc. in a boat — n., pl. **-ries** boat used for ferrying: also **fer'ry-boat'**

fer'tile (furt'l) a. 1 producing abundantly 2 able to produce young, fruit, etc. —**fer·til'i·ty** n.

fer·til'ize' v. 1 make fertile 3 spread fertilizer on 3 make fruitful by introducing a male germ cell —**fer·til·i·za'tion** n.

fer·til'iz·er n. manure, chemicals, etc. to enrich the soil

fer'vent a. intense; ardent

fer'vid a. fervent

fer'vor n. ardor; zeal

fes'ter v. 1 form pus 2 rankle

fes'ti·val n. time or day of celebration

fes'tive a. joyous; merry

fes·tiv'i·ty n., pl. **-ties** 1 gaiety 2 pl. things done in celebration

fes·toon' n. garland, etc. hanging in loops —v. adorn with festoons

fet'a (cheese) n. soft, white cheese

fetch v. 1 go after and bring back; get 2 sell for

fetch'ing a. attractive

fete, fête (fāt, fet) n. festival; outdoor party —v. honor with a fete; entertain

fet'id a. stinking

fet'ish n. 1 object thought to have magic power 2 object of irrational devotion

fet'lock' n. leg joint above a horse's hoof

fet'ter n. ankle shackle —v. restrain as with fetters

fet'tle n. used chiefly in fine fettle, in good condition

fe'tus n. unborn young —**fe'tal** a.

feud (fyo͞od) n. deadly quarrel, as between families —v. engage in a feud

feu'dal·ism' n. medieval system with lords, vassals, and serfs —**feu'dal** a.

fe'ver n. abnormally high body temperature —**fe'ver·ish'** a.

few a. not many —pron., n. a small number

fez n. conical Turkish hat

fi·an·cé (fē'än sā') n. man to whom one is betrothed —**fi'an·**

cée' (-sā') n.fem.

fi·as'co (fē-) n., pl. **-coes** or **-cos** utter failure

fi'at' (fī'-, fē'-) n. a decree

fib n. petty lie —v. **fibbed, fib'bing** tell a fib

fi'ber, fi'bre n. 1 threadlike part(s) forming organic tissue 2 threadlike part(s) used for weaving, etc. —**fi'brous** a.

Fi'ber-glass' trademark material made of fine filaments of glass —n. [f-] this material: also **fiber glass**

fi'ber-op'tic a. of synthetic fibers for transmitting light

fi'broid' a. like or made of fibrous tissue

fi·bro'sis n. abnormal growth of fibrous tissue

fib'u·la (-yo͞o-) n., pl. **-lae'** (-lē') or **-las** thinner bone of lower leg

fick'le a. tending to change one's mind

fic'tion n. literary work(s) with imaginary characters and events —**fic'tion·al** a.

fic·ti'tious (-tish'əs) a. imaginary

fi'cus n., pl. **-cus** tropical plant with leathery leaves

fid'dle n. [Col.] violin —v. 1 [Col.] play a violin 2 fidget (with) —**fid'dler** n.

fi·del'i·ty n. faithfulness

fidg'et (fij'-) v. make nervous movements —**fidg'et·y** a.

fie (fī) int. shame!

field n. 1 piece of open land, esp. one for crops, grazing, etc. 2 expanse 3 area for athletic event 4 sphere of knowledge or activity 5 all contestants

field glasses n.pl. portable, telescopic eyeglasses

fiend (fēnd) n. 1 devil 2 [Col.] addict —**fiend'ish** a.

fierce a. 1 savage; wild 2 violent —**fierce'ly** adv.

fi'er·y a. **-i·er, -i·est** 1 flaming, hot, etc. 2 ardent

fi·es'ta (fē-) n. festival

fife n. small, shrill flute

fif'teen' a., n. five more than ten —**fif'teenth'** a., n.

fifth a. preceded by four others —n. 1 one after the fourth 2 one of five equal parts 3 fifth of a gallon

fif'ty a., n., pl. **-ties** five times ten —**fif'ti·eth** a., n.

fig n. sweet, chewy fruit with seed-filled pulp

fight n., v. **fought, fight'ing** struggle; battle; contest —**fighter** n.

fig'ment n. thing imagined

fig'ur·a·tive' a. using metaphors, similes, etc.

fig'ure n. 1 outline; shape 2 person 3 likeness of a person or thing 4 illustration 5 design 6 a number 7 sum of money —v. 1 compute 2 be conspicuous 3 [Col.] predict —**figure out** solve

fig'ure·head' n. leader with no real power

fig'u·rine' (-rēn') n. small statue

fil'a·ment n. threadlike part

fil'bert n. hazelnut

filch v. steal (something trivial)

file n. 1 container for keeping papers in order 2 orderly arrangement of papers, etc. 3 line of persons or things 4 ridged tool for scraping, etc. —v. 1 put papers, etc. in order 2 move in a file 3 smooth or grind with a file

fi·let (fi lā') n., v. fillet

filet mi·gnon (min yōn') n. thick cut of beef tenderloin

fil'i·bus'ter n. obstruction of a bill in a legislature, as by a long speech —v. obstruct a bill in this way

fil'i·gree' n. lacelike work of fine wire

fil'ings n.pl. small pieces scraped off with a file

fill v. 1 make or become full 2 put into or hold (a job or office) 3 supply things ordered —n. anything that fills —**fill in** 1 make complete 2 substitute —**fill out** 1 make or become larger, etc. 2 complete (a blank form)

fil·let (fi lā') n. boneless piece of fish or meat —v. to bone (fish, etc.)

fill'ing n. thing used to fill something else

fil'lip n. stimulus; tonic

fil'ly n., pl. -lies young mare

film n. 1 thin coating 2 flexible cellulose material used in photography 3 a) series of pictures flashed on a screen in rapid succession so that things in them seem to move b) story in this form —v. make a FILM (n. 3)

film'y a. -i·er, -i·est blurred

fil'ter n. thing used for straining out particles, etc. from a fluid, etc. —v. 1 pass through a filter 2 remove with a filter 3 pass slowly —**fil·tra'tion** n.

filth n. 1 foul dirt 2 obscenity —**filth'i·ness** n. —**filth'y** a., -i·er, -i·est

fin n. winglike, membranous organ on a fish

fi·na·gle v. use, or get by, trickery —**fi·na'gler** n.

fi'nal a. 1 last 2 conclusive —n. pl. last of a series of contests —**fi·nal'i·ty** n. —**fi'nal·ly** adv. —**fi'nal·ist** n. —**fi'nal·ize'** v.

fi·na'le (-nal'ē) n. last part of a musical work

fi·nance' (or fi'nans) n. 1 pl. funds 2 science of managing money matters —v. supply money for —**fi·nan'cial** (-shəl) a. —**fin'an·cier'** (-sir') n.

finch n. small songbird

find v. found, find'ing 1 come upon; discover 2 learn 3 recover (a thing lost) 4 decide —n. something found

fine a. 1 excellent 2 not heavy or coarse 3 sharp 4 discriminating 5 very well —n. money paid as a penalty —v. cause to pay a fine

fine arts n.pl. painting, sculpture, music, etc.

fin'er·y n. showy clothes

fi·nesse' n. skill in handling delicate situations

fin'ger n. any of the parts (five with the thumb) at the end of the hand —v. to handle —**fin'ger·nail'** n. —**fin'ger·tip'** n.

fin'ger·board' n. part of a stringed instrument to which the strings are pressed

fin'ger·print' n. impression of the lines of a fingertip

fin'ick·y a. too particular; fussy

fin'ish v. 1 to end 2 complete 3 use up 4 perfect; polish —n. 1 last part; end 2 polish or perfection 3 way a surface is finished

fi'nite' a. having limits

Finn'ish a., n. (of) the people or language of Finland

fiord (fyôrd) n. sea inlet bordered by steep cliffs

fir n. evergreen tree

fire n. 1 flame 2 thing burning 3 ardor 4 discharge of guns —v. 1 make burn 2 shoot (a gun, etc.) 3 discharge from a job —**on fire** burning —**under fire** under attack —**fire'proof'** a.

fire'arm' n. rifle, pistol, etc.

fire'bomb' n. incendiary bomb —v. attack, etc. with a firebomb

fire'crack'er n. noisy explosive rolled in paper

fire engine n. truck equipped for firefighting

fire'fight'er n. one who fights fires —**fire'fight'ing** n.

fire'fly' n. winged beetle with a glowing abdomen

fire'man n., pl. **-men** 1 firefighter 2 stoker

fire'place' n. place built in a wall for a fire

fire'plug' n. street hydrant

fire'trap' n. building unsafe in the case of fire

fire'wood' n. wood used as fuel

fire'works' n.pl. firecrackers, rockets, etc. for noisy or brilliant displays

firm a. 1 solid 2 fixed; stable 3 strong and steady —v. make firm —n. business company — **firm'ness** n.

fir'ma·ment n. [Poet.] sky

first a., adv. before any others — n. 1 first one 2 beginning

first aid n. emergency care for injuries —**first'-aid'** a.

first'-class' a. of the highest quality —adv. with the best accommodations

first'hand' a., adv. from the source; direct(ly)

first'-rate' a. excellent

fis'cal a. financial

fish n., pl. **fish**; for different kinds, **fish'es** coldblooded animal with gills and fins, living in water —v. 1 to catch fish 2 angle (for) —**fish'er·man** n., pl. **-men** —**fish'er·y** n., pl. **-ies**

fish'y a. **-i·er**, **-i·est** 1 like a fish 2 [Col.] questionable

fis'sion (fish'ən) n. a splitting apart

fis'sure (fish'ər) n. a cleft or crack

fist n. clenched hand

fist'ful n. handful

fist'i·cuffs' n.pl. boxing

fit v. **fit'ted** or **fit**, **fit'ting** 1 be suitable to 2 be the proper size, etc. (for) 3 adjust to fit 4 equip —a. **fit'ter**, **fit'test** 1 suited 2 proper 3 healthy —n. 1 way of fitting 2 seizure as of coughing 3 outburst —**fit'ness** n.

fit'ful a. not regular; spasmodic

fit'ting a. proper —n. 1 adjustment 2 pl. fixtures

five a., n. one more than four

fix v. 1 fasten or set firmly 2 determine 3 adjust or repair 4 prepare (food, etc.) 5 [Col.] influence by bribery, etc. —n. 1 [Col.] predicament 2 [Sl.] clear understanding —**fix up** [Col.] set in order —**fixed** a.

fix·a'tion n. obsession

fix'ings' n.pl. [Col.] accessories or trimmings

fix'ture n. any of the attached furnishings of a house

fizz v., n. (make) a hissing, bubbling sound

fiz'zle v. 1 to fizz 2 [Col.] fail

flab n. [Col.] sagging flesh

flab'ber·gast' v. amaze

flab'by a. **-bi·er**, **-bi·est** 1 limp and soft 2 weak

flac'cid (flak'sid, flas'id) a. flabby

flag n. 1 cloth with colors or designs, used as a national symbol, etc. 2 iris (flower) —v. **flagged**, **flag'ging** 1 to signal with flags 2 grow weak —**flag'pole'**, **flag'staff'** n.

flag'el·late' (flaj'-) v. to whip — **flag'el·la'tion** n.

flag'on (flag'-) n. container for liquids

fla'grant a. glaringly bad —**fla'gran·cy** n.

flag'ship' n. 1 commander's ship 2 chief member of a network

flag'stone' n. flat paving stone

flail n. implement used to thresh grain by hand —v. 1 use a flail 2 beat

flair n. aptitude; knack

flak n. 1 fire of antiaircraft guns 2 [Col.] criticism

flake n. 1 soft, thin mass 2 chip or peeling —v. form into flakes —**flak'y** a., **-i·er**, **-i·est**

flam·bé (fläm bā') a. served with flaming rum, etc.

flam'boy·ant a. showy —**flam'boy·ance** n.

flame n. tongue(s) of fire; blaze —v. burst into flame

fla·men'co n. Spanish gypsy music or dancing

fla·min'go n. pink, long-legged wading bird

flam'ma·ble a. easily set on fire

flange (flanj) n. projecting rim on a wheel, etc.

flank n. 1 side of an animal between the ribs and the hip 2 side of anything —v. be at, or go around, the side of

flan'nel n. soft, napped cloth of wool, etc.

flap n. 1 flat, loose piece 2 motion or sound of a swinging flap —v. flutter

flare v. 1 blaze up 2 spread outward —n. 1 bright, unsteady blaze 2 brief, dazzling signal light 3 sudden outburst 4 a spreading outward

flare'-up' n. sudden outburst

flash v. 1 send out a sudden, brief light 2 sparkle 3 move suddenly 4 [Col.] show briefly —n. 1 sudden, brief light 2 an instant 3 bit of late news

flash'back' n. interruption in a story by a return to some earlier episode

flash'card' n. one of a set of cards used as an aid to memorizing

flash'ing n. metal roofing for joints, etc.

flash'light' n. portable electric light

flash'y a. -i·er, -i·est gaudy; showy

flask n. kind of bottle

flat a. **flat'ter, flat'test** 1 smooth and level 2 broad and thin 3 lying spread out 4 absolute 5 without taste or sparkle 6 dull; lifeless 7 emptied of air 8 Mus. below true pitch —adv. in a flat way —n. 1 flat surface or part 2 deflated tire 3 Mus. note ½ step below another; symbol (b) 4 apartment —**flat'ten** v.

flat'bed' n. trailer, etc. having no sides

flat'car' n. railroad car without sides

flat'fish' n. fish with a very broad, flat body

flat'foot' n. foot with the sole's arch flattened

flat'-out' a. [Col.] 1 at full, speed, effort, etc. 2 absolute

flat'ter v. 1 praise insincerely 2 gratify the vanity of —**flat'ter·y** n.

flat'u·lent (flach'ə-) a. having or making gas in the stomach

flat'ware' n. flat tableware

flaunt (flônt) v. show off

fla'vor n. taste of a substance — v. give flavor to

fla'vor·ing n. added essence, etc. that flavors food

flaw n. defect —**flawed** a. — **flaw'less** a.

flax n. plant with fibers that are spun into linen thread

flax'en a. pale yellow

flay v. strip the skin from

flea n. small jumping insect that is parasitic

fleck n., v. spot

fledg'ling (flej'-) n. young bird just able to fly

flee v. **fled, flee'ing** escape swiftly, as from danger

fleece n. wool covering a sheep —v. to swindle —**fleec'y** a. -i·er, -i·est

fleet n. 1 group of warships under one command 2 any

similar group, as of trucks, planes, etc. —a. swift

fleet'ing a. passing swiftly

flesh n. 1 tissue between the skin and bones 2 pulp of fruits and vegetables 3 the body — **flesh'y** a., -i·er, -i·est

flew v. pt. of FLY

flex v. 1 bend, as an arm 2 contract, as a muscle

flex'i·ble a. 1 easily bent; pliable 2 adaptable

flick n. light, quick stroke —v. strike, throw, etc. with such a stroke

flick'er v. move, burn, or shine unsteadily —n. dart of flame or light

fli'er n. 1 aviator 2 handbill or leaflet

flight n. 1 act or power of flying 2 distance flown 3 group of things flying together 4 trip by airplane 5 set of stairs 6 a fleeing —**flight'less** a.

flight'y a. -i·er, -i·est unsettled; frivolous

flim'sy a. -si·er, -si·est 1 easily broken 2 trivial

flinch v. draw back, as from a blow

fling v. throw with force —n. 1 a flinging 2 [Col.] a try 3 [Col.] brief love affair

flint n. a hard quartz

flip v. **flipped, flip'ping** toss with a quick jerk —a. [Col.] flippant

flip'pant a. frivolous and disrespectful —**flip'pan·cy** n.

flip'per n. flat limb adapted for swimming, as in seals

flirt v. 1 play at love 2 trifle —n. one who plays at love —**flir·ta'tion** n. —**flir·ta'tious** a.

flit v. **flit'ted, flit'ting** move lightly and rapidly

float n. 1 thing that stays on the surface of a liquid 2 flat, decorated vehicle in a parade —v. 1 stay on the surface of a liquid 2 drift gently in air, etc. 3 put into circulation, as a bond issue

flock n. group, esp. of animals — v. gather in a flock

floe n. large sheet of floating ice

flog v. **flogged, flog'ging** beat, thrash, or whip

flood n. 1 overflowing of water on land 2 great outpouring —v. to overflow

flood'light' n. lamp casting a very bright, broad light

floor n. 1 bottom surface of a room, etc. 2 story in a building 3 permission to speak —v. 1

furnish with a floor **2** knock down

floor′ing n. material for making a floor

flop v. **flopped, flop′ping 1** move, drop, or flap about clumsily **2** [Col.] fail —n. a flopping —**flop′py** a.

floppy (disk) n. small, flexible computer disk

flo′ra n. the plants of a region

flo′ral a. of or like flowers

flor′id a. **1** ruddy **2** gaudy

flo′rist n. one who grows or sells flowers

floss n. **1** soft, silky fibers **2** dental floss —v. clean (the teeth) with dental floss

flo·til′la n. small fleet

flot′sam n. floating debris or cargo of a shipwreck

flounce v. move with quick, flinging motions —n. a ruffle

floun′der v. struggle or speak clumsily —n. kind of edible flatfish

flour n. a powdery substance ground from grain

flour′ish v. **1** thrive **2** be in one's prime **3** brandish —n. **1** sweeping motion or stroke **2** fanfare

flout v. mock or scorn

flow v. **1** move as water does **2** move smoothly **3** proceed **4** hang loose —n. a flowing or thing that flows

flow′chart′ n. diagram showing steps in a process

flow′er n. **1** petals and pistil of a plant **2** a plant grown for its blossoms **3** best part —v. **1** to produce blossoms **2** become its best

flow′er·y a. **-i·er, -i·est** showy in expression

flown v. pp. of FLY

flu n. influenza

flub [Col.] v. **flubbed, flub′bing** bungle —n. blunder

fluc′tu·ate′ (-choo-) v. keep changing, as prices

flue n. shaft in a chimney

flu′ent a. speaking or writing easily —**flu′en·cy** n.

fluff n. loose, soft mass —v. **1** make fluffy **2** bungle

fluff′y a. **-i·er, -i·est** soft and light

flu′id a. **1** able to flow **2** not fixed —n. liquid or gas —**flu·id′i·ty** n.

fluke n. **1** anchor blade **2** [Col.] stroke of luck

flung v. pt. & pp. of FLING

flunk v. [Col.] to fail

flunk′y n., pl. **-ies** low, servile person

flu·o·res′cent a. giving off cool light —**flu·o·res′cence** n.

flu·o′ri·date′ (flôr′ə-) v. add fluorides to (water) —**flu·o·ri·da′tion** n.

flu·o·ride′ (flôr′īd′) n. fluorine salt

flu·o·rine (flôr′ēn′) n. yellowish gas, a chemical element

flu′o·ro·scope′ (flôr′ə-) n. kind of X-ray machine

flur′ry n., pl. **-ries 1** gust of wind, rain, or snow **2** sudden commotion

flush v. **1** to redden in the face **2** start up from cover, as a bird **3** wash out —n. a blush; glow —a. **1** well-supplied **2** level (with) **3** direct

flus′ter v. make confused

flute n. tubelike wind instrument —**flut′ist** n.

flut′ed a. grooved

flut′ter v. wave, move, or beat rapidly or irregularly —n. **1** a fluttering **2** confusion —**flut′ter·y** a.

flux n. **1** a flowing **2** constant change **3** substance used to help metals fuse

fly v. **flew** (or v. **5**) **flied, flown** (or v. **5**) **flied, fly′ing 1** move through the air by using wings **2** wave or float in the air **3** move swiftly **4** flee **5** hit a fly in baseball **6** travel in or pilot (aircraft) —n., pl. **flies 1** flap concealing buttons, etc. in a garment **2** baseball batted high **3** winged insect

fly′er n. flier

flying saucer n. unidentified flying object

fly′leaf′ n. blank leaf at the front or back of a book

fly′wheel′ n. wheel that regulates a machine's speed

foal n. young horse

foam n. **1** bubbly mass on liquids **2** spongy mass of rubber, plastic, etc. —v. form foam —**foam′y** a., **-i·er, -i·est**

foam rubber n. rubber foam

fob n. pocket-watch chain or ornament on it

fo′cus n., pl. **-cus·es** or **-ci′** (-sī′) **1** point where rays of light meet **2** adjustment of lens distance for clear image **3** center of activity —v. **1** bring into focus **2** concentrate —**fo′cal** a.

fod'der n. coarse food for cattle, horses, etc.

foe n. enemy

fog n. 1 thick mist 2 mental confusion —v. **fogged**, **fog'ging** make or become foggy —**fog'gy** a., **-gi·er**, **-gi·est** —**fog'gi·ness** n.

fog'horn' n. horn blown to warn ships in a fog

fo·gy (fō'gē) n., pl. **-gies** old-fashioned person

foi'ble n. small weakness in character

foil v. thwart —n. 1 thin fencing sword 2 thin sheet of metal 3 one that enhances another by contrast

foist v. impose by fraud

fold v. 1 double (material) over 2 intertwine 3 wrap up —n. 1 folded layer 2 pen for sheep

-fold suf. times as many

fold'er n. 1 folded sheet of cardboard to hold papers 2 booklet of folded sheets

fo'li·age n. plant leaves

fo'li·o' n., pl. **-os'** largest regular size of book

folk n., pl. **folk** or **folks** people —a. of the common people

folk'lore' n. beliefs, legends, etc. of a people

folk'sy a. **-si·er**, **-si·est** [Col.] friendly or sociable

fol'li·cle n. small sac or gland, as in the skin

fol'low v. 1 come or go after 2 go along 3 take up (a trade) 4 result (from) 5 obey 6 pay attention to 7 understand —**follow out** (or **up**) carry out fully —**fol'low·er** n.

fol'low·ing a. next after —n. group of followers

fol'ly n., pl. **-lies** foolish state, action, belief, etc.

fo·ment' v. incite

fond a. loving; tender —**fond of** liking —**fond'ly** adv.

fon'dle v. to caress

fon·due', fon·du' n. oil, melted cheese, etc. for dipping cubes of meat, bread, etc.

font n. basin for holy water

food n. substance taken in by an animal or plant to enable it to live and grow

fool n. 1 silly person 2 dupe —v. 1 be silly or playful 2 trick

fool'har'dy a. **-di·er**, **-di·est** foolishly daring; rash

fool'ish a. silly; unwise

fool'proof' a. simple, safe, etc.

foot n., pl. **feet** 1 end part of the leg, on which one stands 2 bottom; base 3 measure of length, 12 inches —v. [Col.] pay (a bill) —**on foot** walking —**under foot** in the way

foot'ball' n. 1 team game played on a field with an inflated leather ball 2 this ball

foot'hill' n. low hill at the foot of a mountain

foot'hold' n. place for the feet, as in climbing

foot'ing n. 1 secure placing of the feet 2 basis for relationship

foot'lights' n.pl. lights at the front of a stage floor

foot'loose' a. free to go or do as one likes

foot'note' n. note at the bottom of a page

foot'print' n. mark left by a foot

foot'step' n. 1 sound of a step 2 footprint

foot'stool' n. stool for a seated person's feet

fop n. vain man fussy about his clothes, etc. —**fop'pish** a.

for prep. 1 in place of 2 in the interest of 3 in favor of 4 with the purpose of 5 in search of 6 meant to be received, used, etc. 7 with respect to 8 because of 9 to the extent or duration of —con. because

for'age n. fodder —v. to search for food

for'ay n., v. raid

for·bear' v. **-bore'**, **-borne'**, **-bear'ing** 1 refrain (from) 2 control oneself —**for·bear'ance** n.

for·bid' v. **-bade'** (-bad') or **-bad'**, **-bid'den**, **-bid'ding** not permit; prohibit

for·bid'ding a. frightening

force n. 1 strength; power 2 coercion 3 effectiveness 4 organized group, as an army —v. 1 make do something; compel 2 break open 3 impose, produce, etc. by force —**force'ful** a.

for'ceps n., pl. **-ceps'** small tongs or pincers

for'ci·ble a. with force —**for'ci·bly** adv.

ford n. shallow place in a river —v. cross at a ford

fore adv., a., n. (in or toward) the front part —int. Golf warning shout

fore- pref. before; in front

fore'arm' n. arm between the elbow and wrist

fore'bear' n. ancestor

fore·bode' v. foretell

fore·cast v. **-cast'** or **-cast'ed,** **-cast'ing** predict —n. prediction —**fore'cast'er** n.

fore·cas·tle (fōk'səl, fôr'kas'əl) n. forward deck or front part of a ship

fore·close' v. take away the right to redeem (a mortgage) —**fore·clo'sure** n.

fore·fa·ther n. ancestor

fore·fin·ger n. finger nearest the thumb

fore'front' n. extreme front

fore'go'ing a. preceding

fore·gone' a. previous

fore'ground' n. part of a scene nearest the viewer

fore'hand' n. racket stroke with palm of hand turned forward

fore'head' n. part of the face above the eyebrows

for'eign (-in) a. **1** of or from another country **2** not characteristic —**for'eign-born'** a. —**for'eign·er** n.

fore'leg' n. front leg of animal

fore'man n., pl. **-men 1** man in charge of workers **2** chairman of a jury

fore'most' a., adv. first

fore'noon' n. time before noon

fo·ren'sic a. **1** of or suitable for public debate **2** of scientific techniques of crime investigation

fore'play' n. touching, etc. before sexual intercourse

fore'run'ner n. person or thing foretelling another

fore·see' v. **-saw', -seen', -see'ing** see or know beforehand

fore·shad'ow v. presage

fore'sight' n. **1** power to foresee **2** prudence

fore'skin' n. fold of skin over the end of the penis

for'est n. tract of land covered with trees

fore·stall' v. prevent by acting beforehand

for'est·a'tion n. planting or care of forests

for'est·ry n. science of the care of forests —**for'est·er** n.

fore·tell' v. **-told', -tell'ing** predict

fore'thought' n. foresight

for·ev'er adv. **1** for all time **2** at all times

fore·warn' v. warn beforehand

fore'wom·an n.pl. **-wom·en** woman serving as a foreman

fore'word' n. preface

for'feit (-fit) n. penalty —v. lose as a penalty —**for'fei·ture** (-fə-

forge n. **1** furnace for heating metal to be wrought **2** smith's shop —v. **1** shape by heating and hammering **2** counterfeit (a signature) **3** advance slowly

forg'er·y n., pl. **-ies 1** crime of forging documents, signatures, etc. **2** anything forged

for·get' v. **-got', -got'ten** or **-got', -get'ting 1** be unable to remember **2** neglect —**for·get'ful** a.

for·get'-me-not' n. plant with small, blue flowers

for·give' v. **-gave', -giv'en, -giv'ing** give up wanting to punish; pardon —**for·give'ness** n. —**for·giv'ing** a.

for·go' v. **-went', -gone', -go'ing** do without

fork n. **1** pronged instrument for lifting **2** place of branching —v. to branch

fork'lift' n. mobile lifting device in warehouses, etc.

for·lorn' a. **1** abandoned **2** wretched; miserable

form n. **1** shape; figure **2** mold **3** style; customary behavior **4** document to be filled in —v. **1** to shape **2** develop (habits) **3** constitute —**form'less** a.

for'mal a. **1** according to custom, rule, etc. **2** stiff; prim **3** for use at ceremonies —**for'mal·ize'** v. —**for'mal·ly** adv.

form·al'de·hyde' n. disinfectant and preservative

for·mal'i·ty n. **1** an observing of customs, rules, etc. **2** pl. **-ties** formal act

for'mat' n. general arrangement, as of a book

for·ma'tion n. **1** a forming **2** thing formed; structure —**form'a·tive** a.

for'mer a. **1** of the past **2** being the first mentioned —**for'mer·ly** adv.

for'mi·da·ble a. **1** causing fear **2** hard to handle

for'mu·la n., pl. **-las** or **-lae'** (-lē') **1** fixed expression or rule **2** set of symbols expressing a mathematical equation, chemical compound, etc. —**for'mu·late'** v. —**for'mu·la'tion** n.

for'ni·ca'tion n. sexual intercourse between unmarried people —**for'ni·cate'** v.

for·sake' v. **-sook', -sak'en, -sak'ing** abandon; desert

for·swear' v. **1** swear to give up **2** commit perjury

for·syth′i·a (-sith′-) *n.* shrub with yellow flowers

fort *n.* fortified place for military defense

for·te (fôr′tā′; *n.:* fôrt) *a., adv. Mus.* loud —*n.* what one does well

forth *adv.* 1 forward 2 out; into view

forth′com′ing *a.* 1 about to appear 2 ready at hand

forth′right′ *a.* frank

forth·with′ *adv.* at once

for·ti·fi·ca′tion *n.* 1 a fortifying 2 a fort

for′ti·fy′ *v.* -**fied′**, -**fy′ing** to strengthen, enrich, etc.

for·tis′si·mo′ *a., adv. Mus.* very loud

for′ti·tude *n.* calm courage

fort′night′ *n.* two weeks

for′tress *n.* fortified place

for·tu′i·tous *a.* 1 accidental 2 lucky

for′tu·nate (-chə nət) *a.* lucky — **for′tu·nate·ly** *adv.*

for′tune *n.* 1 luck; fate 2 good luck 3 wealth

for′tune-tell′er *n.* one claiming to foretell others' future — **for′tune-tell′ing** *n.*

for′ty *a., n.,* pl. -**ties** four times ten —**for′ti·eth** *a., n.*

fo′rum *n.* meeting for public discussion

for′ward *a.* 1 at, to, or of the front 2 advanced 3 bold —*adv.* ahead: also **for′wards** —*v.* 1 promote 2 send on

fos′sil *n.* hardened plant or animal remains, as in rock —*a.* 1 of a fossil 2 taken from the earth —**fos′sil·ize′** *v.*

fos′ter *v.* 1 bring up 2 promote —*a.* in a family but not by birth or adoption

fought *v.* pt. & pp. of FIGHT

foul *a.* 1 filthy 2 stormy 3 outside the rules or limits 4 very bad —*n.* foul hit, blow, etc. —*v.* 1 make filthy 2 entangle 3 make a foul

foul′-up′ *n.* [Col.] mix-up; mess

found *v.* 1 pt. & pp. of FIND 2 establish —**found′er** *n.*

foun·da′tion *n.* 1 establishment or basis 2 base of a wall, house, etc. 3 philanthropic fund or institution

foun′der *v.* 1 fall or go lame 2 fill and sink, as a ship

found′ling′ *n.* deserted child

found′ry *n.,* pl. -**ries** place where metal is cast

fount *n.* source

foun′tain *n.* 1 spring of water 2 jet of water or basin for it 3 source

foun′tain-head′ *n.* source

four *a., n.* one more than three —**fourth** *a., n.*

four′score′ *a., n.* eighty

four′some *n.* group of four people

four′square′ *a.* 1 firm 2 frank —*adv.* frankly

four·teen′ *a., n.* four more than ten —**four·teenth′** *a., n.*

fowl *n.* 1 any bird 2 domestic bird, as the chicken

fox *n.* small, wild, doglike animal —*v.* to trick —**fox′y** *a.,* -**i·er,** -**i·est**

fox′glove′ *n.* plant with long spikes of flowers

fox′hole′ *n.* hole dug as protection against gunfire

fox trot *n.* ballroom dance

foy′er *n.* entrance hall

fra′cas (frā′-) *n.* brawl

frac′tion *n.* 1 part of a whole, as ½, ⅓, etc. 2 small part

frac′ture *n.* a break, esp. in a bone —*v.* to break; crack

frag′ile (fraj′əl) *a.* easily broken —**fra·gil′i·ty** *n.*

frag′ment *n.* 1 part broken away 2 incomplete part —**frag′men·tar′y** *a.*

fra′grant *a.* sweet-smelling —**fra′grance** *n.*

frail *a.* 1 fragile 2 delicate or weak —**frail′ty** *n.,* pl. -**ties**

frame *v.* 1 make, form, build, etc. 2 enclose in a border 3 [Sl.] make seem guilty by a plot —*n.* 1 framework 2 framing border or case 3 mood

frame′work′ *n.* supporting or basic structure

franc *n.* Fr. monetary unit

fran′chise′ (-chīz′) *n.* 1 special right 2 right to vote 3 business with right to provide product or service

fran′gi·ble *a.* breakable

frank *a.* 1 outspoken; candid —*v.* send (mail) free —**frank′ly** *adv.* —**frank′ness** *n.*

frank′furt·er *n.* smoked link sausage; wiener

frank′in·cense′ *n.* gum resin burned as incense

fran′tic *a.* wild with anger, worry, etc. —**fran′ti·cal·ly** *adv.*

frap·pé (fra pā′) *n.* dessert of partly frozen fruit juices

fra·ter′nal *a.* 1 brotherly 2 of a fellowship society

fra·ter′ni·ty *n.,* pl. -**ties** 1 broth-

erli·ness 2 college social club for men **3** group with like interests

frat'er·nize' v. be friendly

fraud n. **1** a cheating or tricking; dishonesty **2** hypocrite; cheat

fraud'u·lent (frô'jə-) a. **1** using fraud **2** done by fraud

fraught a. filled (with)

fray n. quarrel or fight —v. make or become ragged

fraz'zle [Col.] v. wear out —n. frazzled state

freak n. abnormal animal or plant —a. abnormal

freck'le n. small brown spot on the skin —v. to spot with freckles

free a. **fre'er, fre'est 1** not under another's control **2** loose, clear, unrestricted, etc. **3** without cost —adv. **1** without cost **2** in a free way —v. **freed, free'ing** make free —**free from** (or of) without

free'boot'er n. a pirate

free'dom n. **1** independence **2** liberty **3** ease of movement **4** a right

free'-for-all' n. a brawl

free'lance', free'-lance' a. selling services to individual buyers

free'load'er n. [Col.] one imposing on others for free food, etc.

free'think'er n. religious skeptic

free'way' n. multiple-lane highway with interchanges

freeze v. **froze, fro'zen, freez'ing 1** to change into, or become covered with, ice **2** make or become very cold **3** kill or damage by cold **4** fix (prices, etc.) at a set level —n. a freezing

freez'er n. refrigerator for freezing and storing foods

freight (frāt) n. **1** goods transported **2** transportation of goods or its cost **3** train for freight

freight'er n. ship for freight

French a., n. (of) the people or language of France —**French'man** n., pl. -men

French fries n.pl. potatoes cut in strips and fried in deep fat

French horn n. brass musical instrument with a coiled tube

fre·net'ic a. frantic

fren'zy n., pl. -zies wild excitement —**fren'zied** a.

fre'quen·cy n., pl. -cies **1** frequent occurrence **2** number of times anything recurs in a given period

fre'quent a. **1** occurring often **2** constant —v. go to habitually

---

fres'co n., pl. -coes or -cos painting done on wet plaster

fresh a. **1** not spoiled, stale, worn out, etc. **2** new **3** refreshing **4** not salt: said of water —**fresh'en** v.

fresh'et n. flooded stream

fresh'man n., pl. -men first-year student in high school or college

fresh'wa'ter a. living in water that is not salty

fret v. **fret'ted, fret'ting;** n. **1** worry **2** ridge on fingerboard of banjo, guitar, etc. —**fret'ful** a.

fret'work n. ornate openwork

fri'a·ble (frī'-) a. easily crumbled

fri'ar n. R.C.Ch. member of a religious order

fric·as·see' n. stewed pieces of meat

fric'tion n. **1** rubbing of one object against another **2** conflict —**fric'tion·al** a.

Fri'day n. sixth day of the week

fried v. pt. & pp. of FRY

friend n. **1** person one knows well and likes **2** ally —**friend'ship'** n.

friend'ly a. -li·er, -li·est kindly; helpful

frieze (frēz) n. decorative band around a wall, etc.

frig'ate (frig'ət) n. fast sailing warship

fright n. sudden fear

fright'en v. **1** make afraid **2** drive (away) with fear

fright'ful a. **1** causing fright **2** disgusting

frig'id (frij'id) a. very cold —**fri·gid'i·ty** n.

frill n. **1** ruffle **2** [Col.] fancy ornament —**frill'y** a.

fringe n. border, as of loose threads —v. to edge, as with a fringe

frisk v. to frolic

frisk'y a. -i·er, -i·est lively —**frisk'i·ness** n.

frit'ter v. waste (money, etc.) bit by bit —n. small fried cake

friv'o·lous a. **1** trivial **2** silly —**fri·vol'i·ty** n., pl. -ties

frizz, friz'zle v. to form tight curls —**friz'zy** a.

fro adv. back: used only in **to and fro,** back and forth

frock n. **1** dress **2** robe

frog n. **1** leaping web-footed animal **2** braided loop —**frog in the throat** hoarseness

frol'ic n. merry time; fun —v. -icked, -ick·ing have fun —**frol'ic·some** a.

from prep. 1 beginning at 2 out of 3 originating with 4 out of the possibility, range, etc. of 5 as not being like 6 because of

frond n. fern or palm leaf

front n. 1 forward part 2 first part 3 land along a street, ocean, etc. 4 outward behavior —a. of or at the front —v. to face —**front'age** n. —**fron'tal** a.

fron·tier' n. 1 border of a country 2 new or unexplored field —**fron·tiers'man** n., pl. **-men**

fron'tis·piece' n. picture facing the title page

front'-run'ner n. leading candidate, runner, etc.

frost n. 1 temperature causing freezing 2 frozen dew or vapor —v. cover with frost or frosting —**frost'y** a., **-i·er, -i·est**

frost'bite' n. injury from intense cold —**frost'bit'ten** a.

frost'ing n. 1 icing 2 dull finish on glass

froth n., v. foam —**froth'y** a., **-i·er, -i·est**

fro'ward a. stubborn

frown v. 1 contract the brows 2 look with disapproval (on) —n. a frowning

frow'zy a. slovenly

froze v. pt. of FREEZE

fro'zen v. pp. of FREEZE

fruc'tose' n. sugar in honey, sweet fruit, etc.

fru'gal a. thrifty or sparing —**fru·gal'i·ty** n.

fruit n. 1 pulpy, edible product of a plant or tree 2 result; product —**fruit'ful** a. —**fruit'less** a.

fruit'cake' n. rich cake with fruit, nuts, etc.

fru·i'tion (-ish'ən) n. 1 the bearing of fruit 2 fulfillment

frump n. dowdy woman —**frump'y** a.

frus'trate' v. thwart; block —**frus·tra'tion** n.

fry v. **fried, fry'ing** cook in hot fat or oil —n. young fish

fuch'sia (fyoo'shə) n. plant with purplish-red flowers —a. purplish-red

fudge n. soft candy made of butter, sugar, etc.

fu'el n. thing burned for heat or power —v. supply with or get fuel

fu'gi·tive a. 1 fleeing 2 fleeting —n. one who has fled from the law, etc.

fugue (fyoog) n. musical work with theme in counterpoint

-ful suf. 1 full of 2 having the

qualities of 3 apt to 4 quantity that will fill

ful'crum n. support on which a lever turns

ful·fill', ful·fil' v. **-filled', -fill'ing** carry out or complete, as a promise or duty —**ful·fill'ment, ful·fil'ment** n.

full a. 1 containing all there is space for 2 having much in it 3 complete 4 ample —n. greatest amount, etc. —adv. 1 completely 2 exactly —**full'ness** n. —**ful'ly** adv.

full'-blown' a. matured

full dress n. formal dress

full'-fledged' a. fully developed; of full status

full'-grown' a. fully grown

full'-scale' a. 1 to the utmost degree 2 of full size

full'-time' a. of work, etc. using all one's regular working hours

ful'mi·nate' (ful'-) v. 1 explode 2 denounce strongly

ful'some (fool'-) a. sickeningly insincere

fum'ble v. grope or handle clumsily —n. a fumbling

fume n. offensive smoke or vapor —v. 1 give off fumes 2 show anger

fu'mi·gate' v. fill with fumes so as to kill vermin, germs, etc.

fun n. 1 lively play; merry time 2 source of gaiety —**make fun of** ridicule

func'tion n. 1 special or typical action, use, duty, etc. 2 formal ceremony or social affair —v. do its work —**func'tion·al** a.

func'tion·ar'y n., pl. **-ies** an official

fund n. 1 supply; store 2 money set aside for a purpose 3 pl. ready money

fun'da·men'tal a., n. basic (thing)

fun'da·men'tal·ism' n. religious beliefs based literally on the Bible —**fun'da·men'tal·ist** n., a.

fu'ner·al n. ceremonies for burial or cremation

funeral director n. manager of place (funeral **home** or **parlor**) for funerals

fu·ne're·al (-nir'ē-) a. sad; gloomy

fun'gus n., pl. **-gi'** (-jī', -gī') or **-gus·es** any of the mildews, molds, mushrooms, etc. —**fun'gous** a.

funk n. [Col.] depressed mood

fun'nel n. 1 slim tube with a cone-shaped mouth 2 ship's

smokestack —v. to pour as through a funnel

fun′ny a. **-ni·er, -ni·est** 1 amusing 2 [Col.] odd

fur n. soft, thick hair on an animal —**fur′ry** a., **-ri·er, -ri·est**

fu′ri·ous a. full of fury

furl v. roll up tightly, as a flag

fur′long′ n. ⅛ of a mile

fur′lough (-lō) n. a military leave of absence —v. grant a furlough to

fur′nace (-nəs) n. structure in which heat is produced

fur′nish v. 1 put furniture into 2 supply

fur′nish·ings n.pl. 1 furniture and fixtures, as for a house 2 things to wear

fur′ni·ture n. chairs, beds, etc. in a room, etc.

fu·ror (fyoor′ôr′) n. 1 widespread enthusiasm 2 fury

fur′ri·er n. one who processes, or deals in, furs

fur′row n. 1 groove made in the ground by a plow 2 deep wrinkle —v. make furrows in

fur′ther a. 1 additional 2 more distant —adv. 1 to a greater extent 2 in addition 3 at or to a greater distance —v. to promote —**fur′ther·ance** n.

fur′ther·more′ adv. besides

fur′thest a. most distant —adv. at or to the greatest distance or extent

fur′tive (-tiv) a. done or acting in a stealthy way

fu′ry n. 1 wild rage 2 violence

fuse v. melt (together) —n. 1 wick that is lighted to set off an explosive 2 safety device that breaks an electric circuit when the current is too strong —**fu′sion** n.

fu′se·lage′ (-läzh′) n. body of an airplane

fu′sil·lade′ (-lād′, -läd′) n. simultaneous discharge of many guns

fuss n. nervous, excited state —v. bustle about or worry over trifles —**fuss′y** a., **-i·er, -i·est**

fus′ty a. **-ti·er, -ti·est** 1 musty 2 old-fashioned

fu·tile (fyoot′'l) a. useless —**fu·til′i·ty** n.

fu′ton (foo′-) n. thin floor mattress

fu′ture a. that is to be or come —n. 1 time that is to come 2 what is going to be; prospects —**fu′tur·is′tic** a.

fuzz n. loose, light particles; fine hairs —**fuzz′y** a., **-i·er, -i·est**

G

gab n., v. **gabbed, gab′bing** [Col.] chatter —**gab′by** a., **-bi·er, -bi·est**

gab′ar·dine′ (-ər dēn′) n. cloth with a diagonal weave

gab′ble v., n. jabber

ga′ble n. triangular wall enclosed by the sloping ends of a roof —**ga′bled** a.

gad v. **gad′ded, gad′ding** roam about restlessly —**gad′a·bout′** n.

gad′fly n. 1 large, stinging fly 2 one who annoys in exciting or stirring others

gadg′et (gaj′-) n. small mechanical device

gaff n. large hook on a pole for landing fish

gaffe n. a blunder

gag v. **gagged, gag′ging** 1 retch or cause to retch 2 keep from speaking, as with a gag —n. 1 something put into the mouth to prevent speech 2 joke

gage n. 1 pledge 2 challenge 3 gauge —v. gauge

gag′gle n. 1 flock of geese 2 any group or cluster

gai′e·ty (gā′-) n. 1 cheerfulness 2 merriment

gai′ly adv. 1 merrily 2 brightly

gain n. 1 increase 2 profit —v. 1 earn 2 win 3 get as an addition or advantage 4 reach 5 make progress —**gain on** draw nearer to, as in a race

gain′ful a. profitable

gain′say′ v. **-said′, -say′ing** deny or contradict

gait n. manner of walking or running

gal n. [Col.] girl

ga′la n. a festive —n. festival

gal′ax·y n., pl. **-ies** very large group of stars —**ga·lac′tic** a.

gale n. 1 strong wind 2 outburst, as of laughter

gall (gôl) n. 1 bile 2 tumor on plant tissue 3 [Col.] impudence —v. annoy

gal′lant a. 1 brave and noble 2 polite to women —**gal′lant·ry** n., pl. **-ries**

gall′blad′der n. sac attached to the liver, in which excess bile is stored

gal′le·on n. large Spanish ship of 15th-16th centuries

gal′le·ri′a n. large arcade or court with a glass roof

gal'ler·y n., pl. **-ies** 1 covered walk 2 outside balcony 3 theater balcony 4 place for art exhibits

gal'ley n., pl. **-leys** 1 ancient sailing ship with oars 2 ship's kitchen

gal'li·vant v. gad about for pleasure

gal'lon n. four quarts

gal'lop n. fastest gait of a horse —v. go or make go at a gallop

gal'lows n., pl. **-lows·es** or **-lows** structure for hanging condemned persons

gall'stone' n. abnormal stony mass in the gallbladder

ga·lore' adv. in great plenty

ga·losh'es n.pl. high overshoes

gal·van'ic a. of electric current, esp. from a battery

gal'va·nize' v. 1 startle 2 plate (metal) with zinc

gam'bit n. opening move in chess

gam'ble v. 1 play games of chance for money 2 take a risk 3 bet —n. risk; chance —**gam'bler** n.

gam'bol v., n. frolic

game n. 1 amusement or sport with competing players 2 wild animals hunted for sport —v. gamble —a. 1 plucky 2 ready (for) 3 [Col.] lame —**the game is up** failure is certain

game plan n. long-range strategy

gam·ete (gam'ēt) n. reproductive cell

gam'ma ray n. electromagnetic radiation with short wavelength

gam'ut n. the entire range, esp. of a musical scale

gam'y (gām'-) a. **-i·er, -i·est** 1 strongly flavored 2 slightly tainted

gan'der n. male goose

gang n. group working or acting together —**gang up on** [Col.] attack as a group

gan'gling a. thin and tall

gan'gli·on n. mass of nerve cells

gang'plank' n. movable ramp from a ship to the dock

gan'grene' n. decay of body tissue from lack of blood supply —**gan'gre·nous** a.

gang'ster n. member of a gang of criminals

gang'way' n. 1 passageway 2 gangplank —int. clear the way!

gant'let (gônt'-, gant'-) n. punishment of being beaten as one runs between two rows of men

gan'try n., pl. **-tries** wheeled framework with a crane, etc.

gaol (jāl) n. Br. sp. of JAIL

gap n. 1 opening or break 2 blank space

gape v. 1 open wide 2 stare with the mouth open

gar n. long fish with a long snout: also **gar'fish**

ga·rage' (-räzh', -räj') n. shelter or repair shop for automobiles, etc.

garb n. clothing; style of dress —v. clothe

gar'bage (-bij) n. waste parts of food

gar'ble v. distort (a story, etc.)

gar'den n. 1 plot for flowers, vegetables, etc. 2 fertile area 3 public park —v. make, or work in, a garden —**gar'den·er** n.

gar·de'ni·a (-dēn'yə) n. waxy white flower

Gar·gan'tu·an, gar·gan'tu·an (-choo-) a. huge

gar'gle v. rinse the throat —n. liquid for gargling

gar'goyle n. gutter spout in the form of a sculptured grotesque creature

gar'ish (gar'-) a. gaudy

gar'land n. wreath of flowers, leaves, etc.

gar'lic n. strong-smelling plant bulb, used to season

gar'ment n. piece of clothing

gar'ner v. gather and store

gar'net n. deep-red gem

gar'nish v. decorate (food) —n. decoration for food

gar·nish·ee' v. attach (a debtor's wages, etc.) to pay the debt

gar'ret (gar'-) n. attic

gar'ri·son n. fort for the troops in it —v. provide with troops

gar·rote' (-rōt', -rät') v. strangle —n. device for strangling

gar'ru·lous (gar'-) a. talking much —**gar·ru'li·ty** n.

gar'ter n. elastic band to hold up a stocking

gas n. 1 fluid substance that can expand; vapor: some gases are used as fuel 2 gasoline —v. gassed, gas'sing attack with gas —**gas'e·ous** a.

gash v. cut deep into —n. deep cut

gas'ket n. rubber or metal ring sealing a joint, etc.

gas'o·hol n. fuel mixture of gasoline and alcohol

gas'o·line' (-lēn) n. liquid fuel from petroleum

gasp v. catch the breath with

effort —n. a gasping

gas′tric a. of the stomach

gas·tri′tis (-trīt′is) n. inflammation of the stomach

gas·tron′o·my n. art of good eating —**gas′tro·nom′i·cal** a.

gate n. 1 hinged door in a fence or wall 2 number of paid admissions

gate′way′ n. entrance with a gate

gath′er v. 1 bring or come together; collect 2 infer 3 draw into pleats —n. a pleat —**gath′er·ing** n.

gauche (gōsh) a. tactless

gaud′y a. **-i·er, -i·est** showy but tasteless —**gaud′i·ly** adv.

gauge (gāj) n. 1 standard measure 2 device for measuring —v. 1 to measure 2 to estimate

gaunt a. haggard; thin

gaunt′let n. 1 long glove with a flaring cuff 2 gantlet —**throw down the gauntlet** challenge

gauze n. loosely woven material —**gauz′y** a.

gave v. pt. of GIVE

gav′el n. chairman's small mallet

gawk v. stare stupidly

gawk′y a. **-i·er, -i·est** clumsy; ungainly

gay a. 1 joyous and lively 2 bright 3 homosexual

gaze v. look steadily; stare —n. steady look

ga·ze′bo (-zē′-, -zā′-) n., pl. **-bos** or **-boes** small, open, roofed building in garden or park

ga·zelle′ n. swift antelope

ga·zette′ n. newspaper

gaz′et·teer′ n. dictionary of geographical names

gaz·pa′cho (gäz pä′-) n. cold, Spanish vegetable soup

gear n. 1 equipment 2 system of toothed wheels that mesh 3 such a wheel —v. 1 connect by gears 2 adjust

gear′shift′ n. device for changing transmission gears

geck′o n., pl. **-os** or **-oes** tropical lizard

gee (jē) int. [Sl.] exclamation of surprise, etc.

geese n. pl. of GOOSE

gee′zer (gē′-) n. [Sl.] eccentric old man

Gei·ger counter (gī′gər) n. instrument for measuring radioactivity

gei′sha (gā′-) n., pl. **-sha** or **-shas** Japanese woman entertainer

gel (jel) n. jellylike substance

gel′a·tin n. jellied substance

extracted from bones, hoofs, vegetables, etc. —**ge·lat′i·nous** a.

geld (geld) v. castrate (a horse, etc.) —**geld′ing** n.

gel′id (jel′-) a. frozen

gem n. precious stone

Gem′i·ni (-nī′, -nē′) third sign of the zodiac; Twins

gen·darme′ (zhän-) n. armed French police officer

gen′der n. classification of words as masculine, feminine, or neuter

gene n. unit of heredity in chromosomes

ge′ne·al′o·gy (jē′nē äl′-) n. history of ancestry —**ge′ne·a·log′i·cal** a.

gen·er·a (jen′ər ə) n. pl. of GENUS

gen′er·al a. 1 of or for all 2 widespread 3 usual 4 not specific —n. high-ranking army officer —**in general** usually —**gen′er·al·ly** adv.

gen′er·al′i·ty n., pl. **-ties** nonspecific idea or statement —**gen′er·al·ize′** v.

gen′er·ate′ v. cause to be; produce —**gen′er·a·tive** a.

gen′er·a′tion n. 1 production 2 all persons born about the same time 3 average time (30 years) between generations —**gen′er·a′tion·al** a.

gen′er·a′tor n. machine for changing mechanical into electrical energy

ge·ner′ic a. 1 inclusive; general 2 of a genus —**ge·ner′i·cal·ly** adv.

gen′er·ous a. 1 giving readily; unselfish 2 ample —**gen′er·os′i·ty** n.

gen′e·sis n. origin —[G-] first book of the Bible

genetic code n. arrangement of chemical substances in DNA molecules transmitting genetic information

ge·net′ics n. study of heredity —**ge·net′ic** a. —**ge·net′i·cist** n.

gen′ial (jēn′-) a. kindly; amiable —**ge′ni·al′i·ty** n.

ge·nie (jē′nē) n. 1 magic spirit that can be summoned 2 jinni

gen′i·tals n.pl. external sex organs —**gen′i·tal** a.

gen′i·tive (-tiv) a., n. Gram. (in) the case showing possession or origin

gen′ius (jēn′yəs) n. 1 great mental or creative ability 2 person having this

gen'o·cide' n. systematic killing of a whole people

gen·re (zhän'rə) n. kind or type

gen·teel' (-tēl') a. (overly) polite, refined, etc.

gen'tile' (-tīl') a., n. [also G-] non-Jewish (person)

gen·til'i·ty n. politeness

gen'tle a. 1 mild; moderate 2 kindly; patient —**gen'tly** adv.

gen'tle·man n., pl. -men 1 well-bred, courteous man 2 any man: polite term

gen'tri·fy' v. -fied', -fy'ing raise to a higher status or condition —**gen'tri·fi·ca'tion** n.

gen'try n. people just below the nobility

gen'u·flect' v. bend the knee, as in worship —**gen'u·flec'tion** n.

gen'u·ine (-in) a. 1 real; true 2 sincere

ge'nus (jē'-) n., pl. **gen'e·a** or sometimes **ge'nus·es** class; kind, esp. in biology

ge'o·cen'tric a. with the earth as a center

ge'o·des'ic a. of a dome with a gridlike framework

ge·og'ra·phy n. science of the earth's surface, climates, plants, animals, etc. —**ge·og'ra·pher** n. —**ge'o·graph'i·cal**, **ge'o·graph'ic** a.

ge·ol'o·gy n. science of the earth's crust and of rocks and fossils —**ge'o·log'i·cal** (-läj'-) a. —**ge·ol'o·gist** n.

ge'o·mag·net'ic a. of the earth's magnetic properties —**ge'o·mag'ne·tism'** n.

ge·om'e·try n. branch of mathematics dealing with plane and solid figures —**ge'o·met'ric**, **ge'o·met'ri·cal** a.

ge'o·phys'ics n. science of the effects of weather, tides, etc. on the earth —**ge'o·phys'i·cal** a.

ge'o·sta'tion·ar·y a. of an orbiting satellite staying above same point over earth's surface: also **ge'o·syn'chro·nous**

ge'o·ther'mic a. of heat inside the earth: also **ge'o·ther'mal**

ge·ra'ni·um n. plant with showy flowers

ger'bil n. small rodent

ger·i·at'rics (jer'-) n. branch of medicine dealing with diseases of old age

germ n. 1 microscopic, disease-causing organism 2 seed, bud, etc. 3 origin

Ger'man n., a. (native or language) of Germany

ger·mane' a. relevant

ger·ma'ni·um n. a chemical element used in transistors, semiconductors, etc.

ger'mi·cide' n. anything used to destroy germs

ger'mi·nate' v. sprout, as from a seed —**ger'mi·na'tion** n.

ger·on·tol'o·gy (jer'-) n. study of aging —**ger·on·tol'o·gist** n.

ger'ry·man'der (jer'-) v. divide (voting area) unfairly to benefit one party

ger'und (jer'-) n. verbal noun ending in -ing

ges·ta'tion (jes-) n. pregnancy

ges·tic'u·late' v. to gesture

ges'ture n. movement of part of the body, to express ideas, feelings, etc. —v. make gestures

get v. got, got or got'ten, get'ting 1 come to have; obtain 2 come, go, or arrive 3 bring 4 make or become 5 [Col.] a) be obliged b) possess c) baffle d) understand —**get along** manage —**get around** circumvent —**get away** escape —**get by** [Col.] survive; manage —**get over** recover from —**get through** 1 finish 2 survive —**get together** 1 assemble 2 [Col.] reach an agreement —**get up** rise (from sleep, etc.)

get'a·way' n. 1 a starting, as in a race 2 an escape

gew'gaw (gyōō'gô') n. trinket

gey·ser (gī'zər) n. gushing hot spring

ghast'ly (gast'-) a. -li·er, -li·est 1 horrible 2 pale as a ghost

gher'kin (gur'-) n. small pickle

ghet·to (get'ō) n. section of a city to which Jews, etc. are restricted

ghost n. supposed disembodied spirit of a dead person —**ghost'ly** a.

ghost'writ'er n. a writer of speeches, etc. for another pretending to be the author

ghoul (gōōl) n. supposed evil spirit that feeds on the dead —**ghoul'ish** a.

GI n., pl. **GI's** or **GIs** [Col.] enlisted soldier

gi'ant n. person or thing of great size, strength, etc. —a. like a giant

gib'ber (jib'-) v. speak incoherently

gib'ber·ish n. confused talk

gib'bet (jib'-) n. a gallows

gib'bon (gib'-) n. small, slender, long-armed ape

gibe (jib) v., n. taunt

gib'let (jib'-) *n.* edible internal part of a fowl

gid'dy *a.* **-di·er, -di·est** 1 dizzy 2 frivolous —**gid'di·ness** *n.*

gift *n.* 1 a present 2 a giving 3 natural ability

gift'ed *a.* talented

gig *n.* [Sl.] job, esp. playing jazz

gi·gan'tic *a.* huge

gig'gle *v.* laugh in a nervous, silly way —*n.* such a laugh

gig'o·lo' (jig'-) *n., pl.* **-los'** man supported by his female lover

Gi·la monster (hē'lə) *n.* stout, poisonous lizard

gild *v.* **gild'ed** or **gilt, gild'ing** 1 to cover with a layer of gold 2 make better than it is

gill (gil; *n.* 2: jil) *n.* 1 breathing organ of a fish 2 ¼ pint

gilt *n.* surface layer of gold

gilt'-edged' *a.* of highest value, quality, etc., as securities

gim'let *n.* small tool for making holes

gim'mick *n.* [Col.] tricky or deceptive device

gin *n.* 1 an alcoholic liquor 2 machine for separating cotton from the seeds

gin'ger *n.* spice from the root of a tropical herb

ginger ale *n.* nonalcoholic drink flavored with ginger

gin'ger·bread' *n.* cake flavored with ginger

gin'ger·ly *a., adv.* careful(ly) or timid(ly)

gin'ger·snap' *n.* crisp ginger cookie

ging·ham (giŋ'əm) *n.* cotton cloth in stripes or checks

gin·gi·vi·tis (jin'jə vīt'is) *n.* inflammation of gums

Gip'sy *n., pl.* **-sies** Gypsy

gi·raffe' *n.* large African animal with a very long neck

gird *v.* **gird'ed** or **girt, gird'ing** 1 encircle 2 prepare for action

gird'er *n.* large beam for supporting a floor, etc.

gir'dle *n.* 1 a belt 2 light, flexible corset

girl *n.* female child or young woman —**girl'ish** *a.*

girl'friend' *n.* 1 sweetheart of a boy or man 2 girl who is one's friend 3 woman friend of a woman

girth *n.* 1 horse's belly band 2 circumference

gist (jist) *n.* main point

give *v.* **gave, giv'en, giv'ing** 1 hand over; deliver 2 cause to have 3 produce 4 utter 5 per-form 6 bend, etc. from pressure —*n.* a bending, etc. under pressure —**give away** [Col.] expose —**give forth** (or **off**) emit —**give in** yield —**give out** 1 make public 2 distribute 3 become worn out —**give up** 1 relinquish 2 stop

give'a·way' *n.* thing given away or sold cheap

giv'en *a.* 1 bestowed 2 accustomed 3 stated

giz'mo, gis'mo *n., pl.* **-mos** [Sl.] gadget or gimmick

giz'zard *n.* muscular second stomach of a bird

gla'cier (-shər) *n.* large mass of ice moving slowly down a slope —**gla'cial** (-shal) *a.*

glad *a.* **glad'der, glad'dest** 1 happy 2 causing joy 3 pleased —**glad'ly** *adv.* —**glad'ness** *n.*

glad'den *v.* make glad

glade *n.* clearing in a forest

glad'i·a'tor *n.* 1 in ancient Rome, a fighter in public shows 2 any fighter

glad'i·o'lus *n.* plant with tall spikes of funnel-shaped flowers: also **glad'i·o'la**

glam'our, glam'or *n.* bewitching charm —**glam'or·ous, glam'our·ous** *a.*

glance *v.* 1 strike and go off at an angle 2 look briefly —*n.* a glimpse

gland *n.* body organ that secretes a substance —**glan'du·lar** (-jə lər) *a.*

glare *v.* 1 shine with a dazzling light 2 stare fiercely —*n.* 1 dazzling light 2 fierce stare 3 glassy surface, as of ice

glar'ing *a.* flagrant

glass *n.* 1 hard, brittle substance, usually transparent 2 drinking vessel, mirror, etc. made of this 3 *pl.* eyeglasses or binoculars

glass'y *a.* **-i·er, -i·est** 1 like glass 2 expressionless

glau·co'ma *n.* eye disease

glaze *v.* 1 furnish with glass 2 give a glossy finish to 3 cover with a sugar coating —*n.* glassy coating

gla'zi·er (-zhər) *n.* one who fits glass in windows

gleam *n.* 1 faint glow of light 2 brief show, as of hope —*v.* send out a gleam

glean *v.* collect slowly, as grain left by reapers

glee *n.* joy —**glee'ful** *a.*

glee club *n.* singing group

glen n. secluded valley

glib a. **glib'ber, glib'best** fluent, esp. in a shallow way

glide v. to move or descend smoothly and easily —n. a smooth, easy flow or descent

glid'er n. engineless airplane carried by air currents

glim'mer v., n. (give) a faint, flickering light

glimpse n. brief, quick view —v. catch a glimpse of

glint v., n. gleam

glis'ten (glis'ən) v., n. sparkle

glitch n. [Sl.] mishap, error, etc.

glit'ter v., n. sparkle

glitz n. [Col.] gaudy showiness —**glitz'y** a., **-i-er, -i-est**

gloat v. feel or show malicious pleasure

glob n. rounded lump

globe n. 1 ball-shaped thing 2 the earth, or a model of it — **glob'al** a.

globe'-trot'ter n. world traveler

glob'u-lar a. 1 spherical 2 of globules

glob'ule n. small drop

gloom n. 1 darkness 2 dark place 3 sadness —**gloom'y** a., **-i-er, -i-est**

glo'ri-fy' v. **-fied', -fy'ing** 1 give glory to; honor 2 make seem greater —**glo'ri-fi-ca'tion** n.

glo'ri-ous a. 1 full of glory 2 splendid

glo'ry n., pl. **-ries** 1 great praise or fame 2 splendor 3 heavenly bliss —v. **-ried, -ry'ing** exult (in)

gloss (glôs) n. 1 surface polish 2 explanation; footnote —v. to smooth (over), as an error — **gloss'y** a., **-i-er, -i-est**

glos'sa-ry n., pl. **-ries** list of difficult terms with definitions, as for a book

glot'tis n. opening between the vocal cords —**glot'tal** a.

glove n. 1 covering for the hand with sheaths for the fingers 2 padded mitt for boxing — **gloved** a.

glow v. 1 give off bright or steady light 2 be elated 3 be bright with color —n. 1 bright or steady light 2 brightness, warmth, etc.

glow'er (glou'-) v., n. stare with sullen anger

glow'worm' n. phosphorescent insect or larva

glu'cose' n. the sugar in fruits and honey

glue n. thick, adhesive liquid —

v. stick together as with glue — **glu'ey** a.

glum a. **glum'mer, glum'mest** gloomy

glut v. **glut'ted, glut'ting** feed, fill, or supply to excess —n. excess

glu'ten n. sticky protein substance in wheat flour

glu'ti-nous a. sticky

glut'ton n. one who eats too much —**glut'ton-ous** a.

glut'ton-y n. overeating

glyc'er-in (glis'-) n. glycerol: also sp. **glyc'er-ine**

glyc'er-ol' n. colorless, syrupy liquid used in lotions, etc.

gly'co-gen (glī'kə-) n. substance in animal tissues that is changed into glucose

gnarl (närl) n. knot on a tree —v. to twist

gnash (nash) v. grind (the teeth) together

gnat (nat) n. small insect

gnaw (nô) v. 1 wear away by biting 2 torment —**gnaw'ing** a.

gnome (nōm) n. dwarf

gnu (nōō, nyōō) n. African antelope

go v. **went, gone, go'ing** 1 move along; pass or proceed 2 depart 3 work, as a clock 4 be or become 5 fit or suit 6 belong in a place —n. 1 a success 2 [Col.] energy 3 [Col.] a try —**go back on** [Col.] break, as a promise —**go in for** [Col.] engage or indulge in —**go off** explode —**go out** 1 be extinguished 2 go to social affairs, etc. —**go over** 1 examine 2 do again —**go through** 1 endure 2 search —**go under** fail —**let go** release one's hold

goad n. 1 pointed stick 2 spur —v. urge on

goal n. 1 place where a race, trip, etc. ends 2 end striven for 3 place to put the ball or puck to score

goal'keep'er n. player guarding a goal: also **goal'ie** or **goal'tend'er**

goat n. cud-chewing horned animal —**get someone's goat** [Col.] annoy someone

goat-ee' n. pointed beard on a man's chin

goat'herd' n. herder of goats

gob n. 1 lump or mass 2 [Sl.] U.S. sailor

gob'ble n. cry of a male turkey —v. 1 make this cry 2 eat greedily —**gob'bler** n.

gob'ble·dy·gook' *n.* [Sl.] pompous, wordy talk or writing with little meaning

go'-be·tween' *n.* one acting between two persons

gob'let *n.* stemmed glass

gob'lin *n.* evil spirit

God monotheistic creator and ruler of the universe —*n.* [g-] any divine being —**god'dess** *n.fem.* —**god'like'** *a.*

god'child' *n.* the person (**god'daugh'ter** or **god'son'**) that a godparent sponsors

god'less *a.* 1 irreligious 2 wicked

god'ly *a.* **-li·er, -li·est** devoted to God; devout

god'par'ent *n.* spiritual sponsor (**god'fa'ther** or **god'moth'er**) of an infant, esp. at baptism

god'send' *n.* something unexpected but much needed

go'fer, go'-fer' *n.* [Sl.] employee who does minor tasks

gog'gle *v.* stare with bulging eyes —*n. pl.* large spectacles to protect the eyes against dust, etc.

go'ing 1 departure 2 degree of ease in traveling —*a.* 1 working 2 current

goi'ter, goi'tre *n.* enlargement of the thyroid gland

gold 1 yellow, precious metal, a chemical element 2 money; wealth 3 bright yellow —*a.* of gold —**gold'en** *a.*

gold'en·rod' *n.* plant with long, yellow flower clusters

gold'finch' *n.* small, yellow American songbird

gold'fish' *n.* small yellowish fish, kept in ponds, etc.

golf *n.* outdoor game in which a small ball is driven, with special clubs, into holes —**golf'er** *n.*

go'nad' *n.* ovary or testicle

gon·do·la (or gän dō'lə) *n.* boat used on the canals of Venice —**gon'do·lier'** (-lir') *n.*

gone *v.* pp. of GO

gon'er *n.* person sure to die, be ruined, etc.

gong *n.* metal disk that resounds loudly when struck

gon'or·rhe'a (-rē'ə) *n.* venereal disease

goo *n.* 1 anything sticky 2 sentimentality

goo'ber *n.* peanut

good *a.* **bet'ter, best** 1 having proper qualities 2 beneficial 3 of moral excellence 4 enjoyable, happy, etc. 5 considerable —*n.* 1 worth or virtue 2 benefit —

good'ness *n.*

good'bye', good'-bye' *int., n.* farewell: also written **good'by'** or **good'-by'**

Good Friday *n.* Friday before Easter

good'-heart'ed *a.* kind

good'-look'ing *a.* handsome

good'ly *a.* rather large

good'-na'tured *a.* pleasant

goods *n.pl.* 1 personal property 2 wares 3 fabric

good'y *n., pl.* **-ies** [Col.] thing good to eat

goof [Sl.] *n.* 1 a blunder 2 stupid or silly person —*v.* 1 to blunder 2 waste time: with *off* —**goof'y** *a.*, **-i·er, -i·est**

gook *n.* [Sl.] sticky or slimy substance

goon *n.* [Sl.] 1 hired thug 2 stupid person

goop *n.* [Sl.] sticky, semiliquid substance

goose *n., pl.* **geese** 1 longnecked water bird like a large duck 2 silly person —**cook one's goose** [Col.] spoil one's chances

goose'ber'ry *n., pl.* **-ries** sour berry used for jam, etc.

goose flesh *n.* rough skin caused by cold, fear, etc.: also **goose bumps**

goose'liv'er *n.* smoked liver sausage

go'pher *n.* burrowing rodent

gore *n.* 1 clotted blood 2 tapered cloth inserted to add width —*v.* 1 pierce as with a tusk 2 insert gores in —**gor'y** *a.*, **-i·er, -i·est**

gorge *n.* deep, narrow pass —*v.* eat or stuff greedily

gor'geous (-jəs) *a.* magnificent

go·ril'la *n.* largest of the apes, native to Africa

gosh *int.* call of surprise

gos'ling (gäz'-) *n.* young goose

gos'pel *n.* 1 [often G-] teachings of Jesus and the Apostles 2 belief proclaimed as true

gos'sa·mer *n.* filmy cobweb or cloth —*a.* filmy

gos'sip *n.* 1 one who chatters about others 2 such idle talk —*v.* indulge in gossip —**gos'sip·y** *a.*

got *v.* pt. & pp. GET

got'ten *v.* alt. pp. of GET

Gou'da (cheese) (gou'-, gōō'-) *n.* mild cheese

gouge (gouj) *n.* 1 chisel for cutting grooves 2 such a groove —*v.* 1 scoop out as with a gouge 2

[Col.] overcharge —**goug'er** n.

gou·lash (gōō'läsh') n. stew seasoned with paprika

gourd (gôrd, goord) n. 1 bulb-shaped fruit of a trailing plant 2 its dried shell hollowed out for use

gour·mand (goor mänd', gôr-) n. one who likes to eat

gour·met (goor mā', gôr-) n. judge of fine foods and drinks

gout n. disease with painful swelling of the joints

gov'ern v. 1 control 2 influence; determine

gov'ern·ess n. woman hired to teach children at home

gov'ern·ment n. 1 control; rule 2 system of ruling 3 those who rule —**gov'ern·men'tal** a.

gov'er·nor n. one who governs; esp., head of a State 2 device to control engine speed automatically

gown n. 1 woman's dress 2 long robe, as for a judge

grab v. **grabbed**, **grab'bing** snatch suddenly —n. a grabbing

grace n. 1 beauty of form, movement, etc. 2 favor; good will 3 delay granted for payment due 4 prayer of thanks at a meal 5 God's love for man — v. graced, grac'ing dignify or adorn —**in the good graces of** in favor with —**grace'ful** a. — **grace'ful·ly** adv.

gra'cious (-shəs) a. kind, polite, charming, pleasing, etc.

grack'le n. small blackbird

gra·da'tion n. 1 arrangement in steps 2 stage in a series

grade n. 1 degree in a scale of rank or quality 2 slope 3 any of the school years through the 12th 4 mark or rating, as on a test —v. 1 classify; sort 2 give a GRADE (n. 4) to 3 make (ground) sloped or level

grade crossing n. place where a road crosses a railroad

grade school n. elementary school

gra'di·ent n. slope, or degree of slope

grad'u·al (graj'-) a. little by little —**grad'u·al·ly** adv.

grad'u·ate (-ət, -āt') n. one who completed a course of study at a school or college —v. 1 give a diploma to (a graduate) 2 become a graduate 3 mark with degrees for measuring —**grad'u·a'tion** n.

graf·fi'ti (-fēt'ē) n.pl., sing. **-to**

crude drawings or writing on a public wall, etc.

graft n. 1 shoot, etc. of one plant inserted in another to grow 2 transplanting of skin, etc. 3 dishonest gain of money by public officers —v. insert (a graft)

gra·ham (grā'əm) a. made of unsifted, whole-wheat flour

grain n. 1 seed of wheat, corn, etc. 2 cereal plants 3 particle, as of salt or sand 4 smallest unit of weight 5 natural markings on wood, leather, etc.

gram n. metric unit of weight ($\frac{1}{28}$ of an ounce)

-gram suf. a writing or drawing

gram'mar n. system of speaking and writing a language —**gram·mar'i·an** (-mer'-) n. —**gram·mat'i·cal** a.

gran'a·ry (grān'-, gran'-) n., pl. **-ries** building for storing grain

grand a. great in size, beauty, importance, etc.; imposing, splendid, etc. —n. [Sl.] a thousand dollars

grand'child' n. child (**grand' daugh'ter** or **grand'son'**) of one's son or daughter

gran'deur (-jər, -dyoor) n. great size, beauty, etc.; splendor

gran·dil'o·quent a. bombastic

gran'di·ose' (-ōs') a. 1 very grand 2 too grand

grand jury n. jury with power to indict persons for trial

grand'par'ent n. parent (**grand' fa'ther** or **grand'moth'er**) of one's father or mother

grand piano n. large piano with a horizontal case

grand slam n. home run hit with a runner on each base

grand'stand' n. structure for spectators of outdoor sports — v. [Col.] show off to get attention or applause

grange (grānj) n. 1 farm 2 [G-] association of farmers

gran'ite (-it) n. very hard crystalline rock

gra·no'la n. breakfast cereal of oats, honey, nuts, etc.

grant v. 1 consent to or give 2 concede —n. something granted —**take for granted** consider as a fact

gran'u·lar a. of or like grains or granules

gran'u·late' v. form into granules —**gran'u·la'tion** n.

gran'ule n. small grain

grape n. small, round fruit growing in clusters

grape'fruit' n. large citrus fruit with a yellow rind

grape'vine' n. **1** woody vine with grapes **2** rumor

graph n. a diagram that shows changes in value

-graph suf. **1** that writes **2** thing written

graph'ic a. **1** vivid; in lifelike detail **2** of the arts of drawing, printing, etc. —**graph'i·cal·ly** adv.

graph'ite' n. soft, black carbon in pencils, etc.

grap'nel n. device with hooks or claws for grasping

grap'ple n. **1** grapnel **2** grip in wrestling —v. **1** grip and hold **2** struggle

grasp v. **1** grip; seize **2** comprehend —n. **1** a grip **2** control **3** power to grasp

grasp'ing a. greedy

grass n. **1** green plant grown for lawns **2** cereal plant **3** pasture —**grass'y** a.

grass'hop'per n. leaping insect with long hind legs

grass'land' n. open land with grass; prairie

grass'-roots' a. of common people having basic political opinions

grate v. **1** form into particles by scraping **2** rub with a harsh sound **3** irritate —n. **1** frame of bars to hold fuel **2** framework of bars over an opening

grate'ful a. thankful

grat'i·fy' v. **-fied', -fy'ing 1** please **2** indulge —**grat'i·fi·ca'tion** n.

grat'ing n. GRATE (n. 2)

gra·tis (grāt'is, grat'-) adv., a. free

grat'i·tude' n. thankful appreciation

gra·tu'i·tous a. **1** free of charge **2** uncalled-for

gra·tu'i·ty n., pl. **-ties** gift of money for a service

grave a. **1** serious **2** solemn —n. burial place, esp. a hole in the ground

grav'el n. bits of rock —v. cover with gravel

grav'el·ly a. hoarse or rasping

grav'en image (grāv'-) n. idol of stone or wood

grave'yard' n. cemetery

grav'i·tate' v. be attracted

grav'i·ta'tion n. Physics force of mutual attraction between masses

grav'i·ty n. **1** seriousness **2** weight **3** Physics gravitation;

esp., the pull on bodies toward earth's center

gra'vy n., pl. **-vies** juice from cooking meat

gray n. mixture of black and white —a. **1** of this color **2** dreary —**gray'ish** a.

gray'beard' n. old man

gray matter n. **1** grayish brain tissue **2** [Col.] intelligence

graze v. **1** feed on growing grass, etc. **2** rub lightly in passing —n. a grazing

grease n. **1** melted animal fat **2** thick oily lubricant —v. put grease on —**greas'y** a., **-i·er, -i·est**

great a. **1** much larger, more, or better than average **2** being one generation removed —**great'ly** adv.

Great Dane n. large, strong dog with short hair

greed n. excessive desire, as for wealth —**greed'y** a., **-i·er, -i·est** —**greed'i·ly** adv.

Greek n., a. (native or language) of Greece

green n. **1** color of grass **2** pl. leafy vegetables **3** smooth turf —a. **1** of the color green **2** unripe **3** inexperienced —**green'ness** n.

green'belt' n. area around a city, reserved for parks or farms

green'er·y n. green foliage

green'horn' n. beginner

green'house' n. heated glass building for growing plants

greet v. address, meet, or receive in a certain way

greet'ing n. act or words of one who greets

gre·gar'i·ous (-ger'-) a. sociable

gre·nade' n. small bomb usually thrown by hand

gren'a·dier' (-dir'-) n. Br. soldier of a special regiment

grew v. pt. of GROW

grey n., a. Br. sp. of GRAY

grey'hound' n. swift dog

grid n. **1** GRATE (n. 2) **2** network of crossed lines, as on a map

grid'dle n. flat pan for cooking pancakes, etc.

grid'i·ron n. **1** framework of bars on which to broil **2** football field

grid'lock' n. traffic jam allowing no movement at all

grief n. deep sorrow —**come to grief** fail

griev'ance n. complaint or a basis for it

grieve v. be or make sad

griev'ous a. **1** causing grief **2**

deplorable —**griev'ous·ly** adv.

grif'fin n. mythical beast, part eagle and part lion

grill n. 1 gridiron 2 restaurant serving grilled foods —v. 1 broil 2 question relentlessly

grille n. open grating forming a screen

grim a. **grim'mer, grim'mest** 1 fierce 2 hideous; ghastly —**grim'ly** adv.

gri·mace (or grim'is) n. twisting of the facial features —v. make grimaces

grime n. sooty dirt —**grim'y** a., **-i·er, -i·est**

grin v. **grinned, grin'ning** smile broadly —n. such a smile

grind v. **ground, grind'ing** 1 crush into bits 2 sharpen, smooth, etc. by friction 3 rub harshly 4 work by cranking —n. hard task

grind'stone' n. revolving stone for sharpening, etc.

grip n. 1 firm hold 2 handclasp 3 a handle 4 a valise —v. **gripped, grip'ping** hold firmly

gripe v. 1 cause pain in the bowels of 2 [Sl.] complain —n. [Sl.] complaint

grippe (grip) n. influenza

gris'ly (griz'-) a. **-li·er, -li·est** ghastly

grist n. grain to be ground

gris'tle (-al) n. cartilage

grit n. 1 rough bits of sand, etc. 2 obstinate courage —v. **grit'ted, grit'ting** grind (the teeth) —**grit'ty** a., **-ti·er, -ti·est**

griz'zled, griz'zly a. gray

grizzly bear n. large, ferocious North American bear

groan v., n. (utter) a deep sound of pain, etc.

gro'cer n. storekeeper who sells food, etc.

gro'cer·y n., pl. **-ies** 1 store of a grocer 2 pl. goods sold by a grocer

grog'gy a. **-gi·er, -gi·est** dazed or sluggish

groin n. fold where the abdomen joins either thigh

groom n. 1 man who tends horses 2 bridegroom —v. 1 make neat 2 train

groove n. 1 narrow furrow 2 channel 3 routine —v. make a groove in

grope v. feel or search about blindly

gross (grōs) a. 1 flagrant 2 coarse 3 total —n. 1 overall total 2 pl. **gross** twelve dozen —

v. earn before deductions —**gross out** [Sl.] disgust, offend, etc.

gro·tesque' (-tesk') a. 1 distorted 2 absurd

grot'to n., pl. **-toes** or **-tos** 1 cave 2 cavelike shrine, place, etc.

grouch n. [Col.] 1 one who grumbles 2 sulky mood —**grouch'y** a., **-i·er, -i·est**

ground v. 1 pt. & pp. of GRIND 2 set or keep on the ground 3 base 4 instruct (in) —n. 1 land; earth 2 pl. tract of land 3 distance 4 often pl. cause or basis 5 background 6 pl. dregs —a. of or on the ground

ground'er n. batted ball that rolls or bounces along the ground

ground hog n. woodchuck: also **ground'hog'**

ground'less a. without reason

ground rule n. any basic rule

ground'work' n. foundation

group n. persons or things gathered or classed together —v. form a group

grouse n. game bird

grove n. small group of trees

grov'el (gruv'-, gräv'-) v. 1 crawl abjectly 2 behave humbly

grow v. **grew, grown, grow'ing** 1 develop 2 increase 3 become 4 raise (crops) —**grow up** to mature

growl n. rumbling sound, as of an angry dog —v. make this sound

grown'-up' (n: -up') a., n. adult

growth n. 1 a growing 2 something that grows

grub v. **grubbed, grub'bing** 1 dig or dig up 2 work hard —n. 1 wormlike larva, esp. of a beetle 2 [Sl.] food

grub'by a. **-bi·er, -bi·est** dirty; untidy

grudge v. begrudge —n. resentment or a reason for this

gru'el n. thin cereal broth

gru'el·ing, gru'el·ling a. very tiring; exhausting

grue'some a. causing loathing and horror

gruff a. 1 rough and surly 2 hoarse —**gruff'ly** adv.

grum·ble v. mutter in discontent —**grum'bler** n.

grump'y a. **-i·er, -i·est** peevish; surly

grun'gy a. **-gi·er, -gi·est** [Sl.] dirty, messy, etc.

grunt v., n. (utter with) the deep sound of a hog

guar·an·tee' (gar'-) n. 1 pledge to replace something sold if faulty 2 assurance 3 pledge or security for another's debt or obligation —v. 1 give a guarantee for 2 assure Also **guar'an·ty —guar'an·tor** n.

guard v. 1 protect; defend 2 keep from escape 3 take precautions (against) —n. 1 a person or thing that guards 2 careful watch

guard'house' n. Mil. jail

guard'i·an n. 1 one legally in charge of a minor, etc. 2 custodian

guard'rail' n. protective railing

gua'va (gwä'-) n. yellow tropical fruit

gu·ber·na·to'ri·al a. of a governor or governor's office

guer·ril'la, gue·ril'la (gə-) n. fighter who makes raids behind enemy lines

guess v. 1 estimate; judge 2 suppose —n. surmise

guess'work' n. 1 a guessing 2 view based on this

guest n. 1 one entertained at another's home, etc. 2 paying customer, as at a hotel —a. 1 for guests 2 performing by invitation

guf·faw' n., v. laugh in a loud, coarse burst

guide v. 1 show the way to 2 control —n. person or thing that guides —**guid'ance** n.

guided missile n. war missile guided by radio or radar

guide'line' n. principle for directing policies, etc.

guild (gild) n. association to promote mutual interests

guile (gīl) n. deceit

guil·lo·tine (gil'ə tēn') n. instrument for beheading

guilt n. 1 fact of having committed an offense 2 painful feeling that one has done a wrong

guilt'y a. -i·er, -i·est having or showing guilt —**guilt'i·ly** adv.

guin·ea (gin'ē) n. former English coin, equal to 21 shillings

guinea fowl (or **hen**) n. speckled domestic fowl

guinea pig n. small rodent used in experiments

guise (gīz) n. assumed or false appearance

gui·tar' n. musical instrument usually with six strings plucked or strummed —**gui·tar'ist** n.

gulch n. deep narrow valley

gulf n. 1 ocean area partly enclosed by land 2 wide chasm 3 vast separation

gull n. 1 gray and white seabird 2 dupe —v. cheat

gul'let n. esophagus

gul'li·ble a. easily tricked —**gul'li·bil'i·ty** n.

gul'ly n., pl. -lies narrow ravine

gulp v. swallow greedily or hastily —n. a gulping

gum n. 1 sticky substance from some plants 2 adhesive 3 flesh around the teeth —v. gummed, gum'ming make sticky —**gum'my** a., -mi·er, -mi·est

gum'bo' n., pl. -bos soup made with okra pods

gum'drop' n. chewy candy

gun n. weapon for shooting projectiles —v. gunned, gun'ning 1 to shoot or hunt with a gun 2 to increase the speed of (an engine)

gung'-ho' a. [Col.] enthusiastic

gunk n. [Sl.] thick, messy substance

gun'man n., pl. -men armed gangster

gun'ner·y n. the making or firing of large guns —**gun'ner** n.

gun'ny n., pl. -nies sack made of coarse fabric

gun'play' n. exchange of gunshots

gun'pow'der n. explosive powder used in guns, etc.

gun'shot' n. shot fired from a gun

gun'smith' n. one who makes or repairs small guns

gun·wale (gun'əl) n. upper edge of a boat's side

gup'py n., pl. -pies tiny tropical fish

gur'gle n. bubbling sound —v. make this sound

gur'ney n. wheeled stretcher or cot used in hospitals

gu'ru' n. Hindu spiritual advisor or teacher

gush v. 1 flow copiously 2 talk too emotionally —n. a gushing —**gush'er** n.

gus'set n. a triangular piece inserted in a garment

gust n. 1 sudden rush of air 2 sudden outburst

gus·ta·to'ry a. of the sense of taste

gus'to n. zest; relish

gut n. 1 intestine 2 cord made of intestines 3 pl. [Col.] courage —v. gut'ted, gut'ting destroy the

gut'less a. lacking courage

guts'y a. **-i·er, -i·est** [Col.] courageous, forceful, etc.

gut'ta-per'cha n. rubberlike substance from some trees

gut'ter n. channel to carry off rain water, etc.

gut'tur·al (-ər əl) a. sounded in the throat; rasping

guy n. **1** rope for steadying **2** [Sl.] boy or man

guz'zle v. drink greedily

gym (jim) n. [Col.] gymnasium

gym·na'si·um n. place for physical training and sports

gym·nas'tics n.pl. **1** exercises for the muscles **2** sport employing acrobatics, etc. —**gym'nast'** n. —**gym·nas'tic** a.

gy·ne·col'o·gy (gī'nə-) n. medical science of women's diseases — **gy·ne·col'o·gist** n.

gyp (jip) n., v. **gypped, gyp'ping** [Col.] swindle

gyp'sum n. calcium sulfate, a white chalky mineral

Gyp'sy n., pl. **-sies** [also **g-**] one of a wandering people

gy'rate' (jī'-) v. to whirl —**gy·ra'tion** n.

gy'ro·scope' n. wheel mounted in a ring and spinning rapidly, used as a stabilizer —**gy'ro·scop'ic** a.

H

ha int. exclamation of surprise, triumph, etc.

ha'be·as cor'pus n. writ requiring a court to decide the legality of a prisoner's detention

hab'er·dash'er n. dealer in men's hats, shirts, etc. —**hab'er·dash'er·y, -ies** n., pl. **-ies**

hab'it n. **1** costume **2** custom **3** fixed practice

hab'it·a·ble a. fit to live in

hab'i·tat' n. natural living place

hab'i·ta'tion n. dwelling

hab'it-form'ing a. resulting in addiction

ha·bit'u·al (-bich'ōō-) a. **1** done by habit **2** constant **3** usual — **ha·bit'u·al·ly** adv.

ha·bit'u·ate' v. accustom

ha·bit'u·é' (-ā') n. constant frequenter of a place

hack v. **1** chop roughly **2** cough harshly —n. **1** gash **2** harsh cough **3** vehicle for hire **4** old, worn-out horse **5** a literary drudge

hack'er n. **1** unskilled golfer **2** talented amateur computer user

hack'les n.pl. hairs on a dog's back that bristle

hack'neyed (-nēd) a. trite; stale

hack'saw' n. saw for cutting metal: also **hack saw** n.

had v. pt. & pp. of HAVE

had'dock n. small ocean fish used as food

Ha·des (hā'dēz') hell

had'n't had not

haft n. handle, as of an ax

hag n. ugly old woman

hag'gard a. having a wasted, worn look; gaunt

hag'gle v. argue about terms, price, etc.

hai'ku (hī'-) n. three-line Japanese poem

hail n. **1** greeting **2** frozen raindrops **3** shower of or like hail — int. shout of greeting, etc. —v. **1** cheer **2** shout to **3** pour down (like) hail

hail'stone' n. piece of hail

hair n. **1** threadlike outgrowth from the skin **2** growth of these, as on the head —**split hairs** quibble —**hair'y** a., **-i·er, -i·est**

hair'breadth' n. very short distance —a. very narrow

hair'cut' n. act or style of cutting the hair

hair'dress'er n. person whose work is arranging hair

hair'piece' n. wig

hair'pin' n. wire for keeping hair in place —a. U-shaped

hair'-rais'ing a. [Col.] horrifying

hair'style' n. special style of hair: also **hair'do'**, pl. **-dos'**

hal'cy·on (-sē ən) a. tranquil

hale a. healthy; robust —v. force to go

half n., pl. **halves** either of the two equal parts of a thing —a. **1** being a half **2** partial —adv. **1** to the extent of a half **2** partially

half'-breed' n. one with parents of different races: offensive term

half brother (or sister) n. brother (or sister) by one parent only

half'heart'ed a. with little enthusiasm or interest

half'tone' n. semitone

half'way' a. **1** midway between points **2** partial —adv. to the halfway point

half'-wit'ted a. feebleminded — **half'-wit'** n.

hal'i·but n. large flounder

hall n. **1** public building with

offices 2 large room for meetings, shows, etc. 3 vestibule 4 passageway

hal'le·lu'jah, hal'le·lu'iah (-ya) int., n. praise (to) God

hall'mark' n. mark of quality

hal'low v. make or regard as holy —hal'lowed a.

Hal'low·een', Hal'low·e'en' n. evening of Oct. 31

hal·lu'ci·na'tion n. apparent perception of sights, etc. not really present —hal·lu'ci·nate' v. —hal·lu'ci·na·to'ry a.

hal·lu'ci·no·gen n. drug that produces hallucinations

hall'way' n. corridor

ha'lo n. ring of light

halt v. 1 to stop 2 to limp 3 hesitate —n. a stop —halt'ing·ly adv.

hal'ter n. 1 rope for tying an animal 2 woman's backless upper garment

halve (hav) v. 1 divide into halves 2 reduce to half

halves n. pl. of HALF

hal'yard (-yərd) n. rope for raising a flag, etc.

ham n. 1 upper part of a hog's hind leg 2 [Col.] amateur radio operator

ham'burg'er n. 1 ground beef 2 cooked patty of such meat, often in a bun Also ham'burg

ham'let n. small village

ham'mer n. tool with a metal head for pounding —v. pound, drive, shape, etc. as with a hammer

ham'mock n. bed of canvas, etc. swung from ropes

ham'per v. hinder; impede —n. large basket

ham'ster n. small rodent kept as a pet

ham'string' n. tendon back of the knee

hand n. 1 end of the arm beyond the wrist 2 side or direction 3 active part 4 handwriting 5 applause 6 help 7 hired worker 8 pointer on a clock 9 cards held by a player in a card game —a. of, for, or by the hand —v. give as with the hand —at hand near —hand down bequeath —hand in hand together —hands down easily —on hand available —hand'ful n.

hand'bag' n. woman's purse

hand'ball' n. game in which players hit a ball against a wall with the hand

hand'bill' n. printed notice passed out by hand

hand'book' n. compact book of instructions or facts

hand'clasp' n. handshake

hand'cuff' n. one of a pair of shackles for the wrists —v. put handcuffs on

hand'gun' n. firearm held with one hand, as a pistol

hand'i·cap' n. 1 difficulty or advantage given to some contestants to equalize their chances 2 hindrance 3 physical disability —v. -capped', -cap' ping hinder

hand'i·craft' n. work calling for skill with the hands

hand'i·work' n. result of one's doing

hand·ker·chief (haŋ'kər chif') n. small cloth for wiping the nose, etc.

han'dle n. part of tool, etc. by which it is held —v. 1 touch, lift, etc. with the hand 2 manage 3 deal with 4 deal in; sell

han'dle·bar' n. often pl. curved bar for steering a bicycle, etc.

hand'made' adv. made by hand, not by machine

hand'out' n. 1 gift to a beggar, etc. 2 leaflet, etc. handed out

hand'rail' n. rail along a staircase, etc.

hand'shake' n. clasping of hands in greeting

hand'some adv. 1 good-looking in a manly or impressive way 2 sizable 3 gracious

hand'spring' n. a turning over in midair with the hands touching the ground

hand'-to-mouth' a. with just enough to live on

hand'writ·ing n. writing done by hand —hand'writ'ten a.

hand'y a. -i·er, -i·est 1 nearby 2 easily used 3 clever with the hands —hand'i·ly adv.

hand'y·man' n., pl. -men' man who does odd jobs

hang v. hung or (v. 3) hanged, hang'ing 1 to attach or be attached from above 2 attach so as to swing freely 3 kill by suspending from a rope about the neck 4 attach to walls 5 droop —n. 1 way a thing hangs 2 way a thing is done —hang around [Col.] loiter —hang back hesitate, as from shyness —hang on 1 keep hold 2 persevere —hang up 1 end a telephone call 2 delay

hang'ar n. aircraft shelter

hang'dog a. abject; cowed

hang'er n. that on which something is hung

hang'nail n. bit of torn skin next to a fingernail

hang'o·ver n. sickness resulting from being drunk

hang'-up' n. [Sl.] personal problem one finds hard to cope with

hank n. skein of yarn

han'ker v. long (for)

Ha·nu·ka (hä'noo kä') n. Jewish festival

hap'haz'ard a. not planned; random —adv. by chance

hap'less a. unlucky

hap'pen v. 1 take place 2 occur by chance 3 have the luck or occasion

hap'pen·ing n. event

hap'py a. **-pi·er, -pi·est** 1 showing pleasure or joy 2 lucky 3 apt —**hap'pi·ly** adv. —**hap'pi·ness** n.

hap'py-go-luck'y a. easygoing

har·a·ki·ri (här'ə kir'ē) n. Japanese ritual suicide

ha·rangue' (-raŋ') v., n. (to address in) a noisy or scolding speech

ha·rass (hə ras', har'əs) v. trouble or attack constantly —**har'ass'ment** n.

har·bin·ger (här'bin jər) n. forerunner

har'bor n. protected inlet for ships —v. 1 to shelter 2 hold in the mind

hard a. 1 firm or solid 2 powerful 3 difficult to do, understand, etc. 4 harsh —adv. 1 with energy 2 with strength 3 firmly —**hard and fast** strict —**hard'en** v.

hard'-bit'ten a. tough; stubborn

hard'-boiled' a. 1 boiled until solid 2 [Col.] tough; unfeeling

hard'-core' adv. absolute

hard'head'ed a. 1 shrewd 2 stubborn

hard'-heart'ed a. cruel

hard'-line' a. politically unyielding

hard'ly adv. 1 barely 2 not likely

hard'-nosed' a. [Col.] tough and stubborn

hard'ship' n. thing hard to bear, as poverty, pain, etc.

hard'ware' n. 1 metal articles, as tools, nails, etc. 2 electronic equipment

hard'wood' n. tough timber with a compact texture

har'dy a. **-di·er, -di·est** 1 bold

and resolute 2 robust —**har'di·ness** n.

hare n. rabbit, esp. one of the larger kind

hare'brained' a. senseless

hare'lip' n. congenital cleft of the upper lip

ha·rem (her'əm) n. 1 quarters for the women in a Muslim's house 2 these women

hark v. [Poet.] listen

hark·en v. hearken

har'le·quin n. masked clown

har'lot n. prostitute

harm n., v. hurt; damage —**harm'ful** a. —**harm'less** a.

har·mon'i·ca n. small wind instrument held to the mouth

har'mo·nize' v. 1 be, sing, etc. in harmony 2 bring into harmony

har'mo·ny n. 1 pleasing agreement of parts 2 agreement in ideas, action, etc. 3 pleasing combination of musical tones —**har·mon'ic** a. —**har·mon'i·cal·ly** adv. —**har·mo'ni·ous** a.

har'ness n. straps, etc. for hitching a horse to a wagon, etc. —v. 1 put harness on 2 control for use

harp n. stringed musical instrument played by plucking —v. keep talking or writing (on) —**harp'ist** n.

har·poon' n. barbed shaft for spearing whales —v. to strike or catch with a harpoon

harp'si·chord' n. early keyboard instrument

har'ri·dan (har'-) n. shrewish old woman

har'row (har'-) n. frame with spikes or disks for breaking up plowed land —v. 1 draw a harrow over 2 distress

har'ry (har'-) v. **-ried, -ry·ing** harass; torment

harsh a. 1 rough to the ear, eye, taste, etc. 2 cruel or severe —**harsh'ly** adv. —**harsh'ness** n.

hart n. male deer; stag

har'vest n. 1 a season's crop or the gathering of it 2 season for this —v. reap

has v. pres. t. of HAVE: used with he, she, or it

hash n. a cooked mixture of chopped meat, potatoes, etc.

hash'ish' (-ēsh') n. narcotic made from Indian hemp

has'n't has not

hasp n. clasplike fastening for a door, lid, etc.

has'sle n. [Col.] annoying or troubling situation —v. [Sl.]

annoy; harass

has'sock n. firm cushion used as a footstool, etc.

hast v. [Ar.] have: with *thou*

haste n. hurry or rush

has·ten (hās'ən) v. to hurry

hast'y a. **-i·er, -i·est** done with haste **—hast'i·ly** adv.

hat n. head covering, often with a brim

hatch v. 1 bring or come forth from (an egg) 2 contrive (a plot) **—n.** hatchway or its lid

hatch'er·y n., pl. **-ies** place for hatching eggs

hatch'et n. short ax

hatch'way' n. opening in a ship's deck, or in a floor

hate v. dislike strongly **—n.** strong dislike: also **ha'tred**

hate'ful a. deserving hate

hath v. [Ar.] has

haugh·ty (hôt'ē) a. **-ti·er, -ti·est** scornfully proud **—haugh'ti·ly** adv. **—haugh'ti·ness** n.

haul v. 1 pull; drag 2 transport by truck, etc. **—n.** 1 amount caught 2 load or distance transported

haunch n. hip, rump, and upper thigh

haunt v. 1 visit often 2 recur often to **—n.** place often visited

haunt'ed a. supposedly frequented by ghosts

have v. **had, hav'ing** 1 hold; possess 2 experience 3 hold mentally 4 get; take 5 beget 6 engage in 7 cause to do, be, etc. 8 permit to be forced *Have* is also an important auxiliary verb **—n.** rich person or nation **— have on** be wearing **—have to do with** deal with

ha'ven n. shelter; refuge

have'-not' n. poor person or nation

have'n't have not

hav'er·sack' n. bag for provisions, worn on the back

hav'oc n. great destruction **— play havoc with** ruin

hawk n. bird of prey **—v.** 1 peddle (goods) in the streets 2 clear the throat

hawk'er n. peddler

haw'ser (-zər) n. cable for anchoring or towing a ship

haw'thorn' n. small tree with red berries

hay n. grass, clover, etc. cut and dried **—hay'stack'** n.

hay fever n. allergy to pollen that affects one like a cold

hay'wire' a. [Col.] wrong or crazy

haz'ard n. 1 chance 2 risk; danger 3 obstacle on a golf course **—v.** to risk **—haz'ard·ous** a.

haze n. 1 mist of fog, smoke, etc. 2 vagueness **—ha'zy** a., **-zi·er, -zi·est**

ha'zel n. 1 tree bearing small nut (**ha'zel·nut'**) 2 reddish brown

H'-bomb' n. hydrogen bomb

he pron. 1 the male mentioned 2 anyone

head n. 1 part of the body above or in front of the neck 2 mind 3 top or front part 4 leader 5 crisis 6 poise **—a.** 1 chief 2 at the head **—v.** 1 to lead 2 set out; go **—head off** intercept **— lose one's head** lose self-control **—not make head or tail of** not understand **—over one's head** beyond one's understanding **—turn one's head** make one vain

head'ache' n. pain in the head

head'dress' n. decorative head covering

head'first' adv. headlong

head'ing n. title; caption

head'light' n. light at the front of a vehicle

head'line' n. title of newspaper article **—v.** feature

head'long' a., adv. 1 with the head first 2 rash(ly)

head'-on' a., adv. 1 with the head or front foremost 2 directly

head'phone' n. often pl. device with tiny speakers worn over the ears

head'quar'ters n.pl. center of operations; main office

head'stone' n. grave marker

head'strong' a. obstinate

head'way' n. progress

head'y a. **-i·er, -i·est** 1 intoxicating 2 rash

heal v. cure or mend

health n. 1 soundness of body and mind 2 physical condition **—health'ful** a. **—health'y** a., **-i·er, -i·est**

heap n., v. pile; mass

hear v. **heard, hear'ing** 1 receive (sounds) through the ear 2 listen to 3 be told **—not hear of** not permit

hear'ing n. 1 ability to hear 2 chance to be heard

heark·en (här'kən) v. listen

hear'say' n. gossip; rumor

hearse (hurs) n. vehicle to carry

a body to the grave

heart n. 1 organ that circulates the blood 2 vital part 3 love, sympathy, courage, etc. 4 figure shaped like ♥ —**by heart** from memory —**take to heart** take (too) seriously

heart'ache' n. sorrow

heart'bro'ken a. overwhelmed with sorrow —**heart'break'ing** a.

heart'burn' n. burning sensation in the stomach

heart'en v. encourage

heart'felt' a. sincere

hearth (härth) n. 1 floor of a fireplace 2 home

heart'less a. unkind

heart'-rend'ing a. agonizing

heart'sick' a. very sad

heart'-to-heart' a. intimate

heart'y a. -i-er, -i-est 1 cordial 2 vigorous 3 strong and healthy 4 nourishing —**heart'i-ly** adv.

heat n. 1 hotness, or the perception of it 2 strong feeling 3 single race, etc. in a series 4 sexual excitement in animals —v. to make or become hot —**heat'ed-ly** adv. —**heat'er** n.

heath n. tract of open wasteland

hea-then (hē'thən) a. n. (of) one not a Jew, Christian, or Muslim

heath'er (heth'-) n. low plant with purple flowers

heave v. **heaved** or **hove**, **heav'ing** 1 lift, or lift and throw, with effort 2 make (a sigh) with effort 3 rise and fall in rhythm 4 retch or vomit —n. act of heaving

heav'en Theol. the place where God and his angels are —n. 1 pl. sky 2 state of bliss —**heav'en-ly** a.

heav'y a. -i-er, -i-est 1 weighing much 2 very great, intense, etc. 3 sorrowful —n., pl. -ies stage villain —**heav'i-ly** adv. —**heav'i-ness** n.

heav'y-du'ty a. made to withstand hard use

heav'y-hand'ed a. awkward

heav'y-set' a. stout; stocky

He'brew' n. language of ancient and modern Israel —a. of the Jews

heck'le v. annoy with questions, taunts, etc. —**heck'ler** n.

hec'tare' n. measure of land, 10,000 sq. meters

hec'tic a. rushed, frenzied, etc. —**hec'ti-cal-ly** adv.

he'd 1 he had 2 he would

hedge n. dense row of shrubs —

v. 1 put a hedge around 2 avoid direct answers

hedge'hog' n. porcupine

he'don-ist n. pleasure-seeker —**he'don-ism'** n. —**he'do-nis'tic** a.

heed n. careful attention —v. pay heed (to) —**heed'ful** a. —**heed'less** a.

heel n. 1 back part of the foot 2 part of shoe, etc. at the heel —v. 1 furnish with heels 2 follow closely 3 lean to one side, as a ship

heft [Col.] n. heaviness —v. to lift —**heft'y** a., -i-er, -i-est

he-gem'o-ny (hi jem'-) n. dominance of one nation over others

heif'er (hef'-) n. young cow

height n. 1 highest point or degree 2 distance from bottom to top 3 altitude 4 pl. high place

height'en v. make or become higher, greater, etc.

Heim'lich maneuver (hīm'lik) n. emergency technique for dislodging an object in the windpipe

hei'nous (hā'-) a. outrageous

heir (er) n. one who inherits another's property, etc. —**heir'ess** n.fem.

heir'loom' n. a possession handed down in a family

heist (hīst) [Sl.] n. a robbery —v. rob or steal

held v. pt. & pp. of HOLD

hel'i-cop'ter n. aircraft with a horizontal propeller above the fuselage

he'li-um n. very light, nonflammable gas, a chemical element

he'll 1 he will 2 he shall

hell Theol. place of torment for sinners after death —n. state of evil or great suffering —**hell'ish** a.

Hel-len'ic a. Greek

hel-lo' int. exclamation of greeting

helm n. 1 tiller or wheel to steer a ship 2 control

hel'met n. protective head covering of metal, etc.

helms'man n., pl. -men man who steers a ship

help v. 1 give assistance (to); aid 2 to remedy 3 avoid 4 serve —n. 1 aid; assistance 2 remedy 3 one that helps 4 hired helper(s) —**help'er** n. —**help'ful** a.

help'ing n. portion of food served to one person

help'less n. 1 unable to help

oneself 2 unprotected

hel'ter-skel'ter *adv.*, *a.* in or showing haste or confusion

hem *v.* **hemmed, hem'ming** 1 fold the edge of and sew down 2 surround or confine 3 clear the throat audibly —*n.* hemmed edge —**hem and haw** hesitate in speaking

hem'i·sphere *n.* 1 half a sphere 2 any of the halves (N or S, E or W) of the earth

hem'lock *n.* 1 evergreen tree 2 poisonous weed

hemo– *pref.* blood

he'mo·glo'bin *n.* coloring matter of red blood cells

he'mo·phil'i·a *n.* inherited condition in which the blood fails to clot —**he'mo·phil'i·ac'** *n.*

hem'or·rhage (-ər ij') *n.* heavy bleeding —*v.* bleed heavily

hem'or·rhoids' (-ər oidz') *n.pl.* swollen veins near the anus —**hem'or·rhoi'dal** *a.*

hemp *n.* tall plant with fibers used to make rope, etc.

hem'stitch' *n.* ornamental stitch, used esp. at a hem

hen *n.* female of the chicken or certain other birds

hence *adv.* 1 from this place or time 2 therefore

hence·forth' *adv.* from now on

hench'man *n.*, *pl.* **-men** helper or follower, esp. of a criminal

hen'na *n.* reddish-brown dye from a tropical shrub

hen'pecked' *a.* nagged or dominated by one's wife

hep'a·ti'tis *n.* inflammation of the liver

her *pron.* objective case of SHE —*a.* of her

her'ald *n.* 1 messenger 2 forerunner —*v.* foretell

her'ald·ry *n.* 1 study of coats of arms, etc. 2 pomp —**he·ral'dic** *a.*

herb (urb, hurb) *n.* nonwoody plant, now esp. one used as seasoning or in medicine —**herb'al** (hur'bal, ur'-) *a.*

her'bi·cide' (hur'-, ur'-) *n.* chemical used to kill plants, esp. weeds

her·biv'o·rous (hər-) *a.* plant-eating

her'cu·le'an *a.* having or involving great strength, courage, etc.

herd *n.* cattle, etc. feeding or living together —*v.* form into a herd or group

herds'man *n.*, *pl.* **-men** one who tends a herd

here *adv.* 1 in, at, or to this place 2 at this point; now —*n.* this place

here'a·bout' *adv.* near here: also **here'a·bouts'**

here·aft'er *adv.* from now on —*n.* state after death

here'by' *adv.* by this means

he·red'i·tar'y *adv.* of, or passed down by, heredity or inheritance

he·red'i·ty *n.* passing on of characteristics to offspring or descendants

here·in' *adv.* in this place, matter, writing, etc.

her'e·sy (her'-) *n.*, *pl.* **-sies** unorthodox opinion or religious belief —**her'e·tic** *n.* —**he·ret'i·cal** *a.*

here·to·fore' *adv.* until now

her'it·a·ble *a.* that can be inherited

her'it·age *n.* tradition, etc. handed down from the past

her·maph'ro·dite' *n.* one with both male and female parts —**her·maph'ro·dit'ic** *a.*

her·met'ic *a.* airtight: also **her·met'i·cal** —**her·met'i·cal·ly** *adv.*

her'mit *n.* one who lives alone in a secluded place

her'ni·a *n.* rupture, as of the abdominal wall

he·ro (hir'ō) *n.*, *pl.* **-roes** 1 brave, noble person, esp. a man 2 central male character in a story —**he·ro'ic** *a.* —**her·o·ine** (her'ō in) *n.fem.* —**her'o·ism'** *n.*

her'o·in *n.* narcotic

her'on *n.* wading bird

her'pes' (-pēz') *n.* viral disease causing blisters

her'ring *n.* food fish of the Atlantic

her'ring·bone' *n.* pattern of parallel, slanting lines

hers *pron.* that or those belonging to her

her·self' *pron.* intensive or reflexive form of SHE

hertz *n.*, *pl.* **hertz** international unit of frequency, as of waves

he's 1 he is 2 he has

hes'i·tate' (hez'-) *v.* 1 feel unsure; waver 2 pause —**hes'i·tan·cy** *n.* —**hes'i·tant** *a.* —**hes'i·ta'tion** *n.*

het'er·o·dox' *a.* unorthodox, as in religious beliefs —**het'er·o·dox'y** *n.*

het'er·o·ge'ne·ous *a.* 1 dissimilar 2 varied

het'er·o·sex'u·al *a.* of or having sexual desire for those of the opposite sex —*n.* heterosexual person

hew v. **hewed, hewed** or **hewn'**, **hew'ing** chop, as with an ax

hex n. spell bringing bad luck; jinx

hex'a·gon' n. figure with 6 angles and 6 sides —**hex·ag'o·nal** a.

hey (hā) int. exclamation to get attention, etc.

hey'day' n. peak period

hi int. [Col.] word of greeting

hi·a'tus n. gap or interruption

hi'ber·nate' v. spend the winter in a sleeplike state —**hi'ber·na'·tion** n. —**hi'ber·na'tor** n.

hi·bis'cus n. plant with large, colorful flowers

hic'cup' n. muscle spasm that stops the breath —v. have a hiccup Also **hic'cough'**

hick n. [Col.] unsophisticated country person: contemptuous term

hick'o·ry n., pl. **-ries** 1 hardwood tree 2 its nut

hide v. **hid, hid'den** or **hid, hid'ing** 1 put, or be, out of sight 2 keep secret —n. animal skin or pelt

hide'a·way' n. [Col.] secluded place

hide'bound' a. narrow-minded

hid'e·ous a. very ugly

hide'-out' n. [Col.] hiding place, as for gangsters

hie v. **hied, hie'ing** or **hy'ing** hasten

hi'er·ar'chy (-är'kē) n., pl. **-chies** (rule by) officials or clergy in graded ranks —**hi'er·ar'chi·cal** a.

hi'er·o·glyph'ics (hī'er ə glif'-, hī'rə glif'-) n.pl. picture writing, as of the ancient Egyptians —**hi'er·o·glyph'ic** a., n.

hi'-fi' a. of high fidelity

high a. 1 tall 2 to, at, or from a height 3 above others in rank, size, cost, etc. 4 raised in pitch; shrill 5 elated 6 [Sl.] drunk or influenced by drugs —adv. in or to a high level, etc. —n. 1 high level, degree, etc. 2 the gear arrangement giving greatest speed —**high'ly** adv.

high'ball' n. liquor mixed with soda water, etc.

high'brow' n., a. [Col.] intellectual

high fidelity n. accurate reproduction of sound

high'-flown' a. too showy

high'hand'ed a. arrogant

high'light' n. brightest or most interesting part, scene, etc.

high'-mind'ed a. having high ideals or principles

high'ness n. 1 height 2 [H-] title of royalty

high'-pres'sure a. using persuasive methods

high'-rise' a. tall building

high school n. school from grades 8 (or 9) through 12

high seas n.pl. ocean waters not belonging to any nation

high'-strung' a. excitable

high'-tech' a. of complex technology

high'-ten'sion a. carrying a high voltage

high'way' n. main road

high'way·man n., pl. **-men** highway robber

hi'jack' v. [Col.] steal (goods in transit) by force

hike v., n. 1 (take) a long walk 2 [Col.] increase

hi·lar'i·ous a. very funny or merry —**hi·lar'i·ty** n.

hill n. mound of land —**hill'y** a., **-i·er, -i·est**

hill·bil'ly n., pl. **-lies** [Col.] native of mountains or backwoods of southern U.S.: sometimes a contemptuous term

hill'ock n. small hill

hilt n. handle of a sword, dagger, etc.

him pron. objective case of HE

him·self' pron. intensive or reflexive form of HE

hind a. back; rear —n. female of the red deer

hin'der v. keep back; stop or thwart —**hin'drance** n.

hind'most' a. farthest back

hind'sight' n. recognition, after the event, of what one should have done

Hin'du n. native or language of India —a. 1 of Hindus 2 of Hinduism

Hin'du·ism' n. main religion of India

hinge n. joint on which a door, etc. swings —v. 1 attach by a hinge 2 depend

hint n. slight indication —v. give a hint

hin'ter·land' n. remote area

hip n. part between the upper thigh and the waist

hip'pie n. [Sl.] young person, esp. of 1960's, alienated from conventional society

hip'po·pot'a·mus n., pl. **-mus·es** or **-mi'** (-mī') large, thick-skinned animal of Africa

hire v. pay for the services or use

of —n. amount paid in hiring

hire'ling n. one who will do almost anything for pay

hir'sute' (hur'-) a. hairy

his pron. that or those belonging to him —a. of him

His·pan'ic n. Spanish-speaking Latin American living in U.S.

hiss n. prolonged s sound —v. 1 make this sound 2 disapprove of by hissing

his'to·ry n., pl. **-ries** study or record of past events —his·to'ri·an n. —his·tor'i·cal, his·tor'ic a.

his'tri·on'ics (-trē-) n.pl. dramatics —his'tri·on'ic a.

hit v. hit, hit'ting 1 come against with force; bump 2 give a blow (to); strike 3 affect strongly 4 come (on or upon) —n. 1 a blow 2 collision 3 successful song, play, etc. —hit'ter n.

hitch v. 1 move with jerks 2 fasten with a hook, knot, etc. — n. 1 a tug; jerk 2 hindrance 3 kind of knot

hitch'hike' v. travel by asking for rides from motorists —hitch'hik'er n.

hith'er adv. to this place

hith'er·to' adv. until now

hive n. 1 colony of bees or its shelter 2 pl. skin allergy with raised, itching patches

hoard n. hidden supply —v. accumulate and store away (money, etc.) —hoard'er n.

hoar'frost' n. frozen dew

hoarse a. sounding rough and husky

hoar'y a. **-i·er, -i·est** 1 white 2 white-haired and old 3 very old

hoax n. a trick; practical joke — v. to fool

hob'ble v. 1 to limp 2 hamper by tying the legs —n. a limp

hob'by n., pl. **-bies** pastime activity —hob'by·ist n.

hob'nail' n. broad-headed nail for shoe soles

hob'nob' v. **-nobbed', -nob'bing** be friendly (with)

ho'bo' n., pl. **-bos'** or **-boes'** a vagrant; tramp

hock n. hind-leg joint that bends backward —v. [Sl.] to pawn

hock'ey n. team game played on ice skates

hod n. 1 trough for carrying bricks, etc. 2 coal scuttle

hodge'podge' n. a jumble

hoe n. garden tool with a thin blade on a long handle —v. hoed, hoe'ing cultivate with a hoe

hog n. 1 pig 2 [Col.] greedy person —v. hogged, hog'ging [Sl.] take all of

hogs'head' n. large barrel

hog'tie' v. [Col.] hinder from action

hog'wash' n. insincere words

hoi pol·loi' (-pə loi') n. the common people

hoist v. raise, esp. with a crane, etc. —n. apparatus for lifting

hok'ey (hōk'-) a. [Sl.] overly sentimental

hold v. held, hold'ing 1 keep in the hands 2 keep in a certain position 3 keep back 4 occupy 5 have (a meeting, etc.) 6 contain 7 regard as 8 remain unyielding —n. 1 grip 2 a strong influence 3 ship's interior below deck —get hold of acquire —hold up 1 delay 2 rob

hold'ings n.pl. property, esp. stocks or bonds, owned

hold'out' n. one who refuses to perform, join in, etc.

hold'o·ver n. [Col.] one staying on from former time

hold'up' n. 1 a delay 2 robbery

hole n. 1 hollow place 2 burrow 3 an opening, tear, etc. —hole up hibernate, as in a hole

hol'i·day' (häl'ə-) n. 1 religious festival 2 work-free day, usually set aside by law

ho'li·ness n. a being holy

hol'lan·daise' sauce (-dāz'-) n. creamy sauce of butter, egg yolks, etc.

hol'ler v., n. [Col.] shout

hol'low a. 1 having a cavity within it 2 concave; sunken 3 insincere 4 deep-toned and dull —n. 1 cavity 2 small valley — v. make or become hollow

hol'ly n. evergreen shrub with red berries

hol'ly·hock' n. tall plant with large, showy flowers

hol·o·caust' (häl'ə kôst') n. great destruction, esp. of people or animals by fire

hol'ster n. leather pistol case

ho'ly a. **-li·er, -li·est** 1 sacred 2 sinless 3 deserving reverence or worship

Holy Communion n. church rite in which bread and wine are received as (symbols of) the body and blood of Jesus

Holy Ghost (or Spirit) third person of the Trinity

hom'age (häm'-, äm'-) n. anything done to show honor or respect

home n. 1 place where one lives 2 household or life around it —a. 1 domestic 2 central —adv. 1 at or to home 2 to the target —**home'less** a. —**home'made'** a.

home'land' n. native land

home'ly a. -li·er, -li·est 1 simple 2 plain; ugly

home plate n. Baseball last base touched in scoring a run

home run n. Baseball hit by which the batter scores a run

home'sick' a. longing for home —**home'sick·ness** n.

home'spun' n. cloth made of yarn spun at home —a. plain or simple

home'stead' (-sted') n. 1 a home and its grounds 2 public land granted as a farm

home'stretch' n. final part of racetrack, project, etc.

home'ward adv., a. toward home: also **home'wards** adv.

home'work' n. schoolwork done outside the classroom

hom'i·cide' n. 1 a killing of one person by another 2 one who kills another —**hom·i·ci'dal** a.

hom'i·let'ics n. art of writing and preaching sermons

hom'i·ly n., pl. -lies sermon

hom'i·ny n. coarsely ground dry corn

homo- pref. same; equal

ho·mo·ge'ne·ous a. 1 similar 2 made up of similar parts

ho·mog'e·nize' (-mäj'-) v. make uniform throughout —**ho·mog'e·nous** a.

hom'o·graph' n. word with same spelling as another but having a different meaning

hom'o·nym' (-nim') n. word pronounced like another but having a different meaning and, usually, spelling

Ho·mo sa·pi·ens (hō'mō sā'pē enz') n. man; human being

ho·mo·sex'u·al a. of or having sexual desire for those of the same sex —n. homosexual person

hon'cho n., pl. -chos' [Sl.] person in charge; chief

hone n. fine whetstone —v. sharpen on a hone

hon'est (än'-) a. 1 not cheating, stealing, or lying; upright 2 sincere or genuine 3 frank and open —**hon'es·ty** n.

hon'ey n. sweet, syrupy substance made by bees (**hon'ey·bees'**)

hon'ey·comb' n. structure of wax cells made by bees to hold their honey, etc. —v. fill with holes

hon'ey·dew melon n. muskmelon with a whitish rind

hon'ey·moon' n. vacation for a newly married couple —v. have a honeymoon

hon'ey·suck'le n. a vine with small, fragrant flowers

honk n. 1 call of a wild goose 2 sound of an auto horn —v. make this sound

hon'ky-tonk' n. [Sl.] cheap, noisy nightclub

hon'or (än'-) n. 1 high regard 2 good reputation 3 adherence to right principles 4 glory or credit 5 [H-] title of certain officials 6 something showing respect 7 source of respect of fame —v. 1 treat with respect or high regard 2 confer an honor on 3 accept as valid

hon'or·a·ble a. deserving honor —**hon'or·a·bly** adv.

hon·o·ra'ri·um (-rer'ē-) n. fee paid for professional services

hon'or·ar'y a. done, given, or held as an honor

hon'our n. Br. sp. of HONOR

hood n. 1 covering for the head and neck 2 cover over an automobile engine 3 [Sl.] hoodlum —**hood'ed** a.

-hood suf. 1 state or quality 2 whole group of

hood'lum n. ruffian

hood'wink' v. deceive

hoof n., pl. hoofs or hooves horny covering on the feet of cattle, horses, etc.

hook n. 1 bent piece of metal used to catch or hold something, spec., one for catching fish 2 sharp curve or curving motion —v. catch, fasten, hit, etc. with a hook —**hook up** connect, as a radio

hook'er n. [Sl.] a prostitute

hook'up' n. connection of parts, as in radio

hook'y n. used only in play hooky, be a truant

hoop n. large, circular band

hoop'la' n. [Col.] excitement

hoo·ray' int., n. hurrah

hoot n. 1 cry an owl makes 2 shout of scorn —v. utter a hoot or hoots

hop v. hopped, hop'ping leap on one foot, or with all feet at once —n. 1 a hopping 2 [Col.] a dance 3 pl. dried cones of a vine, used to flavor beer, etc.

hope n. 1 trust that what is wanted will happen 2 object of this —v. want and expect —**hope'ful** a. —**hope'less** a.

hop'per n. trough from which material is conveyed

horde n. a crowd; pack

ho·ri'zon n. line where sky and earth seem to meet

hor·i·zon'tal a. 1 parallel to the horizon 2 level

hor'mone' n. substance that is formed by a gland and stimulates an organ

horn n. 1 bonelike growth on the head of a cow, etc. 2 brass musical instrument —**horned** a.

hor'net n. large wasp

horn'pipe' n. sailor's dance

horn'y a. -i·er, -i·est 1 hard; callous 2 [Sl.] easily aroused sexually

hor'o·scope' n. chart of the zodiac used by astrologers

hor·ren'dous a. horrible

hor'ri·ble a. 1 causing horror 2 [Col.] very bad, ugly, etc. —**hor'ri·bly** adv.

hor'rid a. horrible

hor'ri·fy' v. -fied', -fy'ing 1 make feel horror 2 [Col.] shock greatly

hor'ror n. 1 strong fear or dislike 2 cause of this

hors d'oeuvre (ôr' dʉrv') n., pl. **hors d'oeuvres'** appetizer

horse n. 1 large animal domesticated for pulling loads, carrying a rider, etc. 2 supporting frame on legs —**horse around** [Sl.] 1 engage in horseplay 2 waste time —**hors'y** a.

horse'back' adv., n. (on) the back of a horse

horse'man n., pl. -men skilled rider of horses —**horse'man·ship'** n. —**horse'wom'an** n., pl. -wom'en

horse'play' n. rough play

horse'pow'er n. unit of power output, as of engines

horse'rad'ish n. plant with a pungent edible root

horse'shoe' n. flat, U-shaped, metal plate nailed to a horse's hoof

hor·ta·to·ry a. exhorting

hor'ti·cul'ture n. art of growing flowers, fruits, etc. —**hor'ti·cul'tur·al** a.

ho·san'na (-zan'-) int., n. shout of praise to God

hose n. 1 pl. hose stocking 2 flexible tube to convey liquids

ho'sier·y (-zhər-) n. stockings

hos'pice (-pis) n. shelter for travelers, sick, poor, etc.

hos'pi·ta·ble (-pit a-) a. friendly to guests —**hos·pi·tal'i·ty** n.

hos'pi·tal n. place of medical care for sick and injured —**hos'pi·tal·ize'** v.

host n. 1 man who entertains guests 2 great number

hos'tage n. person held as a pledge

hos'tel n. lodging place

host'ess n. 1 woman who acts as a host 2 woman in charge of seating in a restaurant

hos'tile (-təl) a. 1 of or like an enemy 2 unfriendly

hos·til'i·ty n., pl. -ties 1 enmity 2 pl warfare

hot a. **hot'ter, hot'test** 1 high in temperature; very warm 2 spicy; peppery 3 angry, violent, eager, etc. 4 close behind 5 [Col.] fresh or new —**hot'ly** adv.

hot'bed' n. glass-covered bed of earth, for forcing plants

hot'-blood'ed a. excitable

hot cake n. pancake

hot dog n. [Col.] wiener

ho·tel' n. place with rooms, etc. for travelers

hot'head'ed a. easily angered —**hot'head'** n.

hot'house' n. greenhouse

hot plate n. small, portable stove

hot rod n. [Sl.] car rebuilt for speed —**hot rod'der** n.

hot'shot' n. [Sl.] one thought of as skillful, important, etc.

hound n. breed of hunting dog —v. keep pursuing

hour n. 1 $\frac{1}{24}$ of a day; 60 minutes 2 a particular time —**hour'ly** a., adv.

hour'glass' n. instrument for measuring time by the flow of sand in it

house (v.: houz) n. 1 building to live in 2 family 3 building for specified use 4 business firm 5 legislative assembly —v. cover, shelter, lodge, etc. —**keep house** take care of a home

house'break'ing n. breaking into another's house to steal

house'bro'ken a. trained to live in a house, as a dog

house'hold' n. 1 all those living in one house 2 home and its affairs

house'hold'er n. 1 owner of a house 2 head of a household

house'keep'er n. a woman who manages a home

house′wife′ *n.*, *pl.* **-wives′** woman running a home

house′work′ *n.* work of cleaning, cooking, etc. in a house

hous′ing (houz′-) *n.* **1** shelter or lodging; houses **2** enclosing frame, box, etc.

hov′el (huv′-) *n.* small, miserable dwelling

hov′er (huv′-) *v.* **1** flutter in the air near one place **2** linger close by

how *adv.* **1** in what way **2** in what condition **3** why **4** to what extent

how·ev′er *adv.* **1** by whatever means **2** to whatever degree —*con.* nevertheless

how′itz·er *n.* short cannon

howl *v.* **1** long, wailing cry of a wolf, dog, etc. **2** similar cry, as of pain —*v.* **1** utter a howl **2** laugh in scorn, mirth, etc.

how′so·ev′er *adv.* however

hub *n.* **1** center of a wheel **2** center of activity, etc.

hub′bub′ *n.* tumult

hu′bris (hyōō′-) arrogance

huck′le·ber′ry *n.*, *pl.* **-ries** edible dark-blue berry

huck′ster *n.* peddler

hud′dle *v.* **1** to crowd close together **2** draw (oneself) up tightly —*n.* confused crowed or heap

hue *n.* color; tint —**hue and cry** loud outcry

huff *v.* to blow; puff —*n.* burst of anger —**huff′y** *a.*, **-i·er**, **-i·est**

hug *v.* **hugged**, **hug′ging 1** embrace **2** keep close to —*n.* embrace

huge *a.* very large; immense

hu′la *n.* native Hawaiian dance

hulk *n.* **1** body of an old, dismantled ship **2** big, clumsy person or thing —**hulk′ing** *a.*

hull *n.* **1** outer covering of a seed or fruit **2** main body of a ship —*v.* remove the hulls from

hul′la·ba·loo′ *n.* clamor

hum *v.* **hummed**, **hum′ming 1** sing with closed lips **2** make a low, steady murmur —*n.* this sound

hu′man *a.* of or like a person or people —*n.* a person: also **human being** —**hu′man·ly** *adv.*

hu·mane′ *a.* kind, merciful, etc. —**hu·mane′ly** *adv.*

hu·man′i·tar′i·an *n.* one devoted to promoting the welfare of humanity —*a.* helping humanity

hu·man′i·ty *n.* **1** a being human

or humane **2** the human race

hu′man·ize′ *v.* make human or humane

hu′man·kind′ *n.* people

hu′man·oid′ *a.*, *n.* nearly human (creature)

hum′ble *a.* **1** not proud; modest **2** lowly; unpretentious —*v.* to make humble —**hum′bly** *adv.*

hum′bug′ *n.* fraud; sham

hum′drum′ *adv.* monotonous

hu′mid *a.* damp; moist

hu·mid′i·fy′ *v.* **-fied′**, **-fy′ing** make humid —**hu·mid′i·fi′er** *n.*

hu·mid′i·ty *n.* **1** dampness **2** amount of moisture in the air

hu′mi·dor′ *n.* jar, etc. for keeping tobacco moist

hu·mil′i·ate′ *v.* lower the pride or dignity of; mortify —**hu·mil′i·a′tion** *n.*

hu·mil′i·ty *n.* humbleness

hum′ming·bird′ *n.* tiny bird able to hover

hum′mock (-ək) *n.* low, rounded hill

hu·mon′gous (-mäŋ′-, -muŋ′-) *a.* [Sl.] huge

hu′mor *n.* **1** comical quality, talk, etc. **2** ability to see or express what is funny **3** mood **4** whim —*v.* indulge Also, Br. sp., **hu′mour** —**hu′mor·ist** *n.* —**hu′mor·ous** *a.*

hump *n.* rounded bulge —*v.* to arch; hunch

hump′back′ *n.* (person having) a back with a hump

hu′mus *n.* dark soil made up of decayed leaves, etc.

hunch *v.* arch into a hump —*n.* **1** a hump **2** feeling not based on facts

hunch′back′ *n.* humpback

hun′dred *a.*, *n.* ten times ten —**hun′dredth** *a.*, *n.*

hung *v.* pt. & pp. of HANG

Hun·gar′i·an (-ger′-) *a.*, *n.* (of) the people or language of Hungary

hun′ger *n.* **1** need or craving for food **2** strong desire —*v.* feel hunger (for) —**hun′gry** *a.*, **-gri·er**, **-gri·est** —**hun′gri·ly** *adv.*

hunk *n.* [Col.] large piece

hun′ker *v.* squat

hunt *v.* **1** search out (game) to catch or kill **2** search; seek **3** chase —*n.* a chase or search —**hunt′er** *n.*

hur′dle *n.* **1** frame for jumping over in a race **2** obstacle —*v.* **1** jump over **2** overcome (an obstacle)

hurl *v.* throw with force or violence —**hurl′er** n.

hurl′y-burl′y n. turmoil

hur-rah′ int., n. shout of joy, approval, etc.

hur-ray′ int., n. hurrah

hur′ri-cane n. violent storm from the tropics

hur′ry v. -ried, -ry·ing move, act, etc. with haste; rush —n. rush; haste —**hur′ried·ly** adv.

hurt v. hurt, hurt′ing 1 cause pain or injury to 2 damage 3 offend 4 have pain —n. pain, injury, or harm —**hurt′ful** a.

hur′tle v. move or throw swiftly or with violence

hus′band n. married man —v. manage thriftily

hus′band·ry n. 1 thrifty management 2 farming

hush v. make or become silent —n. silence; quiet

husk n. dry covering of some fruits and seeds —v. remove the husk from

husk′y a. -i·er, -i·est 1 hoarse 2 big and strong —n. [also H-] arctic dog used for pulling sleds

hus′sy n., pl. -sies bold or shameless woman

hus′tle (-əl) v. 1 shove roughly 2 move, work, etc. quickly or energetically —n. a hustling

hus′tler (-lər) n. [Sl.] 1 one who gets money dishonestly 2 a prostitute

hut n. shedlike cabin

hutch n. 1 chest or cupboard 2 pen or coop for small animals

hy′a·cinth′ n. plant with spikes of flowers

hy′brid n. offspring of two animals or plants of different species, etc.

hy·dran′ge·a (-drān′jə) n. shrub with large clusters of flowers

hy′drant n. large pipe with a valve for drawing water from a water main

hy·drau′lic (-drô′-) a. 1 worked by force of a moving liquid 2 of hydraulics

hy·drau′lics n. study and use of the mechanical properties of liquids

hydro- pref. 1 water 2 hydrogen

hy′dro·car′bon n. compound of hydrogen and carbon

hy′dro·chlo′ric acid (-klôr′ik) n. acid formed of hydrogen and chlorine

hy′dro·e·lec′tric a. of the production of electricity by water power

hy′dro·foil′ n. (winglike structure on) high-speed watercraft that skims just above water

hy′dro·gen n. colorless gas, the lightest chemical element

hy·drog′e·nat·ed (-dräj′-) a. treated with hydrogen

hydrogen bomb n. very destructive atomic bomb

hydrogen peroxide n. liquid bleach and disinfectant

hy′dro·pho′bi·a n. rabies

hy′dro·pon′ics n. science of growing plants in liquid mineral solutions

hy′dro·ther′a·py n. treatment of disease by external use of water

hy·e′na n. wolflike animal of Africa and Asia

hy′giene′ (-jēn′) n. set of principles for health

hy·gi·en′ic (-jē en′-, -jēn′-) a. 1 of hygiene or health 2 sanitary

hy·grom′e·ter n. device for measuring humidity

hy′men n. membrane covering part of the opening of the vagina

hymn (him) n. song of praise, esp. a religious one

hym′nal n. book of hymns: also **hymn′book′**

hype (hīp) n. [Sl.] n. sensational publicity —v. promote in a sensational way —**hype up** stimulate

hyper- pref. over; excessive

hy·per′bo·le (-bə lē) n. exaggeration for effect —**hy′per·bol′ic** a.

hy′per·ten′sion n. abnormally high blood pressure

hy′per·ven′ti·la′tion n. extreme rapid breathing, often causing dizziness, etc.

hy′phen n. mark (-) used between parts or syllables of a word

hy′phen·ate′ v. join or write with a hyphen —**hy′phen·a′tion** n.

hyp·no′sis (hip-) n. sleeplike state in which one responds to the hypnotist's suggestions —**hyp·not′ic** a.

hyp′no·tize′ v. induce hypnosis in —**hyp′no·tism′** n. —**hyp′no·tist** n.

hypo- pref. 1 under 2 less than; deficient in

hy′po·chon′dri·ac′ (-kän′-) n. one who suffers from abnormal anxiety over his or her health

hy·poc′ri·sy (hi-) n., pl. -sies condition of being, or action of a hypocrite

hyp'o·crite (-krit') *n.* one who pretends to have a virtue, feeling, etc. he or she does not have —**hyp'o·crit'i·cal** *a.*

hy'po·der'mic *a.* injected under the skin —*n.* syringe and needle for giving hypodermic injections

hy·pot'e·nuse' (-nōōs') *n.* side of right-angled triangle opposite the right angle

hy·poth'e·sis *n.* tentative explanation

hy'po·thet'i·cal *a.* based on a hypothesis; supposed

hys'ter·ec'to·my (his'-) *n.* surgical removal of the uterus

hys·te'ri·a *n.* outbreak of wild emotion —**hys·ter'i·cal** *a.*

hys·ter'ics *n.pl.* hysteria

I

I *pron.* person speaking or writing

i'bex' *n.* wild goat

i'bis *n.* large wading bird

-ible *suf.* **1** that can or should be **2** tending to

i'bu·pro'fen (i'byōō-) *n.* drug that relieves pain or fever

-ic, -ical *suf.* **1** of or having to do with **2** like **3** produced by **4** containing

ice *n.* **1** water frozen solid by cold **2** frozen dessert of fruit juice, sugar, etc. —*v.* **1** change into ice **2** cool with ice **3** cover with icing —**iced** *a.*

ice'berg' *n.* great mass of ice afloat in the sea

ice'box' *n.* refrigerator, esp. one in which ice is used

ice cream *n.* frozen cream dessert

ice skate *n.* shoe with a metal runner for gliding on the ice —**ice'-skate'** *v.*

ich'thy·ol'o·gy (ik'thē-) *n.* study of fishes —**ich'thy·ol'o·gist** *n.*

i'ci·cle *n.* hanging stick of ice

ic'ing *n.* sweet, soft coating for cakes; frosting

i'con *n.* sacred image or picture

i·con'o·clast' *n.* one who attacks venerated institutions or ideas

-ics *suf.* art or science

i'cy *a.* **i'ci·er, i'ci·est 1** full of or covered with ice **2** very cold —**i'ci·ly** *adv.* —**i'ci·ness** *n.*

id *n.* part of mind thought to be source of psychic energy

I'd 1 I had **2** I would

i·de'a *n.* **1** mental conception; a thought or belief **2** a plan or scheme

i·de'al *n.* **1** conception of something in its perfect form **2** perfect model —*a.* thought of as, or being, an ideal —**i·de'al·ly** *adv.*

i·de'al·ism' *n.* conception of, or striving for, an ideal —**i·de'al·ist** *n.* —**i·de'al·is'tic** *a.*

i·de'al·ize' *v.* regard or show as perfect —**i·de'al·i·za'tion** *n.*

i·den'ti·cal *a.* the same —**i·den'ti·cal·ly** *adv.*

i·den'ti·fy' *v.* **-fied', -fy'ing 1** show to be a certain one **2** associate closely (*with*) —**i·den'ti·fi·ca'tion** *n.*

i·den'ti·ty *n., pl.* **-ties 1** state or fact of being the same **2** individuality

i'de·ol'o·gy (i'dē-, id'ē-) *n., pl.* **-gies** system of beliefs, as of a group —**i'de·o·log'i·cal** *a.*

id'i·om *n.* **1** set phrase with a special meaning **2** usual way of expression in words —**id'i·o·mat'ic** *a.*

id'i·o·syn'cra·sy (-siŋ'-) *n., pl.* **-sies** personal oddity

id'i·ot *n.* foolish or stupid person —**id'i·o·cy** *n.* —**id'i·ot'ic** *a.*

i'dle *a.* **1** useless **2** baseless **3** not busy or working **4** lazy —*v.* **1** loaf **2** be or make idle —**i'dler** *n.* —**i'dly** *adv.*

i'dol *n.* image or object worshiped or adored

i·dol'a·try *n.* worship of idols —**i·dol'a·ter** *n.* —**i·dol'a·trous** *a.*

i'dol·ize' *v.* adore as an idol

i'dyll, i'dyl (-dəl) *n.* short poem about pleasant rural life —**i·dyl'lic** (-dil'-) *a.*

i.e. that is to say

if *con.* **1** in case that **2** although **3** whether —**as if** as it would be

if'fy *a.* [Col.] not definite

ig'loo *n., pl.* **-loos'** Eskimo hut made of snow blocks

ig·ne'ous *a.* **1** of fire **2** produced by great heat

ig·nite' *v.* **1** set fire to **2** catch on fire

ig·ni'tion *n.* **1** an igniting **2** electrical system for igniting the gases in an engine

ig·no'ble *a.* not noble; base

ig·no·min'y *n.* shame; disgrace —**ig'no·min'i·ous** *a.*

ig'no·ra'mus (-rā'məs, -ram'əs) *n., pl.* **-mus·es** ignorant person

ig'no·rant *a.* **1** showing lack of knowledge **2** unaware —**ig'no·rance** *n.*

ig·nore' *v.* pay no attention to

i·gua'na (i gwä'-) *n.* large tropical lizard

ilk *n.* kind; sort

I'll 1 I shall 2 I will

ill *a.* worse, worst 1 bad 2 sick —*n.* an evil or disease —*adv.* worse, worst 1 badly 2 scarcely —**ill at ease** uncomfortable

ill'-ad·vised' *a.* unwise

ill'-bred' *a.* rude; impolite

il·le'gal *a.* against the law —**il·le'gal·ly** *adv.*

il·leg'i·ble *a.* hard or impossible to read —**il·leg·i·bil'i·ty** *n.* —**il·leg'i·bly** *adv.*

il'le·git'i·mate (-mət) *a.* 1 born of unwed parents 2 contrary to law, rules, etc. —**il'le·git'i·ma·cy** *n.*

il·lib'er·al *a.* 1 without culture 2 narrow-minded

il·lic'it (-lis'-) *a.* improper or unlawful

il·lit'er·ate (-ət) *a.* unable to read —*n.* illiterate person —**il·lit'er·a·cy** *n.*

ill'-man'nered *a.* impolite; rude

ill'ness *n.* sickness; disease

il·log'i·cal *a.* not logical

ill'-suit'ed *a.* not appropriate

ill'-tem'pered *a.* irritable

ill'-timed' *a.* inappropriate

ill'-treat' *v.* to treat unkindly, unfairly, etc. —**ill'-treat'ment** *n.*

il·lu'mi·nate' *v.* 1 light up 2 explain 3 decorate —**il·lu'mi·na'tion** *n.*

il·lu'mine *v.* light up

ill'-use' *v.* abuse —*n.* cruel treatment: also **ill'-us'age**

il·lu'sion *n.* 1 false idea 2 misleading appearance —**il·lu'sive, il·lu'so·ry** *a.*

il'lus·trate' *v.* 1 explain, as by examples 2 furnish (books, etc.) with pictures —**il'lus·tra'tion** *n.* —**il·lus'tra·tive** *a.* —**il'lus·tra'tor** *n.*

il·lus'tri·ous *a.* famous

ill will *n.* hate; dislike

I'm I am

im– *pref.* in-: used before *b, m,* or *p*

im'age *n.* 1 a representation, as a statue 2 reflection in a mirror, etc. 3 mental picture; idea 4 copy —*v.* reflect

im'age·ry *n.* 1 images 2 descriptions

i·mag'i·nar'y *a.* existing only in the imagination

i·mag'i·na'tion *n.* 1 power to form mental pictures or ideas 2 thing imagined —**i·mag'i·na-**

tive *a.*

i·mag'ine *v.* 1 conceive in the mind 2 suppose —**i·mag'i·na·ble** *a.*

im·bal'ance *n.* lack of balance in proportion, force, etc.

im'be·cile (-səl) *a.* stupid —*n.* person who is mentally deficient —**im'be·cil'ic** *a.* —**im'be·cil'i·ty** *n.*

im·bed' *v.* embed

im·bibe' *v.* 1 drink (in) 2 absorb into the mind

im·bro'glio (-brōl'yō) *n., pl.* **–glios** involved misunderstanding or disagreement

im·bue' (-byōo') *v.* 1 saturate 2 dye 3 fill, as the mind

im'i·tate' *v.* 1 copy or mimic 2 resemble —**im'i·ta'tion** *n., a.* —**im'i·ta'tor** *n.*

im·mac'u·late (-yōō lət) *a.* 1 perfectly clean 2 without a flaw 3 pure; sinless

im'ma·nent *a.* present everywhere: said of God

im'ma·te'ri·al *a.* 1 unimportant 2 spiritual

im'ma·ture' *a.* not fully grown or developed —**im'ma·tu'ri·ty** *n.*

im·meas'ur·a·ble *a.* boundless; vast —**im·meas'ur·a·bly** *adv.*

im·me'di·ate (-ət) *a.* 1 closest 2 instant 3 direct —**im·me'di·ate·ly** *adv.*

im'me·mo'ri·al *a.* very old

im·mense' *a.* vast; huge —**im·men'si·ty** *n.*

im·merse' *v.* 1 plunge into a liquid 2 engross —**im·mer'sion** *n.*

im'mi·grant *n.* one who immigrates —*a.* immigrating

im'mi·grate' *v.* enter a country, etc. in order to settle there —**im'mi·gra'tion** *n.*

im'mi·nent *a.* likely to happen without delay —**im'mi·nence** *n.*

im·mo'bile (-bəl) *a.* not moving or movable —**im'mo·bil'i·ty** *n.* —**im·mo'bi·lize'** *v.*

im·mod'er·ate (-ət) *a.* without restraint; excessive

im·mod'est *a.* indecent —**im·mod'es·ty** *n.*

im·mor'al *a.* not moral; esp., unchaste —**im'mo·ral'i·ty** *n.*

im·mor'tal *a.* 1 living forever 2 having lasting fame —*n.* immortal being —**im'mor·tal'i·ty** *n.*

im·mov'a·ble *a.* 1 firmly fixed 2 unyielding

im·mune' *a.* exempt from or protected against something bad, as a disease, etc. —**im·mu'ni·ty** *n.*

—**im·mu·ni·za'tion** n. —**im'mu·**
nize' v.

immune system n. system protecting body from disease by
producing antibodies

im·mu·nol'o·gy n. study of
immunity to disease

im·mu'ta·ble a. unchangeable —
im·mu'ta·bly adv.

imp n. 1 young demon 2 mischievous child

im·pact' n. (force of) a collision

im·pact'ed a. describing a tooth
lodged tight in jaw

im·pair' v. make worse, less, etc.
—**im·pair'ment** n.

im·pale' v. pierce through with
something pointed

im·pal'pa·ble a. that cannot be
felt or easily perceived

im·pan'el v. Law choose (a jury)
from a jury list

im·part' v. 1 give 2 tell

im·par'tial a. fair; just —**im·par·**
ti·al'i·ty n.

im·pass'a·ble a. that cannot be
traveled over

im'passe' (–pas) n. deadlock

im·pas'sioned a. passionate;
fiery

im·pas'sive a. calm

im·pa'tient a. annoyed because
of delay, etc. —**im·pa'tience** n.

im·peach' v. try (an official) on a
charge of wrong-doing —**im·**
peach'ment n.

im·pec'ca·ble a. flawless

im·pe·cu'ni·ous a. having no
money; poor

im·ped'ance (–pēd'–) n. total
resistance in a circuit to the flow
of an electric current

im·pede' v. hinder

im·ped'i·ment n. thing that
impedes; spec., a speech defect

im·pel' v. **–pelled', –pel'ling** 1
drive forward 2 force

im·pend' v. be imminent —**im·**
pend'ing a.

im·pen'e·tra·ble a. that cannot
be penetrated

im·per'a·tive a. 1 necessary;
urgent 2 of the mood of a verb
expressing a command

im·per·cep'ti·ble a. not easily
perceived; subtle

im·per'fect a. 1 not complete 2
not perfect

im·per·fec'tion n. 1 a being
imperfect 2 fault

im·pe'ri·al a. (–pir'ē–) a. of an
empire, emperor, or empress

im·pe'ri·al·ism' n. policy of forming and maintaining an empire,
as by subjugating territories,

etc. —**im·pe'ri·al·ist** a., n.

im·per'il v. endanger

im·pe'ri·ous a. domineering

im·per'ish·a·ble a. indestructible

im·per'son·al a. 1 without reference to any one person 2 not
existing as a person

im·per'son·ate' v. 1 assume the
role of 2 mimic —**im·per·son·a'**
tion n.

im·per'ti·nent a. 1 not relevant
2 insolent —**im·per'ti·nence** n.

im·per·turb'a·ble a. calm; impas-
sive

im·per'vi·ous a. 1 incapable of
being penetrated 2 not affected
by: with to

im·pe·ti'go (–tī'–) n. skin disease
with pustules

im·pet'u·ous (–pech'–) a. impul-
sive; rash —**im·pet'u·os'i·ty** n.

im'pe·tus n. 1 force of a moving
body 2 stimulus

im·pinge' v. 1 strike, hit, etc.
(on) 2 encroach (on)

im'pi·ous (–pē–) a. not pious —
im·pi'e·ty (–pī'–) n.

im·pla'ca·ble (–plak'ə–, –plā'kə–)
a. not to be appeased

im·plant' v. 1 plant firmly 2
insert surgically —n. implanted
organ, etc.

im·plau'si·ble a. not plausible

im'ple·ment n. tool or instrument —v. put into effect

im'pli·cate' v. show to be a party
to a crime, etc.

im·pli·ca'tion n. 1 an implying
or implicating 2 something
implied

im·plic'it (–plis'–) a. 1 implied 2
absolute

im·plode' v. burst inward —**im·**
plo'sion n.

im·plore' v. beseech

im·ply' v. **–plied', –ply'ing** hint;
suggest

im·po·lite' a. discourteous

im·port' (n.: im'pôrt') v. 1 bring
(goods) into a country 2 signify
—n. 1 thing imported 2 meaning 3 importance —**im·por·ta'**
tion n.

im·por'tant a. 1 having much
significance 2 having power or
authority —**im·por'tance** n.

im·por·tune' v. urge repeatedly
—**im·por'tu·nate** (–chə nət) a.

im·pose' v. put on (a burden,
tax, etc.) —**impose on** 1 take
advantage of 2 cheat —**im·po·**
si'tion n.

im·pos'ing a. impressive

im·pos'si·ble a. that cannot be
done, exist, etc. —**im·pos·si·bil'**

i·ty n., pl. **-ties**

im·pos'tor n. cheat pretending to be what he is not

im·po'tent (-pə-) a. lacking power; helpless —**im'po·tence** n.

im·pound' v. seize by law

im·pov'er·ish v. make poor

im·prac'ti·ca·ble a. that cannot be put into practice

im·prac'ti·cal a. not practical

im'pre·cate' v. to curse —**im'pre·ca'tion** n.

im·pre·cise' a. not precise; not clear, etc.

im·preg'na·ble a. that cannot be overcome by force

im·preg'nate' v. 1 make pregnant 2 saturate —**im'preg·na'tion** n.

im'pre·sa'ri·o' (-sä'-) n., pl. **-os'** manager, as of concerts

im·press' (n.: im'pres') v. 1 to stamp 2 affect the mind or emotions of 3 to fix in the memory —n. an imprint —**im·pres'sive** a.

im·pres'sion n. 1 a mark 2 effect produced on the mind 3 vague notion

im·pres'sion·a·ble a. sensitive; easily influenced

im·pres'sion·ism' n. style of art, music, etc. reproducing a brief, immediate impression —**im·pres'sion·ist** n. —**im·pres'sion·is'tic** a.

im·pri·ma'tur (-mät'ər) n. permission, esp. to publish

im·print' (n.: im'print') v. mark or fix as by pressing —n. 1 a mark; print 2 characteristic effect

im·pris'on v. put in prison

im·prob'a·ble a. unlikely

im·promp'tu' a., adv. without preparation; offhand

im·prop'er a. not proper

im'pro·pri'e·ty (-pri'-) n., pl. **-ties** improper act

im·prove' v. make or become better or more valuable —**im·prove'ment** n.

im·prov'i·dent a. unthrifty

im'pro·vise' v. 1 compose and perform without preparation 2 make or do with whatever is at hand —**im·prov'i·sa'tion** n.

im·pru'dent a. rash; indiscreet —**im·pru'dence** n.

im'pu·dent (-pyōō-) a. insolent —**im'pu·dence** n.

im·pugn' (-pyōōn') v. to challenge as false

im'pulse n. 1 driving force;

impetus 2 sudden inclination to act —**im·pul'sive** a.

im·pu'ni·ty n. freedom from punishment or harm

im·pure' a. 1 dirty 2 immoral 3 adulterated —**im·pu'ri·ty** n., pl. **-ties**

im·pute' v. attribute

in prep. 1 contained by 2 wearing 3 during 4 at the end of 5 with regard to 6 because of 7 into —adv. to or at the inside —n. 1 pl. those in power 2 [Col.] special access —**in that** because —**in with** associated with

in- pref. 1 in, into, or toward 2 no, not, or lacking: add not or lack of to meaning of base word in list below

in'a·bil'i·ty

in'ac·ces'si·ble

in·ac'cu·ra·cy

in·ac'cu·rate

in·ac'tive

in'ad·e·qua·cy

in'ad·e·quate

in'ad·mis'si·ble

in'ad·vis'a·ble

in·an'i·mate

in·ap'pli·ca·ble

in'ap·pro'pri·ate

in·apt'

in'ar·tic'u·late

in'at·ten'tion

in·au'di·ble

in'aus·pi'cious

in·ca'pa·ble

in'ca·pac'i·ty

in'ci·vil'i·ty

in'co·her'ence

in'co·her'ent

in'com·bus'ti·ble

in'com·pat'i·ble

in'com·pre·hen'si·ble

in'con·ceiv'a·ble

in'con·clu'sive

in·con'gru·ous

in'con·sid'er·a·ble

in'con·sid'er·ate

in'con·sis'ten·cy

in'con·sis'tent

in·con'stant

in·con'ti·nence

in'con·tro·vert'i·ble

in'cor·rect'

in'cor·rupt'i·ble

in·cur'a·ble

in·de'cent

in'de·ci'sion

in'de·ci'sive

in·dec'o·rous

in·def'i·nite

in'di·gest'i·ble

in'di·rect'

in'dis·cern'i·ble

in'dis·creet'

in'dis·cre'tion

in'dis·pu'ta·ble

in'dis·tinct'

in'dis·tin'guish·a·ble

in'di·vis'i·ble

in·ed'i·ble

in'ef·fec'tive

in'ef·fec'tu·al

in·ef'fi·ca·cy

in·ef·fi'cient

in'e·las'tic

in·el'e·gant

in·el'i·gi·ble

in·e·qual'i·ty

in·eq'ui·ta·ble

in·eq'ui·ty

in'ex·act'

in'ex·cus'a·ble

in'ex·haust'i·ble

in'ex·pe'di·ent

in'ex·pen'sive

in'ex·tin'guish·a·ble

in·fer'tile

in·fre'quent

in·glo'ri·ous

in·grat'i·tude

in'har·mo'ni·ous

in·hos'pi·ta·ble

in·hu'mane'

in'ju·di'cious

in·of'fen'sive

in·op'er·a·tive

in·op'por·tune'

in·sep'a·ra·ble

in'sig·nif'i·cance

in'sig·nif'i·cant

in·sol'u·ble

in·solv'a·ble

in'sta·bil'i·ty

in'suf·fi'cient

in'sur·mount'a·ble

in·tan'gi·ble

in·tol'er·a·ble

in·tol'er·ance

in·tol'er·ant

in·var'i·a·ble

in·vul'ner·a·ble

in ab·sen'ti·a (-sen'shə) *adv.* although not present

in·ac'ti·vate' *v.* make no longer active

in'ad·vert'ent *a.* not on purpose; accidental —**in'ad·vert'ence** *n.*

in·a'lien·a·ble (-āl'yən-) *a.* that cannot be taken away

in·ane' *a.* lacking sense; silly —**in·an'i·ty** *n.*

in'as·much' as' *adv.* because

in·au'gu·rate' (-ô'gyə-) *v.* 1 formally induct into office 2 begin; open —**in·au'gu·ral** *a.* —**in·au'gu·ra'tion** *n.*

in'board' *a.* inside the hull of a boat

in'born' *a.* present at birth; natural

in'bound' *a.* going inward

in'breed' *v.* breed by continually mating from the same stock

in·cal'cu·la·ble *a.* too great to be calculated

in'can·des'cent *a.* 1 glowing with heat 2 shining

in'can·ta'tion *n.* words chanted in magic spells

in·ca·pac'i·tate' (-pas'-) *v.* make unable or unfit

in·car'cer·ate' *v.* imprison —**in·car'cer·a'tion** *n.*

in·car'nate (-nət) *a.* in human form; personified —**in·car'na'tion** *n.*

in'cen·di·ar'y (-sen'-) *a.* 1 causing fires 2 stirring up strife —*n.* one who willfully sets fire to property

in'cense' (*v.:* in sens') *n.* 1 substance burned to produce a pleasant odor 2 this odor —*v.* enrage

in·cen'tive *n.* motive or stimulus

in·cep'tion *n.* a beginning

in·ces'sant *a.* constant

in'cest' *n.* sexual intercourse between close relatives —**in·ces'tu·ous** (-chōō əs) *a.*

inch *n.* measure of length, $\frac{1}{12}$ foot —*v.* to move very slowly, by degrees —**every inch** in all respects

in·cho'ate (-kō'ət) *a.* just begun

in'ci·dence *n.* range of occurrence or effect

in'ci·dent *n.* event

in'ci·den'tal *a.* 1 happening along with something more important 2 minor —*n.* 1 something incidental 2 *pl.* miscellaneous items —**in'ci·den'tal·ly** *adv.*

in·cin'er·ate' *v.* burn to ashes

in·cin'er·a'tor *n.* furnace for burning trash

in·cip'i·ent *a.* just beginning to exist or appear

in·cise' (-sīz') *v.* cut into; engrave

in·ci'sion (-sizh'ən) *n.* 1 a cutting into 2 a cut; gash

in·ci'sive (-sī'siv) *a.* piercing; acute

in·ci'sor (-zər) *n.* any of the front cutting teeth

in·cite' *v.* urge to action —**in·cite'ment** *n.*

in·clem'ent *a.* stormy

in·cline' (*n.:* in'klīn') *v.* 1 lean; bend; slope 2 tend 3 have a preference 4 influence —*n.* a slope —**in'cli·na'tion** *n.*

in·close v. enclose

in·clude v. have or take in as part of a whole; contain —**in·clu'sion** n.

in·clu'sive a. 1 including everything 2 including the limits mentioned

in·cog·ni·to (-nē'-) adv., a. disguised under a false name

in'come n. money one gets as wages, salary, rent, etc.

in'com·ing a. coming in

in·com·mu·ni·ca'do (-kä'dō) adv., a. unable to or not allowed to communicate

in·com'pa·ra·ble a. beyond comparison; matchless

in·com'pe·tent n., a. (one) without adequate skill or knowledge —**in·com'pe·tence** n.

in·com·plete' a. lacking a part or parts; unfinished

in·con·se·quen'tial a. unimportant

in·con·sol'a·ble a. that cannot be comforted or cheered

in·con·spic'u·ous a. attracting little attention

in·con'ti·nent a. unable to control one's natural functions —**in·con'ti·nence** n.

in·con·ven'ience n. 1 lack of comfort, etc. 2 inconvenient thing —v. cause bother, etc. to —**in·con·ven'ient** a.

in·cor'po·rate v. 1 combine; include 2 merge 3 form (into) a corporation —**in·cor'po·ra'tion** n.

in·cor'ri·gi·ble a. too bad to be reformed

in·crease' (or in'krēs) v. make or become greater, larger, etc. —n. 1 an increasing 2 amount of this

in·creas'ing·ly adv. more and more

in·cred'i·ble a. too unusual to be believed

in·cred'u·lous (-krej'-) a. showing doubt —**in·cre·du'li·ty** n.

in'cre·ment n. 1 an increasing 2 amount of this

in·crim'i·nate v. involve in, or make appear guilty of, a crime —**in·crim'i·na'tion** n.

in·crust' v. cover with, or form into, a crust

in'cu·bate' v. sit on and hatch (eggs) —**in'cu·ba'tion** n.

in'cu·ba'tor n. 1 heated container for hatching eggs 2 similar device in which premature babies are kept

in·cul'cate v. fix in the mind, as by insistent urging

in·cum'bent a. resting (on or upon one) as a duty —n. holder of an office, etc.

in·cur' v. -curred', -cur'ring bring upon oneself

in·cur'sion n. raid

in·debt'ed a. 1 in debt 2 owing gratitude

in·debt'ed·ness n. 1 a being indebted 2 amount owed

in·de·ci'pher·a·ble (-sī'fər-) a. illegible

in·deed' adv. certainly —int. exclamation of surprise, doubt, sarcasm, etc.

in·de·fat'i·ga·ble a. not tiring; tireless

in·de·fen'si·ble a. that cannot be defended or justified

in·del'i·ble a. that cannot be erased, washed out, etc. —**in·del'i·bly** adv.

in·del'i·cate (-kət) a. lacking propriety; coarse

in·dem'ni·fy' v. repay for or insure against loss —**in·dem'ni·ty** n.

in·dent' v. 1 to notch 2 space in from the regular margin —**in'den·ta'tion** n.

in·den'ture v. bind by a contract to work for another

in·de·pend'ent a. not ruled, controlled, supported, etc. by others —**in·de·pend'ence** n.

in'-depth' a. thorough

in·de·scrib'a·ble a. beyond the power of description

in·de·struct'i·ble a. that cannot be destroyed

in·de·ter'mi·nate (-nət) a. not definite; vague

in'dex n., pl. -dex'es or -di·ces' (-di sēz') 1 the forefinger: also **index finger** 2 indication 3 alphabetical list of names, etc. in a book showing pages where they can be found —v. make an index of or for

In'di·an n., a. 1 (native) of India 2 (member) of any of the aboriginal peoples of the Western Hemisphere: also **American Indian**

in'di·cate' v. 1 point out; show 2 be a sign of —**in'di·ca'tion** n. —**in'di·ca'tive** a. —**in'di·ca'tor** n.

in·dict' (-dīt') v. charge with a crime —**in·dict'ment** n.

in·dif'fer·ent a. 1 neutral 2 unconcerned 3 of no importance 4 fair, average, etc. —**in·dif'fer·ence** n.

in·dig·e·nous (-dij′-) a. native

in′di·gent a. poor; needy —**in′di·gence** n.

in·di·ges′tion n. difficulty in digesting food

in·dig′nant a. angry at unjust or mean action —**in·dig·na′tion** n.

in·dig′ni·ty n., pl. **-ties** an insult to one's pride

in′di·go′ n. 1 blue dye 2 deep violet-blue

in·dis·crim′i·nate (-nət) a. making no distinctions

in·dis·pen′sa·ble a. absolutely necessary

in′dis·posed′ a. 1 slightly ill 2 unwilling

in′dis·sol′u·ble a. that cannot be dissolved or destroyed

in′di·vid′u·al (-vij′-) n. 1 single person, thing, or being —a. 1 single 2 of, for, or typical of an individual —**in′di·vid′u·al·ly** adv.

in′di·vid′u·al·ism′ n. the leading of one's life in one's own way —**in′di·vid′u·al·ist** n.

in′di·vid′u·al′i·ty n. distinct characteristics

in·doc′tri·nate′ v. teach a doctrine or belief to —**in·doc′tri·na′tion** n.

in′do·lent (-də-) a. idle; lazy —**in′do·lence** n.

in·dom′i·ta·ble a. unyielding; unconquerable

in′door′ a. being, belonging, done, etc. in a building

in′doors′ adv. in or into a building

in·du′bi·ta·ble a. that cannot be doubted

in·duce′ v. 1 persuade 2 bring on; cause —**in·duce′ment** n.

in·duct′ v. 1 install in an office, a society, etc. 2 bring into the armed forces —**in·duct·ee′** n.

in·duc′tion n. 1 an inducting 2 a coming to a general conclusion from particular facts

in·dulge′ v. 1 satisfy a desire 2 gratify the wishes of —**in·dul′gence** n. —**in·dul′gent** a.

in·dus′tri·al a. having to do with industries or people working in industry

in·dus′tri·al·ist n. owner or manager of a large industry

in·dus′tri·al·ize′ v. build up industries in

in·dus′tri·ous a. working hard and steadily

in′dus·try n., pl. **-tries** 1 steady effort 2 any branch of manufacture or trade

-ine suf. of or like

in·e′bri·ate′ (-āt′; n.: -ət) v. make drunk —n. drunkard —**in·e′bri·a′tion** n.

in·ef′fa·ble a. too sacred to be spoken

in·ept′ a. 1 unfit 2 foolishly wrong 3 awkward —**in·ep′ti·tude′, in·ept′ness** n.

in·ert′ a. 1 unable to move or act 2 dull; slow 3 without active properties

in·er′ti·a (-shə) n. tendency of matter to remain at rest, or to continue moving in a fixed direction

in′es·cap′a·ble a. that cannot be escaped

in·es′ti·ma·ble a. too great to be estimated

in·ev′i·ta·ble a. certain to happen —**in·ev′i·ta·bil′i·ty** n.

in·ex·o′ra·ble a. unrelenting —**in·ex·o′ra·bly** adv.

in′ex·pe′ri·enced a. lacking experience or skill

in·ex′pert a. not skillful

in·ex′pli·ca·ble a. that cannot be explained

in′ex·tri′ca·ble a. 1 that one cannot get free from 2 that cannot be disentangled

in·fal′li·ble a. never wrong

in′fa·my (-fə mē) n. 1 disgrace 2 great wickedness —**in′fa·mous** a.

in′fant n. baby —a. 1 of infants 2 in an early stage —**in′fan·cy** n. —**in′fan·tile′** a.

in′fan·try n. soldiers trained to fight on foot —**in′fan·try·man** n., pl. **-men**

in·farct′ n. area of dying tissue: also **in·farc′tion**

in·fat′u·ate′ (-fach′ōō-) v. inspire with unreasoning passion —**in·fat′u·a′tion** n.

in·fect′ v. make diseased —**in·fec′tion** n.

in·fec′tious a. 1 caused by microorganisms in the body 2 tending to spread to others

in·fer′ v. **-ferred′, -fer′ring** conclude by reasoning —**in′fer·ence** n.

in·fe′ri·or (-fir′ē-) a. 1 lower in space, order, status, etc. 2 poor in quality —**in·fe′ri·or′i·ty** n.

in·fer′nal a. of hell; hellish

in·fer′no n., pl. **-nos′** hell

in·fest′ v. overrun in large numbers

in′fi·del′ (-fə-) n. one who rejects (a) religion

in′fi·del′i·ty n. unfaithfulness

in'field' n. Baseball area enclosed by base lines —**in'field'er** n.

in'fight·ing n. personal conflict within a group

in·fil'trate v. 1 filter 2 pass through —**in·fil·tra'tion** n.

in'fi·nite (-nit) a. 1 lacking limits; endless 2 vast

in·fin·i·tes'i·mal a. too small to be measured

in·fin'i·tive n. form of a verb without reference to person, tense, etc.

in·fin'i·ty n. unlimited space, time, or quantity

in·firm' a. weak; feeble —**in·fir'mi·ty** n., pl. -ties

in·fir'ma·ry n. hospital

in·flame' v. 1 excite 2 make red, sore, and swollen —**in·flam·ma'tion** n. —**in·flam'ma·to·ry** a.

in·flam'ma·ble a. flammable

in·flate' v. make swell out, as with gas

in·fla'tion n. 1 an inflating 2 increase in the currency in circulation resulting in a fall in its value and a rise in prices —**in·fla'tion·ar'y** a.

in·flect' v. 1 vary the tone of (the voice) 2 change the form of (a word) to show tense, etc. —**in·flec'tion** n.

in·flex'i·ble a. stiff, fixed, unyielding, etc.

in·flict' v. cause to suffer (a wound, punishment, etc.) —**in·flic'tion** n.

in·flu·ence n. 1 power to affect others 2 one with such power —v. have an effect on —**in'flu·en'tial** a.

in·flu·en'za n. acute, contagious viral disease

in'flux' n. a flowing in

in·form' v. give information (to) —**in·form'er** n.

in·for'mal a. 1 not following fixed rules 2 casual; relaxed —**in'for·mal'i·ty** n., pl. -ties

in·for·ma'tion n. news or knowledge imparted —**in·form'a·tive** a.

in·frac'tion n. violation of a law, etc.

in'fra·red' a. of those invisible rays having a penetrating, heating effect

in'fra·struc'ture n. basic installations and facilities, as roads

in·fringe' v. break (a law, etc.) —**infringe** on encroach on (others' rights) —**in·fringe'ment** n.

in·fu'ri·ate v. enrage

in·fuse' v. 1 instill 2 inspire 3 to steep —**in·fu'sion** n.

-ing suf. used to form the present participle

in·gen'ious (-jēn'-) a. clever; resourceful —**in'ge·nu'i·ty** n.

in·gé·nue (an'zhə nōō', än'-) n. role of an inexperienced young woman in a play, etc.

in·gen'u·ous (-jen'-) a. 1 frank 2 naive

in·gest' v. take (food, drugs, etc.) into the body

in'got (iŋ'gət) n. mass of metal cast as a bar, etc.

in·grained' a. firmly fixed

in'grate' n. ungrateful person

in·gra'ti·ate' (-grā'shē-) v. get (oneself) into another's favor

in·gre'di·ent n. component part of a mixture

in'gress' n. entrance

in·hab'it v. live in

in·hab'it·ant n. person or animal inhabiting a place

in·hal'ant n. medicine, etc. to be inhaled

in'ha·la'tor n. 1 apparatus for inhaling medicine 2 respirator

in·hale' v. breathe in —**in'ha·la'tion** n.

in·hal'er n. 1 respirator 2 INHALATOR (n. 1)

in·her'ent (-hir'-, -her'-) a. inborn; natural; basic

in·her'it v. 1 receive as an heir 2 have by heredity —**in·her'it·ance** n.

in·hib'it v. restrain; check —**in·hi·bi'tion** n.

in·hu'man a. cruel, brutal, etc. —**in'hu·man'i·ty** n.

in·im'i·cal a. 1 hostile 2 harmful; adverse

in·im'i·ta·ble a. that cannot be imitated

in·iq'ui·ty (i nik'wə tē) n., pl. -ties sin or wicked act —**in·iq'ui·tous** a.

in·i'tial (i nish'əl) a. first —n. first letter of a name —v. mark with one's initials —**in·i'tial·ly** adv.

in·i'ti·ate' v. 1 begin to use 2 teach the fundamentals to 3 admit as a new member —**in·i'ti·a'tion** n.

in·i'ti·a·tive n. 1 first step 2 ability to get things started

in·ject' v. 1 force (a fluid) into tissue, etc. with a syringe, etc. 2 throw in; insert —**in·jec'tion** n.

in·junc'tion n. order or command, esp. of a court

in·jure v. do harm to; hurt —**ju'ri·ous** a.

in'ju·ry *n.*, *pl.* **-ries** harm or wrong

in·jus'tice *n.* **1** a being unjust **2** unjust act

ink *n.* colored liquid for writing, printing, etc. —*v.* mark or color with ink —**ink'y** *a.*, **-i·er**, **-i·est**

ink'ling *n.* hint or notion

in'land *a.*, *adv.* in or toward a country's interior

in'-law' *n.* [Col.] a relative by marriage

in'lay' *v.* **-laid'**, **-lay'ing** decorate a surface with pieces of wood, etc. set in —*n.*, *pl.* **-lays'** **1** inlaid decoration **2** filling in a tooth

in'let' *n.* narrow strip of water going into land

in'mate' *n.* one kept in a prison, hospital, etc.

in'most' *a.* innermost

inn *n.* hotel or restaurant

in·nate' *a.* inborn; natural

in'ner *a.* **1** farther in **2** more secret

inner city *n.* crowded or blighted central section of a city

in'ner·most' *a.* **1** farthest in **2** most secret

in'ning *n. Baseball* round of play in which both teams have a turn at bat

in'no·cent *a.* **1** without sin **2** not guilty **3** harmless **4** artless —*n.* innocent person —**in'no·cence** *n.*

in·noc'u·ous *a.* harmless

in'no·va'tion *n.* new method, device, etc. —**in'no·va'tor** *n.*

in'nu·en'do (in'yōō-) *n.*, *pl.* **-does** or **-dos** a hint or sly remark

in·nu'mer·a·ble *a.* too numerous to be counted

in·oc'u·late' *v.* inject a vaccine so as to immunize —**in·oc'u·la'tion** *n.*

in·or'di·nate (-nət) *a.* excessive

in'or·gan'ic *a.* not living; not animal or vegetable

in'put' *n.* **1** what is put in, as power into a machine or data into a computer **2** opinion or advice —*v.* feed (data) into a computer —**in'put'ter** *n.*

in'quest' *n.* judicial inquiry, as by a coroner

in·quire' *v.* **1** ask; question **2** investigate (*into*) —**in·quir'y** (in'kwə rē, in kwīr'ē) *n.*, *pl.* **-ies**

in'qui·si'tion *n.* **1** investigation **2** strict suppression, as of heretics by a tribunal —**in·quis'i·tor** *n.*

in·quis'i·tive (-kwiz'-) *a.* asking many questions; prying

in'roads' *n.pl.* an advance, esp. an encroachment

in·sane' *a.* **1** mentally ill; crazy **2** of or for insane people —**in·san'i·ty** *n.*

in·sa'ti·a·ble (-sā'shə bəl) *a.* that cannot be satisfied

in·scribe' *v.* mark or engrave (words, etc.) on —**in·scrip'tion** *n.*

in·scru'ta·ble *a.* that cannot be understood

in'sect' *n.* small animal with six legs, as a fly

in·sec'ti·cide *n.* substance used to kill insects

in·se·cure' *a.* **1** not safe **2** anxious **3** not firm —**in·se·cu'ri·ty** *n.*

in·sem'i·nate' *v.* sow or impregnate —**in·sem'i·na'tion** *n.*

in·sen'sate' *a.* not feeling

in·sen'si·ble *a.* **1** unconscious **2** unaware

in·sen'si·tive *a.* not sensitive or responsive —**in·sen'si·tiv'i·ty** *n.*

in·sert' (*n.:* in'surt') *v.* put into something else —*n.* a thing inserted —**in·ser'tion** *n.*

in'set' *v.* set in —*n.* something inserted

in'side' *n.* inner side or part —*a.* **1** internal **2** secret —*adv.* **1** within **2** indoors —*prep.* in

in·sid'er *n.* one having confidential information

in·sid'i·ous *a.* sly, treacherous, tricky, etc.

in'sight' *n.* understanding of a thing's true nature

in·sig'ni·a *n.pl.* badges, emblems, etc., as of rank or membership

in'sin·cere' *a.* deceptive or hypocritical —**in'sin·cer'i·ty** *n.*

in·sin'u·ate' *v.* **1** hint; imply **2** to get in artfully —**in·sin'u·a'tion** *n.*

in·sip'id *a.* tasteless; dull

in·sist' *v.* **1** demand strongly **2** maintain a stand —**in·sist'ence** *n.* —**in·sist'ent** *a.*

in'so·far' *adv.* to the degree that: with *as*

in'sole' *n.* (removable) inside sole of a shoe

in'so·lent (-sə-) *a.* showing disrespect —**in'so·lence** *n.*

in·sol'vent *a.* bankrupt

in·som'ni·a *n.* abnormal inability to sleep —**in·som'ni·ac'** *n.*

in'so·much' as *adv.* inasmuch as

in·sou'ci·ant (-sōō'sē-) *a.* calm; carefree

in·spect' v. **1** look at carefully **2** examine officially —**in·spec'tion** n. —**in·spec'tor** n.

in·spire' v. **1** stimulate, as to a creative effort **2** arouse (a feeling) **3** inhale —**in'spi·ra'tion** n.

in·stall' v. **1** put formally in office **2** establish in a place **3** fix in place for use —**in'stal·la'tion** n.

in·stall'ment, in·stal'ment n. any of the several parts of a payment, magazine serial, etc.

in'stance n. **1** example **2** occasion **3** instigation

in'stant a. **1** immediate **2** quick to prepare —n. moment —**in'stant·ly** adv.

in'stan·ta'ne·ous a. done or happening in an instant

in·stead' adv. in place of the other

in'step' n. upper surface of the arch of the foot

in'sti·gate' v. urge on to an action; incite —**in'sti·ga'tion** n. —**in'sti·ga'tor** n.

in·still', in·stil' v. put in gradually; implant

in'stinct' n. inborn tendency to do a certain thing; knack —**in·stinc'tive** a.

in'sti·tute' v. establish —n. organization for promoting art, science, etc.

in'sti·tu'tion n. **1** establishment **2** established law, custom, etc. **3** institute —**in'sti·tu'tion·al** a. —**in'sti·tu'tion·al·ize'** v.

in·struct' v. **1** teach **2** direct —**in·struc'tion** n. —**in·struc'tive** a. —**in·struc'tor** n.

in'stru·ment n. **1** means; agent **2** tool or device for doing exact work **3** device producing musical sound

in'stru·men'tal a. **1** serving as a means **2** of, for, or by musical instruments

in'sub·or'di·nate (-nət) a. disobedient

in·suf'fer·a·ble a. intolerable

in'su·lar (-sə-, -syoo-) a. **1** of an island **2** narrow in outlook

in'su·late' v. **1** protect with a material to prevent the loss of electricity, heat, etc. **2** set apart —**in'su·la'tion** n. —**in'su·la'tor** n.

in'su·lin n. pancreatic hormone used to treat diabetes

in·sult' v. act or remark meant to hurt the feelings —v. subject to an insult

in'su·per·a·ble a. that cannot be overcome

in·sur'ance (-shoor'-) n. **1** an insuring **2** contract whereby a company guarantees payment for a loss, death, etc. **3** amount for which a thing is insured

in·sure' v. **1** make sure **2** protect **3** get or give insurance on

in·sur'gent a. rising up in revolt; rebelling —n. a rebel —**in·sur'gence** n.

in'sur·rec'tion n. rebellion

in·tact' a. kept whole

in·ta'glio (-tal'yō) n., pl. **-ios'** design carved below the surface

in'take' n. **1** amount taken in **2** place in a pipe, etc. where fluid is taken in

in'te·ger n. whole number

in'te·gral (or in teg'rəl) a. **1** essential to completeness **2** entire

in'te·grate' v. **1** form into a whole; unify **2** desegregate —**in'te·gra'tion** n.

in·teg'ri·ty n. **1** honesty, sincerity, etc. **2** wholeness

in·teg'u·ment n. skin, rind, shell, etc.

in'tel·lect' n. **1** ability to reason **2** high intelligence

in'tel·lec'tu·al a. **1** of the intellect **2** needing or showing high intelligence —n. one with intellectual interests

in·tel'li·gence n. **1** ability to learn, or solve problems **2** news; information —**in·tel'li·gent** a.

in·tel'li·gi·ble a. that can be understood; clear

in·tem'per·ate (-ət) a. not moderate; excessive

in·tend' v. **1** to plan; purpose **2** to mean

in·tense' a. **1** very strong, great, deep, etc. **2** very emotional —**in·ten'si·fy'** v., **-fied', -fy'ing** —**in·ten'si·fi·ca'tion** n. —**in·ten'si·ty** n.

in·ten'sive a. **1** thorough **2** Gram. emphasizing

in·tent' a. firmly fixed in attention or purpose —n. purpose; intention

in·ten'tion n. thing intended or planned; purpose —**in·ten'tion·al** a.

in·ter' (-tur') v. **-terred', -ter'ring** bury

inter- pref. **1** between; among **2** with each other

in'ter·act' v. to act on one another —**in'ter·ac'tion** n. —**in'ter·ac'tive** a.

in'ter·breed' v. **-bred', -breed'**

ing to cross varieties of in breeding

in·ter·cede' (-sēd') v. **1** plead for another **2** mediate —**in·ter·ces'sion** (-sesh'ən) n.

in·ter·cept' v. seize or interrupt on the way —**in·ter·cep'tion** n.

in·ter·change' (n.: in'tər chānj') v. **1** exchange **2** alternate —n. **1** an interchanging **2** traffic entrance or exit on a freeway —**in·ter·change'a·ble** a.

in·ter·course' n. **1** dealings between people, countries, etc. **2** sexual union

in·ter·de·pend'ence n. mutual dependence —**in·ter·de·pend'ent** a.

in·ter·dict' (n.: in'tər dikt') v. **1** prohibit **2** restrain —n. prohibition —**in·ter·dic'tion** n.

in·ter·est (in'trist) n. **1** feeling of curiosity or concern **2** thing causing this feeling **3** share in something **4** welfare; benefit **5** group with a common concern **6** (rate of) payment for the use of money —v. have the interest or attention of

in'ter·face' n. point or means of interaction —v. interact with

in·ter·fere' (-fir') v. **1** come between; intervene **2** meddle —**interfere with** hinder —**in'ter·fer'ence** n.

in'ter·im n. time between; meantime —a. temporary

in·te'ri·or (-tir'ē-) a. **1** inner **2** inland **3** private —n. **1** interior part **2** domestic affairs of a country

in'ter·ject' v. throw in between; insert

in'ter·jec'tion n. **1** an interjecting **2** thing interjected **3** *Gram.* exclamation

in'ter·lace' v. join as by weaving together

in'ter·lock' v. lock together

in'ter·loc'u·to·ry a. *Law* not final, as a decree

in'ter·lop'er n. intruder

in'ter·lude' n. thing that fills time, as music between acts of a play

in'ter·mar'ry v. **-ried, -ry·ing** marry, as persons of different races, religions, etc. —**in'ter·mar'riage** n.

in'ter·me'di·ar'y a. intermediate —n., pl. **-ies** go-between

in'ter·me'di·ate (-ət) a. in the middle; between

in·ter'ment n. burial

in'ter·mez'zo' (-met'sō') n., pl.

-zos' or **-zi'** (-sē') short musical piece

in·ter'mi·na·ble a. lasting, or seeming to last, forever

in'ter·mis'sion n. interval, as between acts of a play

in'ter·mit'tent a. periodic; recurring at intervals

in·tern' (v.: in turn') n. doctor in training at a hospital —v. confine within an area

in·ter'nal a. **1** inner **2** within a country —**in·ter'nal·ly** v.

internal medicine n. diagnosis and nonsurgical treatment of disease

in'ter·na'tion·al a. **1** among nations **2** for all nations —**in·ter·na'tion·al·ize'** v.

in'ter·ne'cine (-nē'sin) a. destructive to both sides

in'tern·ist n. doctor specializing in internal medicine

in'ter·plan'e·tar'y a. between planets

in'ter·play' n. action or influence on each other

in·ter'po·late' v. to insert (extra words, etc.)

in'ter·pose' v. place or come between; interrupt

in·ter'pret v. explain or translate —**in·ter'pre·ta'tion** n. —**in·ter'pret·er** n.

in'ter·ra'cial a. among or for persons of different races

in'ter·re·lat'ed a. closely connected with one another

in·ter'ro·gate' (-ter'-) v. question formally —**in·ter'ro·ga'tion** n.

in·ter·rog'a·tive n., a. (word) asking a question

in'ter·rupt' v. **1** break in on (talk, etc.) **2** obstruct —**in'ter·rup'tion** n.

in'ter·scho·las'tic a. between or among schools

in'ter·sect' v. **1** divide by passing across **2** cross each other —**in'ter·sec'tion** n.

in'ter·sperse' v. scatter among other things

in'ter·state' a. between or among states of a country

in·ter'stice (-stis) n. crevice

in'ter·twine' v. twist together

in'ter·ur'ban a. going between towns or cities

in'ter·val n. **1** space between things **2** time between events **3** difference in musical pitch —**at intervals** now and then

in'ter·vene' v. **1** come or be between **2** come in so as to help settle something —**in'ter·ven'**

tion *n.*

in'ter·view *n.* meeting of people, as to confer, ask questions, etc. —*v.* have an interview with

in·tes'tate *a.* not having made a will

in·tes'tine (-tin) *n.* usually pl. alimentary canal from the stomach to the anus —**in·tes'tin·al** *a.*

in'ti·mate (-mät'; *a., n.:* -mət) *v.* hint —*a.* 1 most personal 2 very familiar —*n.* an intimate friend —**in'ti·ma·cy** *n., pl.* **-cies** —**in'ti·ma'tion** *n.*

in·tim'i·date' *v.* make afraid as with threats —**in·tim'i·da'tion** *n.*

in'to *prep.* 1 toward and within 2 to the form, state, etc. 3 [Col.] involved in or concerned with

in'to·na'tion *n.* manner of utterance with regard to rise and fall in pitch

in·tone' *v.* utter in a chant

in to'to *adv.* as a whole

in·tox'i·cate' *v.* 1 make drunk 2 excite greatly —**in·tox'i·cant** *n.* —**in·tox'i·ca'tion** *n.*

intra- *pref.* within; inside

in·trac'ta·ble *a.* unruly

in'tra·mu'ral *a.* among members of a school or college

in·tran'si·gent *a.* refusing to compromise —**in·tran'si·gence** *n.*

in·tran'si·tive (-tiv) *a.* not taking a direct object, as some verbs

in'tra·ve'nous *a.* into or within a vein

in·trep'id *a.* fearless

in'tri·cate (-kət) *a.* hard to follow because complicated —**in'tri·ca·cy** *n., pl.* **-cies**

in·trigue' (-trēg') *v.* 1 to plot secretly 2 excite the curiosity of —*n.* 1 secret plot 2 secret love affair

in·trin'sic (sik, -zik) *a.* real; essential —**in·trin'si·cal·ly** *adv.*

in'tro·duce' *v.* 1 insert 2 bring into use 3 make acquainted with 4 give experience of 5 begin —**in'tro·duc'tion** *n.* —**in'tro·duc'to·ry** *a.*

in'tro·spec'tion *n.* a looking into one's own thoughts, feelings, etc.

in'tro·vert' *n.* one more interested in his inner feelings than in external events —**in'tro·ver'sion** *n.* —**in'tro·vert'ed** *a.*

in·trude' *v.* force oneself upon others without welcome —**in·trud'er** *n.* —**in·tru'sion** *n.* —**in·**

tru'sive *a.*

in·tu·i'tion (-ish'ən) *n.* immediate knowledge of something without conscious reasoning —**in·tu'i·tive** *a.*

in'un·date' *v.* flood —**in'un·da'tion** *n.*

in·ure' (-yoor') *v.* accustom to pain, trouble, etc.

in·vade' *v.* enter forcibly, as to conquer —**in·vad'er** *n.* —**in·va'sion** *n.*

in'va·lid *n.* one who is ill or disabled

in·val'id *a.* not valid, sound, etc. —**in·val'i·date'** *v.*

in·val'u·a·ble *a.* priceless

in·vec'tive *n.* strong critical or abusive language

in·veigh' (-vā') *v.* talk or write bitterly (*against*)

in·vei'gle (-vē'-, -vā'-) *v.* trick or lure into an action

in·vent' *v.* 1 produce (a new device) 2 think up —**in·ven'tor** *n.*

in·ven'tion *n.* 1 an inventing 2 power of inventing 3 something invented —**in·ven'tive** *a.*

in'ven·to·ry *n., pl.* **-ries** complete list or stock of goods

in·verse' (or in'vurs') *a.* inverted; directly opposite —*n.* inverse thing

in·vert' *v.* 1 turn upside down 2 reverse —**in·ver'sion** *n.*

in·ver'te·brate (-brət) *n., a.* (animal) having no backbone

in·vest' *v.* 1 install in office 2 furnish with authority 3 put (money) into business, etc. for profit —**in·vest'ment** *n.* —**in·ves'tor** *n.*

in·ves'ti·gate' *v.* search (into); examine —**in·ves'ti·ga'tion** *n.* —**in·ves'ti·ga'tor** *n.*

in·vet'er·ate (-ət) *a.* firmly fixed; habitual

in·vid'i·ous *a.* offensive, as an unfair comparison

in·vig'or·ate' *v.* enliven

in·vin'ci·ble *a.* unconquerable —**in·vin'ci·bil'i·ty** *n.*

in·vi'o·la·ble *a.* not to be profaned or injured

in·vi'o·late *a.* kept sacred or unbroken

in·vis'i·ble *a.* not visible or not evident —**in·vis'i·bil'i·ty** *n.* —**in·vis'i·bly** *adv.*

in'vi·ta'tion *n.* 1 an inviting 2 message or note used in inviting

in·vite' *v.* 1 ask to come somewhere or to do something 2 request 3 give occasion for

in·vit·ing a. alluring

in vi·tro (-vē′-) a. kept alive apart from the organism, as in a test tube

in·vo·ca·tion n. prayer for blessing, help, etc.

in·voice n. itemized list of goods or services provided; bill

in·voke v. call on (God, etc.) for help, etc.

in·vol·un·tary a. 1 not done by choice; unintentional 2 not consciously controlled

in·volve v. 1 complicate 2 draw into difficulty, etc. 3 include 4 require 5 occupy the attention of —**in·volve·ment** n.

in·ward a. 1 internal 2 directed toward the inside —adv. 1 toward the inside 2 into the mind or soul Also **in·wards** adv. —**in·ward·ly** adv.

i·o·dine n. chemical element used in medicine, etc.

i·on (ī′ən, -än′) n. electrically charged atom or group of atoms

-ion suf. 1 act or state of 2 result of

i·on·ize v. separate into ions or become electrically charged —**i·on·i·za·tion** n.

i·on·o·sphere n. outer part of earth's atmosphere

i·o·ta n. a jot

IOU n. signed note acknowledging a debt

ip·e·cac (ip′ə kak′) n. emetic made from a plant root

ip·so fac·to [L.] by that very fact

IQ n. number showing one's level of intelligence, based on a test

I·ra·ni·an (-rā′-, -rä′-) n., a. (native) of Iran

I·ra·qi (i rä′kē, -rak′ē) n., a. (native) of Iraq

i·ras·ci·ble (-ras′ə-) a. easily angered

i·rate a. very angry

ire n. anger; wrath

ir·i·des·cent a. showing a play of rainbowlike colors —**ir·i·des·cence** n.

i·ris n. 1 colored part of the eye, around the pupil 2 plant with sword-shaped leaves and showy flowers

I·rish a., n. (of) the people or language of Ireland —**I·rish·man** n., pl. -men

irk v. annoy; tire out

irk·some a. annoying; tiresome

i·ron (ī′ərn) n. 1 strong metal that is a chemical element 2 device used for smoothing wrin-

kles from cloth 3 pl. iron shackles 4 golf club with metal head —a. 1 of iron 2 strong —v. press with a hot iron —**iron out** smooth away

i·ron·clad′ a. 1 covered with iron 2 difficult to change or break

i·ro·ny (ī′rə nē) n., pl. -nies 1 expression in which what is meant is the opposite of what is said 2 event that is the opposite of what is expected —**i·ron′ic, i·ron′i·cal** a.

ir·ra·di·ate v. 1 expose to X-rays, ultraviolet rays, etc. 2 shine; radiate

ir·ra·tion·al a. lacking reason or good sense

ir·rec·on·cil·a·ble a. that cannot be reconciled or made to agree

ir·re·deem·a·ble a. that cannot be brought back, changed, etc.

ir·re·fut·a·ble (or ir′i fyōōt′-) a. that cannot be disproved —**ir·ref′u·ta·bly** adv.

ir·reg·u·lar a. 1 not conforming to rule, standard, etc. 2 not straight or uniform —**ir·reg·u·lar′i·ty** n.

ir·rel·e·vant a. not to the point —**ir·rel′e·vance** n.

ir·re·li·gious a. not religious

ir·rep·a·ra·ble a. that cannot be repaired or remedied

ir·re·press·i·ble a. that cannot be held back

ir·re·proach·a·ble a. blameless; faultless

ir·re·sist·i·ble a. that cannot be resisted

ir·res·o·lute a. not resolute; wavering

ir·re·spec·tive a. regardless (of)

ir·re·spon·si·ble a. lacking a sense of responsibility

ir·re·triev·a·ble a. that cannot be recovered

ir·rev·er·ent a. showing disrespect —**ir·rev·er·ence** n.

ir·re·vers·i·ble a. that cannot be reversed, annulled, etc.

ir·rev·o·ca·ble a. that cannot be undone or changed —**ir·rev′o·ca·bly** adv.

ir·ri·gate v. 1 supply with water by means of ditches, etc. 2 wash out (a body cavity) —**ir·ri·ga′tion** n.

ir·ri·ta·ble a. easily irritated or angered —**ir·ri·ta·bil′i·ty** n.

ir·ri·tate v. 1 to anger; annoy 2 make sore —**ir′ri·tant** a., n. —**ir′ri·ta′tion** n.

is v. pres. t. of BE: used with *he*, *she*, or *it*

-ise *suf.* chiefly Br. sp. of -IZE

-ish *suf.* 1 like; like that of 2 somewhat

i'sin·glass' (ī'zin-) *n.* 1 gelatin made from fish bladders 2 mica

Is·lam (is'läm', iz'-) *n.* Muslim religion —**Is·lam'ic** *a.*

is·land *n.* land mass surrounded by water —**is'land·er** *n.*

isle (īl) *n.* small island

is·let (ī lət) *n.* very small island

-ism *suf.* 1 theory or doctrine of 2 act or result of 3 condition or qualities of 4 an instance of

isn't is not

i'so·bar' *n.* line on a map connecting points of equal barometric pressure

i'so·late' *v.* place alone —**i'so·la'tion** *n.*

i'so·met'ric *a.* 1 of equal measure 2 of exercises in which muscles tense against each other

i·sos·ce·les (ī säs'ə lēz') *a.* designating a triangle with two equal sides

i'so·tope' *n.* any of two or more forms of an element with different atomic weights

Is·rae·li (iz rā'lē) *n., a.* (native) of Israel

is·sue *n.* 1 result 2 offspring 3 point under dispute 4 an issuing or amount issued —*v.* 1 emerge 2 result 3 put out; give out 4 publish —**at issue** disputed —**take issue** disagree —**is'su·ance** *n.*

-ist *suf.* 1 one who practices 2 adherent of

isth·mus (is'məs) *n.* strip of land connecting two larger bodies of water

it *pron.* the animal or thing mentioned *It* is also used as an indefinite subject or object

I·tal'ian *n., a.* (native or language) of Italy

i·tal'ic *a., n.* (of) type in which the letters slant upward to the right —**i·tal'i·cize'** *v.*

itch *n.* 1 tingling of the skin, with the desire to scratch 2 restless desire —*v.* have an itch —**itch'y** *a.,* **-i·er,** **-i·est**

-ite *suf.* 1 inhabitant of 2 adherent of

i'tem *n.* 1 article; unit 2 bit of news

i'tem·ize' *v.* list the items of

it'er·ate' *v.* repeat —**it'er·a'tion** *n.*

i·tin'er·ant *a.* traveling —*n.* traveler

i·tin'er·ar·y *n., pl.* **-ies** 1 route 2 plan of a journey

-itis *suf.* inflammation of

its *a.* of it

it's 1 it is 2 it has

it·self' *pron.* intensive or reflexive form of IT

-ity *suf.* state or quality

I've I have

-ive *suf.* 1 of, or having the nature of 2 tending to

i'vo·ry *n., pl.* **-ries** 1 hard, white substance in elephants' tusks, etc. 2 tusk of elephant, etc. 3 creamy white

i'vy *n., pl.* **i'vies** climbing evergreen vine

-ize *suf.* 1 make or become 2 unite with 3 engage in

J

jab *v., n.* **jabbed, jab'bing** punch or poke

jab'ber *v.* talk quickly or foolishly —*n.* chatter

jack *n.* 1 device to lift something 2 playing card with picture of male royal attendant 3 *Naut.* small flag 4 electric plug-in receptacle —*v.* used in **jack up,** *a*) lift with a jack *b*) [Col.] raise (prices, etc.)

jack'al' *n.* wild dog of Asia or Africa

jack'ass' *n.* 1 male donkey 2 fool

jack'daw' *n.* European crow

jack'et *n.* 1 short coat 2 outer covering

jack'-in-the-box' *n.* toy consisting of a box with a figure springing out

jack'knife' *n.* large pocketknife —*v.* bend at the middle

jack'pot' *n.* cumulative stakes, as in a poker game

jack rabbit *n.* large hare of W North America

jade *n.* 1 hard, green stone 2 worn-out horse 3 loose woman —*v.* tire or satiate —**jad'ed** *a.*

jag'ged *a.* having sharp points; notched or ragged

jag'uar (-wär) *n.* animal like a large leopard

jail *n.* prison for short-term confinement —*v.* to put or keep in a jail —**jail'er, jail'or** *n.*

ja·la·pe·ño (hä'lə pän'yō) *n.* Mexican hot pepper

ja·lop'y *n., pl.* **-pies** [Sl.] old, worn-out automobile

jal'ou·sie' (-ə sē') *n.* window or door made of slats fixed as in a

Venetian blind

jam v. **jammed, jam'ming** 1 cram; stuff 2 crush or crowd 3 wedge tight —n. 1 a jamming 2 [Col.] a difficult situation 3 spread made by boiling fruit and sugar

jamb (jam) n. side post of a doorway

jam'bo·ree' n. noisy revel

jan'gle v., n. (make or cause to make) a harsh, inharmonious sound

jan'i·tor n. one who takes care of a building —**jan'i·to'ri·al** a.

Jan'u·ar·y n. first month

Jap'a·nese' n., pl. **-ese'**; a. (native or language) of Japan

jar v. **jarred, jar'ring** 1 make a harsh sound 2 jolt —n. 1 jolt 2 wide-mouthed container

jar'gon n. special vocabulary of some work, class, etc.

jas·mine, jas·min (jaz'min) n. shrub with fragrant flowers

jaun·dice (jôn'dis) n. disease that turns the skin, eyeballs, etc. yellow —v. make bitter with envy

jaunt n. short pleasure trip

jaun'ty a. **-ti·er, -ti·est** easy and carefree

jav'e·lin n. light spear thrown in contests

jaw n. either of the two bony parts that hold the teeth —v. [Sl.] to talk

jaw'bone' n. lower bone of jaw —v. try to persuade by using one's high position

jaw'break'er n. piece of hard candy

jay n. 1 bird of the crow family 2 bluejay

jay'walk' v. cross a street heedlessly —**jay'walk'er** n.

jazz n. popular American music with strong rhythms —v. [Sl.] make exciting or elaborate: with up

jazz'y a. **-i·er, -i·est** [Sl.] lively, flashy, etc.

jeal'ous (jel'-) a. 1 resentfully suspicious or envious 2 watchful in guarding —**jeal'ous·y** n., pl. **-ies**

jeans n.pl. trousers or overalls of twilled cotton cloth

jeep n. small, rugged, orig. military automobile

jeer v. ridicule —n. derisive comment

Je·ho'vah God

jell v. 1 become, or make into, jelly 2 [Col.] become definite

jel'ly n., pl. **-lies** 1 soft, gelatinous food made from cooked fruit syrup 2 gelatinous substance

jel'ly·fish' n. jellylike sea animal with tentacles

jeop'ard·ize' (jep'-) v. to risk; endanger

jeop'ard·y n. danger; peril

jerk n. 1 sharp pull 2 muscular twitch 3 [Sl.] disagreeable person —v. 1 move with a jerk 2 twitch —**jerk'y** a., **-i·er, -i·est**

jer'kin n. snug, usually sleeveless jacket

jerk'wa·ter a. [Col.] small, unimportant, etc.

jer'ky n. dried strips of meat

jer'ry-built' a. poorly built

jer'sey n. 1 soft, knitted cloth 2 pl. **-seys** upper garment of this

jest v., n. 1 joke 2 ridicule —**jest'er** n.

Je'sus founder of the Christian religion

jet v. **jet'ted, jet'ting** 1 shoot out in a stream 2 travel by jet airplane —n. 1 liquid or gas in such a stream 2 spout that shoots a jet 3 jet-propelled airplane 4 black mineral —a. 1 jet-propelled 2 black

jet lag n. fatigue, etc. from adjusting to jet travel over great distances

jet'lin'er n. commercial jet passenger plane

jet propulsion n. propulsion by means of gases from a rear vent —**jet'-pro·pelled'** a.

jet'sam n. cargo thrown overboard to lighten a ship

jet'ti·son v. 1 throw (goods) overboard to lighten a ship 2 discard

jet'ty n., pl. **-ties** 1 wall built into the water 2 landing pier

Jew n. 1 descendant of people of ancient Israel 2 believer in Judaism —**Jew'ish** a.

jew'el n. 1 gem 2 small gem used as a watch bearing

jew'el·er, jew'el·ler n. one who deals in jewelry

jew'el·ry n. jewels, or ornaments with jewels

jib n. triangular sail ahead of all other sails

jibe v. 1 shift a sail, or the course, of a ship 2 [Col.] be in accord 3 to gibe —n. a gibe

jif'fy n. [Col.] an instant

jig n. 1 lively dance 2 device to guide a tool —v. **jigged, jig'ging** dance (a jig)

jig′ger n. glass of 1½ oz. for measuring liquor

jig′gle v. move in slight jerks —n. a jiggling —**jig′gly** a.

jig′saw′ n. saw with a narrow blade set in a frame: also **jig saw**

jigsaw puzzle n. picture cut into pieces that are to be fitted together again

jilt v. reject (a lover)

jim′my n., pl. **-mies** short crowbar used by burglars —v. **-mied, -my·ing** pry open

jin′gle v. make light, ringing sounds —n. 1 jingling sound 2 light verse

jin′go·ism′ n. warlike chauvinism —**jin′go·ist** n.

jinn n., pl. **jinn** supernatural being in Muslim folklore

jin·rik′i·sha′ (-rik′shô′) n. two-wheeled Asian carriage pulled by one or two men

jinx [Col.] n. person or thing supposed to cause bad luck —v. bring bad luck to

jit′ter·y [Col.] a. nervous or restless —**the jitters** nervous feeling

jive v. [Sl.] foolish or insincere talk —v. [Col.] be in accord; jibe

job n. 1 a piece of work 2 employment; work —a. done by the job —v. handle (goods) as a middleman

job′ber n. one who buys goods in quantity and sells them to dealers

job lot n. goods, often of various sorts, for sale as one quantity

jock [Sl.] n. 1 disc jockey 2 male athlete

jock′ey n. race-horse rider —v. maneuver for advantage

jo·cose′ a. joking; playful

joc′u·lar a. joking; full of fun —**joc′u·lar′i·ty** n.

joc′und a. genial; gay

jodh′·purs (jäd′pərz) n.pl. riding breeches

jog v. **jogged, jog′ging** 1 nudge; shake 2 move at a slow, steady, jolting pace —n. 1 nudge 2 jogging pace 3 part that changes direction sharply

jog′ging n. steady trotting as exercise —**jog′ger** n.

join v. 1 to connect; unite 2 become a part or member of

joint n. 1 place where two things are joined 2 one of the parts of a jointed whole 3 [Sl.] any building, esp. a cheap bar —a. common to two or more 2 sharing with another —v. connect by a joint —**out of joint** 1 dislocated 2 disordered —**joint′ly** adv.

joist n. any of the parallel timbers holding up planks of a floor, etc.

joke n. 1 anything said or done to arouse laughter 2 thing not to be taken seriously —v. make jokes

jok′er n. 1 one who jokes 2 deceptive clause, as in a contract 3 extra playing card used in some games

jol′ly a. **-li·er, -li·est** merry —**jol′li·ness** n. —**jol′li·ty** n.

jolt v., n. 1 jar; jerk 2 shock or surprise

jon′quil n. narcissus with yellow or white flower

josh v. [Col.] tease, fool, etc.

jos′tle (-əl) v. shove roughly

jot n. very small amount —v. **jot′ted, jot′ting** write (down) briefly

jounce v. jolt or bounce

jour′nal (jur′-) n. 1 diary 2 record of proceedings 3 a newspaper or magazine 4 book for business records 5 part of an axle, etc. that turns in a bearing

jour′nal·ism′ n. newspaper writing and editing —**jour′nal·ist** n. —**jour′nal·is′tic** a.

jour′ney n. a trip —v. to travel

jour′ney·man n., pl. **-men** worker skilled at a trade

joust (joust, just) n., v. fight with lances on horseback

jo′vi·al a. merry; jolly

jowl n. 1 cheek 2 pl. fleshy, hanging part under the jaw

joy n. gladness; delight —**joy′ful** a. —**joy′ous** a.

joy′stick′ n. 1 [Sl.] control stick of airplane 2 manual control device for video games, etc.

ju′bi·lant a. rejoicing —**ju′bi·la′tion** n.

ju′bi·lee′ n. 1 a 50th or 25th anniversary 2 time of rejoicing

Ju′da·ism′ n. Jewish religion

judge v. 1 hear and decide cases in a law court 2 determine the winner 3 appraise or criticize 4 think; suppose —n. one who judges

judg′ment n. 1 a deciding 2 legal decision 3 opinion 4 ability to make wise decisions Also sp. **judge′ment**

judg·men′tal a. making judgments, esp. harsh judgments; critical

ju·di′cial (-dish′əl) a. 1 of judges, courts, etc. 2 careful in thought

ju·di·ci·ar·y (-dish'ē er'ē, -dish'ər ē) *a.* of judges or courts —*n., pl.* **-ries** 1 part of government that administers justice 2 judges collectively

ju·di·cious (-dish'əs) *a.* showing good judgment —**ju·di·cious·ly** *adv.*

ju'do *n.* kind of jujitsu used for self-defense

jug *n.* container for liquids, with a small opening and a handle

jug'ger·naut *n.* relentless irresistible force

jug'gle *v.* 1 do tricks with (balls, etc.) 2 handle in a tricky way —**jug'gler** *n.*

jug'u·lar (vein) *n.* either of two large veins in the neck

juice *n.* liquid from fruit or cooked meat —**juic'y** *a.,* **-i·er,** **-i·est**

ju·jit'su *n.* Japanese wrestling using leverage

ju'jube (-jōōb', -jōō bē') *n.* gelatinous, fruit-flavored candy

juke'box *n.* coin-operated phonograph: also **juke box**

ju'li·enne *a.* cut into strips: said of vegetables, etc.

Ju·ly' *n.* 7th month

jum'ble *v., n.* (mix into) a confused heap

jum'bo *a.* very large

jump *v.* 1 spring from the ground, etc. 2 leap or make leap over 3 move or change suddenly 4 rise or raise suddenly, as prices —*n.* 1 a jumping 2 distance jumped 3 sudden move or change —**jump at** accept eagerly —**jump'er** *n.*

jump'er *n.* sleeveless dress worn over a blouse, etc.

jump'suit' *n.* coveralls, worn for work or leisure

jump'y *a.* **-i·er, -i·est** 1 moving jerkily 2 nervous

junc'tion *n.* 1 a joining 2 place where things join

junc'ture *n.* 1 junction 2 point of time

June *n.* 6th month

jun'gle *n.* dense forest in the tropics

jun·ior (jōōn'yər) *a.* 1 the younger: written *Jr.* 2 of lower rank, etc. —*n.* high school or college student in the next-to-last year

ju'ni·per *n.* small evergreen with berrylike cones

junk *n.* 1 old metal, paper, etc. 2 Chinese ship with flat bottom 3 [Col.] worthless thing(s); rub-

bish —*v.* [Col.] to discard; scrap —**junk'y** *a.,* **-i·er, -i·est**

junk'er *n.* [Sl.] old, worn-out car, etc.

jun'ket *n.* 1 pleasure trip 2 milk thickened as curd

junk'ie, junk'y *n., pl.* **-ies** [Sl.] narcotics addict

jun'ta (hoon'-, jun'-) *n.* military group seizing political power

ju·ris·dic'tion *n.* (range of) authority, as of a court

ju·ris·pru'dence *n.* 1 science or philosophy of law 2 a system of laws

ju'rist *n.* an expert in law

ju'ror *n.* member of a jury

ju'ry *n., pl.* **-ries** group of people chosen to give a decision, esp. in a law case

just *a.* 1 right or fair 2 righteous 3 well-founded 4 correct; exact —*adv.* 1 exactly 2 only 3 barely 4 a very short time ago 5 [Col.] quite; really —**just now** a moment ago —**just'ly** *adv.*

jus'tice (-tis) *n.* 1 a being just 2 reward or penalty as deserved 3 the upholding of what is just 4 a judge

justice of the peace *n.* local magistrate in minor cases

jus'ti·fy *v.* **-fied', -fy'ing** 1 show to be just, right, etc. 2 free from blame —**jus'ti·fi'a·ble** *a.* —**jus'ti·fi·a'bly** *adv.* —**jus'ti·fi·ca'tion** *n.*

jut *v.* **jut'ted, jut'ting** stick out

jute *n.* strong fiber used to make burlap, rope, etc.

ju've·nile' (-və nil', -nəl) *a.* 1 young; immature 2 of or for juveniles —*n.* child or young person

jux'ta·pose' *v.* put side by side —**jux'ta·po·si'tion** *n.*

K

kale *n.* a cabbage with spreading, curled leaves

ka·lei·do·scope' (-li'-) *n.* small tube containing bits of colored glass that change patterns as the tube is turned —**ka·lei·do·scop'ic** (-skäp'-) *a.*

kan'ga·roo' *n.* leaping marsupial of Australia

ka'o·lin *n.* white clay, used to make porcelain, etc.

ka'pok *n.* silky fibers from tropical trees, used for stuffing pillows, etc.

ka·put' (-poot') *a.* [Sl.] ruined,

destroyed, etc.

kar'at n. one 24th part (of pure gold)

ka·ra'te (-rät'ē) n. self-defense by blows with side of open hand

kar'ma n. fate

ka'ty·did n. insect resembling the grasshopper

kay'ak (kī'-) n. Eskimo canoe

ka·zoo' n. toy musical instrument into which one hums

keel n. center piece along the bottom of a ship —**keel over** turn or fall over

keen a. 1 sharp 2 piercing 3 perceptive; acute 4 eager 5 intense —**keen'ly** adv.

keep v. **kept, keep'ing** 1 fulfill; observe 2 protect; take care of 3 preserve 4 retain 5 continue 6 hold and not let go 7 refrain —n. food and shelter —**keep to oneself** 1 avoid others 2 to refrain from telling —**keep'er** n.

keep'ing n. 1 care or protection 2 conformity

keep'sake' n. souvenir

keg n. small barrel

kelp n. brown seaweed

ken n. range of knowledge

ken'nel n. 1 doghouse 2 often pl. place where dogs are bred or kept

ker'chief (-chif) n. 1 cloth worn around the head or neck 2 handkerchief

ker'nel n. 1 grain or seed 2 soft, inner part of a nut or fruit pit

ker'o·sene', ker'o·sine' (-sēn') n. oil distilled from petroleum

ketch n. sailing vessel

ketch'up n. thick sauce of tomatoes, spices, etc.

ket'tle n. 1 pot used in cooking 2 teakettle

ket'tle·drum' n. hemispheric copper drum with an adjustable parchment top

key n. 1 device for working a lock 2 lever pressed in operating a piano, typewriter, etc. 3 thing that explains, as a code 4 controlling factor 5 mood or style 6 low island 7 Mus. scale based on a certain keynote —a. controlling —v. bring into harmony —**key up** excite —**key in** input (data) with a keyboard — **key'hole'** n.

key'board' n. row(s) of keys of a piano, computer terminal, etc.

key'note' n. 1 Mus. lowest, basic note of a scale 2 basic idea

key'stone' n. central, topmost stone of an arch

kha·ki (kak'ē) a., n. yellowish-brown (uniform)

kib·butz' (-bōots') n., pl. **-but·zim'** (-bōō tsēm') Israeli collective farm

kib'itz v. [Col.] act as meddlesome onlooker —**kib'itz·er** n.

kick v. 1 strike (out) with the foot 2 recoil, as a gun 3 [Col.] complain —n. 1 a kicking 2 [often pl.] [Col.] thrill

kick'back' n. [Sl.] forced or secret rebate

kick'off' n. kick in football that begins a play

kick'stand' n. metal bar on a bicycle to hold it upright

kid n. 1 young goat 2 leather from its skin: also **kid'skin'** 3 [Col.] child —v. **kid'ded, kid'ding** [Col.] tease, fool, etc. — **kid'der** n.

kid'nap' v. **-napped', -nap'ping** seize and hold a person, esp. for ransom —**kid'nap'per** n.

kid'ney n., pl. **-neys** the urine-forming gland

kiel·ba·sa (kēl bä'sə) n., pl. **-si** (-sē) or **-sas** smoked Polish sausage

kill v. 1 make die; slay 2 destroy 3 spend (time) idly —n. 1 a killing 2 animal(s) killed — **kill'er** n.

kiln (kil, kiln) n. oven for baking bricks, etc.

ki·lo (kē'lō, kil'ō) n., pl. **-los** kilogram

kilo- pref. one thousand

kil'o·byte' n. 1, 024 bytes

kil'o·cy'cle n. kilohertz

kil'o·gram' n. 1,000 grams

kil'o·hertz' n. 1,000 hertz

kil'o·me·ter (or ki läm'ət ər) n. 1,000 meters

kil'o·watt' n. 1,000 watts

kilt n. skirt worn by men of Northern Scotland

kil'ter n. [Col.] used chiefly in out of kilter, not in working order

ki·mo'no n., pl. **-nos** Japanese robe

kin n. relatives; family

kind n. sort; variety —a. gentle, generous, etc. —**in kind** in the same way —**kind of** [Col.] somewhat —**kind'ly** a., adv. — **kind'ness** n.

kin'der·gar'ten n. class or school for children about four to six years old —**kin'der·gart'ner, kin'der·gar'ten·er** (-gärt'nər) n.

kind'heart'ed a. kind

kin'dle v. 1 set on fire 2 start burning 3 excite

kin'dling n. bits of wood, etc. for starting a fire

kin'dred n. relatives; kin —a. related or similar

ki·net'ic a. of motion

king n. 1 male ruler of a state 2 playing card with a king's picture 3 chess piece that has to be captured

king'dom n. country ruled by a king or queen

king'fish'er n. fish-eating diving bird

kink n., v. curl or twist —**kink'y** a., **-i·er**, **-i·est**

kin'ship' n. 1 family relationship 2 close connection

kins'man n., pl. **-men** male relative —**kins'wom·an** n.fem., pl. **-wom·en**

ki·osk' (kē'äsk') n. small, open structure used as a newsstand, etc.

kip'per n. salted and dried or smoked herring

kis'met (kiz'-) n. fate

kiss v. caress with the lips in affection or greeting —n. 1 act of kissing 2 kind of candy

kit n. 1 set of tools, etc. 2 box or bag for it

kitch'en n. place for preparing and cooking food

kitch'en·ette', **kitch'en·et'** n. small kitchen

kite n. 1 kind of hawk 2 light frame covered with paper, tied to a string, and flown in the wind

kith and kin n. friends and relatives

kitsch (kich) n. pretentious but shallow popular art, etc.

kit'ten n. young cat: also **kit'ty**, pl. **-ties**

kit'ten·ish a. coy

Klee'nex trademark soft tissue paper used as a handkerchief, etc. —n. a piece of such paper

klep·to·ma'ni·a n. persistent impulse to steal —**klep·to·ma'ni·ac'** n.

knack n. special ability

knack·wurst (näk'wʉrst') n. thick, spicy sausage

knap'sack' n. bag to carry supplies on the back

knave n. dishonest person; rogue —**knav'ish** a.

knav'er·y n. dishonesty

knead v. press and squeeze

knee n. joint between thigh and lower leg

knee'cap' n. movable bone at the front of the knee

knee'-jerk' a. [Col.] automatic and predictable

kneel v. **knelt** or **kneeled**, **kneel'ing** rest on the bent knee or knees

knell n. slow tolling of a bell, as at a funeral

knew v. pt. of KNOW

knick'ers n.pl. breeches gathered below the knees: also **knick'er·bock·ers**

knick'knack' n. small, showy article

knife n., pl. **knives** sharp cutting blade set in a handle —v. stab with a knife

knight n. 1 medieval chivalrous soldier 2 British man holding honorary rank 3 chessman like a horse's head —**knight'hood'** n.

knit v. **knit'ted** or **knit**, **knit'ting** 1 make by looping yarn with needles 2 draw or grow together

knob n. round handle, etc. —**knob'by** a., **-bi·er**, **-bi·est**

knock v. 1 hit; strike; rap 2 make a pounding noise 3 [Col.] find fault with —n. 1 hit; blow 2 a pounding noise —**knock down** take apart —**knock off** [Col.] 1 stop working 2 deduct —**knock out** make unconscious —**knock'er** n. —**knock'out'** n.

knoll (nōl) n. little hill; mound

knot n. 1 lump in tangled thread, etc. 2 a tying together of string, rope, etc. 3 small group 4 hard lump in wood where a branch has grown 5 one nautical mile per hour —v. **knot'ted**, **knot'ting** form a knot (in)

knot'ty a. **-ti·er**, **-ti·est** 1 full of knots 2 puzzling

know v. **knew**, **known**, **know'ing** 1 be informed (about) 2 be aware (of) 3 be acquainted with

know'-how' n. [Col.] technical skill

know'ing a. 1 having knowledge 2 shrewd; cunning

knowl'edge (nä'lij) n. things known or learned —**knowl'edge·a·ble** a.

knuck'le n. joint of a finger —**knuckle down** work hard —**knuckle under** surrender

ko·a'la (-ä'-) n. tree-dwelling marsupial of Australia

kohl·ra·bi (kōl'rä'bē) n., pl. **-bies** kind of cabbage

Ko·ran (kə ran', kôr'an') the

sacred book of Muslims

Ko·re'an n., a. (native or language) of Korea

ko'sher a. fit to eat according to Jewish dietary laws

kow·tow' (kou'tou') v. show great deference (to)

ku·chen (kōō'kən) n. breadlike cake, with raisins, etc.

ku'dos' ('-däs', -dōs') n. credit for achievement

kud·zu (kood'zōō') n. fast-growing vine with large leaves

kum'quat' (-kwät') n. small, oval, orangelike fruit

kung' fu' n. system of self-defense like karate

L

lab n. [Col.] laboratory

la'bel n. card, etc. marked and attached to an object to show its contents, etc. —v. 1 attach a label to 2 classify as

la·bi·a n.pl., sing. **-bi·um** liplike folds of the vulva

la'bi·al a. of the lips

la'bor n. 1 work 2 task 3 all workers 4 process of childbirth —v. 1 work hard 2 move with effort

lab'o·ra·to·ry (lab'rə-) n., pl. **-ries** place for scientific work or research

la'bored a. with effort

la'bor·er n. a worker; esp., an unskilled worker

la·bo'ri·ous a. difficult

labor union n. association of workers to further their interests

la'bour n., v. Br. sp. of LABOR

la·bur'num n. shrub with drooping yellow flowers

lab'y·rinth' (-ə-) n. maze

lace n. 1 string used to fasten together parts of a shoe, etc. 2 openwork fabric woven in fancy designs —v. 1 fasten with a lace 2 intertwine 3 whip

lac'er·ate' (las'-) v. tear jaggedly —**lac'er·a'tion** n.

lach'ry·mose' (lak'ri-) a. tearful; sad

lack n. state of not having enough or any —v. have little or nothing of

lack'a·dai'si·cal (-dā'zi-) a. showing lack of interest

lack'ey n., pl. **-eys** 1 menial male servant 2 toady

lack'lus'ter a. dull

la·con'ic a. concise; brief

lac·quer (lak'ər) n. a varnish, often like enamel —v. coat with lacquer

la·crosse' n. ball game using long-handled sticks

lac'tic a. of or like milk

lac'tic a. 1 of milk 2 of an acid in sour milk

lac'tose' n. sugar found in milk

la·cu'na (-kyōō'-) n. gap; space

lac'y a. **-i·er, -i·est** of or like lace —**lac'i·ness** n.

lad n. boy; youth

lad'der n. series of rungs framed by two sidepieces for climbing up or down

lade v. **lad'ed, lad'ed** or **lad'en, lad'ing** to load

lad'en a. 1 loaded 2 burdened

lad'ing n. a load; cargo

la'dle n. long-handled, cuplike spoon for dipping —v. dip out with a ladle

la'dy n., pl. **-dies** 1 well-bred, polite woman 2 any woman — a. female —**la'dy·like'** a.

la'dy·bug' n. small beetle with a spotted back

la'dy·fin'ger n. small finger-shaped spongecake

lag v. **lagged, lag'ging** fall behind —n. 1 a falling behind 2 amount of this

la'ger (beer) (lä'-) n. a beer aged for several months

lag'gard a. backward; slow —n. one who falls behind

la·goon' n. 1 shallow lake joined to a larger body of water 2 water inside an atoll

laid v. pt. & pp. of LAY

laid'-back' a. [Sl.] easygoing

lain v. pp. of LIE (recline)

lair n. animal's den

lais·sez faire (les'ā fer') n. non-interference

la'i·ty n. all laymen, as a group

lake n. large inland body of water

lam n. [Sl.] headlong flight —v. **lammed, lam'ming** [Sl.] flee

la'ma (lä'-) n. Buddhist priest or monk in Tibet

La·maze' (lə mäz') n. training program in natural childbirth

lamb (lam) n. 1 young sheep 2 its flesh as food

lam·baste' (-bāst') v. [Col.] beat or scold soundly

lam'bent a. 1 flickering 2 glowing softly 3 light and graceful

lame a. 1 crippled 2 stiff and painful 3 poor; ineffectual —v. make lame

la·ment' v. feel or show deep sorrow for —n. 1 a lamenting 2 elegy; dirge —**lam'en·ta·ble** a. —**lam'en·ta'tion** n.

lam'i·nate' v. form of or into thin layers —**lam'i·nat·ed** a. —**lam'i·na'tion** n.

lamp n. 1 device for producing light 2 such a device set in a stand

lamp'black' n. fine soot used as a black pigment

lam·poon' n. written satirical attack —v. to attack in a lampoon

lamp'post' n. post supporting a street lamp

lam'prey (-prē) n., pl. **-preys** eel-like water animal

lance n. 1 long spear 2 lancet —v. cut open with a lancet

lan'cet n. surgical knife

land n. 1 solid part of earth's surface 2 country or region 3 ground; soil 4 real estate —v. 1 put or go on shore on land 2 catch 3 [Col.] get or secure

land'ed a. 1 owning land 2 consisting of land

land'fill' n. place for burying garbage

land'ing n. 1 a coming to shore 2 pier; dock 3 platform at the end of stairs 4 an alighting

land'locked' a. 1 surrounded by land 2 confined to fresh water

land'lord' n. man who leases land, houses, rooms, etc. to others —**land'la'dy** n.fem.

land'lub'ber n. one with little experience at sea

land'mark' n. 1 identifying feature of a locality 2 important event

land'mass' n. large area of land

land'scape' n. (picture of) natural scenery —v. plant lawns, bushes, etc. on

land'slide' n. 1 sliding of rocks or earth down a slope 2 overwhelming victory

lane n. narrow path, road, etc.

lan'guage (-gwij) n. 1 speech or writing 2 any means of communicating

lan'guid a. 1 weak 2 listless; sluggish

lan'guish v. 1 become weak 2 long; pine —**lan'guish·ing** a.

lan'guor (-gər) n. lack of vigor —**lan'guor·ous** a.

lank a. tall and lean

lank'y a. **-i·er, -i·est** awkwardly tall and lean

lan'o·lin' n. fatty substance obtained from wool

lan'tern n. transparent case holding a light

lan'yard (-yard) n. Naut. short rope

lap n. 1 front part from the waist to the knees of a sitting person 2 place in which one is cared for 3 one circuit of a race track 4 overlapping part —v. lapped, lap'ping 1 fold or wrap 2 lay or extend partly over 3 dip up with the tongue 4 splash lightly

la·pel' n. fold-back part at the upper front of a coat

lap'i·dar'y (-der'-) n., pl. **-ies** one who cuts and polishes gems

lap'is laz'u·li' (-yōō li') n. azure, opaque semiprecious stone

lapse n. 1 small error 2 a falling into a lower condition 3 passing, as of time —v. 1 fall into a certain state 2 deviate from virtue 3 become void

lar'board (-bərd) n., a. left; port

lar'ce·ny n., pl. **-nies** theft —**lar'ce·nous** a.

larch n. kind of pine tree

lard n. melted fat of hogs —v. cover with lard

lard'er n. (place for keeping) food supplies

large a. of great size or amount —adv. in a large way —**at large** 1 free; not jailed 2 in general —**large'ness** n.

large'ly adv. mainly

large'-scale' a. extensive

lar·gess', lar·gesse' n. generous giving

lar'go a., adv. Mus. slow and stately

lar'i·at n. a rope; esp., a lasso

lark n. 1 any of various songbirds 2 merry time —v. to play or frolic

lark'spur' n. delphinium

lar'va n., pl. **-vae'** (-vē') insect in the earliest stage after hatching —**lar'val** a.

lar·yn·gi·tis (lar'in jīt'is) n. inflammation of the larynx

lar'ynx (-iŋks) n. upper end of the trachea

la·sa'gna (-zän'yə) n. wide noodles baked with layers of cheese, ground meat, tomato sauce, etc.

las·civ'i·ous (lə siv'-) a. showing or exciting lust

la'ser (-zər) n. device that concentrates light rays in an intense beam

lash n. 1 striking part of a whip 2 a stroke as with a whip 3 eyelash —v. 1 strike or drive as with a lash 2 swing sharply 3 tie with a rope, etc. —**lash out** speak angrily

lass n. young woman

las'si·tude' n. weariness

las'so' n., pl. **-sos'** or **-soes'** rope with a sliding noose, for catching cattle, etc. —v. catch with a lasso

last a. 1 after all others 2 only remaining 3 most recent —adv. 1 after all others 2 most recently —n. 1 last one 2 foot-like form for making shoes —v. stay in use, etc. —**at last** finally

last'ly adv. in conclusion

latch n. fastening for a door, window, etc., esp. a bar that fits into a notch —v. fasten with a latch

late a. 1 after the expected time 2 near the end of a period 3 recent 4 recently dead —adv. 1 after the expected time 2 near the end of a period 3 recently —**of late** recently

late'ly adv. recently

la'tent a. undeveloped

lat'er adv. after some time

lat'er·al a. sideways

la'tex' n. milky fluid in certain plants and trees

lath (lath) n. framework for plaster, as thin strips of wood

lathe (lāth) n. machine for shaping wood, metal, etc. with a cutting tool

lath'er n. 1 foam formed by soap and water 2 foamy sweat —v. cover with or form lather

Lat'in n. 1 language of ancient Rome 2 speaker of a Latin language —a. of or derived from Latin

lat'i·tude' n. 1 freedom of opinion, action, etc. 2 distance in degrees from the equator

la·trine' (-trēn') n. toilet for the use of many people

lat'ter a. 1 nearer the end 2 last mentioned of two

lat'tice (-is) n. a structure of crossed strips of wood, etc.

laud (lôd) v., n. praise —**laud'a·to·ry** a.

laud'a·ble a. praiseworthy

laugh (laf) v. make vocal sounds showing mirth, scorn, etc. —n. act of laughing: also **laugh'ter** n. —**laugh'a·ble** a.

laugh'ing·stock' n. object of ridicule

launch v. 1 send into space 2 set afloat 3 begin —n. a large motorboat

laun'der v. wash or wash and iron (clothes, linens, etc.) —**laun'dress** n. fem.

Laun'dro·mat' service mark self-service laundry —n. [l-] such a laundry

laun'dry n., pl. **-dries** 1 place for laundering 2 things (to be) laundered

lau'rel n. 1 evergreen with large, glossy leaves 2 pl. fame; victory

la·va (lä'və, lav'ə) n. rock from a volcano

lav'a·to·ry n., pl. **-ries** 1 washbowl 2 room with toilet and washbowl

lav'en·der n. pale purple

lav'ish n. very generous —v. give or spend freely

law n. 1 any of the rules of conduct made by a government 2 obedience to these 3 profession of lawyers 4 fundamental rule 5 series of natural events taking place in the same way —**law'break'er** n. —**law'mak'er** n.

law'-a·bid·ing a. obeying the law

law'ful a. LEGAL (a. 1)

law'less a. disobeying law

lawn n. grass cut short

law'suit' n. case before a court for decision

law'yer n. person licensed to practice law

lax a. 1 not tight 2 not strict —**lax'i·ty** n.

lax'a·tive n., a. (medicine) making the bowels move

lay v. **laid**, **lay'ing** 1 put down on something 2 set in place 3 put or place 4 produce (an egg) 5 settle; allay 6 to bet 7 devise 8 to present or assert —n. 1 position; arrangement 2 short poem —a. of or for laymen —**lay aside** (or **away** or **by**) save for future use

lay v. pt. of LIE (recline)

lay'a·way' n. method of buying by making a deposit to hold item until full payment

lay'er n. single thickness

lay·ette' n. complete outfit for a newborn baby

lay'man n., pl. **-men** one not belonging to the clergy or to a given profession

lay'off' n. temporary unemployment

lay'out' n. arrangement

la'zy a. **-zi·er**, **-zi·est** 1 not willing to work 2 sluggish —**la'zi·ly** adv. —**la'zi·ness** n.

leach v. extract or lose (a soluble substance)

lead (lēd) v. **led, lead'ing** 1 direct or guide as by going before 2 be at the head of 3 go or pass 4 bring as a result 5 move first in a game, etc. —n. 1 guidance 2 first place 3 distance ahead 4 clue 5 leading role —**lead off** begin —**lead on** lure —**lead up to** prepare the way for —**lead'er** n. —**lead'er·ship'** n.

lead (led) n. 1 heavy, soft metal, a chemical element 2 graphite used in pencils

lead'en (led'-) a. 1 of lead 2 heavy 3 gloomy

lead'ing (lēd'-) a. chief

leaf n., pl. **leaves** 1 flat, thin, usually green part growing from a plant stem 2 sheet of paper, etc. —v. turn the pages of

leaf'let n. 1 small leaf 2 folded printed sheet

leaf'y a. **-i·er, -i·est** having many leaves

league (lēg) n. 1 association of nations, groups, etc. 2 unit of distance, about 3 miles —v. join in a league

leak v. 1 pass or let pass out or in accidentally 2 become known gradually —n. accidental crack that allows leaking —**leak'y** a., **-i·er, -i·est**

leak'age n. 1 a leaking 2 amount that leaks

lean v. 1 bend or slant 2 rely (on) 3 tend to rest against something —a. 1 with little or no fat 2 meager —**lean'ness** n.

lean'-to' n., pl. **-tos'** structure whose sloping roof abuts a wall, etc.

leap v. **leapt** or **lept** or **leaped, leap'ing** jump (over) —n. a jump

leap'frog' n. game in which players leap over the backs of others —v. **-frogged', -frog'ging** leap or skip (over)

leap year n. every fourth year, having 29 days in February

learn v. 1 get knowledge or skill by study 2 hear (of) 3 memorize —**learn'ing** n.

learn'ed a. having or showing much learning

lease n. contract by which property is rented —v. give or get by a lease

leash n. strap or chain for holding a dog, etc. to check

least a. smallest —adv. in the smallest degree —n. smallest in degree, etc. —**at least** at any rate

leath'er n. animal skin that has been tanned —**leath'er·y** a.

leave v. **left, leav'ing** 1 let remain 2 to have remaining behind or after one 3 bequeath 4 go away (from) —n. 1 permission 2 permitted absence from duty —**leave out** omit —**take one's leave** depart

leav'en (lev'-) n. 1 yeast, etc. used to make dough rise: also **leav'en·ing** 2 permeating influence —v. affect with leaven

leaves n. pl. of LEAF

lech'er n. lewd man —**lech'er·ous** a.

lec'i·thin (les'ə-) n. fatty compound in living cells

lec'tern n. reading stand

lec'ture n. 1 informative talk 2 a scolding —v. give a lecture (to) —**lec'tur·er** n.

led v. pt. & pp. of LEAD (guide)

ledge n. 1 shelf 2 projecting ridge of rocks

ledg'er n. book of final entry for transactions

lee a., n. (on) the side away from the wind —**lee'ward** n., a., adv.

leech n. bloodsucking worm

leek n. onionlike vegetable

leer n. malicious or suggestive grin —v. look with a leer

leer'y a. wary

lees n. pl. dregs; sediment

lee'way' n. [Col.] margin of time, of money, etc.

left a. of that side toward the west when one faces north —n. 1 left side 2 liberal or radical party, etc. —adv. toward the left

left v. pt. & pp. of LEAVE

left'-hand'ed a. 1 using the left hand more easily 2 for the left hand 3 insincere —adv. with the left hand

left'ist n., a. liberal or radical

left'o·ver n., a. (something) remaining

leg n. 1 limb used for standing and walking 2 thing like a leg in shape or use

leg'a·cy n., pl. **-cies** something handed down to one, esp. by a will

le'gal a. 1 of, based upon, or permitted by law 2 of lawyers —**le·gal'i·ty** n. —**le'gal·ize'** v. —**le'gal·ly** adv.

le'gal·ese' (-ēz') n. legal jargon, often thought of as incomprehensible

leg'ate (-at) n. papal envoy

le·ga'tion n. envoy with staff and

headquarters

le·ga·to (li gät′ō) *a.*, *adv. Mus.* in a smooth, even style

leg·end *n.* 1 traditional tale 2 inscription, title, etc. —**leg′end·ar′y** *a.*

leg′er·de·main′ *n.* sleight of hand

leg′gings *n.pl.* coverings for protecting the legs

leg′i·ble *a.* that can be read — **leg′i·bly** *adv.*

le·gion (-jən) *n.* 1 large body of soldiers 2 great number

le·gion·naire′ *n.* member of a legion

leg′is·late′ *v.* 1 make laws 2 bring (about) by laws —**leg′is·la′tion** *n.* —**leg′is·la′tive** *a.* —**leg′is·la′tor** *n.*

leg′is·la·ture *n.* group of persons who make laws

le·git′i·mate (-mət) *a.* 1 born of a married couple 2 lawful 3 reasonable

le·git′i·mize′ *v.* legalize, authorize, justify, etc.

leg·ume (leg′yōōm′) *n.* plant with pods, as the pea and bean —**le·gu′mi·nous** *a.*

lei (lā) *n.*, *pl.* **leis** garland or wreath with flowers

lei·sure (lē′zhər, lezh′ər) *a.*, *n.* free (time) for rest, play, etc.

lei′sure·ly *a.* slow —*adv.* in an unhurried manner

lem′ming *n.* small arctic rodent

lem′on *n.* small, sour, yellow citrus fruit

lem·on·ade′ *n.* drink of lemon juice, sugar, and water

le·mur (lē′-) *n.* small mammal related to the monkey

lend *v.* **lent**, **lend′ing** 1 let another use (a thing) temporarily 2 let out (money) at interest 3 impart —**lend′er** *n.*

length *n.* 1 distance from end to end 2 extent in space or time 3 long stretch —**at length** finally —**length′wise′** *a.*, *adv.*

length′en *v.* make or become longer

length′y *a.* **-i·er**, **-i·est** long; esp., too long

le′ni·ent *a.* merciful; gentle —**le′ni·en·cy, le′ni·ence** *n.*

lens *n.* 1 curved piece of glass, plastic, etc. for adjusting light rays passing through it: used in cameras, telescopes, etc. 2 similar part of the eye

Lent *n.* period of 40 weekdays before Easter

lent *v.* pt. & pp. of LEND

len′til *n.* small edible seed of a pealike plant

Le′o *n.* fifth sign of the zodiac; Lion

le′o·nine *a.* like a lion

leop′ard (lep′-) *n.* large, black-spotted wildcat of Asia and Africa

le′o·tard *n.* a dancer's tight-fitting, one-piece garment

lep′er *n.* one having leprosy

lep′re·chaun (-kôn′) *n.* Irish fairy in the form of a little man who can reveal hidden treasure

lep′ro·sy *n.* disease with skin ulcers, scaling, etc.

les′bi·an (lez′-) *a.*, *n.* female homosexual

le′sion (-zhən) *n.* injury of an organ or tissues

less *a.* not so much, so great, etc. —*adv.* to a smaller extent —*n.* a smaller amount —*prep.* minus

-less *suf.* 1 without 2 that does not 3 that cannot be

les·see′ *n.* one to whom property is leased

less′en *v.* make or become less

less′er *a.* smaller, less, etc.

les′son *n.* 1 exercise for a student to learn 2 something learned by experience

les′sor *n.* one giving a lease

lest *con.* for fear that

let *v.* 1 allow; permit 2 leave 3 rent 4 cause to flow, as blood — *n.* hindrance *Let* is also used as an auxiliary verb —**let down** 1 lower 2 disappoint —**let up** 1 relax 2 cease

let′down′ *n.* a disappointment

le′thal *a.* fatal; deadly

leth′ar·gy *n.* lack of energy —**le·thar′gic** *a.*

let′ter *n.* 1 a character of the alphabet 2 message sent by mail 3 literal meaning 4 *pl.* literature —*v.* mark with letters — **let′tered** *a.*

let′ter·head′ *n.* 1 name, etc. of a person or firm as a heading on letter paper 2 a sheet of this paper

let′ter·per′fect *a.* entirely correct

let′ter·qual′i·ty *a.* producing printed characters of similar quality to typewritten characters

let′tuce (-əs) *n.* plant with crisp, green leaves used in salads

let′up′ *n.* [Col.] 1 a slackening 2 stop or pause

leu·ke′mi·a (lōō-) *n.* disease characterized by an abnormal increase in the white blood corpuscles

lev'ee *n.* river embankment to prevent flooding

lev'el *n.* 1 instrument for determining the horizontal 2 horizontal plane, line, etc. 3 height 4 position, rank, etc. —*a.* 1 flat and even 2 even in height (*with*) —*v.* 1 make or become level 2 demolish —**lev'el·er** *n.*

lev'el-head'ed *a.* sensible

lev'er (or **lē'var**) *n.* bar turning on a fulcrum, used to lift or move weights

lev'er·age *n.* action or power of a lever

le·vi'a·than (-vī'-) *n.* 1 *Bible* sea monster 2 huge thing

lev'i·tate' *v.* (make) rise and float in the air —**lev'i·ta'tion** *n.*

lev'i·ty *n.* improper gaiety; frivolity

lev'y *v.* -**ied**, -**y·ing** 1 impose (a tax, etc.) 2 enlist (troops) 3 wage (war) —*n.*, *pl.* -**ies** a levying or something levied

lewd (lōōd) *a.* indecent

lex'i·cog'ra·phy *n.* work of writing a dictionary —**lex'i·cog'ra·pher** *n.*

lex'i·con *n.* dictionary

li·a·bil'i·ty *n.*, *pl.* -**ties** 1 a being liable 2 debt 3 disadvantage

li'a·ble *a.* 1 legally responsible 2 subject to 3 likely

li·ai·son (lē·ā'zän') *n.* 1 communication between military units 2 illicit love affair

li'ar *n.* one who tells lies

li'bel *n.* statement in writing that may unjustly hurt a reputation —*v.* make a libel against —**li'bel·ous, li'bel·lous** *a.*

lib'er·al *a.* 1 generous 2 not strict 3 tolerant 4 favoring reform —*n.* person who favors reform —**lib'er·al·ism'** *n.* —**lib'er·al'i·ty** *n.* —**lib'er·al·ize'** *v.*

liberal arts *n.pl.* literature, philosophy, history, etc.

lib'er·ate' *v.* set free; release —**lib'er·a'tion** *n.* —**lib'er·a'tor** *n.*

lib'er·tine' (-tēn') *n.* sexually promiscuous person

lib'er·ty *n.*, *pl.* -**ies** 1 freedom from slavery, etc. 2 a particular right 3 *pl.* excessive familiarity —**at liberty** 1 not confined 2 permitted (*to*)

li·bi'do (-bē'-) *n.* sexual urge —**li·bid'i·nous** *a.*

Li'bra (lē'-) seventh sign of the zodiac; Scales

li'brar'y *n.*, *pl.* -**ies** collection of

books or a place for it —**li·brar'i·an** *n.*

li·bret'to *n.*, *pl.* -**tos** or -**ti** (-ē) text of an opera, etc. —**li·bret'tist** *n.*

lice *n.* pl. of LOUSE

li'cense *n.* 1 legal permit 2 freedom from rules 3 freedom that is abused —*v.* permit formally Also, Br. sps., **li'cence**

li·cen'tious (-shəs) *a.* morally unrestrained

li'chen (lī'kən) *n.* mosslike plant growing on rocks, trees, etc.

lick *v.* 1 pass the tongue over 2 [Col.] beat or conquer —*n.* 1 a licking 2 small quantity —**lick up** consume by licking

lic·o·rice (lik'ər ish) *n.* 1 black flavoring from a plant root 2 candy with this flavoring

lid *n.* 1 movable cover 2 eyelid —**lid'ded** *a.*

lie *v.* **lay, lain, ly'ing** 1 be horizontal or rest horizontally 2 be or exist —*n.* position; lay

lie *v.* **lied, ly'ing** make a false statement knowingly —*n.* thing said in lying

lie detector *n.* polygraph

liege (lēj) *n.* feudal lord or vassal

lien (lēn) *n.* legal claim on another's property until a debt is paid

lieu (lōō) *n.* used chiefly in **in lieu of**, instead of

lieu·ten'ant *n.* 1 low-ranking commissioned officer 2 deputy —**lieu·ten'an·cy** *n.*, *pl.* -**cies**

life *n.*, *pl.* **lives** 1 active existence of plants and animals 2 living things 3 time of being alive 4 way of living 5 a biography 6 liveliness —**life'less** *a.* —**life'like'** *a.*

life'boat' *n.* small rescue boat carried by a ship

life'guard' *n.* swimmer employed to prevent drownings

life'long' *a.* lasting for life

life pre·serv'er *n.* device for keeping a body afloat

life'sav'er *n.* [Col.] person or thing that gives help in time of need

life'-size' *a.* as big as the thing represented

life'style' *n.* individual's way of life: also sp. **life style**

life'time' *a.*, *n.* (lasting for) the length of one's life

lift *v.* 1 bring higher; raise 2 go up; rise 3 [Sl.] steal —*n.* 1 a lifting 2 lifting force 3 raising of one's spirits 4 help; aid 5

ride in the direction one is going
6 [Br.] elevator
lift′off′ n. vertical takeoff of a
spacecraft, etc.
lig′a·ment n. connective tissue
for bones or organs
lig′a·ture n. 1 a thing for tying,
as surgical thread 2 letters
united, as fl
light n. 1 radiant energy by
which one sees 2 brightness 3
lamp, lantern, etc. 4 daylight 5
thing to ignite something 6
aspect 7 knowledge —a. 1
bright 2 pale; fair 3 not heavy
or do 6 happy 7 dizzy 8 moderate —adv. 1 palely 2 lightly
—v. **light′ed** or **lit**, **light′ing** 1
ignite 2 furnish with light 3
brighten 4 be lighted 5 come to
rest 6 happen (on) —**in the
light of** considering
light′en v. make or become
brighter, less heavy, etc.
light′heart′ed a. free from care;
cheerful
light′house′ n. tower with a light
to guide ships
light′ly adv. 1 gently 2 very little 3 cheerfully 4 carelessly
light′ning n. flash of light in the
sky from a discharge of atmospheric electricity
lightning bug n. firefly
lightning rod n. metal rod to
divert lightning
light′-year′ n. distance that light
travels in a year, about 6 trillion
miles
lik′a·ble, **like′a·ble** a. pleasant,
friendly, etc.
like a. similar; equal —prep. 1
similar(ly) to 2 typical of 3 in
the mood for 4 indicative of —
con. [Col.] 1 as 2 as if —v. 1
be fond of; enjoy 2 wish —n. 1
an equal 2 pl. preferences —
like crazy (or **mad**) [Col.] wildly
—**lik′ing** n.
-like suf. like
like′ly a. 1 credible 2 probable;
expected 3 suitable —adv.
probably —**like′li·hood** n.
lik′en (līk′-) v. compare
like′ness n. 1 a being like 2 picture; copy
like′wise′ adv. 1 in the same
way 2 also; too
li′lac′ n. shrub with tiny, pale-
purple flower clusters
lilt n. light, swingy rhythm
lil′y n., pl. **-ies** plant with
trumpet-shaped flowers
lily of the valley n., pl. **lilies of**
the **valley** plant with a spike of
bell-shaped flowers
li′ma bean (lī′-) n. large, flat,
edible bean in pods
limb (lim) n. 1 arm, leg, or wing
2 large tree branch
lim′ber v., a. (make or become)
flexible
lim′bo′ n. place of oblivion
Lim′burg·er (cheese) n. white,
strong-smelling cheese
lime n. 1 white substance
obtained from limestone 2 a
green, lemonlike fruit
lime′light′ n. prominent position
before the public
lim′er·ick n. rhymed, funny
poem of five lines
lime′stone′ n. rock used in building, making lime, etc.
lim′it n. 1 point where something ends 2 pl. bounds —v. set
a limit to —**lim′i·ta′tion** n.
lim′it·ed a. confined
limn (lim) v. portray in pictures
or words
lim′ou·sine′ (-ə zēn′) n. large,
luxury automobile: also [Col.]
lim′o, pl. **-os**
limp v., a. (walk with) lameness
—a. not firm
lim′pet′ n. shellfish that clings to
rocks, etc.
lim′pid a. transparent
lin′den n. tree with heart-shaped
leaves
line n. 1 cord, rope, etc. 2 wire,
pipe, etc. 3 long, thin mark 4
boundary 5 outline 6 a row or
series 7 conformity 8 transportation system 9 route; course
10 stock of goods 11 short letter —v. 1 mark with lines 2
form a line: with up 3 put, or
serve as, a lining in
lin·e·age (lin′ē ij) n. line of
descent; ancestry
lin′e·al a. 1 directly descended 2
linear
lin′e·a·ment n. distinctive facial
feature
lin′e·ar a. 1 of a line or lines 2
of length
line′man n., pl. **-men** person
who puts up telephone or other
electric lines
lin′en n. 1 cloth of flax 2 things
of linen or cotton
lin′er (līn′-) n. ship or airplane of
a LINE (n. 8)
line′up′ n. a row of persons or
things
lin′ger v. 1 continue to stay 2
loiter
lin·ge·rie (län′zhə rā′) n.

women's underwear

lin'go n., pl. **-goes** unfamiliar jargon

lin·gui'ne (-gwē'nē) n. flat, narrow spaghetti: also **lin·gui'ni**

lin'guist (-gwist) n. one adept in several languages

lin·guis'tics n. science of (a) language

lin'i·ment n. medicated liquid for the skin

lin'ing (līn'-) n. material covering an inner surface

link n. 1 loop in a chain 2 thing that connects —v. join; connect —**link'age** n.

link'up' n. a joining

li·no'le·um n. hard, smooth floor covering

lin'seed' oil n. yellow oil from seed of flax

lint n. bits of thread, fluff, etc. from cloth —**lint'y** a., **-i·er**, **-i·est**

lin'tel n. horizontal piece over a door or window

li'on n. 1 large animal of the cat family, found in Africa and SW Asia 2 very strong, brave person 3 a celebrity —**li'on·ess** n.fem.

li'on·ize' v. treat as a celebrity

lip n. 1 upper or lower edge of the mouth 2 thing like a lip, as a cup's rim

lip'stick' n. small stick of rouge to color the lips

liq'ue·fy' (lik'wi-) v. **-fied'**, **-fy'ing** change to a liquid

li·queur (li kur', -koor') n. sweet alcoholic liquor

liq'uid a. 1 readily flowing 2 readily changed into cash —n. substance that flows easily

liq'ui·date' v. 1 settle the accounts of (a business) 2 pay (a debt) 3 change into cash —**liq'ui·da'tion** n.

liq'uor (-ər) n. alcoholic drink, as whiskey

lisle (līl) n. fabric woven of strong cotton thread

lisp v. to substitute the sounds "th" and "th" for the sounds of "s" and "z" —n. act or sound of lisping

lis'some, **lis'som** a. lithe and graceful

list n. series of names, words, etc. set forth in order —v. put in a list

list v. tilt to one side, as a ship —n. a listing

lis'ten (-ən) v. 1 try to hear 2 pay attention

list'less a. indifferent because ill, sad, etc.

list price n. retail price

lit v. pt. & pp. of LIGHT

lit'a·ny n., pl. **-nies** prayer with responses

li'ter (lē'-) n. metric unit of capacity (61.025 cubic inches)

lit'er·al a. 1 precise; exact; strict 2 prosaic 3 restricted to fact —**lit'er·al·ly** adv.

lit'er·ar'y a. having to do with literature

lit'er·ate (-ət) a. educated; esp., able to read and write —**lit'er·a·cy** n.

lit'er·a·ture' n. 1 all the valuable writings of a specific time, nation, etc. 2 all writings on some subject

lithe (līth) a. bending easily

lith'i·um n. the lightest metal, a chemical element

lith'o·graph' n. print made from stone or metal treated with grease and water —**li·thog'ra·phy** n.

lit'i·gant n. party to a lawsuit

lit'i·gate' v. to contest in a lawsuit —**lit'i·ga'tion** n.

lit'mus paper n. treated paper that turns blue in bases and red in acids

li'tre n. Br. sp. of LITER

lit'ter n. 1 portable couch 2 stretcher 3 young person at one time by a dog, cat, etc. 4 things lying about in disorder —v. make untidy

lit'ter·bug' n. one who litters public places with rubbish

lit'tle a. 1 small in size or amount 2 short; brief 3 not important —adv. 1 slightly 2 not at all —n. small amount or short time —**little by little** gradually —**not a little** very

lit'ur·gy n., pl. **-gies** ritual for public worship —**li·tur'gi·cal** a.

liv'a·ble a. fit or pleasant to live in

live (liv) v. 1 have life 2 stay alive; endure 3 pass one's life in a certain way 4 have a full life 5 feed (on) 6 reside

live (līv) a. 1 having life 2 energetic 3 of interest now 4 still burning 5 unexploded 6 carrying electrical current 7 broadcast while happening

live'li·hood' n. means of supporting oneself

live'long' (liv'-) a. whole

live'ly a. **-li·er**, **-li·est** 1 full of life 2 exciting 3 cheerful 4 having much bounce —**live′li·ness** n.

liv′en (liv′-) v. cheer (up)

liv′er n. organ in vertebrates that makes bile

liv′er-wurst′ n. sausage made of ground liver

liv′er·y n., pl. **-ies** 1 uniform as of a servant 2 business of renting horses and carriages

lives v. pl. of LIFE

live′stock′ n. animals kept or raised on a farm

liv′id a. 1 discolored by a bruise; black-and-blue 2 grayish-blue

liv′ing a. 1 having life 2 in active use 3 of persons alive 4 true; lifelike 5 of life 6 enough to live on —n. 1 a being alive 2 livelihood 3 way that one lives

living room n. room for lounging, entertaining, etc.

liz′ard n. reptile with a long tail and four legs

lla′ma (lä′-) n. South American camellike animal

lo int. look! see!

load n. 1 amount carried 2 burden —v. 1 put (a load) in or on 2 burden 3 put ammunition into

load′stone′ n. lodestone

loaf n., pl. **loaves** bread, etc. baked in one piece —v. waste (time) —**loaf′er** n.

loam n. rich soil

loan n. 1 act of lending 2 something lent, esp. money at interest —v. lend

loath (lōth) a. reluctant

loathe (lōth) v. abhor —**loath′some** a.

lob v. **lobbed, lob′bing** toss or hit (a ball) in a high curve —n. a toss or hit made this way

lob′by n., pl. **-bies** 1 entrance hall 2 group of lobbyists —v. **-bied, -by·ing** act as a lobbyist

lob′by·ist n. one who tries to influence legislators

lobe n. rounded projection

lob′ster n. edible sea animal with large pincers

lo′cal a. of or for a particular place or area —n. 1 bus, etc. making all stops 2 branch, as of a labor union —**lo′cal·ly** adv.

lo·cale′ (-kal′) n. a place or setting for events, etc.

lo·cal′i·ty n., pl. **-ties** place or district

lo′cal·ize′ v. limit or trace to a certain place

lo′cate′ v. 1 establish in a certain place 2 find or show the position of

lo·ca′tion n. 1 a locating 2 position; place

lock n. 1 device for fastening a door, etc. as with a key 2 part of a canal between gates 3 curl of hair —v. 1 fasten with a lock 2 shut (in or out) 3 jam or link together

lock′er n. chest, closet, etc. that can be locked

lock′et n. little case worn on a necklace

lock′jaw′ n. tetanus

lock′out′ n. a locking out of employees to force agreement to employer's terms

lock′smith′ n. one who makes or repairs locks and keys

lock′up′ n. a jail

lo′co a. [Sl.] crazy; insane

lo′co·mo′tion n. act or power of moving about

lo′co·mo′tive n. engine for a railroad train

lo′cust n. 1 grasshopper-like insect 2 cicada 3 tree with white flowers

lo·cu′tion (-kyōō′-) n. phrase or phraseology

lode n. vein or stratum of metallic ore

lode′stone′ n. magnetic iron ore

lodge n. 1 a house for special use 2 chapter of a society —v. 1 to house or dwell for a time 2 put in 3 come to rest —**lodg′er** n.

lodg′ing n. 1 place to live 2 pl. rented rooms

loft n. 1 space below a roof 2 upper story of a warehouse, etc. 3 gallery —v. send (a ball) high into the air

loft′y a. **-i·er, -i·est** 1 very high 2 noble 3 haughty —**loft′i·ness** n.

log n. 1 section cut from a tree trunk 2 daily record of a ship's, etc. progress 3 logarithm —v. **logged, log′ging** 1 cut down trees and remove the logs 2 enter in a ship's log —**log on** (or off) enter information to begin (or end) activity on a computer terminal

lo′gan·ber′ry n., pl. **-ries** purple-red berry

log′a·rithm (-rith əm) n. Math. power to which a base number must be raised to get a given number

loge (lōzh) n. theater box

log′ic (läj′-) n. 1 science of reasoning 2 (correct) reasoning —

lo·gi·cian (lō jish'ən) n.

log'i·cal a. 1 using or used in logic 2 expected as a result — **log'i·cal·ly** adv.

lo·gis'tics n. military science of moving and supplying troops

log'jam' n. obstacle or deadlock

lo'go' n. distinctive symbol, etc., as a trademark

-logy suf. science or study of

lo'gy (-gē) a. **-gi·er, -gi·est** [Col.] dull or sluggish

loin n. 1 lower back from ribs to hipbone 2 pl. hips and lower abdomen

loi'ter v. 1 spend time idly 2 move slowly

loll (läl) v. 1 lounge about 2 droop or let hang loosely

lol'li·pop', lol'ly·pop' n. piece of candy on a stick

lol'ly·gag' v. **-gagged', -gag'ging** [Col.] waste time aimlessly

lone a. by oneself or itself

lone'ly a. **-li·er, -li·est** 1 alone and unhappy 2 unfrequented — **lone'li·ness** n.

lon'er (lōn'-) n. [Col.] one who avoids the company of others

lone'some a. having or causing a lonely feeling

long a. 1 measuring much 2 in length 3 of great length 4 tedious 5 far-reaching 6 well supplied —adv. 1 for a long time 2 for the time of 3 at a remote time —v. to wish earnestly; yearn —**as** (or **so**) **long as** 1 while 2 since 3 provided that —**before long** soon

lon·gev'i·ty (-jev'-) n. 1 long life 2 length of time

long'hand' n. 1 ordinary handwriting

long'ing n. earnest desire

lon'gi·tude' n. distance, in degrees, east or west of a line through Greenwich, England

lon'gi·tu'di·nal a. 1 of length 2 of longitude

long jump n. a jump for distance

long'-lived' (-līvd', -livd') a. having a long life span

long'-range' a. covering a long distance or time

long'shore'man n., pl. **-men** one whose work is loading and unloading ships

long'-term' a. for a long time

long ton n. 2,240 pounds

long'ways' adv. lengthwise

long'-wind'ed (-win'dəd) a. wordy and tiresome

look v. 1 direct the eyes so as to see 2 search 3 seem —n. 1 an

act of looking 2 appearance 3 [Col.] pl. personal appearance —int. 1 see! 2 pay attention! —**look after** care for —**look into** investigate —**look up to** admire

look'ing glass n. glass mirror

look'out' n. 1 careful watching 2 guard; sentry

loom n. machine for weaving — v. come into sight suddenly

loon n. ducklike bird

loon'y a. **-i·er, -i·est** [Sl.] crazy; insane

loop n. line, figure, etc. that curves back to cross itself —v. make a loop

loop'hole' n. means of evading something

loose (lōōs) a. 1 free 2 not firm or tight 3 inexact 4 sexually immoral —v. 1 to free 2 make less tight, etc. 3 release —**on the loose** not confined; free — **loose'ly** adv. —**loos'en** v.

loot n., v. plunder —**loot'er** n.

lop v. lopped, lop'ping cut off

lope v., n. (move with) a long, swinging stride

lop'sid'ed a. heavier, lower, etc. on one side

lo·qua'cious (-kwā'shəs) a. very talkative

lord n. 1 master 2 Br. nobleman —[L-] 1 God 2 Jesus Christ

lore n. knowledge

lor·gnette (lôrn yet') n. eyeglasses on a handle

lor'ry n., pl. **-ries** [Br.] motor truck

lose (lōōz) v. lost, los'ing 1 become unable to find 2 have taken from one by accident, death, etc. 3 fail to keep 4 fail to win

loss n. 1 a losing, or damage, etc. resulting from losing something 2 person, thing, etc. lost

lost a. 1 ruined 2 missing or mislaid 3 wasted

lot n. 1 deciding of a matter by chance 2 fate 3 piece of land 4 group 5 [Col.] often pl. great amount or number —adv. very much

lo'tion n. liquid for softening or healing the skin

lot'ter·y n., pl. **-ies** game in which numbered chances on prizes are sold

lot'to n. a game like bingo

lo'tus n. tropical waterlily

loud a. 1 strong in sound 2 noisy 3 [Col.] flashy —adv. in a

loud way —**loud'ly** adv. —**loud'-ness** n.

loud'speak'er n. device, as in a radio, for changing electric waves into sound and amplifying it

lounge v. 1 sit in a relaxed way 2 to be idle —n. 1 room furnished for lounging 2 couch

louse (lous) n., pl. **lice** small insect parasite —**louse up** [Sl.] botch; ruin

lous·y (lou'zē) a. -i·er, -i·est 1 infested with lice 2 [Sl.] inferior, contemptible, etc. 3 [Sl.] well supplied (with)

lout n. stupid fellow

lou'ver (lōō'-) n. 1 an opening with boards slanted to let in air and keep out rain 2 such a board

love n. 1 strong affection 2 object of this 3 in tennis, a score of zero —v. feel love (for) —**in love** feeling love —**make love** woo, embrace, etc. —**lov'a·ble, love'a·ble** a. —**lov'er** n. —**lov'ing·ly** adv.

love'lorn' a. pining from love

love'ly a. -li·er, -li·est 1 beautiful 2 [Col.] very enjoyable —**love'li·ness** n.

low a. 1 not high 2 below others in rank, size, cost, etc. 3 gloomy 4 deep in pitch 5 vulgar 6 not loud —adv. in or to a low level, etc. —n. 1 low level, degree, etc. 2 gear arrangement giving least speed 3 moo —**lay low** kill —**lie low** stay hidden

low'brow' n., a. [Col.] nonintellectual

low'-cal' a. having few calories

low'down' (a.: lō'doun') n. [Sl.] pertinent facts: with the —a. [Col.] mean or contemptible

low'er (lō'-) a. below in rank, etc. —v. 1 let or put down 2 make or become less in amount, value, etc.

low'er (lou'-) v. 1 to scowl 2 appear threatening

low'er·case' a., n. (of or in) small, rather than capital, letters

low'-key' a. subdued; not intense

low'ly a. 1 of low rank 2 humble —**low'li·ness** n.

low'-mind'ed a. having a coarse, vulgar mind

lox n. smoked salmon

loy'al a. faithful to one's friends, country, etc. —**loy'al·ly** adv. —

loy'al·ty n., pl. -ties

loz'enge n. cough drop, small piece of hard candy, etc.

lu·au (lōō'ou') n. Hawaiian feast

lube n. [Col.] a lubrication or lubricant

lu'bri·cant a. that lubricates —n. oil, grease, etc.

lu'bri·cate' v. apply oil or grease to reduce friction —**lu'bri·ca'-tion** n.

lu'cid a. 1 clear 2 sane 3 shining —**lu·cid'i·ty** n. —**lu'cid·ly** adv.

luck n. 1 chance; fortune 2 good fortune —**luck'less** a.

luck'y a. -i·er, -i·est having, resulting in, or thought to bring good luck —**luck'i·ly** adv.

lu'cra·tive a. profitable

lu'cre (-kər) n. riches; money: chiefly humorously derogatory

lu'di·crous (-krəs) a. so incongruous as to be funny

luff v. head a ship toward the wind

lug v. **lugged, lug'ging** carry with effort —n. 1 earlike handle or support 2 bolt, used with lug to mount a wheel

luge (lōōzh) n. racing sled

lug'gage n. suitcases, trunks, etc.

lu·gu'bri·ous (la gōō'-) a. mawkishly mournful

luke'warm' a. 1 slightly warm 2 lacking enthusiasm

lull v. 1 soothe by gentle sound or motion 2 calm —n. short period of calm

lull'a·by' n., pl. -bies' song for lulling a baby to sleep

lum·ba'go n. pain in the lower back

lum'bar (-bär', -bər) a. of or near the loins

lum'ber n. wood sawed into beams, boards, etc. —v. move heavily and clumsily —**lum'ber-ing** a.

lum'ber·jack' n. man who cuts timber for the sawmill

lum'ber·man n., pl. -men lumber dealer

lu'mi·nar'y n., pl. -ies famous person

lu'mi·nes'cence (-əns) n. giving off light without heat —**lu'mi·nes'cent** a.

lu'mi·nous a. bright; shining —**lu'mi·nos'i·ty** n.

lum'mox (-əks) n. [Col.] clumsy person

lump n. 1 a mass of something 2 a swelling —a. in a lump or lumps —v. to group together —

lump'y *a.*, **-i'er**, **-i'est**

lu'nar (-nər) *a.* of the moon

lu'na·tic *a.* 1 insane 2 utterly foolish —*n.* an insane person —**lu'na·cy** *n.*

lunch *n.* midday meal —*v.* eat lunch

lunch'eon (lun'chən) *n.* formal lunch

lunch'eon·ette' *n.* small restaurant serving light lunches

lung *n.* organ in the chest for breathing

lunge *n.* 1 sudden thrust 2 forward plunge —*v.* make a lunge

lu'pus *n.* disease with skin lesions

lurch *v.* sway suddenly to one side —*n.* 1 lurching movement 2 danger; trouble

lure (loor) *n.* 1 thing that attracts 2 fish bait —*v.* attract; entice

lu'rid (loor'id) *a.* 1 shocking 2 glowing strangely

lurk *v.* 1 to stay or be hidden, ready to attack 2 to move furtively

lus·cious (lush'əs) *a.* 1 delicious 2 pleasing

lush *a.* of or having luxuriant growth

lust *n.* 1 strong sexual desire 2 strong desire, as for power —*v.* feel an intense desire —**lust'ful** *a.*

lus'ter *n.* 1 gloss; brightness 2 brilliant fame —**lus'trous** (-trəs) *a.*

lust'y *a.*, **-i'er**, **-i'est** vigorous; robust —**lust'i·ly** *adv.*

lute *n.* a stringed, guitarlike instrument

lux·u'ri·ant (lug zhoor'-, luk shoor'-) *a.* 1 growing in abundance 2 richly ornamented —**lux·u'ri·ance** *n.*

lux·u'ri·ate *v.* 1 live in luxury 2 revel (*in*)

lux·u'ri·ous *a.* 1 giving a feeling of luxury 2 fond of luxury

lux'u·ry *n.*, *pl.* **-ries** costly comfort(s) or pleasure(s) —*a.* characterized by luxury

-ly *suf.* 1 like 2 in a specified way, or at a specified time or place 3 in sequence 4 every

lye (lī) *n.* strong alkaline substance

ly'ing *v.* ppr. of LIE

ly'ing-in' *a.* 1 *n.* (of or for) childbirth

lymph (limf) *n.* clear, yellowish body fluid —**lym·phat'ic** *a.*

lynch (linch) *v.* kill by mob action, without lawful trial, as by hanging

lynx (links) *n.* North American wildcat

lyre (līr) *n.* ancient instrument like a small harp

lyr'ic (lir'-) *a.* 1 suitable for singing 2 expressing the poet's emotions —*n.* 1 lyric poem 2 *pl.* words of a song

lyr'i·cal *a.* 1 lyric 2 very enthusiastic, etc. —**lyr'i·cal·ly** *adv.*

M

ma *n.* [Col.] mother

ma'am *n.* [Col.] madam

ma·ca'bre (-käb'rə, -käb') *a.* grim and horrible

mac'ad·am *n.* 1 small broken stones, used to make some roads 2 such a road

mac'a·ro'ni *n.* tubes of flour paste, cooked for food

mac'a·roon' *n.* cookie made with almonds or coconut

ma·caw' *n.* large parrot

mace *n.* 1 heavy, spiked club 2 official's staff 3 spice made from ground nutmeg shell —**[M-]** *trademark* combined tear gas and nerve gas

mac'er·ate (mas'-) *v.* soften by soaking

ma·che'te (-shet'ē) *n.* large, heavy knife

Mach'i·a·vel'li·an (mak'-) *a.* crafty, deceitful, etc.

mach'i·na'tion (mak'-) *n.* wily or evil scheme

ma·chine' (-shēn') *n.* 1 device with moving parts, for doing work 2 group in control of a political party —*a.* of or done by machines —*v.* to shape, etc. by machinery

machine gun *n.* automatic gun

ma·chin'er·y *n.* 1 machines 2 working parts

ma·chin'ist *n.* one who makes or operates machines

ma'cho *a.* overly virile, domineering, etc.

mack'er·el *n.* edible fish of N Atlantic

mack'i·naw' (coat) *n.* short, heavy wool coat, often plaid

mack'in·tosh' *n.* raincoat of rubberized cloth

mac'ra·mé (-mā') *n.* coarse yarn, etc. knotted in designs

macro- *pref.* large

mac'ro·cosm' *n.* universe

mad *a.* **mad'der**, **mad'dest** 1

insane 2 frantic 3 foolish 4 angry —**mad'ly** *adv.* —**mad'ness** *n.*

mad'am *n.* polite title for a woman

ma·dame (mə dăm') *n.*, *pl.* **mes·dames'** (mā'dăm') married woman: Fr. for *Mrs.*

mad'cap' *a.* reckless; wild

mad'den *v.* make mad —**mad'den·ing** *a.*

mad'der *n.* 1 vine with berries 2 red dye made from its root

made *v.* pt. & pp. of MAKE

ma·de·moi·selle (măd'ə mə zel') *n.* unmarried woman: Fr. for *Miss*

mad'house' *n.* 1 insane asylum 2 place of turmoil

mad'man' *n.*, *pl.* -**men'** insane person

Ma·don'na *n.* picture or statue of the Virgin Mary

ma'dras *n.* fine cotton cloth, usually striped

mad'ri·gal *n.* part song for small group

mael'strom (māl'-) *n.* violent whirlpool

maes'tro (mīs'-) *n.* master, as in music

Ma'fi·a *n.* secret, criminal society

mag·a·zine' (-zēn') *n.* 1 periodical publication 2 storage place, as for military supplies 3 supply chamber, as in a rifle

ma·gen'ta *n.* purplish red

mag'got *n.* wormlike larva —**mag'got·y** *a.*

Ma·gi (mā'jī') *n.pl.* wise men in the Bible

mag'ic *n.* 1 use of charms, spells, etc. 2 sleight of hand —*a.* of or as if by magic: also **mag'i·cal** —**mag'i·cal·ly** *adv.*

ma·gi'cian (-jish'ən) *n.* one who does magic

mag·is·te'ri·al (maj'-) *a.* authoritative

mag'is·trate' (maj'-) *n.* official who administers the law —**mag'is·tra·cy** *n.*

mag'ma *n.* molten rock

mag·nan'i·mous *a.* generous in forgiving; noble —**mag·na·nim'i·ty** *n.*

mag'nate *n.* influential person in business

mag·ne'sia (-zhə) *n.* white powder (magnesium oxide) used as a laxative

mag·ne'si·um (-zē əm) *n.* light, silvery metal, a chemical element

mag'net *n.* piece of iron, steel, etc. that attracts iron or steel

magnetic tape *n.* thin plastic tape magnetized for recording

mag'net·ism' *n.* 1 properties of magnets 2 personal charm —**mag·net'ic** *a.*

mag'net·ize' *v.* 1 make a magnet of 2 to charm

mag·ne'to *n.*, *pl.* -**tos** small electric generator

mag·nif'i·cent *a.* 1 grand and stately; splendid 2 exalted —**mag·nif'i·cence** *n.*

mag'ni·fy' *v.* -**fied'**, -**fy'ing** 1 increase apparent size of, as with a lens 2 exaggerate —**mag'ni·fi·ca'tion** *n.* —**mag'ni·fi'er** *n.*

mag'ni·tude' *n.* greatness of size, extent, or importance

mag·no'li·a *n.* tree with large, fragrant flowers

mag'pie' *n.* noisy bird of the crow family

ma·ha·ra'jah, ma·ha·ra'ja *n.* in India, a prince, formerly the ruler of a native state —**ma·ha·ra'ni, ma·ha·ra'nee** *n.fem.*

mah-jongg', mah'jong' *n.* Chinese game played with small tiles

ma·hog'a·ny *n.* reddish-brown wood of a tropical tree

maid *n.* 1 an unmarried, esp. young, woman 2 woman or girl servant

maid'en *n.* [Now Rare] young unmarried woman —*a.* 1 of or for a maiden 2 unmarried 3 first; earliest —**maid'en·hood'** *n.* —**maid'en·ly** *a.*

mail *n.* 1 letters, etc. sent by postal service 2 postal system 3 metal mesh armor —*v.* of mail —*v.* send by mail —**mail'box'** *n.* —**mail'man'** *n.*, *pl.* -**men'**

maim *v.* cripple; disable

main *a.* chief; leading; principal —*n.* 1 chief pipe in a system 2 [Poet.] ocean —**in the main** mostly —**with might and main** with all one's strength —**main'ly** *adv.*

main'frame' *n.* large computer connected to several terminals

main'land' *n.* main part of a continent

main'spring' *n.* chief spring in a clock, etc.

main'stay' *n.* main support

main'stream' *n.* prevailing trend

main·tain' *v.* 1 keep up; carry on 2 keep in working condition 3 declare to be true 4 support

main'te·nance *n.* 1 a maintaining 2 means of support

maî·tre d'hô·tel (me'trə dō'tel') *n.* [Fr.] chief of waiters

maize (māz) *n.* corn

maj·es·ty *n.* 1 grandeur; dignity 2 [M-] title for a sovereign — **ma·jes·tic** *a.* — **ma·jes·ti·cal·ly** *adv.*

ma·jor *a.* 1 greater in size, rank, etc. 2 *Mus.* semitone higher than the minor —*n.* 1 military officer above a captain 2 main field of study —*v.* specialize (*in* a subject)

ma·jor-do·mo *n.* man in charge of a great house

major general officer above brigadier general

ma·jor·i·ty *n.* 1 more than half 2 full legal age

make *v.* **made, mak'ing** 1 bring into being; build, create, etc. 2 cause to be 3 amount to; equal 4 acquire; earn 5 cause success of 6 execute, do, etc. 7 force; compel 8 [Col.] get a place on (a team) —*n.* 1 act of making 2 style or build —**make away with** steal —**make believe** pretend —**make out** 1 see 2 succeed —**make over** change —**make up** 1 put together 2 invent 3 compensate 4 stop quarreling —**mak'er** *n.*

make'shift' *a., n.* (as) a temporary substitute

make'up', make'-up' *n.* 1 way a thing is put together 2 cosmetics

mal- *pref.* bad or badly

mal'ad·just'ed *a.* badly adjusted, as to one's environment —**mal'ad·just'ment** *n.*

mal·a·droit' *a.* clumsy

mal·a·dy *n., pl.* **-dies** illness

ma·laise' (-lāz') *n.* vague feeling of illness

mal·a·prop'ism' *n.* ridiculous misuse of words

ma·lar·i·a (-ler'-) *n.* disease with chills and fever, carried by mosquitoes

mal'con·tent' *a., n.* dissatisfied (person)

male *a.* 1 of the sex that fertilizes the ovum 2 of, like, or for men or boys —*n.* a male person, animal, or plant

male·dic'tion *n.* a curse

male·fac'tor *n.* evildoer —**mal'e·fac'tion** *n.*

ma·lev·o·lent *a.* wishing harm to others —**ma·lev'o·lence** *n.*

mal·fea'sance (-fē'zəns) *n.* wrongdoing in public office

mal'for·ma'tion *n.* faulty formation —**mal-formed'** *a.*

mal'ice (-is) *n.* ill will; wish to harm —**ma·li'cious** (-lish'əs) *a.*

ma·lign' (-līn') *v.* speak evil of —*a.* evil; harmful

ma·lig'nant *a.* 1 evil 2 very harmful 3 likely to cause death —**ma·lig'nan·cy** *n.*

ma·lin'ger *n.* feign illness to escape duty —**ma·lin'ger·er** *n.*

mall *n.* 1 shaded public walk 2 enclosed shopping center

mal'lard *n.* wild duck

mal'le·a·ble *a.* that can be hammered or pressed into shape —**mal'le·a·bil'i·ty** *n.*

mal'let *n.* hammer with a wooden head

mal'low *n.* family of plants including the hollyhock

mal'nu·tri'tion *n.* faulty diet; lack of nourishment

mal·o'dor·ous *a.* having a bad smell; stinking

mal·prac'tice *n.* improper practice, as by a doctor

malt *n.* barley, etc. soaked and dried for use in brewing and distilling

malt'ed (milk) *n.* drink of milk, malt, ice cream, etc.

mal·treat' *v.* to abuse —**mal·treat'ment** *n.*

ma'ma, mam'ma *n.* mother: child's word

mam'mal *n.* any vertebrate the female of which suckles its offspring

mam'ma·ry *a.* of milk-secreting glands

mam'moth *n.* huge, extinct elephant —*a.* huge

man *n.* 1 human being; person 2 adult male person 3 human race —*v.* **manned, man'ning** furnish with men for work, etc. — **to a man** with no exception

man'a·cle *n., v.* handcuff

man·age *v.* 1 to control or guide 2 have charge of 3 succeed in doing —**man'age·ment** *n.* — **man'ag·er** *n.*

man'a·ge'ri·al (-jir'ē-) *a.* of a manager

man'a·tee' *n.* large mammal living in tropical waters

man'da·rin *n.* 1 high official of former Chinese empire 2 [M-] main Chinese dialect

man'date' *n.* 1 an order; command 2 the will of voters as expressed in elections 3 commission given to a nation to administer a region 4 such a region —**man'da·to'ry** *a.*

man'di·ble n. lower jaw

man'do·lin' n. musical instrument with from 8 to 12 strings

man'drake' n. root formerly used in medicine

mane n. long hair on the neck of a horse, lion, etc.

ma·neu·ver (-nōō'-) n. **1** a planned movement of troops, warships, etc. **2** scheme —v. **1** perform maneuvers **2** get, etc. by some scheme

man'ga·nese' n. grayish metal in alloys, a chemical element

mange (mānj) n. parasitic skin disease of animals —**man'gy** a., -**gi·er, -gi·est**

man·ger (mān'jər) n. box from which livestock feed

man'gle v. **1** mutilate by hacking, etc. **2** botch **3** press in a mangle —n. machine with rollers for ironing

man'go n., pl. -**goes** or -**gos** yellow-red tropical fruit

man'grove n. tropical tree with branches that send down roots to form trunks

man'han'dle v. handle roughly

man'hole' n. hole for entering a sewer, etc.

man'hood' n. **1** time of being a man **2** manly qualities

man'-hour' n. one hour of work by one person

ma'ni·a n. **1** wild insanity **2** obsession —**man'ic** a.

ma'ni·ac' n. violently insane person —**ma·ni'a·cal** (-nī'-) a.

man'i·cure' v., n. trim, polish, etc. (of) the fingernails —**man'i·cur·ist** n.

man'i·fest' a. obvious —v. reveal; show —n. list of a ship's cargo —**man'i·fes·ta'tion** n.

man'i·fes'to n., pl. -**toes** or -**tos** public declaration

man'i·fold' a. of many parts, sorts, etc. —n. pipe with several outlets, as for carrying exhaust from an engine

man'i·kin n. mannequin

Ma·nil'a (paper) n. tan paper for wrapping, etc.

ma·nip'u·late' v. **1** handle skillfully **2** manage unfairly or dishonestly —**ma·nip'u·la'tion** n. —**ma·nip'u·la'tive** a.

man'kind' n. **1** human race **2** all human males

man'ly a. -**li·er, -li·est** of, like, or fit for a man —**man'li·ness** n.

man'-made' a. synthetic; artificial

man'na n. thing provided as by a

miracle

man'ne·quin (-kin) n. model of the human body, as for displaying clothes

man'ner n. **1** way; style **2** habit **3** pl. (polite) ways of behaving **4** kind; sort

man'ner·ism' n. (affected) peculiarity of manner

man'ner·ly a. polite

man'nish a. masculine

man'-of-war' n. warship

man'or n. large estate

man'pow'er n. **1** human physical strength **2** the collective strength of a nation, etc.

man'sard (roof) (-särd) n. roof with two slopes on each side

manse n. residence of a minister or clergyman

man'sion n. large, imposing house

man'slaugh'ter n. unintentional killing of a person

man'tel n. frame around or shelf above a fireplace

man·til'la n. woman's scarf for the hair and shoulders

man'tis n. large, predatory insect

man'tle n. **1** sleeveless cloak **2** thing that covers —v. to cover

man'u·al a. made or done by hand —n. handbook

man'u·fac'ture n. making of goods by machinery —v. make, esp. by machinery —**man'u·fac'tur·er** n.

ma·nure' n. animal waste as fertilizer

man'u·script' n. written or typed book, article, etc.

man'y a. more, most numerous —n., pron. large number (of persons or things)

map n. drawing of the features of a region, the earth's surface, the sky, etc. —v. mapped, map'ping **1** to make a map of **2** plan

ma'ple n. **1** large shade tree **2** its hard wood **3** flavor of syrup or sugar made from its sap

mar v. marred, mar'ring damage; spoil

ma·ra'ca n. pebble-filled musical rattle

mar'a·schi'no cherry (-skē'-, -shē'-) n. cherry in a syrup

mar'a·thon' n. **1** foot race of about 26 mi. **2** any endurance contest

ma·raud'er n. raider —**ma·raud'ing** a.

mar'ble n. hard limestone, white or colored —a. of or like marble

March n. third month

march v. 1 walk with regular steps 2 advance steadily —n. 1 a marching 2 progress 3 distance marched 4 marching music

Mar·di Gras' (-grä') n. last day before Lent begins

mare n. female horse, mule, donkey, etc.

mar·ga·rine (-rin) n. a spread like butter, of vegetable oil and skim milk

mar·gin n. 1 edge, as the blank border of a page 2 extra amount in reserve —**mar'gin·al** a.

mar·i·gold' n. plant with yellow or orange flowers

mar·i·jua'na, mar·i·hua'na (-wä'nə) n. narcotic from the hemp plant

ma·rim'ba n. kind of xylophone

ma·ri'na (-rē'-) n. small harbor with docks

mar·i·nade' n. spiced pickling solution for meat, fish, etc.

mar·i·nate' v. soak in spiced vinegar, brine, etc.

ma·rine' a. of or in the sea, ships, etc. —n. member of the Marine Corps

mar·i·ner n. sailor

mar·i·o·nette' n. puppet

mar·i·tal a. of marriage

mar·i·time' a. 1 on or near the sea 2 of sailing

mar·jo·ram n. plant used for flavoring

mark n. 1 spot, scratch, etc. 2 sign or label 3 sign of quality 4 grade 5 impression 6 target; goal —v. 1 put a mark on 2 show by a mark 3 characterize 4 listen to 5 rate —**mark'er** n.

mark'down' n. price decrease

marked a. 1 having a mark 2 noticeable

mar·ket n. 1 place where goods are sold 2 store selling food 3 buying and selling 4 demand for (goods, etc.) —v. buy or sell —**mar'ket·a·ble** a. —**mar'ket·er** n.

mar'ket·place' n. 1 an outdoor market 2 the world of business

mark'ing n. arrangement of marks, as on fur, etc.

marks'man n., pl. **-men** one who shoots well —**marks'man·ship'** n.

mark'up' n. price increase

mar·lin n. large, slender, deepsea fish

mar'ma·lade' n. preserve of oranges or other fruits

mar'mo·set' n. small monkey

mar'mot n. thick-bodied rodent, as the woodchuck

ma·roon' n., a. dark brownish red —v. put (a person) ashore in a lonely place

mar·quee' (-kē') n. rooflike projection over an entrance

mar'quis (-kwis) n. nobleman above an earl or count —**marquise'** (-kēz') n.fem.

mar'riage (-ij) n. 1 married life 2 wedding —**mar'riage·a·ble** a.

mar'row n. 1 soft core inside bones 2 central part

mar'ry v. **-ried, -ry·ing** 1 join as husband and wife 2 take as spouse 3 unite

marsh n. swamp —**marsh'y** a., **-i·er, -i·est**

mar'shal n. 1 highest ranking officer in some armies 2 Federal officer like a sheriff 3 head of a police or fire department —v. arrange (troops, ideas, etc.)

marsh'mal'low n. soft, white, spongy candy

mar·su'pi·al n. animal with a pouch for carrying its young

mart n. market

mar'ten n. 1 weasellike animal 2 its fur; sable

mar'tial (-shəl) a. 1 of war 2 military 3 warlike

martial art n. system of self-defense from Japan, etc.: usually used in pl.

martial law n. military rule over civilians

mar'tin n. kind of swallow

mar·ti·net' n. strict disciplinarian

mar·ti'ni n., pl. **-nis** cocktail

mar'tyr (-tər) n. one who suffers or dies for his beliefs —v. treat as a martyr —**mar'tyr·dom** n.

mar'vel n. wonderful thing —v. be amazed —**mar'vel·ous** a.

Marx'ism' n. doctrine of socialism —**Marx'ist** a., n.

mar'zi·pan' n. candy of ground almonds, egg white, etc.

mas·ca'ra (-kar'ə) n. cosmetic to color eyelashes

mas'cot n. animal or thing kept for good luck

mas'cu·line (-kyŏŏ lin) a. of or like men or boys; male —**mas'cu·lin'i·ty** n.

mash n. 1 grain crushed in water for brewing, etc. 2 moist feed mixture for horses, etc. —v. crush into a soft mass

mask n., v. cover to conceal or protect the face

mas'o·chist (-ə kist) n. one who

gets pleasure from being hurt — **mas'o·chism'** n. —**mas'o·chis'tic** a.

ma'son n. construction worker in brick, stone, etc.

ma'son·ry n. mason's work

masque (mask) n. 1 MASQUERADE (n. 1) 2 elaborate verse play —v. be equal (to) 2 put in opposition 2

mas·quer·ade' (-kər-) n. 1 party with masks and costumes 2 disguise —v. be disguised

mass n. 1 quantity of matter 2 large number 3 size 4 [M-] R.C.Ch. service of the Eucharist —v. gather into a mass —**the masses** the common people

mas'sa·cre (-kər) n. indiscriminate killing —v. kill in large numbers

mas·sage' (mə säzh') n. rubbing and kneading of part of the body —v. give a massage to

mas·seur' (mə sur') n. a man whose work is massaging — **mas·seuse'** (-sōoz') n.fem.

mas'sive a. big and heavy

mass production n. production in large quantities

mast n. tall, upright pole on a ship, supporting sails

mas·tec'to·my n., pl. -mies surgical removal of a breast

mas'ter n. 1 man who rules others or is in control 2 expert —a. 1 of a master 2 chief; main —v. 1 control 2 become expert in

mas'ter·ful a. 1 domineering 2 expert; skillful: also **mas'ter·ly**

mas'ter·mind' v., n. (be) an ingenious planner of (a project)

Master of Arts (or Science, etc.) n. advanced college degree

mas'ter·piece' n. thing made or done with expert skill

mas'ter·y n. 1 control 2 victory 3 expert skill

mast'head' n. part of a newspaper, etc. giving address, publisher, etc.

mas'ti·cate' v. chew up —**mas'ti·ca'tion** n.

mas'tiff n. big, strong dog

mas'to·don' n. extinct animal like the elephant

mas'toid a., n. (of) a bony projection behind the ear

mas'tur·bate' v. practice genital self-excitation —**mas'tur·ba'tion** n.

mat n. 1 flat piece, as of woven straw, for protecting a floor, etc. 2 thick tangled mass 3 border around a picture —v. **mat'ted**, **mat'ting**

matting 1 cover with a mat 2

weave or tangle together

mat'a·dor' n. bullfighter

match n. 1 short sliver with a tip that catches fire by friction 2 person or thing like another 3 contest 4 marriage —v. 1 be equal (to) 2 put in opposition 3 get an equivalent for

match'less a. without equal

match'mak'er n. arranger of marriages

mate n. 1 one of a pair 2 husband or wife 3 lower officer on a ship —v. join, as in marriage

ma·te'ri·al n. 1 what a thing is made of 2 fabric —a. 1 physical 2 essential

ma·te'ri·al·ism' n. 1 concern with physical things only 2 belief that everything has a physical cause —**ma·te'ri·al·is'tic** a.

ma·te'ri·al·ize' v. give or take material form

ma·te'ri·al·ly adv. 1 physically 2 considerably

ma·te'ri·el' n. military supplies

ma·ter'nal a. of, like, or from a mother

ma·ter'ni·ty n. motherhood —a. for pregnant women

math n. [Col.] mathematics

math'e·mat'ics n. science dealing with quantities and forms, their relationships, etc. —**math'e·mat'i·cal** a. —**math'e·ma·ti'cian** (-tish'ən) n.

mat·i·nee', **mat·i·née** (mat'n ā') n. afternoon performance of a play, etc.

mat'ins n.pl. morning prayer

ma'tri·arch' (-ärk') n. woman who rules her family or tribe — **ma'tri·ar'chal** a.

ma·tric'u·late' v. enroll, as in college —**ma·tric'u·la'tion** n.

mat'ri·mo'ny n. marriage —**mat'ri·mo'ni·al** a.

ma'trix' n., pl. -**tri·ces'** (-trə sēz') or -**trix·es** that within which a thing develops

ma'tron n. 1 wife or widow 2 woman manager of domestic affairs, as of a prison

mat'ter n. 1 physical substance of a thing 2 thing or affair 3 occasion 4 importance 5 trouble —v. be of importance —**as a matter of fact** really —**no matter** regardless of

mat'ter-of-fact' a. sticking to facts; literal

mat'ting n. woven straw, etc. used as for mats

mat'tock (-ək) n. kind of pickax

mat'tress n. casing filled with cotton, springs, etc., for use on a bed

ma·ture' (-toor', -choor') a. 1 fully grown, developed, etc. 2 due for payment —v. make or become mature —**ma·tu'ri·ty** n.

maud'lin a. foolishly sentimental

maul v. handle roughly

mau·so·le'um n. large, imposing tomb

mauve (mōv, môv, mäv) n. pale purple

mav'er·ick n. 1 lost, unbranded calf 2 political independent

maw n. 1 bird's crop 2 throat, gullet, jaws, etc.

mawk'ish a. sentimental in a sickening way

max·il'la n. upper jawbone

max'im n. concise saying that is a rule of conduct

max'i·mize' v. to increase to a maximum

max'i·mum n., a. greatest possible (quantity or degree)

May n. fifth month

may v. pt. **might** auxiliary verb showing: 1 possibility 2 permission

may'be adv. possibly

may'fly' n., pl. -**flies'** delicate winged insect

may'hem n. 1 crime of maiming a person intentionally 2 deliberate destruction or violence

may'o n. [Col.] mayonnaise

may·on·naise' (-nāz') n. creamy salad dressing

may'or n. head of a city —**may'or·al·ty** n.

maze n. confusing network of paths

me pron. objective case of I

mead n. alcoholic liquor made from honey

mead·ow (med'ō) n. level field of grass

mea'ger a. 1 poor; scanty 2 thin Br. sp. **mea'gre**

meal n. 1 any of the times for eating 2 food served then 3 coarsely ground grain, etc. — **meal'y** a.

meal'y-mouthed' a. not sincere

mean v. **meant** (ment), **mean'ing** 1 intend 2 intend to express 3 signify 4 have a certain importance —a. 1 low in quality or rank 2 poor or shabby 3 ignoble, petty, unkind, etc. 4 stingy 5 halfway between extremes —n. 1 middle point 2 pl. [sing. or pl. v.] that by which a thing is gotten or done 3 pl. wealth —

by all (or **no**) **means** certainly (not) —**by means of** by using —**mean'ly** adv. —**mean'ness** n.

me·an'der v. 1 wind back and forth 2 wander idly

mean'ing n. what is meant, indicated, etc. —**mean'ing·ful** a. —**mean'ing·less** a.

mean'time' adv., n. (during) the intervening time: also **mean' while'**

mea'sles (-zəlz) n. contagious disease, usually of children

mea'sly a. -**sli·er**, -**sli·est** [Col.] slight, worthless, etc.

meas·ure (mezh'-) v. 1 find out the extent, dimensions, etc. of 2 mark of a certain amount 3 be a thing for measuring 4 be of specified dimensions —n. 1 dimensions, capacity, etc. 2 unit of measuring 3 system of measuring 4 instrument for measuring 5 definite quantity 6 course of action 7 a law 8 notes and rests between two bars on a musical staff —**meas' ur·a·ble** a. —**meas'ure·less** a. —**meas'ure·ment** n.

meat n. 1 flesh of animals used as food 2 edible part 3 essence —**meat'y** a., -**i·er**, -**i·est**

me·chan'ic (-kan'-) n. worker who repairs machines

me·chan'i·cal a. 1 of or run by machinery 2 machinelike — **me·chan'i·cal·ly** adv.

me·chan'ics n. 1 science of motion and the effect of forces on bodies 2 knowledge of machinery 3 technical aspect

mech'a·nism' (mek'-) n. 1 working parts of a machine 2 system of interrelated parts

mech'a·nize' v. 1 to make mechanical 2 to equip with machinery, trucks, etc. — **mech'a·ni·za'tion** n.

med'al n. flat, inscribed piece of metal given as an honor or reward

me·dal'lion (-yən) n. 1 large medal 2 a round, medallike design

med'dle v. interfere in another's affairs —**med'dler** n. —**med' dle·some** a.

me'di·a n. alt. pl. of MEDIUM

me'di·an n., a. (number, point, etc.) in the middle

me'di·ate' v. (try to) settle (differences) between two parties — **me'di·a'tion** n. —**me'di·a'tor** n.

med'ic n. [Col.] 1 doctor 2 army medical corpsman

Med'ic·aid' [*also* m-] State and Federal program helping the poor pay medical bills

med'i·cal *a.* having to do with the practice or study of medicine —**med'i·cal·ly** *adv.*

Med'i·care' [*also* m-] Federal program helping the elderly pay medical bills

med'i·cate' *v.* treat with medicine —**med'i·ca'tion** *n.*

me·dic'i·nal (-dis'-) *a.* that is or is used as a medicine

med'i·cine (-san) *n.* **1** science of treating and preventing disease **2** drug, etc. used in treating disease

medicine man among North American Indians, etc., a man supposed to have healing powers

me·di·e'val (mē'dē-, med'ē-) *a.* of or like the Middle Ages

me'di·o'cre (-kər) *a.* ordinary; average —**me'di·oc'ri·ty** (äk'-) *n.*, *pl.* **-ties**

med'i·tate' *v.* **1** think deeply **2** plan —**med'i·ta'tion** *n.* —**med'i·ta'tive** *a.*

me'di·um *a.* intermediate in amount, degree, etc. —*n.*, *pl.* **-di·ums** *or* **-di·a 1** medium thing or state **2** thing through which a force acts **3** means, agency, etc. **4** surrounding substance

med'ley *n.* **1** mixture of unlike things **2** musical piece made up of several songs

meek *a.* **1** patient and mild **2** easily imposed on

meet *v.* **met, meet'ing 1** come upon **2** be present at the arrival of **3** be introduced (to) **4** come into contact (with) **5** come together **6** satisfy **7** pay —*n.* a meeting —*a.* suitable

meet'ing *n.* **1** a coming together **2** a gathering of people **3** junction

meg'a·byte' *n.* million bytes

meg'a·hertz' *n.*, *pl.* **-hertz'** million hertz

meg'a·lo·ma'ni·a *n.* delusion of grandeur or power

meg'a·phone' *n.* funnel-shaped device to increase the volume of the voice

meg'a·ton' *n.* explosive force of a millions tons of TNT

mel'an·chol'y (-käl'ē) *n.* sadness and mental depression —*a.* sad or saddening

mé·lange (mā lônzh') *n.* mixture or medley

mel'a·nin *n.* dark pigment of skin, etc.

mel'a·no'ma *n.*, *pl.* **-mas** *or* **-ma·ta** skin tumor

meld *v.* to blend; merge

me·lee, mê·lée (mā'lā') *n.* brawling group fight

mel'io·rate' (mēl'yə-) *v.* make or become better

mel·lif'lu·ous *a.* smooth and sweet, as sounds: also **mel·lif'lu·ent** —**mel·lif'lu·ence** *n.*

mel'low *a.* full, rich, gentle, etc.; not harsh —*v.* make or become mellow

me·lo'di·ous *a.* **1** having melody **2** pleasing to hear

mel'o·dra'ma *n.* sensational, extravagant drama —**mel'o·dra·mat'ic** *a.*

mel'o·dy *n.*, *pl.* **-dies** a tune, song, etc. —**me·lod'ic** *a.*

mel'on *n.* large, juicy, many-seeded fruit

melt *v.* **1** change from solid to liquid, as by heat **2** dissolve **3** disappear or merge gradually **4** soften

melt'down' *n.* dangerous melting of fuel in a nuclear reactor

melting pot *n.* place in which various immigrants are assimilated

mem'ber *n.* **1** distinct part, as an arm **2** person in an organization

mem'ber·ship' *n.* **1** state of being a member **2** all the members

mem'brane' *n.* thin tissue lining an organ or part —**mem'bra·nous** *a.*

me·men'to *n.*, *pl.* **-tos** *or* **-toes** souvenir

mem'o *n.*, *pl.* **-os** memorandum

mem'oirs' (-wärz') *n.pl.* account of one's past life

mem'o·ra·ble *a.* worth remembering

mem'o·ran'dum *n.*, *pl.* **-dums** *or* **-da** short note to remind one of something

me·mo'ri·al *n.* anything meant to help people remember a person or event

mem'o·rize' *v.* to commit to memory

mem'o·ry *n.*, *pl.* **-ries 1** power or act of remembering **2** something or everything remembered **3** commemoration **4** device in a computer, etc. that stores information

men *n.* pl. of MAN

men'ace *n.* a threat —*v.* to

threaten

me·nag'er·ie (-naj'-, -nazh'-) *n.* collection of wild animals

mend *v.* 1 repair 2 make or become better —*n.* mended place —**on the mend** improving —**mend'er** *n.*

men·da'cious *a.* lying —**men·dac'i·ty** *n.*

men'di·cant *n.* beggar

me'ni·al *a.* servile —*n.* servant

men·in·gi'tis (-jīt'is) *n.* inflammation of membranes of the brain and spinal cord

me·nis'cus *n.* curved upper surface of a column of liquid

men'o·pause *n.* permanent cessation of menstruation

me·no'rah *n.* Jewish candelabrum

men'ses' (-sēz') *n.pl.* monthly menstrual flow

men'stru·ate' *v.* have a flow of blood monthly from the uterus —**men'stru·al** *a.* —**men'stru·a'tion** *n.*

men·su·ra'tion (-shə-) *n.* a measuring

-ment *suf.* 1 result of 2 a means for 3 act of 4 state of being

men'tal *a.* 1 of or in the mind 2 for the mentally ill —**men'tal·ly** *adv.*

men·tal'i·ty *n.* mental power, attitude, outlook, etc.

men'thol' (-thôl') *n.* derivative of oil of peppermint —**men'tho·lat'ed** *a.*

men'tion *n.* brief reference —*v.* refer to briefly

men'tor *n.* wise advisor

men'u *n., pl.* **-us** list of choices of meals, computer functions, etc.

me·ow', me·ou' *v., n.* (make) the sound of a cat

mer'can·tile' (-til', -tēl') *a.* of merchants or trade

mer'ce·nar'y *a.* thinking mainly of money —*n., pl.* **-ies** soldier paid to serve in a foreign army

mer'cer·ized' *a.* treated, as cotton, to strengthen it

mer'chan·dise' (-dīz'; *also* -dīs') *v.* buy and sell —*n.* things bought and sold

mer'chant *n.* 1 dealer in goods 2 storekeeper

merchant marine *n.* ships of a nation used in trade

mer·ci (mer sē') *int.* [Fr.] thank you

mer·cu'ri·al (-kyoor'ē-) *a.* changeable, fickle, etc.

mer'cu·ry *n.* silvery liquid metal,

a chemical element

mer'cy *n., pl.* **-cies** 1 kindness; forbearance 2 power to forgive —**at the mercy of** in the power of —**mer'ci·ful** *a.* —**mer'ci·less** *a.*

mere *a.* **mer'est** no more than; only

mere'ly *adv.* only; simply

mer'e·tri'cious (-trish'əs) *a.* flashy; tawdry

mer·gan'ser *n.* large duck

merge *v.* unite or combine so as to lose identity

merg'er *n.* a merging, or thing formed by merging

me·rid'i·an *n.* 1 highest point 2 circle through the earth's poles

me·ringue' (-rang') *n.* egg whites and sugar beaten stiff

mer'it *n.* 1 worth; value 2 something deserving praise —*v.* deserve

mer'i·to'ri·ous *a.* deserving reward, praise, etc.

mer'maid' *n.* imaginary creature like a woman with a fish's tail

mer'ry *a.* **-ri·er, -ri·est** full of fun —**make merry** have fun —**mer'ri·ly** *adv.* —**mer'ri·ment** *n.* —**mer'ry·mak'ing** *n.*

mer'ry-go-round' *n.* revolving platform with seats, as in amusement parks

me'sa (mā'-) *n.* high plateau with steep sides

mesh *n.* (cord or wire of) a net or network —*v.* 1 to entangle 2 interlock

mes'mer·ize' (mez'-) *v.* hypnotize —**mes'mer·ism'** *n.* —**mes'**

mes·quite', mes·quit' (-kēt') *n.* spiny shrub

mess *n.* 1 a jumble 2 trouble 3 untidy condition 4 communal meal as in the army —*v.* 1 make dirty, jumbled, etc. 2 meddle —**mess'i·ness** *n.* —**mess'y** *a.*, **-i·er, -i·est**

mes'sage *n.* 1 a communication 2 important idea

mes'sen·ger *n.* one who carries a message, etc.

Mes·si'ah (-sī'-) 1 *Judaism* expected deliverer of the Jews 2 *Christianity* Jesus —*n.* [m-] expected savior or liberator —**Mes'si·an'ic** *a.*

mes·ti'zo (-tē'-) *n., pl.* **-zos** *or* **-zoes** one of American Indian and Spanish parentage

met *v.* pt. & pp. of MEET

me·tab'o·lism' *n.* changing of food by organisms into energy, cells, etc. —**met'a·bol'ic** *a.*

met'al *n.* **1** shiny, usually solid, chemical element **2** an alloy —*a.* of metal —**me·tal'lic** *adv.*

met'al·lur'gy *n.* science of refining metals —**met'al·lur'gi·cal** *a.* —**met'al·lur'gist** *n.*

met'a·mor'pho·sis *n., pl.* **-ses'** (-sēz') **1** change in form **2** any change

met'a·phor' *n.* word for one thing used for another —**met'a·phor'ic, met'a·phor'i·cal** *a.*

met'a·phys'ics *n.* [*sing. v.*] philosophy that deals with first principles —**met'a·phys'i·cal** *a.*

me·tas'ta·sis *n., pl.* **-ses'** (-sēz') spread of cancer cells through the bloodstream —**me·tas'ta·size'** *v.*

met'a·tar'sal *a.* of the part of the foot between the ankle and toes

mete (mēt) *v.* allot

me'te·or *n.* fiery meteoroid traveling through the earth's atmosphere —**me'te·or'ic** *a.*

me'te·or·ite' *n.* part of a meteor fallen to earth

me'te·or·oid' *n.* small, solid body traveling through outer space at high speed

me'te·or·ol'o·gy *n.* science of weather, climate, etc. —**me'te·or·o·log'i·cal** *a.* —**me'te·or·ol'o·gist** *n.*

me'ter *n.* **1** rhythmic pattern in verse **2** metric unit of length (39.37 in.) **3** device to measure flow of fluid —**met'ric** *a.* —**met'ri·cal** *a.*

meth'a·done' (-dōn') *n.* synthetic narcotic used in medicine

meth'ane' *n.* colorless, odorless, inflammable gas

meth'a·nol' (-nôl') *n.* toxic liquid used as fuel, antifreeze, etc.

meth'od *n.* **1** way; process **2** system

me·thod'i·cal *a.* orderly

meth'od·ol'o·gy *n., pl.* **-gies** system of methods

me·tic'u·lous *a.* very careful about details; fussy

mé·tier (mā tyā') *n.* one's trade, etc.

me'tre *n.* Br. sp. of METER

metric system *n.* decimal system of weights and measures

met'ro·nome' *n.* device that beats time at a set rate

me·trop'o·lis *n.* main or important city —**met'ro·pol'i·tan** *a.*

met'tle *n.* spirit; courage —on one's mettle ready to do one's best

mew *v., n.* meow

Mex'i·can *n., adv.* (native) of Mexico

mez'za·nine' (-nēn') *n.* **1** low story built between two main stories **2** first few rows of balcony seats

mez'zo-so·pra'no (met'sō-) *n.* voice or singer between soprano and contralto

mi·as'ma (mī az'-) *n.* vapor from swamps, once believed poisonous

mi'ca (mī'-) *n.* mineral that forms into thin, heat-resistant layers

mice *n. pl. of* MOUSE

micro- *pref.* small

mi'crobe' *n.* minute organism, esp. one causing disease

mi'cro·chip' *n.* electronic circuit on a tiny piece of semiconductor material

mi'cro·com·put'er *n.* small computer for home use, etc.

mi'cro·cosm' *n.* universe on a small scale

mi'cro·film' *n.* film on which documents, etc. are recorded in a reduced size

mi·crom'e·ter *n.* instrument for measuring very small distances, angles, etc.

mi'cron' *n.* one millionth of a meter

mi'cro·or'gan·ism' *n.* microscopic organism

mi'cro·phone' *n.* instrument for changing sound waves into electric impulses

mi'cro·scope' *n.* device for magnifying minute objects

mi'cro·scop'ic *a.* so small as to be invisible except through a microscope

mi'cro·wave' *n.* radio or infrared wave used in radar, cooking, etc. —*v., a.* (to cook) using microwaves

mid, 'mid *prep.* [Poet.] amid

mid- *pref.* middle of

mid'air' *n.* point not in contact with any surface

mid'day' *n., a.* noon

mid'dle *a.* halfway between two points, etc. —*n.* middle point or part

mid'dle-aged' *a.* in the time between youth and old age

Middle Ages a period in Europe, A.D. 476 – c. 1450

mid'dle·man' *n., pl.* **-men'** **1** one who buys from a producer and sells at wholesale or retail **2** go-between

middle school *n.* school with, usually, grades five through eight

mid′dling *a.* of middle size, quality, etc.

mid′dy *n., pl.* **-dies** loose blouse with a sailor collar

midge *n.* small gnat

midg′et *n.* very small person — *adv.* miniature

mid′land *a., n.* (of) the middle region of a country

mid′night *n.* twelve o'clock at night

mid′riff *n.* part of body between abdomen and chest

mid′ship′man *n., pl.* **-men** naval officer trainee

midst *n.* the middle —*prep.* [Poet.] in the midst of

mid′sum′mer *n.* period about June 21

mid′way′ *a., adv.* in the middle; halfway —*n.* location for side shows, etc. at a fair

mid′wife′ *n., pl.* **-wives′** woman who helps others in childbirth —**mid′wife′ry** *n.*

mien (mēn) *n.* one's manner

miff *v.* [Col.] offend

might *v. pt. of* MAY: might is also used to show less possibility or permission than *may* —*n.* strength; force

might′y *a.* **-i-er, -i-est** powerful, great, etc. —*adv.* [Col.] very —**might′i-ly** *adv.*

mi′graine′ *n.* periodic headache

mi′grate′ *v.* move from one place or region to another, as with the change in season —**mi′grant** *a., n.* —**mi·gra′tion** *n.* —**mi′gra-to′ry** *a.*

mi·ka·do (mi kä′-) *n., pl.* **-dos** emperor of Japan

mike *n.* [Col.] microphone

mil *n.* .001 of an inch

mild *a.* **1** gentle **2** weak in taste —**mild′ly** *adv.*

mil′dew′ *n.* whitish fungus on plants, damp cloth, etc.

mile *n.* unit of measure, 5,280 ft.

mile′age *n.* **1** total miles traveled **2** allowance per mile for traveling expenses

mile′stone′ *n.* significant event

mi·lieu (mēl yoo′) *n.* surroundings; environment

mil′i·tant *a.* ready to fight —**mil′i·tan·cy** *n.*

mil′i·ta·rism′ *n.* **1** warlike spirit **2** maintenance of strong armed forces —**mil′i·ta·rist** *n.* —**mil′i·ta·ris′tic** *a.*

mil′i·tar′y *a.* of soldiers, war, etc. —*n.* the army

mil′i·tate′ *v.* work (*for* or *against*)

mi·li′tia (-lish′ə) *n.* citizens trained for emergency military service

milk *n.* **1** white liquid secreted by female mammals for suckling their young **2** any liquid like this —*v.* draw milk from (a mammal) —**milk′y** *a.*, **-i-er, -i-est** —**milk′i·ness** *n.*

milk′man′ *n., pl.* **-men′** man who sells or delivers milk

milk′shake′ *n.* frothy drink of milk, flavoring, and ice cream

milk′weed′ *n.* plant with a milky juice

mill *n.* **1** place for grinding grain into flour **2** machine for grinding **3** factory **4** $\frac{1}{10}$ of a cent —*v.* **1** grind by or in a mill **2** move (*around* or *about*) confusedly, as a crowd —**mill′er** *n.*

mill′age *n.* taxation in mills per dollar of valuation

mil·len′ni·um *n., pl.* **-ni·ums** or **-ni·a 1** *Theol.* 1,000-year period of Christ's future reign on earth **2** period of peace and joy

mil′let *n.* cereal grass

milli- *pref.* $\frac{1}{1000}$ part of

mil′li·gram′ *n.* one thousandth of a gram

mil′li·li′ter *n.* one thousandth of a liter

mil′li·me′ter *n.* one thousandth of a meter

mil′li·ner *n.* one who makes or sells women's hats

mil′li·ner′y *n.* **1** women's hats **2** business of a milliner

mil′lion *n., a.* a thousand thousands —**mil′lionth** *a., n.*

mil′lion·aire′ *n.* one having at least a million dollars

mill′stone′ *n.* **1** flat, round stone used for grinding grain, etc. **2** heavy burden

mill′wright′ *n.* worker who installs or repairs heavy machinery

mime *n., v.* clown or mimic

mim′e·o·graph′ *n.* machine for making stenciled copies of typewritten matter —*v.* make (such copies) of

mim′ic *v.* **-icked, -ick·ing 1** imitate, as to ridicule **2** to copy closely —*n.* one who mimics —**mim′ic·ry** *n.*

mi·mo′sa *n.* flowering tree or shrub of warm climates

min′a·ret′ *n.* mosque tower

mince *v.* **1** cut into small pieces **2** lessen the force of (words) **3**

act with affected daintiness —
minc'ing a.

mince'meat' n. pie filling of raisins, spices, suet, etc.

mind n. 1 center of thought, feeling, etc. 2 intellect 3 sanity 4 memory 5 opinion, intention, etc. —v. 1 observe 2 obey 3 take care of 4 be careful about 5 object to —**bear (or keep) in mind** remember —**have in mind** intend —**make up one's mind** reach a decision —**put in mind** remind

mind'ful a. aware (of)

mine pron. that or those belonging to me —n. 1 large excavation from which to extract ores, coal, etc. 2 great source of supply 3 explosive device hidden under land or water —v. 1 dig (ores, etc.) from a mine 2 hide mines in —**min'er** n.

min'er·al n. ore, rock, etc. found naturally in the earth —a. of or containing minerals

min'er·al'o·gy n. science of minerals —**min'er·al'o·gist** n.

mi·ne·stro·ne (min'ə strō'nē) n. thick vegetable soup

min'gle v. 1 mix or become 2 join with others

mini- pref. miniature; very small; very short

min'i·a·ture n. tiny copy, model, painting, etc. —a. miniature

min'i·a·tur·ize' v. make in a small, compact form

min'i·bike' n. small motorcycle

min'i·cam' n. portable TV camera

min'i·com·put'er n. computer between a mainframe and a microcomputer in power, etc.

min'i·mize' v. reduce to or estimate at a minimum

min'i·mum n. 1 smallest quantity possible 2 lowest degree reached —a. lowest or least possible —**min'i·mal** a.

min'ing n. work of removing ores, etc. from a mine

min'ion (-yən) n. faithful or servile follower

min'is·cule' a. minuscule: a misspelling

min'is·ter n. 1 head of a governmental department 2 diplomatic official below an ambassador 3 one who conducts religious services —v. give help; serve —**min'is·tra'tion** n. —**min'is·te'ri·al** (-tir'ē-) a.

min'is·try n., pl. -tries 1 office of a clergyman 2 clergy 3 government department headed by a minister 4 a ministering

mink n. 1 weasellike mammal 2 its valuable fur

min'now (-ō) n. very small fresh-water fish

mi'nor a. 1 lesser in size, rank, etc. 2 Mus. semitone lower than the major —n. 1 one under full legal age 2 secondary field of study

mi·nor'i·ty n., pl. -ties 1 smaller part or number 2 racial, religious, etc. group that differs from the larger groups 3 time of being a minor

min'strel n. 1 traveling singer of the Middle Ages 2 entertainer in an old-style U.S. variety show

mint n. 1 place where the government make coins 2 large amount 3 aromatic plant with leaves used for flavoring —v. coin (money)

min'u·end' n. number from which another is to be subtracted

min'u·et' n. slow, stately dance of 18th c.

mi'nus prep. less —a. 1 negative 2 less than —n. sign (-) showing subtraction or negative quantity

mi·nus·cule (min'ə skyōōl') a. tiny; minute

min·ute (min'it) n. 1 sixtieth part of an hour 2 moment 3 pl. official record

mi·nute (mī nōōt', -nyōōt') a. 1 very small 2 exact —**mi·nute'ly** adv.

mi·nu·ti·ae (mi nōō'shə, -nyōō'-) n.pl. trifling details

mir'a·cle n. 1 event that seems to contradict scientific laws 2 remarkable thing —**mi·rac'u·lous** a.

mi·rage (mi räzh') n. optical illusion caused by reflection of light

mire n. deep mud or slush —v. stick or cause to get stuck as in mire

mir'ror n. coated glass that reflects images

mirth n. gaiety with laughter —**mirth'ful** a.

mis- pref. wrong(ly); bad(ly)

mis'ad·ven'ture n. bad luck

mis'an·thrope' n. one who hates all people: also **mis·an'thro·pist** —**mis·an·throp'ic** a. —**mis·an'thro·py** n.

mis'ap·pre·hend' v. understand wrongly —**mis'ap·pre·hen'sion** n.

mis·ap·pro'pri·ate' v. use (funds, etc.) dishonestly —**mis·ap·pro'pri·a'tion** n.

mis·be·got'ten a. illegitimate

mis·be·have' v. behave badly —**mis·be·hav'ior** n.

mis·cal'cu·late' v. misjudge —**mis·cal·cu·la'tion** n.

mis·car'ry v. 1 go wrong 2 lose a fetus before full term —**mis·car'riage** (or **mis'kar'ij**) n.

mis·cast' v. cast (an actor) in an unsuitable role

mis·ce·ge·na'tion (mis'i jə-) n. interracial marriage

mis·cel·la'ne·ous a. of various kinds; mixed

mis·cel·la'ny n., pl. **-nies** collection of various kinds

mis·chance' n. bad luck

mis'chief (-chif) n. 1 harm or damage 2 prank 3 teasing —**mis'chie·vous** (-chə-) a.

mis'ci·ble (mis'ə-) a. that can be mixed

mis·con·ceive' v. misunderstand —**mis·con·cep'tion** n.

mis·con'duct n. wrong conduct

mis·con·strue' v. misinterpret

mis'cre·ant n. villain

mis·deed' n. crime, sin, etc.

mis·de·mean'or n. Law minor offense

mi'ser (-zər) n. stingy hoarder of money —**mi'ser·ly** a.

mis'er·a·ble (miz'-) a. 1 in misery 2 causing misery 3 bad, poor, etc. —**mis'er·a·bly** adv.

mis'er·y n., pl. **-ies** pain, poverty, distress, etc.

mis·fire' v. fail to go off

mis·fit' v. fit improperly —n. 1 improper fit 2 maladjusted person

mis·for'tune n. 1 trouble 2 mishap, calamity, etc.

mis·giv'ings n.pl. feelings of fear, doubt, etc.

mis·guide' v. mislead

mis·han'dle v. abuse

mis'hap n. misfortune

mish'mash' n. a jumble

mis·in·form' v. give wrong information to

mis·in·ter'pret v. to interpret wrongly —**mis·in·ter·pre·ta'tion** n.

mis·judge' v. judge wrongly

mis·lay' v. **-laid'**, **-lay'ing** put in a place later forgotten

mis·lead' v. 1 lead astray 2 deceive

mis·man'age v. manage badly

mis·no'mer n. name wrongly applied

mi·sog'y·nist (-säj'ə-) n. one who hates women —**mi·sog'y·ny** n.

mis·place' v. put in a wrong place

mis·print' n. printing error

mis·pri'sion (-prizh'ən) n. misconduct by a public official

mis·pro·nounce' v. pronounce wrongly

mis·quote' v. quote incorrectly

mis·read' (-rēd') v. **-read'** (-red'), **-read'ing** read wrongly and so misunderstand

mis·rep·re·sent' v. give a false idea of

mis·rule' (or mis rōōl') n. bad government

miss v. 1 fail to hit, meet, do, see, hear, etc. 2 avoid 3 note or feel the loss of —n. 1 failure to hit, etc. 2 unmarried woman 3 [M—] title used before her name

mis'sal (-əl) n. R.C.Ch. prayer book for Mass for the year

mis·shap'en (-shāp'-) a. badly shaped; deformed

mis'sile (-əl) n. object to be thrown or shot

miss'ing a. absent; lost

mis'sion n. 1 special task or duty 2 group or station of missionaries 3 diplomatic delegation

mis'sion·ar'y n., pl. **-ies** person sent by a church to make converts, esp. abroad

mis'sive n. letter or note

mis·spell' v. spell incorrectly

mis·state' v. state wrongly —**mis·state'ment** n.

mis'step' n. 1 wrong step 2 mistake in conduct

mist n. mass of water vapor; thin fog —**mist'y** a., **-i·er**, **-i·est**

mis·take' v. **-took'**, **-tak'en**, **-tak'ing** understand or perceive wrongly —n. error

mis·tak'en a. wrong or incorrect

mis'ter n. title before a man's name: usually Mr.

mis'tle·toe' (mis'əl-) n. evergreen plant with white berries

mis·treat' v. treat badly —**mis·treat'ment** n.

mis'tress n. 1 woman in charge or control 2 woman who has sexual intercourse with and is supported by a man without marriage

mis·tri'al n. Law trial made void by an error, etc.

mis·trust' n. lack of trust —v. have no trust in; doubt

mis'un·der·stand' v. **-stood'**, **-stand'ing** understand incorrectly

mis·un·der·stand·ing *n.* **1** failure to understand **2** a quarrel

mis·use' (-yōoz'; *n.:* -yōos') *v.* **1** use improperly **2** abuse —*n.* incorrect use

mite *n.* **1** tiny, parasitic arachnid **2** tiny amount

mi'ter *n.* **1** tall cap of a bishop **2** corner joint of two pieces cut at an angle

mit'i·gate' *v.* make or become less severe —**mit'i·ga'tion** *n.*

mi·to'sis *n.* process of cell division

mitt *n.* **1** padded baseball glove **2** [Sl.] hand

mit'ten *n.* glove without separate finger pouches

mix *v.* **mixed** or **mixt, mix'ing 1** stir or come together in a single mass **2** make by mixing ingredients **3** combine —*n.* mixture, or its ingredients —**mix up 1** confuse **2** involve (*in*)

mixed *a.* **1** blended **2** of different kinds **3** of both sexes

mix'ture *n.* **1** a mixing **2** thing mixed

mix'-up' *n.* confusion

mne·mon'ic (nē-) *a.* of or helping the memory

moan *n.* low, mournful sound —*v.* **1** utter (with) a moan **2** complain

moat *n.* deep, usually water-filled ditch around a castle

mob *n.* crowd, esp. a disorderly one —*v.* **mobbed, mob'bing** crowd around and attack

mo'bile (-bəl, -bil'; *n.:* -bēl') *a.* **1** readily movable or adaptable **2** easy in changing social status —*n.* abstract sculpture suspended to move in the air —**mo·bil'i·ty** *n.*

mo'bi·lize' *v.* make or become ready, as for war —**mo'bi·li·za'tion** *n.*

moc'ca·sin *n.* heelless slipper of soft leather

mo'cha (-ka) *n.* kind of coffee

mock *v.* **1** ridicule **2** mimic and deride —*a.* false

mock'er·y *n., pl.* **-ies 1** a mocking **2** poor imitation

mock'ing·bird' *n.* small bird with imitative call

mock'-up' *n.* full-scale model

mode *n.* **1** way of acting or doing **2** fashion

mod'el *n.* **1** small copy of something **2** one to be imitated **3** style **4** one who poses for an artist **5** one who displays clothes by wearing them —*a.* serving as a model —*v.* **1** plan or form **2** work as a model

mo'dem *n.* device converting computer data for transmission, as by telephone

mod'er·ate (-ət; *v.:* -āt') *a.* avoiding extremes; moderate person —*v.* **1** to make or become moderate **2** preside over (a debate, etc.) —**mod'er·ate·ly** *adv.* —**mod'er·a'tion** *n.* —**mod'er·a'tor** *n.*

mod'ern *a.* of recent times; up-to-date —*n.* modern person —**mod'ern·is'tic** *a.* —**mod'ern·ize'** *v.*

mod'est *a.* **1** not conceited **2** decent **3** moderate —**mod'es·ty** *n.*

mod'i·cum *n.* small amount

mod'i·fy' *v.* **-fied', -fy'ing** change or limit slightly —**mod'i·fi·ca'tion** *n.* —**mod'i·fi'er** *n.*

mod'ish (mōd'-) *a.* fashionable

mod'u·late' (mäj'ə-) *v.* adjust or vary, as the pitch of the voice —**mod'u·la'tion** *n.*

mod·ule (mäj'ōol) *n.* detachable section with a special function —**mod'u·lar** *a.*

mo'gul *n.* important person

mo'hair' *n.* goat-hair fabric

Mo·ham'med·an *a., n.* Muslim —**Mo·ham'med·an·ism'** *n.*

moist *a.* slightly wet

mois'ten (-ən) *v.* make moist

mois'ture *n.* slight wetness

mo'lar *n.* back tooth

mo·las'ses *n.* dark syrup left after sugar is refined

mold *n.* **1** hollow form in which a thing is shaped **2** thing shaped **3** furry, fungous growth —*v.* **1** make in a mold **2** shape **3** become moldy

mold'er *v.* crumble

mold'ing *n.* decorative strip of wood, etc.

mold'y *a.* **-i·er, -i·est** of or covered with MOLD (*n.* 3)

mole *n.* **1** small, dark, congenital spot on the skin **2** small, burrowing animal

mol'e·cule' *n.* smallest particle of a substance that can exist alone —**mo·lec'u·lar** *a.*

mole'hill' *n.* small ridge made by a burrowing mole

mole'skin' *n.* strong cotton fabric with soft nap

mo·lest' *v.* to trouble or harm —**mo'les·ta'tion** *n.*

mol'li·fy' *v.* **-fied', -fy'ing** soothe; make calm

mol'lusk, mol'lusc n. invertebrate with soft body in a shell

mol'ly·cod'dle v. pamper

molt v. shed hair, skin, etc. before getting a new growth

mol'ten (-'n) a. melted by heat

mom n. [Col.] mother

mo'ment n. brief period of, or certain point in, time

mo'men·tar'i·ly adv. 1 for a short time 2 at any moment

mo'men·tar'y a. lasting for only a moment

mo·men'tous a. very important

mo·men'tum n. impetus of a moving object

mom'my n., pl. -mies etc.: child's word

mon'arch (-ərk, -ärk') n. hereditary ruler —**mo·nar'chi·cal** (-när'ki-) a.

mon'ar·chy n., pl. -ies government by a monarch —**mon'ar·chist** n.

mon'as·ter'y n., pl. -ies residence for monks

mo·nas'tic a. of or like monks or nuns — n. monk —**mo·nas'ti·cism'** n.

mon·au'ral (-ôr'əl) a. of sound reproduction using one channel

Mon'day n. second day of the week

mon'e·tar'y a. 1 of currency 2 of money

mon'ey n., pl. -eys or -ies 1 metal coins or paper notes used as the legal medium of exchange 2 wealth —**make money** to become wealthy

mon'eyed (-ēd) a. rich

Mon'gol·oid' n., a. (member) of the large human group including most of the Asian people

mon'goose n., pl. -goos'es ferretlike animal of India

mon'grel n., a. (animal or plant) of mixed breed

mon'i·tor n. 1 student who helps keep order, etc. 2 TV receiver or computer video screen —v. watch, or check on

monk n. man who is a member of an ascetic religious order

mon'key n., pl. -keys small, long-tailed primate —v. [Col.] meddle; trifle

monkey wrench n. wrench with an adjustable jaw

mon'o n. mononucleosis

mono- pref. one; alone

mon'o·cle n. eyeglass for one eye

mo·nog'a·my n. practice of being married to only one person at a time —**mo·nog'a·mous**

a.

mon'o·gram' n. initials of a name, made into a design

mon'o·graph' n. book or article on a single subject

mon'o·lith' n. pillar, statue, etc. made of a single, large stone —**mon'o·lith'ic** a.

mon'o·logue', mon'o·log' n. 1 long speech 2 skit for one actor only

mon'o·ma'ni·a n. excessive interest in one thing —**mon'o·ma'ni·ac'** n.

mon'o·nu'cle·o'sis n. acute viral disease with fever, tiredness, etc.

mo·nop'o·ly n., pl. -lies 1 total control of something, esp. of a product or service 2 company having this —**mo·nop'o·lis'tic** a. —**mo·nop'o·lize'** v.

mon'o·rail' n. railway with cars on a single rail

mon'o·syl'la·ble n. word of one syllable —**mon'o·syl·lab'ic** a.

mon'o·the·ism' n. belief that there is only one God —**mon'o·the·is'tic** a.

mon'o·tone' n. sameness of tone, pitch, color, etc.

mo·not'o·ny n. 1 lack of variety 2 tiresome sameness —**mo·not'o·nous** a.

mon·ox'ide n. oxide with one oxygen atom per molecule

mon·sieur (mə syur') n., pl. **mes·sieurs** (mes'ərz, mā syur') gentleman: Fr. for Mr.

Mon·si'gnor (-sēn'yər) n. R.C.Ch. title of high rank

mon·soon' n. wind bringing rainy season to S Asia

mon'ster n. huge or very abnormal plant or animal

mon'strous a. 1 horrible 2 huge 3 very abnormal —**mon·stros'i·ty** n., pl. -ties

mon·tage' (-täzh') n. superimposing of images, as in a movie

month n. any of the 12 divisions of the year

month'ly a. happening, appearing, etc. every month —n., pl. -lies monthly periodical —adv. every month

mon'u·ment n. 1 memorial statue, building, etc. 2 famous work —**mon'u·men'tal** a.

moo v., n. (make) the vocal sound of a cow

mooch [Sl.] v. get by begging, etc. —**mooch'er** n.

mood n. 1 state of mind 2 verb form to express a fact, wish, or order

mood'y *adv.* **-i·er, -i·est** 1 changing in mood 2 gloomy

moon *n.* body that revolves around a planet, spec. around the earth —*v.* look dreamy or listless —**moon'beam'** *n.* — **moon'light'** *a.*

moon'lit *a.* lighted by the moon

moon'shine' *n.* 1 moonlight 2 [Col.] whiskey made illegally — **moon'shin'er** *n.*

moon'stone' *n.* milky-white gem

Moor *n.* Muslim of NW Africa —**Moor'ish** *a.*

moor *n.* open wasteland —*v.* to secure by cables, ropes, etc.

moor'ings *n.pl.* cables, or place, for mooring a ship

moose *n., pl.* **moose** largest animal of the deer family

moot *a.* debatable

mop *n.* rags, sponge, etc. on a stick, as for washing floors —*v.* **mopped, mop'ping** clean up, as with a mop

mope *v.* be gloomy

mo'ped' *n.* bicycle with a small motor

mop'pet *n.* [Col.] little child

mo·raine' *n.* heap of rocks, etc. left by a glacier

mor'al *a.* 1 of or dealing with right and wrong 2 good; virtuous 3 giving sympathy, but no active help —*n.* 1 moral lesson 2 *pl.* moral rules or standards — **mor'al·ly** *adv.*

mo·rale' (-ral') *n.* degree of courage, discipline, etc.

mo·ral'i·ty *n.* 1 moral quality 2 virtue

mor'al·ize' *v.* discuss moral questions —**mor'al·ist** *n.*

mo·rass' *n.* bog; swamp

mor'a·to'ri·um *n.* authorized delay or stopping of some activity

mo'ray (**eel**) *n.* voracious eel

mor'bid *a.* 1 diseased 2 gloomy or unwholesome —**mor·bid'i·ty** *n.*

mor'dant *a.* sarcastic

more *a.,* **1** greater (in) amount or degree 2 (something) additional —*adv.* 1 to a greater degree 2 in addition — **more or less** somewhat

more·o'ver *adv.* besides

mo·res (môr'ēz', -āz') *n.pl.* customs with the force of law

morgue (môrg) *n.* place where bodies of accident victims, etc. are taken, as for autopsy

mor'i·bund' *a.* dying

morn *n.* [Poet.] morning

morn'ing *n.* first part of the day, till noon

morning glory *n.* vine with trumpet-shaped flowers

morning sickness *n.* nausea during pregnancy

mo·roc'co *n.* fine, soft leather made of goatskin

mo'ron' *n.* person who is mentally somewhat deficient —**mo·ron'ic** *a.*

mo·rose' (-rōs') *a.* gloomy

mor'phine' (-fēn') *n.* opium drug used to relieve pain

mor'row *n.* [Poet.] 1 morning 2 the following day

Morse code *n.* code of dots and dashes used in telegraphy

mor'sel *n.* bit, as of food

mor'tal *a.* 1 that must die 2 causing death 3 very great; extreme —*n.* human being — **mor'tal·ly** *adv.*

mor·tal'i·ty *n.* 1 a being mortal 2 death rate

mor'tar *n.* 1 bowl for pulverizing things with a pestle 2 small cannon 3 cement mixture used between bricks, etc.

mort'gage (môr'gij) *n.* deed pledging property as security for a debt —*v.* pledge (property) by a mortgage

mor·ti'cian (-tish'ən) *n.* undertaker

mor'ti·fy' *v.* **-fied', -fy'ing** 1 shame; humiliate 2 control (desires) by fasting, etc. —**mor'ti·fi·ca'tion** *n.*

mor'tise (môr'tis) *n.* hole cut for a tenon to fit in

mor'tu·ar'y (-choo-) *n., pl.* **-ies** place to keep dead bodies before burial

mo·sa'ic (-zā'-) *n.* design made of colored stones inlaid in mortar

mo'sey (-zē) *v.* [Sl.] amble along

Mos'lem (mäz'-) *a., n.* Muslim

mosque (mäsk) *n.* Muslim place of worship

mos·qui·to (mə skēt'ō) *n., pl.* **-toes** or **-tos** small biting insect that sucks blood

moss *n.* tiny green plant growing in clusters on rocks, etc. — **moss'y** *a.*

most *a.* 1 greatest in amount or number 2 almost all —*n.* the greatest amount or number — *adv.* to the greatest degree — **make the most of** take full advantage of

most'ly *adv.* 1 mainly; chiefly 2

usually; generally

mote *n.* speck, as of dust

mo·tel *n.* roadside hotel for motorists

moth *n.* four-winged insect like a butterfly

moth'ball' *n.* small ball of crystalline substance: its fumes repel moths

moth·er *n.* 1 female parent 2 woman head of a convent: in full **mother superior** —*a.* 1 of or like a mother 2 native —*v.* be a mother to —**moth'er·hood'** *n.* —**moth'er·ly** *a.*

moth·er-in-law' *n., pl.* **moth'ers-** mother of one's husband or wife

moth'er·land' *n.* one's native land

moth'er-of-pearl' *n.* hard, shiny lining of some shells

mo·tif' (-tēf') *n.* main theme of an artistic work

mo·tile (-til) *a.* that can move — **mo·til'i·ty** *n.*

mo'tion *n.* 1 a moving; change of position 2 gesture 3 proposal made at a meeting —*v.* make, or direct by, gestures — **mo'tion·less** *a.*

motion picture *n.* a FILM (*n.* 3)

mo'ti·vate' *v.* provide with motive —**mo'ti·va'tion** *n.* —**mo'ti·va'tor** *n.*

mo'tive *n.* reason for doing something —*adv.* of motion

mot'ley *a.* of many different elements; varied

mo'tor *n.* 1 machine using electricity to make something work 2 engine; esp., a gasoline engine —*a.* 1 of or run by a motor 2 of or for motor vehicles 3 producing motion 4 of muscular movements —*v.* to travel in an automobile —**mo'tor·ist** *n.*

mo'tor·boat' *n.* boat propelled by a motor

mo'tor·car' *n.* automobile

mo'tor·cy'cle *n.* two-wheeled, engine-powered vehicle

mot'tle *v.* to blotch

mot'to *n., pl.* **-toes** or **-tos** maxim or phrase, as used on seals, coins, etc., that shows one's ideals, etc.

mould (mōld) *n., v.* chiefly Br. sp. of MOLD —**mould'y** *a.*, **-i·er**, **-i·est**

moult (mōlt) *v.* chiefly Br. sp. of MOLT

mound *n.* heap of earth, etc.

mount *v.* 1 climb; go up 2 get up on 3 increase in amount 4

fix on or in a mounting —*n.* 1 act of mounting 2 horse to ride 3 mounting 4 mountain

moun'tain *n.* very high rise of land on earth's surface

moun'tain·eer' *n.* 1 mountain dweller 2 mountain climber

mountain lion *n.* cougar

moun'tain·ous *a.* 1 full of mountains 2 very big

moun'te·bank' *n.* charlatan

mount'ed *a.* 1 with a mounting 2 on horseback

Mount'ie, Mount'y *n., pl.* **-ies** [Col.] member of the Royal Canadian Mounted Police

mount'ing *n.* a backing, support, setting, etc.

mourn (môrn) *v.* feel or show grief or sorrow (for) —**mourn'er** *n.* —**mourn'ful** *a.*

mourn'ing *n.* 1 grief at a death 2 mourners' black clothes

mouse (mous) *n., pl.* **mice** 1 small rodent 2 timid person 3 hand-held device for controlling images on a computer video screen —**mous'y, mous'ey** *a.*, **-i·er**, **-i·est**

mousse (mōōs) *n.* chilled dessert of egg, gelatin, etc.

mous'tache' *n.* mustache

mouth (mouth; *v.:* mouth) *n.* 1 opening in the face for food 2 any opening —*v.* form (words) with the mouth soundlessly — **mouth'ful** *n.*

mouth organ *n.* harmonica

mouth'piece' *n.* 1 part held in or near the mouth 2 spokesman for another

mouth'wa'ter·ing *a.* tasty

move *v.* 1 change the place of 2 set or keep in motion 3 change one's residence 4 be active or take action 5 cause 6 stir emotionally 7 propose (a resolution) —*n.* 1 movement or action 2 *Games* one's turn — **mov'a·ble, move'a·ble** *a., n.* — **mov'er** *n.*

move'ment *n.* 1 a moving or way of moving 2 action toward a goal 3 moving parts of a clock, etc. 4 *Mus.* main division of a composition

mov'ie *n.* a FILM (*n.* 3) —**the movies** 1 film industry 2 a showing of a film

mow (mō) *v.* **mowed**, **mowed** or **mown**, **mow'ing** 1 cut down (grass) 2 kill; knock down — **mow'er** *n.*

mow (mou) *n.* heap of hay, esp. in a barn

moz'za·rel'la (mät'sa-) n. soft, white cheese with mild flavor

Mr. title used before a man's name

Mrs. title used before a married woman's name

Ms. (miz) title used instead of *Miss* or *Mrs.*

much a. more, most great in quantity, degree, etc. —adv. 1 greatly 2 nearly —n. 1 great amount 2 something great

mu·ci·lage (myōo'si lij') n. gluey or gummy adhesive

muck n. 1 black earth 2 dirt; filth

muck'rake' v. expose corruption in politics and business —**muck'rak'er** n.

mu'cous (myōo'-) a. 1 of or secreting mucus 2 slimy

mucous membrane n. membrane lining body cavities

mu'cus n. slimy secretion of mucous membranes

mud n. soft, wet earth

mud'dle v. 1 mix up; confuse 2 act confusedly —n. mess, confusion, etc.

mud'dy a. -di·er, -di·est 1 full of or covered with mud 2 clouded or obscure —v. -died, -dy·ing make or become muddy

mud'sling'ing n. unfair verbal attack

mu·ez'zin (myōo'-) n. crier calling Muslims to prayer

muff n. cylindrical covering to warm the hands —v. bungle; miss

muf'fin n. bread baked in a small cupcake mold

muf'fle v. 1 wrap up warmly 2 deaden (sound), as on an automobile

muf'fler n. 1 thick scarf 2 device to deaden noise, as on an automobile

muf'ti n. civilian clothes

mug n. 1 heavy drinking cup 2 [Sl.] face 3 official photograph of a criminal or suspect: in full **mug shot**

mug'gy a. -gi·er, -gi·est hot and humid

mu·lat·to (mə lät'ō) n., pl. -toes or -tos one with a black parent and a white parent

mul'ber·ry n., pl. -ries tree with berrylike fruit

mulch v., n. (use) a cover of leaves, peat, etc. around plants

mule n. 1 offspring of a male donkey and a female horse 2 lounging slipper

mul'ish (myōol'-) a. stubborn

mull v. 1 ponder 2 heat and flavor, as wine

mul'lein (-in) n. tall plant with downy leaves

mul'let n. an edible fish

multi- pref. of or having many or several

mul'ti·far'i·ous a. of many kinds; varied

mul'ti·ple a. having many parts, etc. —n. product of two numbers, one specified

mul'ti·ple-choice' a. listing several answers to choose from

mul'ti·plex' a. of a system for combining signals sent over one circuit, etc.

mul'ti·pli·cand' n. the number to be multiplied by another

mul'ti·plic'i·ty (-plis'-) n. great number

mul'ti·ply' v. -plied', -ply'ing 1 to increase in number, degree, etc. 2 find the product (of) by adding a certain number a certain number of times —**mul'ti·pli·ca'tion** n. —**mul'ti·pli'er** n.

mul'ti·tude' n. large number

mul'ti·tu'di·nous a. many

mum n. [Col.] chrysanthemum —a. silent

mum'ble v. speak or say indistinctly —n. mumbled utterance

mum'bo jum'bo n. meaningless ritual or talk

mum'my n., pl. -mies ancient embalmed body

mumps n. disease in which the salivary glands swell

munch v. chew noisily

mun'dane' a. of the world

mu·nic'i·pal (-nis'-) a. of a city or town

mu·nic'i·pal'i·ty n., pl. -ties of city or town having its own local government

mu·nif'i·cent a. very generous —**mu·nif'i·cence** n.

mu·ni'tions n.pl. weapons and ammunition for war

mu·ral (myoor'al) a. of or on a wall —n. picture painted on a wall

mur'der v. kill (a person) unlawfully and with malice —n. act of murdering —**mur'der·er** n.

mur'der·ous a. 1 of or like murder 2 guilty of, or ready to, murder

murk n. darkness; gloom —**murk'y** a., -i·er, -i·est

mur'mur n. 1 low, steady sound 2 mumbled complaint —v. 1 make a murmur 2 say in a low voice

mur'rain (-in) *n.* a plague, esp. of cattle

mus'cle (-əl) *n.* 1 tissue forming the fleshy parts that move the body 2 any single part of this tissue 3 strength

mus'cu·lar *a.* 1 of or done by muscle 2 strong

muse *v.* think deeply —*n.* spirit inspiring an artist

mu·se'um *n.* place for displaying artistic, historical, or scientific objects

mush *n.* 1 thick, soft mass 2 boiled cornmeal 3 [Col.] maudlin sentimentality —*int.* shout urging on sled dogs —*v.* travel over snow —**mush'y** *a.*, **-i·er, -i·est**

mush'room' *n.* fleshy, umbrella-shaped fungus, often edible —*v.* grow rapidly

mu'sic *n.* 1 songs, symphonies, etc. 2 art of composing or performing these

mu'si·cal *a.* of, fond of, or set to music —*n.* play or film with singing and dancing —**mu'si·cal·ly** *adv.*

mu·si'cian (-zish'ən) *n.* person skilled in music

musk *n.* strong-smelling animal secretion, used in perfumes —**musk'y** *a.*, **-i·er, -i·est**

mus'kel·lunge' *n.* large, edible pike: also **mus'kie**

mus'ket *n.* long gun —**mus'ket·eer'** *n.*

musk'mel'on *n.* cantaloupe

musk'rat' *n.* water rodent

Mus'lim (muz'-, mooz'-) *n.* follower of the religion of Mohammed —*a.* of Islam or Muslims

mus'lin (muz'-) *n.* strong cotton cloth, as for sheets

muss *v.* make messy —*n.* [Col.] mess —**muss'y** *a.*

mus'sel *n.* bivalve mollusk

must *v.* auxiliary verb showing: 1 obligation 2 probability 3 certainty —*n.* [Col.] thing that must be done

mus·tache' (-tash') *n.* hair grown out on the upper lip of men

mus'tang' *n.* small, wild horse

mus'tard *n.* yellow, spicy powder or paste

mus'ter *v.* 1 to bring or come together, as troops 2 summon —*n.* a mustering

mus'ty *a.* **-ti·er, -ti·est** stale and moldy

mu'ta·ble *a.* changeable

mu'tant *n.* animal or plant dif-

ferent from parents

mu·ta'tion *n.* a change, esp. a sudden variation in a plant or animal —**mu'tate'** *v.*

mute *a.* 1 silent 2 not able to speak —*n.* 1 one unable to speak; spec., a deaf-mute 2 device to mute a musical instrument —*v.* soften the sound of

mu'ti·late' *v.* cut off or damage part of

mu'ti·ny *n.*, *pl.* **-nies**; *v.* **-nied, -ny·ing** revolt, as against one's military superiors —**mu'ti·neer'** *n.* —**mu'ti·nous** *a.*

mutt *n.* [Sl.] mongrel dog

mut'ter *v.* 1 speak or say in low, indistinct tones 2 grumble —*n.* muttered utterance

mut'ton *n.* flesh of (grown) sheep used as food

mu'tu·al (-choo-) *a.* 1 of or for one another 2 in common —**mu'tu·al·ly** *adv.*

muz'zle *n.* 1 snout 2 device for an animal's mouth to prevent biting 3 front end of a gun barrel —*v.* 1 put a muzzle on 2 prevent from talking

my *a.* of me

my·e·li'tis (mī'ə lit'is) *n.* inflammation of bone marrow or spinal cord

my'na, my'nah *n.* Asian starling

my·o'pi·a *n.* nearsightedness —**my·op'ic** (-äp'-) *a.*

myr'i·ad (mir'-) *n.* great number —*a.* very many

myrrh (mur) *n.* resin used in incense, perfume, etc.

myr'tle *n.* 1 evergreen shrub 2 creeping evergreen plant

my·self' *pron.* intensive or reflexive form of I

mys'ter·y *n.*, *pl.* **-ies** 1 unexplained or unknown thing 2 obscurity or secrecy —**mys·te'ri·ous** *a.*

mys'tic *a.* 1 of mysticism 2 occult or mysterious —*n.* believer in mysticism

mys'ti·cal *a.* 1 spiritually symbolic 2 mystic

mys'ti·cism *n.* belief that God can be known directly

mys'ti·fy *v.* **-fied', -fy'ing** perplex or puzzle —**mys'ti·fi·ca'tion** *n.*

mys·tique' (-tēk') *n.* mystical or fascinating quality of a person, etc.

myth *n.* 1 traditional story explaining some phenomenon 2 fictitious person or thing —**myth'i·cal** *a.*

my·thol·o·gy n., pl. **-gies 1** study of myths **2** myths of a certain people —**myth·o·log·i·cal** a.

N

nab v. [Col.] seize or arrest

na'dir n. lowest point

nag v. **nagged, nag'ging** scold or urge constantly —n. **1** one who nags **2** inferior horse

nail n. **1** horny layer at the ends of the fingers and toes **2** narrow, pointed piece of metal driven into pieces of wood to hold them —v. fasten as with nails

na·ive, na·ïve (nä ēv') a. innocent; simple —**na·ive·té', na·ïve·té'** (-tā') n.

na'ked a. **1** without clothing or covering **2** plain

nam'by-pam'by a.; n., pl. **-bies** insipid, indecisive (person)

name n. **1** word or words for a person, thing, or place **2** reputation —a. well-known —v. **1** give a name to **2** mention or identify by name **3** appoint

name'less a. **1** without a name **2** obscure; vague

name'ly adv. that is to say

name'sake' n. person named after another

nap v. **napped, nap'ping** sleep briefly —n. **1** short sleep **2** fuzzy surface of fibers on cloth

na'palm' (-päm') n. jellylike gasoline used in bombs, etc.

nape n. back of the neck

naph'tha (naf'-, nap'-) n. oily liquid used as a solvent, etc.

nap'kin n. small piece of paper or cloth to protect clothes while eating

narc n. [Sl.] police agent enforcing narcotics laws

nar·cis'sism' (-sə-) n. self-love —**nar'cis·sist** n.

nar·cis'sus (-sis'-) n. flowering bulbous plant

nar·cot'ic n. drug that causes deep sleep and lessens pain —a. of or like a narcotic

nar'rate' v. tell a story —**nar'ra·tor** n.

nar·ra'tion n. **1** a narrating **2** a narrative

nar'ra·tive a. in story form —n. story; account

nar'row a. **1** not wide **2** intolerant **3** limited in size, degree, etc. —v. lessen in width, extent, etc.

nar'row-mind'ed a. bigoted

nar'y a. [Dial.] used in **nary a,** not any

na'sal (-zəl) a. of or through the nose

nas·tur'tium (-shəm) n. yellowish-red flower

nas'ty a. **-ti·er, -ti·est 1** dirty **2** obscene **3** unpleasant; mean —**nas'ti·ly** adv. —**nas'ti·ness** n.

na'tal a. of (one's) birth

na'tion n. **1** a people with history, language, etc. in common **2** people under one government

na'tion·al a. of a whole nation —n. citizen

na'tion·al·ism' n. **1** patriotism **2** advocacy of national independence —**na'tion·al·ist** a., n. —**na'tion·al·is'tic** a.

na'tion·al'i·ty n., pl. **-ties** nation, esp. of one's birth or citizenship

na'tion·al·ize' v. transfer control of to a government —**na'tion·al·i·za'tion** n.

na'tive a. **1** belonging to a region or country by birth, source, etc. **2** being or of the place of one's birth **3** inborn —n. native person, animal, or plant

na'tive-born' a. born in a specified place

na·tiv'i·ty n. birth

nat'ty a. **-ti·er, -ti·est** neat and stylish

nat'u·ral (nach'-) a. **1** of or dealing with nature **2** not artificial **3** innate **4** lifelike; usual **5** to be expected **6** Mus. neither sharp nor flat —**nat'u·ral·ly** adv.

natural history n. study of nature

nat'u·ral·ist n. one who studies plants and animals

nat'u·ral·ize' v. confer citizenship upon (an alien) —**nat'u·ral·i·za'tion** n.

na'ture n. **1** basic quality of a thing **2** inborn character **3** kind; sort **4** physical universe or [also N-] its forces **5** natural scenery

naught (nôt) n. **1** nothing **2** zero

naugh'ty a. **-ti·er, -ti·est 1** mischievous **2** not nice or proper —**naugh'ti·ly** adv. —**naugh'ti·ness** n.

nau·se·a (-shə, -zhə) n. **1** feeling of wanting to vomit **2** disgust —**nau·se·ate'** (-shē-, -zē-) v.

nau'seous (-shəs) a.

nau'ti·cal a. of sailors, ships, or navigation

nautical mile n. unit of linear measure used in navigation, equal to c. 6,076 ft.

nau'ti·lus n. tropical mollusk

na'val a. of or for a navy, its ships, etc.

nave n. main, long part of some churches

na'vel n. small, abdominal scar where the umbilical cord was attached

nav'i·ga·ble a. 1 wide or deep enough for ship travel 2 that can be steered

nav'i·gate' v. 1 travel through or on (air, sea, etc.) in a ship or aircraft 2 steer (a ship, etc.) — **nav'i·ga'tion** n. — **nav'i·ga'tor** n.

na'vy n., pl. **-vies** 1 entire fleet of warships, etc. of a nation 2 very dark blue: also **navy blue**

navy bean n. small, white bean

nay n. 1 denial 2 negative vote or voter

Na·zi (nät'sē) n., a. (adherent) of the German fascist party (1933-45) — **Na'zism'** n.

neap tide n. lowest high tide, occurring twice a month

near adv. at a short distance —a. 1 close in distance, time, etc. 2 intimate 3 stingy —v. to draw near to —prep. close to —**near'ness** n.

near'by' a., adv. near; close at hand

near'ly adv. almost

near'sight'ed a. seeing only near objects distinctly

neat a. 1 tidy; clean 2 skillful 3 trim in form —**neat'ly** adv. — **neat'ness** n.

neb'u·la n., pl. **-lae** (-lē) or **-las** cloudlike patch seen in the night sky —**neb'u·lar** a.

neb'u·lous a. vague

nec·es·sar'i·ly adv. 1 because of necessity 2 as a necessary result

nec'es·sar'y a. 1 that must be had or done; essential 2 inevitable —n., pl. **-ies** necessary thing

ne·ces'si·tate' v. make (something) necessary

ne·ces'si·ty n., pl. **-ties** 1 great need 2 something necessary 3 poverty

neck n. 1 part that joins the head to the body 2 narrow part, as of a bottle —v. [Sl.] to hug, kiss, and caress passionately —**neck and neck** very close as to outcome

neck'er·chief n. kerchief worn around the neck

neck'lace (-ləs) n. chain of gold, beads, etc. worn around the neck

neck'tie' n. decorative neck band worn with a shirt

ne·crol'o·gy (ne-) n. list of people who have died

nec'tar n. 1 sweet liquid in flowers 2 delicious drink

nec·tar·ine' (-tə rēn') n. smooth-skinned peach

nee, née (nā) a. born

need n. 1 lack of something required; also, the thing lacking 2 poverty or distress —v. 1 have need of 2 to be obliged —Need is also used as an auxiliary verb —**if need be** if it is required

need'ful a. necessary

nee'dle n. 1 a very slender, pointed piece, as for sewing, knitting, playing phonograph records, etc. 2 anything needle-shaped —v. [Col.] goad; tease

nee'dle·point' n. embroidery of woolen threads on canvas

need'less a. unnecessary

nee'dle·work' n. sewing, embroidery, crocheting, etc.

need'y a. **-i·er, -i·est** very poor; destitute

ne'er-do-well' (ner'-) a., n. lazy and irresponsible (person)

ne·far'i·ous (-fer'-) a. very wicked

ne·gate' v. deny or nullify —**ne·ga'tion** n.

neg'a·tive a. 1 saying "no" 2 not positive 3 of the electricity made by friction on resin 4 being less than zero —n. 1 a negative word, reply, etc. 2 battery plate of lower potential 3 photographic plate or film in which light and shadow are reversed

ne·glect' v. 1 fail to do 2 fail to care for properly —n. a neglecting —**ne·glect'ful** a.

neg·li·gee' (-zhā') n. woman's dressing gown

neg'li·gent a. habitually careless —**neg'li·gence** n.

neg'li·gi·ble a. trivial

ne·go'ti·ate' (-shē āt') v. 1 discuss so as to agree on 2 arrange for (a loan, etc.) 3 transfer or sell 4 move across —**ne·go'ti·a·ble** a. —**ne·go'ti·a'tion** n. —**ne·go'ti·a'tor** n.

Ne'gro a., n., pl. **-groes** (of) a member of dark-skinned peoples of Africa, or a person having African ancestors; black —

Ne'groid' a.

neigh (nā) v., n. (utter) the cry of a horse

neigh'bor n. 1 one that lives or is near another 2 fellow human being —a. nearby —v. live or be near

neigh'bor·hood n. one part of a city or the people in it —**in the neighborhood of** [Col.] near or nearly

neigh'bor·ly a. friendly

nei'ther (nē'-, nī'-) a., pron. not one or the other (of two) —con. correlative used with neither

nem'e·sis n. inevitable cause of one's downfall or defeat

neo- pref. new; recent

ne'o·co·lo'ni·al ism' n. exploiting of a supposedly independent region by a foreign power

ne·ol'o·gism' (-äl'ə jiz'əm) n. new word

ne'on' n. inert gas used in electric signs, a chemical element

ne'o·phyte' (-fīt') n. novice

neph'ew (nef'yōō) n. 1 son of one's brother or sister 2 son of one's brother-in-law or sister-in-law

ne·phri'tis (-frīt'is) n. inflammation of the kidneys

nep'o·tism' n. giving of jobs, etc. to relatives

nerd n. [Sl.] one regarded as dull, ineffective, etc.

nerve n. 1 cordlike fiber carrying impulses to and from the brain 2 courage 3 pl. nervousness 4 [Col.] impudence —**get on someone's nerves** [Col.] make someone nervous or annoyed

nerve gas n. poisonous liquid that paralyzes: used in warfare

nerve'-rack'ing a. very trying to one's composure or patience: also sp. **nerve'-wrack'ing**

nerv'ous a. 1 of nerves 2 easily upset; restless 3 fearful —**nerv'ous·ness** n.

nervous system n. all the nerve cells and nervous tissues of an organism

-ness suf. quality; state

nest n. 1 place where a bird or other animal raises its young 2 cozy place 3 set of things in increasing sizes —v. make a nest

nest egg n. money put aside

nes'tle (-əl) v. 1 settle down or hold close for comfort 2 lie sheltered

net n. 1 openwork fabric as of string, for snaring fish, etc. 2 fine net to hold the hair 3 netlike cloth 4 net amount —a. left over after deductions, etc. —v. gain

net'ted, net'ting 1 to snare 2 to gain

neth'er a. under

net'ting n. net fabric

net'tle n. weed with stinging hairs —v. annoy

net'work' n. 1 arrangement of wires or threads as in a net 2 system of roads, computers, etc. 3 chain of radio or TV stations

neu'ral (noor'əl, nur'-) a. of a nerve or nerves

neu·ral'gia (-jə) n. pain along a nerve path

neu·ri'tis (-rīt'is) n. inflammation of nerves —**neu·rit'ic** a.

neuro- pref. of nerves

neu·rol'o·gy n. branch of medicine dealing with the nervous system —**neu·rol'o·gist** n.

neu'ron' n. nerve cell and its processes

neu·ro'sis n., pl. **-ses'** (-sēz') mental disorder with abnormally intense anxieties, obsessions, etc. —**neu·rot'ic** a., n.

neu'ter a. neither masculine nor feminine —v. castrate or spay (an animal)

neu'tral a. 1 supporting neither side in a war or quarrel 2 not one or the other 3 having no decided color —n. 1 neutral nation, etc. 2 position of disengaged gears —**neu·tral'i·ty** n.

neu'tral·ize' v. counteract the effectiveness of

neu'tron' n. uncharged particle of an atom

nev'er adv. 1 at no time 2 in no way

nev'er·the·less' adv., con. in spite of that; however

new a. 1 appearing, thought of, made, etc. for the first time 2 unfamiliar or foreign 3 fresh 4 unused 5 modern; recent 6 more 7 beginning again —adv. 1 again 2 recently

new'born' a. 1 just born 2 reborn

new'com'er n. recent arrival

new'fan'gled a. new and strange

new'ly adv. recently

new'ly·wed' n. recently married person

news n. 1 new information 2 (reports of) recent events

news'boy' n. boy who sells or delivers newspapers

news'cast' n. radio or TV news

broadcast —**news'cast'er** n.

news'let'ter n. special group's news bulletin, issued regularly

news'man' n., pl. **-men'** male newscaster or reporter —**news'wom'an** n., pl. **-wom'en**

news'pa'per n. daily or weekly news publication

news'print' n. cheap paper used for newspapers, etc.

news'stand' n. a stand for the sale of newspapers, etc.

newt n. small salamander

New Testament second part of the Christian Bible

New Year's (Day) n. January 1

next a. nearest; closest —adv. in the nearest time, place, etc.

next'-door' a. in or at the next house, building, etc.

nex'us n., pl. **-us·es** or **-us** connection or link

ni'a·cin n. nicotinic acid

nib n. 1 bird's beak 2 (pen) point

nib'ble v. eat with quick, small bites —n. small bite

nice a. 1 pleasant, kind, good, etc. 2 precise; accurate 3 refined —**nice'ly** adv.

ni'ce·ty n., pl. **-ties** 1 accuracy 2 refinement 3 small detail; fine point 4 something choice or dainty

niche (nich) n. 1 recess in a wall for a statue, etc. 2 especially suitable position

nick v. make a small cut, chip, etc. in or on —n. small cut, chip, etc. —**in the nick of time** exactly when needed

nick'el n. 1 rust-resistant metal, a chemical element 2 nickel and copper coin worth 5 cents

nick'name' n. 1 a substitute name, as "Slim" 2 familiar form of a proper name, as "Bob" —v. give a nickname to

nic'o·tine' (-tēn') n. poisonous liquid in tobacco leaves

nic'o·tin'ic acid (-tin'-) n. member of the vitamin B complex

niece (nēs) n. 1 daughter of one's sister or brother 2 daughter of one's sister-in-law or brother-in-law

nig'gard·ly a. stingy; miserly

nigh (nī) adv., a., prep. [Dial.] near

night n. period of darkness between sunset and sunrise —**night'time'** n.

night'cap' n. 1 cap worn in bed 2 [Col.] alcoholic drink taken just before bedtime

night'club' n. place for eating, drinking, dancing, etc. at night

night'gown' n. sleeping gown for women and children

night'hawk' n. 1 night bird 2 night owl

night'ie n. [Col.] nightgown

night'in·gale' n. a European thrush that sings at night

night'ly a., adv. (done or happening) every night

night'mare' n. frightening dream or experience

night owl n. one who stays up late

night'shade' n. belladonna or related plant

night'shirt' n. shirtlike nightgown, esp. for men

ni·hil·ism (nī'ə liz'əm, nē'-) n. general rejection of usual beliefs in morality, religion, etc. —**ni'hil·ist** n.

nil n. nothing

nim'ble a. quick in movement or thought —**nim'bly** adv.

nim'bus n. 1 rain cloud 2 halo

nin'com·poop' n. fool

nine a., n. one more than eight —**ninth** a., n.

nine'teen' a., n. nine more than ten —**nine'teenth'** a., n.

nine'ty a., n., pl. **-ties** nine times ten —**nine'ti·eth** a., n.

nin'ja n. in former times, a trained Japanese assassin

nin'ny n., pl. **-nies** a fool

nip v. **nipped, nip'ping** 1 pinch or bite 2 pinch off 3 spoil, as by frost —n. 1 stinging cold 2 small drink of liquor —**nip and tuck** very close as to outcome

nip'per n. 1 pliers, pincers, etc. 2 claw of a crab or lobster

nip'ple n. 1 protuberance on a breast or udder 2 thing shaped like this

nip'py a. **-pi·er, -pi·est** sharp; biting

nir·va·na (-vä'-) n. Buddhism perfect, passionless bliss

nit n. egg of a louse

ni'ter n. salt used in explosives, fertilizer, etc.: also, Br. sp., **ni'tre**

nit'-pick'ing a. fussy —**nit'pick'er** n.

ni'trate' n. salt of nitric acid

ni'tric acid n. corrosive acid containing nitrogen

ni'tro·gen n. colorless, odorless gas, a chemical element —**ni·trog'e·nous** (-träj'-) a.

ni'tro·glyc'er·in, ni'tro·glyc'er·ine (-glis'ər in) n. thick, explosive oil, used in dynamite

nit′wit′ *n.* stupid person

nix *int.* [Sl.] no! stop!

no *adv.* 1 not at all 2 not so —*a.* not a —*n., pl.* **noes** 1 refusal 2 negative vote

no·bil′i·ty *n., pl.* **-ties** 1 noble state or rank 2 people of noble rank

no′ble *a.* 1 highly moral 2 grand; splendid 3 of high hereditary rank —*n.* person of high rank —**no′ble·man** *n., pl.* **-men** —**no′bly** *adv.*

no′bod′y *pron.* no one —*n., pl.* **-ies** unimportant person

noc·tur′nal *a.* 1 of the night 2 done, happening, etc. at night

noc′turne′ *n.* romantic musical composition

nod *v.* **nod′ded, nod′ding** 1 bend the head quickly (assent) thus 3 let the head fall forward in dozing —*n.* a nodding

node *n.* 1 knob; swelling 2 point on a stem from which a leaf grows

nod·ule (näj′ōōl′) *n.* small knot or rounded lump

No·el, No·ël (nō el′) *n.* Christmas

no′-fault′ *a.* of car insurance paying for damages without blame being fixed

nog′gin *n.* [Col.] the head

no′-good′ *a.* [Sl.] despicable

noise *n.* sound, esp. a loud, unpleasant sound —*v.* spread (a rumor) —**noise′less** *a.*

noi′some *a.* 1 unhealthful 2 foul-smelling

nois′y *a.* **-i·er, -i·est** 1 making noise 2 full of noise —**nois′i·ly** *adv.* —**nois′i·ness** *n.*

no′mad′ *n.* 1 member of a wandering tribe 2 wanderer —**no·mad′ic** *a.*

no′men·cla′ture (-klā′chər) *n.* system of names

nom′i·nal *a.* 1 in name only 2 relatively small —**nom′i·nal·ly** *adv.*

nom′i·nate′ *v.* 1 appoint; name 2 name as a candidate —**nom′i·na′tion** *n.*

nom′i·na·tive *a., n. Gram.* (in) the case of the subject of a verb

nom′i·nee′ *n.* a person who is nominated

non- *pref.* not: see list below

non′ab·sorb′ent

non′ac′tive

non′ag·gres′sion

non′al·co·hol′ic

non′be·liev′er

non′com·bus′ti·ble

non′com·mer′cial

non′con·form′ist

non′con·ta′gious

non′es·sen′tial

non′ex·ist′ent

non·fac′tu·al

non·fa′tal

non·fic′tion

non′flow′er·ing

non′fly′ing

non·func′tion·al

non′in·ter·fer′ence

non′in·ter·ven′tion

non·ir′ri·tat·ing

non·ma·lig′nant

non′me·tal′lic

non·mil′i·tar·y

non′of·fi′cial

non′pay′ment

non·per′ish·a·ble

non·poi′son·ous

non′po·lit′i·cal

non·po′rous

non′pro·duc′tive

non′pro·fes′sion·al

non·prof′it·a·ble

non′re·li′gious

non′res·i·den′tial

non·smok′er

non′sup·port′ing

non′sus·tain′ing

non·tax′a·ble

non·tech′ni·cal

non·tox′ic

non·age (-ij) *n.* state of being under legal age

nonce *n.* the present time

non′cha·lant′ (-shə länt′) *a.* casually indifferent —**non′cha·lance′** *n.*

non′com′bat·ant *n.* 1 civilian in wartime 2 soldier not in combat

non′com·mis′sioned officer *n.* enlisted person in the armed forces

non′com·mit′tal *a.* not taking a definite stand

non·con·duc′tor *n.* thing that does not conduct electricity, heat, etc.

non′de·script′ *a.* of no definite class or type

none (nun) *pron.* 1 no one 2 not any —*adv.* not at all

non·en′ti·ty *n., pl.* **-ties** unimportant person

none′the·less′ *adv.* nevertheless: also **none the less**

non·fer′rous *a.* of metals other than iron

non′pa·reil′ (-pə rel′) *a.* without equal; peerless

non′par·ti·san *a.* not of any single party, faction, etc.

non'plus' v. **-plused'** or **-plussed', -plus'ing** or **-plus'sing** thoroughly bewilder

non'prof'it a. not for profit

non'res'i·dent n., a. (person) not living in the locality of his work, etc.

non'sec·tar'i·an a. not connected with a specific religion

non'sense' n. absurd or meaningless words or acts —**non·sen'si·cal** a.

non' se'qui·tur (-sek'wi-) n. remark having no relation to something just said

non'stop' a., adv. without a stop

non'sup·port' n. failure to support a legal dependent

non'un'ion a. not belonging to, or done by, a labor union

non'vi'o·lent a. not using violence —**non'vi'o·lence** n.

noo'dle n. flat strip of dry dough

nook n. 1 corner 2 small secluded spot

noon n. twelve o'clock in the daytime; midday: also **noon'day'** or **noon'time'**

no one pron. no person

noose n. loop with a slipknot for tightening it

nor con. and not (either)

norm n. standard or model

nor'mal a. 1 usual; natural 2 average —n. what is normal; usual state —**nor'mal·cy, nor·mal'i·ty** n.

nor'mal·ly adv. 1 in a normal way 2 usually

north n. direction or region to the right of one facing the sunset —a., adv. in, toward, or from the north —**north'er·ly** a., adv. —**north'ern** a. —**north'ern·er** n. —**north'ward** a., adv. —**north'wards** adv.

north'east' n. direction or region between north and east —a., adv. in, toward, or from the northeast —**north'east'er·ly** a., adv. —**north'east'ern** a. —**north'east'ward** a., adv. —**north'east'wards** adv.

northern lights n.pl. aurora borealis

North Pole northern end of the earth's axis

North Star bright star almost directly above the North Pole

north'west' n. direction or region between north and west —a., adv. in, toward, or from the northwest —**north'west'er·ly** a., adv. —**north'west'ern** a.

—**north'west'ward** a., adv. —**north'west'wards** adv.

nose n. 1 part of the face with two openings for breathing and smelling 2 sense of smell 3 thing like a nose —v. 1 find, as by smell 2 push with the front forward 3 meddle (in) —**nose out** defeat narrowly

nose dive n. 1 swift downward plunge of an airplane, nose first 2 sharp drop, as of prices

nose'gay' n. bunch of flowers

nos·tal'gi·a (-jə) n. a longing for something past or far away —**nos·tal'gic** a.

nos'tril n. either of two outer openings of the nose

nos'trum n. quack medicine

nos'y, nos'ey (nōz'-) a. **-i·er, -i·est** [Col.] inquisitive

not adv. in no manner, degree, etc.

no'ta·ble a., n. remarkable or outstanding (person) —**no'ta·bly** adv.

no'ta·rize' v. certify (a document) as a notary

no'ta·ry n., pl. **-ries** one authorized to certify documents, etc.: in full **notary public**

no·ta'tion n. 1 (use of) a system of symbols, as in music 2 a note

notch n. 1 a V-shaped cut 2 [Col.] a step; degree —v. to cut notches in

note n. 1 brief writing, comment, letter, etc. 2 notice; heed 3 written promise to pay 4 musical tone or its symbol 5 importance —v. 1 to notice 2 make a note of —**compare notes** exchange views

note'book' n. book for keeping memorandums, etc.

not'ed a. renowned; famous

note'wor'thy a. outstanding

noth'ing n. 1 no thing 2 unimportant person or thing 3 zero —adv. not at all —**for nothing** 1 free 2 in vain 3 without reason —**noth'ing·ness** n.

no'tice n. 1 announcement or warning 2 a short review 3 attention —v. observe —**take notice** observe

no'tice·a·ble a. 1 easily seen 2 significant —**no'tice·a·bly** adv.

no'ti·fy' v. **-fied', -fy'ing** give notice to; inform —**no'ti·fi·ca'tion** n.

no'tion n. 1 general idea 2 belief; opinion 3 whim 4 pl. small wares

no·to'ri·ous a. widely known,

esp. unfavorably —**no'to·ri'e·ty** n.

not'with·stand'ing prep., adv. in spite of (that)

nou'gat (nōo'-) n. candy of sugar paste with nuts

nought (nôt) n. 1 nothing 2 zero

noun n. word that names a person, thing, etc.

nour'ish (nur'-) a. feed to promote life and growth —**nour'ish·ment** n.

nov'el a. new and unusual —n. long fictional narrative

nov'el·ist n. writer of novels

nov'el·ty n., pl. **-ties** 1 newness 2 novel thing 3 small, cheap toy, etc.

No·vem'ber n. 11th month

nov'ice n. 1 one in a religious order before taking final vows 2 beginner

no·vi'ti·ate (nō vish'ē ət) n. period of being a novice: also, Br. sp., **no·vi'ci·ate**

No'vo·cain' trademark procaine: also sp. **No'vo·caine'**

now adv. 1 at this moment; at present 2 at that time; then 3 with things as they are —con. since —n. the present time —**now and then** occasionally: also **now and again**

now'a·days' adv. in these days; at the present time

no'where' adv. not in, at, or to any place

nox'ious (näk'shəs) a. harmful to health or morals

noz'zle n. small spout at the end of a hose, etc.

nu'ance (-äns') n. slight change in color, meaning, etc.

nub'by a. **-bi·er**, **-bi·est** rough and knotty, as cloth

nu'bile (-bil, -bil') a. sexually attractive: said of a young woman

nu'cle·ar a. of, like, or forming a nucleus or nuclei

nuclear fission n. splitting of nuclei of atoms, with the release of much energy, as in the atomic bomb

nuclear fusion n. fusion of nuclei of atoms, with the release of much energy, as in the hydrogen bomb

nu'cle·us n., pl. **-cle·i'** (-klē ī') or **-cle·us·es** central part, spec. of an atom or of a living cell

nude a. naked (figure) —**nu'di·ty** n.

nudge v. push gently, as with the

elbow to get someone's attention —n. gentle push

nud'ism' n. practice or cult of going nude —**nud'ist** a., n.

nug'get n. lump of gold ore

nui'sance (nōo'-) n. annoying act, person, etc.

nuke v., n. [Sl.] (attack with) nuclear weapon

null a. without legal force: also **null and void**

nul'li·fy v. **-fied'**, **-fy'ing** 1 make null 2 make useless —**nul'li·fi·ca'tion** n.

numb (num) a. not able to feel —v. make numb

num'ber n. 1 symbol or word showing how many or what place in a series 2 total 3 often pl. many 4 quantity 5 single issue of a periodical 6 one part of a program of entertainment 7 form of a word showing it to be singular or plural —v. 1 to count 2 give a number to 3 include 4 to total or come

num'ber·less a. countless

nu'mer·al n. figure, letter, or word expressing a number

nu'mer·a'tor n. part above the line in a fraction

nu·mer'i·cal a. 1 of, in, or having to do with number(s) 2 (expressed) by numbers Also **nu·mer'ic** —**nu·mer'i·cal·ly** adv.

nu'mer·ous a. 1 very many 2 large in number

nu'mis·mat'ics n. study or collecting of coins —**nu·mis'ma·tist** n.

num'skull' n. stupid person

nun n. woman living in a convent under vows

nun'ci·o' (-shē ō') n., pl. **-os'** papal ambassador

nun'ner·y n., pl. **-ies** [Ar.] convent

nup'tial (-shəl) a. of marriage or a wedding —n. pl. a wedding

nurse n. 1 one trained to care for the sick, help doctors, etc. 2 nursemaid —v. 1 take care of (an invalid, etc.) 2 try to cure; treat 3 suckle 4 protect or conserve 5 nourish

nurse'maid' n. woman hired to care for children

nurs'er·y n., pl. **-ies** 1 room set aside for children 2 place where trees and plants are raised for sale

nursery school n. school for children about three to five years old

nur'ture n. training; care —v. 1

nourish 2 train; rear

nut n. 1 dry fruit with a kernel inside a hard shell 2 the kernel 3 small metal block for screwing onto a bolt, etc. 4 [Sl.] odd or silly person 5 [Sl.] fan; devotee

nut'hatch' n. small songbird

nut'meat n. kernel of a nut

nut'meg' n. aromatic seed grated and used as a spice

nu'tri·ent a., n. nutritious (substance)

nu'tri·ment n.

nu·tri'tion (-trish'ən) n. 1 process of taking in and assimilating food 2 food —**nu'tri·tive** (-tiv) a.

nu·tri'tious a. nourishing

nuts a. [Sl.] crazy; silly

nut'shell' n. shell of a nut

nut'ty a. **-ti·er, -ti·est** 1 containing nuts 2 tasting like nuts 3 [Sl.] crazy, enthusiastic, etc.

nuz'zle v. 1 to push against with the nose 2 snuggle

ny'lon' n. 1 synthetic material made into thread, etc. 2 pl. stockings of this

nymph (nimf) n. minor Greek or Roman nature goddess

nym'pho·ma'ni·a n. uncontrollable sexual desire in a woman —**nym'pho·ma'ni·ac'** a., n.

O

O int. 1 exclamation in direct address 2 oh

oaf n. stupid, clumsy fellow —**oaf'ish** a.

oak n. hardwood tree bearing acorns —**oak'en** a.

oa'kum n. hemp fiber used to caulk seams in boats

oar n. pole with a broad blade at one end, for rowing —**oars'man** n., pl. **-men**

oar'lock' n. device supporting an oar in rowing

o·a'sis n., pl. **-ses'** fertile place with water in the desert

oat n. usually pl. 1 a cereal grass 2 its grain —**oat'en** a.

oath n. 1 sworn declaration to tell the truth, etc. 2 word used in cursing

oat'meal' n. ground or rolled oats, cooked as porridge

ob'bli·ga'to (-gät'ō) n., pl. **-tos** or **-ti** 1 elaborate musical accompaniment to a piece

ob'du·rate (-dər ət) a. 1 stubborn; unyielding; inflexible 2 not repenting —**ob'du·ra·cy** n.

o·be'di·ent a. obeying or willing to obey —**o·be'di·ence** n. —**o·be'di·ent·ly** adv.

o·bei'sance (-bā'-, -bē'-) n. 1 bow, curtsy, etc. 2 homage

ob'e·lisk n. slender, tapering, four-sided pillar

o·bese' a. very fat —**o·be'si·ty** n.

o·bey' v. 1 carry out orders (of) 2 be guided by

ob·fus'cate v. to obscure; confuse —**ob·fus·ca'tion** n.

o·bit'u·ar·y (-bich'ōō-) n., pl. **-ies** notice of death, often with a short biography: also **o'bit**

ob·ject' (v.: əb jekt') n. 1 thing that can be seen or touched 2 person or thing to which action, etc. is directed 3 purpose; goal 4 Gram. word receiving the action of the verb or governed by a preposition —v. feel or express opposition or disapproval —**ob·jec'tor** n.

ob·jec'tion n. 1 expression of disapproval 2 a reason for objecting

ob·jec'tion·a·ble a. offensive; disagreeable

ob·jec'tive a. 1 real or actual; not subjective 2 without bias 3 Gram. of the case of an object of a preposition or verb —n. goal —**ob'jec·tiv'i·ty** n. —**ob·jec'tive·ly** a.

ob·jet d'art (äb'zhä där') n., pl. **ob'jets d'art'** (-zhä-) small object of artistic value

ob'jur·gate' v. rebuke; upbraid —**ob'jur·ga'tion** n.

ob'li·gate' v. bind by a promise, sense of duty, etc. —**ob'li·ga'tion** n. —**ob·lig'a·to'ry** a.

o·blige' (-blīj') v. 1 compel, as by law or duty 2 make indebted; do a favor for

o·blig'ing a. helpful

ob·lique' (ō blēk') a. 1 slanting 2 not direct —**ob·liq'ui·ty** n.

ob·lit'er·ate' v. 1 blot out 2 destroy —**ob·lit'er·a'tion** n.

ob·liv'i·on n. 1 state of being forgotten 2 forgetful state

ob·liv'i·ous a. not aware

ob'long' a. rectangular and longer than broad —n. oblong figure

ob'lo·quy (-kwē) n. widespread censure or disgrace

ob·nox'ious (-näk'shəs) a. offensive

o'boe n. double-reed woodwind instrument

ob·scene' (-sēn') a. offensive to decency —**ob·scen'i·ty** (-sen'ī-)

n., pl. **-ties**

ob·scure' *a.* **1** dim **2** not clear or distinct **3** not well-known —*v.* make obscure —**ob·scu'ri·ty** *n.*

ob'se·quies' (-kwēz') *n.pl.* funeral rites

ob·se'qui·ous (-kwē-) *a.* servile

ob·serv'ance (-zurv'-) *n.* **1** the observing of a law, etc. **2** customary act, rite, etc.

ob·serv'ant *a.* **1** attentive **2** perceptive; alert

ob·serv'a·to'ry *n., pl.* **-ries** building for astronomical research

ob·serve' *v.* **1** adhere to (a law, etc.) **2** celebrate (a holiday, etc.) **3** notice; watch **4** to remark —**ob·serv'a·ble** *a.* —**ob'ser·va'tion** *n.* —**ob·serv'er** *n.*

ob·sess' *v.* haunt in mind; preoccupy greatly

ob·ses'sion *n.* idea, etc. that obsesses one

ob·sid'i·an *n.* hard, dark volcanic glass

ob'so·les'cent *a.* becoming obsolete —**ob'so·les'cence** *n.*

ob'so·lete' *a.* no longer used

ob'sta·cle *n.* obstruction

ob·stet'rics *n.* branch of medicine dealing with childbirth —**ob·stet'ric, ob·stet'ri·cal** *a.* —**ob'ste·tri'cian** *n.*

ob'sti·nate (-nat) *a.* **1** stubborn **2** hard to treat or cure —**ob'sti·na·cy** *n.*

ob·strep'er·ous *a.* unruly

ob·struct' *v.* **1** block **2** hinder —**ob·struc'tion** *n.* —**ob·struc'tive** *a.*

ob·tain' *v.* **1** get by trying **2** prevail; be in effect

ob·trude' *v.* **1** push out **2** to force oneself upon others —**ob·tru'sive** *a.*

ob·tuse' *a.* **1** more than 90°: said of an angle **2** blunt **3** slow to understand

ob·verse' (*n.:* äb'vurs) *a.* facing the observer —*n.* front or main side of a coin, etc.

ob'vi·ate' *v.* prevent, as by proper measures

ob'vi·ous *a.* easy to understand —**ob'vi·ous·ly** *adv.*

oc'a·ri'na (-rē'-) *n.* small, oval musical toy

oc·ca'sion *n.* **1** happening **2** special event **3** opportunity **4** cause —*v.* to cause —**on occasion** sometimes

oc·ca'sion·al *a.* **1** for special times **2** infrequent —**oc·ca'sion·al·ly** *adv.*

Oc'ci·dent (äk'sə-) Europe and the Western Hemisphere —**Oc'ci·den'tal** *a., n.*

oc·clude' *v.* to close or shut

oc·clu'sion *n.* the way the upper and lower teeth come together

oc·cult' *a.* **1** secret **2** mysterious **3** magical

oc'cu·pan·cy *n., pl.* **-cies** an occupying —**oc'cu·pant** *n.*

oc'cu·pa'tion *n.* **1** an occupying **2** work; vocation —**oc'cu·pa'tion·al** *a.*

oc'cu·py' *v.* **-pied', -py'ing 1** take possession of **2** dwell in **3** employ

oc·cur' *v.* **-curred', -cur'ring 1** exist **2** come to mind **3** happen —**oc·cur'rence** *n.*

o·cean (ō'shən) *n.* **1** body of salt water covering much of the earth **2** one of its four main divisions —**o·ce·an'ic** (ō'shē-) *a.*

o'ce·an·og'ra·phy (ō'shə näg'-) *n.* study of the ocean environment

o'ce·lot (äs'ə-) *n.* large, spotted wildcat

o'cher, o·chre (ō'kər) *n.* yellow or red clay pigment

o'clock' *adv.* by the clock

oc'ta·gon *n.* figure with eight sides and eight angles —**oc·tag'o·nal** *n.*

oc'tane' number *n.* number representing certain property of a gasoline

oc'tave (-tiv) *n.* eight full steps of a musical scale

oc·tet', oc·tette' *n.* group of eight, esp. of musical performers

Oc·to'ber *n.* tenth month

oc'to·ge·nar'i·an *n., a.* (person) between 80 and 90 years old

oc'to·pus *n.* mollusk with soft body and eight arms

oc'u·lar (-yōō-) *a.* of, for, or by the eye

oc'u·list *n.* [Ar.] ophthalmologist

OD *n., v.* [Sl.] overdose, esp. fatal(ly)

odd *a.* **1** having a remainder of one when divided by two; not even **2** left over, as from a pair **3** with a few more **4** occasional **5** peculiar; strange —**odd'ly** *adv.*

odd'ball' *a., n.* [Sl.] peculiar (person)

odd'i·ty *n.* **1** odd quality **2** *pl.* **-ties** odd person or thing

odds *n.pl.* **1** advantage **2** betting ratio based on chances —**at odds** quarreling

odds and ends *n.pl.* remnants

odds'-on' a. having a very good chance of winning

ode n. lofty poem in praise

o'di·ous a. disgusting

o'di·um n. 1 hatred 2 disgrace

o·dom'e·ter n. device that measures distance traveled

o'dor n. smell; aroma —**o'dor·ous** a.

o'dor·if'er·ous a. giving off a strong odor

o'dour n. Br. sp. of ODOR

od·ys·sey (äd'ə sē) n. long journey with adventures

o'er (ō'ər) prep., adv. [Poet.] over

oeu·vre (ʉ'vr') n., pl. **oeu'vres** [Fr.] all the works of a writer, composer, etc.

of prep. 1 being or coming from 2 belonging to 3 having or containing 4 concerning; about 5 during

off adv. 1 farther away in space or time 2 so as to be no longer on 3 so as to be less —prep. 1 not on 2 dependent on 3 away from 4 below the standard of —a. 1 not on 2 on the way 3 away from work; absent 4 below standard 5 provided for 6 in error; wrong —**off and on** now and then

of·fal (ôf'əl) n. refuse; garbage

off'beat' a. [Col.] unconventional

off'-col'or a. not quite proper; risqué

of·fend' v. 1 commit an offense 2 make angry; displease —**of·fend'er** n.

of·fense' (or ô'fens') n. 1 sin or crime 2 an offending 3 an attacking —**give offense** make angry; insult —**take offense** become offended

of·fen'sive a. 1 attacking 2 disgusting —n. position for attacking

of'fer v. 1 to present or give 2 suggest —n. thing offered —**of'fer·ing** n.

of'fer·to·ry n., pl. **-ries** [often O-] 1 offering of bread and wine at Mass 2 collection of money at church service

off'hand' adv. without preparation —a. 1 said offhand 2 rude; curt Also **off'hand'ed**

of'fice n. 1 a favor 2 post of authority 3 place for doing business 4 rite

of'fice·hold'er n. government official

of'fi·cer n. 1 one having a position of authority in business, the

armed forces, etc. 2 policeman

of·fi'cial (-fish'əl) a. 1 authorized 2 formal —n. one holding an office —**of·fi'cial·ly** adv.

of·fi'ci·ate (-fish'ē-) v. perform official duties or functions

of·fi'cious (-fish'əs) a. meddlesome

off'ing n. used chiefly in **in the offing**, at some future time

off'-key' a. not harmonious

off'-lim'its a. not to be gone to

off'-line' a. not connected to a computer's CPU

off'-price' a. selling high-quality clothing, etc. at a price lower than the retail price

off'set' v. **-set'**, **-set'ting** compensate for

off'shoot' n. anything that comes from a main source

off'shore' a., adv. (moving) away from shore

off'spring' n. child or children

off'-white' a. grayish-white or yellowish-white

oft adv. [Poet.] often

of·ten (ôf'ən) adv. many times: also **of'ten·times'**

o·gle (ō'gəl) v. look at in a boldly desirous way —n. ogling look

o'gre (-gər) n. 1 Folklore man-eating giant 2 cruel man

oh (ō) int., n., pl. **oh's** or **ohs** exclamation of surprise, fear, wonder, pain, etc.

ohm (ōm) n. unit of electrical resistance

-oid suf. like; resembling

oil n. 1 any greasy liquid 2 petroleum —v. lubricate with oil —a. of, from, or like oil —**oil'y** a.

oil'cloth' n. cloth waterproofed with oil or paint

oink v., n. (make) the vocal sound of a pig

oint'ment n. oily cream for healing the skin

OK, O.K. a., adv., int. all right —n. approval —v. **OK'd, O.K.'d, OK'ing, O.K.'ing** to approve Also sp. **o'kay'**

o'kra n. plant with green pods used in soups

old a. 1 having lived or existed for a long time 2 of a specified age 3 not new 4 former —n. time long past —**old'ness** n.

Old English n. English language before A.D. 1100

old'-fash'ioned a. of the past; out-of-date

old hand n. experienced person

old hat a. [Sl.] 1 old-fashioned

2 trite

Old Testament Bible of Judaism, or the first part of the Christian Bible

old'-tim'er n. [Col.] longtime member, worker, etc.

o·le·an'der n. flowering evergreen shrub

o'le·o·mar'ga·rine, o'le·o'mar'ga·rin n. margarine: also **o'le·o'**

ol·fac'to·ry a. of the sense of smell

ol'i·gar'chy (-gär'kē) n., pl. -ies 1 state rule by a few people 2 these people

ol'ive (-iv) n. 1 evergreen tree 2 its small, oval fruit 3 yellowish green

om'buds·man n., pl. -men official who investigates complaints against an organization, etc.

o·me'ga n. last letter of the Greek alphabet

om·e·lette, om·e·let (äm'lət) n. eggs beaten up and cooked as a pancake

o'men n. sign of something to come

om'i·nous a. threatening

o·mis'sion n. an omitting or thing omitted

o·mit' v. **o·mit'ted, o·mit'ting** 1 leave out 2 fail to do

omni- pref. all; everywhere

om'ni·bus a. providing for, or including, many things at once

om·nip'o·tent a. all-powerful — **om·nip'o·tence** n.

om·ni·pres·ent (-nish'ənt) a. present everywhere

om·nis'cient (-nish'ənt) a. knowing all things — **om·nis'cience** n.

om·niv'o·rous a. 1 eating both animal and vegetable foods 2 taking in everything — **om·ni·vore'** n.

on prep. 1 held up by, covering, or attached to 2 near to 3 at the time of 4 connected with 5 in a state of 6 by using 7 concerning 8 [Sl.] using; addicted to —adv. 1 in a situation of touching, covering, or being held up by 2 toward 3 forward 4 continuously 5 into operation —a. in action

once adv. 1 one time 2 at any time 3 formerly —n. one time —**at once** 1 immediately 2 simultaneously

on·col'o·gy n. branch of medicine dealing with tumors — **on·col'o·gist** n.

on'com'ing a. approaching

one a. 1 being a single thing 2 united a certain 4 some —n.

1 lowest number 2 single person or thing —pron. a person or thing —**one by one** individually

one'ness n. unity; identity

on'er·ous a. oppressive

one·self' pron. one's own self; himself or herself —**be oneself** function normally —**by oneself** alone

one'-sid'ed a. 1 unequal 2 partial

one'-way' a. in one direction only

on·ion (un'yən) n. bulblike, sharp-tasting vegetable

on'-line' a. connected to a computer's CPU

on·look'er n. spectator

on'ly a. 1 alone of its or their kind 2 best —adv. 1 and no other 2 merely —con. [Col.] except that —**only too** very

on'rush' n. strong onward rush

on·set' n. 1 attack 2 start

on'slaught' n. violent attack

on·to prep. to and upon

o'nus n. 1 burden 2 blame

on'ward adv. forward: also **onwards** —a. advancing

on·yx (-iks) n. kind of agate

ooze v. flow out slowly —n. 1 something that oozes 2 soft mud or slime

o'pal n. iridescent gem

o·paque' (-pāk') a. not transparent —**o·pac'i·ty** (-pas'-) n.

o'pen a. 1 not closed, covered, etc. 2 not enclosed 3 unfolded 4 free to be entered, used, etc. 5 not restricted 6 available 7 frank —v. 1 to cause to be or become open 2 begin 3 start operating —**open to** glad to consider —**o'pen·er** n. —**o'pen·ly** adv.

o'pen-faced' a. 1 having a frank, honest face 2 without a top slice of bread

o'pen-hand'ed a. generous

o'pen·ing n. 1 open place 2 beginning 3 favorable chance 4 unfilled job

o'pen-mind'ed a. impartial

o'pen·work' n. ornamental work with openings in it

op'er·a n. play set to music and sung with an orchestra —**op'er·at'ic** a.

op'er·a·ble a. that can be treated by surgery

op'er·ate' v. 1 be or keep in action 2 have an effect 3 perform an operation 4 manage — **op'er·a'tor** n.

op·er·a'tion n. 1 act or way of

operating 2 a being in action 3 one process in a series 4 surgical treatment for an illness —**op·er·a·tion·al** a.

op'er·a·tive a. 1 operating 2 efficient

op'er·et'ta n. light opera

oph·thal·mol·o·gy (äf'-) n. branch of medicine dealing with diseases of the eye —**oph·thal·mol'o·gist** n.

o'pi·ate (-pē ət) n. narcotic drug containing opium

o·pin'ion (-yən) n. 1 what one thinks true 2 estimation 3 expert judgment

o·pin'ion·at·ed a. obstinate in holding an opinion

o'pi·um n. narcotic drug made from a certain poppy

o·pos'sum n. small, tree-dwelling mammal

op·po'nent n. person against one in a fight, etc.

op'por·tune' adv. timely

op'por·tun'ist n. one willing to get ahead unethically —**op'por·tun'ism'** n. —**op'por·tun·is'tic** a.

op'por·tu'ni·ty n., pl. **–ties** fit time to do something

op·pose' v. 1 to place opposite 2 fight or resist —**op'po·si'tion** (-zish'ən) n.

op'po·site (-zit) a. 1 entirely different 2 opposed to —n. anything opposed —prep. across from

op·press' v. 1 weigh down 2 rule in a cruel way —**op·pres'sion** n. —**op·pres'sor** n.

op·pres'sive a. 1 burdensome 2 cruel and unjust

op·pro'bri·ous a. 1 abusive 2 disgraceful

op·pro'bri·um n. disgrace

opt v. make a choice (for) —**opt out (of)** choose not to be or continue (in)

op'tic a. of the eye

op'ti·cal a. 1 of vision 2 aiding sight 3 of optics

op·ti'cian (-tish'ən) n. maker or seller of eyeglasses

op'tics n. science dealing with light and vision

op'ti·mism' n. tendency to be cheerful about life —**op'ti·mist** n. —**op'ti·mis'tic** a.

op'ti·mize' v. make the greatest use of

op'ti·mum n., a. (the) best: also **op'ti·mal** a.

op'tion n. choice or right to choose —**op'tion·al** a.

op·tom'e·trist n. one who tests and fits eyeglasses —**op·tom'e·try** n.

op'u·lent a. 1 wealthy 2 abundant —**op'u·lence** n.

o'pus n., pl. **o'pe·ra** or **o'pus·es** a work, esp. of music

or con. word introducing an alternative, synonym, etc.

-or suf. person or thing that

or'a·cle n. ancient Greek or Roman priestess or priest who acted as prophet —**o·rac'u·lar** a.

o·ral (ôr'al) a. 1 spoken 2 of the mouth —**o'ral·ly** adv.

or'ange n. 1 sweet, round, reddish-yellow citrus fruit 2 reddish yellow

or·ange·ade' n. drink of orange juice, water, and sugar

o·rang'u·tan' n. large ape

o·ra'tion n. formal public speech —**or'a·tor** n.

or'a·to'ri·o' n., pl. **-os'** vocal and orchestral composition on a religious theme

or'a·to·ry n. skill in public speaking —**or'a·tor'i·cal** a.

orb n. (celestial) sphere

or'bit n. path of one heavenly body around another —v. put or go in an orbit

or'chard n. grove of fruit trees

or'ches·tra (-kis-) n. 1 group of musicians playing together 2 main floor of a theater —**or·ches'tral** (-kes'-) a.

or'ches·trate' v. arrange music for an orchestra —**or·ches·tra'tion** n.

or'chid (-kid) n. 1 plant having flowers with three petals, one of which is enlarged 2 light bluish red

or·dain' v. 1 to decree 2 admit to the ministry

or·deal' n. difficult or painful experience

or'der n. 1 peaceful, orderly, or proper state 2 monastic or fraternal brotherhood 3 general condition 4 a command 5 (a request for) items to be supplied 6 class; kind —v. 1 arrange 2 command 3 request (supplies) —**in order that** so that —**in short order** quickly —**on the order of** 1 similar to 2 approximately

or'der·ly a. 1 neatly arranged 2 well-behaved —n., pl. **-lies** 1 soldier acting as an officer's servant 2 male hospital attendant —**or'der·li·ness** n.

or'di·nal number n. number

used to show order in a series, as *first, second,* etc.

or'di·nance *n.* statute, esp. of a city government

or'di·nar·y *a.* 1 customary; usual; regular 2 common; average —**or'di·nar'i·ly** *adv.*

or·di·na'tion *n.* an ordaining or being ordained

ord'nance *n.* Mil. heavy guns, ammunition, etc.

ore *n.* rock or mineral containing metal

o·reg'a·no *n.* plant with fragrant leaves used as seasoning

or'gan *n.* 1 keyboard musical instrument with pipes, reeds, or electronic tubes 2 animal or plant part with a special function 3 agency or medium —**or'gan·ist** *n.*

or'gan·dy, or'gan·die *n.* sheer, stiff cotton cloth

or·gan'ic *a.* 1 of a body organ 2 systematically arranged 3 of or from living matter 4 of chemical compounds containing carbon

or'gan·ism' *n.* living thing

or'gan·i·za'tion *n.* 1 act of organizing 2 group organized for some purpose

or'gan·ize' *v.* 1 arrange according to a system 2 form into a group, union, etc. —**or'gan·iz'er** *n.*

or'gasm' *n.* climax of a sexual act

or'gy (-jē) *n., pl.* **-gies** 1 wild merrymaking, esp. with sexual activity 2 unrestrained indulgence

o'ri·ent *v.* adjust (oneself) to a specific situation —[O-] E Asia —**O'ri·en'tal** *a.,* *n.* —**o'ri·en·ta'tion** *n.*

or'i·fice (-fis) *n.* mouth; opening

or'i·gin *n.* 1 beginning 2 parentage 3 source

o·rig'i·nal *a.* 1 first 2 new; novel 3 inventive —*n.* an original work, form, etc. —**o·rig'i·nal'i·ty** *n.* —**o·rig'i·nal·ly** *adv.*

o·rig'i·nate' *v.* 1 create; invent 2 begin; start —**o·rig'i·na'tion** *n.* —**o·rig'i·na'tor** *n.*

o'ri·ole' *n.* bird with bright orange and black plumage

Or'lon' *trademark* synthetic fiber —*n.* [o-] this fiber

or'na·ment (-mənt; *v.:* -ment') *n.* decoration —*v.* decorate —**or'na·men'tal** *a.* —**or'na·men·ta'tion** *n.*

or·nate' *a.* showy —**or·nate'ly** *adv.*

or·ner·y *a.* **-i·er, -i·est** [Col.] mean; obstinate

or·ni·thol'o·gy *n.* study of birds —**or·ni·thol'o·gist** *n.*

o'ro·tund' *a.* 1 full and deep in sound 2 bombastic

or'phan *n.* child whose parents are dead —*v.* cause to be an orphan —**or'phan·age** *n.*

or·tho·don'tics *n.* dentistry of teeth straightening: also **or'tho·don'ti·a** (-sha) —**or·tho·don'tist** *n.*

or'tho·dox' *a.* 1 holding to the usual or fixed beliefs; conventional 2 [O-] of a large eastern Christian church —**or'tho·dox'y** *n.*

or·tho·pe'dics *n.* surgery dealing with bones —**or·tho·pe'dic** *a.* —**or·tho·pe'dist** *n.*

-ory *suf.* 1 of or like 2 place or thing for

os'cil·late' (äs'ə-) *v.* 1 swing to and fro 2 fluctuate —**os'cil·la'tion** *n.*

os·cil'lo·scope' (ə sil'ə-) *n.* instrument showing an electrical wave on a fluorescent screen

os·mo'sis *n.* diffusion of fluids through a porous membrane

os'prey (-prē) *n., pl.* **-preys** large, fish-eating hawk

os'si·fy' *v.* **-fied', -fy'ing** change into bone

os·ten'si·ble *a.* seeming; apparent —**os·ten'si·bly** *adv.*

os·ten·ta'tion *n.* showiness —**os'ten·ta'tious** *a.*

os'te·op'a·thy *n.* a school of medicine and surgery emphasizing interrelationship of muscles and bones —**os'te·o·path'** *n.*

os'te·o·po·ro'sis *n.* a disorder marked by porous, brittle bones

os'tra·cize' *v.* banish; shut out —**os'tra·cism'** *n.*

os'trich *n.* large, nonflying bird

oth'er *a.* 1 being the one(s) remaining 2 different 3 additional —*pron.* 1 the other one 2 some other one —*adv.* otherwise —**every other** every alternate

oth'er·wise' *adv.* 1 differently 2 in all other ways 3 if not; else —*a.* different

oth'er·world'ly *a.* apart from earthly interests

ot'ter *n.* weasellike animal

ot'to·man *n.* low, cushioned seat or footstool

ouch *int.* cry of pain

ought *v.* auxiliary verb showing: 1 duty 2 desirability 3 probability

ounce *n.* **1** unit of weight, $\frac{1}{16}$ pound **2** fluid ounce, $\frac{1}{16}$ pint

our *a.* of us

ours *pron.* that or those belonging to us

our·selves' *pron.* intensive or reflexive form of WE

-ous *suf.* having; full of; characterized by

oust *v.* force out; expel

oust'er *n.* dispossession

out *adv.* **1** away from a place, etc. **2** outdoors **3** into being or action **4** thoroughly **5** from a group —*a.* **1** not used, working, etc. **2** having lost —*n.* **1** [Sl.] excuse **2** *Baseball* retirement of a batter or runner from play —*v.* become known —*prep.* out of —**on the outs** [Col.] quarreling —**out for** trying to get or do —**out of 1** from inside of **2** beyond **3** from (material) **4** because of **5** no longer having **6** so as to deprive

out- *pref.* **1** outside **2** outward **3** better or more than

out'age (-ij) *n.* accidental suspension of operation

out'-and-out' *a.* thorough

out'bid' *v.* **-bid'**, **-bid'ding** bid or offer more than (someone else)

out'board' *a.* located on the outer surface of a boat

out'break' *n.* a breaking out, as of disease or rioting

out'build'ing *n.* building apart from the main one

out'burst' *n.* sudden show of feeling, energy, etc.

out'cast' *a., n.* shunned (person)

out'class' *v.* surpass

out'come' *n.* result

out'crop' *n.* exposed rock layer

out'cry' *n., pl.* **-cries'** **1** a crying out **2** strong protest

out·dat'ed *a.* out-of-date

out'dis'tance *v.* leave behind, as in a race

out·do' *v.* do better than

out'door' *a.* in the open

out·doors' *adv.* in or into the open; outside —*n.* the outdoor world

out'er *a.* on or closer to the outside

out'er·most' *a.* farthest out

outer space *n.* space beyond the earth's atmosphere

out'field' *n. Baseball* the area beyond the infield —**out'field'er** *n.*

out'fit' *n.* **1** equipment for some activity **2** group; esp., military

unit —*v.* **-fit'ted**, **-fit'ting** equip

out'flank' *v.* go around and beyond the flank of (troops)

out'fox' *v.* outwit

out'go' *n.* expenditure

out'go'ing *a.* **1** leaving or retiring **2** sociable

out'grow' *v.* grow too large for

out'growth' *n.* **1** result **2** an offshoot

out'guess' *v.* outwit

out'ing *n.* picnic, trip, etc.

out·land'ish *a.* **1** strange **2** fantastic

out·last' *v.* endure longer than

out'law' *n.* notorious criminal —*v.* declare illegal

out'lay' *n.* money spent

out'let' *n.* **1** passage or way out **2** market for goods

out'line' *n.* **1** bounding line **2** sketch showing only outer lines **3** general plan

out·live' *v.* live longer than

out'look' *n.* **1** viewpoint **2** prospect

out'ly'ing *a.* remote

out·mod'ed (-mōd'-) *a.* obsolete; old-fashioned

out·num'ber *v.* be greater in number than

out'-of-date' *a.* obsolete

out'-of-doors' *a.* outdoor —*n., adv.* outdoors

out'-of-the-way' *a.* secluded

out'pa'tient *n.* hospital patient treated without lodging or meals

out'post' *n.* remote settlement or military post

out'put' *n.* **1** total quantity produced in a given period **2** information from a computer **3** current or power delivered

out'rage' *n.* **1** shocking act or crime **2** deep insult —*v.* commit an outrage on —**out·ra'geous** *a.*

out'right' *a.* complete —*adv.* entirely

out'set' *n.* beginning

out'side' *n.* **1** the exterior **2** area beyond —*a.* **1** outer **2** from some other **3** slight —*adv.* on or to the outside —*prep.* on or to the outside of

out·sid'er *n.* one not of a certain group

out'skirts' *n.pl.* outlying districts of a city, etc.

out·smart' *v.* outwit

out·spo'ken *a.* frank; bold

out·stand'ing *a.* **1** prominent **2** unpaid

out'stretched' *a.* extended

out·strip' *v.* **-stripped'**, **-strip'**

ping excel

out'take' *n.* faulty recording, film scene, etc. not used in the final version

out'ward *a.* 1 outer 2 visible — *adv.* toward the outside Also **out'wards** —**out'ward·ly** *adv.*

out'wear' *v.* **-wore'**, **-worn'**, **-wear'ing** outlast

out·wit' *v.* **-wit'ted**, **-wit'ting** to overcome by cleverness

o'va *n.* pl. of OVUM

o'val *a.*, *n.* egg-shaped (thing)

o'va·ry *n.*, *pl.* **-ries** 1 female gland where ova are formed 2 part of a flower where the seeds form —**o·var'i·an** (-ver'-) *a.*

o·va'tion *n.* loud and long applause or cheering

ov'en (uv'-) *n.* compartment for baking, drying, etc.

o'ver *prep.* 1 above 2 on; upon 3 across 4 during 5 more than 6 about —*adv.* 1 above or across 2 more 3 down 4 other side up 5 again —*a.* 1 finished 2 on the other side

over- *pref.* excessive or excessively: see list below

o'ver·a·bun'dance
o'ver·ac'tive
o'ver·anx'ious
o'ver·bur'den
o'ver·cau'tious
o'ver·con'fi·dent
o'ver·cook'
o'ver·crowd'
o'ver·eat'
o'ver·em'pha·size'
o'ver·es'ti·mate'
o'ver·ex·ert'
o'ver·ex·pose'
o'ver·heat'
o'ver·in·dulge'
o'ver·pop'u·late'
o'ver·pro·duc'tion
o'ver·ripe'
o'ver·stim'u·late'
o'ver·stock'
o'ver·sup·ply'

o'ver·a·chieve' *v.* 1 do better in school than expected 2 drive oneself beyond reasonable goals

o'ver·all' *a.* 1 end to end 2 total —*n. pl.* work trousers with attached bib

o'ver·awe' *v.* subdue by inspiring awe

o'ver·bear'ing *a.* bossy

o'ver·blown' *a.* 1 excessive 2 pompous

o'ver·board' *adv.* from a ship into the water

o'ver·cast' *a.* cloudy; dark

o'ver·coat' *n.* coat worn over the usual clothing

o'ver·come' *v.* get the better of; master

o'ver·do' *v.* 1 do too much 2 cook too long

o'ver·dose' (*n.*: ō'vər dōs') *v.*, *n.* (take) too large a dose

o'ver·draw' *v.* draw on in excess of the amount credited to one — **o'ver·draft'** *n.*

o'ver·dress' *v.* dress too warmly, showily, or formally

o'ver·drive' *n.* gear that reduces an engine's power without reducing its speed

o'ver·due' *a.* past the time for payment, arrival, etc.

o'ver·flow' (*n.*: ō'vər flō') *v.* 1 flood; run over 2 fill beyond capacity —*n.* 1 an overflowing 2 vent for overflowing liquids

o'ver·grow' *v.* 1 grow over all of 2 grow too much

o'ver·hand' *a.*, *adv.* with the hand held higher than the elbow

o'ver·haul' *v.* check thoroughly and make needed repairs

o'ver·head' *a.*, *adv.* above the head —*n.* continuing business costs, as of rent

o'ver·hear' *v.* hear a speaker without his knowledge

o'ver·joyed' *a.* delighted

o'ver·kill' *n.* much more than is needed, suitable, etc.

o'ver·land' *a.*, *adv.* by or across land

o'ver·lap' *v.* lap over

o'ver·look' *v.* 1 look down on 2 fail to notice 3 neglect 4 excuse

o'ver·ly *adv.* too much

o'ver·night' (*a.*: ō'vər nīt') *adv.* during the night —*a.* of or for a night

o'ver·pass' *n.* bridge over a river, road, etc.

o'ver·pow'er *v.* subdue

o'ver·rate' *v.* estimate too highly

o'ver·re·act' *v.* react in an overly emotional way

o'ver·ride' *v.* overrule

o'ver·rule' *v.* 1 set aside 2 prevail over

o'ver·run' *v.* 1 spread out over 2 swarm over

o'ver·seas' *a.*, *adv.* 1 across or beyond the sea 2 foreign

o'ver·see' *v.* supervise —**o'ver·se'er** *n.*

o'ver·shad'ow *v.* be more important than

o'ver·shoe' *n.* boot worn over the regular shoe to ward off dampness, etc.

o'ver·sight' *n.* 1 failure to see 2 careless omission

o'ver·sim'pli·fy' *v.* simplify to the point of distortion —**o'ver·sim'pli·fi·ca'tion** *n.*

o'ver·size' *a.* 1 too large 2 larger than usual Also **o'ver·sized'**

o'ver·sleep' *v.* sleep longer than intended

o·vert' (or ō'vʉrt') *a.* 1 open; public 2 done openly

o'ver·take' *v.* 1 catch up with 2 come upon suddenly

o'ver·tax' *v.* 1 tax too much 2 put a strain on

o'ver-the-count'er *a.* sold without prescription, as some drugs

o'ver·throw' (*n.:* ō'vər thrō') *v., n.* defeat

o'ver·time' *n.* 1 time beyond a set limit 2 pay for overtime work —*a., adv.* of or for overtime

o'ver·tone' *n. Mus.* higher tone heard faintly when a main tone is played

o'ver·ture *n.* 1 *Mus.* introduction 2 proposal

o'ver·turn' *v.* 1 turn over 2 conquer

o'ver·ween'ing *a.* haughty

o'ver·weight' *a.* above the normal or allowed weight

o'ver·whelm' *v.* 1 cover over completely 2 crush

o'ver·work' *v.* work too hard —*n.* too much work

o'ver·wrought' (-rôt') *a.* too nervous or excited

o·void' *a.* egg-shaped

ov'u·late' (äv'yōo-) *v.* make and release ova —**ov'u·la'tion** *n.*

ov·ule *n.* 1 immature ovum 2 part of a plant that develops into a seed

o'vum *n., pl.* **-va** mature female germ cell

owe *v.* 1 be in debt (to) for a certain sum 2 feel obligated to give

ow'ing (ō'-) *a.* due; unpaid — **owing to** resulting from

owl *n.* night bird of prey with large eyes —**owl'ish** *a.*

own *a.* belonging to oneself or itself —*n.* what one owns —*v.* 1 possess 2 confess —**own'er** *n.* —**own'er·ship'** *n.*

ox *n., pl.* **ox'en** 1 a cud-chewing animal, as a cow, bull, etc. 2 castrated bull

ox'blood' *n.* deep-red color

ox'ford (-fərd) *n.* low shoe laced over the instep

ox'ide' *n.* oxygen compound

ox'i·dize' *v.* unite with oxygen — **ox·i·da'tion** *n.*

ox'y·gen *n.* colorless gas, commonest chemical element

ox'y·gen·ate' *v.* treat or combine with oxygen

oys'ter *n.* edible mollusk with hinged shell

o'zone' *n.* form of oxygen with a strong odor

P

pa *n.* [Col.] father

pab'lum *n.* simplistic or tasteless writing, ideas, etc.

pace *n.* 1 a step or stride 2 rate of speed 3 gait —*v.* 1 to walk back and forth across 2 measure by paces 3 set the pace for

pace'mak'er *n.* 1 one leading the way: also **pace'set'ter** 2 electronic device placed in the body to regulate heart beat

pach'y·derm' (pak'ə-) *n.* large, thick-skinned animal

pa·cif'ic *a.* peaceful; calm

pac'i·fism' (pas'-) *n.* opposition to all war —**pac'i·fist** *n.*

pac'i·fy' *v.* **-fied', -fy'ing** make calm —**pac'i·fi·ca'tion** *n.* — **pac'i·fi'er** *n.*

pack *n.* 1 bundle of things 2 package of a set number 3 a group of animals, etc. —*v.* 1 put (things) in a box, bundle, etc. 2 crowd; cram 3 fill tightly 4 send (*off*)

pack'age *n.* packed thing —*v.* make a package of

pack'et *n.* small package

pact *n.* compact; agreement

pad *n.* 1 soft stuffing or cushion 2 sole of an animal's foot 3 water lily leaf 4 paper sheets fastened at one edge —*v.* **pad'ded, pad'ding** 1 stuff with material 2 walk softly

pad'dle *n.* 1 oar for a canoe 2 similar thing for games, etc. —*v.* 1 propel with a paddle 2 spank

pad'dock *n.* small enclosure for horses

pad'dy *n., pl.* **-dies** rice field

pad'lock' *n.* a lock with a U-shaped arm —*v.* fasten with a padlock

pae'an (pē'ən) *n.* song of joy

pa'gan *n., a.* heathen —**pa'gan·ism'** *n.*

page *n.* 1 one side of a leaf of a book, etc. 2 the leaf 3 boy attendant —*v.* 1 number the pages of 2 try to find (a person) by calling his or her name

pag·eant (paj′ənt) *n.* elaborate show, parade, play, etc. —**pag′eant·ry** *n.*

pag·i·na′tion (paj′-) *n.* numbering of pages

pa·go′da *n.* towerlike temple of the Orient

paid *v.* pt. & pp. of PAY

pail *n.* bucket —**pail′ful** *n.*

pain *n.* 1 hurt felt in body or mind 2 *pl.* great care —*v.* cause pain to —**pain′ful** *a.* —**pain′less** *a.*

pains′tak′ing *a.* careful

paint *n.* pigment mixed with oil, water, etc. —*v.* 1 make pictures (of) with paint 2 cover with paint —**paint′er** *n.* —**paint′ing** *n.*

pair *n.* two things, persons, etc. that match or make a unit —*v.* form pairs (of)

pais′ley (pāz′-) *a.* [*also* P-] having a complex pattern of swirls, etc.

pa·ja′mas (-jä′məz, -jam′əz) *n.pl.* matching trousers and top for sleeping

pal *n.* [Col.] close friend

pal′ace (-əs) *n.* 1 monarch's residence 2 magnificent building —**pa·la′tial** (-shəl) *a.*

pal′at·a·ble *a.* pleasing to the taste

pal′ate (-ət) *n.* 1 roof of the mouth 2 taste

pale *a.* 1 white; colorless 2 not bright or intense —*v.* 1 pointed fence stake 2 boundary —*v.* turn pale

pa·le·on·tol′o·gy *n.* study of fossils —**pa·le·on·tol′o·gist** *n.*

pal′ette (-ət) *n.* thin board on which artists mix paint

pal·i·sade′ (pal′ə sād′) *n.* 1 fence of large pointed stakes for fortification 2 *pl.* steep cliffs

pall (pôl) *v.* **palled, pall′ing** become boring —*n.* dark covering as for a coffin

pall′bear′er *n.* bearer of a coffin at a funeral

pal′let *n.* straw bed

pal′li·ate′ *v.* 1 relieve; ease 2 make seem less serious —**pal′li·a′tion** *n.* —**pal′li·a′tive** *a.*, *n.*

pal′lid *a.* pale —**pal′lor** *n.*

palm (päm) *n.* 1 tall tropical tree topped with a bunch of huge leaves 2 its leaf: symbol of victory 3 inside of the hand —**palm off** [Col.] get rid of, sell, etc. by fraud

pal·met′to *n., pl.* **-tos** or **-toes** small palm tree

palm′is·try *n.* fortunetelling from the lines, etc. on a person's palm —**palm′ist** *n.*

palm′y *a.* **-i·er, -i·est** prosperous

pal·o·mi′no (-mē′-) *n., pl.* **-nos** pale-yellow horse with white mane and tail

pal′pa·ble *a.* 1 that can be touched, felt, etc. 2 obvious —**pal′pa·bly** *adv.*

pal′pi·tate′ *v.* to throb —**pal′pi·ta′tion** *n.*

pal′sy (pôl′zē) *n.* paralysis in part of the body, often with tremors —**pal′sied** *a.*

pal′try (pôl′trē) *a.* **-tri·er, -tri·est** trifling; petty

pam′pas (pam′pəz) *n.pl.* treeless plains of Argentina

pam′per *v.* to be overindulgent with

pam′phlet (-flət) *n.* a thin, unbound booklet

pan *n.* broad, shallow container used in cooking, etc. —*v.* **panned, pan′ning** 1 move camera to view a panorama 2 [Col.] criticize adversely —**pan out** [Col.] turn out (well)

pan- *pref.* all; of all

pan·a·ce′a (-sē′-) *n.* supposed remedy for all diseases or problems

pa·nache′ (-nash′) *n.* dashing, elegant manner or style

pan′cake′ *n.* thin cake of batter fried in a pan

pan′cre·as (-krē əs) *n.* gland that secretes a digestive juice —**pan′cre·at′ic** *a.*

pan′da *n.* white-and-black, bearlike animal of Asia

pan·dem′ic *n., a.* (disease) that is epidemic in a large area

pan·de·mo′ni·um *n.* wild disorder or noise

pan′der *v.* 1 act as a pimp 2 help others satisfy their desires —*n.* pimp

pane *n.* sheet of glass

pan·e·gyr′ic (-jir′-) *n.* speech or writing of praise

pan′el *n.* 1 flat section set off on a wall, door, etc. 2 group chosen for judging, discussing, etc. —*v.* provide with panels —**pan′el·ing** *n.* —**pan′el·ist** *n.*

pang *n.* sudden, sharp pain

pan′han′dle *v.* [Col.] beg on the streets

pan′ic *n.* sudden, wild fear —*v.* **-icked, -ick·ing** fill with panic —**pan′ick·y** *a.*

pan′ic-strick′en *a.* badly frightened

pan′o·ply (-plē) *n., pl.* **-plies** 1 suit of armor 2 splendid display

pan′o·ram′a *n.* 1 unlimited view 2 constantly changing scene —**pan′o·ram′ic** *a.*

pan′sy (-zē) *n., pl.* **-sies** small plant with velvety petals

pant *v.* 1 breathe in pants 2 long (*for*) 3 gasp out —*n.* rapid, heavy breath

pan′ta·loons′ *n.pl.* trousers

pan′the·on′ *n.* temple for all the gods

pan′ther *n.* 1 cougar 2 jaguar 3 leopard

pant′ies *n.pl.* women's or children's short underpants

pan′to·mime′ *v., n.* (make) use of gestures without words to present a play

pan′try *n., pl.* **-tries** a room for food, pots, etc.

pants *n.pl.* trousers

pant′y·hose′ *n.* women's hose joined and extending to the waist: also **pant′y hose**

pap *n.* soft food

pa′pa *n.* father: child's word

pa′pa·cy (pā′-) *n.* position, authority, etc. of the Pope

pa′pal *a.* of the Pope or the papacy

pa·paw′ (pô′pô′) *n.* tree with yellow fruit

pa·pa·ya (pə pī′ə) *n.* tropical palmlike tree with large, orange fruit

pa′per *n.* 1 thin material in sheets, used to write or print on, wrap, etc. 2 sheet of this 3 essay 4 newspaper 5 wallpaper 6 *pl.* credentials —*a.* of or like paper —*v.* cover with wallpaper —**pa′per·y** *a.*

pa′per·back′ *n.* book bound in paper

pa′per·boy′ *n.* boy who sells or delivers newspapers —**pa′per·girl′** *n.fem.*

pa′pier-mâ·ché′ (-pər mə shā′) *n.* wet paper pulp, molded into various objects

pa·poose′ *n.* North American Indian baby

pa·pri·ka (-prē′-) *n.* ground, mild, red seasoning

Pap test *n.* test for uterine cancer

pa·py′rus *n.* 1 paper made by ancient Egyptians from a water plant 2 this plant

par *n.* 1 equal rank 2 average 3 face value of stocks, etc. 4 expert score in golf

par- *pref.* 1 beside; beyond 2 helping; secondary

par′a·ble *n.* short, simple story with a moral

pa·rab′o·la *n.* curve formed when a cone is sliced parallel to its side

par′a·chute′ *n.* umbrellalike device used to slow down a person or thing dropping from an aircraft —*v.* drop by parachute —**par′a·chut′ist** *n.*

pa·rade′ *n.* 1 showy display 2 march or procession —*v.* 1 march in a parade 2 show off

par′a·digm′ (-dīm′) *n.* example

par′a·dise′ *n.* place or state of great happiness —[P-] heaven

par′a·dox′ *n.* contradictory statement that is or seems false —**par′a·dox′i·cal** *a.*

par′af·fin′ *n.* white, waxy substance used for making candles, sealing jars, etc.

par′a·gon′ *n.* model of perfection or excellence

par′a·graph′ *n.* distinct section of a piece of writing, begun on a new line and often indented

par′a·keet′ *n.* small parrot

par′a·le′gal *a., n.* (of) a lawyer's assistant

par′al·lel′ *a.* 1 in the same direction and at a fixed distance apart 2 similar —*n.* 1 parallel line, surface, etc. 2 one like another 3 imaginary line parallel to the equator, representing degrees of latitude —*v.* be parallel with

par′al·lel′o·gram′ *n.* four-sided figure with opposite sides parallel and equal

pa·ral′y·sis *n.* 1 loss of power to move any part of the body 2 crippling —**par′a·lyt′ic** (-lit′-) *a., n.*

par′a·lyze′ (-līz′) *v.* 1 to cause paralysis in 2 to make ineffective

pa·ram′e·ter *n.* boundary or limit

par′a·mount′ *a.* supreme

par′a·mour′ (-moor′) *n.* illicit lover or mistress

par′a·noi′a *n.* mental illness of feeling persecuted —**par′a·noid′** *a., n.*

par′a·pet′ *n.* wall for protection from enemy fire

par′a·pher·na′li·a *n.pl.* [*sing.* or *pl. v.*] belongings or equipment

par′a·phrase′ *n.* rewording —*v.* reword

par′a·ple′gi·a (-plē′jē ə, -jə) *n.*

paralysis of the lower body — **par′a·ple′gic** *a., n.*

par′a·pro·fes′sion·al *n.* worker trained to assist a professional

par′a·site *n.* plant or animal that lives on or in another — **par′a·sit′ic** *a.*

par′a·sol (-sôl′) *n.* light umbrella used as a sunshade

par′a·troops′ *n.pl.* unit of soldiers trained to parachute from airplanes behind enemy lines — **par′a·troop′er** *n.*

par′boil *v.* boil until partly cooked

par′cel (-səl) *n.* **1** package **2** piece (of land) — *v.* apportion: with *out*

parcel post *n.* postal branch which delivers parcels

parch *v.* **1** make hot and dry **2** make thirsty

parch′ment *n.* **1** skin of a sheep, etc. prepared as a surface for writing **2** paper resembling this

par′don *v.* **1** to release from punishment **2** excuse; forgive — *n.* act of pardoning — **par′don·a·ble** *a.*

pare *v.* **1** peel **2** reduce gradually

par′e·gor′ic *n.* medicine with opium, for diarrhea, etc.

par′ent *n.* **1** father or mother **2** source — **pa·ren′tal** *a.* — **par′ent·hood′** *n.* — **par′ent·ing** *n.*

par′ent·age *n.* descent from parents or ancestors

pa·ren′the·sis *n., pl.* **-ses′** (-sēz′) **1** word of explanation put into a sentence **2** either of the marks ( ) used to set this off — **paren·thet′i·cal, par′en·thet′ic** *a.*

par·fait′ (-fā′) *n.* ice cream dessert in a tall glass

pa·ri′ah (-rī′ə) *n.* outcast

par′ing (per′-) *n.* strip peeled off

par′ish *n.* **1** part of a diocese under a priest, etc. **2** church congregation

pa·rish′ion·er *n.* member of a parish

par′i·ty *n., pl.* **-ties** equality of value at a given ratio between moneys, commodities, etc.

park *n.* public land for recreation or rest — *v.* leave (a vehicle) temporarily

par′ka *n.* hooded coat

Par′kin·son′s disease *n.* disease causing tremors

park′way′ *n.* broad road lined with trees

par′lance *n.* mode of speech

par′lay *v.* **1** bet (wager plus winnings from one race, etc.) on another **2** exploit (an asset) successfully — *n.* bet or bets made by parlaying

par′ley (-lē) *v., n.* talk to settle differences, etc.

par′lia·ment (-lə-) *n.* legislative body, spec. [**P-**] of Great Britain, Canada, etc. — **par′lia·men′ta·ry** *a.*

par′lor *n.* **1** living room **2** business establishment, as a shop where hair is styled

pa·ro′chi·al (-kē əl) *a.* **1** of a parish **2** limited; narrow

par′o·dy *v.* **-died, -dy·ing;** *n., pl.* **-dies** (write) a farcical imitation of a work

pa·role′ *v., n.* release from prison on condition of future good behavior

pa·rol′ee′ *n.* one on parole

par′ox·ysm′ (-əks iz′əm) *n.* spasm or outburst

par·quet′ (-kā′) *n.* flooring of parquetry

par′quet·ry (-kə trē) *n.* inlaid flooring of geometric forms

par′rot *n.* brightly colored bird that can imitate speech — *v.* repeat or copy without full understanding

par′ry *v.* **-ried, -ry·ing 1** ward off **2** evade

parse *v.* analyze (a sentence) grammatically

par′si·mo′ny *n.* stinginess — **par′si·mo′ni·ous** *a.*

pars′ley *n.* plant with leaves used to flavor some foods

pars′nip′ *n.* sweet white root used as a vegetable

par′son *n.* minister or clergyman

par′son·age *n.* parson's dwelling, provided by the church

part *n.* **1** portion, piece, element, etc. **2** duty **3** role **4** music for a certain voice or instrument in a composition **5** *usually pl.* region **6** dividing line formed in combing the hair — *v.* **1** divide; separate **2** go away from each other — *a.* less than whole — **part with** give up — **take part** participate

par·take′ *v.* **-took′, -tak′en, -tak′ing 1** participate (in) **2** eat or drink (of)

par′tial (-shəl) *a.* **1** favoring one over another **2** not complete — **partial to** fond of — **par′ti·al′i·ty** (-shē al′-) *n.* — **par′tial·ly** *adv.*

par·tic′i·pate′ (-tis′-) *v.* have or take a share with others (in) — **par·tic′i·pant** *n.* — **par·tic′i·pa′tion** *n.*

par·ti·ci·ple n. verb form having the qualities of both a verb and adjective

par·ti·cle n. 1 tiny fragment of matter 2 preposition, article, or conjunction

par·tic·u·lar a. 1 of one; individual 2 specific 3 hard to please —n. a detail —**par·tic·u·lar·ly** adv.

part'ing a., n. 1 dividing 2 departing

par·ti·san n. 1 strong supporter; adherent 2 guerrilla —a. of a partisan

par·ti·tion (-tish'ən) n. 1 division into parts 2 thing that divides —v. divide into parts

part'ly adv. not fully

part'ner n. one who undertakes something with another; associate; mate —**part'ner·ship** n.

part of speech n. class of word, as noun, verb, etc.

par'tridge n. game bird, as the pheasant, quail, etc.

part time n. part of the usual time —**part'-time'** a.

par·tu·ri·tion (-rish'ən) n. childbirth

par'ty n., pl. **-ties** 1 group working together for a political cause, etc. 2 social gathering 3 one involved in a lawsuit, crime, etc. 4 [Col.] person —v. **-tied, -ty·ing** take part in social activity, esp. boisterously

pas'chal (-kal) a. of the Passover or Easter

pass v. 1 go by, beyond, etc. 2 go or change from one form, place, etc. to another 3 cease; end 4 approve or be approved 5 take a test, etc. successfully 6 cause or allow to go, move, qualify, etc. 7 throw 8 spend time 9 happen 10 give as an opinion, judgment, etc. —n. 1 a passing 2 free ticket 3 brief military leave 4 PASSAGE (n. 4) —**pass'a·ble** a.

pas'sage n. 1 a passing 2 right to pass 3 voyage 4 road, opening, etc. 5 part of something written

pas'sage·way' n. narrow way, as a hall, alley, etc.

pass'book' n. booklet recording depositor's bank account

pas·sé (pa sā') a. out-of-date

pas'sen·ger n. one traveling in a train, car, etc.

pass'er-by' n., pl. **pass'ers·by'** one who passes by

pass'ing a. 1 that passes 2 cas-

ual —**in passing** incidentally

pas'sion n. 1 strong emotion, as hate, love, etc. 2 an object of strong desire —**pas'sion·ate** a.

pas'sive a. 1 inactive, but acted upon 2 yielding; submissive —**pas·siv'i·ty** n.

pass'key' n. key that fits a number of locks

Pass'o'ver n. Jewish holiday in the spring

pass'port' n. government document identifying a citizen traveling abroad

pass'word' n. secret word given to pass a guard

past a. 1 gone by 2 of a former time —n. 1 history 2 time gone by —prep. beyond in time, space, etc. —adv. to and beyond

pas'ta (päs'-) n. spaghetti, macaroni, etc.

paste n. 1 moist, smooth mixture 2 adhesive mixture with flour, water, etc. —v. make adhere, as with paste

paste'board' n. stiff material of pasted layers of paper

pas·tel' a., n. soft and pale (shade)

pas'teur·ize' (-chər-, -tər-) v. kill bacteria (in milk, etc.) by heating —**pas'teur·i·za'tion** n.

pas·tiche' (-tēsh') n. artistic composition made up of bits from several sources

pas'time' n. way to spend spare time

pas'tor n. clergyman in charge of a congregation

pas'to·ral a. 1 of a pastor 2 simple and rustic

pas·tra'mi (pə strä') n. spiced, smoked beef

pas'try (pās'-) n., pl. **-tries** fancy baked goods

pas'ture n. ground for grazing: also **pas'tur·age** —v. let (cattle) graze

past'y a. **-i·er, -i·est** of or like paste

pat n. 1 gentle tap with something flat 2 small lump, as of butter —v. **pat'ted, pat'ting** give a gentle pat to —a. suitable

patch n. 1 piece of material used to mend a hole, etc. 2 spot —v. 1 put a patch on 2 to make crudely

patch'work' n. quilt made of odd patches of cloth

pate (pāt) n. top of the head

pâ·té (pä tā') n. meat paste or spread

pa·tel'la n., pl. **-las** or **-lae** (-ē)

kneecap

pat'ent (pat'-; *a.* 2: pāt'-) *n.* document granting exclusive rights over an invention —*a.* 1 protected by patent 2 obvious —*v.* get a patent for

pat'ent leather (pat'-) *n.* leather with a hard, glossy finish

pa·ter'nal *a.* 1 fatherly 2 on the father's side —**pa·ter'nal·ism'** *n.* —**pa·ter'nal·is'tic** *a.*

pa·ter'ni·ty *n.* fatherhood

path *n.* 1 way worn by footsteps 2 line of movement 3 course of conduct

pa·thet'ic *a.* arousing pity —**pa·thet'i·cal·ly** *adv.*

pa·thol'o·gy *n.* study of the nature and effect of disease —**path'o·log'i·cal** *a.* —**pa·thol'o·gist** *n.*

pa·thos (pā'thäs') *n.* the quality in a thing which arouses pity

path'way' *n.* path

pa'tient (-shant) *a.* 1 enduring pain, delay, etc. without complaint 2 persevering —*n.* one receiving medical care —**pa'tience** *n.* —**pa'tient·ly** *adv.*

pat'i·na *n.* green oxidized coating on bronze or copper

pa'ti·o' *n., pl.* -os' 1 courtyard 2 paved lounging area next to house

pa·tri·arch' (-ärk') *n.* 1 father and head of a family or tribe 2 dignified old man —**pa'tri·ar'chal** *a.*

pa·tri'cian (-trish'ən) *a., n.* aristocratic (person)

pat'ri·mo'ny *n.* inheritance from one's father

pa'tri·ot *n.* one who shows love and loyalty for his or her country —**pa'tri·ot'ic** *a.* —**pa'tri·ot·ism'** *n.*

pa·trol' *v.* -trolled', -trol'ling make trips around in guarding —*n.* a patrolling, or a group that patrols

pa·trol'man *n., pl.* -men policeman who patrols a certain area

pa'tron *n.* 1 a sponsor 2 regular customer

pa'tron·age *n.* 1 help given by a patron 2 customers, or their trade 3 political favors

pa'tron·ize' *v.* 1 sponsor 2 be condescending to 3 be a regular customer of

pat'ter *n.* 1 series of rapid taps 2 glib talk —*v.* make or utter (a) patter

pat'tern *n.* 1 one worthy of imitation 2 plan used in making

things 3 design or decoration 4 usual behavior, procedure, etc. —*v.* copy as from a pattern

pat'ty *n., pl.* -ties flat cake of ground meat, etc.

pau'ci·ty (pô'-) *n.* 1 fewness 2 scarcity

paunch *n.* fat belly

pau'per *n.* very poor person

pause *v., n.* (make a) temporary stop

pave *v.* surface (a road, etc.), as with asphalt

pave'ment *n.* paved road, sidewalk, etc.

pa·vil'ion (-yan) *n.* 1 large tent 2 building for exhibits, etc., as at a fair

paw *n.* foot of an animal with claws —*v.* 1 to touch, etc. with paws or feet 2 handle roughly

pawl *n.* a catch for the teeth of a ratchet wheel

pawn *v.* give as security for a loan —*n.* 1 chessman of lowest value 2 person who is subject to another's will

pawn'bro'ker *n.* one licensed to lend money on things pawned —**pawn'shop'** *n.*

pay *v.* **paid, pay'ing** 1 give (money) to (one) for goods or services 2 settle, as a debt 3 give, as a compliment 4 make, as a visit 5 be profitable (to) —*n.* wages —*a.* operated by coins, etc. —**pay out** *pt.* **payed** out let out, as a rope —**pay'ee** *n.* —**pay'er** *n.* —**pay'ment** *n.*

pay'a·ble *a.* 1 that can be paid 2 due to be paid

pay'check' *n.* check in payment of wages or salary

pay'load' *n.* load carried by an aircraft, missile, etc.

pay'mas·ter *n.* official in charge of paying employees

pay'off' *n.* 1 reckoning or payment 2 [Col.] bribe

pay'roll' *n.* 1 list of employees to be paid 2 amount due them

PC *n.* personal computer, or microcomputer

pea *n.* plant with pods having round, edible seeds

peace *n.* 1 freedom from war or strife 2 agreement to end war 3 law and order 4 calm —**peace'a·ble** *a.*

peace'ful *a.* 1 not fighting 2 calm of a time of peace —**peace'ful·ly** *adv.*

peach *n.* round, juicy, orange-yellow fruit

pea'cock' *n.* male of a large bird

(pea'fowl'), with a long showy tail —**pea'hen'** n.fem.

peak n. 1 pointed end or top 2 mountain with pointed summit 3 highest point —v. come or bring to a peak

peak'ed a. thin and drawn

peal n. 1 loud ringing of bell(s) 2 loud, prolonged sound —v. to ring; resound

pea'nut' n. 1 vine with underground pods and edible seeds 2 the pod or a seed

pear n. soft, juicy fruit

pearl (purl) n. 1 smooth, roundish stone formed in oysters, used as a gem 2 mother-of-pearl 3 bluish gray —**pearl'y** a., **-i·er**, **-i·est**

peas'ant (pez'-) n. farm worker of Europe, etc. —**peas'ant·ry** n.

peat n. decayed plant matter in bogs, dried for fuel

peb'ble n. small, smooth stone —**peb'bly** a., **-bli·er**, **-bli·est**

pe·can' n. edible nut with a thin, smooth shell

pec·ca·dil'lo n., pl. **-loes** or **-los** minor or petty sin

pec'ca·ry n., pl. **-ries** wild piglike animal with tusks

peck v. strike as with a beak —n. 1 stroke made as with a beak 2 dry measure equal to 8 quarts

pec'tin n. substance in some fruits causing jelly to form

pec'to·ral a. of the chest

pe·cu'liar (-kyōōl'yər) a. 1 of only one; exclusive 2 special 3 odd —**pe·cu'li·ar'i·ty** (-er'-) n., pl. **-ties**

pe·cu'ni·ar'y (-kyōō'nē-) a. of money

ped'a·gogue', ped'a·gog' (-gäg') n. teacher —**ped'a·gog'y** (-gä'jē) n. —**ped'a·gog'ic** a. —**ped'a·gog'i·cal** a.

ped'al n. lever worked by the foot —v. work by pedals —a. of the foot

ped'ant n. one who stresses trivial points of learning —**pe·dan'tic** a. —**ped'ant·ry** n.

ped'dle v. go from place to place selling —**ped'dler** n.

ped'es·tal n. base, as of a column, statue, etc.

pe·des'tri·an a. 1 going on foot 2 dull and ordinary —n. one who goes on foot

pe·di·at'rics n. medical care and treatment of babies and children —**pe·di·a·tri'cian** (-trish'ən) n.

ped'i·cure' n. a trimming, polishing, etc. of the toenails

ped'i·gree' n. ancestry; descent —**ped'i·greed'** a.

pe·dom'e·ter n. device measuring a distance walked

peek v. glance quickly and furtively —n. glance

peel v. 1 cut away (the rind, etc.) of 2 shed skin, bark, etc. 3 come off in layers or flakes —n. rind or skin of fruit

peel'ing n. rind peeled off

peep v. 1 make the chirping cry of a young bird 2 look through a small opening 3 peek 4 appear partially —n. 1 peeping sound 2 furtive glimpse —**peep'hole'** n.

peer n. 1 an equal 2 British noble —v. look closely —**peer'age** n.

peer'less a. without equal

peeve [Col.] v. make peevish —n. annoyance

pee'vish a. irritable

pee'wee' n. [Col.] something very small

peg n. 1 short pin or bolt 2 step or degree —v. pegged, peg'ging fix or mark as with pegs

pe·jo'ra·tive a. derogatory

Pe'king·ese' (-ka nēz') n., pl. **-ese'** small dog with pug nose: also **Pe'kin·ese'**

pe'koe n. a black tea

pel'i·can n. water bird with a pouch in its lower bill

pel·la'gra (-lā'-) n. a disease caused by vitamin deficiency

pel'let n. little ball

pell'-mell', pell'mell' adv. in reckless haste

pel·lu'cid (-lōō'-) a. clear

pelt v. 1 throw things at 2 beat steadily —n. skin of a fur-bearing animal

pel'vis n. cavity formed by bones of the hip and part of the backbone —**pel'vic** a.

pem'mi·can n. dried food concentrate

pen n. 1 enclosure for animals 2 device for writing with ink 3 [Sl.] penitentiary —v. penned, pent, pen'ning 1 enclose as in a pen 2 write with a pen

pe'nal a. of or as punishment

pe'nal·ize' (or pen'al-) v. punish

pen'al·ty n., pl. **-ties** 1 punishment 2 handicap

pen'ance n. voluntary suffering to show repentance

pence [Br.] pl. of PENNY (n. 2)

pen'chant n. strong liking

pen'cil n. device with a core of

graphite, etc. for writing, etc. —
v. write with a pencil

pend v. await decision

pend'ant n. hanging object used as an ornament

pend'ent a. suspended

pend'ing a. not decided —*prep.* 1 during 2 until

pen'du·lous (-jə ləs, -dyə-) a. hanging freely

pen'du·lum n. weight hung so as to swing freely

pen'e·trate' v. 1 enter by piercing 2 to affect throughout 3 understand —**pen'e·tra·ble** a. —**pen'e·tra'tion** n.

pen'guin (-gwin) n. flightless bird of the antarctic

pen'i·cil'lin n. antibiotic drug obtained from a mold

pen·in'su·la n. land area almost surrounded by water —**pen·in'su·lar** a.

pe'nis n. male sex organ

pen'i·tent a. willing to atone — n. a penitent person —**pen'i·tence** n.

pen'i·ten'tia·ry (-shə rē) n., pl. -ries prison

pen'knife' n. small pocketknife

pen'man·ship' n. quality of handwriting

pen name n. pseudonym

pen'nant n. 1 long, narrow flag 2 championship

pen'ni·less a. very poor

pen'non n. flag or pennant

pen'ny n. pl. -nies cent 2 pl. **pence** Br. coin, $\frac{1}{100}$ pound (formerly, $\frac{1}{12}$ shilling)

pe·nol'o·gy n. study of prison management and reform

pen'sion n. regular payment to a retired or disabled person —v. pay a pension to

pen'sive (-siv) a. thoughtful; reflective

pent a. shut in; kept in: often with up

pen'ta·gon' n. figure with five angles and five sides

pen·tam'e·ter n. line of verse of five metrical feet

pent'house' n. apartment on the roof of a building

pent'-up' a. confined; checked

pe·nul'ti·mate a. next to last

pe·nu'ri·ous (pe nyoor'ē-) a. stingy

pen'u·ry n. extreme poverty

pe'on' n. Latin American worker —**pe'on·age** n.

pe'o·ny n., pl. -nies plant with large showy flowers

peo'ple (pē'-) n.pl. 1 human beings 2 a populace 3 one's family —n., pl. -ples a nation, race, etc. —v. populate

pep [Col.] n. energy; vigor —v. pepped, pep'ping fill with pep: with up —**pep'py** a., -pi·er, -pi·est

pep'per n. 1 plant with a red or green, hot or sweet pod 2 the pod 3 spicy seasoning made from berries (**pep·per·corns**) of a tropical plant —v. 1 season with pepper 2 pelt with small objects

pep'per·mint' n. mint plant yielding an oily flavoring

pep'per·o'ni n. highly spiced Italian sausage

pep'sin n. stomach enzyme that helps digest proteins

pep'tic a. of digestion

per prep. 1 by means of 2 for each

per·am'bu·late' v. walk through or over

per an'num a., adv. by the year

per·cale' (-kāl') n. cotton cloth used for sheets

per cap'i·ta a., adv. for each person

per·ceive' (-sēv') v. 1 grasp mentally 2 become aware (of) through the senses

per·cent' adv., a. out of every hundred: also **per cent** —n. [Col.] percentage

per·cent'age n. 1 rate per hundred 2 portion

per·cen'tile' n. any of 100 equal parts

per·cep'ti·ble a. that can be perceived

per·cep'tion n. 1 ability to perceive 2 knowledge got by perceiving —**per·cep'tu·al** (-chōo-) a.

per·cep'tive a. able to perceive readily

perch n. 1 small food fish 2 a pole or branch that birds roost on —v. rest on a perch

per'co·late' v. 1 filter 2 make in a percolator

per'co·la'tor n. pot in which boiling water filters through ground coffee

per·cus'sion (-kush'ən) n. 1 hitting of one thing against another 2 musical instruments played by striking, as drums — **per·cus'sion·ist** n.

per·di'tion (-dish'ən) n. 1 hell 2 loss of one's soul

per·emp'to·ry a. 1 overbearing 2 not to be refused

per·en·ni·al a. 1 lasting a year 2 living more than two years —n. plant living more than two years

per·fect (v.: pər fekt') a. 1 complete 2 excellent 3 completely accurate —v. make perfect —**per·fect·i·ble** a. —**per·fec·tion** n. —**per·fect·ly** adv.

per·fec·tion·ist n. one who strives for perfection

per·fi·dy n., pl. —**dies** treachery —**per·fid·i·ous** a.

per·fo·rate v. pierce with a hole or holes —**per·fo·ra·tion** n.

per·force' adv. necessarily

per·form' v. 1 do; carry out 2 act a role, play music, etc.

per·form'ance n. 1 a doing or thing done 2 display of one's skill or talent

per·fume' (or pur'fyoom') n. 1 scent with perfume —n. 1 fragrance 2 liquid with a pleasing odor

per·func·to·ry a. done without care or interest

per·haps' adv. possibly; probably

per·i·gee' (-jē') n. point nearest earth in a satellite's orbit

per·il n., n. (put in) danger or risk —**per·il·ous** a.

pe·rim·e·ter n. outer boundary of a figure or area

pe·ri·od n. 1 portion of time 2 mark of punctuation (.)

pe·ri·od·ic a. recurring at regular intervals

pe·ri·od·i·cal n. magazine published every week, month, etc. —a. periodic —**pe·ri·od·i·cal·ly** adv.

per·i·o·don·tal a. around a tooth and affecting the gums

per·i·pa·tet·ic a. moving or walking about; itinerant

pe·riph·er·y (-rif'-) n., pl. —**ies** outer boundary or part —**pe·riph·er·al** a.

per·i·scope n. tube with mirrors, etc., for seeing over or around an obstacle

per·ish v. be destroyed; die

per·ish·a·ble n., a. (food) liable to spoil

per·i·to·ni·tis (-nīt'is) n. inflammation of the membrane (**per·i·to·ne'um**) lining the abdominal cavity

per·i·win·kle n. MYRTLE (n. 2)

per·jure v. tell a lie while under oath —**per·jur·er** n. —**per·ju·ry** n., pl. —**ries**

perk v. 1 raise or liven (up) 2 make stylish or smart 3 [Col.] percolate —n. [Col.] perquisite

—**perk'y** a., -i·er, -i·est

perm [Col.] n. a permanent —v. give a permanent to

per'ma·frost n. permanently frozen subsoil

per'ma·nent a. lasting indefinitely —n. long-lasting hair wave —**per'ma·nence** n. —**per'ma·nent·ly** adv.

per'me·ate v. diffuse; penetrate (through or among) —**per·me·a·ble** a.

per·mis·si·ble a. allowable

per·mis·sion n. consent

per·mis·sive a. not restricting

per·mit' (n.: pur'mit) v. -mit'ted, -mit'ting allow —n. document giving permission

per·mu·ta·tion (-myoo-) n. a change, as in order

per·ni·cious (-nish'əs) a. very harmful or damaging

per·o·ra·tion n. last part or summation of a speech

per·ox·ide n. hydrogen peroxide

per·pen·dic·u·lar a. 1 at right angles to a given line or plane 2 vertical —n. perpendicular line

per·pe·trate v. do (something evil, wrong, etc.) —**per·pe·tra'tion** n. —**per·pe·tra·tor** n.

per·pet·u·al (-pech'-) a. 1 lasting forever 2 constant

per·pet·u·ate (-pech'-) v. cause to continue or be remembered —**per·pet·u·a'tion** n.

per·pe·tu·i·ty (-pə tōō'-) n. existence forever

per·plex' v. confuse or puzzle —**per·plex'i·ty** n., pl. —**ties**

per·qui·site (-kwi zit) n. privilege or profit incidental to one's employment

per se' (-sā') by (or in) itself

per'se·cute v. torment continuously for one's beliefs, etc. —**per·se·cu'tion** n. —**per'se·cu'tor** n.

per'se·vere' (-vir') v. to continue in spite of difficulty —**per·se·ver'ance** n.

Per'sian (-zhən) n. domestic cat with long, thick coat

per'si·flage (-fläzh) n. playful or joking talk

per·sim'mon n. an orange-red, plumlike fruit

per·sist' v. continue insistently or steadily —**per·sist'ent** a. —**per·sist'ence** n.

per'son n. 1 human being 2 the body or self 3 Gram. any of the three classes of pronouns indicating the identity of the subject, as I, you, he, etc.

-person *suf.* person (without regard to sex)

per·son·a·ble *a.* pleasing in looks and manner

per·son·age *n.* (important) person

per·son·al *a.* **1** private; individual **2** of the body **3** of the character, conduct, etc. of a person **4** indicating person in grammar **5** other than real estate: said of property —**per·son·al·ize** *v.* —**per·son·al·ly** *adv.*

personal computer *n.* microcomputer

per·son·al·i·ty *n., pl.* **-ties 1** distinctive or attractive character of a person **2** notable person

per·so'na non gra'ta (-grät'ə) *a.* [L.] unwelcome person

per·son·i·fy *v.* **-fied', -fy'ing 1** represent as a person **2** typify —**per·son·i·fi·ca'tion** *n.*

per·son·nel' *n.* persons employed in any work, etc.

per·spec'tive *n.* **1** appearance of objects from their relative distance and positions **2** sense of proportion

per·spi·ca'cious *a.* having keen insight

per·spire' *v.* to sweat —**per·spi·ra'tion** *n.*

per·suade' *v.* to cause to do or believe by urging, etc. —**per·sua'sive** *a.*

per·sua'sion *n.* **1** a persuading **2** belief

pert *a.* saucy; impudent

per·tain' *v.* **1** belong **2** have reference

per·ti·na'cious (-nā'shəs) *a.* persistent —**per·ti·nac'i·ty** (-nas'-) *n.*

per'ti·nent *a.* relevant; to the point —**per'ti·nence** *n.*

per·turb' *v.* alarm; upset

pe·ruse' (-rōōz') *v.* read —**pe·rus'al** *n.*

per·vade' *v.* spread or be prevalent throughout —**per·va'sive** *a.*

per·verse' *a.* **1** stubbornly contrary **2** erring **3** wicked —**per·ver'si·ty** *n., pl.* **-ties**

per·vert' (*n.:* pur'vurt) *v.* lead astray; corrupt —*n.* one who engages in abnormal sexual acts —**per·ver'sion** *n.*

pes'ky *a.* **-ki·er, -ki·est** [Col.] annoying

pe'so (pā'-) *n., pl.* **-sos** monetary unit of Mexico, Cuba, etc.

pes'si·mism' *n.* tendency to expect the worst —**pes'si·mist** *n.* —**pes'si·mis'tic** *a.*

pest *n.* person or thing that causes trouble, etc.

pes'ter *v.* annoy; vex

pes'ti·cide' *n.* chemical for killing insects, weeds, etc.

pes'ti·lence *n.* virulent or contagious disease —**pes'ti·lent** *a.*

pes·tle (-əl, -tal) *n.* tool used to pound or grind substances

pet *n.* **1** domesticated animal treated fondly **2** favorite **3** bad humor —*v.* **pet'ted, pet'ting** stroke gently

pet'al *n.* leaflike part of a blossom

pet'cock' *n.* small valve for draining pipes, etc.

pe·tite' (-tēt') *a.* small and trim in figure

pe·ti'tion *n.* solemn, earnest request, esp. in writing —*v.* address a petition to

pet'rel *n.* small sea bird

pet'ri·fy *v.* **-fied', -fy'ing 1** change into stony substance **2** stun, as with fear

pet'rol *n.* [Br.] gasoline

pe·tro·la'tum *n.* greasy, jellylike substance used for ointments: also petroleum jelly

pe·tro'le·um *n.* oily liquid found in rock strata: it yields kerosene, gasoline, etc.

pet'ti·coat' *n.* skirt worn under an outer skirt

pet'ty *a.* **-ti·er, -ti·est 1** of little importance **2** narrow-minded **3** low in rank

pet'u·lant (pech'ə-) *a.* impatient or irritable —**pet'u·lance** *n.*

pe·tu'ni·a (-tōōn'yə) *n.* plant with funnel-shaped flowers

pew (pyōō) *n.* row of fixed benches in a church

pew'ter *n.* alloy of tin with lead, brass, or copper

pha'e·ton (fā'-) *n.* light, four-wheeled carriage

pha'lanx *n.* massed group of individuals

phal'lus *n.* image of the penis —**phal'lic** *a.*

phan'tom *n.* **1** ghost; specter **2** illusion —*a.* unreal

Phar·aoh (far'ō) *n.* title of ancient Egyptian rulers

phar'i·see' (far'-) *n.* self-righteous person

phar·ma·ceu'ti·cal (fär'mə sōō'-) *a.* **1** of pharmacy **2** of or by drugs —*n.* a drug or medicine

phar'ma·cist *n.* one whose profession is pharmacy

phar·ma·col'o·gy *n.* study of drugs —**phar'ma·col'o·gist** *n.*

phar·ma·cy n., pl. **-cies 1** science of preparing drugs and medicines **2** drugstore

phar·yn·gi·tis (far'in jīt'is) n. inflammation of the pharynx; sore throat

phar·ynx (-iŋks) n. cavity between mouth and larynx

phase n. **1** aspect; side **2** one of a series of changes

phase'out' n. gradual withdrawal

pheas·ant (fez'-) n. game bird with a long tail

phe·no·bar·bi·tal' n. white compound used as a sedative

phe·nom'e·non n., pl. **-na 1** observable fact or event **2** anything very unusual **—phe·nom'e·nal** a.

phi'al (fī'-) n. vial

phi·lan'der (fi-) v. make love insincerely **—phi·lan'der·er** n.

phi·lan'thro·py n. **1** desire to help mankind **2** pl. **-pies** thing done to help mankind **—phil'an·throp'ic** a. **—phi·lan'thro·pist** n.

phi·lat'e·ly n. collection and study of postage stamps **—phi·lat'e·list** n.

phi·lis·tine (fil'i stēn') n. one who is smugly conventional

phil'o·den'dron n. tropical American climbing plant

phi·los'o·pher n. one learned in philosophy

phi·los'o·phize' v. to reason like a philosopher

phi·los'o·phy n. **1** study of ultimate reality, ethics, etc. **2** pl. **-phies** system of principles **3** mental calmness **—phil'o·soph'ic, phil'o·soph'i·cal** a.

phle·bi·tis (fli bīt'is) n. inflammation of a vein

phlegm (flem) n. mucus in the throat, as during a cold

phleg·mat'ic (fleg-) a. sluggish, unexcitable, etc.

phlox (fläks) n. plant with clusters of flowers

pho·bi·a n. irrational, persistent fear of something

phoe·be (fē'bē) n. small bird

phoe'nix Egyptian myth. immortal bird

phone n., v. [Col.] telephone

pho'neme' n. a set of speech sounds heard as one sound

pho·net'ics n. science of speech sounds and the written representation of them **—pho·net'ic** a.

phon'ics n. phonetic method of teaching reading

pho'no·graph' n. instrument that reproduces sound from grooved records

pho'ny a., n. **-ni·er, -ni·est** [Col.] fake

phos'phate' n. **1** salt of phosphoric acid **2** fertilizer containing phosphates

phos'pho·res'cent a. giving off light without heat **—phos'pho·res'cence** n.

phos'pho·rus n. phosphorescent, waxy chemical element **—phos·phor'ic, phos'pho·rous** a.

pho'to n., pl. **-tos** photograph

pho'to·cop'y n., pl. **-ies** copy made by photographic device (pho'to·cop'i·er)

pho'to·e·lec'tric a. of the electric effects produced by light on some substances

pho'to·en·grav'ing n. reproduction of photographs in relief on printing plates **—pho'to·en·grav'er** n.

pho'to·gen'ic (-jen'-) a. attractive to photograph

pho'to·graph' n. picture made by photography **—v.** take a photograph of **—pho·tog'ra·pher** n.

pho·tog'ra·phy n. process of producing images on a surface sensitive to light **—pho'to·graph'ic** a.

pho'ton' n. unit of light or energy

Pho'to·stat' trademark device for making photographic copies of printed matter, etc. **—n.** [p-] copy so made **—v.** [p-] make a photostat of **—pho'to·stat'ic** a.

pho'to·syn'the·sis (-sin'-) n. formation of carbohydrates in plants by the action of sunlight

phrase n. **1** a short, colorful expression **2** group of words, not a sentence or clause, conveying a single idea **—v.** express in words

phra'se·ol'o·gy n. wording

phy'lum (fī'-) n., pl. **-la** basic division of plants or animals

phys'ic (fiz'-) n. cathartic

phys'i·cal adv. **1** of matter **2** of physics **3** of the body **—n.** physical examination **—phys'i·cal·ly** adv.

physical therapy n. treatment of disease by massage, exercise, etc.

phy·si'cian (-zish'ən) n. doctor of medicine

phys'ics n. science that deals with matter and energy **—phys'i·cist** n.

phys'i·og'no·my n., pl. **-mies** the face

phys'i·ol'o·gy n. science of the functions of living organisms — **phys'i·o·log'i·cal** a. —**phys'i·ol'o·gist** n.

phys'i·o·ther'a·py n. physical therapy

phy·sique' (-zēk') n. form or build of the body

pi (pī) n. symbol (π) for the ratio of circumference to diameter, about 3.1416

pi'a·nis·si·mo' (pē'-) a., adv. Mus. very soft

pi'an·ist (or pē·an'ist) n. piano player

pi·an'o (a., adv.: -än'-) n., pl. **-nos** keyboard instrument with hammers that strike steel wires: also **pi·an'o·forte'** —a., adv. Mus. soft

pi·az·za (pē·ät'sə, n. 2: -az'ə) n. 1 in Italy, a public square 2 veranda

pi'ca (pī'-) n. size of printing type

pic'a·resque' (-resk'-) a. of adventurous vagabonds

pic'a·yune' a. trivial

pic·ca·lil'li n. relish of vegetables, mustard, etc.

pic·co·lo' n., pl. **-los** small flute

pick v. 1 scratch or dig at with something pointed 2 gather, pluck, etc. 3 choose; select 4 provoke (a fight) —n. 1 choice 2 the best 3 pointed tool for breaking up soil, etc. 4 plectrum —**pick at** eat sparingly — **pick on** [Col.] criticize; tease — **pick out** choose —**pick up** 1 lift 2 get, find, etc. 3 gain (speed) 4 improve —**pick'er** n.

pick'ax', pick'axe' n. pick with one end of the head pointed, the other axlike

pick'er·el n. fish with a narrow, pointed snout

pick'et n. 1 pointed stake 2 soldier(s) on guard duty 3 striking union member, etc. stationed outside a factory, etc. — v. place or be a picket at

pick'ings n.pl. scraps

pick'le v. preserve in vinegar, brine, etc. —n. cucumber, etc. so preserved

pick'pock'et n. one who steals from pockets

pick'up' n. 1 power of speeding up 2 small truck

pick'y a. **-i·er, -i·est** [Col.] very fussy

pic'nic n. outing with an outdoor meal —v. **-nicked, -nick·ing** to hold a picnic —**pic'nick·er** n.

pic·to'ri·al a. of or expressed in pictures

pic'ture n. 1 likeness made by painting, photography, etc. 2 description 3 a FILM (n. 3) —v. 1 make a picture of 2 describe 3 imagine

pic'tur·esque' (-esk') a. 1 having natural beauty 2 quaint 3 vivid

pid'dle v. dawdle; trifle

pid'dling a. insignificant

pid'dly a. piddling

pidg'in English (pij'-) n. mixture of English and Chinese

pie n. fruit, meat, etc. baked on or in a crust

pie'bald' a. covered with patches of two colors

piece n. 1 part broken off or separated 2 part complete in itself 3 single thing —v. join (together) the pieces of

piece'meal' a., adv. (made or done) piece by piece

piece'work' n. work which one is paid for by the piece

pier (pir) n. 1 landing place built out over water 2 heavy, supporting column

pierce v. 1 pass through as a needle does 2 make a hole in 3 sound sharply —**pierc'ing** a.

pi'e·ty (pī'-) n. devotion to religious duties, etc.

pif'fle n. [Col.] insignificant or nonsensical talk, etc.

pig n. 1 fat farm animal; swine 2 greedy or filthy person —**pig'gish** a.

pi·geon (pij'ən) n. plump bird with a small head

pi'geon·hole' v., n. (put in) a compartment, as in a desk, for filing papers

pi'geon-toed' a. having the toes or feet turned inward

pig'gy·back' adv. on the back

pig'head'ed a. stubborn

pig iron n. molten iron

pig'ment n. coloring matter

pig'men·ta'tion n. coloration in plants or animals

pig'my a., n., pl. **-mies** pygmy

pig'pen' n. a pen for pigs: also **pig'sty'**, pl. **-sties'**

pig'skin' n. 1 leather made from the skin of a pig 2 [Col.] a football

pig'tail' n. braid of hair hanging down the back

pike n. 1 slender, freshwater fish 2 turnpike 3 metal-tipped

pik'er n. [Sl.] petty or stingy person

pi·laf, pi·laff (pē′läf′) n. boiled, seasoned rice with meat, etc.

pi·las'ter n. column projecting from a wall

pile n. 1 mass of things heaped together 2 thick nap, as on a rug 3 heavy, vertical beam —v. 1 heap up 2 accumulate 3 to crowd

piles n.pl. hemorrhoids

pile'up' n. 1 accumulation 2 [Col.] collision of several cars

pil'fer v. steal; filch

pil'grim n. traveler to a holy place —**pil'grim·age** n.

pill n. pellet of medicine to be swallowed whole

pil'lage v., n. plunder

pil'lar n. upright support

pil'lion (-yən) n. extra seat on a horse or motorcycle

pil'lo·ry n., pl. **-ries** device with holes for head and hands, in which offenders were locked —v. **-ried, -ry·ing** expose to public scorn

pil'low n. bag of soft material, to support the head, as in sleeping —v. rest as on a pillow

pil'low·case' n. removable covering for a pillow: also **pil'low·slip'**

pi'lot n. 1 one whose job is steering ships in harbors, etc. 2 one who flies an airplane 3 guide —v. be pilot of, in etc.

pi·men'to n., pl. **-tos** sweet, bell-shaped red pepper: also **pi·mien'to** (-myen′-)

pimp v., n. (act as) a prostitute's agent

pim'ple n. small, sore swelling of the skin —**pim'ply** a., **-pli·er, -pli·est**

pin n. 1 pointed piece of wire to fasten things together 2 thin rod to hold things with 3 thing like a pin 4 ornament with a pin to fasten it 5 club at which a ball is bowled —v. pinned, pin' ning fasten as with a pin

pin'a·fore' n. apronlike garment for girls

pin'cers n.pl. 1 tool for gripping things 2 claw of a crab, etc. Also **pinch'ers**

pinch v. 1 squeeze between two surfaces 2 to make look thin, gaunt, etc. 3 be stingy —n. 1 squeeze 2 small amount 3 an emergency

pinch'-hit' v. **-hit', -hit'ting** substitute (for someone)

pin'cush'ion n. small cushion to stick pins in

pine n. 1 evergreen tree with cones and needle-shaped leaves 2 its wood —v. 1 waste (away) through grief, etc. 2 yearn

pine'ap'ple n. large, juicy tropical fruit

pin'feath'er n. an undeveloped feather

ping n. sound of a bullet striking something sharply

Ping'-Pong' trademark table tennis equipment —n. [p- p-] table tennis

pin'ion (-yən) n. 1 small cogwheel 2 wing or wing feather —v. bind the wings or arms of

pink n. 1 plant with pale-red flowers 2 pale red 3 finest condition —v. cut a saw-toothed edge on (cloth)

pink'eye' n. acute, contagious conjunctivitis

pink'ie, pink'y n., pl. **-ies** smallest finger

pin'na·cle n. 1 slender spire 2 mountain peak 3 highest point

pi'noch'le (-nuk′-, -näk′-) n. card game using a double deck above the eight

pin'point' v. show the precise location of

pin stripe n. fabric pattern of very narrow stripes

pint n. ½ quart

pin'to a., n. piebald (horse)

pinto bean n. mottled, kidney-shaped bean

pin'up' n. [Col.] picture of a sexually attractive person

pi'o·neer' n. early settler, first investigator, etc. —v. be a pioneer

pi'ous a. having, showing, or pretending religious devotion —**pi'ous·ly** adv.

pip n. 1 seed of an apple, etc. 2 [Old Sl.] one much admired

pipe n. 1 long tube for conveying water, gas, etc. 2 tube with a bowl at one end, for smoking tobacco 3 tube for making musical sounds —v. 1 utter in a shrill voice 2 convey (water, etc.) by pipes 3 play (a tune) on a pipe —**pip'er** n.

pip'ing n. 1 music made by pipes 2 shrill sound 3 pipelike cloth trimming

pip'pin n. kind of apple

pip'squeak' n. [Col.] insignificant person or thing

pi·quant (pē′kənt) a. 1 agreeably pungent 2 stimulating —

pi'quan·cy n.

pi·qué, pi·que (pē kā′) n. cotton fabric with vertical cords

pique (pēk) n. resentment at being slighted —v. 1 offend 2 excite

pi·ra·nha (pə rän′ə) n., pl. **-nhas** or **-nha** small fish that hunts in schools

pi'rate (-rət) n. 1 one who robs ships at sea 2 one who uses a copyrighted or patented work without authorization —v. take, use, etc. by piracy —**pi'ra·cy** n.

pi·ro·gi (pi rō′gē) n.pl. small pastry filled with meat, etc.

pir·ou·ette' (-ōo et′) n. a whirling on the toes —v. **-et'ted, -et'ting** do a pirouette

pis·ca·to'ri·al a. of fishing

Pis·ces (pī′sēz′) 12th sign of the zodiac; Fish

pis·tach·i·o (pi stash′ē ō′) n., pl. **-os'** greenish nut

pis'til n. seed-bearing organ of a flower

pis'tol n. small firearm held with one hand

pis'ton n. part that moves back and forth in a hollow cylinder from pressure caused by combustion, etc.

pit n. 1 stone of a plum, peach, etc. 2 hole in the ground 3 small hollow in a surface 4 section for the orchestra in front of the stage —v. **pit'ted, pit'ting** 1 remove the pit from (a fruit) 2 mark with pits 3 set in competition (*against*)

pi'ta (pē′-) n. round, flat bread of Middle East: also **pita bread**

pitch v. 1 set up (tents) 2 throw 3 plunge forward 4 set at some level, key, etc. 5 rise and fall, as a ship —n. 1 throw 2 point or degree 3 degree of slope 4 highness or lowness of a musical sound 5 black, sticky substance from coal tar, etc. —**pitch in** [Col.] begin working hard

pitch'blende' n. dark, uranium-bearing mineral

pitch'er n. 1 container for holding and pouring liquids 2 baseball player who pitches to the batters

pitch'fork' n. large fork for lifting and tossing hay

pit'e·ous a. deserving pity —**pit'e·ous·ly** adv.

pit'fall' n. 1 covered pit as a trap 2 hidden danger

pith n. 1 soft, spongy tissue in the center of plant stems 2 essential part

pith'y a. **-i·er, -i·est** full of meaning or force

pit'i·a·ble a. 1 deserving pity 2 deserving contempt —**pit'i·a·bly** adv.

pit'i·ful a. 1 arousing or deserving pity 2 contemptible —**pit'i·ful·ly** adv.

pit'i·less a. without pity

pit'tance n. small amount, esp. of money

pit'ter-pat'ter n. rapid series of tapping sounds

pi·tu'i·tar·y a. of a small endocrine gland (**pituitary gland**) attached to the brain

pit'y n. 1 sorrow for another's misfortune 2 cause for sorrow or regret —v. **-ied, -y·ing** feel pity (for)

piv'ot n. 1 person or thing on which something turns or depends 2 pivoting motion —v. provide with or turn on a pivot —**piv'ot·al** a.

pix'el n. any of the dots making up a TV image

pix'ie, pix'y n., pl. **-ies** fairy; sprite

pi·zazz', piz·zazz' n. [Col.] 1 vitality 2 stylishness

piz·za (pēt′sa) n. baked dish of thin dough topped with cheese, tomato sauce, etc.

piz·zi·ca·to (pit′si kät′ō) adv., a. *Mus.* with the strings plucked

plac'ard v., n. (put up) a sign in a public place

pla'cate' v. appease

place n. 1 space 2 region 3 city or town 4 residence 5 particular building, site, part, position, etc. 6 job or its duties —v. 1 put in a certain place 2 identify by some relationship —**in place of** rather than —**take place** occur

pla·ce'bo n., pl. **-bos** or **-boes** harmless preparation without medicine given to humor a patient

place'ment n. a placing, esp. in a job

pla·cen'ta n., pl. **-tas** or **-tae** (-tē) organ in the uterus to nourish the fetus

plac'id (plas′-) a. calm

plack'et n. slit at the waist of a skirt or dress

pla'gi·a·rize' (-jə rīz′) v. present another's writings as one's own —**pla'gi·a·rism'** n. —**pla'gi·a·rist** n.

plague (plāg) n. 1 affliction 2

deadly epidemic disease —*v.* vex; trouble

plaid (plad) *n., a.* (cloth) with crisscross pattern

plain *a.* 1 clear 2 outspoken 3 obvious 4 simple 5 homely 6 not fancy 7 common —*n.* an extent of flat land —*adv.* clearly —**plain'ly** *adv.* —**plain'ness** *n.*

plain'clothes' man *n.* policeman who does not wear a uniform

plaint *n.* complaint

plain'tiff *n.* one who brings a suit into a court of law

plain'tive (-tiv) *a.* sad; mournful

plait *v., n.* 1 braid 2 pleat

plan *n.* 1 outline; map 2 way of doing; scheme —*v.* **planned, plan'ning** 1 make a plan of or for 2 intend —**plan'ner** *n.*

plane *a.* flat —*n.* 1 flat surface 2 level or stage 3 airplane 4 carpenter's tool for leveling or smoothing —*v.* smooth or level with a plane

plan'et *n.* any of nine heavenly bodies revolving around the sun —**plan'e·tar'y** *a.*

plan'e·tar'i·um (-ter'-) *n.* large domed room for projecting images of the heavens

plank *n.* 1 long, broad, thick board 2 a principle in a political platform —*v.* cover with planks

plank'ton *n.* tiny animals and plants floating in bodies of water

plant *n.* 1 living thing that cannot move, as a tree, flower, etc. 2 factory —*v.* 1 to put in the ground to grow 2 set firmly in place

plan'tain (-tin) *n.* 1 weed with broad leaves 2 banana plant with coarse fruit

plan'tar (-tər) *a.* of the sole of the foot

plan·ta'tion *n.* estate with its workers living on it

plant'er *n.* container for plants

plaque (plak) *n.* 1 flat, decorative piece of wood or metal 2 thin film of bacteria on teeth

plas'ma (plaz'-) *n.* fluid part of blood or lymph

plas'ter *n.* lime, sand, and water, mixed as a coating that hardens on walls —*v.* cover as with plaster

plaster of Paris *n.* paste of gypsum and water that hardens quickly

plas'tic *a.* 1 that shapes or can be shaped 2 of plastic —*n.* substance that can be molded and

hardened —**plas·tic'i·ty** (-tis'-) *n.*

plastic surgery *n.* surgical grafting of skin or bone

plat *n.* 1 map 2 PLOT (*n.* 1)

plate *n.* 1 shallow dish 2 plated dinnerware 3 cast of molded type 4 engraved illustration 5 denture 6 home plate —*v.* coat with metal

pla·teau (pla tō') *n.* 1 tract of high, level land 2 period of no progress

plat'form' *n.* 1 raised horizontal surface 2 political party's stated aims

plat'i·num *n.* silvery, precious metal, a chemical element

plat'i·tude' *n.* trite remark

pla·ton'ic *a.* spiritual or intellectual, not sexual

pla·toon' *n.* small group, as of soldiers

plat'ter *n.* large serving dish

plat'y·pus *n., pl.* **-pus·es** or **-pi'** (-pī') duckbill

plau'dits (plô'-) *n.pl.* applause

plau'si·ble (-za-) *a.* credible —**plau·si·bil'i·ty** *n.*

play *v.* 1 have fun 2 do in fun 3 take part in a game or sport 4 perform on a musical instrument 5 make a tape or disc machine give out sounds or images 6 trifle 7 cause 8 act in a certain way 9 act the part of —*n.* 1 recreation 2 fun 3 motion or freedom for motion 4 move in a game 5 drama —**play up** [Col.] emphasize —**play'er** *n.*

play'back' *n.* playing of tape or disc that has been recorded

play'bill' *n.* program, poster, etc. for a play

play'boy' *n.* rich man given to pleasure-seeking

play'ful *a.* full of fun; frisky —**play'ful·ly** *adv.* —**play'ful·ness** *n.*

play'ground' *n.* outdoor place for games and play

playing cards *n.pl.* cards in four suits for playing games

play'off' *n.* final match played to break a tie

play on words *n.* pun

play'wright' (-rīt') *n.* one who writes plays

pla·za (plä'zə, plaz'ə) *n.* public square

plea *n.* 1 appeal; request 2 statement in defense

plead *v.* 1 beg; entreat 2 argue (a law case) 3 offer as an excuse

pleas'ant a. pleasing; agreeable —**pleas'ant·ly** adv.

pleas'ant·ry n., pl. **-ries** 1 jocular remark 2 a polite social remark

please v. 1 satisfy 2 be the wish of 3 be obliging enough to: used in polite requests —**pleased** a.

pleas'ing a. giving pleasure —**pleas'ing·ly** adv.

pleas'ure (plezh'-) n. 1 delight or satisfaction 2 one's choice —**pleas'ur·a·ble** a.

pleat n. fold made by doubling cloth —v. make pleats in

ple·be'ian (-bē'ən) a., n. common (person)

pleb'i·scite' (-sit') n. direct popular vote on an issue

plec'trum n., pl. **-trums** or **-tra** small device for plucking a banjo, etc.

pledge n. 1 thing given as security for a contract, etc. 2 promise —v. 1 give as security 2 promise

ple'na·ry a. full or fully attended

plen'i·po·ten'ti·ar'y (-shē-) a. having full authority —n., pl. **-ies** ambassador

plen'i·tude' n. 1 fullness 2 abundance

plen'ti·ful a. abundant: also **plen'te·ous**

plen'ty n. 1 prosperity 2 ample amount

pleth'o·ra n. overabundance

pleu·ri·sy (ploor'ə sē) n. inflammation of membrane lining the chest cavity

Plex'i·glas' trademark transparent plastic

plex'i·glass' n. material like Plexiglas

pli'a·ble a. easily bent; flexible —**pli'a·bil'i·ty** n.

pli'ant a. 1 flexible 2 compliant —**pli'an·cy** n.

pli'ers n.pl. small pincers

plight n. condition, esp. a bad or dangerous one —v. 1 pledge 2 betroth

plod v. **plod'ded, plod'ding** 1 trudge 2 work steadily —**plod'der** n.

plop n. sound of object falling into water —v. **plopped, plop'ping** fall with a plop

plot n. 1 piece of ground 2 diagram, plan, etc. 3 plan of action of a play, etc. 4 secret, esp. evil, scheme —v. **plot'ted, plot'ting** 1 make a map, plan, etc. of 2 scheme —**plot'ter** n.

plov'er (pluv'-) n. shore bird

with long, pointed wings

plow (plou) n. 1 implement for cutting and turning up soil 2 machine for removing snow —v. 1 use a plow (on) 2 make one's way Also [Br.] **plough** —**plow'man** n., pl. **-men**

plow'share' n. blade of a plow

ploy n. ruse; trick

pluck v. 1 pull off or out 2 pull at and release quickly —n. 1 a pull 2 courage

pluck'y a. **-i·er, -i·est** brave; spirited

plug n. 1 stopper 2 device for making electrical contact 3 [Col.] insinuated advertisement 4 [Sl.] worn-out horse —v. **plugged, plug'ging** 1 stop up with a plug 2 [Col.] advertise with a plug 3 [Col.] work doggedly 4 [Sl.] hit with a bullet

plum n. 1 smooth-skinned, juicy fruit 2 choice thing

plum'age (plōōm'-) n. a bird's feathers

plumb (plum) n. weight on a line for checking a vertical wall or sounding a depth —a. perpendicular —adv. 1 straight down 2 [Col.] entirely —v. 1 test with a plumb 2 solve

plumb'er n. one who fits and repairs water pipes, etc. —**plumb'ing** n.

plume n. feather or tuft of feathers —v. 1 adorn with plumes 2 preen

plum'met v. fall straight downward —n. plumb

plump a. full and rounded —v. drop heavily —adv. suddenly; heavily

plun'der v. rob by force —n. goods plundered

plunge v. 1 thrust suddenly (into) 2 dive or rush —n. dive or fall

plung'er n. 1 rubber suction cup to open drains 2 part that moves with a plunging motion

plunk v. 1 strum (a banjo), etc. 2 put down heavily —n. sound of plunking

plu·ral (ploor'əl) a. more than one —n. Gram. word form designating more than one —**plu'ral·ize'** v.

plu·ral'i·ty n. 1 majority 2 excess of winner's votes over his nearest rival's

plus prep. added to —a. 1 designating a sign (+) showing addition 2 positive 3 more than —n. something added

plush n. fabric with a long pile —a. [Col.] luxurious

plu'to·crat' n. wealthy person with great influence —**plu·toc'ra·cy** n.

plu·to'ni·um n. radioactive chemical element

ply n., pl. **plies** one layer in plywood, folded cloth, etc. —v. **plied, ply'ing** 1 work at (a trade) or with (a tool) 2 keep supplying (with) 3 travel back and forth (between)

ply'wood' n. board made of glued layers of wood

p.m., P.M. after noon

pneu·mat'ic a. 1 of or containing air or gases 2 worked by compressed air

pneu·mo'ni·a n. acute disease of the lungs

poach v. 1 cook (an egg without its shell) in water 2 hunt or fish illegally —**poach'er** n.

pock'et n. 1 little bag or pouch, esp. when sewn into clothing 2 pouchlike cavity or hollow —a. that can be carried in a pocket —v. 1 put into a pocket 2 hide; suppress —**pock'et·ful'** n.

pock'et·book' n. purse

pock'et·knife' n., pl. **-knives** small knife with folding blades

pock'mark' n. scar left by a pustule: also **pock**

pod n. shell of peas, beans, etc. containing the seeds

po·di'a·try (-dī'-) n. treatment of foot ailments —**po·di'a·trist** n.

po'di·um n., pl. **-di·a** platform for an orchestra conductor

po'em n. piece of imaginative writing in rhythm, rhyme, etc.

po'et n. writer of poems —**po'et·ess** n.fem.

po'et·ry n. 1 writing of poems 2 poems 3 rhythms, deep feelings, etc. of poems —**po·et'ic, po·et'i·cal** a.

poi n. Hawaiian dish of taro paste

poign·ant (poin'yant) a. 1 painful to the feelings 2 keen —**poign'an·cy** n.

poin·set'ti·a (-set'ə, -set'ē ə) n. plant with petallike red leaves

point n. 1 a dot 2 specific place or time 3 a stage or degree reached 4 item; detail 5 special feature 6 unit, as of a game score 7 sharp end 8 cape (land) 9 purpose; object 10 essential idea 11 mark showing direction on a compass —v. 1 sharpen to a point 2 call attention (to) 3

show 4 aim —**at the point of** very close to —**beside the point** irrelevant —**to the point** pertinent

point'-blank' a., adv. 1 (aimed) straight at a mark 2 direct(ly)

point'ed a. 1 sharp 2 aimed at someone, as a remark

point'er n. 1 long, tapered rod for pointing 2 indicator 3 large hunting dog 4 [Col.] hint; suggestion

point'less a. without meaning —**point'less·ly** adv.

point of view n. way something is viewed or thought of

poise (poiz) n. 1 balance 2 ease and dignity of manner —v. balance

poi'son n. substance which can cause illness or death —v. 1 harm or kill with poison 2 put poison into 3 corrupt —**poi'son·ous** a.

poison ivy n. plant that can cause severe skin rash

poke v. 1 prod, as with a stick 2 search (about or around) 3 move slowly (along) —n. jab; thrust —**poke fun (at)** ridicule

pok'er n. 1 gambling game with cards 2 iron bar for stirring a fire

pok'y a. **-i·er, -i·est** [Col.] slow; dull: also **pok'ey**

po'lar a. 1 having opposite magnetic poles 2 opposite in character, nature, etc. —**po·lar'i·ty** n. —**po'lar·i·za'tion** n. —**po'lar·ize'** v.

polar bear n. large white bear of arctic regions

pole n. 1 long, slender piece of wood, metal, etc. 2 end of an axis, as of the earth 3 either of two opposed forces, as the ends of a magnet —v. propel (a boat) with a pole

pole'cat' n. 1 weasellike animal of Europe 2 skunk

po·lem'ics n. art or practice of disputation —**po·lem'ic** a., n.

pole vault n. a leap for height by vaulting with aid of a pole —**pole'-vault'** v.

po·lice' n. 1 department of a city, etc. for keeping law and order 2 [with pl. v.] members of such a department —v. control, etc. with police

po·lice'man n., pl. **-men** member of a police force —**po·lice'wom'an** n.fem., pl. **-wom'en**

pol'i·cy n., pl. **-cies** 1 governing principle, plan, etc. 2 insurance contract

po·li·o·my·e·li·tis (-lit'is) n. virus disease often resulting in paralysis: also **po·li·o'**

Pol·ish (pōl'-) n., a. (language) of Poland

pol·ish (päl'-) v. **1** smooth and brighten, as by rubbing **2** refine (manners, etc.) —n. **1** surface gloss **2** elegance **3** substance used to polish

po·lite' a. **1** showing good manners; courteous **2** refined —**po·lite'ly** adv.

pol'i·tic' adv. wise or shrewd

po·lit'i·cal a. of government, politics, etc. —**po·lit'i·cize'** v.

pol'i·ti'cian (-tish'ən) n. one active in politics

pol'i·tics n.pl. [sing. or pl. v.] **1** science of government **2** political affairs, methods, opinions, scheming, etc.

pol'i·ty n., pl. **-ties 1** system of government **2** a state

pol'ka (pōl'-) n. fast dance for couples

pol'ka dot n. any of a pattern of dots on cloth

poll (pōl) n. **1** a counting or listing as of voters **2** number of votes recorded **3** pl. voting place **4** survey of opinion —v. **1** take the votes or opinions of **2** receive, as votes

pol'len n. powderlike sex cells on flower stamens

pol'li·nate' v. put pollen on the pistil of —**pol'li·na'tion** n.

pol'li·wog n. tadpole

poll'ster n. taker of opinion polls

pol·lute' v. make unclean or impure —**pol·lut'ant** n. —**pol·lu'tion** n.

po'lo n. team game played on horseback

pol·troon' n. coward

poly- pref. much; many

pol'y·es'ter n. synthetic substance used in plastics, fibers, etc.

po·lyg'a·my (-lig'-) n. a being married to more than one person at one time —**po·lyg'a·mist** n. —**po·lyg'a·mous** a.

pol'y·gon' n. figure with more than four angles and sides

pol'y·graph' n. device measuring bodily changes, used on one suspected of lying

pol'y·mer n. substance of giant molecules formed from smaller molecules of same kind

pol'y·p (-ip) n. **1** slender water animal with tentacles **2** growth

on a mucous membrane

pol'y·syl'la·ble n. word of more than three syllables —**pol'y·syl·lab'ic** a.

pol'y·the·ism' (-thē-) n. belief in more than one god —**pol'y·the·is'tic** a.

pol'y·un·sat'u·rat'ed a. of fats with low cholesterol

po·made' n. perfumed ointment for the hair

pome'gran'ate (päm'-, päm'a-) n. round, red fruit with a hard rind and many seeds

pom'mel (pum'-) n. rounded, upward-projecting front part of a saddle —v. pummel

pomp n. stately or ostentatious display

pom'pa·dour' (-dôr') n. hair style with the hair brushed up high from the forehead

pom'pom' n. tuft of fabric decorating hats, waved by cheerleaders, etc.: also **pom'pon'**

pom'pous a. pretentious —**pom·pos'i·ty** n.

pon'cho n., pl. **-chos** cloak like a blanket

pond n. small lake

pon'der v. think deeply (about)

pon'der·ous a. heavy; clumsy

pone n. corn meal bread

pon·gee' n. soft, silk cloth

pon'iard (-yard) n. dagger

pon'tiff n. **1** bishop **2** [P-] the Pope —**pon·tif'i·cal** a.

pon·tif'i·cate v. be dogmatic or pompous

pon·toon' n. one of the floats supporting a bridge or airplane on water

po'ny n., pl. **-nies** small horse

po'ny·tail' n. hairstyle in which hair is tied to hang in back

poo'dle n. curly-haired dog

pooh int. exclamation of contempt, disbelief, etc.

pool n. **1** small pond **2** puddle **3** tank for swimming **4** billiards on a table with pockets **5** common fund of money, etc. —v. put into a common fund

poop n. raised deck at the stern of a sailing ship

poor a. **1** having little money **2** below average; inferior **3** worthy of pity —**poor'ly** adv.

pop n. **1** light, explosive sound **2** flavored soda water —v. popped, pop'ping **1** make, or burst with, a pop **2** cause to pop **3** move, go, etc. suddenly **4** bulge —adv. like a pop —a. **1** of music popular with many people

2 intended for popular taste

pop'corn' n. corn with kernels that pop when heated

Pope n. head of the Roman Catholic Church

pop'lar n. tall tree

pop'lin n. ribbed cloth

pop'o'ver n. hollow muffin

pop'py n., pl. **-pies** plant with showy flowers

pop'u·lace (-ləs) n. the common people

pop'u·lar a. 1 of, by, or for people generally 2 very well liked —**pop'u·lar'i·ty** n. —**pop'u·lar·ize'** v.

pop'u·late' v. inhabit

pop'u·la'tion n. total number of inhabitants

pop'u·lism' n. movement to advance interests of common people —**pop'u·list** a., n.

pop'u·lous a. full of people

por'ce·lain (-lin) n. hard, fine, glazed earthenware

porch n. open or screen-enclosed room on the outside of a building

por'cine (-sīn') a. of or like pigs

por'cu·pine' n. gnawing animal with long, sharp spines in its coat

pore v. study or ponder (over) —n. tiny opening, as in the skin, for absorbing or discharging fluids

pork n. flesh of a pig used as food

por·nog'ra·phy n. writings, pictures, etc. intended to arouse sexual desire: also [Sl.] **por'no** or **porn** —**por·no·graph'ic** a. —**por·nog'ra·pher** n.

po'rous a. full of pores or tiny holes —**po·ros'i·ty** n.

por'poise (-pəs) n. 1 sea mammal with a blunt snout 2 dolphin

por'ridge n. cereal or meal boiled in water or milk

por'rin·ger (-jər) n. bowl for porridge, etc.

port n. 1 harbor 2 city with a harbor 3 sweet, dark-red wine 4 left side of a ship as one faces the bow 5 porthole 6 opening, as in a valve face

port'a·ble a. that can be carried —**port'a·bil'i·ty** n.

por'tage n. 1 carrying of boats and supplies overland between waterways 2 route so used

por'tal n. doorway; gate

por·tend' v. be an omen or warning of —**por'tent'** n. —**por·ten'-**

tous a.

por'ter n. 1 doorman 2 attendant who carries luggage, sweeps up, etc.

por'ter·house' (steak) n. beef steak

port·fo'li·o n., pl. **-os'** brief case

port'hole' n. window in a ship's side

por'ti·co' n., pl. **-coes'** or **-cos'** porch consisting of a roof supported by columns

por·tiere', por·tière' (-tyer') n. curtain hung in a doorway

por'tion n. part; share —v. divide or give out in portions

port'ly a. stout and stately

por'trait (-trit) n. a painting, photograph, etc. of a person

por·tray' v. 1 make a portrait of 2 describe 3 represent on the stage —**por·tray'al** n.

Por'tu·guese' (-chə gēz') n., pl. **-guese'**; a. (native or language) of Portugal

pose v. 1 present, as a question 2 assume a bodily posture, a false role, etc. —n. assumed posture, etc. —**pos'er, po·seur'** (-zur') n.

posh a. [Col.] luxurious and fashionable

pos'it v. postulate

po·si'tion n. 1 way of being placed 2 opinion 3 place; location 4 status 5 job —v. to place

pos'i·tive a. 1 explicit; definite 2 sure or too sure 3 affirmative 4 real; absolute 5 of the electricity made by friction on glass 6 Gram. of an adjective, etc. in its uncompared degree 7 Math. greater than zero —n. 1 anything positive 2 battery plate of higher potential —**pos'i·tive·ly** adv.

pos'se (-ē) n. body of men called to help a sheriff

pos·sess' v. 1 own 2 have as a quality, etc. 3 control —**pos·ses'sor** n.

pos·ses'sion n. 1 a possessing 2 thing possessed

pos·ses'sive a. 1 showing or desiring possession 2 Gram. indicating a form, etc. indicating possession

pos'si·ble a. that can be, can happen, etc. —**pos'si·bil'i·ty** n., pl. **-ties** —**pos'si·bly** adv.

pos'sum n. opossum —**play possum** feign sleep, ignorance, etc.

post n. 1 piece of wood, etc. set upright as a support 2 place where a soldier or soldiers are stationed 3 job; position 4 mail —v. 1 put up (a notice, etc.) 2 assign to a post 3 to mail 4 inform

post- *pref.* after; following

post'age *n.* amount charged for mailing a letter, etc.

post'al *a.* of (the) mail

post'card' *n.* card, often a picture card, sent by mail

post'date' *v.* 1 mark with a later date 2 be later than

post'er *n.* large sign or notice posted publicly

pos-te'ri-or (-tir'ē-) *a.* 1 at the back 2 later —*n.* buttocks

pos-ter'i-ty *n.* all future generations

post'grad'u-ate *a.* of study after graduation

post'haste' *adv.* speedily

post'hu-mous (päs'tyōō-, päs'chōō-) *a.* after one's death

post'man *n., pl.* **-men** mailman

post'mark' *v., n.* mark to show the date and place of mailing at the post office

post'mas'ter *n.* person in charge of a post office

post'-mor'tem *a.* after death — *n.* autopsy

post office *n.* place where mail is sorted, etc.

post'op'er-a-tive *a.* after surgery

post'paid' *a.* with the sender paying the postage

post'par'tum *a.* of the time after childbirth

post'pone' *v.* put off; delay — **post'pone'ment** *n.*

post'script' *n.* note added at the end of a letter, etc.

pos-tu-late (päs'cha lāt'; *n.:* -lət) *v.* assume to be true, real, etc. — *n.* something postulated

pos'ture *n.* way one holds the body —*v.* pose

post'war' *a.* after the war

po'sy (-zē) *n., pl.* **-sies** flower or bouquet

pot *n.* round container for cooking, etc.—*v.* **pot'ted, pot'ting** put into a pot —**go to pot** go to ruin

po'ta-ble *a.* drinkable

pot'ash' (pät'-) *n.* white substance obtained from wood ashes

po-tas'si-um *n.* soft, white, metallic chemical element

po-ta'to *n., pl.* **-toes** starchy tuber of a common plant, used as a vegetable

pot'bel'ly *n., pl.* **-lies** belly that sticks out

po'tent *a.* 1 powerful 2 effective —**po'ten-cy** *n.*

po'ten-tate' *n.* person having great power; ruler, etc.

po-ten'tial (-shəl) *a.* that can be; possible; latent —*n.* 1 something potential 2 voltage at a given point in a circuit —**po-ten'ti-al'i-ty** (-shē al'-) *n., pl.* **-ties** —**po-ten'tial-ly** *adv.*

po'tion *n.* a drink, esp. of medicine or poison

pot'luck' *n.* whatever is available

potluck dinner (or **supper**) *n.* dinner in which everyone brings a dish of food to share

pot-pour-ri (pō'pər ē') *n.* mixture

pot'sherd' *n.* piece of broken pottery

pot'shot' *n.* random shot, attack, etc.

pot'ter *n.* one who makes pots, dishes, etc. of clay

pot'ter-y *n.* earthenware

pouch *n.* 1 small sack or bag 2 baglike part

poul-tice (pōl'tis) *n.* hot, soft mass applied to a sore part of the body

poul'try *n.* domestic fowls

pounce *v.* leap or swoop down, as if to seize —*n.* a pouncing

pound *n.* 1 unit of weight, 16 ounces 2 British monetary unit 3 enclosure for stray animals — *v.* 1 hit hard 2 beat to pulp, powder, etc. 3 throb

pour (pôr) *v.* 1 flow or make flow steadily 2 rain heavily

pout *v.* 1 push out the lips, as in sullenness 2 sulk —*n.* a pouting

pov'er-ty *n.* 1 being poor; need 2 inadequacy

pov'er-ty-strick'en *a.* very poor

pow'der *n.* dry substance of fine particles —*v.* 1 put powder on 2 make into powder —**pow'der-y** *a.*

pow'er *n.* 1 ability to act or do 2 strength or energy 3 authority 4 powerful person, nation, etc. 5 result of multiplying a number by itself —*a.* operated by electricity, fuel engine, etc.

pow'er-less *a.*

pow'er-ful *a.* strong; mighty — **pow'er-ful-ly** *adv.*

pow'wow' *n.* conference of or with North American Indians

prac'ti-ca-ble (-kə-) *a.* that can be done —**prac'ti-ca-bil'i-ty** *n.*

prac'ti-cal *a.* 1 of or obtained through practice 2 useful 3 sensible 4 virtual —**prac'ti-cal'**

i·ty n. —**prac'ti·cal·ly** adv.

prac'tice (-tis) v. 1 do repeatedly so as to gain skill 2 make a habit of 3 work at as a profession —n. 1 a practicing 2 acquired skill 3 the work or business of a professional Also, chiefly Br. sp., **practise**

prac'ticed a. skilled

prac·ti·tion·er (-tish'ən-) n. one who practices a profession, etc.

prag·mat'ic a. 1 practical 2 tested by results

prai·rie (prer'ē) n. large area of grassy land

prairie dog n. small squirrellike animal

praise v. 1 to say good things about 2 worship —n. a praising —**praise'wor'thy** a.

prance v. 1 move along on the hind legs, as a horse 2 strut —**pranc'er** n.

prank n. mischievous trick —**prank'ster** n.

prate v. talk foolishly

prat'tle v., n. chatter or babble

prawn n. shellfish like a shrimp but larger

pray v. 1 implore 2 ask for by prayer 3 say prayers

pray'er n. 1 a praying 2 words of worship or entreaty to God 3 thing prayed for —**prayer'ful** a.

praying mantis n. mantis

pre- pref. before

preach v. 1 give (a sermon) 2 urge or advise as by preaching —**preach'er** n.

pre·am'ble n. introduction

pre'ar·range' v. arrange beforehand

pre·car'i·ous a. not safe or sure; risky

pre·cau'tion n. care taken beforehand, as against danger —**pre·cau'tion·ar'y** a.

pre·cede' v. go or come before

prec'e·dence (pres'-) n.

prec'e·dent n. earlier case that sets an example

pre'cept' n. rule of ethics

pre·cep'tor n. teacher

pre'cinct' (-sinkt') n. 1 subdivision of a city, ward, etc. 2 pl. grounds or environs

pre·cious (presh'əs) a. 1 of great value 2 beloved 3 too refined —**pre'cious·ly** adv.

prec'i·pice (-pis) n. steep cliff

pre·cip'i·tate' v. 1 bring on; hasten 2 hurl down 3 to separate out as a solid from solution —a. hasty; rash —n. precipitated substance

pre·cip'i·ta'tion n. 1 a precipitating 2 (amount of) rain, snow, etc.

pre·cip'i·tous a. 1 steep; sheer 2 hasty; rash

pré·cis' (prā sē') n. summary

pre·cise' a. 1 exact; definite; accurate 2 strict; scrupulous —**pre·cise'ly** adv. —**pre·ci'sion** (-sizh' ən) n.

pre·clude' v. make impossible, esp. in advance

pre·co'cious (-shəs) a. advanced beyond one's age —**pre·coc'i·ty** (-käs'-) n.

pre'-Co·lum'bi·an a. of any period in the Americas before 1492

pre'con·ceive' v. form an opinion of beforehand —**pre'con·cep'tion** n.

pre·cur'sor n. forerunner

pred'a·to'ry a. 1 plundering 2 preying on other animals

pre·des'tine (-tin) v. destine or determine beforehand —**pre·des'ti·na'tion** n.

pre'de·ter'mine v. set or decide beforehand

pre·dic'a·ment n. difficult situation

pred'i·cate' (-kāt'; a., n.: -kət) v. base upon facts, conditions, etc. —a., n. Gram. (of) the word or words that make a statement about the subject

pre·dict' v. tell about in advance —**pre·dict'a·ble** a. —**pre·dic'tion** n.

pre'di·lec'tion n. special liking; partiality

pre'dis·pose' v. make likely to get, etc.; incline —**pre'dis·po·si'tion** n.

pre·dom'i·nate' v. be greater in amount, power, etc.; prevail —**pre·dom'i·nance** n. —**pre·dom'i·nant** a.

pre·em'i·nent, pre-em'i·nent a. most outstanding —**pre·em'i·nence, pre-em'i·nence** n.

pre·empt', pre-empt' v. 1 to seize before anyone else can 2 to replace a scheduled radio or TV program —**pre·emp'tive, pre-emp'tive** a.

preen v. 1 groom (its feathers): said of a bird 2 groom (oneself)

pre'fab' n. [Col.] prefabricated building

pre'fab·ri·cat'ed a. made in sections ready for quick assembly, as a house

pref'ace (-əs) *n.* introduction to a book, speech, etc. —*v.* give or be a preface to —**pref'a·to'ry** *a.*

pre'fect' *n.* administrator

pre·fer' *v.* **-ferred', -fer'ring 1** like better **2** bring (charges) before a court —**pref'er·a·ble** *a.*

pref'er·ence *n.* **1** a preferring **2** thing preferred **3** advantage given to one over others —**pref'er·en'tial** *a.*

pre·fer'ment *n.* promotion

pre'fix' *n.* syllable(s) added to the beginning of a word to alter its meaning

preg'nant *a.* **1** bearing a fetus in the uterus **2** filled (*with*) —**preg'nan·cy** *n., pl.* **-cies**

pre·hen'sile (-səl) *a.* adapted for grasping, as the hand

pre'his·tor'ic *a.* of times before recorded history

pre·judge' *v.* judge beforehand

prej'u·dice (-dis) *n.* **1** preconceived idea **2** hatred or intolerance of other races, etc. **3** disadvantage —*v.* **1** harm **2** fill with prejudice —**prej'u·di'cial** *a.*

prel'ate (-ət) *n.* high-ranking clergyman

pre·lim'i·nar·y *a.* leading up to the main action —*n., pl.* **-ies** preliminary step

prel'ude (prel'yōod', prā'lōod') *n.* preliminary part, as of a musical piece

pre·mar'i·tal *a.* before marriage

pre'ma·ture' *a.* before the proper or usual time

pre·med'i·tate' *v.* think out or plan beforehand —**pre'med'i·ta'tion** *n.*

pre·men'stru·al *a.* before a menstrual period

pre·mier' (-mir') *a.* foremost —*n.* prime minister

pre·mière', pre·miere' (-mir') *n.* first performance of a play, etc.

prem'ise (-is) *n.* **1** a basic assumption **2** *pl.* piece of real estate

pre'mi·um *n.* **1** prize **2** extra charge **3** a payment **4** high value

prem'o·ni'tion *n.* feeling of imminent evil

pre·na'tal *a.* before birth

pre·oc'cu·py' *v.* **-pied', -py'ing** engross; absorb —**pre·oc'cu·pa'tion** *n.*

prep *a.* preparatory —*v.* **prepped, prep'ping** prepare (a patient) for surgery

preparatory school *n.* private school preparing students for college

pre·pare' *v.* **1** make or get ready **2** equip **3** to put together —**prep'a·ra'tion** *n.* —**pre·par'a·to'ry** *a.* —**pre·par'ed·ness** *n.*

pre'pay' *v.* pay in advance —**pre'pay'ment** *n.*

pre·pon'der·ate' *v.* predominate —**pre·pon'der·ance** *n.* —**pre·pon'der·ant** *a.*

prep'o·si'tion (-zish'ən) *n.* word that connects a noun or pronoun to another word —**prep'o·si'tion·al** *a.*

pre'pos·sess'ing *a.* making a good impression

pre·pos'ter·ous *a.* absurd

prep'py, prep'pie *n., pl.* **-pies** (former) student at a preparatory school

pre're·cord'ed *a.* of a magnetic tape on which sound, etc. has been recorded before its sale

pre·req'ui·site (-rek'wə zit) *n., a.* (something) required beforehand

pre·rog'a·tive *n.* exclusive privilege

pres'age (*v.:* prē sāj') *n.* **1** warning **2** foreboding —*v.* **1** warn about **2** predict

pre'school' *a.* younger than school age

pres'ci·ence (presh'əns) *n.* foresight —**pres'ci·ent** *a.*

pre·scribe' *v.* **1** to order **2** order to take a certain medicine or treatment

pre'script' *n.* prescribed rule —**pre·scrip'tive** *a.*

pre·scrip'tion *n.* **1** a prescribing, esp. by a doctor **2** medicine prescribed

pres'ence *n.* **1** a being present **2** one's appearance

presence of mind *n.* ability to think and act quickly in an emergency

pres'ent (*v.:* prē zent') *a.* **1** being at a certain place **2** of or at this time —*n.* **1** present time **2** gift —*v.* **1** introduce **2** show **3** offer for consideration **4** give (to)

pre·sent'a·ble *a.* **1** fit to present **2** properly dressed

pres'en·ta'tion *n.* **1** a presenting **2** thing presented

pre·sen'ti·ment *n.* premonition

pres'ent·ly *adv.* **1** soon **2** now

pre·sent'ment *n.* presentation

pre·serve' *v.* **1** keep from harm, spoiling, etc. **2** maintain —*n.* **1** *pl.* fruit cooked with sugar —**pre·serv'a·tive** *a., n.* —**pres'er·**

va'tion n.

pre·set' v. set (controls) beforehand

pre'shrunk' a. shrunk to minimize shrinkage in laundering

pre·side' (-zīd') v. 1 act as chairman 2 have control

pres'i·dent n. chief executive of a republic, company, etc. — **pres'i·den·cy** n., pl. **-cies** — **pres'i·den'tial** (-shal) a.

press v. 1 push against; squeeze 2 iron, as clothes 3 force 4 entreat 5 urge on 6 keep moving 7 crowd —n. 1 pressure 2 crowd 3 machine for crushing, printing, etc. 4 newspapers 5 journalists

press'ing a. urgent

pres·sure (presh'ər) n. 1 a pressing 2 distress 3 strong influence 4 urgency 5 force of weight —v. try to influence

pres'sur·ize' v. keep nearly normal air pressure inside (aircraft, etc.) at high altitude

pres'ti·dig'i·ta'tion (-dij'-) n. sleight of hand

pres·tige' (-tēzh') n. earned fame and respect

pres'to adv., a. fast

pre·sume' v. 1 dare 2 suppose 3 take liberties — **pre·sump'-tion** n. — **pre·sump'tive** a.

pre·sump'tu·ous (-chōō əs) a. too bold or daring

pre'sup·pose' v. assume beforehand

pre'teen' n. child nearly a teenager

pre·tend' v. 1 claim falsely 2 make believe 3 lay claim: with to

pre·tense' (or prē'tens') n. 1 claim 2 false claim or show 3 a making believe

pre·ten'sion n. 1 claim 2 pretext 3 showy; display

pre·ten'tious a. showy; flashy

pre'ter·nat'u·ral a. supernatural

pre'text' n. false reason used to hide the real one

pret'ty a. **-ti·er, -ti·est** attractive and dainty —adv. somewhat — **pret'ti·ly** adv. — **pret'ti·ness** n.

pret'zel n. hard, salted biscuit, twisted in a knot

pre·vail' v. 1 win out or be successful 2 become more common

prev'a·lent a. common; general — **prev'a·lence** n.

pre·var'i·cate' v. evade the truth; lie — **pre·var'i·ca'tion** n. — **pre·var'i·ca'tor** n.

pre·vent' v. stop or keep from

doing or happening — **pre·vent'-a·ble, pre·vent'i·ble** a. — **pre·ven'tion** n.

pre·ven'tive n., a. (something) that prevents: also **pre·vent'a·tive**

pre'view' n. advance showing of (scenes from) a movie

pre'vi·ous a. coming before; prior — **pre'vi·ous·ly** adv.

prey (prā) n. 1 animal seized by another for food 2 victim —v. 1 hunt as prey 2 plunder; rob 3 harass

price n. 1 sum asked or paid for a thing 2 value —v. get or put a price on

price'less a. beyond price

prick v. 1 pierce with a sharp point 2 pain sharply 3 raise (the ears) —n. 1 a pricking 2 sharp pain — **prick up one's ears** listen closely

prick'le n. thorn or spiny point —v. tingle — **prick'ly** a., **-li·er, -li·est**

pride n. 1 too high opinion of oneself 2 self-respect 3 satisfaction in one's achievements 4 person or thing one is proud of — **pride oneself on** be proud of

priest n. one who conducts religious rites — **priest'ess** n.fem. — **priest'hood** n. — **priest'ly** a.

prig n. smug, moralistic person — **prig'gish** a.

prim a. **prim'mer, prim'mest** stiffly proper — **prim'ly** adv.

pri'ma·cy n. supremacy

pri'ma don'na (prē'-) n. 1 chief woman singer in an opera 2 [Col.] one temperamental, vain, etc.

pri'ma·ry a. 1 most important 2 basic 3 first in order —n., pl. **-ies** preliminary election — **pri·mar'i·ly** adv.

pri'mate' n. 1 archbishop 2 member of the order of mammals having hands and feet with five digits; man, ape, etc.

prime a. first in rank, importance, or quality —n. best period or part —v. make ready

prime minister n. chief official in some countries

prim'er (prim-) n. 1 explosive used to set off a larger explosive 2 preliminary coat of paint, etc.

prim'er (prim'-) n. elementary textbook, esp. for reading

pri·me'val a. of the first age or ages

prim'i·tive a. 1 of earliest times 2 crude; simple —n. primitive person or thing

primp v. groom oneself fussily

prim'rose' n. plant with tubelike flowers in clusters

prince n. 1 monarch's son 2 ruler of a principality — **prince'ly** a. — **prin'cess** n.fem.

prin'ci·pal a. chief; main — n. 1 principal person or thing 2 head of a school 3 sum owed, etc. aside from interest — **prin'ci·pal·ly** adv.

prin'ci·pal'i·ty n., pl. **-ties** land ruled by a prince

prin'ci·ple n. 1 basic truth, rule, action, etc. 2 rule of conduct 3 integrity

print n. 1 cloth stamped with a design 2 impression made by inked type, plates, etc. 3 photograph — v. 1 to impress inked type, etc. on paper 2 publish in print 3 write in letters like printed ones — **print'er** n.

print'ing n., a.

print'out' n. printed or typed computer output

pri'or a. preceding in time, order, or importance — n. head of a monastery or order — **pri'or·ess** n.fem. — **pri'o·ry** n., pl. **-ries**

pri·or'i·ty n., pl. **-ties** 1 precedence 2 prior right

prism n. clear glass, etc. of angular form, for dispersing light into its spectrum — **pris·mat'ic** a.

pris'on n. place of confinement — **pris'on·er** n.

pris'sy a. **-i·er, -i·est** [Col.] very prim or prudish

pris'tine' (-tēn') n. fresh and untouched

pri'vate a. 1 of or for a particular person or group; not public 2 secret — n. Mil. lowest rank of enlisted man — **pri'va·cy** n. — **pri'vate·ly** adv.

pri'va·teer' n. private ship commissioned to attack enemy ships

pri·va'tion n. lack of necessities

pri'va·tize' v. turn over (public property, etc.) to private interests

priv'et n. evergreen shrub

priv'i·lege (-lij) n. special right, favor, etc. — v. grant a privilege to

priv'y a. private — n., pl. **-ies** outhouse — **privy to** privately informed about

prize v. value highly — n. 1 thing given to the winner of a contest, etc. 2 valued possession

pro adv. on the affirmative side — n. 1 pl. **pros** reason or vote for 2 professional

pro- pref. in favor of

prob'a·ble a. likely to occur or to be so — **prob·a·bil'i·ty** n., **-ties** — **prob'a·bly** adv.

pro'bate' v. establish the validity of (a will) — a. of such action — n. a probating

pro·ba'tion n. 1 trial of ability, etc. 2 conditional suspension of a jail sentence — **pro·ba'tion·ar'y** a.

probe n. 1 a slender surgical instrument for exploring a wound 2 investigation 3 spacecraft, etc. used to get information about an environment — v. 1 explore with a probe 2 investigate — **prob'er** n.

pro'bi·ty (prō'bə-) n. honesty

prob'lem n. 1 question to be solved 2 difficult matter, etc.

prob'lem·at'ic a. 1 hard to solve or deal with 2 uncertain Also **prob'lem·at'i·cal**

pro·bos'cis n. elephant's trunk, or similar snout

pro'caine' n. drug used as a local anesthetic

pro·ce'dure (-jər) n. act or way of doing something

pro·ceed' v. 1 go on after stopping 2 carry on an action 3 come forth

pro·ceed'ing n. 1 course of action 2 pl. transactions 3 pl. legal action

pro·ceeds' n.pl. money from a business deal

proc'ess' n. 1 series of changes in developing 2 act or way of doing something 3 court summons 4 projecting part — v. prepare by a special process

pro·ces'sion n. group moving forward, as in a parade

pro·ces'sion·al n. hymn or music for a procession

pro·claim' v. announce officially — **proc'la·ma'tion** n.

pro·cliv'i·ty n., pl. **-ties** inclination; tendency

pro·cras'ti·nate' v. put off; delay — **pro·cras'ti·na'tion** n. — **pro·cras'ti·na'tor** n.

pro'cre·ate' v. produce (young) — **pro'cre·a'tion** n.

proc'tor n. one supervising students, as during a test

pro·cure' v. get; obtain — **pro·cur'a·ble** a. — **pro·cure'ment** n. — **pro·cur'er** n.

prod n., v. **prod'ded, prod'ding**

prod'i·gal a. very wasteful or generous —n. spendthrift —**prod'i·gal'i·ty** n.

pro·di'gious (-dij'əs) a. 1 amazing 2 enormous —**pro·di'gious·ly** adv.

prod'i·gy n., pl. **-gies** remarkable person or thing

pro·duce' (n.: prō'dōōs) v. 1 show 2 bring forth 3 manufacture 4 cause 5 get (a play, etc.) ready for the public —n. farm products —**pro·duc'er** n. —**pro·duc'tion** n.

prod'uct n. 1 thing produced 2 result 3 result of multiplying numbers

pro·duc'tive a. 1 producing much 2 causing —**pro·duc'tiv'i·ty** n.

pro·fane' a. 1 not religious 2 scornful of sacred things —v. treat irreverently —**pro·fane'ly** adv.

pro·fan'i·ty n., pl. **-ties** swearing

pro·fess' v. 1 declare openly 2 claim to have or be 3 declare one's belief in

pro·fes'sion n. 1 occupation requiring special study 2 its members 3 avowal

pro·fes'sion·al n., a. (one) of a profession, or (one) paid to play in games, etc. —**pro·fes'sion·al·ly** adv.

pro·fes'sor n. college teacher —**pro·fes·so'ri·al** a.

prof'fer v., n. offer

pro·fi'cient (-fish'ənt) a. skilled —**pro·fi'cien·cy** n.

pro'file n. 1 side view of the face 2 outline

prof'it n. 1 gain; benefit 2 net income from business —v. benefit —**prof'it·a·ble** a. —**prof'it·a·bly** adv. —**prof'it·less** a.

prof'it·eer' n. one who makes excessive profits

prof'li·gate (-gət) a. 1 dissolute 2 wasteful —**prof'li·ga·cy** n.

pro·found' a. 1 very deep 2 complete —**pro·fun'di·ty** n., pl. **-ties**

pro·fuse' (-fyōōs') a. abundant —**pro·fuse'ly** adv. —**pro·fu'sion** n.

pro·gen'i·tor n. ancestor

prog'e·ny (präj'-) n. offspring

pro·ges'ter·one n. hormone secreted in the ovary

prog·no'sis n., pl. **-ses** (-sēz') prediction

prog·nos'ti·cate v. predict —**prog·nos'ti·ca'tion** n. —**prog·**

nos'ti·ca'tor n.

pro'gram n. 1 list of things to be performed 2 plan of procedure 3 scheduled radio or TV broadcast 4 logical sequence of operations for electronic computer —v. 1 schedule in a program 2 plan a computer program for 3 furnish with a program Br. sp. **pro'gramme** —**pro'gram'ma·ble** a.

prog'ress (prō gres'; n.: präg'res) v. advance, develop, or improve —n. a progressing —**pro·gres'sion** n.

pro·gres'sive a. 1 progressing 2 favoring progress, reform, etc. —n. progressive person —**pro·gres'sive·ly** adv.

pro·hib'it v. 1 forbid, as by law 2 prevent —**pro·hib'i·tive, pro·hib'i·to'ry** a.

pro'hi·bi'tion (-bish'ən) n. a forbidding, esp. of the making or selling of liquor —**pro'hi·bi'tion·ist** n.

proj·ect' (v.: prə jekt') n. 1 scheme 2 undertaking —v. 1 propose 2 stick out 3 cause (a light, etc.) to fall upon a surface —**pro·jec'tion** n. —**pro·jec'tor** n.

pro·jec'tile (-təl) n. object to be shot forth, as a bullet

pro·jec'tion·ist n. operator of a film or slide projector

pro·le·tar'i·at n. working class —**pro·le·tar'i·an** a., n.

pro·lif'er·ate v. increase rapidly —**pro·lif'er·a'tion** n.

pro·lif'ic a. producing much

pro·lix' a. wordy —**pro·lix'i·ty** n.

pro'logue' (-lôg') n. introduction to a poem, play, etc.

pro·long' v. lengthen —**pro'lon·ga'tion** n.

prom n. formal dance at a college, etc.

prom'e·nade' (-nād', -näd') n. 1 walk for pleasure 2 public place for walking —v. take a promenade

prom'i·nent a. 1 projecting 2 conspicuous; very noticeable 3 famous —**prom'i·nence** n.

pro·mis'cu·ous (-kyōō-) a. not discriminating —**prom'is·cu'i·ty** n.

prom'ise n. 1 agreement to do or not do something 2 sign as of future success —v. 1 to make a promise of or to 2 to cause to expect

prom'is·ing a. showing signs of future success

prom·is·so·ry *a.* containing or being a promise

prom·on·to·ry *n., pl.* **-ries** peak of high land jutting out into the sea

pro·mote' *v.* 1 raise in rank 2 further the growth or sale of — **pro·mo'tion** *n.* —**pro·mot'er** *n.*

prompt *a.* ready; quick —*v.* 1 help with a cue 2 inspire or urge —**prompt'er** *n.* —**prompt'ly** *adv.*

promp'ti·tude *n.* quality of being prompt

prom·ul·gate' *v.* proclaim; publish —**prom'ul·ga'tion** *n.*

prone *a.* 1 lying face downward 2 apt or likely

prong *n.* projecting point, as of a fork —**pronged** *a.*

pro'noun *n.* word used in place of a noun —**pro·nom'i·nal** *a.*

pro·nounce' *v.* 1 declare officially 2 utter the sounds of — **pro·nounce'a·ble** *a.* —**pro·nounce'ment** *n.*

pro·nounced' *a.* definite; unmistakable

pro·nun'ci·a'tion *n.* act or way of pronouncing words

proof *n.* 1 convincing evidence 2 a test 3 strength of a liquor — *a.* strong enough to resist

-proof *suf.* impervious to

proof'read' *v.* to read in order to correct errors

prop *n.* 1 a support or aid 2 propeller —*v.* propped, prop'ping to support or lean against

prop·a·gan'da *n.* 1 systematic spreading of ideas 2 ideas so spread —**prop'a·gan'dist** *a., n.* —**prop'a·gan'dize** *v.*

prop'a·gate' *v.* 1 produce offspring 2 raise; breed 3 spread (ideas) —**prop'a·ga'tion** *n.*

pro'pane' *n.* a gas used as a fuel

pro·pel' *v.* **-pelled', -pel'ling** drive forward

pro·pel'lant, pro·pel'lent *n.* fuel for a rocket

pro·pel'ler *n.* blades on end of a revolving shaft for propelling a ship or aircraft

pro·pen'si·ty *n., pl.* **-ties** natural tendency

prop'er *a.* 1 suitable; fit 2 correct 3 genteel; respectable 4 belonging (to) 5 actual —**prop'er·ly** *adv.*

prop'er·ty *n., pl.* **-ties** 1 thing owned 2 characteristic

proph'e·cy (-sē) *n., pl.* **-cies** prediction

proph'e·sy' (-sī') *v.* **-sied', -sy'-**

ing to predict; foretell —**pro·phet'ic** *a.*

proph'et *n.* 1 leader regarded as divinely inspired 2 one who predicts

pro·phy·lac'tic (-fə-) *n., a.* (medicine, device, etc.) that prevents disease, etc.

pro·pin'qui·ty *n.* nearness

pro·pi'ti·ate' (-pish'ē-) *v.* to appease

pro·pi'tious *a.* favorable

pro·po'nent *n.* supporter

pro·por'tion *n.* 1 part in relation to the whole 2 ratio 3 symmetry 4 *pl.* dimensions —*v.* 1 make symmetrical 2 make fit —**pro·por'tion·al, pro·por'tion·ate** *a.*

pro·pose' *v.* 1 suggest for considering 2 plan 3 offer marriage —**pro·pos'al** *n.*

prop·o·si'tion *n.* 1 a plan 2 subject for debate

pro·pound' *v.* suggest for consideration

pro·pri'e·tar'y *a.* held under a patent, etc.

pro·pri'e·tor *n.* owner

pro·pri'e·ty *n.* fitness; correctness

pro·pul'sion *n.* a propelling or a force that propels —**pro·pul'sive** *a.*

pro·rate' *v.* divide or assess proportionally

pro·sa'ic (-zā'-) *a.* commonplace

pro·scribe' *v.* forbid

prose *n.* nonpoetic language

pros'e·cute' *v.* 1 engage in 2 take legal action against —**pros'e·cu'tion** *n.* —**pros'e·cu'tor** *n.*

pros'e·lyte' (-līt) *n., v.* convert —**pros'e·lyt·ize'** *v.*

pros'pect *n.* 1 outlook 2 likely customer, etc. 3 *pl.* apparent chance for success —*v.* search (for) —**pros'pec·tor** *n.*

pro·spec'tive *a.* expected

pro·spec'tus *n.* report outlining a new work, etc.

pros'per *v.* thrive

pros·per'i·ty *n.* wealth —**pros'per·ous** *a.* —**pros'per·ous·ly** *adv.*

pros'tate' *a.* of a gland at the base of the bladder in males

pros·the'sis *n., pl.* **-ses** (-sēz) (use of) artificial body part(s) — **pros·thet'ic** *a.*

pros'ti·tute' *n.* one who engages in sexual intercourse for pay — *v.* sell (one's talents, etc.) for base purposes —**pros'ti·tu'tion** *n.*

pros'trate' *a.* 1 lying flat, esp. face downward 2 overcome —*v.* 1 lay flat 2 overcome —**pros·tra'tion** *n.*

pro·tag'o·nist *n.* main character or leading figure

pro·tect' *v.* shield from harm —**pro·tec'tion** *n.* —**pro·tec'tive** *a.* —**pro·tec'tor** *n.*

pro·tec'tor·ate (-ət) *n.* territory controlled and protected by a strong state

pro·té·gé (prōt'ə zhā') *n.* one under another's patronage

pro'te·in' (-tēn') *n.* nitrogenous substance essential to diet

pro·test' (*n.:* prō'test') *v.* 1 to object 2 assert —*n.* objection —**prot'es·ta'tion** *n.* —**pro·test'er, pro·tes'tor** *n.*

Prot'es·tant *n.* Christian not of the Roman Catholic or Eastern Orthodox Church —**Prot'es·tant·ism'** *n.*

pro'to·col' (-kôl') *n.* code of etiquette among diplomats, etc.

pro'ton' *n.* positive particle in the nucleus of an atom

pro'to·plasm' *n.* essential matter in all living cells —**pro'to·plas'mic** *a.*

pro'to·type' *n.* first thing of its kind

pro'to·zo'an *n.,* *pl.* **-zo'a** one-celled animal

pro·tract' *v.* draw out; prolong —**pro·trac'tion** *n.*

pro·trac'tor *n.* device for drawing and measuring angles

pro·trude' *v.* jut out —**pro·tru'sion** *n.*

pro·tu'ber·ance *n.* bulge —**pro·tu'ber·ant** *a.*

proud *a.* 1 haughty 2 feeling or causing pride 3 splendid —**proud of** highly pleased with —**proud'ly** *adv.*

prove (prōōv) *v.* proved, proved or prov'en, prov'ing 1 test by experiment 2 establish as true

prov'en·der *n.* fodder

prov'erb *n.* wise saying —**pro·ver'bi·al** *a.*

pro·vide' *v.* 1 supply; furnish (with) 2 prepare (*for* or *against*) 3 stipulate —**pro·vid'er** *n.*

pro·vid'ed *con.* on condition (*that*): also **pro·vid'ing**

prov'i·dence *n.* 1 prudent foresight 2 guidance of God or Nature —[**P**—] God —**prov'i·dent** *a.* —**prov'i·den'tial** (-shəl) *a.*

prov'ince *n.* 1 division of a country 2 *pl.* parts of a country

outside major cities 3 sphere; field

pro·vin'cial (-shəl) *a.* 1 of a province 2 narrow-minded —**pro·vin'cial·ism'** *n.*

pro·vi'sion (-vizh'ən) *n.* 1 a providing 2 *pl.* stock of food 3 stipulation —*v.* supply with provisions

pro·vi'sion·al *a.* temporary

pro·vi'so' *n.,* *pl.* **-sos'** or **-soes'** stipulation

prov'o·ca'tion *n.* 1 a provoking 2 thing that provokes —**pro·voc'a·tive** *a.*

pro·voke' *v.* 1 anger 2 stir up or evoke

prow (prou) *n.* forward part of a ship

prow'ess *n.* 1 bravery; valor 2 superior skill, etc.

prowl *v.* roam or stalk furtively

prox·im'i·ty *n.* nearness

prox'y *n.,* *pl.* **-ies** (one with) authority to act for another

prude *n.* one overly modest or proper —**prud'er·y** *n.* —**prud'ish** *a.*

pru'dent *a.* wisely careful —**pru'dence** *n.* —**pru·den'tial** (-shəl) *a.*

prune *n.* dried plum —*v.* trim twigs, etc. from

pru'ri·ent (proor'ē-) *a.* lustful —**pru'ri·ence** *n.*

pry *n.,* *pl.* **pries** lever —*v.* pried, pry'ing 1 raise with a lever 2 look closely or inquisitively

psalm (säm) *n.* sacred song or poem —**psalm'ist** *n.*

pseu'do (sōō'dō) *a.* false

pseu'do·nym' (-nim') *n.* fictitious name assumed by an author, etc.

pshaw (shô) *int., n.* exclamation of disgust, etc.

pso·ri'a·sis (sə rī'ə-) *n.* skin disease with scaly, reddish patches

psych (sīk) *v.* [Sl.] 1 probe behavior psychologically so as to outwit or control: often with *out* 2 prepare (oneself) psychologically: with *up*

psy·che (sī'kē) *n.* 1 soul 2 mind

psy·chi'a·try (-kī'-) *n.* branch of medicine dealing with mental illness —**psy·chi·at'ric** (-kē-) *a.* —**psy·chi'a·trist** *n.*

psy'chic (-kik) *a.* 1 of the mind 2 supernatural Also **psy'chi·cal** —*n.* one sensitive to psychic phenomena

psy'cho (-kō) [Col.] *n.,* *pl.* **-chos** psychopath —*a.* psychopathic

psycho– *pref.* mind; mental

processes: also **psych–**

psy·cho·a·nal'y·sis n. method of treating neuroses —**psy'cho·an'a·lyst** n. —**psy'cho·an'a·lyze'** v.

psy·chol'o·gy n. science dealing with the mind and behavior — **psy'cho·log'i·cal** a. —**psy'cho·log'i·cal·ly** adv. —**psy·chol'o·gist** n.

psy·cho·path'ic a. of mental disorder —**psy'cho·path'** n.

psy·cho'sis n., pl. **-ses'** (-sēz') severe mental illness —**psy·chot'ic** a., n.

psy·cho·so·mat'ic a. of a physical disorder caused by emotional disturbance

psy·cho·ther'a·py n. treatment of mental illness —**psy·cho·ther'a·pist** n.

ptar'mi·gan (tär'-) n. northern grouse

pto'maine' (tō'-) n. a substance in decaying matter

pub n. [Br. Col.] bar; tavern: in full public house

pu'ber·ty (pyoo'-) n. time of maturing sexually

pu'bic a. of or in the region of the groin

pub'lic a. 1 of people as a whole 2 for everyone 3 known by all —n. the people —**in public** in open view —**pub'lic·ly** adv.

pub·li·ca'tion n. 1 printing and selling of books, etc. 2 thing published

pub'li·cist n. publicity agent

pub·lic'i·ty (-lis'-) n. 1 public attention 2 information meant to bring one this —**pub'li·cize'** v.

pub'lish v. 1 issue (a printed work) for sale 2 announce — **pub'lish·er** n.

puce n. brownish purple

puck n. hard rubber disk used in ice hockey

puck'er n., v. wrinkle

puck'ish a. mischievous

pud'ding (pood'-) n. soft food of flour, milk, eggs, etc.

pud'dle n. small pool of water

pudg'y a. **-i·er, -i·est** short and fat

pueb'lo (pweb'-) n., pl. **-los** American Indian village of SW U.S.

pu·er·ile (pyoor'il) a. childish — **pu'er·il'i·ty** n.

puff n. 1 brief burst of wind, etc. 2 draw at a cigarette 3 light pastry shell 4 soft pad —v. 1 blow in puffs 2 breathe rapidly

3 smoke 4 swell —**puff'i·ness** n. —**puff'y** a., **-i·er, -i·est**

puf'fin n. northern seabird

pug n. small dog

pu·gil·ism (pyoo'jə liz'əm) n. sport of boxing —**pu'gil·ist** n. — **pu·gil·is'tic** a.

pug·na'cious a. quarrelsome — **pug·na'cious·ly** adv. —**pug·nac'i·ty** (-nas'-) n.

pug nose n. a short, thick nose that is turned up at the end — **pug'-nosed'** a.

puke n., n. [Col.] vomit

pul'chri·tude' (-krə-) n. beauty

pull v. 1 to make (something) move toward one 2 pluck out 3 rip 4 strain 5 [Col.] do; perform 6 move (away, ahead, etc.) —n. 1 act or effort of pulling 2 handle, etc. 3 [Col.] influence —**pull for** [Col.] cheer on —**pull off** accomplish —**pull out** 1 depart 2 quit or withdraw — **pull over** drive toward, and stop at, the curb —**pull through** [Col.] get over (an illness, etc.)

pul'let (pool'-) n. young hen

pul'ley n., pl. **-leys** wheel with a grooved rim in which a rope runs, for raising weights

Pull'man (car) n. railroad car with berths for sleeping

pull'out' n. removal, withdrawal, etc.

pull'o·ver n. sweater, etc. to be pulled over the head

pul'mo·nar'y a. of the lungs

pulp n. 1 soft, inside part, as of fruit 2 moist wood fiber, ground to make paper —**pulp'y** a., **-i·er, -i·est**

pul'pit n. clergyman's platform for preaching

pul'sar n. celestial object emitting pulses of radiation

pul'sate' v. throb —**pul·sa'tion** n.

pulse n. regular beat, as of blood in the arteries

pul'ver·ize' v. grind or crush into powder

pu'ma (pyoo'-, poo'-) n. cougar

pum'ice n. light, spongy rock, used for cleaning, etc.

pum'mel v. hit with repeated blows, esp. with the fist

pump n. 1 machine that forces fluids in or out 2 low-cut, strapless shoe —v. 1 move or empty (fluids) with a pump 2 move like a pump 3 question persistently

pum'per·nick'el n. coarse, dark rye bread

pump'kin n. large, round, orange-yellow gourd

pun n. humorous use of different words that sound alike —v. **punned, pun'ning** make puns

punch n. 1 tool for piercing, etc. 2 fruit drink 3 energy with the fist —v. 1 pierce, etc. with a punch 2 hit with the fist

punch'y a. **-i-er, -i-est** [Col.] forceful 2 dazed

punc-til'i-ous a. 1 careful in behavior 2 precise

punc'tu-al (-choō əl) a. on time —**punc'tu-al'i-ty** n.

punc'tu-ate' v. use periods, commas, etc. in (writing) —**punc'tu-a'tion** n.

punc'ture n. hole made by a sharp point —v. pierce as with a point

pun'dit n. very learned person

pun'gent a. 1 sharp in taste or smell 2 keen and direct —**pun'gen-cy** n.

pun'ish v. make suffer pain, loss, etc. as for a crime or offense —**pun'ish·a·ble** a. —**pun'ish·ment** n.

pu'ni-tive a. of or inflicting punishment

punk n. 1 substance that smolders, used to light fireworks 2 [Sl.] insignificant young person

pun'ster n. one who makes puns: also **pun'ner**

punt v. 1 kick a dropped football before it touches the ground 2 move (a boat) using a long pole —n. 1 a punting 2 square, flat-bottomed boat

pu'ny a. **-ni-er, -ni-est** small or weak

pup n. young dog, wolf, etc.

pu'pa (pyoō'-) n., pl. **-pae** (-pē) or **-pas** insect just before the adult stage

pu'pil n. 1 person being taught 2 contracting opening in iris of the eye

pup'pet n. 1 doll moved manually by strings, etc. 2 person controlled by another —**pup'pet-eer'** n.

pup'py n., pl. **-pies** young dog

pup tent n. small, portable tent

pur'chase (-chəs) v. buy —n. 1 thing bought 2 act of buying —**pur'chas-er** n.

pure a. 1 unmixed 2 clean 3 mere 4 faultless 5 chaste 6 abstract —**pure'ly** adv. —**pu'ri-fy'** v. —**pu'ri-fi-ca'tion** n. —**pu'ri-ty** n.

pure'bred' a. belonging to a breed of unmixed descent

pu-rée, pu-ree (pyoō rā') n. 1 mashed, strained food 2 thick soup

pur'ga-tive (-gə-) a. purging —n. a laxative

pur'ga-to'ry R.C.Ch. state or place for expiating sins after death

purge v. 1 cleanse; make pure 2 move (the bowels) 3 get rid of —n. 1 a purging 2 a laxative

pur'ist n. person who strictly observes rules in art, etc.

pu'ri-tan (pyoor'ə-) n. one very strict in morals and religion —**pu'ri-tan'i-cal, pu'ri-tan'ic** a.

pur-lieu (purl'yoō') n. outlying part; suburb

pur'loin' v. steal

pur'ple n., a. bluish red

pur-port' (n.: pur'pôrt) v. seem or claim to mean or be —n. meaning

pur'pose (-pəs) n. 1 intention; aim 2 determination —**on purpose** intentionally —**pur'pose-ful** a. —**pur'pose-less** a. —**pur'pose-ly** adv.

purr v., n. (make) the sound of a cat at ease

purse n. 1 small bag for money 2 woman's handbag 3 prize money —v. to pucker (the lips)

purs'er n. ship's officer in charge of accounts, etc.

pur'su-ant a. following —**pursuant to** according to

pur-sue' v. 1 try to overtake; chase 2 go on with 3 seek —**pur-su'ance** n.

pur-suit' n. 1 a pursuing 2 occupation

pur-vey' (-vā') v. supply, as food —**pur-vey'or** n.

pur'view' n. scope or extent of control, activity, etc.

pus n. yellowish matter forming in infections

push v. 1 to move by pressing against 2 urge on —n. 1 a pushing 2 an advance

push'er n. [Sl.] one who sells drugs illegally

push'o'ver n. [Sl.] 1 anything easy to do 2 one easily persuaded, defeated, etc.

push'-up', push'up' n. exercise of raising one's prone body by pushing down on the palms

push'y a. **-i-er, -i-est** [Col.] annoyingly aggressive

pu'sil-lan'i-mous a. cowardly; timid

puss (poos) n. [Col.] cat: also

puss'y, puss'y·cat'

puss'y·foot' v. [Col.] 1 move cautiously 2 avoid taking a stand

pussy willow n. willow with soft, silvery catkins

pus'tule (-tyōōl′, -chōōl′) n. inflamed, pus-filled pimple

put v. put, put'ting 1 make be in some place, state, relation, etc. 2 impose or assign 3 express 4 go (in, out, etc.) —**put down** 1 repress 2 [Sl.] belittle or humiliate —**put in for** apply for —**put off** 1 postpone 2 perturb —**put on** 1 pretend 2 [Sl.] to hoax —**put out** 1 extinguish 2 inconvenience —**put up** 1 preserve (fruits, etc.) 2 give lodgings to 3 provide (money) — **put upon** impose on —**put up with** tolerate —**stay put** [Col.] remain; stay

put′-down′ n. [Sl.] belittling remark

put′-on′ n. [Sl.] hoax

pu′tre·fy′ v. -fied′, -fy′ing rot — **pu′tre·fac′tion** n.

pu′trid a. rotten; stinking

putt v., n. Golf (make) a stroke to roll the ball into the hole

put′ter v. busy oneself aimlessly —n. Golf club for putting

put′ty n. pliable substance to fill cracks, etc. —v. -tied, -ty·ing fill with putty

puz′zle v. perplex —n. 1 thing that puzzles 2 problem to test cleverness

pyg′my (pig′-) n., pl. -mies dwarf

py·ja′mas n.pl. Br. sp. of PAJAMAS

py′lon′ (pi-) n. towerlike shaft

py·or·rhe·a, py·or·rhoe·a (pi′ə rē′ə) n. infection of the gums and tooth sockets

pyr′a·mid (pir′-) n. solid figure or structure with triangular sides meeting at a point —v. build up —**py·ram′i·dal** a.

pyre (pir) n. pile of wood for burning a dead body

py·ro·ma′ni·a n. compulsion to start fires —**py′ro·ma′ni·ac′** a.

py′ro·tech′nics n.pl. 1 display of fireworks 2 dazzling display

py′thon′ n. large snake that crushes its prey to death

Q

quack v. utter the cry of a duck —n. 1 this cry 2 one who prac-

tices medicine fraudulently — **quack′er·y** n.

quad′ran′gle n. 1 plane figure with four angles and four sides 2 four-sided area surrounded by buildings: also **quad**

quad′rant n. quarter section of a circle

quad′ri·lat′er·al a., n. four-sided (figure)

qua·drille′ n. dance in which four couples form a square, etc.

quad′ri·ple′gi·a (-plē′jē ə) n. paralysis of the body from the neck down —**quad′ri·ple′gic** a., n.

quad′ru·ped′ n. four-footed animal

quad·ru′ple a., adv. four times as much —v. make or become quadruple

quad·ru′plet n. any of four children born at one birth

quaff (kwäf) v. drink deeply —n. a quaffing

quag′mire′ n. a bog

quail v. draw back in fear —n. game bird

quaint a. pleasingly odd or old-fashioned —**quaint′ly** adv. — **quaint′ness** n.

quake v. shake —n. 1 a quaking 2 earthquake

qual′i·fy′ v. -fied′, -fy′ing 1 make or be fit for a job, etc. 2 modify; restrict 3 moderate — **qual′i·fi·ca′tion** n. —**qual′i·fi′er** n.

qual′i·ty n., pl. -ties 1 characteristic 2 kind 3 degree of (excellence) —**qual′i·ta′tive** a.

qualm (kwäm) n. scruple; misgiving

quan′da·ry n., pl. -ries state of perplexity; dilemma

quan′ti·ty n., pl. -ties 1 amount 2 large amount 3 number or symbol expressing measure — **quan′ti·ta′tive** a.

quan′tum n., pl. -ta Physics basic unit of energy, etc.

quar′an·tine′ (-tēn′) n. isolation to keep contagious disease from spreading —v. place under quarantine

quar′rel v., n. (have) an argument or disagreement —**quar′rel·some** a.

quar′ry n., pl. -ries 1 animal, etc. being hunted down 2 place where stone is excavated —v. -ried, -ry·ing excavate from a quarry

quart n. ¼ gallon

quar′ter n. 1 any of four equal

parts; 1/4 25-cent coin 3 district 4 *pl.* lodgings 5 mercy —*v.* 1 divide into quarters 2 provide lodgings for —**at close quarters** at close range

quar'ter·back' *n. Football* back who calls signals and passes the ball

quar'ter·ly *a.* occurring regularly four times a year —*adv.* once every quarter of the year —*n.*, *pl.* **-lies** publication issued quarterly

quar'ter·mas·ter *n.* army officer in charge of supplies

quar·tet', quar·tette' *n.* musical composition for four performers

quar'to *n.* book-page size about 9 X 12 in.

quartz *n.* bright mineral

qua'sar *n.* a distant celestial object that emits immense quantities of light and radio waves

quash (kwäsh) *v.* 1 annul 2 suppress

qua·si (kwä'zī', kwä'zē') *a.*, *adv.* seeming(ly)

quat'rain' *n.* stanza of four lines

qua'ver *v.* 1 tremble 2 be tremulous: said of the voice —*n.* tremulous tone

quay (kē) *n.* wharf

quea'sy (kwē'-) *a.* **-si·er, -si·est** feeling nausea

queen *n.* 1 wife of a king 2 woman monarch 3 female in an insect colony 4 playing card with a queen's picture 5 most powerful chess piece

queer *a.* 1 odd 2 [Col.] eccentric —**queer'ly** *adv.*

quell *v.* subdue or quiet

quench *v.* 1 extinguish 2 satisfy —**quench'less** *a.*

quer'u·lous (kwer'-) *a.* 1 fretful 2 complaining

que'ry (kwir'-) *n.*, **-ries**; *v.* **-ried, -ry·ing** question

quest *n.* a seeking —*v.* seek

ques'tion *n.* 1 inquiry 2 thing asked 3 doubt 4 problem 5 point being debated —*v.* 1 inquire 2 doubt 3 challenge —**out of the question** impossible —**ques'tion·er** *n.*

ques'tion·a·ble *a.* 1 doubtful 2 not well thought of

question mark *n.* mark of punctuation (?)

ques'tion·naire' *n.* list of questions for gathering information

queue (kyōō) *n.* 1 pigtail 2 line of persons

quib'ble *v.* evade a point by carping

quiche (kēsh) *n.* hot custard pie made with cheese, spinach, etc.

quick *a.* 1 swift 2 prompt —*adv.* rapidly —*n.* 1 the living 2 one's deepest feelings —**quick'ly** *adv.*

quick'en *v.* 1 enliven 2 hasten

quick'lime' *n.* unslaked lime

quick'sand' *n.* wet, deep sand that engulfs heavy things

quick'sil·ver *n.* mercury

quick'-wit'ted *a.* alert

qui·es·cent (kwi-) *a.* quiet; inactive

qui'et *a.* 1 still 2 silent 3 gentle —*n.* 1 stillness 2 silence —*v.* make or become quiet —**qui'et·ly** *adv.* —**qui'et·ness** *n.*

quill *n.* 1 large feather 2 pen made from this 3 spine of a porcupine

quilt *v., n.* (make) a bedcover stitched in layers

quince *n.* yellowish fruit

qui'nine' *n.* alkaloid used in treating malaria

quin·tes'sence *n.* 1 pure essence 2 perfect example

quin·tet', quin·tette' *n.* musical composition for five performers

quin·tu'plet (-tup'lət) *n.* any of five children born at one birth

quip *v., n.* **quipped, quip'ping** (make) a witty remark

quire *n.* set of 24 or 25 sheets of the same paper

quirk *n.* peculiarity

quirt *n.* riding whip with braided leather lash

quis'ling (kwiz'-) *n.* traitor

quit *v.* **quit, quit'ted, quit'ting** 1 give up 2 leave 3 stop —*a.* free

quit'claim' *n.* deed resigning a claim, as to property

quite *adv.* 1 completely 2 really 3 very or fairly —**quite a few** [Col.] many

quits *a.* on even terms —**call it quits** [Col.] stop working, being friendly, etc.

quit'tance *n.* 1 discharge of a debt 2 recompense

quit'ter *n.* [Col.] one who gives up easily

quiv'er *v.* tremble —*n.* 1 tremor 2 case for arrows

quix·ot'ic *a.* idealistic but impractical

quiz *n., pl.* **quiz'zes** test of knowledge —*v.* **quizzed, quiz'zing** give a quiz to

quiz'zi·cal *a.* 1 comical 2 perplexed —**quiz'zi·cal·ly** *adv.*

quoit *n.* 1 ring thrown to encircle an upright peg 2 *pl.* game so played

quon′dam *a.* former

Quon′set hut *trademark* metal shelter with a curved roof

quo′rum *n.* minimum number needed to transact business at an assembly

quo′ta *n., pl.* **-tas** share assigned to each one

quo·ta′tion *n.* 1 a quoting 2 words quoted 3 current price of a stock or bond

quotation marks *n.* marks ("...") around quoted words

quote *v.* 1 repeat (the words of) 2 state (the price of) —*n.* [Col.] 1 quotation 2 quotation mark —**quot′a·ble** *a.*

quoth (kwōth) *v.* [Ar.] said

quo′tient (-shənt) *n.* number got by dividing one number into another

R

rab′bi (-ī) *n., pl.* **-bis** ordained teacher of the Jewish law —**rab·bin′i·cal** *a.*

rab′bit *n.* burrowing rodent with soft fur and long ears

rab′ble *n.* a mob

rab′ble-rous′er *n.* one who tries to incite others to anger or violence

rab′id *a.* 1 fanatical 2 of or having rabies

ra′bies *n.* disease of dogs, etc., transmitted by biting

rac·coon′ *n.* small, furry mammal with black-ringed tail

race *n.* 1 a competition, esp. of speed 2 swift current 3 division of mankind, esp. based on skin color 4 any group or class —*v.* 1 be in a race 2 move swiftly — **rac′er** *n.* —**ra′cial** (-shəl) *a.*

ra·ceme′ *n.* flower cluster

rac′ism′ *n.* racial discrimination or persecution —**rac′ist** *a., n.*

rack *n.* 1 framework for holding things 2 ancient torture device 3 great torment 4 toothed bar meshing with a gearwheel —*v.* to torture —**rack one's brain** think hard

rack′et *n.* 1 noisy confusion 2 dishonest scheme 3 netted frame used as a bat in tennis: also sp. **rac′quet**

rack′et·eer′ *n.* one who gets money by fraud, extortion, etc. —**rack′et·eer′ing** *n.*

rac′on·teur′ (-tur′) *n.* one clever at telling stories

rac′quet·ball′ *n.* game like handball played with rackets

rac·y (rā′sē) *a.* **-i·er, -i·est** 1 lively 2 risqué

ra′dar′ *n.* device for locating objects by their reflection of radio waves

ra′di·al *a.* of or like a ray or rays

radial (ply) tire *n.* tire with ply cords at right angles to the center line of tread

ra′di·ant *a.* 1 beaming 2 shining bright 3 issuing in rays —**ra′di·ance** *n.*

ra′di·ate′ *v.* 1 send out rays, as of heat or light 2 branch out as from a center

ra′di·a·tion *n.* 1 a radiating 2 rays sent out 3 nuclear particles

ra′di·a·tor *n.* device for radiating heat

rad′i·cal *a.* 1 basic 2 favoring extreme change —*n.* 1 one with radical views 2 *Chem.* group of atoms acting as one —**rad′i·cal·ism′** *n.* —**rad′i·cal·ly** *adv.*

ra′di·o′ *n., pl.* **-os′** 1 way of sending sounds through space by electromagnetic waves 2 set for receiving radio waves 3 broadcasting by radio —*a.* of radio —*v.* **-oed′, -o′ing** send by radio

ra′di·o·ac′tive *a.* emitting radiant energy by the disintegration of atomic nuclei —**ra′di·o·ac·tiv′i·ty** *n.*

ra′di·ol′o·gy *n.* medical use of radiant energy —**ra′di·ol′o·gist** *n.*

rad′ish *n.* edible pungent root of certain plant

ra′di·um *n.* radioactive metallic chemical element

ra′di·us *n., pl.* **-di·i′** (-dē ī′) or **-di·us·es** straight line from the center to the outside of a circle or sphere

ra′don′ *n.* radioactive gas, a chemical element

raf′fi·a *n.* fiber from leaves of a palm, used in weaving

raf′fle *n.* lottery —*v.* offer as a prize in a raffle

raft *n.* floating platform of logs fastened together

raf′ter *n.* beam in a roof

rag *n.* 1 piece of torn or waste cloth 2 *pl.* tattered clothes — **rag′ged** *a.*

rag′a·muf′fin *n.* dirty, ragged child

rage *n.* 1 furious anger 2 craze; fad —*v.* 1 show violent anger 2 be unchecked

rag'lan n. designating a sleeve that continues in one piece to the collar

ra·gout (ra gōō') n. stew

rag'time' n. early jazz

rag'weed' n. common weed whose pollen causes hay fever

raid n. sudden attack or invasion —v. make a raid on

rail n. 1 bar put between posts as a guard or support 2 either of the bars of a railroad track 3 railroad 4 small wading bird —v. speak bitterly

rail'ing n. fence made of rails and posts

rail'ler·y n. playful teasing

rail'road' n. 1 road with steel rails for trains 2 system of such roads —v. [Col.] rush through unfairly

rail'way' n. 1 [Br.] railroad 2 track with rails for cars

rai'ment (rā'-) n. [Ar.] attire

rain n. water falling in drops from the clouds —v. fall as or like rain —**rain'drop'** n. —**rain'fall'** n. —**rain'storm'** n. —**rain'y** a., -i·er, -i·est

rain'bow' n. arc of colors formed by sunshine on rain

rain'coat' n. waterproof coat

raise v. 1 lift up 2 increase in amount, degree, etc. 3 build or put up 4 bring up 5 collect 6 make grow —n. a pay increase

rai'sin n. sweet, dried grape

rake n. 1 long-handled tool with teeth at one end 2 debauched man —v. 1 gather (leaves, etc.) with a rake 2 search carefully 3 sweep with gunfire

rak'ish (rāk'-) a. jaunty

ral'ly v. -lied, -ly·ing 1 regroup 2 to set in order 3 revive —n., pl. -lies 1 a rallying 2 mass meeting

ram n. 1 male sheep 2 battering ram —v. rammed, ram'ming 1 strike against with force 2 force into place

RAM (ram) n. computer memory allowing direct access of data: also ran'dom-ac'cess memory

ram'ble v. 1 stroll; roam 2 talk or write aimlessly 3 spread, as vines —n. a stroll —**ram'bler** n.

ram·bunc'tious (-shəs) a. disorderly; unruly

ram'i·fy' v. -fied', -fy'ing spread out into branches —**ram'i·fi·ca'tion** n.

ramp n. sloping passage joining

different levels

ram·page' (n.: ram'pāj) v. rush wildly about —n. wild, angry action: usually in **on the** (or **a**) **rampage**

ramp'ant a. 1 raging; wild 2 rearing up

ram'part' n. fortified embankment

ram'rod' n. rod for ramming down a charge in a gun

ram·shack'le a. rickety

ran v. pt. of RUN

ranch n. large farm for raising livestock —**ranch'er, ranch'man** n., pl. **-men**

ran'cid a. stale, as oil or fat; spoiled

ran'cor n. bitter hate or ill will —**ran'cor·ous** a.

ran'dom a. haphazard —**at ran·dom** haphazardly

rang v. pt. of RING

range v. 1 set in rows 2 roam about 3 extend —n. 1 row or line, esp. of mountains 2 effective distance 3 extent 4 open land 5 place for shooting practice 6 cooking stove

rang'er n. 1 trooper who patrols a region 2 warden who patrols forests

rang·y (rān'jē) a. -i·er, -i·est long-limbed and thin

rank n. 1 row; line 2 class or grade 3 pl. enlisted soldiers —v. 1 to place in, or hold, a certain rank 2 outrank —a. 1 growing wildly 2 bad in taste or smell 3 utter —**rank and file** 1 enlisted men and women 2 common people

ran'kle v. cause mental pain, resentment, etc.

ran'sack' v. 1 search thoroughly 2 plunder; loot

ran'som n. 1 the freeing of a captive by paying money 2 price asked —v. buy a captive's freedom

rant v. talk wildly; rave

rap v. **rapped, rap'ping** 1 strike or knock sharply 2 [Sl.] to chat; talk —n. quick, sharp knock

ra·pa'cious (-shəs) a. greedy voracious —**ra·pac'i·ty** n.

rape n. 1 crime of attacking sexually 2 plant whose leaves are used for fodder —v. commit rape (on) —**rap'ist** n.

rap'id a. swift —**ra·pid'i·ty** n. —**rap'id·ly** adv.

rap'ids n.pl. part of a river with very swift current

ra·pi·er n. light, sharp sword

rap·ine (rap'in) n. plunder

rap·port' (-pôr') n. sympathetic relationship; harmony

rap·proche·ment (ra'prōsh män') n. an establishing of friendly relations

rapt a. engrossed (in)

rap'ture n. ecstasy

rare a. 1 scarce; uncommon 2 very good 3 not dense 4 partly raw —**rare'ness** n. —**rar'i·ty** n., pl. -**ties**

rare'bit n. Welsh rabbit

rar·e·fy' v. -**fied'**, -**fy'ing** make or become less dense

rare'ly adv. seldom

ras'cal n. 1 rogue 2 mischievous child —**ras·cal'i·ty** n.

rash a. too hasty; reckless —n. red spots on the skin —**rash'ly** adv.

rasp v. 1 scrape harshly 2 irritate —n. 1 rough file 2 grating sound

rasp'ber·ry n., pl. -**ries** 1 shrub with red or black berries 2 the berry

rat n. long-tailed rodent, larger than a mouse —v. **rat'ted**, **rat'ting** [Sl.] inform on others

ratch'et n. wheel or bar with slanted teeth that catch on a pawl

rate n. 1 relative amount or degree 2 price per unit 3 rank —v. 1 appraise 2 rank 3 [Col.] deserve

rath'er adv. 1 preferably 2 with more reason 3 more truly 4 on the contrary 5 somewhat

raths'kel·ler n. restaurant below street level

rat'i·fy' v. -**fied'**, -**fy'ing** approve formally —**rat'i·fi·ca'tion** n.

rat'ing n. 1 rank 2 appraisal

ra'tio (-shō, -shē ō') n., pl. -**tios** relation of one thing to another in size, etc.

ra·tion (rash'ən, rā'shən) n. fixed share, as of food —v. to give in rations —**ra'tion·ing** n.

ra'tion·al (rash'-) a. 1 able to reason 2 reasonable —**ra·tion·al'i·ty** n. —**ra'tion·al·ly** adv.

ra·tion·ale (rash'ə nal') n. reasons or explanation

ra'tion·al·ize' v. give plausible explanations for —**ra·tion·al·i·za'tion** n.

rat·tan' n. palm stems used in wickerwork, etc.

rat'tle v. 1 make or cause to make a series of sharp, short sounds 2 chatter 3 [Col.] upset —n. 1 a rattling 2 baby's toy that rattles

rat'tle·snake' n. snake with a tail that rattles: also **rat'tler**

rau·cous (rô'kəs) a. loud or rowdy

rav'age v., n. ruin

rave v. 1 talk wildly 2 praise greatly —n. [Sl.] enthusiastic praise

rav'el v. untwist; fray

ra'ven n. large black crow —a. black and shiny

rav'e·nous a. greedily hungry —**rav'e·nous·ly** adv.

ra·vine' (-vēn') n. long, deep hollow in the earth

ra·vi·o'li (ravē-) n. dough casings holding meat, cheese, etc.

rav'ish v. 1 fill with great joy 2 rape

rav'ish·ing a. delightful

raw a. 1 uncooked 2 unprocessed 3 inexperienced 4 sore and inflamed 5 cold and damp 6 [Sl.] unfair —**raw'ness** n.

raw'hide' n. untanned cattle hide

ray n. 1 thin beam of light 2 stream of radiant energy 3 tiny amount 4 broad, flat fish

ray'on n. fabric made from cellulose

raze v. demolish

ra'zor n. sharp-edged instrument for shaving

razz v. [Sl.] make fun of

re (rē) prep. regarding

re- pref. 1 back 2 again: add *again* to meaning of base word in list below

re'ad·just'

re'af·firm'

re'ap·pear'

re'ap·point'

re·arm'

re'as·sem'ble

re'as·sign'

re'a·wak'en

re·born'

re·build'

re·cap'ture

re'con·sid'er

re'con·struct'

re'dis·cov'er

re·do'

re·dou'ble

re·ed'u·cate'

re'e·lect'

re'en·act'

re·en'ter

re'en·list'

re'ex·am'ine

re·fill'

re·fu'el

re·heat'

re'in·vest'

re·load'

re·lo'cate'

re·make'

re·mar'ry

re·o'pen

re·or'der

re·phrase'

re·play'

re·print'

re·read'

re·tell'

re·u·nite'

reach v. 1 extend the hand, etc. 2 touch 3 get to 4 influence 5 get in touch with 6 try to get —n. act or extent of reaching

re·act' v. 1 respond to stimulus 2 return to an earlier state 3 act with another substance in a chemical change —**re·ac'tion** n.

re·ac'tion·ar'y a.; n., pl. **-ies** ultraconservative

re·ac'ti·vate' v. make or become active again

re·ac'tor n. device for producing atomic power

read (rēd) v. **read** (red), **read'ing** 1 understand or utter (written or printed matter) 2 to study 3 to register, as a gauge 4 access computer data —**read'er** n.

read'ing n. 1 act of one that reads 2 thing to be read 3 interpretation

read'out' n. displayed information

read'y a. **-i·er, -i·est** 1 prepared to act 2 willing 3 available —v. **-ied, -y·ing** prepare —**read'i·ly** adv. —**read'i·ness** n.

read'y-made' a. ready for use or sale at once

re·a'gent n. chemical used to detect or convert another

re·al' a. 1 actual; true 2 genuine —adv. [Col.] very —**re·al'ly** adv.

real estate n. land, including buildings, etc., on it

re'al·ism' n. awareness of things as they really are —**re'al·ist** n. —**re'al·is'tic** a. —**re'al·is'ti·cal·ly** adv.

re·al'i·ty n., pl. **-ties** 1 state of being real 2 real thing; fact

re'al·ize' v. 1 achieve 2 understand fully 3 make real 4 gain —**re'al·i·za'tion** n.

realm (relm) n. 1 kingdom 2 region; sphere

Re'al·tor trademark certified real estate broker —n. [r-] real estate agent

re'al·ty n. real estate

ream n. quantity of 480 to 516 sheets of paper —v. enlarge (a hole) —**ream'er** n.

reap v. cut and gather (grain, etc.) —**reap'er** n.

re'ap·por'tion v. adjust the representation pattern of (a legislature) —**re'ap·por'tion·ment** n.

rear n. back part or place —a. of or at the rear —v. 1 bring up; raise 2 rise on the hind legs above a plantation

rear admiral n. naval officer above a captain

re'ar·range' v. arrange in a different way —**re'ar·range'ment** n.

rea'son n. 1 explanation 2 cause 3 power to think 4 good sense —v. think or argue with logic —**rea'son·ing** n.

rea'son·a·ble a. 1 fair 2 sensible 3 not expensive —**rea'son·a·bly** adv.

re·as·sure' v. restore to confidence —**re'as·sur'ance** n.

re'bate v., n. return (of) part of a payment

reb'el (v.: rē bel') n. one who openly resists authority —a. rebellious —v. **re·bel'**, **-belled'**, **-bel'ling** resist authority —**re·bel'lion** n. —**re·bel'lious** a.

re·bound' v., n. recoil

re·buff' v., n. snub

re·buke' ('-byōōk') v. to scold sharply —n. sharp scolding

re'bus n. puzzle in which pictures stand for words

re·but' v. **-but'ted**, **-but'ting** contradict formally —**re·but'tal** n.

re·cal'ci·trant a. refusing to obey —**re·cal'ci·trance** n.

re·call' (n.: rē'kôl) v. 1 call back 2 remember 3 revoke —n. a recalling

re·cant' v. to renounce (one's beliefs)

re'cap (v.: 1. also rē kap') v. **-capped'**, **-cap'ping** 1 put new tread on (worn tire) 2 recapitulate —n. 1 a recapped tire 2 recapitulation

re'ca·pit'u·late' ('-pich'ə-) v. summarize —**re'ca·pit'u·la'tion** n.

re·cede' v. move or slope backward

re·ceipt' ('-sēt') n. 1 a receiving 2 written acknowledgment of sum received 3 pl. amount received

re·ceiv'a·ble a. due

re·ceive' v. 1 get; be given 2 greet (guests) 3 react to

re·ceiv'er n. 1 one who receives

2 one holding in trust property in bankruptcy, etc. **3** apparatus that converts electrical signals into sound or light, as in radio and TV

re'cent *a.* of a short time ago — **re'cent·ly** *adv.*

re·cep'ta·cle *n.* container

re·cep'tion *n.* **1** a receiving or being received **2** social function **3** the receiving of signals on radio or TV

re·cep'tion·ist *n.* employee who receives callers, etc.

re·cep'tive *a.* ready to receive suggestions

re'cess (*or* rē ses') *n.* **1** hollow in a wall **2** break from work — *v.* **1** take a recess **2** set back

re·ces'sion *n.* temporary falling off of business

rec'i·pe (res'ə pē) *n.* directions for preparing dish or drink

re·cip'i·ent *n.* one that receives

re·cip'ro·cal *a.* **1** done, etc. in return **2** mutual —**re·cip'ro·cal·ly** *adv.* —**re·cip'ro·cate'** *v.* —**rec'i·proc'i·ty** (-präs'-) *n.*

re·cit'al (-sīt'-) *n.* **1** account told **2** musical program

re·cite' *v.* **1** repeat something memorized **2** narrate —**rec'i·ta'tion** *n.*

reck'less *a.* heedless; rash — **reck'less·ly** *adv.* —**reck'less·ness** *n.*

reck'on *v.* **1** count **2** estimate **3** [Col.] suppose —**reckon with** deal with

reck'on·ing *n.* **1** a figuring out **2** settlement of accounts

re·claim' *v.* restore for use —**rec'la·ma'tion** *n.*

re·cline' *v.* lie down or lean back

rec'og·nize' *v.* **1** to identify as known before **2** to perceive **3** acknowledge; notice formally — **rec'og·ni'tion** *n.* —**rec'og·niz'a·ble** *a.*

re·coil' (*n.:* rē'koil) *v.* pull back —*n.* a recoiling

rec'ol·lect' *v.* remember —**rec'ol·lec'tion** *n.*

rec'om·mend' *v.* **1** suggest as fit or worthy **2** advise —**rec'om·men·da'tion** *n.*

rec'om·pense' *v.* pay or pay back —*n.* compensation

rec'on·cile' (-sīl') *v.* **1** make friendly again **2** settle (a quarrel) **3** to make agree or fit **4** to make acquiescent (*to*) —**rec'on·cil'a·ble** *a.* —**rec'on·cil'i·a'tion** (-sil'-) *n.*

rec'on·dite' *a.* abstruse

re·con·di'tion *v.* put back in good condition

re·con'nais·sance (-kän'ə səns) *n.* a spying on an area

rec'on·noi'ter *v.* examine or spy on an area

re·cord' (*n., a.:* rek'ərd) *v.* **1** keep a written account of **2** show on a dial, etc. **3** put (sound, images, etc.) on a disc, tape, etc. —*n.* **1** official account **2** known facts **3** a disc with recorded sound **4** the best yet done —*a.* best

re·cord'er *n.* **1** a person or machine that records **2** early form of flute

re·cord'ing *n.* **1** what is recorded on a disc, tape, etc. **2** the record itself

re·count' *v.* narrate

re'count' (*n.:* rē'kount) *v.* count again —*n.* second count

re·coup' (-kōōp') *v.* make up for, as a loss

re'course' *n.* **1** a turning for aid **2** source of aid

re·cov'er (-kuv'-) *v.* **1** get back; regain **2** become normal **3** keep from a fall **4** reclaim —**re·cov'er·y** *n., pl.* **-ies**

rec're·a'tion *n.* refreshing play —**rec're·a'tion·al** *a.*

re·crim'i·nate' *v.* accuse one's accuser —**re·crim'i·na'tion** *n.*

re·cruit' *n.* new member, soldier, etc. —*v.* enlist (recruits) —**re·cruit'ment** *n.*

rec'tan·gle *n.* four-sided figure with four right angles —**rec·tan'gu·lar** *a.*

rec'ti·fy' *v.* **-fied', -fy'ing 1** to correct **2** convert (alternating current) to direct current —**rec'ti·fi·ca'tion** *n.* —**rec'ti·fi'er** *n.*

rec'ti·tude' *n.* honesty

rec'tor *n.* head of some schools or parishes

rec'to·ry *n., pl.* **-ries** rector's residence

rec'tum *n.* lowest part of the intestine —**rec'tal** *a.*

re·cum'bent *a.* lying down

re·cu'per·ate' *v.* recover health, losses, etc. —**re·cu'per·a'tion** *n.*

re·cur' *v.* **-curred', -cur'ring 1** occur again **2** return in talk, etc. —**re·cur'rence** *n.* —**re·cur'rent** *a.*

re·cy'cle *v.* **1** pass through a cycle again **2** use (metal, paper, etc.) again (and again)

red *n.* **1** color of blood **2** [R-] communist —*a.* **red'der, red'dest** of the color red —**in the**

red losing money —**red'dish** a. —**red'ness** n.

red'cap' n. porter in a railroad or bus station

red'den v. make or become red

re·deem' v. **1** buy back **2** pay off **3** turn in for a prize **4** free, as from sin **5** atone for —**re·deem'a·ble** a. —**re·deem'er** n. —**re·demp'tion** n.

red'-hand'ed a. while committing a crime

red'head' n. person with red hair —**red'head'ed** a.

red'-hot' a. **1** glowing hot **2** very excited **3** very new

red'-let'ter a. memorable

red'o·lent a. **1** fragrant **2** smelling (of) **3** suggesting —**red'o·lence** n.

re·doubt' (-dout') n. stronghold

re·doubt'a·ble a. **1** formidable **2** deserving respect

re·dound' v. have a result

re·dress' (n.: rē'dres') v. correct and make up for —n. a redressing

red snapper n. ocean food fish

red tape n. rules and details that waste time and effort

re·duce' v. **1** lessen; decrease **2** change the form of **3** lower **4** lose weight —**re·duc'tion** n.

re·dun'dant a. **1** excess; superfluous **2** wordy —**re·dun'dan·cy** n., pl. -**cies**

red'wood' n. **1** giant evergreen **2** its reddish wood

reed n. **1** a hollow-stemmed grass **2** musical pipe made of this **3** vibrating strip in some musical instruments —**reed'y** a., -**i·er**, -**i·est**

reef n. ridge of land near the surface of water —v. take in part of a sail

reek v., n. (emit) a strong, offensive smell

reel n. **1** spool or frame on which thread, film, etc. is wound **2** amount wound on it **3** lively dance —v. **1** wind (in or out) on a reel **2** tell fluently: with off **3** stagger

re·fec'to·ry n., pl. -**ries** dining hall, as in a college

re·fer' v. -**ferred'**, -**fer'ring 1** go to, or direct someone to, for aid, information, etc. **2** allude (to)

ref·er·ee' n. **1** one chosen to decide something **2** a judge in sports —v. act as referee in

ref'er·ence n. **1** a referring **2** relation or connection **3** mention of a source of information **4** recommendation, or person giving it —**make reference to** mention

ref'er·en'dum n. submission of a law to direct popular vote

re·fer'ral n. **1** a referring or being referred **2** person referred to another person

re·fine' v. free from impurities, coarseness, etc. —**re·fine'ment** n.

re·fined' a. **1** purified **2** cultivated or elegant

re·fin'er·y n., pl. -**ies** plant for purifying materials

re·flect' v. **1** throw back, as an image or sound **2** result in (credit, etc.) —**reflect on** (or upon) **1** ponder **2** cast blame —**re·flec'tion** n. —**re·flec'tive** a. —**re·flec'tor** n.

re'flex' a., n. (designating or of) an involuntary reaction to a stimulus

re·flex'ive a. **1** designating a verb whose subject and object are the same **2** designating a pronoun used as object of such a verb

re·form' v. **1** improve **2** behave or make behave better —n. improvement —**re·form'er** n.

ref·or·ma'tion n. a reforming —**the Reformation** 16th-c. movement establishing the Protestant churches

re·form'a·to'ry n., pl. -**ries** institution for reforming young lawbreakers

re·fract' v. bend (a light ray, etc.) —**re·frac'tion** n.

re·frac'to·ry a. obstinate

re·frain' v. hold back (from) —n. repeated verse of a song

re·fresh' v. make fresh or stronger; renew or revive

re·fresh'ing a. **1** that refreshes **2** pleasingly new or different

re·fresh'ment n. **1** a refreshing **2** pl. food or drink

re·frig'er·ate' (-frij'-) v. make cold, as to preserve —**re·frig'er·a'tion** n. —**re·frig'er·ant** n.

re·frig'er·a'tor n. box or room for refrigerating

ref'uge (-yōoj) n. protection from danger or pursuit

ref·u·gee' n. one who flees to seek refuge

re·fund' (n.: rē'fund') v. give back (money, etc.) —n. amount refunded

re·fur'bish v. renovate

re·fuse (rē fyōoz'; n.: ref'yōos) v. **1** reject **2** decline (to do, etc.) —

n. rubbish —**re·fus′al** *n.*

re·fute′ *v.* prove wrong —**refu·ta′tion** *n.*

re·gain′ *v.* get back; recover

re·gal′ *a.* royal

re·gale′ *v.* entertain, as with a feast

re·ga′li·a *n.pl.* insignia or decorations, as of a rank

re·gard′ *n.* 1 concern 2 affection and respect 3 reference 4 *pl.* good wishes —*v.* 1 to gaze upon 2 think of; consider 3 concern —**as regards** concerning —**re·gard′ful** *a.* —**re·gard′less** *a., adv.*

re·gard′ing *prep.* about

re·gat′ta (-gät′-) *n.* boat race

re·gen′er·ate *v.* 1 give new life to; renew 2 improve —**re·gen′er·a′tion** *n.*

re′gent *n.* interim ruler in place of a monarch —**re′gen·cy** *n., pl.* -cies

reg·gae (reg′ā) *n.* type of popular Jamaican music

re·gime (rā zhēm′) *n.* political or ruling system

reg′i·men *n.* system of diet, exercise, etc.

reg′i·ment *n.* section of an army division —*v.* to control and discipline strictly —**reg′i·men′tal** *a.* —**reg′i·men·ta′tion** *n.*

re′gion *n.* area, division, or part —**re′gion·al** *a.*

reg′is·ter *n.* 1 list of names, etc. 2 recording device, as for cash transactions 3 a device for adjusting passage of air 4 musical range —*v.* 1 enter in a list 2 show 3 make an impression —**reg′is·trant** (-trənt) *n.* —**reg′is·tra′tion** *n.*

reg′is·trar′ (-trär′) *n.* keeper of records, as in a college

re·gress′ *v.* go backward —**re·gres′sion** *n.* —**re·gres′sive** *a.*

re·gret′ *v.* -gret′ted, -gret′ting be sorry for (a mistake, etc.) —*n.* a being sorry —**re·gret′ful** *a.* —**re·gret′ta·ble** *a.*

reg′u·lar *a.* 1 according to rule; orderly 2 usual 3 unchanging —**reg′u·lar′i·ty** *n.* —**reg′u·lar·ize′** *v.* —**reg′u·lar·ly** *adv.*

reg′u·late′ *v.* 1 control 2 adjust to a standard, etc. —**reg′u·la′tor** *n.* —**reg′u·la·to′ry** *a.*

reg′u·la′tion *n.* 1 a regulating 2 a rule —*a.* usual

re·gur′gi·tate′ (-jə-) *v.* bring up from the stomach —**re·gur′gi·ta′tion** *n.*

re′ha·bil′i·tate′ *v.* restore to ear-

lier state —**re′ha·bil′i·ta′tion** *n.*

re′hash′ *v.* repeat; go over again —*n.* a rehashing

re·hearse′ (-hurs′) *v.* 1 recite 2 practice for a performance —**re·hears′al** *n.*

reign (rān) *n.* (period of) a sovereign's rule —*v.* rule as sovereign

re′im·burse′ *v.* pay back —**re′im·burse′ment** *n.*

rein (rān) *n.* 1 strap hooked to a bit for controlling a horse 2 *pl.* means of controlling —**give (free) rein to** free from restraint

re′in·car·na′tion *n.* rebirth (of the soul) —**re′in·car′nate** *v.*

rein′deer′ *n., pl.* -deer′ large northern deer

re′in·force′ *v.* strengthen —**re′in·force′ment** *n.*

re′in·state′ *v.* restore —**re′in·state′ment** *n.*

re·it′er·ate′ *v.* repeat —**re·it′er·a′tion** *n.*

re·ject′ (*n.:* rē′jekt) *v.* 1 refuse to accept 2 discard —*n.* thing rejected —**re·jec′tion** *n.*

re·joice′ *v.* be or make happy —**re·joic′ing** *n.*

re·join′ *v.* 1 join again 2 answer —**re·join′der** *n.*

re·ju′ve·nate′ *v.* make young again —**re·ju′ve·na′tion** *n.*

re·lapse′ (*n.:* also rē′laps) *v., n.* fall back into a past state

re·late′ *v.* 1 narrate 2 connect, as in meaning 3 have reference (to)

re·lat′ed *a.* of the same family or kind

re·la′tion *n.* 1 a relating or being related 2 kinship 3 a relative 4 *pl.* dealings, as between people —**re·la′tion·ship′** *n.*

rel′a·tive *a.* 1 related 2 relevant 3 comparative —*n.* related person

rel′a·tiv′i·ty *n.* 1 a being relative 2 modern theory of the universe

re·lax′ *v.* 1 loosen up 2 rest, as from work —**re′lax·a′tion** *n.*

re′lay′ *n.* fresh group of workers, runners, etc. —*v.* get and pass on

re·lease′ *v.* 1 set free 2 allow to be issued —*n.* 1 a releasing 2 device to release a catch

rel′e·gate′ *v.* 1 exile 2 put into a lower position 3 assign —**rel′e·ga′tion** *n.*

re·lent′ *v.* become less stern

re·lent′less *a.* 1 pitiless 2 persistent

rel′e·vant *a.* pertinent —**rel′e·vance, rel′e·van·cy** *n.*

re·li·a·ble *a.* that can be relied on —**re·li·a·bil·i·ty** *n.* —**re·li·a·bly** *adv.*

re·li·ance *n.* trust or confidence —**re·li·ant** *a.*

rel·ic *n.* 1 something from the past 2 sacred object

re·lief *n.* 1 a relieving 2 thing that relieves 3 public aid, as to the poor 4 sculpted figures projecting from a flat surface

re·lieve *v.* 1 to ease; comfort 2 give aid to 3 to free by replacing 4 bring a pleasant change to

re·li·gion *n.* 1 belief in God or gods 2 system of worship —**re·li·gious** *a.*

re·lin·quish *v.* let go

rel·ish *n.* 1 pleasing flavor 2 enjoyment 3 pickles, etc. served with a meal —*v.* enjoy

re·live *v.* experience again

re·luc·tant *a.* unwilling —**re·luc·tance** *n.* —**re·luc·tant·ly** *adv.*

re·ly *v.* **-lied', -ly'ing** to trust; depend *on* or *upon*

re·main' *v.* 1 be left when part is gone 2 stay 3 continue —**re·main·der** *n.*

re·mains' *n.pl.* 1 part left 2 dead body

re·mand' *v.* send back

re·mark' *v., n.* (make) a brief comment or observation

re·mark·a·ble *a.* unusual —**re·mark·a·bly** *adv.*

re·me·di·al *a.* corrective

rem·e·dy *n., pl.* **-dies** thing that corrects, etc.

re·mem'ber *v.* 1 think of again 2 to bear in mind —**re·mem'brance** *n.*

re·mind' *v.* cause to remember —**re·mind'er** *n.*

rem·i·nis·cence *n.* 1 memory 2 *pl.* an account of remembered events —**rem·i·nisce'** (-nis') *v.* —**rem·i·nis'cent** *a.*

re·miss' *a.* careless; negligent

re·mit' *v.* **-mit'ted, -mit'ting** 1 forgive 2 refrain from exacting 3 slacken 4 send money —**re·mis'sion** *n.* —**re·mit'tance** *n.*

rem'nant *n.* part left over

re·mod'el *v.* rebuild

re·mon'strate *v.* say in protest —**re·mon'strance** *n.*

re·morse' *n.* deep sense of guilt —**re·morse'ful** *a.*

re·mote' *a.* 1 distant 2 slight —**re·mote'ly** *adv.*

remote control *n.* 1 control from a distance 2 hand-held device for controlling TV, etc.

re·move' *v.* 1 take away 2 dis-

miss 3 get rid of —**re·mov'a·ble** *a.* —**re·mov'al** *n.*

re·mu·ner·ate' (-myŏŏ'-) *v.* pay for; reward —**re·mu·ner·a'tion** *n.* —**re·mu'ner·a·tive** *a.*

ren·ais·sance (-ə säns') *n.* rebirth; revival: also **re·nas'cence** —**the Renaissance** period in Europe, 14th-16th c.

re·nal *a.* of the kidneys

rend *v.* **rent, rend'ing** tear; split apart

ren'der *v.* 1 submit 2 give in return 3 cause to be 4 perform 5 translate 6 melt (fat) —**ren·di'tion** *n.*

ren·dez·vous (rän'dā vōō') *n.* appointed meeting (place) —*v.* meet as agreed

ren'e·gade *n.* traitor

re·nege' (-nig') *v.* go back on a promise

re·new' *v.* 1 make new again 2 begin again 3 replenish (a supply) —**re·new'al** *n.*

re·nounce' *v.* 1 give up (a claim, etc.) 2 disown —**re·nounce'ment** *n.*

ren'o·vate' *v.* make like new; restore —**ren'o·va'tion** *n.* —**ren'o·va'tor** *n.*

re·nown' *n.* fame —**re·nowned'** *a.*

rent *n.* 1 payment for the use of property 2 a rip —*v.* get or give rent (for)

rent'al *n.* 1 rate of rent 2 thing for rent —*a.* of or for rent

re·nun·ci·a'tion *n.* a renouncing, as of a right

rep *n.* [Col.] a representative

re·pair' *v.* 1 fix; mend 2 make amends for 3 go (*to*) —*n.* a repairing or being repaired

rep·a·ra'tion *n.* 1 a making of amends 2 *often pl.* compensation, as for war damage

rep·ar·tee' (-tē', -tā') *n.* quick, witty reply or conversation

re·past' *n.* a meal

re·pa·tri·ate' *v.* return to country of birth, etc. —**re·pa·tri·a'tion** *n.*

re·pay' *v.* **-paid', -pay'ing** pay back —**re·pay'ment** *n.*

re·peal' *v.* revoke; annul (a law) —*n.* revocation

re·peat' *v.* say or do again —*n.* 1 a repeating 2 thing repeated —**re·peat'ed·ly** *adv.* —**re·peat'er** *n.*

re·pel' *v.* **-pelled', -pel'ling** 1 force back 2 disgust —**re·pel'lent** *a., n.*

re·pent' *v.* feel sorry for (a sin, etc.) —**re·pent'ance** *n.* —**re·**

pent′ant *a.*

re′per·cus′sion (-kush′ən) *n.* 1 echo 2 reaction, often an indirect one

rep′er·toire′ (-twär′) *n.* stock of plays, songs, etc. one is prepared to perform: also **rep′er·to′ry,** *pl.* **-ries**

rep′e·ti′tion (-tish′ən) *n.* 1 a repeating 2 thing repeated —**rep′e·ti′tious** *a.* —**re·pet′i·tive** *a.*

re·place′ *v.* 1 put back 2 take the place of 3 put another in place of —**re·place′ment** *n.*

re·plen′ish *v.* fill again —**re·plen′ish·ment** *n.*

re·plete′ *a.* filled —**re·ple′tion** *n.*

rep′li·ca *n.* exact copy

re·ply′ *v.* **-plied′, -ply′ing;** *n., pl.* **-plies′** answer

re·port′ *v.* 1 give an account of 2 tell as news; announce 3 denounce (an offender, etc.) to someone in authority 4 present oneself —*n.* 1 statement or account 2 rumor 3 explosive noise —**re·port′ed·ly** *adv.*

re·port′er *n.* one who gathers and reports news

re·pose′ *v., n.* rest

re·pos′i·to·ry *n., pl.* **-ries** a place where things may be put for safekeeping

re·pos·sess′ *v.* take back from a defaulting buyer

rep′re·hen′si·ble *a.* deserving scolding or blame

rep′re·sent′ *v.* 1 portray or describe 2 symbolize 3 act in place of 4 be an example of —**rep′re·sen·ta′tion** *n.*

rep′re·sent′a·tive *a.* 1 representing 2 typical —*n.* 1 typical example 2 one chosen to act for others 3 [R-] Congressional or State legislator

re·press′ *v.* 1 hold back 2 subdue 3 force (painful ideas, etc.) into the unconscious —**re·pres′sion** *n.* —**re·pres′sive** *a.*

re·prieve′ *n., v.* delay (in) the execution of (one sentenced to die)

rep′ri·mand′ *n., v.* rebuke

re·pris′al (-prī′zal) *n.* injury done for injury received

re·proach′ *v.* blame; rebuke —*n.* 1 disgrace 2 a scolding or blaming —**re·proach′ful** *a.*

rep′ro·bate′ *a., n.* depraved (person)

re′pro·duce′ *v.* produce copies, offspring, etc. —**re′pro·duc′tion** *n.* —**re′pro·duc′tive** *a.*

re·proof′ *n.* a reproving; rebuke: also **re·prov′al**

re·prove′ *v.* find fault with

rep′tile *n.* coldblooded, creeping vertebrate, as a snake, lizard, etc. —**rep·til′i·an** *a.*

re·pub′lic *n.* government by elected representatives —**re·pub′li·can** *a., n.*

re·pu′di·ate′ *v.* disown; cast off —**re·pu′di·a′tion** *n.*

re·pug′nant *a.* 1 opposed 2 distasteful; offensive —**re·pug′nance** *n.*

re·pulse′ *v.* 1 repel 2 rebuff —**re·pul′sion** *n.*

re·pul′sive *a.* disgusting

rep′u·ta·ble *a.* having a good reputation

rep′u·ta′tion *n.* 1 others′ opinion of one 2 good character 3 fame

re·pute′ *v.* consider to be —*n.* reputation —**re·put′ed** *a.* —**re·put′ed·ly** *adv.*

re·quest′ *n.* 1 an asking for 2 thing asked for —*v.* ask for

Re′qui·em′ (rek′wē-, rā′kwē-) *n.* R.C.Ch. [also r-] Mass for the dead

re·quire′ *v.* 1 demand 2 need —**re·quire′ment** *n.*

req′ui·site (rek′wə zit) *n., a.* (something) necessary

req′ui·si′tion *n.* written order —*v.* to demand or take

re·quite′ *v.* repay for —**re·quit′al** *n.*

re·route′ *v.* send by a different route

re·run′ *n.* showing of a movie, etc. after the first showing

re·scind′ (-sind′) *v.* cancel; repeal —**re·scis′sion** *n.*

res′cue *v.* free or save —*n.* a rescuing —**res′cu·er** *n.*

re·search′ (*or* rē surch′) *v., n.* (do) careful study in a subject

re·sem′ble *v.* be like —**re·sem′blance** *n.*

re·sent′ *v.* feel anger at —**re·sent′ful** *a.* —**re·sent′ment** *n.*

res′er·va′tion *n.* 1 a reserving, as of a hotel room 2 public land set aside, as for North American Indians

re·serve′ *v.* keep back; set aside —*n.* 1 thing reserved 2 limitation 3 reticence 4 *pl.* troops subject to call —**re·served′** *a.*

res′er·voir′ (-vwär′, -vôr′) *n.* 1 place for storing water 2 large supply

re·side′ *v.* 1 live (*in* or *at*) 2 be present (*in*)

res'i·dence n. 1 a residing 2 home —**res'i·dent** a., n. —**res'i·den'tial** (-shəl) a.

res'i·den·cy n., pl. **-cies** period of advanced medical training

res'i·due n. part that is left —**re·sid'u·al** (-zij'-) a.

re·sign' v. 1 give up, as a claim, position, etc. 2 be submissive —**res'ig·na'tion** n. —**re·signed'** a.

re·sil'i·ent a. bouncing back; elastic —**re·sil'i·ence, re·sil'i·en·cy** n.

res'in n. 1 substance from trees used in varnish, etc. 2 rosin —**res'in·ous** a.

re·sist' v. 1 withstand 2 to fight against

re·sist'ance n. 1 power to resist 2 opposition to another force —**re·sist'ant** a.

re·sis'tor n. device in electrical circuit providing resistance

res'o·lute a. firm; determined —**res'o·lute'ly** adv.

res'o·lu'tion n. 1 a resolving 2 formal statement 3 determination

re·solve' v. 1 decide 2 solve 3 change —n. fixed purpose —**re·solved'** a.

res'o·nant a. 1 resounding 2 intensifying sound —**res'o·nance** n.

re·sort' v. 1 go often 2 turn for help (to) —n. 1 place for a vacation, etc. 2 source of help

re·sound' (-zound') v. make an echoing sound

re·sound'ing a. 1 reverberating 2 complete

re'source' (or ri sôrs') n. 1 emergency supply 2 pl. wealth 3 resourcefulness

re·source'ful a. able to handle problems, etc. effectively

re·spect' v. 1 think highly of 2 show concern for —n. 1 honor 2 concern 3 pl. regards 4 reference —**re·spect'ful** a. —**re·spect'ful·ly** adv.

re·spect'a·ble a. 1 of good reputation 2 good enough —**re·spect'a·bil'i·ty** n.

re·spect'ing prep. concerning; about

re·spec'tive a. of or for each separately —**re·spec'tive·ly** adv.

res'pi·ra'tion n. act or process of breathing —**res'pi·ra·to'ry** a.

res'pi·ra'tor n. device to aid breathing artificially

res'pite (-pit) n. 1 a delay 2 period of relief or rest

re·splend'ent a. dazzling

re·spond' v. 1 to answer 2 react —**re·spond'ent** n.

re·sponse' n. 1 a reply 2 reaction —**re·spon'sive** a.

re·spon'si·ble a. 1 obliged to do or answer for 2 involving duties 3 dependable —**re·spon'si·bil'i·ty** n., pl. **-ties**

rest n. 1 ease or inactivity 2 peace 3 a support 4 a pause 5 remainder —v. 1 get, or be at, ease 2 become still 3 lie or lay 4 depend —**rest'ful** a.

res'tau·rant (-tə ränt', -tränt') n. place for buying and eating meals

res'ti·tu'tion n. 1 a giving back 2 reimbursement

rest'ive a. restless

rest'less a. 1 uneasy 2 disturbed 3 active

re·store' v. 1 give back 2 return to a former position, condition, etc. —**res'to·ra'tion** n. —**re·stor'a·tive** a., n.

re·strain' v. to hold back from action; suppress

re·straint' n. 1 a restraining 2 thing that restrains 3 self-control

re·strict' v. limit; confine —**re·stric'tion** n. —**re·stric'tive** a.

rest'room' n. public room with toilets and washbowls: also **rest room**

re·struc'ture v. plan or provide a new structure, etc. for

re·sult' v. 1 happen as an effect 2 to end (in) —n. 1 what is caused; outcome 2 mathematical answer —**re·sult'ant** a.

re·sume' v. 1 take again 2 continue after interrupting —**re·sump'tion** n.

ré·su·mé (rez'ə mā') n. summary, esp. of one's employment history

re·sur'face v. 1 put a new surface on 2 come to the surface again

re·sur'gent a. rising again —**re·sur'gence** n.

res'ur·rect' v. bring back to life, use, etc. —**res'ur·rec'tion** n.

re·sus'ci·tate' (-sus'ə-) v. revive, as one almost dead —**re·sus'ci·ta'tion** n.

re'tail' n. sale of goods in small amounts to consumers —a. of such a sale —v. sell at retail —**re'tail'er** n.

re·tain' v. 1 keep in possession, use, etc. 2 keep in mind 3 hire (a lawyer)

re·tain'er n. 1 servant to a rich person or family 2 fee paid to hire a lawyer

re·tal'i·ate v. return injury for injury —re·tal·i·a'tion n. —re·tal'i·a·to·ry a.

re·tard' v. slow down; delay —re'tar·da'tion n.

re·tard'ant n. substance delaying chemical reaction

re·tard'ed a. slowed in development, esp. mentally

retch v. strain to vomit

re·ten'tion n. 1 a retaining 2 ability to retain —re·ten'tive a.

ret'i·cent a. disinclined to speak —ret'i·cence n.

ret'i·na n. cells lining the interior of the eyeball, on which images are formed

ret'i·nue n. attendants on a person of rank

re·tire' v. 1 withdraw or retreat 2 withdraw from one's career, etc. 3 go to bed —re·tire'ment n.

re·tired' a. no longer working because of age, etc.

re·tir·ee' n. one who has retired from work, business, etc.

re·tir'ing a. shy; modest

re·tool' v. adapt (factory machinery) for different use

re·tort' v. reply sharply or cleverly —n. 1 sharp or clever reply 2 container for distilling, etc.

re·touch' v. touch up

re·trace' v. go back over

re·tract' v. 1 draw back or in 2 withdraw, as a charge —re·trac'tion n.

re·tread' (n.: rē'tred') v., n. recap

re·treat' v. 1 withdraw, esp. under attack 2 quiet place 3 period of contemplation —v. withdraw

re·trench' v. economize —re·trench'ment n.

ret'ri·bu'tion n. deserved punishment

re·trieve' v. 1 get back or bring back 2 make good (a loss or error)

ret'ro·ac·tive a. effective as of a prior date

ret'ro·grade' a. 1 moving backward 2 getting worse

ret'ro·spect' n. contemplation of the past —ret'ro·spec'tive a.

re·turn' v. 1 go or come back 2 bring or send back 3 repay (a visit, etc.) 4 yield (profit) —n. 1 a going or coming back 2 something returned 3 recurrence 4 requital 5 often pl.

yield or profit 6 official report —a. of or for a return —in return as a return

re·u'ni·fy v. -fied', -fy'ing unify again —re·u'ni·fi·ca'tion n.

re·un'ion n. a coming together again

rev v. revved, rev'ving [Col.] increase engine speed: with up

re·vamp' v. renovate; redo

re·veal' v. 1 make known, as a secret 2 show

rev·eil·le (rev'ə lē) n. Mil. morning signal to wake up

rev'el v. 1 make merry 2 take pleasure (in) —n. merrymaking —rev'el·ry n., pl. -ries

rev·e·la'tion n. 1 a revealing 2 striking disclosure

re·venge' v., n. harm in retaliation —re·venge'ful a.

rev'e·nue n. a government's income from taxes, etc.

re·ver'ber·ate' v. 1 to echo again; resound 2 have repercussions —re·ver'ber·a'tion n.

re·vere' v. show deep respect or love for —rev'er·ence n. —rev'er·ent a.

rev·er·end a. respected: [R-] used with the for a member of the clergy

rev'er·ie (-ē) n. daydream(ing)

re·verse' a. opposite —n. 1 the opposite 2 the back of a coin, etc. 3 change for the worse 4 gear for reversing —v. 1 turn about or inside out 2 revoke 3 go or make go in the opposite direction —re·ver'sal n. —re·vers'i·ble a.

re·vert' v. go back to a former state, owner, etc. —re·ver'sion n.

re·view' n. 1 general survey 2 reexamination 3 a criticism of a book, play, etc. 4 formal inspection —v. 1 to survey 2 study again 3 to inspect formally 4 write a review of (a book, etc.) —re·view'er n.

re·vile' v. use abusive language (to or about)

re·vise' v. change, esp. after reading —re·vi'sion n.

re·viv'al n. 1 a reviving 2 meeting to stir up religious feeling —re·viv'al·ist n.

re·vive' v. return to life, health, use, etc.

re·voke' v. put an end to; cancel —rev'o·ca·ble a. —rev'o·ca'tion n.

re·volt' v. 1 to rebel 2 disgust or be disgusted —n. a rebellion —

re·volt'ing a.

rev·o·lu'tion n. 1 movement in an orbit 2 complete cycle 3 complete change 4 overthrow of a government, etc. —**rev'o·lu'tion·ar'y** a.; n., pl. **-ies** —**rev·o·lu'tion·ist** n.

rev·o·lu'tion·ize' v. make a drastic change in

re·volve' v. 1 rotate 2 move in an orbit 3 think about

re·volv'er n. pistol with a revolving cylinder for bullets

re·vue' n. musical show

re·vul'sion n. disgust

re·ward' n. thing given in return for something done —v. give a reward to or for

re·wind' v. **-wound', -wind'ing** wind (film or tape) back on reel

re·word' v. put into other words

re·write' v. **-wrote', -writ'ten, -writ'ing** revise

rhap'so·dize' (rap'-) v. speak or write ecstatically

rhap'so·dy n., pl. **-dies** 1 ecstatic speech or writing 2 a musical piece of free form —**rhap·sod'i·cal, rhap·sod'ic** a.

rhe·a (rē'ə) n. large, ostrichlike bird

rhe'o·stat' n. device for regulating electric current

rhe'sus (monkey) n. small, brownish monkey of India

rhet'o·ric n. effective or showy use of words —**rhe·tor'i·cal** a. —**rhet'o·ri'cian** (-rish'ən) n.

rhetorical question n. question with an obvious answer

rheu·mat'ic fever n. disease with fever, aching joints, etc.

rheu'ma·tism' (rōō'-) n. painful condition of the joints, etc. —**rheu·mat'ic** a., n. —**rheu'ma·toid'** a.

Rh factor n. antigen group in some human blood

rhine'stone' (rīn'-) n. artificial gem of glass, etc.

rhi·ni'tis (rī-) n. inflammation in the nose

rhi'no n., pl. **-nos** rhinoceros

rhi·noc'er·os n. large mammal with one or two horns on the snout

rhi'zome' n. creeping stem with leaves near its tips and roots growing underneath

rho·do·den'dron (rō'-) n. shrub with showy flowers

rhom'boid' (räm'-) n. a parallelogram with oblique angles and only opposite sides equal

rhom'bus n., pl. **-bus·es** or **-bi'** (-bī') equilateral parallelogram with oblique angles

rhu'barb' (rōō'-) n. 1 plant with edible leafstalks 2 [Sl.] heated argument

rhyme (rīm) n. 1 likeness of end sounds in words 2 verse using this —v. make (a) rhyme

rhythm (rith'əm) n. pattern of regular beat, accent, etc. —**rhyth'mi·cal, rhyth'mic** a. —**rhyth'mi·cal·ly** adv.

rib n. 1 any of the curved bones around the chest 2 anything riblike —v. **ribbed, rib'bing** 1 form with ribs 2 [Sl.] tease

rib'ald a. coarsely joking —**rib'ald·ry** n.

rib'bon n. 1 narrow strip, as of silk, etc. 2 pl. shreds

ri'bo·fla'vin n. a vitamin in milk, eggs, etc.

rice n. food grain grown in warm climates

rich a. 1 wealthy 2 well supplied 3 costly 4 full of fats or sugar 5 full and deep 6 producing much —**the rich** wealthy people —**rich'ly** adv. —**rich'ness** n.

rich'es n.pl. wealth

rick n. stack of hay, etc.

rick'ets n. disease causing a softening of the bones

rick'et·y a. weak; shaky

rick'sha, rick'shaw n. jinrikisha

ric'o·chet' (-shā') n., v. **-cheted'** (-shād'), **-chet'ing** (-shā'iŋ) rebound at an angle

ri·cot'ta (ri-) n. soft Italian cheese

rid v. **rid** or **rid'ded, rid'ding** to free or relieve of —**get rid of** dispose of —**rid'dance** n.

rid'dle n. puzzling question, thing, etc. —v. perforate

ride v. **rode, rid'den, rid'ing** 1 sit on and make go 2 move along, as in a car 3 be carried along on or by 4 dominate 5 [Col.] tease —n. 1 a riding 2 thing to ride in at an amusement park

rid'er n. 1 one who rides 2 addition to a contract or legislative bill

ridge n. 1 crest 2 narrow, raised strip —v. form into ridges

rid'i·cule' n. remarks meant to make fun of another —v. make fun of

ri·dic'u·lous a. foolish; absurd —**ri·dic'u·lous·ly** adv.

rife a. 1 widespread 2 abounding

riff n. constantly repeated musical phrase in jazz

riff'raff n. people thought of as low, common, etc.

ri'fle n. gun with spiral grooves in the barrel —v. rob —**ri'fle·man** n., pl. **-men**

rift n., v. crack; split

rig v. **rigged**, **rig'ging** 1 equip 2 arrange dishonestly —n. 1 equipment 2 arrangement of sails

rig'ging n. ropes, etc. to work the sails of a ship

right a. 1 straight 2 just and good 3 correct 4 suitable 5 normal 6 of that side toward the east when one faces north —n. 1 what is right 2 right side 3 power or privilege 4 conservative party, etc. —adv. 1 directly 2 properly 3 completely 4 toward the right —**right away** at once —**right'ful** a.

right angle n. 90-degree angle

right·eous (rī'chəs) a. 1 virtuous 2 morally right —**right'eous·ly** adv. —**right'eous·ness** n.

right'-hand'ed a. 1 using the right hand more easily 2 for the right hand

right'ist n., a. conservative or reactionary

right of way n. legal right to proceed, pass over, etc.

rig'id (rij'-) a. 1 stiff and firm 2 severe; strict —**ri·gid'i·ty** n.

rig'ma·role' n. nonsense

rig'or n. strictness; hardship —**rig'or·ous** a.

rig'or mor'tis n. stiffening of muscles after death

rile v. [Col.] to anger

rill n. little brook

rim n. edge, esp. of something round —v. **rimmed**, **rim'ming** form a rim around

rime n., v. rhyme

rime n. white frost

rind n. firm outer layer

ring v. **rang**, **rung** 1 make, or cause to make, the sound of a bell 2 seem 3 resound 4 encircle —n. 1 sound of a bell 2 band for the finger 3 hollow circle 4 group with selfish aims 5 enclosed area —**ring'er** n.

ring'lead'er n. leader of a group, as of lawbreakers

ring'let n. long curl

ring'side' n. space just outside the ring at boxing match, etc.

ring'worm n. skin disease

rink n. smooth area for skating

rinse v. 1 wash lightly 2 wash soap from —n. rinsing or liquid for this

ri'ot v., n. (take part in) mob violence —**ri'ot·er** n. —**ri'ot·ous** a.

rip v. **ripped**, **rip'ping** 1 tear apart roughly 2 become torn —n. torn place

ripe a. 1 ready to be harvested, eaten, etc. 2 ready —**rip'en** v. —**ripe'ness** n.

rip'-off' n. [Sl.] a stealing, cheating, etc.

ri·poste', **ri·post'** (ri-) n. sharp retort

rip'ple v. to form small surface waves —n. small wave

rise v. **rose**, **ris'en**, **ris'ing** 1 stand up 2 come or go up 3 increase 4 begin 5 revolt —n. 1 ascent 2 upward slope 3 increase 4 origin

ris·er (rī'zər) n. vertical piece between steps

risk n. chance of harm, loss, etc. —v. 1 put in danger 2 take the chance of —**risk'y** a., **-i·er**, **-i·est**

ris·qué' (-kā') a. almost indecent

rite n. ceremonial act

rit'u·al (rich'-) a. of a rite —n. system of rites

ri'val n. competitor —v. compete with —**ri'val·ry** n., pl. **-ries**

riv'er n. large stream —**riv'er·side'** n., a.

riv'et n. metal bolt used to fasten by hammering the ends into heads —v. fasten firmly —**riv'et·er** n.

riv·u·let (-yōō-) n. little stream

roach n. cockroach

road n. 1 way made for traveling 2 way; path —**road'side'** n., a.

road'block' n., v. blockade

road'show' n. touring theatrical show

roam v. wander about; rove

roan a. reddish-brown, etc. thickly sprinkled with white —n. roan horse

roar v., n. 1 (make) a loud, deep, rumbling sound 2 (burst out in) loud laughter

roast v. cook (meat, etc.) in an oven or over an open fire —n. roasted meat —a. roasted —**roast'er** n.

rob v. **robbed**, **rob'bing** take property from unlawfully by force —**rob'ber** n. —**rob'ber·y** n., pl. **-ies**

robe n. 1 long, loose, outer garment 2 covering —v. dress as in a robe

rob'in n. red-breasted North American thrush

ro'bot' n. automatic manlike device

ro·bust' a. strong and healthy — **ro·bust'ness** n.

rock n. 1 mass or pieces of stone 2 popular music based on jazz, folk music, etc. —v. move back and forth —**on the rocks** [Col.] 1 in serious trouble 2 served with ice cubes —**rock'i·ness** n. —**rock'y** a., -i·er, -i·est

rock'-and-roll' n. popular music with a strong rhythm

rock bottom n. lowest level

rock'er n. chair mounted on curved pieces for rocking: also **rock'ing chair**

rock'et n. projectile propelled by the thrust of escaping gases

ro·co'co a. full of elaborate decoration

rod n. 1 straight stick or bar 2 linear measure, 5½ yd.

rode v. pt. of RIDE

ro'dent n. gnawing mammal, as a rat, rabbit, etc.

ro·de·o' n., pl. **-os'** public exhibition of the skills of cowboys

roe n. 1 fish eggs 2 pl. **roe** or **roes** small deer

roent·gen (rent'gən) n. unit for measuring radiation

rogue (rōg) n. 1 scoundrel 2 mischievous person —**ro'guish** (-gish) a.

roil v. make muddy or cloudy

role, rôle n. 1 part played by an actor 2 function taken on by someone

roll v. 1 move by turning 2 move on wheels 3 wind into a ball or cylinder 4 flatten with a roller 5 rock 6 trill —n. 1 a rolling 2 scroll 3 list of names 4 small cake of bread 5 a swaying motion 6 loud, echoing sound —**roll'er** n.

roller coaster n. ride with cars on tracks that dip and curve sharply

roller skate n. frame or shoe with four small wheels, for gliding on floor, etc. —**roll'er·skate'** v.

rol'lick·ing (räl'-) a. lively and carefree

rolling pin n. cylinder used to roll out dough

ro'ly-po'ly a. pudgy

ROM n. computer memory that can be read but not altered

ro·maine' n. type of lettuce having long leaves and head

Ro'man a. of Rome —n. 1 a native of Rome 2 [r-] type with non-slanting letters

Roman Catholic a. of the Christian church headed by the Pope —n. member of this church

ro·mance' a. [R-] of any language derived from Latin —n. 1 tale of love, adventure, etc. 2 exciting quality 3 love affair —v. [Col.] make love to

Roman numerals n.pl. Roman letters used as numerals: I=1, V=5, X=10, L=50, C=100, D=500, M=1,000

ro·man'tic a. 1 of romance 2 visionary 3 full of feelings of romance —n. a romantic person —**ro·man'ti·cal·ly** adv. —**ro·man'ti·cism'** n.

ro·man'ti·cize' v. act in a romantic way

romp v. play boisterously —n. a romping

romp'ers n.pl. loose, one-piece outer garment for a small child

roof n., pl. **roofs** outside top covering of a building —v. cover as with a roof

rook n. 1 European crow 2 chess piece moving horizontally or vertically

rook'ie n. [Sl.] beginner

room n. 1 enough space 2 space set off by walls 3 pl. living quarters; apartment —v. to lodge —**room'er** n. —**room'ful** n. —**room'mate** n. —**room'y** a., -i·er, -i·est

roost n. perch for birds —v. perch on a roost

roost'er n. male chicken

root (rōōt, root) n. 1 underground part of a plant 2 embedded part, as of a tooth 3 cause 4 quantity multiplied by itself —v. 1 take root 2 place firmly 3 dig (up or out) with snout or muzzle about 5 [Col.] support a team, etc.: with for —**take root** 1 grow by putting out roots 2 become fixed

root beer n. carbonated drink made of root extracts

rope n. strong cord of twisted strands —v. 1 mark off with a rope 2 catch with a lasso

ro'sa·ry n., pl. **-ries** string of beads used when praying

rose n. 1 sweet-smelling flower that has a prickly stem 2 pinkish red —**rose'bud'** n. —**rose' bush'** n. —**rose'-col'ored** a.

ro·sé' (-zā') n. a pink wine

ro'se·ate (-zē-) a. rose-colored

rose'mar'y n. fragrant herb used in cooking

ro·sette' n. roselike ornament

rose'wood' n. reddish wood

ros'in (räz'-) n. hard resin

ros'ter n. list; roll

ros'trum n. speakers' platform

ros'y a. **-i·er, -i·est 1** rose red or pink **2** bright or promising —**ros'i·ly** adv. —**ros'i·ness** n.

rot v. **rot'ted, rot'ting** decay; spoil —n. **1** a rotting **2** plant disease

ro'ta·ry a. **1** rotating **2** having rotating parts

ro'tate' v. **1** turn around, as a wheel **2** alternate —**ro·ta'tion** n.

rote n. fixed routine —**by rote** by memory alone

ro·tis'se·rie (-ē) n. electric grill with a turning spit

ro'tor n. rotating blades on a helicopter, etc.

rot'ten a. **1** decayed **2** corrupt —**rot'ten·ness** n.

ro·tund' a. round; plump —**ro·tun'di·ty** n.

ro·tun'da n. round building with a dome

rouge (rōozh) n. **1** cosmetic to redden cheeks and lips **2** red polish for jewelry —v. put rouge on

rough a. **1** not smooth; uneven **2** disorderly **3** harsh **4** not perfected **5** [Col.] difficult —adv. in a rough way —n. rough part —v. **1** treat roughly: with up **2** shape roughly —**rough it** live without comforts —**rough'en** v.

rough'age n. coarse food

rou·lette' (rōo let') n. gambling game played with a ball in a whirling bowl

round a. **1** that forms a circle or curve **2** complete **3** that is a whole number **4** vigorous —n. **1** thigh of beef **2** a course or series **3** often pl. regular circuit **4** single gun shot **5** period of action or time **7** simple song for three or four voices —v. **1** make round **2** finish **3** turn **4** pass around —adv. **1** in a circle **2** through a cycle **3** from one to another **4** in the opposite direction —prep. **1** so as to encircle **2** near **3** in a circuit through —**round up** collect in a herd, etc.

round'a·bout' a. indirect

round'house' n. round building for repairing and storing locomotives

round table n. group discussion

round'-the-clock' a., adv. without interruption

round trip n. trip to a place and back

round'up' n. a bringing together, esp. of cattle

round'worm' n. unsegmented worm

rouse (rouz) v. **1** excite **2** wake

roust'a·bout' n. unskilled, transient worker

rout n. **1** confused flight **2** crushing defeat —v. **1** make flee **2** defeat **3** force out **4** gouge out

route (rōot, rout) n. course traveled, as to make deliveries —v. send by a certain route

rou·tine' (rōo tēn') n. regular procedure —a. regular; customary —**rou·tine'ly** adv.

rove v. roam —**rov'er** n.

row (rō) n. **1** line of people, seats, etc. **2** a trip by rowboat —v. move (in) a boat with oars

row (rou) n., v. quarrel; brawl

row'boat' n. boat to row

row'dy a. **-di·er, -di·est** rough, disorderly, etc. —n., pl. **-dies** rowdy person —**row'di·ness** n.

row'el (rou'-) n. small wheel with points, as on a spur

roy'al a. of a monarch, kingdom, etc. —**roy'al·ist** n. —**roy'al·ly** adv.

roy'al·ty n., pl. **-ties 1** royal rank, person, or persons **2** set payment for use of copyright or patent

rub v. **rubbed, rub'bing 1** move over a surface with pressure and friction **2** spread on, erase, injure, etc. by rubbing —n. **1** a rubbing **2** difficulty; trouble

rub down v. to massage

rub'ber n. **1** elastic substance **2** an overshoe —**rub'ber·ize'** v. —**rub'ber·y** a.

rubber stamp n. **1** rubbery printing stamp **2** [Col.] automatic or routine approval —**rub'ber-stamp'** v.

rub'bish n. **1** trash; worthless material **2** nonsense

rub'ble n. broken stones, bricks, etc.

rub'down' n. a massage

ru·bel'la n. contagious disease with red skin spots

ru'ble n. monetary unit of U.S.S.R. and Russia

ru'bric n. title of a chapter, section, etc.

ru'by n., pl. **-bies** deep-red precious stone

ruck'sack' n. knapsack

ruck'us n. [Col.] noisy confusion; disturbance

rud'der n. steering piece at ship's stern or aircraft's tail

rud'dy a. **-di·er, -di·est** 1 healthily red 2 reddish —**rud'di·ness** n.

rude a. 1 coarse; crude 2 impolite —**rude'ly** adv. —**rude'ness** n.

ru'di·ment n. 1 first principle of a subject 2 trace —**ru'di·men'ta·ry** a.

rue v. regret —**rue'ful** a.

ruff n. 1 high, frilled collar 2 raised ring of feathers or fur about a bird's or beast's neck

ruf'fi·an n. brutal, lawless person

ruf'fle v. 1 to ripple 2 make ruffles in or on 3 make (feathers, etc.) stand up 4 disturb —n. narrow, pleated cloth trimming

rug n. floor covering of thick fabric in one piece

rug'by n. English game like football

rug'ged a. 1 uneven; rough 2 harsh; severe 3 strong

ru'in n. 1 anything destroyed, etc. 2 pl. remains of this 3 downfall; destruction —v. bring or come to ruin —**ru'in·a'tion** n. —**ru'in·ous** a.

rule n. 1 a set guide for conduct, etc. 2 custom; usage 3 government 4 RULER (n. 2) 5 straight line —v. 1 to guide or govern 3 decide officially 4 mark lines on —**as a rule** usually —**rule out** exclude —**rul'ing** a., n.

rul'er n. 1 one who governs 2 straight-edged strip for drawing lines, measuring, etc.

rum n. alcoholic liquor made from molasses, etc.

rum'ba n. Cuban dance

rum'ble v., n. (make) a deep rolling sound

ru'mi·nant a. cud-chewing —n. cud-chewing mammal

ru'mi·nate' v. 1 chew the cud 2 meditate —**ru'mi·na'tion** n.

rum'mage v. search thoroughly

rummage sale n. sale of miscellaneous articles

rum'my n. card game

ru'mor n. unconfirmed report or story —v. spread as a rumor

rump n. 1 animal's hind part 2 buttocks

rum'ple n., v. wrinkle

rum'pus n. [Col.] uproar

run v. **ran, run, run'ning** 1 go by

moving the legs fast 2 make a quick trip 3 compete (in) 4 unravel 5 spread (over) 6 continue 7 operate 8 follow (a course) 9 undergo 10 cause to run —n. 1 act or period of running 2 journey; trip 3 brook 4 watch 5 enclosed area 6 freedom 7 unraveled part in a fabric 8 *Baseball* point scored by a circuit of the bases —**run across** happen on —**run down** 1 cease operating 2 knock down, capture, or kill 3 disparage —**run out** expire —**run out of** use up —**run over** 1 ride over 2 overflow

run'a·round' n. [Col.] series of evasions

run'a·way' n. person or animal that has run away or fled —a. 1 running away 2 out of control

run'down' n. quick summary

run'-down' a. 1 not wound, as a watch 2 in poor condition

rung v. pp. of RING —n. rodlike step of a ladder, etc.

run'-in' n. [Col.] a quarrel

run'ner n. 1 one that runs 2 long, narrow rug 3 unraveled part 4 either of the pieces on which a sled slides

run'ner-up' n. the second to finish in a contest

run'ning a. 1 that runs 2 measured straight 3 continuous —adv. in succession —n. act of one that runs —**in (or out of) the running** in (or out of) competition

running mate n. lesser candidate, as for Vice President

run'-of-the-mill' a. ordinary

runt n. stunted animal or plant

run'-through' n. a complete rehearsal

run'way' n. a landing strip

rup'ture n. 1 a breaking apart 2 hernia —v. 1 burst 2 induce a hernia

ru'ral a. of or living in the country

ruse (rōōz) n. artful trick

rush v. 1 move, push, attack, etc. swiftly 2 hurry —n. 1 a rushing 2 busyness 3 grassy marsh plant

rus'set n., a. yellowish (or reddish) brown

Rus'sian n., a. (native or language) of Russia

rust n. 1 reddish-brown coating formed on iron, etc. 2 plant disease —v. 1 form rust on 2 deteriorate, as through disuse —

rust'y a., **-i·er**, **-i·est**

rus'tic a. 1 rural 2 plain or rough —n. country person

rus'tle (-əl) v. 1 steal cattle 2 make soft sounds of slight motion, as stirring leaves —n. these sounds —**rus'tler** n.

rut n. 1 groove as made by wheels 2 fixed routine 3 sexual excitement in animals —v. **rut'ted**, **rut'ting** make ruts in

ru·ta·ba·ga n. yellow turnip

ruth'less a. without pity

RV n., pl. **RVs** recreational vehicle for camping trips, etc.

-ry suf. -ERY

rye (rī) n. 1 cereal grass 2 its grain, used for flour

S

Sab'bath (-əth) n. day of rest and worship; Saturday for Jews, Sunday for many Christians

sa'ber, sa'bre n. cavalry sword

sa'ble n. animal like the weasel, with dark fur

sab'o·tage' (-täzh') n. destruction of factories, etc. by enemy agents, strikers, etc. —v. destroy by sabotage

sab'o·teur' (-tur') n. one who commits sabotage

sac n. pouchlike part

sac·cha·rin (sak'ə rin) n. sugar substitute

sac'cha·rine' (-rin') a. very sweet —n. saccharin

sa·chet (sa shā') n. small bag of perfumed powder

sack n. 1 bag 2 large, coarse bag 3 plunder 4 [Sl.] bed —v. 1 put in sacks 2 plunder 3 [Sl.] dismiss from a job —**hit the sack** [Sl.] go to sleep

sack'cloth' n. coarse cloth worn to show sorrow

sac'ra·ment n. sacred Christian rite, as Communion —**sac'ra·men'tal** a.

sa'cred a. 1 consecrated to a god or God 2 venerated 3 inviolate —**sa'cred·ly** adv. —**sa'cred·ness** n.

sac'ri·fice' v. 1 offer (something) to a deity 2 give up something for another 3 take a loss in selling —n. a sacrificing —**sac'ri·fi'cial** (-fish'əl) a.

sac'ri·lege (-lij) n. desecration of the sacred things —**sac'ri·le'gious** (-lij'əs) a.

sac'ro·il'i·ac' n. joint at lower end of the spine

sac'ro·sanct' a. very holy

sad a. **sad'der**, **sad'dest** showing or causing sorrow; unhappy —**sad'ness** n.

sad'den v. make sad —**sad'ly** adv. —**sad'ness** n.

sad'dle n. seat for a rider on a horse, etc. —v. 1 put a saddle on 2 burden

sa'dist n. one who gets pleasure from hurting others —**sa'dism'** n. —**sa·dis'tic** a.

sad'o·mas'o·chist (-kist) n. one who gets pleasure from causing or being hurt —**sad'o·mas'o·chism'** n. —**sad'o·mas'o·chis'tic** a.

sa·fa'ri n. hunting trip, esp. in Africa

safe a. 1 free from danger 2 unharmed 3 trustworthy 4 cautious —n. metal box with a lock —**safe'ly** adv. —**safe'ty** n.

safe'-de·pos'it a. of a bank box, etc. for storing valuables: also **safe'ty-de·pos'it**

safe'guard' n. protection; precaution —v. protect

safe'keep'ing n. protection

saf'flow'er n. plant whose seeds yield an edible oil

saf'fron n. orange-yellow dye and seasoning

sag v. **sagged**, **sag'ging** 1 sink in the middle 2 hang unevenly 3 lose strength —n. place that sags

sa'ga (sä'-) n. long story of heroic deeds

sa·ga'cious (-gā'shəs) a. very wise or shrewd —**sa·gac'i·ty** (-gas'-) n.

sage a. very wise —n. 1 very wise old man 2 green leaves used as seasoning 3 sagebrush

sage'brush' n. shrub of the western plains of the U.S.

Sag'it·tar'i·us (saj'-) n. ninth sign of the zodiac; Archer

sa·hib (sä'ib', -ēb') n. title for a European, once used in India

said v. pt. & pp. of SAY —a. aforesaid

sail n. 1 canvas sheet to catch the wind and move a vessel 2 boat trip —v. 1 move by means of sails 2 travel on water 3 glide —**set sail** begin a trip by water —**sail'boat** n.

sail'fish' n. ocean fish with a tall dorsal fin

sail'or n. 1 enlisted man in the navy 2 one who sails

saint n. holy person —**saint'ly** a., **-li·er**, **-li·est** —**saint'li·ness** n.

saith (seth) v. [Ar.] says

sake n. 1 motive; cause 2 behalf

sa·ke (sä′kē) n. Japanese alcoholic beverage

sa·laam (sə läm′) n. Oriental greeting of bowing low

sal·a·ble, sale·a·ble a. that can be sold

sa·la·cious (-lā′shəs) a. obscene

sal·ad n. mixture of vegetables, fruit, etc., with salad dressing

sal·a·man·der n. amphibian resembling a lizard

sa·la·mi n. spiced, salted sausage

sal·a·ry n., pl. **-ries** fixed payment at regular intervals for work —**sal′a·ried** a.

sale n. 1 a selling 2 special selling of goods at reduced prices —**for sale** to be sold —**on sale** for sale at a reduced price

sales′clerk′ n. one employed to sell goods in a store

sales′man n., pl. **-men** man employed to sell goods or services —**sales′wom·an** n.fem., pl. **-wom·en** —**sales′man·ship′** n.

sales′per·son n. one employed to sell goods or services

sal·i·cyl·ic acid (-sil′-) n. pain-relieving compound, as in aspirin

sa·li·ent (sāl′yənt) a. 1 prominent; conspicuous 2 jutting —**sa′lience** n.

sa·line (-līn, -lēn) a. salty

sa·li·va n. watery fluid secreted by glands in the mouth —**sal′i·var′y** a.

sal·low a. sickly yellow

sal·ly n., pl. **-lies** 1 sudden rush forward 2 quip 3 short trip —v. **-lied, -ly·ing** start out briskly

salm·on (sam′-) n. large, edible ocean fish

sal·mo·nel·la (sal′mə-) n. bacillus causing food poisoning and typhoid

sa·lon′ n. 1 parlor 2 gathering of notables

sa·loon′ n. 1 public place where liquor is sold and drunk 2 large public room

sal·sa (säl′-) n. sauce made with chilies, tomatoes, etc.

salt n. 1 white substance found in the earth, sea water, etc., used to flavor food 2 a compound formed from an acid 3 [Col.] sailor —a. containing salt —v. add salt to —**salt′i·ness** n. —**salt′y** a., **-i·er, -i·est**

salt′wa·ter a. of salt water, or of the sea

sa·lu·bri·ous a. healthful

sal′u·tar′y (-yōō-) a. 1 healthful 2 beneficial

sal·u·ta·tion n. act or form of greeting

sa·lute′ n. formal gesture, act, etc. expressing respect —v. to greet with a salute

sal·vage (-vij) n. 1 rescue of a ship, etc. from shipwreck 2 reclaimed property or goods —v. 1 save from shipwreck, etc. 2 utilize (damaged goods, etc.) —**sal′vage·a·ble** a.

sal·va·tion n. 1 a saving or being saved 2 one that saves 3 saving of the soul

salve (sav) n. soothing ointment —v. soothe

sal·ver n. tray

sal′vo′ n., pl. **-vos′** or **-voes′** discharge of a number of guns together

sam′ba n. Brazilian dance, or music for it

same a. 1 being the very one 2 alike 3 unchanged 4 before-mentioned —pron. the same person or thing —adv. in like manner —**all** (or **just**) **the same** nevertheless —**same′ness** n.

sam′o·var n. metal urn to heat water for tea

sam′pan n. small Oriental boat, rowed with a scull

sam′ple n. 1 part typical of a whole 2 example —v. take a sample of

sam′pler n. cloth embroidered with designs, etc.

sam′u·rai′ (-ə rī′) n., pl. **-rai′** member of a military class in feudal Japan

san·a·to′ri·um n. [Chiefly Br.] sanitarium

sanc′ti·fy v. to make holy or free from sin —**sanc′ti·fi·ca′tion** n.

sanc′ti·mo′ni·ous a. pretending to be pious —**sanc′ti·mo′ny** n.

sanc′tion n. 1 authorization 2 approval 3 punitive measure against a nation: often used in pl. —v. 1 authorize 2 approve

sanc′ti·ty n. 1 holiness 2 sacredness

sanc′tu·ar′y (-chōō-) n., pl. **-ies** 1 holy place, as a church 2 place of refuge

sanc′tum n. 1 sacred place 2 one's own private room

sand n. 1 loose grains of disintegrated rock 2 pl. area of sand —v. to sandpaper —**sand′er** n.

san′dal n. open shoe with sole tied to the foot by straps

san′dal·wood′ n. tree with sweet-smelling wood

sand'blast' v. clean with a blast of air and sand

sand'box' n. box with sand, as for children to play in

sand'lot' a. of baseball played by amateurs

sand'man' n. mythical bringer of sleep to children

sand'pa'per n. paper coated with sand —v. to smooth or polish with sandpaper

sand'pip'er n. shore bird with a long bill

sand'stone' n. kind of rock much used in building

sand'storm' n. windstorm with clouds of blown sand

sand'wich n. slices of bread with meat, etc. between them —v. squeeze in or between

sand'y a. -i·er, -i·est 1 of or like sand 2 dull yellow

sane a. 1 mentally healthy 2 sensible —**sane'ly** adv.

sang v. pt. of SING

san'gui·nar'y (-gwi-) a. 1 of or with bloodshed 2 bloodthirsty

san'guine (-gwin) a. 1 blood-red 2 cheerful or optimistic

san'i·tar'i·um n. institution for invalids, etc.

san'i·tar'y a. 1 of health 2 clean and healthful —**san'i·tize'** v.

san'i·ta'tion n. 1 hygienic conditions 2 sewage disposal

san'i·ty n. soundness of mind or judgment

sank v. pt. of SINK

sans prep. without

sap n. 1 juice of a plant 2 vigor 3 [Sl.] a fool —v. 1 undermine 2 weaken —**sap'py** a., -pi·er, -pi·est

sa'pi·ent a. wise —**sa'pi·ence** n.

sap'ling n. young tree

sap·phire (saf'ir) n. deep-blue precious stone

sap'suck'er n. small woodpecker

sar'casm' n. taunting, ironic remark(s) —**sar·cas'tic** a.

sar·co'ma n., pl. -mas or -ma·ta malignant tumor

sar·coph'a·gus (-käf'-) n., pl. -gi' (-jī') or -gus·es stone coffin

sar·dine' (-dēn') n. small herring preserved in oil

sar·don'ic a. bitterly sarcastic

sa·ri (sä'rē) n. long, draped outer garment of Hindu women

sa·rong' n. skirtlike garment of East Indies

sar'sa·pa·ril'la (sas'pə-) n. sweetened, root-flavored drink

sar·to'ri·al a. 1 of tailors 2 of (men's) clothing

sash n. 1 band worn over the shoulder or around the waist 2 sliding frame for glass in a window

sass v., n. [Col.] (use) impudent talk

sas'sa·fras' n. tree whose root bark is used for flavoring

sass'y a. -i·er, -i·est [Col.] impudent

sat v. pt. & pp. of SIT

Sa'tan the Devil —**sa·tan'ic** a.

Sa'tan·ism' n. worship of Satan —**Sa'tan·ist** n.

satch'el n. small traveling bag

sate v. 1 satisfy fully 2 satiate

sa·teen' n. satinlike cotton cloth

sat'el·lite' n. 1 small planet revolving around a larger one 2 man-made object orbiting in space 3 small state dependent on a larger one

sa'ti·ate' (-shē-) v. give too much to, causing disgust —**sa·ti'e·ty** (-tī'-) n.

sat'in n. smooth and glossy silk, nylon, or rayon cloth

sat'ire' n. 1 use of ridicule, irony, etc. to attack vice or folly 2 literary work in which this is done —**sa·tir'i·cal** (-tir'-), **sa·tir'ic** a. —**sat'i·rist** n.

sat'i·rize' v. attack with satire

sat'is·fy' v. -fied', -fy'ing 1 fulfill the needs and desires of 2 fulfill the requirements of 3 convince 4 pay in full —**sat'is·fac'tion** n. —**sat'is·fac'to·ry** a.

sat'u·rate' (sach'-) v. 1 soak thoroughly 2 fill completely —**sat'u·rat'ed** a. —**sat'u·ra'tion** n.

Sat'ur·day n. seventh day of the week

sat'ur·nine' a. gloomy

sa·tyr (sāt'ər) n. Gr. myth. woodland god with goat's legs

sauce n. 1 tasty, liquid or soft dressing for food 2 mashed, stewed fruit 3 flavored syrup

sauce'pan' n. metal cooking pot with a long handle

sau'cer n. shallow dish, esp. one for holding a cup

sau'cy a. -ci·er, -ci·est 1 impudent 2 lively and bold —**sau'ci·ly** adv. —**sau'ci·ness** n.

sau·er·kraut (sour'krout') n. chopped, fermented cabbage

sau'na n. bath with exposure to hot, dry air

saun'ter v., n. stroll

sau'sage n. chopped, seasoned pork, etc., often stuffed into a casing

sau·té (sō tā') v. fry quickly in a

little fat

sav'age a. 1 fierce; untamed 2 primitive; barbarous —n. an uncivilized or brutal person —**sav'age·ly** adv. —**sav'age·ry** n.

sa·van'na, sa·van'nah n. treeless, grassy plain

sa·vant' (sə vänt') n. scholar

save v. 1 rescue; keep safe 2 keep or store (up) for future use 3 avoid waste (of) —prep., con. except; but

sav'ing a. that saves —n. 1 reduction in time, cost, etc. 2 pl. money saved

sav'ior, sav'iour (-yər) n. one who saves or rescues —[S—] Jesus Christ

sa·voir-faire' (sav'wär fer') n. social poise; tact

sa'vor v., n. (have) a special taste, smell, or quality

sa'vor·y a. -i·er, -i·est tasting or smelling good

sav'vy [Sl.] n. shrewdness —a. shrewd

saw n. 1 thin, metal blade with sharp teeth, for cutting 2 proverb —v. 1 pt. of SEE 2 cut with a saw —**saw'yer** n.

saw'dust n. fine bits of wood formed in sawing wood

saw'horse n. rack to hold wood while sawing it: also **saw'buck'**

sax'o·phone' n. single-reed, metal wind instrument

say v. said, say'ing 1 speak 2 to state 3 suppose —n. 1 chance to speak 2 power to decide —**that is to say** in other words

say'ing n. proverb

say'-so' n. [Col.] 1 (one's) word, assurance, etc. 2 power to decide

scab n. 1 crust over a healing sore 2 worker who rejects union or breaks a strike —v. scabbed, scab'bing form a scab

scab'bard (-ərd) n. sheath for a sword, dagger, etc.

sca'bies (skā'-) n. itch caused by mites

scaf'fold n. 1 framework to hold workmen, painters, etc. 2 platform on which criminals are executed

scald (skôld) v. 1 burn with hot liquid or steam 2 heat almost to a boil —n. burn caused by scalding

scale n. 1 series of gradations or degrees 2 ratio of a map, etc. to the thing represented 3 any of the thin, hard plates on a fish, snake, etc. 4 flake 5 either pan of a balance 6 often pl. balance or weighing machine 7 Mus. series of consecutive tones —v. 1 climb up 2 set according to a scale 3 scrape scales from 4 flake off in scales —**scal'y** a., -i·er, -i·est —**scal'i·ness** n.

scal'lion (-yan) n. green onion

scal'lop n. 1 edible mollusk 2 any of the curves forming a fancy edge —v. 1 to edge in scallops 2 to bake with a milk sauce, etc.

scalp n. skin on top of the head —v. 1 cut the scalp from 2 [Col.] sell (tickets, etc.) above current prices —**scalp'er** n.

scal'pel n. sharp knife used in surgery, etc.

scam n. [Sl.] a trick or swindle

scamp n. rascal

scam'per v. run quickly —n. quick dash

scam'pi n., pl. -pi or -pies large, edible prawns

scan v. scanned, scan'ning 1 look at quickly 2 examine 3 analyze the meter in verse

scan'dal n. 1 disgrace or thing that disgraces 2 gossip —**scan'dal·ous** a.

scan'dal·ize' v. outrage one's feeling of decency

scan'dal·mon'ger (-muŋ'-, -män'-) n. one who spreads gossip

scant a. not enough —**scant'y** a., -i·er, -i·est —**scant'i·ly** adv. —**scant'i·ness** n.

scape'goat' n. one who is blamed for others' mistakes

scap'u·la n. shoulder bone

scar n. mark left after a wound has healed —v. scarred, scar'ring to mark with or form a scar

scar'ab (skar'-) n. beetle

scarce a. 1 not common 2 hard to get —adv. scarcely —**scarce'ness** n. —**scar'ci·ty** n., pl. -ties

scarce'ly adv. hardly

scare v. frighten —n. sudden fear —[Col.] **scar'y** a., -i·er, -i·est

scare'crow' n. human figure set up to scare away birds from crops

scarf n., pl. scarfs or scarves long or broad cloth piece for the neck, etc.

scar'let n. bright red

scarlet fever n. contagious disease with fever and a rash

scat int. [Col.] go away!

scath'ing (skāth'-) a. harsh; bitter —**scath'ing·ly** adv.

scat·o·log·i·cal *a.* of obscenity

scat'ter *v.* 1 throw about 2 move in several directions

scat'ter·brain' *n.* one incapable of clear thinking —**scat'ter·brained'** *a.*

scav'eng·er *n.* 1 one who collects refuse 2 animal that eats decaying matter —**scav'enge** *v.*

sce·nar'i·o' (sə ner'-, -när'-) *n., pl.* -**os'** 1 movie script 2 outline for proposed action

scene (sēn) *n.* 1 place; setting 2 view 3 division of a play, film, etc. 4 show of emotion

scen'er·y *n., pl.* -**ies** 1 painted backdrops for a stage play 2 outdoor views

sce'nic *a.* 1 of scenery 2 picturesque

scent (sent) *v.* 1 to suspect 2 of perfume —*n.* 1 odor 2 perfume 3 sense of smell

scep'ter (sep'-) *n.* a staff as symbol of a ruler's power: also [Chiefly Br.] **scep'tre**

scep'tic (skep'-) *n.* chiefly Br. sp. of SKEPTIC

sched·ule (ske'jool) *n.* 1 timetable 2 timed plan of list of details —*v.* to place in a schedule

scheme (skēm) *n.* 1 plan; system 2 plot; intrigue 3 diagram —*v.* plot —**sche·mat'ic** *a.* —**schem'er** *n.*

schism (siz'əm) *n.* split, esp. in a church, over doctrine —**schis·mat'ic** *a.*

schist (shist) *n.* rock in layers

schiz·o·phre'ni·a (skits·ə frē'-) *n.* severe mental illness —**schiz·o·phren'ic** (-fren'-) *a., n.*

schlock *n.* [Sl.] cheap or inferior (thing)

schmaltz *n.* [Sl.] very sentimental music, writing, etc.

schnau'zer (shnou'-) *n.* small terrier

schol'ar (skä'lər) *n.* 1 learned person 2 student —**schol'ar·ly** *a.*

schol'ar·ship' *n.* 1 academic knowledge; learning 2 money given to help a student

scho·las'tic *a.* of schools, students, teachers, etc.

school *n.* 1 place for teaching and learning 2 its students and teachers 3 education 4 group with the same beliefs 5 group of fish —*v.* train; teach —*a.* of, in, or for school —**school'mate'** *n.* —**school'teach'er** *n.*

school board *n.* group in charge

of local public schools

schoon'er *n.* ship with two or more masts

schwa (shwä) *n.* vowel sound in an unaccented syllable: symbol (ə)

sci·at'i·ca (sī-) *n.* neuritis in the hip and thigh

sci'ence *n.* systematized knowledge or a branch of it —**sci·en·tif'ic** *a.* —**sci·en·tif'i·cal·ly** *adv.*

science fiction *n.* imaginative fiction involving scientific phenomena

sci'en·tist *n.* expert in science

scim'i·tar (sim'-) *n.* curved sword

scin·til'la (sin-) *n.* tiny bit

scin'til·late' *v.* 1 sparkle 2 be clever and witty —**scin'til·la'tion** *n.*

sci'on (sī'-) *n.* 1 a bud or shoot 2 descendant

scis'sors (siz'-) *n.pl.* cutting tool with two opposing blades that move on a pivot

scle·ro'sis (skli-) *n.* a hardening of body tissues

scoff *n.* scornful remark —*v.* mock or jeer (at)

scoff'law' *n.* [Col.] habitual violator of traffic laws, etc.

scold *v.* find fault with angrily —*n.* one who scolds

sconce *n.* wall bracket for candles

scone *n.* small tea cake

scoop *n.* 1 small, shovellike utensil 2 bucket of a dredge, etc. 3 a scooping —*v.* 1 take up with a scoop 2 hollow out

scoot *v.* [Col.] scurry off

scoot'er *n.* 1 child's two-wheeled vehicle 2 small motorcycle

scope *n.* 1 range of understanding, action, etc. 2 chance

-scope *suf.* instrument, etc. for seeing

scorch *v.* 1 burn slightly 2 parch —*n.* surface burn

score *n.* 1 points made in a game, etc. 2 grade on a test 3 piece of music showing all parts 4 scratch or mark 5 twenty 6 *pl.* very many 7 debt —*v.* 1 make a score or scores 2 evaluate 3 achieve 4 keep score 5 upbraid —**scor'er** *n.*

score'board' *n.* large board or screen posting scores, etc., as in a stadium

score'less *a.* having scored no points

scorn *n.* contempt; disdain —*v.* 1 treat with scorn 2 refuse —

scorn'ful a. —**scorn'ful·ly** adv.

Scor'pi·o' eighth sign of the zodiac; Scorpion

scor'pi·on n. arachnid with a poisonous sting

Scotch n. whiskey made in Scotland —a. Scottish —v. [s-] put an end to

scot'-free' a. unpunished

Scot'tish a., n. (of) the people or language of Scotland

scoun'drel n. villain

scour v. 1 to clean by rubbing with abrasives 2 go through thoroughly, as in search

scourge (skurj) n., v. 1 whip 2 torment; plague

scout n., v. (one sent ahead) to spy, search, etc.

scow n. flat-bottomed boat

scowl v., n. (to have) an angry frown

scrag'gly a. -**gli·er**, -**gli·est** rough; jagged

scram'ble v. 1 climb, crawl, etc. hurriedly 2 struggle for something 3 to mix; jumble 4 stir and cook (eggs) 5 make (signals) unclear —n. a scrambling

scrap n. 1 fragment 2 discarded material 3 pl. bits of food —a. discarded —v. **scrapped, scrap'ping** 1 discard 2 [Col.] fight —**scrap'py** a., -**pi·er**, -**pi·est**

scrap'book' n. book in which to paste pictures, etc.

scrape v. 1 rub smooth or rub away 2 scratch 3 gather bit by bit —n. 1 scraped place 2 harsh sound 3 predicament —**scrap'er** n.

scratch v. 1 cut the surface 2 scrape or dig with one's nails 3 scrape noisily 4 cross out —n. mark from scratching —a. for hasty notes, etc. —**from scratch** from nothing —**scratch'y** a., -**i·er**, -**i·est**

scrawl v. write carelessly —n. poor handwriting

scraw'ny a. -**ni·er**, -**ni·est** lean; thin

scream v., n. (make) a loud, shrill cry or noise

screech v., n. (give) a harsh, high shriek

screen n. 1 thing used to shield, conceal, etc. 2 wire mesh in a frame 3 surface for showing video images, films, etc. —v. 1 conceal or shelter 2 sift or sift out

screen'play' n. script for a motion picture

screw n. 1 naillike fastener with

a spiral groove 2 propeller —v. 1 to turn; twist 2 fasten, as with a screw

screw'ball' a., n. [Sl.] erratic or unconventional (person)

screw'driv·er n. tool for turning screws

screw'y a. -**i·er**, -**i·est** [Sl.] 1 crazy 2 peculiar or eccentric

scrib'ble v. 1 write carelessly 2 draw marks —n. scribbled writing

scribe n. writer; author

scrim'mage (-ij) n. Football 1 play that follows the pass from center 2 practice game —v. take part in a scrimmage

scrimp v. spend or use as little as possible

scrip n. certificate redeemable for stocks, money, etc.

script n. 1 handwriting 2 working copy of a play

Scrip'ture n. 1 often pl. the Bible 2 [s-] any sacred writing —**Scrip'tur·al** a.

scrod n. young cod or haddock

scrof'u·la n. tuberculosis of the lymphatic glands

scroll n. 1 roll of paper, etc. with writing on it 2 coiled or spiral design

scro'tum n. skin pouch containing the testicles

scrounge v. [Col.] hunt around for and take; pilfer

scrub v. **scrubbed, scrub'bing** rub hard, as in washing —n. 1 a scrubbing 2 a growth of stunted trees or bushes —a. 1 inferior 2 undersized —**scrub'by** a., -**bi·er**, -**bi·est**

scruff n. back of the neck; nape

scruff'y a. -**i·er**, -**i·est** shabby or unkempt

scrunch v. 1 crumple or crunch 2 huddle, squeeze, press

scru'ple n. a doubt as to what is right, proper, etc. —v. hesitate from doubt

scru'pu·lous a. 1 showing or having scruples 2 precise

scru'ti·nize' v. examine closely —**scru'ti·ny** n.

scu'ba n. equipment, as an air tank, for breathing underwater

scud v. **scud'ded, scud'ding** move swiftly

scuff v. 1 scrape with the feet 2 wear a rough place on —n. worn spot

scuf'fle n. rough, confused fight —v. be in a scuffle

scull n. 1 large oar at the stern of a boat 2 light rowboat for racing —v. propel with a scull

scul'ler·y n., pl. **-ies** room for rough kitchen work

sculp'ture v. carve wood, stone, etc. into statues, etc. —n. art of sculpturing or work sculptured —**sculp'tor** n. —**sculp'tur·al** a.

scum n. 1 surface impurities on a liquid 2 [Col.] vile person or people —**scum'my** a., **-mi·er**, **-mi·est**

scup'per n. side opening for water to run off a deck

scur'ril·ous a. vulgarly abusive —**scur·ril'i·ty** n., pl. **-ties**

scur'ry v., n. **-ried**, **-ry·ing** scamper

scur'vy a. **-vi·er**, **-vi·est** low; mean —n. disease due to vitamin C deficiency

scut'tle n. bucket for coal —v. **-tled**, **-tling** 1 scamper 2 cut holes in (a ship) to sink it

scut'tle·butt' n. [Col.] rumor

scythe (sith) n. long-bladed tool to cut grass, etc.

sea n. 1 the ocean 2 a smaller body of salt water 3 large body of fresh water 4 heavy wave

sea'bird' n. bird that lives near the sea, as a gull

sea'board' n. land along the sea: also **sea'coast'**

sea'far·ing (-fer'-) a., n. (of) sea travel or a sailor's work —**sea'far·er** n.

sea'food' n. ocean fish or shellfish used as food

sea gull n. a gull (bird)

sea horse n. small fish with a head like that of a horse

seal n. 1 sea mammal with flippers 2 official design stamped on a letter, etc. 3 thing that seals —v. 1 certify as with a seal 2 close tight 3 settle finally

seal'ant n. substance, as wax, plastic, etc. used for sealing

sea level n. mean level of the sea's surface

sea lion n. seal of N Pacific

seam n. 1 line where two pieces are sewn or welded together 2 layer of ore or coal —v. join with a seam

sea'man n., pl. **-men** 1 sailor 2 navy enlisted man

seam'stress n. woman whose work is sewing

seam'y a. **-i·er**, **-i·est** unpleasant or sordid

sé·ance (sā'äns) n. spiritualists' meeting

sea'plane' n. airplane which can land on water

sea'port' n. port for ocean ships

sear a. withered —v. 1 wither 2 burn the surface of

search v. look through or examine to find something —n. a searching

search'light' n. strong light 2 device to project it

sea'shell' n. mollusk shell

sea'shore' n. land along the sea

sea'sick·ness n. nausea caused by a ship's rolling —**sea'sick'** a.

sea'son n. 1 any of the four divisions of the year 2 special time —v. 1 to flavor 2 age 3 accustom —**sea'son·al** a.

sea'son·a·ble a. timely

sea'son·ing n. flavoring for food

seat n. 1 place to sit 2 thing or part one sits on 3 right to sit as a member 4 chief location —v. 1 set on a seat 2 have seats for

seat belt n. strap across the hips to protect a seated passenger

sea'way' n. inland waterway for ocean-going ships

sea'weed' n. any sea plant(s)

seb'or·rhe'a, seb'or·rhoe'a (-rē'ə) n. oily skin condition

se·cede' (-sēd') v. withdraw formally from a group, etc. —**se·ces'sion** (-sesh'ən) n.

se·clude' v. isolate —**se·clu'sion** n.

sec'ond a. 1 next after the first 2 another, like the first —n. 1 one that is second 2 thing not of the first quality 3 assistant 4 $\frac{1}{60}$ of a minute —v. support (a suggestion, motion, etc.) —adv. in the second place, etc. —**sec'ond·ly** adv.

sec'ond·ar'y a. 1 second in order 2 less important 3 derivative

secondary school n. high school

sec'ond-class' a. 1 of the class, rank, etc. next below the highest 2 inferior

sec'ond-guess' v. [Col.] use hindsight in judging

sec'ond-hand' a. 1 not from the original source 2 used before

second nature n. deeply fixed, acquired habit

sec'ond-rate' a. inferior

se'cret a. 1 kept from being known by others 2 hidden —n. secret fact, etc. —**se'cre·cy** n. —**se'cret·ly** adv.

sec're·tar'i·at (-ter'-) n. staff headed by a secretary

sec're·tar'y n., pl. **-ies** 1 one who keeps records, writes letters, etc. for a person or group 2 head of a department of govern-

ment 3 tall desk —**se′cre·tar′i·**
al a.

se·crete′ v. 1 to hide 2 make (a
body substance), as a gland —
se·cre′tion n.

se′cre·tive a. not frank or open
—**se′cre·tive·ly** adv.

sect n. group having the same
beliefs, esp. in religion

sec·tar′i·an (-ter′-) a. 1 of or like
a sect 2 narrow-minded

sec′tion n. distinct part —v.
divide into sections —**sec′tion·**
al a.

sec′tor n. 1 part of a circle like a
pie slice 2 district for military
operations

sec′u·lar a. not connected with
church or religion

se·cure′ a. 1 free from danger,
care, etc. 2 firm; stable 3 sure
—v. 1 make secure 2 get —**se·**
cure′ly adv.

se·cu′ri·ty n., pl. -**ties** 1 secure
state or feeling 2 protection 3
thing given as a pledge of repay-
ment, etc. 4 pl. stocks, bonds,
etc.

se·dan′ n. closed automobile
with front and rear seats

se·date′ a. quiet and dignified —
se·date′ly adv.

sed′a·tive (-tiv) a. making one
calmer —n. sedative medicine
—**se·da′tion** n.

sed′en·tar′y a. characterized by
much sitting

sedge n. coarse, grasslike plant
of marshes

sed′i·ment n. matter that settles
from a liquid —**sed′i·men′ta·ry**
a.

se·di′tion (-dish′ən) n. stirring
up a rebellion —**se·di′tious** a.

se·duce′ v. 1 to lead astray 2
entice into sexual intercourse,
esp. for the first time —**se·**
duc′er n. —**se·duc′tion** n. —**se·**
duc′tive a.

see v. **saw**, **seen**, **see′ing** 1 look
at 2 understand 3 find out 4
make sure 5 escort 6 meet;
visit with 7 consult 8 have the
power of sight —n. office or district of a bishop —**see to** attend
to

seed n., pl. **seeds** or **seed** 1 the
part of a plant from which a new
one will grow 2 source 3 sperm
—v. 1 plant with seed 2 take
the seeds from —**seed′less** a.

seed′ling n. young plant grown
from a seed

seed′y a. -**i·er**, -**i·est** 1 full of
seeds 2 shabby; untidy

see′ing con. considering

seek v. **sought**, **seek′ing** 1
search for 2 try to get

seem v. look, feel, etc. (to be)

seem′ing a. not actual —**seem′**
ing·ly adv.

seep v. leak through; ooze —
seep′age n.

seer n. prophet

seer′suck·er n. crinkled fabric

see′saw′ n. balanced plank rid-
den at the ends for swinging up
and down —v. to move up and
down or back and forth

seethe (sēth) v. boil

seg′ment (-mənt; v.: -ment) n.
section —v. divide into seg-
ments

seg′re·gate′ v. set apart —**seg′re·**
ga′tion n.

seis′mic (sīz′-) a. of an earthquake

seis′mo·graph′ n. instrument to
record earthquakes

seize (sēz) v. 1 take suddenly or
by force 2 attack 3 capture —
sei′zure n.

sel′dom adv. rarely

se·lect′ a. 1 chosen with care 2
exclusive —v. choose; pick out
—**se·lec′tion** n. —**se·lec′tive** a.

selective service n. compulsory
military training

se·lect′man n., pl. -**men** New
England town official

self n., pl. **selves** one's own person, welfare, etc.

self- pref. of, by, in, to, or with
oneself or itself: see list below

self′-ad·dressed′

self′-ap·point′ed

self′-de·ni′al

self′-dis·ci·pline

self′-ed′u·cat·ed

self′-es·teem′

self′-ex·plan′a·to·ry

self′-ex·pres′sion

self′-in·dul′gence

self′-pit′y

self′-pres′er·va′tion

self′-re·li′ance

self′-re·spect′

self′-sat′is·fied

self′-sup·port′ing

self′-taught′

self′-as·sur′ance n. self-confi-
dence

self′-cen′tered a. selfish

self′-con·fi′dent a. sure of oneself —**self′-con′fi·dence** n.

self′-con′scious a. ill at ease

self′-con·tained′ a. 1 self-con-
trolled 2 reserved 3 self-suffi-
cient

self′-con·trol′ n. control of one's

emotions, actions, etc. —**self'-con·trolled'** a.

self'-de·fense' n. defense of oneself or of one's rights, etc.

self'-de·ter·mi·na'tion n. 1 free will 2 right to choose one's government

self'-ev'i·dent a. evident without proof

self'-im'age n. one's idea of oneself, one's worth, etc.

self'-im·por'tance n. pompous conceit —**self'-im·por'tant** a.

self'-in'ter·est n. (selfish) interest in one's own welfare

self'ish a. caring too much about oneself —**self'ish·ly** adv. —**self'ish·ness** n.

self'less a. unselfish

self'-made' a. successful, rich, etc. through one's own efforts

self'-pos·ses'sion n. full control over one's actions, etc. —**self'-pos·sessed'** a.

self'-re·straint' n. self-control —**self'-re·strained'** a.

self'-right'eous a. feeling more righteous than others

self'same' a. identical

self'-serv'ice a. practice of serving oneself in a store, cafeteria, etc.

self'-serv'ing a. serving one's selfish interests

self'-styled' a. so called by oneself

self'-suf·fi'cient a. independent —**self'-suf·fi'cien·cy** n.

self'-willed' a. stubborn

sell v. **sold, sell'ing** 1 exchange for money 2 offer for sale 3 be sold (for) —**sell out** 1 sell completely 2 [Col.] betray

sell'out' n. [Col.] show, game, etc. for which all seats have been sold

sel'vage, sel'vedge (-vij) n. edge woven to prevent raveling

se·man'tics n. study of words —**se·man'tic** a.

sem'a·phore' n. flags or lights for signaling

sem'blance n. outward show

se'men n. reproductive fluid of the male

se·mes'ter n. either of the terms in a school year

sem'i' (-ī') n. semitrailer: also used of semitrailer and its attached TRACTOR (n. 2)

semi- pref. 1 half 2 partly 3 twice in some period (**sem'i·an'nu·al, sem'i·month'ly, sem'i·week'ly**)

sem'i·cir'cle n. half circle

sem'i·co'lon n. mark of punctuation (;)

sem'i·con·duc'tor n. substance, as silicon, used in transistors, etc. to control current flow

sem'i·fi'nal n., a. (contest) just before the finals

sem'i·nal a. primary

sem'i·nar' (-när') n. supervised course of research

sem'i·nar'y (-ner'-) n., pl. -**ies** 1 school for women 2 school to train ministers, etc.

sem'i·pre'cious a. less valuable than precious gems

sem'i·skilled' a. of manual work requiring little training

sem'i·tone' n. Mus. half of a whole tone

sem'i·trail'er n. detachable trailer attached to a TRACTOR (n. 2)

sem·o·li'na (-lē'-) n. ground durum

sen'ate n. 1 lawmaking assembly 2 [S-] upper branch of Congress or a State legislature

sen'a·tor n. —**sen'a·to'ri·al** a.

send v. **sent, send'ing** 1 cause to go or be carried 2 impel; drive —**send for** summon —**send'er** n.

send'-off' n. [Col.] farewell demonstration for someone leaving

se'nile a. 1 of old age 2 weak in mind and body —**se·nil'i·ty** n.

sen'ior (-yar) a. 1 the older: written Sr. 2 of higher rank, etc. —n. high school or college student in the last year

sen·ior'i·ty (-yôr'-) n. status gained by length of service

se·ñor' (se nyôr') n. [Sp.] Mr.

se·ño'ra n. [Sp.] Mrs.

se·ño·ri'ta n. [Sp.] Miss

sen·sa'tion n. 1 sense impression or the power to receive it 2 exciting thing

sen·sa'tion·al a. shocking —**sen·sa'tion·al·ism'** n.

sense n. 1 power to see, hear, taste, feel, etc. 2 sound judgment 3 meaning —v. perceive —**in a sense** to some extent —**make sense** be intelligible

sense'less a. 1 unconscious 2 foolish or stupid

sen'si·bil'i·ty n., pl. -**ties** 1 power of feeling 2 pl. delicate feelings

sen'si·ble a. 1 reasonable; wise 2 aware 3 noticeable —**sen'si·bly** adv.

sen'si·tive (-tiv') a. 1 quick to feel, notice, etc. 2 susceptible to stimuli **3** tender or sore **4** touchy —**sen'si·tiv'i·ty** n.

sen'si·tize' v. make sensitive

sen'sor n. device for detecting heat, light, etc.

sen'so·ry a. of the senses

sen'su·al (-shōō-) a. of or enjoying the pleasures of the body —**sen'su·al·ly** adv. —**sen'su·al'i·ty** n.

sen'su·ous a. having to do with the senses

sent v. pt. & pp. of SEND

sen'tence n. **1** group of words stating something **2** court decision **3** punishment —v. pronounce punishment on

sen·ten'tious a. **1** pithy **2** pompously boring

sen'tient (-shənt) a. conscious

sen'ti·ment n. **1** a feeling **2** opinion **3** tender feelings **4** maudlin emotion —**sen'ti·men'tal** a. —**sen'ti·men'tal·ist** n. —**sen'ti·men·tal'i·ty** n. —**sen'ti·men'tal·ly** adv.

sen'ti·nel n. guard; sentry

sen'try n., pl. **-tries** guard posted to protect a group

se'pal n. leaf at the base of a flower

sep'a·rate' (-rāt'; a.: -rət) v. **1** divide; set apart **2** keep apart **3** go apart —a. set apart; distinct —**sep'a·ra·ble** a. —**sep'a·rate·ly** adv. —**sep'a·ra'tion** n. —**sep'a·ra'tor** n.

se'pi·a n., a. reddish brown

sep'sis n. blood infection —**sep'tic** a.

Sep·tem'ber n. ninth month

septic tank n. tank into which house waste drains

sep'tum n., pl. **-tums** or **-ta** Biol. partition, as in the nose

sep'ul·cher (-kər) n. tomb: also, Br. sp., **sep'ul·chre** —**se·pul'chral** a.

se'quel n. **1** result **2** book, etc. that continues an earlier one

se'quence n. **1** succession or the order of this **2** series **3** scene; episode

se·ques'ter v. hide; isolate —**se'ques·tra'tion** n.

se'quin n. small, shiny disk for decorating cloth

se·quoi'a (-kwoi'-) n. giant evergreen tree

se·ra·pe (sə rä'pē) n. blanket worn over the shoulders

ser'aph (-əf) n., pl. **-aphs** or **-a·phim'** angel of the highest rank —**se·raph'ic** a.

ser'e·nade' v., n. (perform)

music sung or played at night, esp. by a lover

ser'en·dip'i·ty n. the making of lucky discoveries by chance

se·rene' (-rēn') a. undisturbed; calm —**se·rene'ly** adv. —**se·ren'i·ty** (-ren'-) n.

serf n. feudal farmer, almost a slave —**serf'dom** n.

serge n. twilled, worsted fabric

ser'geant (sär'jənt) n. **1** low-ranking police officer **2** non-commissioned officer above a corporal

ser'geant-at-arms' n., pl. **ser'geants-at-arms'** one who keeps order, as in a court

se'ri·al (sir'ē-) a. of, in, or published in a series —n. serial story —**se'ri·al·i·za'tion** n. —**se'ri·al·ize'** v.

se'ries n., pl. **se'ries** number of similar things coming one after another

se'ri·ous a. **1** earnest **2** important **3** dangerous

ser'mon n. **1** religious speech by a clergyman **2** serious talk on duty, etc.

ser'pent n. snake

ser'pen·tine' (-tēn', -tīn') a. winding

ser'rate' a. edged like a saw: also **ser'rat'ed**

ser'ried (-ēd) a. placed close together

se·rum (sir'əm) n. **1** yellowish fluid in blood **2** antitoxin from the blood of an immune animal —**se'rous** a.

serv'ant n. one hired to work in another's home

serve v. **1** be a servant to **2** aid **3** do official service **4** spend a prison term **5** offer (food, etc.) **6** to be used by **7** deliver **8** hit a ball to start play —n. a hitting of a ball in tennis, etc. —**serv'er** n.

serv'ice n. **1** a serving **2** governmental work **3** armed forces **4** religious ceremony **5** set of silverware, etc. **6** aid —v. **1** supply **2** repair —**of service** helpful —**serv'ice·a·ble** a.

serv'ice·man' n., pl. **-men'** member of the armed forces

service mark n. mark used like a trademark by supplier of services

ser'vile (-vəl, vīl) a. humbly submissive —**ser·vil'i·ty** n.

ser'vi·tude' n. slavery

ses'a·me' n. edible seeds

ses'qui·cen·ten'ni·al (ses'kwi-)

n. 150th anniversary

ses'sion *n.* meeting of a court, legislature, class, etc.

set *v.* **set, set'ting** 1 put; place 2 put in the proper condition, position, etc. 3 make or become firm or fixed 4 establish; fix 5 sit on eggs, as a hen 6 start 7 mount (gems) 8 furnish (an example) 9 sink below the horizon 10 fit (words) to music —*a.* 1 fixed 2 obstinate 3 ready — *n.* 1 way in which a thing is set 2 scenery for a play 3 group of like persons or things 4 assembled parts, as of a radio —**set about (or in or to) begin —set forth** state —**set off** 1 show by contrast 2 explode —**set on (or upon)** attack —**set up** 1 erect 2 establish

set'back' *n.* relapse

set·tee' *n.* small sofa

set'ter *n.* long-haired hunting dog

set'ting *n.* 1 that in which a thing is set 2 time, place, etc., as of a story 3 surroundings

set'tle *v.* 1 put in order 2 set in place firmly or comfortably 3 go to live in 4 deposit sediment, etc. 5 calm 6 decide 7 pay, as a debt 8 come to rest 9 sink — **set'tler** *n.*

set'tle·ment *n.* 1 a settling 2 a colonizing of new land 3 colony 4 village 5 an agreement 6 payment

set'up' *n.* details or makeup of organization, equipment, plan, etc.

sev'en *a., n.* one more than six —**sev'enth** *a., n.*

sev'en·teen' *a., n.* seven more than ten —**sev'en·teenth'** *a., n.*

sev'en·ty *a.; n., pl.* **-ties** seven times ten —**sev'en·ti·eth** *a., n.*

sev'er *v.* cut off; separate —**sev'er·ance** *n.*

sev'er·al *a.* 1 more than two but not many 2 separate —*n.* several persons or things —**sev'er·al·ly** *adv.*

se·vere' *a.* 1 harsh; strict 2 grave 3 very plain 4 intense — **se·vere'ly** *adv.* —**se·ver'i·ty** *n.*

sew (sō) *v.* **sewed, sewn** or **sewed, sew'ing** fasten, make, etc. by means of needle and thread —**sew'er** *n.* —**sew'ing** *n.*

sew'age (sōō'-) *n.* waste matter carried off by sewers

sew'er *n.* underground drain for water and waste matter

sex *n.* 1 either of the two divi-

sions of organisms, male or female 2 character of being male or female 3 attraction between the sexes 4 sexual intercourse —**sex'u·al** *a.* —**sex·u·al·ly** *adv.*

sex'ism' *n.* unfair treatment of one sex by the other, esp. of women by men —**sex'ist** *a.*

sex'tant *n.* ship's instrument for navigation

sex'ton *n.* official who maintains church property

sex'y *a.* **-i·er, -i·est** [Col.] exciting sexual desire

shab'by *a.* **-bi·er, -bi·est** 1 worn out 2 clothed poorly 3 mean — **shab'bi·ly** *adv.* —**shab'bi·ness** *n.*

shack *n.* shanty

shack'le *n.* metal fastening for a prisoner's wrist or ankle —*v.* 1 put shackles on 2 restrain

shad *n.* saltwater fish

shade *n.* 1 partial darkness caused by cutting off light rays 2 device to cut off light 3 degree of darkness of a color 4 small difference —*v.* 1 to screen from light 2 change slightly 3 represent shade in (a painting, etc.) —**shad'y** *a.,* **-i·er, -i·est**

shad'ow *n.* 1 shade cast by a body blocking light rays 2 sadness 3 small amount —*v.* follow in secret —**shad'ow·y** *a.*

shad'ow-box' *v.* spar with imaginary boxing opponent

shaft *n.* 1 arrow or spear, or its stem 2 long, slender part or thing 3 vertical opening 4 bar that transmits motion to a mechanical part

shag *n.* long nap on cloth

shag'gy *a.* **-gi·er, -gi·est** 1 having long, coarse hair 2 unkempt

shah (shä) *n.* title of former rulers of Iran

shake *v.* **shook, shak'en, shak'ing** 1 move quickly up and down, back and forth, etc. 2 tremble 3 weaken, disturb, upset, etc. 4 clasp (another's hand), as in greeting —*n.* a shaking —**shake off** get rid of —**shake up** 1 mix by shaking 2 jar 3 reorganize —**shak'y** *a.,* **-i·er, -i·est**

shake'down' *n.* [Sl.] extortion of money

shake'-up' *n.* extensive reorganization

shale *n.* rock of hard clay

shall *v. pt.* **should** auxiliary verb showing: 1 future time 2 determination or obligation

shal·lot' n. onionlike plant

shal·low a. not deep —n. shoal

shalt v. [Ar.] shall: used with *thou*

sham n., a. (something) false or fake —v. **shammed, sham'ming** pretend

sham'ble v. walk clumsily —n. pl. scene of great destruction

shame n. 1 guilt, embarrassment, etc. felt for a wrong act 2 dishonor 3 a misfortune —v. 1 make ashamed 2 dishonor 3 force by a sense of shame — **shame'ful** a.

shame'faced' a. 1 bashful 2 ashamed

shame'less a. showing no shame or modesty

sham·poo' v. wash (the hair, etc.) —n. a shampooing, or soap, etc. used for this

sham'rock' n. cloverlike plant with three leaflets

shang·hai' (-hī') v. **-haied', -hai'ing** to kidnap for service aboard ship

shank n. the leg, esp. between the knee and ankle

shan't shall not

shan'ty n., pl. **-ties** small, shabby dwelling

shape n. 1 outer form 2 definite form 3 [Col.] condition —v. form or adapt —**shape up** [Col.] 1 come to definite form 2 behave as one should —**take shape** become definite —**shape'less** a.

shape'ly a. **-li·er, -li·est** wellshaped

shard n. broken piece

share n. 1 part each gets or has 2 equal part of stock in a corporation —v. 1 give in shares 2 have a share (*in*) 3 use in common with

share'crop' v. **-cropped', -crop'ping** work (land) for a share of the crop —**share'crop'per** n.

share'hold'er n. an owner of share(s) of corporation stock

shark n. a large, fierce fish

shark'skin' n. smooth, silky cloth

sharp a. 1 having a fine point or cutting edge 2 abrupt 3 distinct 4 clever or shrewd 5 vigilant 6 harsh or intense 7 *Mus.* above the true pitch —n. *Mus.* a note one half step above another: symbol (♯) —adv. 1 in a sharp way 2 precisely —v. **sharp'en** v. —**sharp'en·er** n. — **sharp'ly** adv. —**sharp'ness** n.

sharp'shoot'er n. good marksman

shat'ter v. 1 break into pieces 2 damage badly —**shat'ter·proof'** a.

shave v. **shaved, shaved** or **shav'en, shav'ing** 1 cut thin slices from 2 cut the hair or beard (of) to the skin —n. act of shaving —**close shave** [Col.] narrow escape —**shav'er** n.

shav'ing n. 1 act of one who shaves 2 thin piece shaved off

shawl n. cloth covering for the head and shoulders

she pron. the female mentioned

sheaf n., pl. **sheaves** bundle of stalks, papers, etc.

shear v. **sheared, sheared** or **shorn, shear'ing** 1 cut or cut off as with shears 2 clip hair from —n. pl. large scissors

sheath (shēth) n. 1 case for a knife blade, etc. 2 any covering like this

sheathe (shēth) v. put into or cover with a sheath

shed n. small shelter or storage place —v. **shed, shed'ding** 1 make flow 2 radiate 3 throw or cast off

she'd 1 she had 2 she would

sheen n. luster; gloss

sheep n., pl. **sheep** cud-chewing animal with heavy wool — **sheep'skin'** n.

sheep'ish a. bashful or embarrassed

sheer v. to swerve —a. 1 very thin 2 absolute 3 very steep —adv. completely

sheet n. 1 large cloth of cotton, etc. used on beds 2 piece of paper 3 broad, thin piece of glass, etc. 4 rope to control a sail

sheet'ing n. cloth material for sheets

sheik, sheikh (shēk, shāk) n. Arab chief

shek'el n. ancient Hebrew coin

shelf n., pl. **shelves** 1 thin, flat board for holding things 2 ledge or reef

shell n. 1 hard outer covering, as of an egg 2 narrow rowboat for racing 3 missile from a large gun 4 cartridge —v. 1 remove the shell from 2 bombard

she'll 1 she will 2 she shall

shel·lac', shel·lack' n. thin varnish of resin and alcohol —v. **-lacked', -lack'ing** 1 put shellac on 2 [Sl.] to beat

shell'fish' n. aquatic animal with a shell

shel′ter n. something that covers or protects —v. give shelter to

shelve v. 1 put on a shelf 2 lay aside

shelv′ing n. 1 material for shelves 2 shelves

she·nan′i·gans n.pl. [Col.] mischief; trickery

shep′herd (-ərd) n. 1 one who herds sheep 2 religious leader —v. be a shepherd —**shep′herd·ess** n.fem.

sher′bet n. frozen dessert of fruit juice, milk, etc.

sher′iff n. chief law officer of a county

sher′ry n., pl. -ries a strong wine

she's 1 she is 2 she has

shib′bo·leth′ n. password

shield n. 1 armor carried on the arm 2 thing that protects —v. protect

shift v. 1 move or change from one person, place, direction, etc. to another 2 get along —n. 1 a shifting 2 time at work 3 trick

shift′less a. lazy

shift′y a. -i·er, -i·est tricky; evasive

shill n. [Sl.] one who pretends to buy, bet, etc. to lure others

shil·le·lagh (shi lā′lē) n. Irish cudgel

shil′ling n. former British coin, $\frac{1}{20}$ of a pound

shil′ly-shal′ly v. -lied, -ly·ing hesitate

shim n. wedge for filling space

shim′mer v., n. (shine with) a wavering light

shim′my n., v. -mied, -my·ing shake or wobble

shin n. front of the leg between knee and ankle —v. shinned 2

shin′ning climb, as a rope, with hands and legs: also **shin′ny**, -**nied**, -**ny·ing**

shin′dig′ n. [Col.] informal party, dance, etc.

shine v. shone or (esp. for v. 3) shined, shin′ing 1 be or make be bright 2 excel 3 make shiny by polishing —n. 1 brightness 2 polish

shin′gle n. 1 piece of wood, slate, etc. for roofing 2 [Col.] small signboard —v. put shingles on (a roof)

shin′gles n. virus skin disease along a nerve

shin′splints′ n. muscle strain of lower leg

shin′y a. -i·er, -i·est bright; shining

ship n. 1 large water craft 2 aircraft —v. shipped, ship′ping 1 put or go in a ship 2 transport —**on shipboard** on a ship —**ship′load′** n. —**ship′ment** n.

ship′per n.

-ship suf. 1 state of 2 rank of 3 skill as

ship′mate′ n. fellow sailor

ship′shape′ a. neat; trim

ship′wreck′ v., n. (cause) loss or ruin of a ship

ship′yard′ n. place where ships are built and repaired

shire n. county in England

shirk v. to neglect (a duty) —**shirk′er** n.

shirr v. 1 pull stitches tight in rows 2 bake (eggs) with crumbs

shirt n. 1 upper garment for men 2 undershirt

shish′ ke·bab′ (-kə bäb′) n. dish of small chunks of meat and vegetables broiled on a skewer

shiv′er v. 1 shake or tremble 2 shatter —n. 1 a trembling 2 sliver

shoal n. 1 school of fish 2 shallow place in water

shock n. 1 sudden blow or jar 2 sudden emotional upset 3 effect of electric current on the body 4 bundle of grain 5 thick mass of hair —v. 1 astonish; horrify 2 give an electric shock to

shod′dy a. -di·er, -di·est inferior —**shod′di·ness** n.

shoe n. 1 outer covering for the foot 2 horseshoe 3 part of a brake that presses on the wheel —v. shod, shoe′ing put shoes on

shoe′horn′ n. device to help slip a shoe on the foot

shoe′lace′ n. LACE (n. 1)

shoe′string′ n. 1 shoelace 2 small amount of capital

shoe tree n. form put in a shoe to hold its shape

sho′gun′ n. hereditary governor of Japan: absolute rulers until 1867

shone v. pt. & pp. of SHINE

shoo int. go away! —v. drive away abruptly

shoo′-in′ n. [Col.] one expected to win easily

shook v. pt. of SHAKE

shoot v. shot, shoot′ing 1 send out, or move, with force, speed, etc. 2 send a bullet, etc. from 3 wound or kill with a bullet, etc. 4 to photograph 5 to score (a point, etc.) in sports 6 grow rapidly 7 to mark in spots, etc. (with color) —n. new growth; sprout —**shoot′er** n.

shop n. 1 place where things are sold 2 manufacturing place —v. buy goods in shops —**shop'per** n.

shop'lift'er n. one who steals from a store during shopping hours —**shop'lift** v.

shop'talk' n. 1 specialized words for certain work 2 talk about work after hours

shore n. 1 land next to water 2 prop; support —v. prop (up)

short a. 1 not measuring much 2 not tall 3 brief 4 brusque 5 less than enough —n. 1 short movie 2 pl. short pants 3 short circuit —adv. abruptly or briefly —v. short-circuit —**in short** briefly —**short'en** v. —**short'ness** n.

short'age n. 1 lack; deficiency 2 deficit

short'cake' n. light biscuit or sweet cake

short'change' v. [Col.] give less change than is due

short circuit n. side circuit of low resistance that deflects electric current —**short'-cir'cuit** v.

short'com'ing n. defect

short'cut' n. 1 shorter route 2 way of saving time, etc.

short'en·ing n. fat used to make baked goods flaky

short'hand' n. system of symbols for writing fast

short'hand'ed a. short of workers or helpers

short'-lived' (-līvd', -livd') a. lasting only a short time

short'ly adv. 1 briefly 2 soon 3 curtly

short shrift n. little attention

short'sight'ed a. lacking in foresight

short'stop' n. Baseball infielder between second and third basemen

short'-tem'pered a. easily angered

short'-term' a. for a short time

short'wave' n. radio wave 60 meters or less in length

short'-wind'ed (-wind'əd) a. easily put out of breath

shot v. pt. & pp. of SHOOT —n. 1 act of shooting 2 range; scope 3 attempt 4 throw, etc., as of a ball 5 projectile(s) for a gun 6 marksman 7 photograph 8 dose or drink —a. worn out —**shot'gun'** n.

shot put n. track event in which a heavy metal ball is thrown

should v. pt. of SHALL: *should* is used to express obligation, probability, etc.

shoul'der n. 1 part of the body to which an arm or foreleg is connected 2 edge of a road —v. 1 push with the shoulder 2 assume the burden of

shout v., n. (utter) a loud, sudden cry or call

shove v. 1 push along a surface 2 push roughly —n. a push

shov'el n. tool with a broad scoop and a handle —v. move or dig with a shovel —**shov'el·ful'** n., pl. **-fuls**

show v. **showed**, **shown** or **showed**, **show'ing** 1 bring into sight; reveal 2 appear 3 be noticeable 4 guide 5 point out 6 prove; explain —n. 1 display, performance, etc. 2 pompous display 3 pretense —**show off** make a display of —**show up** 1 expose 2 arrive —**show'case'** n. —**show'room'** n.

show'down' n. [Col.] disclosure of facts to force a settlement

show'er n. 1 brief fall of rain 2 any sudden fall or flow 3 party with gifts for a bride, etc. 4 bath of fine water spray —v. 1 to spray with water 2 give, or fall, abundantly 3 bathe under a shower —**show'er·y** a.

show'man n., pl. **-men** one who produces shows skillfully —**show'man·ship'** n.

show'y a. **-i·er**, **-i·est** 1 of striking appearance 2 gaudy; flashy —**show'i·ly** adv. —**show'i·ness** n.

shrap'nel n. fragments of an exploded artillery shell

shred n. 1 torn strip 2 fragment —v. **shred'ded** or **shred**, **shred'ding** cut or tear into shreds

shrew n. 1 small, mouselike mammal 2 nagging woman —**shrew'ish** a.

shrewd a. clever or sharp in practical affairs —**shrewd'ly** adv. —**shrewd'ness** n.

shriek (shrēk) v., n. (utter) a loud, piercing cry

shrill a. high-pitched and piercing in sound —**shrill'ness** n. —**shril'ly** adv.

shrimp n. 1 small, long-tailed, edible shellfish 2 [Col.] small person

shrine n. saint's tomb or other sacred place

shrink v. **shrank** or **shrunk**, **shrunk** or **shrunk'en**, **shrink'ing**

1 lessen in size; contract 2 draw back —**shrink'age** n.

shriv'el v. dry up; wither

shroud n. 1 cloth used to wrap a corpse 2 cover; veil 3 pl. ropes supporting ship's masts —v. hide; cover

shrub n. bush —**shrub'ber·y** n.

shrug v., n. shrugged, shrug'ging (draw up the shoulders in) a gesture of doubt, indifference, etc.

shtick n. [Sl.] 1 comic act 2 attention-getting device

shuck v., n. husk; shell

shud'der v. shake, as in horror —n. a shuddering

shuf'fle v. 1 walk with feet dragging 2 mix or jumble together —n. a shuffling

shuf'fle·board' n. game in which disks are pushed toward numbered squares

shun v. shunned, shun'ning keep away from

shunt v. 1 move to one side 2 switch or shift

shush int. be quiet! —v. say "shush" to

shut v. shut, shut'ting 1 close (a door, etc.) 2 prevent entrance to —a. closed —**shut down** cease operating —**shut off** prevent passage of or on —**shut out** prevent from scoring —**shut up** 1 enclose 2 [Col.] stop talking

shut'-eye' n. [Sl.] sleep

shut'-in' a. confined indoors by illness —n. invalid

shut'out' n. game in which a team is kept from scoring

shut'ter n. 1 movable window cover 2 light-controlling device on a camera lens

shut'tle n. device to carry thread back and forth in weaving —v. move rapidly to and fro

shut'tle·cock' n. feathered cork ball in badminton

shy a. shy'er or shi'er, shy'est or shi'est 1 timid 2 bashful 3 distrustful 4 [Sl.] lacking —v. shied, shy'ing 1 be startled 2 hesitate 3 fling sideways —**shy'ly** adv. —**shy'ness** n.

shy'ster (shī'-) n. [Sl.] dishonest lawyer

Si'a·mese' twins n. pair of twins born joined

sib'i·lant a. hissing (sound) —**sib'i·lance** n.

sib'ling n. a brother or sister

sib'yl (-əl) n. prophetess of ancient Greece or Rome

sic v. sicked, sick'ing to urge to attack

sick a. 1 having disease; ill 2 nauseated 3 of or for sick people 4 disgusted 5 [Col.] morbid —v. sic —**the sick** sick people —**sick'ness** n.

sick'en v. make or become sick —**sick'en·ing** a.

sick'le n. curved blade with a short handle, for cutting tall grass

sick'ly a. -li·er, -li·est 1 in poor health 2 faint or weak

side n. 1 right or left half 2 a bounding line 3 a surface 4 aspect 5 relative position 6 party; faction —a. 1 of, at, or to a side 2 secondary —**side with** support —**take sides** support one faction

side'arm' a., adv. with the arm from the side, below the shoulder

side arms n.pl. weapons worn at the side

side'board' n. dining-room cabinet for linen, etc.

side'burns' n.pl. hair on the cheeks, beside the ears

side'kick' n. [Sl.] 1 close friend 2 partner

side'light' n. bit of incidental information

side'line' n. secondary line of merchandise, work, etc. —v. remove from active participation —**on the sidelines** not actively participating

side'long' adv., a. toward or to the side

si·de're·al (-dir'ē-) a. of or measured by the stars

side'show' n. small show connected to main show

side'step' v. avoid as by stepping aside

side'swipe' v. hit along the side in passing —n. such a hit

side'track' v. turn aside from a course, subject, etc.

side'walk' n. path for pedestrians alongside a street

side'wall' n. side of a tire

side'ways' a., adv. 1 to or from one side 2 side first Also **side'wise'**

sid'ing (sīd'-) n. 1 outside boards, etc. on a building 2 short railroad track off the main track

si'dle v. move sideways cautiously

siege (sēj) n. 1 encircling of a place to effect its capture 2 persistent attack

si·es'ta (sē-) n. brief rest or nap, esp. in the afternoon

sieve (siv) n. strainer with many small holes

sift v. 1 pass through a sieve, as to separate 2 examine with care, as evidence

sigh (sī) v. 1 let out a deep breath, as in sorrow 2 long (for) —n. a sighing

sight n. 1 something seen 2 act or power of seeing 3 range of vision 4 aiming device —v. 1 to see 2 aim (a gun, etc.) —at (or on) **sight** as soon as seen — **sight'less** a.

sight'ly a. **-li·er, -li·est** pleasing to look at

sign n. 1 mark or symbol 2 meaningful gesture 3 signboard, road marker, etc. 4 trace; vestige —v. write one's name (on) —**sign off** stop broadcasting — **sign'er** n.

sig'nal n. 1 gesture, device, etc. to warn, order, etc. 2 radio wave —a. notable —v. make signals (to)

sig'nal·ize' v. 1 make noteworthy 2 point out

sig'na·to'ry n., pl. **-ries** one signing a pact, etc.

sig'na·ture n. one's name written by oneself

sign'board' n. board bearing advertising

sig'net n. small official seal

sig·nif'i·cance n. 1 meaning 2 importance —**sig·nif'i·cant** a.

sig·ni·fy' v. **-fied', -fy'ing** 1 to mean 2 make known, as by a sign —**sig'ni·fi·ca'tion** n.

si'lage n. green fodder preserved in a silo

si'lence n. absence of sound —v. 1 make silent 2 repress —int. be silent!

si'lent a. 1 not speaking 2 still; quiet 3 inactive —**si'lent·ly** adv.

sil'hou·ette' (-ōō-) v., n. (make) a dark shape against a light background

sil'i·ca n. glassy mineral found as sand, etc.

sil'i·con' n. chemical element forming silica, etc.

sil'i·cone' n. silicon compound resistant to water, etc.

sil'i·co'sis n. chronic lung disease from inhaling silica dust

silk n. thread or fabric of soft fiber made by silkworms — **silk'en** a. —**silk'y, -i·er, -i·est**

silk'worm' n. moth caterpillar

that spins silk fiber

sill n. bottom of a door frame or window frame

sil'ly a. **-li·er, -li·est** foolish; absurd —**sil'li·ness** n.

si'lo n., pl. **-los** tower for storing green fodder

silt n. fine particles of soil floating in or left by water —v. fill with silt

sil'ver n. 1 white, precious metal, a chemical element 2 silver coins 3 silverware 4 grayish white —a. of silver —v. cover as with silver —**sil'ver·y** a.

sil'ver·fish' n. wingless insect found in damp places

silver lining n. hope or comfort in the midst of despair

sil'ver·smith' n. one who makes things of silver

sil'ver·ware' n. tableware of or plated with silver

sim'i·an n. ape or monkey

sim'i·lar a. nearly alike —**sim'i·lar'i·ty** n., pl. **-ties** —**sim'i·lar·ly** adv.

sim'i·le' (-lē') n. a likening of dissimilar things

si·mil'i·tude' n. likeness

sim'mer v., n. (keep at or near) a gentle boiling

sim'per v. smile in a silly way — n. silly smile

sim'ple a. 1 having only one or a few parts 2 easy to do or understand 3 plain 4 natural 5 common 6 foolish —**sim·plic'i·ty** n., pl. **-ties**

sim'ple-mind'ed a. 1 naive 2 foolish 3 mentally retarded

sim'ple·ton n. fool

sim'pli·fy' v. **-fied', -fy'ing** make easier —**sim'pli·fi·ca'tion** n.

sim·plis'tic a. oversimplifying or oversimplified

sim'ply adv. 1 in a simple way 2 merely 3 completely

sim'u·late' v. pretend —**sim'u·la'tion** n.

si'mul·ta'ne·ous a. done, etc. at the same time —**si'mul·ta'ne·ous·ly** adv.

sin n. 1 breaking of religious or moral law —v. sinned, sin'ning commit a sin —**sin'ful** a. —**sin'ner** n.

since adv., prep. 1 from then until now 2 at some time between then and now —con. 1 after the time that 2 because

sin·cere' a. 1 without deceit 2 genuine —**sin·cere'ly** adv. — **sin·cer'i·ty** n.

si'ne·cure' n. well-paid job with

little work

sin'ew (-yōō) n. 1 tendon 2 strength —**sin'ew·y** a.

sing v. **sang, sung, sing'ing** 1 make musical sounds with the voice, etc. 2 perform by singing 3 hum, buzz, etc. 4 tell in song —n. [Col.] group singing —**sing'er** n.

singe v. **singed, singe'ing** burn superficially —n. a singeing

sin'gle a. 1 one only 2 of or for one person or family 3 unmarried —v. select others: with out —n. 1 single person or thing 2 pl. tennis game with only two players 3 Baseball hit on which the batter reaches first base —**sin'gle·ness** n.

single file n. column of persons one behind the other

sin'gle-hand'ed a. without help

sin'gle-mind'ed a. with only one purpose

sin'gly adv. 1 alone 2 one by one

sing'song' a., n. (having) a monotonous cadence

sin'gu·lar a. 1 unique 2 separate 3 exceptional 4 unusual —n. Gram. word form designating only one —**sin'gu·lar'i·ty** n. —**sin'gu·lar·ly** adv.

sin'is·ter a. 1 threatening 2 wicked or evil

sink v. **sank or sunk, sunk, sink'ing** 1 go or put beneath the surface of water, etc. 2 go down slowly 3 become lower 4 pass gradually (into sleep, etc.) 5 invest 6 defeat —n. basin with a drain pipe —**sink in** [Col.] be understood fully

sink'er n. lead weight used on a fishing line

sin'u·ous a. 1 bending or winding in and out 2 crooked

si'nus n., pl. **-nus·es** any air cavity in the skull opening into the nasal cavities

si'nus·i'tis n. inflammation of the sinuses

sip v. **sipped, sip'ping** drink a little at a time —n. a small amount sipped

si'phon n. tube for carrying liquid from one container to another being it —v. drain through a siphon

sir n. 1 polite title for a man 2 [S-] title for a knight or baronet

sire n. male parent —v. be the male parent of

si'ren n. 1 warning device with a wailing sound 2 a seductive woman

sir'loin' n. choice cut of beef from the loin

sir'up n. syrup —**sir'up·y** a.

sis n. [Col.] sister

si'sal n. strong rope fiber

sis'sy n., pl. **-sies** [Col.] unmanly boy or man —**sis'si·fied** a.

sis'ter n. 1 female related to one by having the same parents 2 female fellow member 3 nun —**sis'ter·hood'** n. —**sis'ter·ly** a.

sis'ter-in-law' n., pl. **sis'ters-in-law'** 1 sister of one's spouse 2 brother's wife

sit v. **sat, sit'ting** 1 rest on one's buttocks or haunches 2 perch 3 be in session 4 pose, as for a portrait 5 be located 6 baby-sit —**sit down** take a seat —**sit in** take part —**sit out** take no part in —**sit'ter** n.

site n. location; scene

sit'-in' n. strike or demonstration in which participants refuse to work or leave

sit·u·ate (sich'ōō-) v. put or place; locate

sit·u·a'tion n. 1 location 2 condition 3 job

six a., n. one more than five —**sixth** a., n.

six'teen' a., n. six more than ten —**six'teenth'** a., n.

sixth sense n. intuitive power

six'ty a., n., pl. **-ties** six times ten —**six'ti·eth** a., n.

siz'a·ble, size'a·ble a. fairly large

size n. 1 dimensions 2 any of a series of measures, often numbered 3 pasty glaze: also **siz'ing** —v. 1 arrange by SIZE (n. 2) 2 apply SIZE (n. 3) —**size up** [Col.] 1 to estimate 2 meet requirements

siz'zle v. to hiss when hot —n. such a sound

skate n. 1 ice skate 2 roller skate —v. glide or roll on skates

skein (skān) n. coil of yarn or thread

skel'e·ton n. framework, as of the bones of a body —**skel'e·tal** a.

skep'tic n. one who questions matters generally accepted —**skep'ti·cal** a. —**skep'ti·cism'** n.

sketch n. 1 rough drawing or design 2 outline —v. make a sketch (of) —**sketch'y** a., **-i·er, -i·est**

skew (skyōō) v. slant

skew'er n. long pin to hold meat together as it cooks

ski (skē) n., pl. **skis** long, flat runner fastened to the shoe for snow travel —v. travel on skis —**ski'er** n.

skid n. 1 plank, log, etc. on which to support or slide something heavy 2 act of skidding —v. **skid'ded, skid'ding** slide sideways

skid row n. city area where vagrants gather

skiff n. small sailboat

skill n. 1 great ability 2 art or craft involving use of the hands or body —**skilled** a. —**skill'ful**, **skil'ful** a.

skil'let n. frying pan

skim v. **skimmed, skim'ming** 1 take floating matter from a liquid 2 read quickly 3 glide lightly

skim milk n. milk with the cream removed

skimp v. [Col.] scrimp

skimp'y a. **-i·er, -i·est** [Col.] barely enough; scanty

skin n. 1 tissue covering the body 2 pelt 3 covering like skin, as fruit rind —v. **skinned,** **skin'ning** remove the skin from

skin'flint' n. miser

skin'ny a. **-ni·er, -ni·est** very thin —**skin'ni·ness** n.

skip v. **skipped, skip'ping** 1 move by hopping on alternate feet 2 leap lightly (over) 3 bounce 4 omit —n. act of skipping

skip'per n. ship's captain

skir'mish v., n. (take part in) a small, brief battle

skirt n. 1 part of a dress, coat, etc. below the waist 2 woman's garment that hangs from the waist —v. go along the edge of

skit n. short, funny play

skit'tish a. 1 lively; playful 2 very nervous

skiv'vies n.pl. [Sl.] men's underwear

skul·dug'ger·y n. [Col.] mean trickery

skulk v. to move or lurk in a stealthy way

skull n. bony framework of the head

skunk n. small mammal that ejects a smelly liquid

sky n., pl. **skies** often pl. upper atmosphere or space around the earth

sky diving n. parachute jumping

sky'lark' n. lark of Europe and Asia, famous for its song

sky'light' n. window in a roof or ceiling

sky'line' n. outline of a city, etc. seen against the sky

sky'rock'et n. fireworks rocket —v. rise fast

sky'scrap'er n. very tall building

sky'ward a., adv. toward the sky: also **sky'wards** adv.

slab n. flat, thick piece

slack a. 1 loose 2 not busy 3 slow; sluggish —n. slack part or time —**slack off** (or **up**) slacken

slack'en v. 1 slow down 2 loosen

slack'er n. one who shirks

slacks n.pl. trousers

slag n. smelting refuse

slain v. pp. of SLAY

slake v. 1 satisfy (thirst) 2 mix (lime) with water

sla'lom n. downhill ski race over a zigzag course

slam v. **slammed, slam'ming** shut, hit, etc. with force —n. heavy impact

slan'der n. spoken falsehood harmful to another —v. speak slander against —**slan'der·ous** a.

slang n. vigorous, short-lived, informal language

slant v., n. 1 incline; slope 2 (show) a special attitude

slap n. a blow with something flat —v. **slapped, slap'ping** strike with a slap

slap'dash' a., adv. hurried(ly) or careless(ly)

slap'stick' n. crude comedy

slash v. 1 cut with a knife 2 cut slits in 3 reduce —n. a slashing; cut

slat n. narrow strip

slate n. 1 bluish-gray rock in thin layers 2 tile, etc. of slate 3 list of candidates —v. designate

slat'tern n. untidy woman —**slat'tern·ly** a., adv.

slaugh'ter v. 1 kill (animals) for food 2 kill (people) brutally —n. a slaughtering

slaugh'ter·house' n. place for butchering animals

slave n. human being owned by another —v. to toil —**slav'ish** a.

slav'er (slav'-) v. drool

slav'er·y n. 1 condition of slaves 2 ownership of slaves 3 drudgery

Slav'ic (släv'-) a. of the Russians, Poles, Slovaks, etc.

slay v. **slew, slain, slay'ing** kill by violent means —**slay'er** n.

sleaze n. [Sl.] 1 sleaziness 2 something or someone sleazy

slea'zy a. **-zi·er, -zi·est** 1 flimsy;

thin **2** morally low, shabby, shoddy, etc. —**slea'zi·ness** n.

sled n. vehicle with runners, for snow —v. **sled'ded, sled'ding** ride a sled

sledge n. **1** long, heavy hammer **2** heavy sled

sleek a. **1** glossy **2** well-groomed —v. make sleek

sleep n. natural regular rest, as at night —v. **slept, sleep'ing** to be in a state of sleep —**sleep'less** a.

sleep'er n. **1** one who sleeps **2** railway car with berths

sleep'y a. **-i·er, -i·est 1** drowsy **2** dull; quiet

sleet n. partly frozen rain —v. to shower as sleet

sleeve n. **1** part of a garment covering the arm **2** protective cover —**sleeve'less** a.

sleigh (slā) n. vehicle on runners for travel on snow

sleight of hand (slīt) n. **1** skill in doing tricks with the hands **2** such tricks

slen'der a. **1** long and thin **2** small in size or force

slept v. pt. & pp. of SLEEP

sleuth (slooth) n. [Col.] detective

slew v. pt. of SLAY —n. [Col.] large number or amount

slice n. **1** thin, broad piece cut off **2** share —v. cut into slices or as a slice —**slic'er** n.

slick v. make smooth —a. **1** smooth **2** slippery **3** clever —n. smooth area, as of oil on water

slick'er n. loose, waterproof coat

slide v. **slid, slid'ing 1** move along a smooth surface **2** glide **3** slip —n. **1** a sliding **2** inclined surface to slide on **3** picture for projection on a screen —**let slide** fail to take proper action

slide fastener n. fastener with interlocking tabs worked by a sliding part

slid'er n. Baseball fast pitch that curves sharply

slight a. **1** slender **2** unimportant **3** small or weak —v., n. neglect or snub —**slight'ly** adv.

slim a. **slim'mer, slim'mest 1** long and thin **2** small —v. **slimmed, slim'ming** make or become slim

slime n. soft, wet, sticky matter —**slim'y** a., **-i·er, -i·est**

sling n. **1** device for hurling stones **2** band or looped cloth for raising or supporting —v. **slung, sling'ing** hurl as with a

sling'shot' n. Y-shaped piece with elastic band for shooting stones, etc.

slink v. **slunk, slink'ing** move in a sneaking way

slink'y a. **-i·er, -i·est** [Sl.] sinuous and graceful in movement, line, etc.

slip v. **slipped, slip'ping 1** go quietly **2** put or pass smoothly or quickly **3** slide accidentally **4** escape from **5** become worse **6** err —n. **1** dock for ships **2** woman's undergarment **3** a falling down **4** error: also [Col.]

slip'-up' n. **5** plant stem or root, for planting, etc. **6** small piece of paper

slip'knot' n. knot that can slip along a rope

slip'per n. light, low shoe

slip'per·y a. **-i·er, -i·est 1** that can cause slipping **2** tending to slip **3** tricky

slip'shod' a. careless

slit v. **slit, slit'ting** cut or split open —n. a straight, narrow opening

slith'er (slith'-) v. slide or glide along

sliv'er n. thin, pointed piece cut or split off

slob n. [Col.] sloppy or coarse person

slob'ber v., n. drool

sloe n. dark-blue fruit

slog v. **slogged, slog'ging** plod

slo'gan n. motto or phrase, as for advertising purposes

sloop n. boat with one mast

slop n. **1** spilled liquid **2** slush **3** watery food **4** often pl. liquid waste —v. **slopped, slop'ping** splash

slope n. **1** rising or falling surface, line, etc. **2** amount of this —v. have a slope

slop'py a. **-pi·er, -pi·est 1** slushy **2** careless

slot n. narrow opening

sloth (slôth, slōth) n. **1** laziness **2** South American mammal living in trees —**sloth'ful** a.

slouch n. **1** a lazy person **2** drooping posture —v. have a drooping posture

slough (sluf; n.: sloō) v. to shed; discard —n. swamp

slov'en (sluv'-) n. slovenly person

slov'en·ly a. careless or untidy

slow a. **1** taking longer than usual **2** low in speed **3** behind the right time **4** stupid **5** sluggish —v. make or become slow —adv. in a slow way —slow'ly adv. —slow'ness n.

slow'-mo'tion a. of film or video showing action slowed down

slow'poke' n. [Sl.] one who acts slowly

slow'-wit'ted a. mentally slow; dull

sludge n. 1 mud or mire 2 slimy waste

slug n. 1 small mollusk 2 bullet 3 false coin —v. slugged, slug'ging [Col.] hit hard —slug'ger n.

slug'gard n. lazy person

slug'gish a. slow-moving

sluice (sloos) n. water channel or gate to control it

slum n. populous area with very poor living conditions

slum'ber v., n. sleep

slump v. 1 fall suddenly 2 to slouch —n. sudden fall

slur v. slurred, slur'ring 1 pass over quickly 2 pronounce indistinctly 3 insult —n. 1 a slurring 2 insult

slurp [Sl.] v. drink or eat noisily —n. loud sipping or sucking sound

slush n. partly melted snow — slush'y a.

slut n. immoral woman

sly a. sli'er or sly'er, sli'est or sly'est 1 cunning; crafty 2 playfully mischievous —on the sly secretly —sly'ly adv.

smack n. 1 slight taste 2 sharp noise made by parting the lips suddenly 3 sharp slap 4 loud kiss 5 fishing boat —v. 1 have a trace 2 make a smack with one's lips 3 slap loudly —adv. directly

small a. 1 little in size, extent, etc. 2 trivial 3 mean; petty —n. small part —small'ish a.

small'pox' n. contagious disease with fever and sores

smart v. 1 cause or feel stinging pain 2 suffer —a. 1 that smarts 2 brisk; lively 3 bright; clever 4 neat 5 stylish —smart'ly adv.

smart al'eck, smart al'ec n. [Col.] conceited, insolent person

smash v. 1 break violently 2 crash 3 to destroy —n. 1 a smashing 2 wreck; collision

smash'up' n. very damaging collision

smat'ter·ing n. a little knowledge

smear v. 1 make greasy, dirty, etc. 2 spread 3 slander —n. a smearing

smell v. smelled or [Br.] smelt, smell'ing 1 catch the odor of 2 sniff 3 have an odor —n. 1 power to smell 2 thing smelled; odor

smell'y a. -i·er, -i·est having a bad smell

smelt n. small, silvery food fish —v. melt (ore or metal) so as to remove the impurities — smelt'er n.

smidg·en (smij'an) n. [Col.] tiny amount

smile v. 1 to show pleasure, amusement, etc. by curving the mouth upward 2 show with a smile —n. act of smiling

smirch v., n. smear

smirk v. to smile in a conceited or annoyingly complacent way —n. such a smile

smite v. smote, smit'ten, smit'ing 1 hit or strike hard 2 affect strongly

smith n. one who makes or repairs metal objects

smith'er·eens' n.pl. [Col.] bits; fragments

smith'y n., pl. -ies blacksmith's shop

smock n. loose, protective outer garment

smog n. fog and smoke —smog'gy a. -gi·er, -gi·est

smoke n. vapor, as from something burning —v. 1 give off smoke 2 use cigarettes, a pipe, etc. 3 cure (meats, etc.) with smoke —smoke'less a. — smok'er n. —smok'y a., -i·er, -i·est

smoke'stack' n. tall chimney

smol'der v. 1 burn without flame 2 exist suppressed Br. sp. smoul'der

smooch n., v. [Sl.] kiss

smooth a. 1 having no roughness or bumps; even 2 with no trouble 3 ingratiating —v. to make smooth —adv. in a smooth way —smooth'ness n.

smor·gas·bord' (-gas-) n. variety of tasty foods served buffet style

smoth·er (smuth'-) v. 1 suffocate 2 cover thickly

smudge n. 1 dirty spot 2 fire with dense smoke —v. to smear —smudg'y a.

smug a. smug'ger, smug'gest too self-satisfied —smug'ly adv.

smug·gle v. bring in or take out secretly or illegally —smug'gler n.

smut n. 1 dirt 2 obscene matter 3 plant disease —smut'y a., -tier, -ti·est

snack n. light meal

snag n. 1 sharp projection 2 tear made by this 3 hidden difficulty —v. snagged, snag'ging 1 tear on a snag 2 hinder

snail n. mollusk with a spiral shell

snake n. long, legless reptile —v. twist like a snake —snak'y a., -i·er, -i·est

snap v. snapped, snap'ping 1 bite or grasp suddenly 2 shout (at) 3 break suddenly 4 make a cracking sound 5 move quickly 6 take a snapshot of —n. 1 sharp sound 2 fastening that clicks shut 3 [Sl.] easy job —a. quick —snap'per n. —snap'pish a.

snap'drag'on n. plant with red or yellow flowers

snap'py a. -pi·er, -pi·est [Col.] 1 lively; brisk 2 stylish; smart

snap'shot' n. picture taken with a hand camera

snare n. 1 trap for small animals 2 dangerous lure 3 string across the bottom of a drum —v. to trap

snarl v. 1 growl, baring the teeth 2 speak sharply 3 tangle —n. 1 a snarling 2 tangle; disorder

snatch v. seize; grab —n. 1 brief time 2 fragment

sneak v. move, do, etc. secretly —n. one who sneaks —sneak'y a., -i·er, -i·est

sneak'er n. canvas shoe with a rubber sole

sneer v. show scorn —n. sneering look or remark

sneeze v. expel breath from the nose and mouth in a sudden, uncontrolled way —n. act of sneezing

snick'er v., n. (give) a silly, partly stifled laugh

snide a. slyly malicious

sniff v. inhale forcibly through the nose, as in smelling —n. act of sniffing

snif'fle v., n. sniff to check mucus flow —the sniffles [Col.] a head cold

snif'ter n. goblet with a small opening, as for brandy

snip v. snipped, snip'ping cut in a quick stroke —n. small piece cut off

snipe n. wading bird —v. shoot at from a hidden place —snip'er n.

snip'pet n. small piece; bit

snip'py a. -pi·er, -pi·est [Col.]

insolently curt

snitch [Sl.] v. inform; tattle (on) —n. informer; tattler

sniv'el v. 1 cry and sniffle 2 whine

snob n. one who disdains his supposed inferiors —snob'bish a. —snob'ber·y n.

snood n. kind of hair net

snoop [Col.] v. pry in a sneaky way —n. one who snoops: also snoop'er

snoot'y a. -i·er, -i·est [Col.] snobbish

snooze v., n. (take) a nap

snore v. breathe noisily while asleep —n. a snoring

snor'kel v. -keled, -kel·ing; n. (use) a breathing tube for swimming underwater

snort v. force breath audibly from the nose —n. a snorting

snot n. [Sl.] 1 nasal mucus 2 insolent young person —snot'ty a., -ti·er, -ti·est

snout n. projecting nose and jaws of an animal

snow n. flakes of frozen water vapor from the sky —v. 1 fall as snow 2 cover with snow 3 [Sl.] deceive —snow under overwhelm or defeat —snow'drift' n. —snow'fall' n. —snow'flake' n. —snow'storm' n. —snow'y a., -i·er, -i·est

snow'ball' n. ball of packed snow —v. increase rapidly

snow'bound' a. confined by snow

snow'man' n., pl. -men' crude human figure made of packed snow

snow'mo·bile' n. motor vehicle for snow travel, with runners and tractor treads

snow'plow' n. machine for removing snow

snow'shoe' n. racketlike footgear for walking on snow

snub v. snubbed, snub'bing 1 treat with scorn 2 stop abruptly —n. a slight —a. short and turned up, as a nose

snuff v. put out (a candle, etc.) —n. powdered tobacco —up to snuff [Col.] up to the usual standard

snug a. snug'ger, snug'gest 1 cozy 2 compact 3 tight in fit

snug'gle v. nestle

so adv. 1 in such a way 2 to such a degree 3 very 4 therefore 5 more or less 6 also 7 then 8 [Col.] very much —con. 1 in order (that) 2 [Col.] with the result (*that*) —*int.* word showing surprise —**and so on** (or **forth**) and the rest

soak *v.* 1 make wet 2 stay in liquid —**soak up** absorb

soap *n.* substance that makes suds in water for washing —*v.* rub with soap —**soap'y** *a.*, **-i·er**, **-i·est**

soap'box' *n.* improvised platform for public speaking

soar *v.* fly high in the air

sob *v.* **sobbed, sob'bing** weep aloud with short gasps —*n.* act of sobbing

so'ber *a.* 1 not drunk 2 serious; sedate 3 plain —*v.* make or become sober —**so·bri'e·ty** *n.*

so'-called' *a.* called thus, but usually inaccurately

soc'cer *n.* kind of football

so'cia·ble (-sha-) *a.* friendly; agreeable —**so·cia·bil'i·ty** *n.* —**so'cia·bly** *adv.*

so'cial *a.* 1 of society 2 living in groups 3 sociable 4 of social work —*n.* a party —**so'cial·ly** *adv.*

so'cial·ism' *n.* public ownership of the means of production —**so'cial·ist** *n., a.* —**so'cial·is'tic** *a.*

so'cial·ite' *n.* person prominent in fashionable society

so'cial·ize' *v.* 1 put under public ownership 2 take part in social affairs

social science *n.* field of study dealing with society

social security *n.* federal insurance for old age, unemployment, etc.

social work *n.* work of clinics, agencies, etc. to improve living conditions

so·ci'e·ty *n., pl.* **-ties** 1 community of people 2 all people 3 companionship 4 organized group 5 the fashionable class

so'ci·ol'o·gy (-sē-) *n.* study of the organization, problems, etc. of society —**so'ci·o·log'i·cal** *a.* —**so'ci·ol'o·gist** *n.*

sock *n.* 1 short stocking 2 [Sl.] a blow —*v.* [Sl.] hit with force

sock'et *n.* hollow part into which something fits

sod *n.* earth surface with grass —*v.* **sod'ded, sod'ding** cover with sod

so'da *n.* 1 substance containing sodium 2 soda water 3 beverage of soda water and ice cream

soda cracker *n.* crisp cracker

soda water *n.* carbonated water

sod'den *a.* soaked or soggy

so'di·um *n.* silver-white metallic chemical element

sodium bi·car'bon·ate (-ət) *n.* baking soda

sodium chloride *n.* common salt

sod'om·y *n.* sexual intercourse held to be abnormal

so'fa *n.* couch with back and arms

soft *a.* 1 not hard; easy to crush, cut etc. 2 not harsh; mild, gentle, etc. 3 without minerals that hinder lathering 4 weak 5 nonalcoholic —*adv.* gently —**soft'ly** *adv.* —**soft'ness** *n.*

soft'ball' *n.* game like baseball played with a larger and softer ball

soft'-boiled' *a.* boiled briefly to keep the egg's yolk soft

soft drink *n.* nonalcoholic drink, esp. one carbonated

soft'en (sôf'-) *v.* make or become soft —**soft'en·er** *n.*

soft'ware' *n.* programs, etc. for a computer or other electronic equipment

sog'gy *a.* **-gi·er, -gi·est** very wet and heavy; soaked

soil *n.* earth or ground, esp. the surface layer —*v.* make or become dirty

soi·ree, soi·rée (swä rā') *n.* an evening social

so'journ (-jurn) *n., v.* visit, as in a foreign land

sol'ace *n.* relief or comfort —*v.* comfort

so'lar *a.* of or having to do with the sun

so·lar'i·um *n.* glassed-in room for sunning

solar system *n.* the sun and all its planets

sold *v.* pt. & pp. of SELL

sol'der (säd'ər) *n.* metal alloy for joining metal parts —*v.* join with solder

sol'dier (sōl'jər) *n.* member of an army, esp. one who is not an officer —*v.* be a soldier

sole *n.* 1 bottom of the foot, or of a shoe 2 sea flatfish —*v.* put a sole on (a shoe) —*a.* one and only

sole'ly *adv.* 1 alone 2 only

sol'emn (-əm) *a.* 1 formal 2 serious —**sol'emn·ly** *adv.*

so·lem'ni·ty *n., pl.* **-ties** 1 solemn ritual 2 seriousness

sol'em·nize' *v.* celebrate or perform formally

so·lic'it (-lis'-) *v.* ask for —**so·lic'i·ta'tion** *n.*

so·lic'i·tor *n.* 1 one who solicits

trade, etc. 2 in England, lawyer not a barrister 3 in U.S., lawyer for a city, etc.

so·lic'i·tous *a.* 1 showing concern 2 anxious —**so·lic'i·tude'** *n.*

sol'id *a.* 1 firm or hard 2 not hollow 3 three-dimensional 4 of one piece, color, etc. 1 firm or hard substance 2 three-dimensional object —**sol·id'i·fy'** *v.*, **-fied', -fy'ing** —**so·lid'i·ty** *n.*

sol·i·dar'i·ty *n.* firm unity

so·lil'o·quy (-kwē) *n.*, *pl.* **-quies** a talking to oneself —**so·lil'o·quize'** *v.*

sol'i·taire' (-ter') *n.* 1 gem set by itself 2 card game for one person

sol'i·tar'y *a.* 1 alone; lonely 2 single

sol'i·tude' *n.* loneliness

so'lo *n.*, *a.* (piece of music) for one performer —**so'lo·ist** *n.*

sol'stice (-stis) *n.* longest day (June 21 or 22) or shortest day (Dec. 21 or 22)

sol'u·ble *a.* 1 that can be dissolved 2 solvable —**sol·u·bil'i·ty** *n.*

so·lu'tion *n.* 1 solving of a problem 2 explanation or answer 3 liquid with something dissolved in it

solve *v.* find the answer to —**solv'a·ble** *a.*

sol'vent *a.* 1 able to pay one's debts 2 able to dissolve a substance —*n.* substance used to dissolve another —**sol'ven·cy** *n.*

som'ber *a.* 1 dark and gloomy 2 sad Br. sp. **som'bre**

som·bre'ro (-brer'ō) *n.*, *pl.* **-ros** broad-brimmed hat

some *a.* 1 certain but unspecified 2 of indefinite quantity 3 about —*pron.* indefinite quantity —*adv.* 1 approximately 2 [Col.] somewhat 3 [Col.] to a great extent

-some *suf.* tending to (be)

some'bod'y *n.*, *pl.* **-ies** important person —*pron.* person not named or known

some'day' *adv.* sometime

some'how' *adv.* in some way

some'one' *pron.* somebody

som'er·sault (sum'ər sôlt') *n.*, *v.* (perform) a turning of the body, heels over head

some'thing *n.* thing not named or known

some'time' *adv.* at some unspecified time —*a.* former

some'times' *adv.* at times

some'what' *n.* some part, amount, etc. —*adv.* a little

some'where' *adv.* in, to, or at some unnamed place

som·nam'bu·lism' *n.* act of walking while asleep

som'no·lent *a.* sleepy —**som'no·lence** *n.*

son *n.* male in relation to his parents

so·na'ta *n.* piece of music for one or two instruments

song *n.* 1 music, or poem, to be sung 2 singing sound

song'bird' *n.* bird that makes vocal sounds like music

song'ster *n.* singer —**song'stress** *n.fem.*

son'ic *a.* of or having to do with sound

son'-in-law' *n.*, *pl.* **sons'-** husband of one's daughter

son'net *n.* 14-line poem

so·no'rous *a.* resonant —**so·nor'i·ty** *n.*

soon *adv.* 1 in a short time 2 early 3 readily

soot *n.* black particles in smoke —**soot'y** *a.*, **-i·er, -i·est**

soothe (sōōth) *v.* 1 make calm, as by kindness 2 ease, as pain —**sooth'ing·ly** *adv.*

sooth'say'er (sōōth'-) *n.* one who pretends to prophesy

sop *n.* bribe —*v.* **sopped, sop'ping** soak (up)

so·phis'ti·cat'ed *a.* 1 knowledgeable, subtle, etc. 2 highly complex; advanced —**so·phis'ti·cate** (-kət) *n.* —**so·phis'ti·ca'tion** *n.*

soph'ist·ry, soph'ism' *n.* clever but misleading reasoning —**soph'ist** *n.*

soph'o·more' *n.* second-year student in high school or college

soph'o·mor'ic *a.* immature

sop'o·rif'ic *n.*, *a.* (drug) causing sleep

sop'ping *a.* very wet: also **sop'py, -i·er, -i·est**

so·pra'no (-pran'ō, -prä'nō) *n.*, *pl.* **-nos** highest female voice

sor·bet' (-bā') *n.* tart ice, as of fruit juice

sor'cer·y *n.* witchcraft —**sor'cer·er** *n.* —**sor'cer·ess** *n.fem.*

sor'did *a.* 1 dirty; filthy 2 mean; selfish

sore *a.* 1 painful 2 sad 3 [Col.] angry —*n.* injured body tissue —**sore'ness** *n.*

sore'ly *adv.* greatly

sor'ghum (-gəm) *n.* grass grown for grain, syrup, etc.

so·ror'i·ty *n.*, *pl.* **-ties** social club

for women

sor'rel *n.* **1** reddish brown **2** horse of this color

sor'row *n.* (feel) sadness — **sor'row·ful** *a.*

sor'ry *a.* **-ri·er, -ri·est 1** full of sorrow, regret, etc. **2** pitiful; wretched

sort *n.* kind; class —*v.* arrange according to kind —**of sorts** or **of a sort** of an inferior kind — **out of sorts** [Col.] slightly ill — **sort of** [Col.] somewhat

sor'tie (-tē) *n.* **1** raid by besieged troops **2** one mission by a single military plane

SOS *n.* signal of distress

so'-so' *a., adv.* fair or fairly well: also so so

sot *n.* habitual drunkard

souf·flé (sōō flā') *n.* food made puffy by being baked with beaten egg whites

sought *v.* pt. & pp. of SEEK

soul *n.* **1** spiritual part of a person **2** vital part **3** person — **soul'ful** *a.*

sound *n.* **1** that which is heard **2** strait or inlet of the sea —*v.* **1** (cause) to make a sound **2** seem **3** measure the depth of water **4** seek the opinion of: often with **out** —*a.* **1** free from defect; healthy, secure, wise, etc. **2** deep or thorough —*adv.* in a sound way —**sound'ly** *adv.* — **sound'ness** *n.*

sound'proof' *v., a.* (make) impervious to sound

sound'track' *n.* sound record along one side of a film

soup *n.* liquid food with meat, vegetables, etc. in it

sour *a.* **1** having an acid taste **2** fermented **3** unpleasant —*v.* make or become sour —**sour'ness** *n.*

source *n.* **1** starting point **2** place of origin

souse *n.* **1** pickled food **2** brine **3** [Sl.] drunkard —*v.* **1** to pickle **2** soak in liquid

south *n.* direction or region to the left of one facing the sunset —*a., adv.* in, toward, or from the south —**south'er·ly** *a., adv.* —**south'ern** *a.* —**south'ern·er** *n.* —**south'ward** *a., adv.* — **south'wards** *adv.*

south'east' *n.* direction or region between south and east —*a., adv.* in, toward, or from the southeast —**south'east'er·ly** *a., adv.* —**south'east'ern** *a.* — **south'east'ward** *a., adv.* —

south'east'wards *adv.*

south'paw' *n.* [Sl.] left-handed person, esp. a baseball pitcher

South Pole southern end of the earth's axis

south'west' *n.* direction or region between south and west —*a., adv.* in, toward, or from the southwest —**south'west'er·ly** *a., adv.* —**south'west'ern** *a.* —**south'west'ward** *a., adv.* — **south'west'wards** *adv.*

sou·ve·nir (sōō'və nir') *n.* thing kept as a reminder

sov·er·eign (säv'rən) *a.* **1** chief; supreme **2** independent —*n.* **1** monarch **2** former Br. gold coin —**sov'er·eign·ty** *n., pl.* **-ties**

sow (sou) *n.* adult female pig

sow (sō) *v.* **sowed, sown** or **sowed, sow'ing** scatter, or plant with, seed for growing

soy *n.* sauce from soybeans

soy'bean' *n.* seed of a plant of the pea family

spa *n.* (resort having) a mineral spring

space *n.* **1** limitless expanse containing all things **2** distance or area **3** interval of time —*v.* divide by spaces

space'craft' *n., pl.* **-craft'** vehicle or satellite for outer-space travel, exploration, etc.

space'ship' *n.* spacecraft, esp. if manned

spa'cious (-shəs) *a.* having much space; vast

Spack·le *trademark* paste that dries hard, used to fill holes in wood, etc. —*n.* [s-] this substance

spade *n.* **1** flat-bladed digging tool **2** playing card marked with a ♠ —*v.* dig with a spade

spa·ghet'ti (-get'-) *n.* (cooked) strings of dried flour paste

span *n.* **1** nine inches **2** extent **3** period of time —*v.* extend over

span'gle *n.* shiny decoration, as a sequin —*v.* to decorate with spangles

span'iel (-yəl) *n.* dog with large drooping ears

Span'ish *a., n.* (of) the people or language of Spain

spank *v., n.* slap on the buttocks

spar *n.* pole supporting a ship's sail —*v.* **sparred, spar'ring** box cautiously

spare *v.* **1** save or free from something **2** avoid using **3** give up, as time or money —*a.* **1** extra **2** lean; meager —*n.* extra thing

spare'ribs n.pl. thin end of pork ribs

spar'ing a. frugal

spark n. 1 small glowing piece from a fire 2 particle 3 flash from an electrical discharge across a gap —v. 1 make sparks 2 excite

spar'kle v. 1 give off sparks 2 glitter 3 effervesce —n. glitter —**spar'kler** n.

spark plug n. piece in an engine cylinder, that ignites the fuel mixture

spar'row n. small songbird

sparse a. thinly spread —**sparse'ly** adv. —**spar'si·ty, sparse'ness** n.

Spar'tan a. brave; hardy

spasm (spaz'əm) n. 1 involuntary muscular contraction 2 short, sudden burst of activity —**spas·mod'ic** a.

spas'tic n., a. (one) having muscular spasms

spat v. pt. & pp. of SPIT —n. 1 [Col.] a brief quarrel 2 cloth ankle covering

spate n. unusually large outpouring, as of words

spa'tial (-shəl) a. of, or existing in, space

spat'ter v. 1 spurt out in drops 2 splash —n. mark made by spattering

spat'u·la (spach'ə-) n. tool with a broad, flexible blade

spawn n. 1 eggs of fishes, etc. 2 offspring —v. produce (spawn)

spay v. sterilize (a female animal)

speak v. **spoke, spo'ken, speak' ing** 1 utter words 2 tell; express 3 make a speech 4 use (a language) in speaking —**speak for** ask for

speak'er n. 1 one who speaks 2 loudspeaker

spear n. long, slender sharp-pointed weapon —v. pierce or stab as with a spear

spear'head' n. leading person or group, as in an attack

spear'mint' n. fragrant mint

spe'cial (spesh'əl) a. 1 distinctive 2 unusual 3 main; chief 4 for a certain use —n. special thing —**spe'cial·ly** adv.

spe'cial·ize' v. concentrate on a certain type of study, work, etc. —**spe'cial·ist** n. —**spe'cial·i·za' tion** n.

spe'cial·ty n., pl. **-ties** 1 special feature, interest, etc. 2 special

article

spe'cie (-shē, -sē) n. metal money

spe'cies n., pl. **-cies** distinct kind of plant or animal

spe·cif'ic a. definite; explicit —**spe·cif'i·cal·ly** adv.

spec'i·fi·ca'tion n. 1 a specifying 2 pl. detailed description

spec'i·fy' v. **-fied', -fy'ing** state explicitly

spec'i·men n. sample

spe'cious (-shəs) a. plausible but not genuine

speck n. small spot or bit —v. mark with specks

speck'le n., v. speck

specs n.pl. [Col.] specifications

spec'ta·cle n. 1 unusual sight 2 public show 3 pl. eyeglasses

spec·tac'u·lar a. showy; striking

spec'ta·tor n. one who watches

spec'ter n. ghost: Br. sp. **spec'tre** —**spec'tral** a.

spec'tro·scope' n. instrument that forms spectra for study

spec'trum n., pl. **-tra** or **-trums** row of colors formed by diffraction

spec'u·late' v. 1 ponder 2 take risky chances in business —**spec·u·la'tion** n. —**spec'u·la'tor** n.

speech n. 1 act or way of speaking 2 power to speak 3 something said 4 public talk —**speech'less** a.

speed n. 1 rapid motion 2 rate of movement —v. **sped, speed' ing** 1 move fast 2 aid —**speed'y** a., **-i·er, -i·est**

speed·om'e·ter n. device to indicate speed

spell n. 1 supposedly magic words 2 fascination; charm 3 period of work, duty, etc. —v. 1 give in order the letters of (a word) 2 mean 3 [Col.] relieve (another)

spell'bound' a. fascinated

spell'ing n. 1 a forming words from letters 2 way a word is spelled

spe·lunk'er n. cave explorer

spend v. **spent, spend'ing** 1 use up 2 pay out (money) 3 pass (time)

spend'thrift' n. one who wastes money —a. wasteful

sperm n. 1 semen 2 any of the germ cells in it

spew v. throw up; vomit

sphere (sfir) n. 1 globe; ball 2 place or range of action —**spher'i·cal** (sfer'-, sfir'-) a.

sphe·roid (sfir'oid) *n.* almost spherical body

spice *n.* 1 any aromatic seasoning 2 stimulating quality —*v.* add spice to —**spic'y** *a.*, **-i·er**, **-i·est**

spick'-and-span' *a.* fresh or tidy

spi'der *n.* arachnid that spins webs

spig'ot *n.* faucet or tap

spike *n.* 1 sharp-pointed projection 2 long, heavy nail 3 ear of grain 4 long flower cluster —*v.* 1 fasten or pierce as with a spike 2 thwart

spill *v.* **spilled** or **spilt**, **spill'ing** 1 let run over 2 overflow 3 shed (blood) 4 [Col.] make fall —*n.* a fall

spill'way' *n.* channel for excess water

spin *v.* **spun**, **spin'ning** 1 twist fibers into thread 2 make a web, cocoon, etc. 3 tell (a story) 4 to whirl 5 move fast —*n.* 1 whirling movement 2 fast ride

spin'ach *n.* plant with dark-green, edible leaves

spi'nal *a.* of the spine

spinal column *n.* long row of connected bones in the back

spinal cord *n.* cord of nerve tissue in the spinal column

spin'dle *n.* 1 rod used in spinning thread 2 rod that acts as an axis

spin'dly *a.* **-dli·er**, **-dli·est** long and thin: also **spin'dling**

spine *n.* 1 thorn, quill, etc. 2 spinal column —**spin'y** *a.*, **-i·er**, **-i·est**

spine'less *a.* 1 having no spine 2 weak or cowardly

spin'et *n.* small upright piano

spin'off' *n.* secondary benefit, product, etc.

spin'ster *n.* unmarried, older woman

spi'ral *a.* circling around a center —*n.* spiral curve or coil —*v.* move in a spiral

spire *n.* tapering, pointed part, as of a steeple

spir'it *n.* 1 soul 2 ghost, angel, etc. 3 *pl.* mood 4 courage 5 loyalty 6 essential quality 7 *pl.* alcoholic liquor —*v.* carry away secretly

spir'it·ed *a.* lively

spir'it·u·al *a.* 1 of the soul 2 religious; sacred —*n.* Negro religious song —**spir'it·u·al'i·ty** *n.*

spir'it·u·al·ism' *n.* seeming communication with the dead —**spir'it·u·al·ist** *n.*

spit *n.* 1 thin rod to roast meat on 2 shoreline narrowed to a point 3 saliva —*v.* **spit'ted** or (*v.* 2) **spit** or [Br.] **spat**, **spit'ting** 1 fix as on a spit 2 eject (saliva, etc.) from the mouth

spite *n.* malice —*v.* annoy; hurt —**in spite of** regardless of —**spite'ful** *a.*

spit'tle *n.* spit; saliva

spit·toon' *n.* container to spit into

splash *v.* dash liquid, etc. (on) —*n.* 1 a splashing 2 a spot made by splashing —**make a splash** [Col.] attract great attention

splash'y *a.* **-i·er**, **-i·est** [Col.] spectacular

splat'ter *n.*, *v.* splash

splay *v.*, *a.* spread out

spleen *n.* 1 large abdominal organ 2 malice; spite —**sple·net'ic** *a.*

splen'did *a.* magnificent; grand —**splen'dor** *n.*

splice *v.*, *n.* (make) a joint with ends overlapped

splint *n.* stiff strip to hold a broken bone in place

splin'ter *n.* thin, sharp piece —*v.* split in splinters

split *v.* **split**, **split'ting** separate into parts —*n.* break; crack —*a.* divided

split'-lev'el *a.* having adjacent floor levels staggered about a half story apart

split'ting *a.* severe

splotch *n.*, *v.* spot; stain —**splotch'y** *a.*, **-i·er**, **-i·est**

splurge *v.*, *n.* [Col.] (make) a showy display, etc.

splut'ter *v.* 1 make spitting sounds 2 speak confusedly —*n.* a spluttering

spoil *v.* **spoiled** or **spoilt**, **spoil'-ing** to damage, ruin, decay, etc. —*n.pl.* plunder —**spoil'age** *n.*

spoil'sport' *n.* one who ruins the fun of others

spoke *v.* pt. of SPEAK —*n.* rod from hub to rim

spo'ken *v.* pp. of SPEAK —*a.* oral; voiced

spokes'man *n.*, *pl.* **-men** one who speaks for another —**spokes'per·son** *n.*

sponge *n.* 1 absorbent substance made from a sea animal, plastic, etc. 2 the sea animal —*v.* 1 clean, etc. with a sponge 2 [Col.] live off others —**spon'gy** *a.*, **-gi·er**, **-gi·est**

sponge'cake' *n.* light, spongy cake without shortening

spon'sor n. 1 promoter; supporter 2 advertiser who pays for a radio or TV program —v. be sponsor for

spon·ta'ne·ous a. 1 without effort 2 within or by itself —**spon·ta·ne'i·ty** (-nē-', -nā'-) n.

spoof n. light satire —v. satirize playfully

spook n. [Col.] ghost —**spook'y** a., -i·er, -i·est

spool n. cylinder upon which thread, etc. is wound

spoon n. small bowl with a handle, used in eating —**spoon'ful** n., pl. **-fuls**

spoon'-feed' v. pamper

spoor n. wild animal's trail or track

spo·rad'ic a. not regular —**spo·rad'i·cal·ly** adv.

spore n. tiny reproductive cell of mosses, fern, etc.

sport n. 1 athletic game 2 fun 3 abnormal plant or animal —v. 1 [Col.] display 2 play —a. for play

sport'ing a. 1 of sports 2 fair 3 risky

sports a. sport

sports (or **sport**) **car** n. small, expensive car with powerful engine

sports'man n., pl. **-men** 1 participant in sports 2 one who plays fair —**sports'man·like'** a.

sport'y a. -i·er, -i·est [Col.] flashy or showy

spot n. 1 stain; mark 2 place —v. **spot'ted, spot'ting** 1 mark with spots 2 see —a. made at random —**spot'less** a.

spot'-check' v. check at random —n. such a checking

spot'light' n. 1 strong beam of light, or lamp that throws it 2 public notice

spot'ty a. -ti·er, -ti·est 1 spotted 2 not uniform

spouse n. husband or wife —**spous·al** (spou'zal) n.

spout n. 1 pipe, etc. by which a liquid pours 2 stream of liquid —v. 1 shoot out with force 2 talk loudly and on

sprain v. twist a muscle or ligament in a joint —n. injury caused by this

sprang v. pt. of SPRING

sprat n. small herring

sprawl v. sit or spread out in a relaxed or awkward way —n. sprawling position

spray n. 1 mist or stream of tiny liquid drops 2 branch with leaves, flowers, etc. 3 spray gun —v. apply, or emit in, a spray

spray gun n. device that sprays a liquid, as paint

spread v. spread, spread'ing 1 open out 2 extend in time or space 3 make known 4 cover 5 go or make go —n. 1 act or extent of spreading 2 a cloth cover 3 butter, jam, etc.

spread'sheet' n. computer program organizing data into rows and columns on a video screen

spree n. 1 lively time 2 drinking bout

sprig n. little twig

spright'ly a. -li·er, -li·est brisk; lively —adv. briskly

spring v. sprang or sprung, sprung, spring'ing 1 leap 2 grow; develop 3 snap back or shut 4 make or become bent, split, etc. 5 make known —n. 1 a leap 2 resilience 3 resilient coil of wire, etc. 4 flow of water from the ground 5 source 6 season after winter —a. of, for, or in the season of spring —**spring'y** a., -i·er, -i·est

spring'board' n. springy board, as to dive from

sprin'kle v. 1 scatter drops of or on 2 rain lightly —n. a sprinkling

sprint v., n. race at full speed for a short distance

sprite n. elf, fairy, etc.

sprock'et n. any tooth in a series on a wheel made to fit the links of a chain

sprout v. begin to grow —n. new growth; shoot

spruce n. evergreen tree —v., a. (make) neat or trim

spry a. spri'er or spry'er, spri'est or spry'est lively

spume n. foam; froth

spu·mo'ni n. Italian ice cream

spun v. pt. and pp. of SPIN

spunk [Col.] n. courage —**spunk'y** a., -i·er, -i·est

spur n. 1 pointed device on a shoe to prick a horse 2 stimulus 3 projecting part —v. **spurred, spur'ring** 1 to prick with spurs 2 urge on

spu'ri·ous (spyoor'-) a. false; not genuine

spurn v. reject in scorn

spurt v. 1 shoot forth; squirt 2 make a sudden effort —n. a spurting

sput'ter v. 1 speak in a fast, confused way 2 spit out bits 3 make hissing sounds —n. a sputtering

spu'tum n. saliva

spy v. **spied, spy'ing 1** watch closely and secretly **2** see —n., pl. **spies** one who spies, esp. to get another country's secrets

squab (skwäb) n. young pigeon

squab'ble v., n. quarrel over a small matter

squad n. small group

squad'ron n. unit of warships, aircraft, etc.

squal'id a. **1** foul; unclean **2** wretched —**squal'or** n.

squall n. **1** brief, violent windstorm **2** harsh, loud cry —v. cry loudly

squan'der v. spend or use wastefully

square n. **1** rectangle with all sides equal **2** area with streets on four sides **3** tool for making right angles **4** product of a number multiplied by itself **5** [Sl.] person who is SQUARE (a. 6) —v. **1** make square **2** make straight, even, etc. **3** settle; adjust **4** multiply by itself —a. **1** shaped like a square **2** forming a right angle **3** straight, level, or even **4** just; fair **5** [Col.] filling, as a meal **6** [Sl.] old-fashioned, unsophisticated, etc. —adv. in a square way —**square'ly** adv. —**square'ness** n.

square dance n. lively dance with couples grouped in a square, etc.

square root n. quantity that when squared produces another, given quantity

squash v. **1** press into a soft, flat mass **2** to suppress —n. **1** a squashing **2** game played with rackets in a walled court **3** fleshy vegetable growing on a vine

squat v. **squat'ted, squat'ting 1** crouch **2** settle on land without title to it —a. short and heavy —n. position of squatting —**squat'ter** n.

squaw n. a North American Indian woman or wife: now considered offensive

squawk v. **1** utter a loud, harsh cry **2** [Col.] complain —n. a squawking —**squawk'er** n.

squeak v. make a sharp, high-pitched sound —n. such a sound —**squeak'y** a., **-i-er, -i-est**

squeal v., n. **1** (utter) a long, shrill cry

squeam'ish a. **1** easily nauseated **2** easily shocked

squee'gee (-jē) n. rubber-edged tool used in washing windows

squeeze v. **1** press hard **2** extract by pressure **3** force by pressing **4** hug —n. a squeezing —**squeez'er** n.

squelch v. suppress or silence completely

squid n. long, slender sea mollusk with ten arms

squig'gle n. short, wavy line —**squig'gly** a.

squint v. **1** peer with eyes partly closed **2** be cross-eyed —n. a squinting

squire n. English country gentleman —v. escort

squirm v. twist and turn

squir'rel n. tree-dwelling rodent with a bushy tail

squirt v., n. (shoot out in) a jet or spurt

squish [Col.] v., n. **1** (make) a soft, splashing sound when squeezed **2** SQUASH (v. 1, n. 1) —**squish'y** a., **-i-er, -i-est**

stab v. **stabbed, stab'bing** pierce or wound as with a knife —n. **1** a thrust, as with a knife **2** [Col.] a try

sta·bi·lize' v. **1** make stable, or firm **2** keep from changing —**sta·bi·li·za'tion** n. —**sta'bi·liz'er** n.

sta'ble a. not apt to change; firm —n. building for horses or cattle —v. keep in a stable —**sta·bil'i·ty** n.

stac·ca·to (stä kät'ō) a., adv. Mus. with abrupt tones

stack n. **1** orderly pile **2** smokestack **3** set of bookshelves —v. to pile in a stack

sta'di·um n. place for outdoor games, surrounded by tiers of seats

staff n., pl. (n. 1, 2, 3) **staffs** or (n. 1 & 3) **staves 1** stick or rod used for support, etc. **2** group of people assisting a leader **3** the five lines on and between which music is written —v. provide with workers

stag n. full-grown male deer —a. for men only

stage n. **1** platform, esp. one on which plays are presented **2** the theater **3** part of a journey **4** period in growth or development —v. **1** to present as on a stage **2** carry out

stage'coach' n. horse-drawn public coach for long trips

stage fright n. fear of speaking before an audience

stage′hand *n.* one who sets up scenery, etc. for a play

stage′-struck *a.* eager to become an actor or actress

stag′ger *v.* **1** (cause to) totter, reel, etc. **2** shock **3** arrange alternately —*n.* a staggering

stag′ger·ing *a.* astonishing

stag′nant *a.* **1** not flowing, therefore foul **2** sluggish

stag′nate′ *v.* become stagnant —**stag·na′tion** *n.*

staid *a.* sober; sedate

stain *v.* **1** discolor; spot **2** dishonor **3** color (wood, etc.) with a dye —*n.* **1** a spot; mark **2** dishonor **3** dye for wood, etc. —**stain′less** *a.*

stair *n.* **1** one of a series of steps between levels **2** *usually pl.* flight of stairs: also **stair′case′** or **stair′way′**

stair′well′ *n.* shaft containing a staircase

stake *n.* **1** pointed stick to be driven into the ground **2** *often pl.* money risked as a wager —*v.* **1** mark the boundaries of **2** wager —**at stake** being risked

sta·lac′tite *n.* stick of lime hanging from a cave roof

sta·lag′mite *n.* stick of lime built up on a cave floor

stale *a.* **1** no longer fresh **2** trite

stale′mate′ *n.* deadlock

stalk *v.* **1** stride haughtily **2** track secretly —*n.* **1** a stalking **2** plant stem —**stalk′er** *n.*

stall *n.* **1** section for one animal in a stable **2** market booth —*v.* **1** put in a stall **2** stop **3** delay by evading

stal′lion (-yən) *n.* uncastrated male horse

stal′wart *a.* strong or brave —*n.* stalwart person

sta′men *n.* pollen-bearing part of a flower

stam′i·na *n.* endurance

stam′mer *v., n.* pause or halt in speaking

stamp *v.* **1** put the foot down hard **2** pound with the foot **3** cut out with a die **4** impress a design on **5** put a stamp on —*n.* **1** a stamping **2** gummed piece of paper, as for postage **3** a stamped mark **4** stamping device —**stamp out 1** crush or put out by treading on **2** suppress or put down

stam·pede′ *n.* sudden, headlong rush, as of a herd —*v.* move in a stampede

stance *n.* way one stands

stanch (stônch, stanch) *v.* check the flow of blood from a wound —*a.* staunch

stan′chion (-chən) *n.* upright support

stand *v.* **stood, stand′ing 1** be or get in an upright position **2** place or be placed **3** hold a certain opinion **4** halt **5** endure or resist —*n.* **1** a halt **2** a position **3** platform, rack, counter, etc. **4** a growth (of trees) —**stand by** be ready to help —**stand for 1** represent **2** [Col.] tolerate —**stand in for** be a substitute for —**stand out** to project, be prominent, etc. —**stand up 1** prove valid, durable, etc. **2** [Sl.] fail to keep a date with

stand′ard *n.* **1** flag, banner, etc. **2** thing set up as a rule or model **3** upright support —*a.* **1** that is a standard or rule **2** proper

stand′ard·ize′ *v.* make standard or uniform

stand′-in′ *n.* a substitute

stand′ing *n.* **1** status or rank **2** duration —*a.* **1** upright **2** continuing

stand′off′ *n.* tie in a contest

stand′off′ish *a.* aloof

stand′point′ *n.* viewpoint

stand′still′ *n.* a stop or halt

stan′za *n.* group of lines making a section of a poem

staph′y·lo·coc′cus *n., pl.* **-ci′** (-sī′) kind of spherical bacteria

sta′ple *n.* **1** main product, part, etc. **2** basic trade item, as flour **3** U-shaped metal fastener —*v.* fasten with a staple —*a.* regular or principal —**sta′pler** *n.*

star *n.* **1** celestial body seen as a point of light at night **2** flat figure with five or more points **3** asterisk **4** one who excels or plays a leading role as in acting —*v.* **starred, star′ring 1** mark with stars **2** present in, or play, a leading role —**star′ry** *a.*, **-ri·er**, **-ri·est**

star′board (-bərd) *n.* right side of a ship, etc. as one faces the bow

starch *n.* **1** white food substance in potatoes, etc. **2** powdered form of this —*v.* stiffen (laundry) with starch —**starch′y** *a.*, **-i·er, -i·est**

star′dom *n.* status of a STAR (*n.* 4)

stare *v.* gaze steadily —*n.* long, steady look

star′fish′ *n.* small, star-shaped sea animal

stark *a.* **1** bleak **2** complete;

utter —*adv.* entirely —**stark'ly** *adv.*

star'ling *n.* bird with shiny, black feathers

start *v.* 1 begin to go, do, etc. 2 set in motion 3 jump or jerk — *n.* 1 a starting 2 a jump or jerk 3 place or time of beginning 4 a lead; advantage —**start in** begin to do —**start out** (or **off**) begin a trip, etc. —**start'er** *n.*

star'tle *v.* 1 frighten suddenly 2 surprise —**star'tling** *a.*

starve *v.* 1 suffer or die from lack of food 2 cause to starve —**star·va'tion** *n.*

stash [Col.] *v.* hide away —*n.* something hidden

stat *n.* [Col.] statistic

state *n.* 1 the way a person or thing is 2 formal style 3 nation 4 [often S-] a unit of a federal government —*v.* to express in words

stat'ed *a.* fixed; set

state'ly *a.* **-li·er, -li·est** grand or dignified

state'ment *n.* 1 a stating 2 something stated 3 report, as of money owed

state'room' *n.* private room in a ship or railroad car

states'man *n., pl.* **-men** person skillful in government

stat'ic *a.* 1 at rest 2 of electricity caused by friction —*n.* electrical disturbances in radio reception

sta'tion *n.* 1 assigned place 2 stopping place 3 place for radio or TV transmission 4 social rank —*v.* assign to a station

sta'tion·ar'y *a.* not moving or changing

sta'tion·er'y *n.* writing materials

sta·tis'tics *n.* analysis of numerical data —*n.pl.* the data —**sta·tis'ti·cal** *a.* —**stat·is·ti'cian** (-tish'ən) *n.*

stat'u·ar'y *n.* statues

stat·ue (stach'ōō) *n.* likeness done in stone, metal, etc.

stat'u·esque' ('-esk') *a.* tall and stately

stat'u·ette' *n.* small statue

stat·ure (stach'ər) *n.* 1 person's height 2 level of attainment or esteem

sta'tus *n.* 1 rank 2 condition

status quo *n.* existing state of affairs

stat'ute (stach'-) *n.* a law

stat'u·to'ry *a.* authorized, or punishable, by statute

staunch (stônch) *a.* firm, loyal,

etc. —*v.* stanch

stave *n.* 1 any of the wooden side strips of a barrel 2 staff 3 stanza —*v.* **staved** or **stove, stav'ing** smash (**in**) —**stave off** hold off

staves *n.* 1 alt. pl. of STAFF (*n.* 1 & 3) 2 pl. of STAVE

stay *v.* 1 remain 2 dwell 3 stop or delay 4 to support —*n.* 1 a staying 2 prop 3 guy rope 4 stiffening strip

stead (sted) *n.* place for a substitute

stead'fast' *a.* constant; firm

stead'y *a.* **-i·er, -i·est** 1 firm 2 regular 3 calm 4 reliable —*v.* **-ied, -y·ing** make or become steady

steak *n.* slice of meat or fish

steal *v.* **stole, stol'en, steal'ing** 1 take dishonestly and secretly 2 move stealthily

stealth (stelth) *n.* secret action —**stealth'i·ly** *adv.* —**stealth'y** *a.*, **-i·er, -i·est**

steam *n.* water changed to a vapor by boiling; source of heat and power —*a.* using steam —*v.* 1 expose to steam 2 cook with steam 3 give off steam —**steam'boat', steam'ship'** *n.* —**steam'y** *a.*, **-i·er, -i·est**

steam'er *n.* thing run by steam

steed *n.* [Poet.] riding horse

steel *n.* hard alloy of iron with carbon —*a.* of steel —*v.* make strong —**steel'y** *a.*

steel wool *n.* steel shavings used for cleaning, etc.

steep *a.* having a sharp rise or slope —*v.* soak or saturate

stee'ple *n.* high tower

stee'ple·chase' *n.* horse race over a course with obstacles

steer *v.* guide; direct —*n.* male of beef cattle; ox

steer'age *n.* part of a ship for passengers paying least

stein (stīn) *n.* beer mug

stel'lar *a.* 1 of or like a star 2 most important

stem *n.* 1 stalk of a plant, flower, etc. 2 stemlike part 3 prow of a ship 4 root of a word —*v.* **stemmed, stem'ming** 1 remove the stem of 2 advance against 3 stop 4 derive

stench *n.* offensive smell

sten'cil *n.* sheet cut with letters, etc. to print when inked over —*v.* mark with a stencil

ste·nog'ra·phy *n.* transcription of dictation in shorthand —**ste·nog'ra·pher** *n.*

sten·to·ri·an (-tôr′ē-) *adv.* very loud

step *n.* 1 one foot movement, as in walking 2 footstep 3 way of stepping 4 stair tread 5 degree; rank 6 act in a series —*v.* 1 move with a step 2 press the foot down —**in** (or **out of**) **step** (not) in rhythm with others —**step up** 1 advance 2 increase in rate

step′broth′er *n.* stepparent's son

step′child′ *n.* spouse's child (**step′daugh′ter** or **step′son′**) by a former marriage

step′lad′der *n.* four-legged ladder with flat steps

step′par′ent *n.* the spouse (**step′fa′ther** or **step′moth′er**) of one's remarried parent

steppe (step) *n.* great plain

step′sis′ter *n.* a stepparent's daughter

ster·e·o′ *n.*, *pl.* **-os′** stereophonic system, etc. —*a.* stereophonic

ster′e·o·phon′ic *a.* of a blend of sounds reproduced through separate speakers

ster′e·o·scope′ *n.* device for giving three-dimensional effect to pictures

ster′e·o·type′ *v.*, *n.* (express or conceive in) a set, trite form —**ster′e·o·typ′i·cal, ster′e·o·typ′ic** *a.*

ster′ile (-əl) *a.* 1 not able to reproduce itself or oneself 2 free of germs —**ste·ril′i·ty** *n.*

ster′i·lize′ *v.* to make sterile —**ster′i·li·za′tion** *n.*

ster′ling *a.* 1 (made) of silver at least 92.5% pure 2 of British money 3 excellent

stern *a.* severe; unyielding —*n.* rear end of a ship, etc.

ster′num *n.* front chest bone to which ribs are joined

ster′oid′ *n.* any of a group of compounds including cholesterol, sex hormones, etc.

steth′o·scope′ *n.* instrument for hearing chest sounds

ste′ve·dore′ *n.* one hired to load and unload ships

stew *v.* cook by boiling slowly —*n.* meat with vegetables, cooked in this way

stew′ard *n.* 1 one put in charge of funds, supplies, etc. 2 servant on a ship, airplane, etc. —**stew′ard·ess** *n.fem.*

stick *n.* 1 small branch broken or cut off 2 long, thin piece, as of wood —*v.* **stuck, stick′ing** 1 pierce 2 attach or be attached as by pinning or gluing 3 extend 4 become fixed, jammed, etc. 5 persevere 6 hesitate 7 be puzzled

stick′er *n.* gummed label

stick′-in-the-mud′ *n.* [Col.] one who resists change, etc.

stick′ler *n.* one who is stubbornly fussy

stick′y *a.* **-i·er, -i·est** adhesive —**stick′i·ness** *n.*

stiff *a.* 1 hard to bend or move 2 thick; dense 3 strong, as a wind 4 difficult 5 tense —**stiff′en** *v.* —**stiff′ly** *adv.*

sti′fle *v.* 1 suffocate 2 suppress; restrain

stig′ma *n.*, *pl.* **-mas** or **-ma·ta** 1 sign of disgrace 2 upper tip of a pistil

stig′ma·tize′ *v.* mark as disgraceful

stile *n.* step(s) for climbing over a fence or wall

sti·let′to *n.*, *pl.* **-tos** or **-toes** small, thin dagger

still *a.* 1 quiet 2 motionless 3 calm —*n.* device to distill liquor —*adv.* 1 until then or now 2 even; yet 3 nevertheless —*con.* nevertheless —*v.* to make or become still —**still′ness** *n.*

still′born′ *a.* dead at birth —**still′birth′** *n.*

stilt *n.* supporting pole, esp. one of a pair for walking high off the ground

stilt′ed *a.* pompous

stim′u·lant *n.* thing that stimulates, as a drug

stim′u·late′ *v.* make (more) active —**stim′u·la′tion** *n.*

stim′u·lus *n.*, *pl.* **-li′** (-lī′) anything causing activity

sting *v.* **stung, sting′ing** 1 hurt with a sting 2 cause or feel sharp pain —*n.* 1 a stinging, or pain from it 2 sharp part in some plants, bees, etc. that pricks: also **sting′er**

stin′gy (-jē) *a.* **-gi·er, -gi·est** miserly; grudging

stink *v.* **stank** or **stunk, stunk, stink′ing;** (have) a strong, unpleasant smell

stint *v.* restrict to a small amount —*n.* 1 limit 2 assigned task

sti′pend *n.* regular payment

stip′ple *v.* paint or draw in small dots

stip′u·late′ *v.* specify as an essential condition

stir *v.* **stirred, stir′ring** 1 move, esp. slightly 2 move around as with a spoon 3 excite —*n.* 1 a stirring 2 commotion

stir'-cra'zy a. [Sl.] mentally affected by long confinement

stir-fry' v. fry (vegetables, meat, etc.) quickly while stirring

stir'rup n. ring hung from a saddle as a footrest

stitch n. 1 single movement or loop made by a needle in sewing, knitting, etc. 2 sudden pain — v. sew

stock n. 1 tree trunk 2 ancestry 3 biological breed 4 rifle part holding the barrel 5 pl. frame with holes for feet and hands, once used for punishment 6 broth from meat or fish 7 livestock 8 goods on hand 9 shares in a business — v. supply or keep in stock — a. 1 kept in stock 2 common —in (or out of) stock (not) available

stock-ade' n. defensive wall of tall stakes

stock'bro'ker n. a broker for stocks and bonds

stock exchange, stock market n. place of sale for stocks and bonds

stock'hold'er n. one owning stock in a company

stock'ing n. knitted covering for the leg and foot

stock'pile' v., n. (accumulate) a reserve supply

stock'-still' a. motionless

stock'y a. -i·er, -i·est short and heavy

stock'yard' n. place to pen livestock till slaughtered

stodg·y (stä'jē) a. -i·er, -i·est 1 dull; uninteresting 2 stubbornly conventional

sto'gie, sto'gy n., pl. -gies long cigar

sto'ic a., n. stoical (person)

sto'i·cal a. indifferent to grief, pain, etc. —**sto'i·cism'** n.

stoke v. stir up and feed fuel to (a fire) —**stok'er** n.

stole v. pt. of STEAL —n. long fur piece worn by women around the shoulders

stol'en v. pp. of STEAL

stol'id (stäl'-) a. unexcitable

stom·ach (stum'ək) n. 1 digestive organ into which food passes 2 abdomen 3 appetite —v. tolerate

stomp v. STAMP (v. 1 & 2)

stone n. 1 solid nonmetallic mineral matter 2 piece of this 3 seed of certain fruits 4 abnormal stony mass in the kidney, etc. 5 pl. stone [Br.] 14 pounds

—v. throw stones at

stone'wall' v. [Col.] impede by refusing to help, cooperate, etc.

ston'y a. -i·er, -i·est 1 full of stones 2 unfeeling

stood v. pt. & pp. of STAND

stooge (stōōj) n. [Col.] lackey

stool n. 1 single seat with no back or arms 2 feces

stoop v. 1 bend the body forward 2 lower one's dignity —n. 1 position of stooping 2 small porch

stop v. stopped, stop'ping 1 close by filling, shutting off, etc. 2 cease; end; halt 3 to block; obstruct 4 stay —n. 1 a stopping 2 place stopped at 3 obstruction, plug, etc. —stop off stop for a while —stop'page n.

stop'gap' n. temporary substitute

stop'per n. something inserted to close an opening

stop'watch' n. watch that can be started and stopped instantly, as to time races

stor'age n. 1 a storing 2 place for, or cost of, storing goods

store n. 1 supply; stock 2 establishment where goods are sold —v. put aside for future use — in store set aside for the future

store'front' n. front room or ground floor, for use as retail store

store'house' n. warehouse

store'keep'er n. a person in charge of a store

store'room' n. a room where things are stored

stork n. large, long-legged wading bird

storm n. 1 strong wind with rain, snow, etc. 2 any strong disturbance 3 strong attack — v. 1 blow violently, rain, etc. 2 rage 3 rush or attack violently —**storm'y** a., -i·er, -i·est

sto'ry n., pl. -ries 1 a telling of an event 2 fictitious narrative 3 one level of a building 4 [Col.] a falsehood —**sto'ried** a.

stout a. 1 brave 2 firm; strong 3 fat —n. strong, dark beer —**stout'ly** adv.

stove n. apparatus for heating, cooking, etc. —v. alt. pt. & pp. of STAVE

stow (stō) v. pack or store away —**stow away** hide aboard a ship, etc. for a free ride —**stow'a·way'** n.

strad'dle v. 1 sit or stand astride

2 take both sides of (an issue)

strafe v. attack with machine guns from aircraft

strag'gle v. 1 wander from the group 2 spread out unevenly —**strag'gler** n.

straight a. 1 not crooked, bent, etc. 2 direct 3 in order 4 honest or frank 5 undiluted 6 [Sl.] conventional 7 [Sl.] heterosexual —adv. 1 in a straight line 2 directly 3 without delay — **straight away** (or **off**) without delay —**straight'en** v.

straight'a·way' n. straight part of a track, road, etc. —adv. at once

straight face n. facial expression showing no emotion — **straight'-faced'** a.

straight'for'ward a. 1 direct 2 honest

strain v. 1 stretch tight or to the utmost 2 strive hard 3 sprain 4 filter — n. 1 a straining or being strained 2 excessive demand on one's emotions, etc. 3 ancestry 4 inherited tendency 5 trace; streak 6 often pl. tune —**strain'er** n.

strait n. often pl. 1 narrow waterway 2 distress

strait'ened a. impoverished

strait'jack'et n. coatlike device for restraining a person

strait'-laced' a. strict

strand v. 1 any of the threads, wires, etc. that form a string, cable, etc. 2 string, as of pearls 3 shore —v. put into a helpless position

strange a. 1 unfamiliar 2 unusual 2 peculiar; odd — **strange'ly** adv.

stran'ger n. 1 newcomer 2 person not known to one

stran'gle v. 1 choke to death 2 stifle —**stran'gler** n.

strap n. narrow strip of leather, etc., as for binding things —v. **strapped, strap'ping** fasten with a strap —**strap'less** a.

strapped a. [Col.] without money

strap'ping a. [Col.] robust

strat'a·gem (-jəm) n. tricky ruse or move to gain an end

strat'e·gy n., pl. -**gies** 1 science of military operations 2 artful managing 3 plan —**stra·te'gic** a. —**stra·te'gi·cal·ly** adv. —**strat'e·gist** n.

strat'i·fy v. form in layers — **strat'i·fi·ca'tion** n.

strat'o·sphere' n. upper atmos-

phere from 12 to 31 miles

stra'tum n., pl. -**ta** or -**tums** any of a series of layers

stra·tus (strat'əs) n., pl. -**ti** long, low, gray cloud layer

straw n. 1 grain stalk or stalks after threshing 2 tube for sucking a drink

straw'ber'ry n., pl. -**ries** small, red, juicy fruit of a vinelike plant

straw vote n. unofficial poll of public opinion

stray v. 1 wander; roam 2 deviate —a. 1 lost 2 isolated —n. lost domestic animal

streak n. 1 long, thin mark 2 layer 3 tendency in behavior 4 spell, as of luck —v. 1 mark with streaks 2 go fast

stream n. 1 small river 2 steady flow, as of air — 3 flow in a stream 2 move swiftly

stream'er n. long, narrow flag or strip

stream'line' v., a. (to make) streamlined

stream'lined' a. 1 shaped to move easily in air, etc. 2 made more efficient

street n. road in a city

street'car' n. passenger car on rails along streets

street'walk'er n. prostitute

street'wise' a. [Col.] knowing how to deal with conditions in crowded, dangerous, etc. urban areas

strength n. 1 force; power; vigor 2 durability 3 intensity 4 potency —**on the strength of** based upon or relying on — **strength'en** v.

stren'u·ous a. needing or showing much energy

strep'to·coc'cus (-käk'əs) n., pl. -**coc'ci'** (-käk'sī') kind of spherical bacteria

strep'to·my'cin (-mī'sin) n. antibiotic drug

stress n. 1 strain; pressure 2 importance; emphasis 3 special force on a syllable, etc. —v. 1 to strain 2 accent 3 emphasize

stretch v. 1 reach out 2 draw out to full extent 3 strain 4 exaggerate —n. 1 a stretching 2 ability to be stretched 3 extent

stretch'er n. 1 canvas-covered frame to carry the sick 2 one that stretches

strew v. **strewed, strewed** or **strewn, strew'ing** 1 scatter 2 cover as by scattering

stri'at'ed a. striped

strick'en a. struck, wounded, afflicted, etc.

strict a. 1 exact or absolute 2 rigidly enforced or enforcing —**strict'ly** adv. —**strict'ness** n.

stric'ture n. strong criticism

stride v. strode, strid'den, strid'ing walk with long steps —n. 1 long step 2 pl. progress

stri'dent a. shrill; grating

strife n. a quarrel(ing)

strike v. struck, struck or strick'en, strik'ing 1 hit 2 sound by hitting some part 3 ignite (a match) 4 make by stamping 5 attack 6 reach or find 7 occur to 8 assume (a pose) 9 take down or apart 10 stop working until demands are met —n. 1 a striking 2 Baseball a pitched ball struck at but missed, etc. 3 Bowling a knocking down of all the pins at once —**strike out** 1 erase 2 Baseball put or go out on three strikes —**strike up** begin —**strik'er** n.

strik'ing a. very attractive, impressive, etc.

string n. 1 thick thread, etc. used as for tying 2 numbers of things on a string or in a row 3 thin cord bowed, etc. to make music, as on a violin 4 pl. condition attached to a plan, offer, etc. —v. strung, string'ing 1 provide with strings 2 put on a string 3 extend —**pull strings** use influence to gain advantage —**string'y** a., -i·er, -i·est

string bean n. thick bean pod, eaten as a vegetable

strin'gent (-jant) a. strict

strip v. stripped, strip'ping 1 take off clothing, covering, etc. (of) 2 make bare 3 break the teeth (of a gear, etc.) —n. long, narrow piece

stripe n. 1 narrow band of different color or material 2 kind; sort —v. mark with stripes

strip'ling n. a youth

strive v. strove or strived, striv'en or strived, striv'ing 1 try very hard 2 struggle

strobe (light) n. electronic tube emitting rapid, bright flashes of light

strode v. pt. of STRIDE

stroke n. 1 sudden blow, attack, action, etc. 2 a single movement of the arm, a tool, etc. 3 striking sound —v. draw one's hand, etc. gently over

stroll n. leisurely walk —v. 1 take a stroll 2 wander

stroll'er n. chairlike cart for a baby

strong a. 1 powerful 2 healthy 3 durable 4 intense —**strong'ly** adv.

strong'hold' n. fortress

stron'ti·um (-sham) n. chemical element with radioactive isotope

struck v. pt. & pp. of STRIKE

struc'ture n. 1 thing built 2 plan, design, etc. —**struc'tur·al** a.

stru'del n. pastry of thin dough and filling, rolled up and baked

strug'gle v. 1 fight 2 strive —n. a struggling

strum v. strummed, strum'ming play (a guitar, etc.) with long strokes, often casually

strung v. pt. & pp. of STRING

strut v. strut'ted, strut'ting walk arrogantly —n. 1 strutting walk 2 rod used as a support

strych'nine (strik'-) n. poisonous drug used as a stimulant

stub n. short, leftover, or blunt part —v. stubbed, stub'bing bump (one's toe)

stub'ble n. 1 short grain stumps 2 short growth

stub'born a. obstinate —**stub'born·ness** n.

stub'by a. -bi·er, -bi·est short and thick

stuc'co v. -coed, -co·ing; n. (cover with) rough plaster

stuck v. pt. & pp. of STICK

stuck'-up' a. [Col.] snobbish

stud n. 1 decorative nail 2 removable button 3 upright support in a wall 4 breeding stallion —v. stud'ded, stud'ding be set thickly in

stu'dent n. one who studies

stud'ied a. done on purpose

stu'di·o' n., pl. -os' 1 artist's work area 2 place for producing movies, radio or TV programs, etc.

stu'di·ous a. 1 fond of study 2 attentive

stud'y v. -ied, -y·ing 1 learn by reading, thinking, etc. 2 investigate —n., pl. -ies 1 act of studying 2 pl. education 3 deep thought 4 place to study

stuff n. 1 material; substance 2 (worthless) objects —v. 1 fill 2 cram —**stuffed shirt** [Col.] pompous person

stuff'y a. -i·er, -i·est 1 poorly ventilated 2 stopped up 3 [Col.] dull

stul'ti·fy' v. -fied', -fy'ing make seem foolish, etc.

stum'ble v. 1 walk unsteadily; trip 2 speak confusedly 3 come by chance —n. a stumbling

stum'bling block n. difficulty

stump n. part left after cutting off the rest —v. 1 make a speaking tour 2 walk heavily 3 [Col.] perplex

stun v. stunned, stun'ning 1 make unconscious, as by a blow 2 shock deeply

stung v. pt. & pp. of STING

stunk v. pp. & alt. pt. of STINK

stun'ning a. [Col.] very attractive

stunt v. keep from growing —n. daring show of skill

stu'pe·fy' v. -fied', -fy'ing stun —stu'pe·fac'tion n.

stu·pen'dous a. overwhelming

stu'pid a. 1 not intelligent 2 foolish 3 dull —stu·pid'i·ty n., pl. -ties

stu'por n. dazed condition

stur'dy a. -di·er, -di·est 1 firm 2 strong

stur'geon (-jən) n. food fish

stut'ter n., v. stammer

sty n., pl. **sties** pigpen

sty, stye n., pl. **sties** swelling on the rim of the eyelid

style n. 1 way of making, writing, etc. 2 fine style 3 fashion —v. 1 name 2 design the style of

styl'ish a. fashionable

styl'ize v. design or depict in a style rather than naturally

sty'lus n. 1 pointed writing tool 2 phonograph needle

sty'mie v. -mied', -mie·ing to obstruct; block

styp'tic (stip'-) a. that halts bleeding; astringent

Sty'ro·foam' trademark rigid, light, porous plastic —n. [s-] this substance

suave (swäv) a. smoothly polite —suav'i·ty n.

sub- pref. 1 under; below 2 somewhat 3 being a division

sub'a·tom'ic a. smaller than an atom

sub·con'scious a., n. (of) one's feelings, wishes, etc. of which one is unaware

sub'cu·ta'ne·ous (-kyōō-) a. beneath the skin

sub'di·vide' v. 1 divide again 2 divide (land) into small sections for sale —sub'di·vi'sion n.

sub·due' v. 1 get control over 2 make less intense

sub'ject (v.: səb jekt') a. 1 that is a subject 2 liable 3 contin-

gent upon —n. 1 one controlled by another 2 topic of discussion or study 3 Gram. word or words about which something is said —v. 1 bring under the control of 2 make undergo —sub·jec'tion n.

sub·jec'tive a. of one's feelings rather than from facts —sub'jec·tiv'i·ty n.

sub'ju·gate' v. conquer

sub'lease' (v.: sub lēs') n. lease granted by a lessee —v. grant or hold a sublease of

sub·let' v. 1 sublease 2 let out work one has contracted to do

sub'li·mate' v. 1 to sublime 2 express (unacceptable impulses) in acceptable forms —sub'li·ma'tion n.

sub·lime' a. noble; lofty —v. purify (a solid) by heating and then condensing —sub·lim'i·ty n.

sub·lim'i·nal a. below the threshold of awareness

sub'ma·chine' gun n. portable, automatic firearm

sub'ma·rine' n. warship operating under water

sub·merge' v. put or go under water —sub·mer'gence n.

sub·merse' v. submerge —sub·mer'sion n.

sub·mis'sion n. 1 a submitting 2 obedience —sub·mis'sive a.

sub·mit' v. -mit'ted, -mit'ting 1 to present for consideration, etc. 2 surrender

sub·nor'mal a. below normal, as in intelligence

sub·or'di·nate (-nət; v.: -nāt') a. lower in rank; secondary —n. subordinate person —v. to make subordinate

sub·orn' v. induce (another) to commit perjury

sub·poe'na, sub·pe·na (sə pē'na) n. legal paper ordering one to appear in court —v. to order with a subpoena

sub·scribe' v. 1 give support or consent (to) 2 promise to contribute (money) 3 agree to take and pay for a periodical, etc.: with to —sub·scrip'tion n.

sub'se·quent a. following

sub·ser'vi·ent a. servile

sub·side' v. 1 to sink lower 2 become quieter

sub·sid'i·ar·y a. helping in a lesser way —n., pl. -ies company controlled by another

sub'si·dize' v. support with a subsidy

sub'si·dy *n.*, *pl.* **-dies** (government) grant of money

sub·sist' *v.* continue to live or exist

sub·sist'ence *n.* **1** a subsisting **2** livelihood

sub'soil' *n.* layer of soil beneath the surface soil

sub'stance *n.* **1** essence **2** physical matter **3** central meaning **4** wealth

sub·stand'ard *a.* below standard

sub·stan'tial (-shəl) *a.* **1** material **2** strong **3** large **4** wealthy **5** in essentials

sub·stan'ti·ate (-shē-) *v.* prove to be true or real

sub'sti·tute' *n.* one that takes the place of another —*v.* use as or be a substitute —**sub'sti·tu'tion** *n.*

sub'ter·fuge' *n.* scheme used to evade something

sub'ter·ra'ne·an *a.* **1** underground **2** secret

sub'text' *n.* underlying meaning, theme, etc.

sub'ti·tle *n.* **1** secondary title **2** line translating dialogue, etc. as at the bottom of a film image

sub'tle (sut''l) *a.* **1** keen; acute **2** crafty **3** delicate **4** not obvious —**sub'tle·ty** *n.*, *pl.* **-ties** —**sub'tly** *adv.*

sub·tract' *v.* take away, as one number from another —**sub·trac'tion** *n.*

sub'tra·hend' *n.* quantity to be subtracted from another

sub'urb *n.* district, town, etc. on the outskirts of a city —**sub·ur'ban** *a.* —**sub·ur'ban·ite'** *n.*

sub·ur'bi·a *n.* suburbs or suburbanites collectively

sub·vert' *v.* overthrow (something established) —**sub·ver'sion** *n.* —**sub·ver'sive** *a.*, *n.*

sub'way' *n.* underground electric railroad in a city

suc·ceed' *v.* **1** come next after **2** have success

suc·cess' *n.* **1** favorable result **2** the gaining of wealth, fame, etc. **3** successful one —**suc·cess'ful** *a.* —**suc·cess'ful·ly** *adv.*

suc·ces'sion *n.* **1** a coming after another **2** series —**suc·ces'sive** *a.*

suc·ces'sor *n.* one who succeeds another, as in office

suc·cinct' (-siŋkt') *a.* terse

suc'cor (-ər) *v.*, *n.* help

suc'co·tash' *n.* beans and corn kernels cooked together

suc'cu·lent *a.* juicy

suc·cumb' (-kum') *v.* **1** give in; yield **2** die

such *a.* **1** of this or that kind **2** whatever **3** so much —*pron.* such a one —**such as** for example

suck *v.* **1** draw into the mouth **2** suck liquid from **3** dissolve in the mouth **4** act of sucking

suck'er *n.* **1** one that sucks or clings **2** sprout **3** lollipop **4** [Sl.] dupe

suck'le *v.* give or get milk from the breast or udder

su'crose' *n.* sugar found in sugar cane, sugar beets, etc.

suc'tion *n.* creation of a vacuum that sucks in fluid, etc. —*a.* worked by suction

sud'den *a.* **1** unexpected **2** hasty —**sud'den·ly** *adv.*

suds *n.pl.* foam on soapy water —**suds'y** *a.*, **-i·er**, **-i·est**

sue *v.* **1** begin a lawsuit against **2** petition

suede (swād) *n.* **1** leather with one side buffed into a nap **2** cloth like this

su'et *n.* hard animal fat

suf'fer *v.* **1** undergo or endure (pain, injury, etc.) **2** tolerate —**suf'fer·ance** *n.*

suf·fice' *v.* be enough

suf·fi'cient (-fish'ənt) *a.* enough —**suf·fi'cien·cy** *n.* —**suf·fi'cient·ly** *adv.*

suf'fix *n.* syllable(s) added at the end of a word to alter its meaning, etc.

suf'fo·cate' *v.* **1** kill by cutting off air **2** die from lack of air **3** stifle —**suf'fo·ca'tion** *n.*

suf'frage *n.* right to vote

suf·fuse' (-fyoōz') *v.* overspread, as with color

sug'ar *n.* sweet carbohydrate found in sugar cane, etc.

sugar beet *n.* beet with a white root of high sugar content

sugar cane *n.* tall tropical grass grown for its sugar

sug'ar·coat' *v.* make seem more pleasant

sug·gest' *v.* **1** bring to mind **2** propose as a possibility **3** imply —**sug·ges'tion** *n.*

sug·gest'i·ble *a.* readily influenced by suggestion

sug·ges'tive *a.* suggesting ideas, esp. indecent ideas

su'i·cide' *n.* **1** act of killing oneself intentionally **2** one who commits suicide —**su'i·ci'dal** *a.*

suit *n.* **1** coat and trousers (or skirt) **2** any of the four sets of playing cards **3** lawsuit **4** a suing, pleading, etc. —*v.* **1** be suitable for **2** make suitable **3** please —**follow suit** follow the example set

suit'a·ble *a.* appropriate; fitting —**suit'a·bly** *adv.*

suit'case' *n.* traveling bag

suite (swēt) *n.* **1** group of connected rooms **2** set of matched furniture

suit'or *n.* man who courts a woman

su·ki·ya·ki (-kē yä'kē) *n.* Japanese dish of thinly sliced meat and vegetables

sul'fa *n.* of a family of drugs used in combating certain bacterial infections

sul'fate' *n.* salt of sulfuric acid

sul'fide' *n.* compound of sulfur

sul'fur *n.* yellow solid substance, a chemical element —**sul·fu'ric** (-fyoor'ik), **sul'fu·rous** *a.*

sulfuric acid *n.* acid formed of hydrogen, sulfur, and oxygen

sulk *v.* be sulky —*n.* sulky mood: also **the sulks**

sulk'y *a.* **-i·er, -i·est** sullen; glum —*n., pl.* **-ies** light, two-wheeled carriage —**sulk'i·ly** *adv.*

sul'len *a.* **1** showing ill-humor by morose withdrawal **2** gloomy —**sul'len·ly** *adv.*

sul'ly *v.* **-lied, -ly·ing** soil, stain, defile, etc.

sul'phur *n.* Br. sp. of SULFUR

sul'tan *n.* Muslim ruler

sul'try *a.* **-tri·er, -tri·est 1** hot and humid **2** inflamed, as with passion

sum *n.* **1** amount of money **2** summary **3** total —*v.* **summed, sum'ming** summarize

su·mac, su·mach (shōō' mak, sōō'-) *n.* plant with lance-shaped leaves and red fruit

sum'ma·rize' *v.* make or be a summary of

sum'ma·ry *n., pl.* **-ries** brief report; digest —*a.* **1** concise **2** prompt —**sum·mar'i·ly** *adv.*

sum·ma'tion *n.* summarizing of arguments, as in a trial

sum'mer *n.* warmest season of the year —*a.* of or for summer —*v.* pass the summer —**sum'mer·y** *a.*

sum'mit *n.* highest point

sum'mon *v.* **1** call together **2** send for **3** rouse

sum'mons *n.* official order to appear in court

su·mo (wrestling) *n.* Japanese wrestling by large, extremely heavy men

sump'tu·ous (-choo əs) *a.* costly; lavish

sun *n.* **1** incandescent body about which (the) planets revolve **2** heat or light of the sun —*v.* **sunned, sun'ning** to expose to sunlight

sun'bathe' *v.* expose the body to sunlight or a sunlamp —**sun'bath** *n.* —**sun'bath'er** *n.*

sun'beam' *n.* beam of sunlight

sun'burn' *n.* inflammation of the skin from exposure to the sun —*v.* give or get sunburn

sun'dae *n.* ice cream covered with syrup, nuts, etc.

Sun'day first day of the week

sun'der *v.* break apart

sun'di'al *n.* instrument that shows time by the shadow cast by the sun

sun'down' *n.* sunset

sun'dries *n.pl.* sundry items

sun'dry *a.* various

sun'fish' *n.* **1** small freshwater fish **2** large sea fish

sun'flow'er *n.* tall plant with big, daisylike flowers

sung *v.* pp. of SING

sun'glass'es *n.pl.* eyeglasses with tinted lenses

sunk *v.* pp. & alt. pt. of SINK

sunk'en *a.* **1** sunk in liquid **2** depressed; hollow

sun'lamp' *n.* an ultraviolet-ray lamp, used for tanning the body, etc.

sun'light' *n.* light of the sun

sun'lit *a.* lighted by the sun

sun'ny *a.* **-ni·er, -ni·est** full of sunshine **2** cheerful

sun'rise' *n.* daily rising of the sun in the east

sun'roof' *n.* car roof with a panel to let in air and light

sun'screen' *n.* chemical used in creams, etc. to block ultraviolet rays and reduce sunburn

sun'set' *n.* daily setting of the sun in the west

sun'shine' *n.* **1** shining of the sun **2** light from the sun —**sun'shin'y** *a.*

sun'spot' *n.* temporary dark spot on sun

sun'stroke' *n.* illness from over-exposure to the sun

sun'tan' *n.* skin darkened by exposure to the sun

sup *v.* **supped, sup'ping** have supper

su'per *a.* [Col.] outstanding

super– *pref.* **1** over; above **2** very; very much **3** greater than others 4 extra

su'per·an'nu·at·ed a. 1 retired on a pension 2 too old to work or use

su·perb' a. excellent

su'per·charge' v. increase an engine's power

su'per·cil'i·ous (-sil'-) a. disdainful; haughty

su'per·con·duc·tiv'i·ty n. lack of electrical resistance in some metals at low temperatures

su'per·fi'cial (-fish'əl) a. 1 of or on the surface 2 shallow; hasty —**su'per·fi'cial·ly** adv.

su·per'flu·ous a. unnecessary —**su'per·flu'i·ty** n.

su'per·high'way n. expressway

su'per·hu'man a. 1 divine 2 greater than normal

su'per·im·pose' v. put on top of something else

su'per·in·tend' v. direct or manage —**su'per·in·tend'ent** n.

su·pe'ri·or a. 1 higher in rank, etc. 2 above average 3 haughty —n. one that is superior —**superior to** unaffected by —**su·pe'ri·or'i·ty** n.

su·per'la·tive a. of the highest degree; supreme —n. 1 highest degree 2 third degree in the comparison of adjectives and adverbs

su'per·man' n., pl. **-men** seemingly superhuman man

su'per·mar'ket n. large, self-service food store

su'per·nat'u·ral a. beyond known laws of nature —**the supernatural** supernatural things

su'per·nu'mer·ar'y a.; n., pl. **-ies** extra (person or thing)

su'per·script' n. figure, letter, etc. written above and to the side of another

su'per·sede' v. replace, succeed, or supplant

su'per·son'ic a. 1 traveling faster than sound 2 ultrasonic

su'per·star' n. famous athlete, entertainer, etc.

su'per·sti'tion n. belief or practice based on fear or ignorance —**su'per·sti'tious** a.

su'per·struc'ture n. 1 part above a ship's deck 2 upper part of a building

su'per·tank'er n. extremely large oil tanker

su'per·vene' v. come unexpectedly

su'per·vise' v. oversee or direct —**su'per·vi'sion** n. —**su'per·vi'sor** n. —**su'per·vi'so·ry** a.

su·pine' a. 1 lying on the back 2 lazy

sup'per n. evening meal

sup·plant' v. take the place of, esp. by force

sup'ple a. flexible

sup'ple·ment n. something added —v. add to —**sup'ple·men'tal, sup'ple·men'ta·ry** a.

sup'pli·cate' v. implore —**sup'pli·ant, sup'pli·cant** n., a. —**sup'pli·ca'tion** n.

sup·ply' v. **-plied', -ply'ing** 1 furnish; provide 2 make up for —n., pl. **-plies'** 1 amount available 2 pl. materials —**sup·pli'er** n.

sup·port' v. 1 hold up 2 help 3 provide for 4 help prove —n. 1 a supporting 2 that which supports

sup·port'ive a. giving support, help, or approval

sup·pose' v. 1 take as true; assume 2 guess; think 3 expect —**sup·posed'** a. —**sup'po·si'tion** n.

sup·pos'i·to·ry n., pl. **-ries** medicated substance put in the rectum or vagina

sup·press' v. 1 put down by force 2 keep back; conceal —**sup·pres'sion** n.

sup'pu·rate' (-yōō-) v. become filled with pus

su·prem'a·cy n. supreme power or authority

su·preme' a. highest in rank, power, or degree

sur'charge' n. 1 extra charge 2 overload —v. put a surcharge in or on

sure a. 1 reliable; certain 2 without doubt 3 bound to happen or do —adv. [Col.] surely —**for sure** certainly —**sure enough** [Col.] without doubt

sure'-fire' a. [Col.] sure to be successful

sure'-foot'ed a. not likely to stumble, err, etc.

sure'ly adv. 1 with confidence 2 without doubt

sure'ty n., pl. **-ties** 1 security 2 guarantor of another's debts

surf n. ocean waves breaking on a shore or reef

sur'face n. 1 outside of a thing 2 any face of a solid 3 outward look —a. superficial —v. 1 give a surface to 2 rise to the surface

surf'board' n. long board used in riding the surf

sur'feit (-fit) n. 1 excess, as of food 2 sickness caused by this

—v. overindulge

surf'ing n. sport of riding the surf on a surfboard

surge v., n. (move in) a large wave or sudden rush

sur'geon n. doctor who practices surgery

sur'ger·y n. 1 treatment of disease or injury by operations 2 a room for this —**sur'gi·cal** a.

sur'ly a. **-li·er, -li·est** bad-tempered; uncivil

sur·mise' (-mīz') n., v. guess

sur·mount' v. 1 to overcome 2 climb over 3 top —**sur·mount' a·ble** a.

sur'name n. family name

sur·pass' v. 1 excel 2 go beyond the limit of

sur'plice (-plis) n. clergyman's loose, white tunic

sur'plus n., a. (quantity) over what is needed or used

sur·prise' v. 1 come upon unexpectedly 2 astonish —n. 1 a surprising or being surprised 2 thing that surprises —**sur·pris' ing** a.

sur·re'al a. fantastic or bizarre

sur·re'al·ism' n. art depicting the unconscious mind —**sur·re'al·ist** a., n.

sur·ren'der v. 1 give oneself up 2 give up; abandon —n. act of surrendering

sur'rep·ti'tious (-tish'əs) a. secret; stealthy

sur'rey n., pl. **-reys** light, four-wheeled carriage

sur'ro·gate (-gət) n., a. (a) substitute

sur·round' v. encircle on all sides

sur·round'ings n.pl. things, conditions, etc. around a person or thing

sur'tax' n. extra tax on top of the regular tax

sur·veil'lance (-vā'-) n. watch kept over a person

sur·vey' (n.: sur'vā') v. 1 examine in detail 2 determine the form, boundaries, etc. of a piece of land —n. 1 general or comprehensive study 2 act of surveying an area —**sur·vey'or** n.

sur·vive' v. 1 outlive 2 continue to live —**sur·viv'al** n. —**sur·vi' vor** n.

sus·cep'ti·ble (sə sep'-) a. easily affected; sensitive

su'shi n. Japanese dish of rice cakes, raw fish, etc.

sus·pect' (n.: sus'pekt') v. 1 believe to be guilty on little evidence 2 distrust 3 surmise —n.

one suspected

sus·pend' v. 1 exclude, stop, etc. for a time 2 hold back (judgment, etc.) 3 hang —**sus·pen' sion** n.

sus·pend'ers n.pl. shoulder straps to hold up trousers

sus·pense' n. tense uncertainty

sus·pi·cion (sə spish'ən) n. 1 a suspecting or being suspected 2 feeling of one who suspects 3 trace —**sus·pi'cious** a.

sus·tain' v. 1 maintain; prolong 2 provide for 3 support 4 suffer 5 uphold as valid 6 confirm

sus'te·nance n. 1 means of livelihood 2 food

su'ture (-chər) n. stitching up of a wound, or stitch so used

svelte a. 1 slender and graceful 2 suave

swab n. 1 a mop 2 piece of cotton, etc. used to medicate or clean the throat, etc. —v. **swabbed, swab'bing** clean with a swab

swad'dle v. wrap (a baby) in narrow bands of cloth

swag'ger v. 1 walk with a bold stride 2 brag loudly —n. swaggering walk

swal'low v. 1 pass (food, etc.) from the mouth into the stomach 2 take in; absorb 3 tolerate 4 suppress —n. 1 act of swallowing 2 amount swallowed 3 small, swift-flying bird

swam v. pt. of SWIM

swa'mi n. Hindu religious teacher

swamp n. piece of wet, spongy ground —v. 1 flood with water 2 overwhelm —**swamp'y** a., **-i· er, -i·est**

swan n. large water bird with a long graceful neck

swank a. [Col.] ostentatiously stylish: also **swank'y, -i·er, -i· est**

swan song n. last act, final work, etc. of a person

swap n., v. **swapped, swap'ping** [Col.] trade

swarm n. 1 colony of bees 2 large, moving mass of insects, etc. —v. move in a swarm

swarth·y (swôr'thē) a. **-i·er, -i· est** dark-skinned

swash'buck·ler n. swaggering fighting man

swas'ti·ka n. cross with bent arms: Nazi emblem

swat v. **swat'ted, swat'ting** (hit with) a quick, sharp blow —**swat'ter** n.

swatch n. sample bit of cloth

swath n. a strip cut by a scythe, mower, etc.

swathe (swäth, swäth) v. 1 wrap up in a bandage 2 envelop

sway v. 1 swing from side to side or to and fro 2 incline 3 influence —n. 1 a swaying 2 influence

swear v. **swore, sworn, swear'ing** 1 make a solemn declaration or promise 2 curse 3 make take an oath

swear'word n. profane or obscene word or phrase

sweat n. 1 salty liquid given off through the skin 2 moisture collected on a surface —v. **sweat** or **sweat'ed, sweat'ing** 1 give forth sweat 2 work so hard as to cause sweating —**sweat'y** a., **-i-er, -i-est**

sweat'er n. knitted garment for the upper body

sweat shirt n. heavy jersey worn to absorb sweat

sweat'shop' n. shop having many hours of work at low wages

Swed'ish a., n. (of) the people or language of Sweden

sweep v. **swept, sweep'ing** 1 clean, or clear away, with a broom 2 carry away or pass over swiftly 3 extend in a long line —n. 1 a sweeping 2 range or extent —**sweep'ing** a.

sweep'ings n.pl. things swept up

sweep'stakes' n., pl. **-stakes'** lottery on a horse race

sweet a. 1 tasting of sugar 2 pleasant 3 fresh —n. a candy —**sweet'en** v. —**sweet'ly** adv.

sweet'bread n. calf's pancreas or thymus, used as food

sweet'bri'er, sweet'bri'ar n. kind of rose

sweet'en-er n. sugar substitute

sweet'heart' n. loved one

sweet pea n. climbing plant with fragrant flowers

sweet potato n. thick, yellow root of a tropical vine

sweet tooth n. [Col.] fondness for sweet foods

swell v. **swelled, swelled** or **swol'len, swell'ing** 1 bulge 2 increase in size, force, etc. 3 fill, as with pride —n. 1 a swelling 2 large wave —a. [Sl.] excellent

swell'ing n. 1 swollen part 2 increase

swel'ter v. feel oppressed with great heat

swel'ter-ing a. very hot

swept v. pt. & pp. of SWEEP

swerve v., n. (make) a quick turn aside

swift a. 1 moving fast 2 prompt —n. swallowlike bird —**swift'ly** adv.

swig [Col.] v. **swigged, swig'ging** drink in large gulps —n. large gulp

swill v. drink greedily —n. garbage fed to pigs

swim v. **swam, swum, swim'ming** 1 move in water by moving the limbs, fins, etc. 2 float on a liquid 3 overflow 4 be dizzy —n. a swimming —**swim'mer** n.

swim'suit' n. garment worn for swimming

swin'dle v. defraud; cheat —n. a swindling

swine n., pl. **swine** pig or hog —**swin'ish** a.

swing v. **swung, swing'ing** 1 sway back and forth 2 turn, as on a hinge 3 manage to get, win, etc. 4 to strike (at) —n. 1 a swinging 2 a sweeping blow 3 musical rhythm 4 seat hanging from ropes

swipe n. [Col.] hard, sweeping blow —v. 1 [Col.] hit with a swipe 2 [Sl.] steal

swirl v., n. whirl; twist

swish v., n. (move with) a hissing or rustling sound

Swiss a., n. (of) the people of Switzerland

Swiss (cheese) n. pale-yellow cheese with large holes

switch n. 1 thin stick used for whipping 2 control device for an electric circuit 3 movable section of railroad track 4 shift; change —v. 1 to whip 2 jerk 3 turn a light, etc. on or off 4 move a train to another track 5 shift

switch'blade' (knife) n. jackknife opened by a spring release

switch'board' n. control panel for electric switches

swiv'el n. fastening with free-turning parts —v. turn as on a swivel

swol'len (swō'lən) v. alt. pp. of SWELL —a. bulging

swoon v., n. faint

swoop v. sweep down or pounce upon —n. a swooping

sword (sôrd) n. weapon with a handle and a long blade

sword'fish' n. large ocean fish with a swordlike jaw

sworn v. pp. of SWEAR —a. bound by an oath

swum v. pp. of SWIM

syc′a·more (sik′-) n. shade tree with shedding bark

syc·o·phant (sik′ə fənt) n. flatterer

syl·lab′i·fy′ v. -fied′, -fy′ing divide into syllables: also **syl·lab′i·cate** —**syl·lab′i·fi·ca′tion** n.

syl′la·ble n. **1** single vocal sound **2** written form of this —**syl·lab′ic** a.

syl′la·bus n., pl. **-bus·es** or **-bi′** (-bī′) summary or outline

syl′lo·gism′ (-jiz′əm) n. two premises and a conclusion

sylph (silf) n. slender, graceful woman

syl′van a. of, living in or covered with trees

sym·bi·ot′ic (-bī-, -bē-) a. mutually dependent

sym′bol n. object, mark, etc. that represents another object, an idea, etc. —**sym·bol′ic, sym·bol′i·cal** a. —**sym′bol·ize′** v.

sym′bol·ism′ n. **1** use of symbols **2** set of symbols

sym′me·try n. balance of opposite parts in position or size —**sym·met′ri·cal** a.

sym·pa·thet′ic a. of, in, or feeling sympathy —**sym′pa·thet′i·cal·ly** adv.

sym′pa·thize′ v. feel or show sympathy

sym′pa·thy n., pl. **-thies 1** sameness of feeling **2** agreement **3** compassion

sym′pho·ny n., pl. **-nies** full orchestra or composition for it —**sym·phon′ic** a.

sym·po′si·um n., pl. **-ums** or **-a** meeting for discussion

symp′tom n. indication or sign, as of disease —**symp′to·mat′ic** a.

syn′a·gogue′ (-gäg′) n. building where Jews worship

sync, synch (sink) v. synced or synched, sync′ing or synch′ing synchronize —n. synchronization

syn′chro·nize′ v. **1** move or occur at the same time or rate **2** make agree in time or rate —**syn′chro·ni·za′tion** n.

syn′co·pate′ v. Mus. shift the beat to unaccented notes —**syn′co·pa′tion** n.

syn′di·cate (-kət; v.: -kāt′) n. **1** business association of bankers, corporations, etc. **2** organization selling news stories, etc. —v. publish through a syndicate

syn′drome′ n. set of symptoms characterizing a disease or condition

syn′od n. council of churches or church officials

syn′o·nym (-nim) n. word meaning the same as another —**syn·on′y·mous** a.

syn·op′sis n., pl. **-ses′** (-sēz′) summary

syn′tax′ n. the way words are arranged in a sentence —**syn·tac′ti·cal** a.

syn′the·sis n., pl. **-ses′** (-sēz′) combining of parts into a whole —**syn′the·size′** v.

syn′the·siz′er n. an electronic device for producing musical sounds without instruments

syn·thet′ic a. **1** of or using synthesis **2** artificial; not natural —n. synthetic thing —**syn·thet′i·cal·ly** adv.

syph′i·lis (sif′-) n. infectious venereal disease —**syph′i·lit′ic** a., n.

sy·ringe′ (sə rinj′) n. ball with a tube, for ejecting fluids

syr′up n. sweet, thick liquid, as of sugar boiled in water —**syr′up·y** a.

sys′tem n. **1** whole formed of related things **2** set of organized facts, rules, etc. **3** orderly way of doing things —**sys′tem·a·tize′** v.

sys·tem·at′ic a. orderly; methodical —**sys·tem·at′i·cal·ly** adv.

sys·tem′ic a. of or affecting the body as a whole

T

tab n. small flap or tag —**keep tab on** —**keep tabs on** [Col.] keep informed about

tab′by n., pl. **-bies** pet cat

tab′er·nac′le (-nak′əl) n. large place of worship

ta′ble n. **1** flat surface set on legs **2** table set with food **3** orderly list or arrangement —v. postpone

tab·leau′ (-lō′) n., pl. **-leaux′** (-lōz′) or **-leaus′** scene by persons posing in costume

ta′ble·land′ n. plateau

ta′ble·spoon′ n. spoon holding ½ fluid ounce —**ta′ble·spoon·ful** n., pl. **-fuls**

tab′let n. **1** flat, inscribed piece of stone, metal, etc. **2** writing pad **3** flat, hard cake of medicine

table tennis *n.* game like tennis, played on a table

ta·ble·ware' *n.* dishes, forks, etc. used for eating

tab·loid' *n.* small newspaper with sensational news stories

ta·boo, ta·bu' *n.* sacred or social prohibition —*v.* prohibit

tab·u·lar *a.* of or arranged in a table or list

tab·u·late *v.* put in tabular form —**tab·u·la'tion** *n.*

ta·chom·e·ter (tə käm'-) *n.* a device showing rate of rotation of a shaft

tac'it (tas'-) *a.* not expressed openly, but implied

tac'i·turn' (tas'-) *a.* usually silent —**tac'i·tur'ni·ty** *n.*

tack *n.* 1 short, flat-headed nail 2 a course of action 3 ship's direction relative to position of sails —*v.* 1 fasten with tacks 2 add 3 change course

tack'le *n.* 1 equipment 2 set of ropes and pulleys 3 a tackling —*v.* 1 undertake 2 *Football* bring down (the ball carrier)

tack'y *a.* **-i·er, -i·est** 1 slightly sticky 2 [Col.] in poor taste —**tack'i·ness** *n.*

ta'co (tä'-) *n., pl.* **-cos** folded, fried tortilla, filled with meat, etc.

tact *n.* skill in dealing with people —**tact'ful** *a.* —**tact'less** *a.*

tac'tic *n.* skillful method

tac'tics *n.* science of battle maneuvers —**tac'ti·cal** *a.* —**tac·ti'cian** (-tish'ən) *n.*

tad *n.* small amount

tad'pole' *n.* frog or toad in an early stage

taf'fe·ta *n.* stiff silk cloth

taf'fy *n.* a chewy candy

tag *n.* 1 hanging end 2 card, etc. attached as a label 3 children's chasing game —*v.* 1 provide with a tag 2 touch as in game of tag 3 [Col.] follow closely: with *along, after,* etc.

tail *n.* 1 appendage at rear end of an animal's body 2 hind or end part —*v.* [Col.] follow closely —*a.* at or from the rear —**tail'less** *a.*

tail'bone' *n.* coccyx

tail'gate' *n.* hinged door or gate at the back of a truck, etc. —*v.* to drive too closely behind (another vehicle)

tail'light' *n.* red light at the back of a vehicle

tai'lor *n.* one who makes or alters clothes —*v.* 1 make by a tailor's

work 2 form, alter, etc. to suit

tail'spin' *n.* sharp downward plunge of a plane with tail spinning in circles

taint *v.* 1 spoil; rot 2 make corrupt or depraved —*n.* trace of contamination

take *v.* **took, tak'en, tak'ing** 1 grasp 2 capture, seize, win, etc. 3 obtain, select, assume, etc. 4 use, consume, etc. 5 buy; rent 6 travel by 7 deal with 8 occupy 9 derive from 10 write down 11 make (a photograph) 12 require 13 engage in 14 understand 15 have or feel 16 carry, lead, etc. 17 remove 18 subtract —*n.* amount taken —**take after** act or look like —**take in** 1 admit; receive 2 make smaller 3 understand 4 trick —**take over** begin managing —**take up** 1 make tighter or shorter 2 absorb 3 engage in

take'off' *n.* 1 a leaving the ground, as for flight 2 [Col.] mocking imitation; caricature Also **take'-off'**

tal'cum (powder) *n.* powder for the body and face made from a soft mineral (talc)

tale *n.* 1 story 2 lie 3 gossip

tal'ent *n.* special, natural ability —**tal'ent·ed** *a.*

tal'is·man *n., pl.* **-mans** anything supposed to have magic power

talk *v.* 1 say words; speak 2 gossip 3 confer 4 discuss —*n.* 1 a talking 2 conversation 3 speech 4 conference 5 gossip —**talk back** answer impertinently —**talk'er** *n.*

talk'a·tive *a.* talking a great deal: also **talk'y**

tall *a.* high, as in stature

tal'low *n.* hard animal fat used in candles and soap

tal'ly *n., pl.* **-lies** record, account, etc. —*v.* 1 record; score 2 add 3 agree

tal'ly·ho' *int.* fox hunter's cry —*n., pl.* **-hos'** coach drawn by four horses

Tal·mud (täl'mood) *n.* body of early Jewish law

tal'on *n.* claw of a bird of prey

tam *n.* tam-o'-shanter

ta·ma'le (-mä'lē) *n.* peppery chopped meat rolled in corn meal

tam'a·rack' *n.* swamp larch

tam'bou·rine' (-bə rēn') *n.* small, shallow drum with metal disks around it

tame *a.* 1 trained from a wild

state 2 gentle 3 not lively; dull —v. make tame —**tame'ly** adv. —**tam'er** n.

tam'–o'–shan·ter n. flat, round Scottish cap

tamp v. pack down by tapping —**tamp'er** n.

tam'per v. interfere (with)

tam'pon' n. plug of cotton for absorbing blood, etc.

tan n. yellowish brown —a. **tan'ner, tan'nest** yellowish-brown —v. **tanned, tan'ning** 1 make (hide) into leather by soaking in tannic acid 2 brown by sun's rays

tan'bark' n. tree bark containing tannic acid

tan'dem adv. one behind another

tang n. strong taste or odor —**tang'y** a., -i·er, -i·est

tan'gent a. touching a curve at one point —n. a tangent curve, line, etc. —**go off at** (or **on**) **a tangent** change suddenly to another line of action —**tan·gen'tial** (-jen'shəl) a.

tan'ge·rine' (-jə rēn') n. small, loose-skinned orange

tan'gi·ble a. 1 real or solid 2 definite

tan'gle v. 1 make or become knotted, confused, etc. 2 catch, as in a snare —n. tangled mass or condition

tan'go n., pl. -gos South American dance —v. dance the tango

tank n. 1 large container for liquid or gas 2 armored vehicle carrying guns

tank'ard n. large drinking cup with a hinged lid

tank'er n. ship for transporting liquids, esp. oil

tan'ner·y n., pl. -ies place where leather is made by tanning hides —**tan'ner** n.

tannic acid n. acid used in tanning, dyeing, etc.: also **tan'nin**

tan'ta·lize' v. show but withhold something; tease

tan'ta·mount' a. equal (to)

tan'trum n. fit of rage

tap v. **tapped, tap'ping** 1 hit lightly 2 make a hole in 3 draw off, as liquid 4 connect into —n. 1 light blow 2 faucet or spigot 3 plug or cork 4 place for connection

tape n. narrow strip of cloth, paper, etc. —v. 1 to bind with a tape 2 record on tape

tape measure n. tape with marks for measuring

ta'per v. decrease or lessen gradually in thickness, loudness, etc. —n. 1 a tapering 2 slender candle

tape recorder n. recording device using magnetic tape

tap'es·try n., pl. -tries cloth with woven designs

tape'worm' n. tapelike worm found in the intestines

tap·i·o'ca n. starchy substance from cassava roots

ta'pir (-pər) n. hoglike animal

tap'root' n. main root

taps n. bugle call for funerals and the end of the day

tar n. 1 black liquid distilled from wood or coal 2 [Col.] sailor —v. **tarred, tar'ring** cover with tar —**tar'ry** a.

ta·ran'tu·la (-chə lə) n. large, hairy spider

tar'dy a. -di·er, -di·est 1 slow 2 late

tare n. 1 a weed 2 container's weight

tar'get n. thing aimed at, shot at, or attacked

tar'iff n. 1 tax on exports or imports 2 list of prices, charges, etc.

tar'nish v. stain; discolor —n. dullness; stain

ta·ro (ter'ō) n. tropical plant with edible root

tar·ot (tar'ō) n. [often T-] any of a set of fortunetelling cards

tar·pau'lin (-pô'-) n. waterproofed canvas

tar'pon n. large ocean fish

tar'ra·gon' (tar'ə-) n. seasoning of fragrant leaves of wormwood

tar'ry (tar'ē) v. -ried, -ry·ing 1 linger 2 delay

tart a. 1 sour; acid 2 sharp in meaning —n. pastry filled with jam, etc. —**tart'ly** adv. —**tart'ness** n.

tar'tan n. plaid cloth

tar'tar n. hard deposit forming on the teeth

tartar sauce n. sauce of mayonnaise with chopped pickles, olives, etc.

task n. work that must be done —v. burden; strain —**take to task** scold

task'mas·ter n. one who assigns severe tasks

tas'sel n. 1 bunch of threads hanging from a knob 2 tuft of corn silk

taste v. 1 notice or test the flavor of in one's mouth 2 eat or drink sparingly 3 have a certain flavor —n. 1 sense for telling flavor 2 flavor 3 small amount 4 sense of the beautiful, proper, etc. 5 liking —taste'ful a. —taste'less a.

tast'y a. -i·er, -i·est that tastes good

tat v. tat'ted, tat'ting make lace with a hand shuttle

tat'ter n. 1 rag; shred 2 pl. ragged clothes —tat'tered a.

tat'tle v. 1 tell secrets 2 gossip —n. gossip —tat'tler n.

tat'tle-tale' n. informer

tat·too' v. -tooed', -too'ing make designs on the skin —n., pl. -toos' 1 tattooed design 2 steady beating, as on a drum

taught v. pt. & pp. of TEACH

taunt v. mock; tease —n. scornful remark

taupe (tōp) n. dark, brownish gray

Tau'rus second sign of the zodiac; Bull

taut a. 1 tightly stretched 2 tense

tau·tol'o·gy (tô-) n. statement that is true by definition —tau'to·log'i·cal a.

tav'ern n. saloon or inn

taw'dry a. -dri·er, -dri·est gaudy and cheap

taw'ny a. -ni·er, -ni·est dark yellow or tan

tax n. 1 compulsory payment to a government 2 burden; strain —v. 1 levy, or make pay, a tax 2 burden 3 accuse; charge —tax'a·ble a. —tax·a'tion n. —tax'pay'er n.

tax'i n., pl. -is taxicab —v. -ied, -i·ing or -y·ing 1 go in a taxicab 2 move along the ground or water, as an airplane

tax'i·cab' n. automobile for passengers who pay

tax'i·der'my n. art of stuffing animal skins —tax'i·der'mist n.

TB tuberculosis

tea n. 1 leaves of an Asian shrub 2 drink made from these 3 similar drink made from other plants, etc. 4 afternoon party with tea —tea'cup' n.

teach v. taught, teach'ing give lessons (in) —teach'er n.

teak n. East Indian tree

tea'ket'tle n. kettle with a spout, used to heat water

teal n. 1 wild duck 2 grayish or greenish blue

team n. 1 two or more animals harnessed together 2 group working or playing together —v.

join in a team —team'mate' n. —team'work' n.

tea'pot' n. pot with spout and handle for brewing tea

tear v. tore, torn, tear'ing 1 pull apart, up, etc. by force 2 make by tearing 3 move fast —n. 1 a tearing 2 torn place —tear down wreck

tear (tir) n. drop of liquid from the eye: also tear'drop' —in tears weeping —tear'ful, tear'y a.

tear gas n. gas that blinds the eyes with tears: used in warfare

tease v. 1 annoy by poking fun at, etc. 2 fluff up, as hair —n. one who teases

tea'spoon' n. small spoon —tea'spoon·ful' n., pl. -fuls'

teat n. nipple on a breast or udder

tech'ni·cal (tek'-) a. 1 dealing with industrial arts or skills 2 of a specific arts, science, etc. 3 of technique —tech'ni·cal·ly adv.

tech'ni·cal'i·ty n., pl. -ties 1 technical detail 2 minute, formal point

tech·ni'cian (-nish'ən) n. one skilled in a technique or in a technical area

tech·nique' (-nēk') n. method of procedure, as in art

tech'no·crat' n. one who believes in government by scientists, etc. —tech·noc'ra·cy n.

tech·nol'o·gy n. study of applied arts and sciences —tech'no·log'i·cal a.

te'di·ous a. tiring; boring

te'di·um n. a being tedious

tee Golf n. 1 small peg to rest the ball on 2 starting place for each hole —v. teed, tee'ing hit a ball from a tee: with off

teem v. abound; swarm

teen n. 1 pl. numbers or years from 13 through 19 2 teenager —a. teenage

teen'age' a. 1 in one's teens 2 of or for those in their teens —teen'ag'er n.

tee'pee n. tepee

tee'ter v., n. seesaw

tee'ter-tot'ter n., v. seesaw

teeth n. pl. of TOOTH

teethe (tēth) v. have teeth growing through the gum

tee'to·tal·er, tee'to'tal·ler n. one who never drinks liquor

Tef'lon trademark nonsticking coating for cookware, etc. —n.

[t-] this finish

tel'e·cast' v. **-cast'** or **-cast'ed,** **-cast'ing;** n. broadcast over television

tel'e·com·mu·ni·ca'tion n. [also pl., with sing. or pl. v.] electronic communication using radio, computers, etc.

tel'e·gram' n. message sent by telegraph

tel'e·graph' n. device or system for sending messages by electric signals through a wire —v. send a message by telegraph —**te·leg'ra·pher** n. —**tel·e·graph'ic** a. —**te·leg'ra·phy** n.

te·lep'a·thy n. supposed communication between minds without help of speech, sight, etc. —**tel'e·path'ic** a.

tel'e·phone' n. device or system for talking over distances through wires —v. talk (to) by telephone

tel'e·pho'to a. of a camera lens producing a large image of a distant object

tel'e·scope' n. device with lenses that magnify distant objects —v. slide one into another —**tel'e·scop'ic** a.

tel'e·thon' n. televised campaign seeking donations

tel'e·vise' v. transmit by television

tel'e·vi'sion n. way of sending pictures through space by radio waves to a receiving set 2 such a set

tell v. **told, tell'ing** 1 report; narrate 2 put into words 3 show 4 inform 5 recognize 6 order —**tell off** [Col.] criticize sharply

tell'er n. 1 one who tells 2 cashier at a bank

tell'tale' a. revealing what is meant to be secret

te·mer'i·ty n. rashness; boldness

tem'per v. 1 make less intense 2 make hard, as steel —n. 1 state of mind 2 self-control 3 rage 4 tendency to become angry

tem'per·a n. painting with pigments mixed with egg, etc.

tem'per·a·ment (-prə mənt, -pər-) n. (moody or excitable) disposition —**tem·per·a·men'tal** a.

tem'per·ance n. 1 self-restraint; moderation 2 abstinence from liquor

tem'per·ate (-ət) a. 1 moderate; self-restrained 2 neither very hot nor very cold

tem'per·a·ture (-prə chər) n. 1 degree of hotness or coldness 2 fever

tem'pered a. having a certain kind of temper

tem'pest n. wild storm —**tem·pes'tu·ous** (-chōō-) a.

tem'ple n. 1 a building for worship service or for some special purpose 2 area between the eye and ear

tem'po n., pl. **-pos** or **-pi** (-pē) rate of speed, esp. for playing music

tem'po·ral a. 1 worldly 2 of time

tem'po·rar'y a. lasting only a while —**tem·po·rar'i·ly** adv.

tempt v. 1 entice, esp. to an immoral act 2 provoke 3 to incline strongly —**temp·ta'tion** n.

tem·pu'ra (-poor'ə) n. Japanese dish of deep-fried fish, vegetables, etc.

ten a., n. one more than nine —**tenth** a., n.

ten'a·ble a. that can be defended or believed

te·na'cious (-shəs) a. 1 holding firmly 2 retentive 3 stubborn —**te·nac'i·ty** (-nas'-) n.

ten'ant n. occupant (who pays rent) —**ten'an·cy** n.

tend v. 1 take care of 2 be apt; incline 3 lead

tend'en·cy n., pl. **-cies** a being likely to move or act in a certain way

ten'der a. 1 soft or delicate 2 sensitive 3 loving 4 young —n. 1 thing offered, as in payment 2 car with locomotive's coal 3 one who tends —v. give to one to take —**ten'der·ly** adv.

ten'der·foot' n., pl. **-foots'** or **-feet'** newcomer, esp. one not used to hardships

ten'der·ize' v. make tender

ten'der·loin' n. tenderest part of a loin of meat

ten'don n. cord of tissue binding a muscle to a bone

ten'dril n. threadlike, clinging part of a climbing plant

ten'e·ment n. apartment house, esp. an old one

ten'et n. opinion or belief

ten'nis n. game played by hitting a ball over a net with a racket

ten'on n. projecting part to fit in a mortise

ten'or n. 1 highest male voice 2 general course 3 meaning

tense a. 1 taut 2 anxious —v.

make or become tense —n. verb form showing tense

ten'sile (-səl) a. of or under tension

ten'sion n. 1 a stretching 2 stress from this 3 nervous strain 4 voltage

tent n. shelter of canvas, nylon, etc. supported by poles and stakes

ten'ta·cle n. slender growth on an animal's head, for feeling, grasping, etc.

ten'ta·tive a. not final

ten'u·ous (-yōō-) a. 1 thin; fine 2 not dense 3 flimsy

ten'ure (-yər) n. right or duration of holding a position, etc.

te'pee n. cone-shaped tent

tep'id a. lukewarm

te·qui'la (-kē'-) n. strong alcoholic liquor of Mexico

term n. 1 fixed time period 2 pl. conditions of a contract, etc. 3 pl. personal relationship 4 word or phrase 5 either part of a fraction, etc. —v. name —**come to terms** arrive at an agreement —**in terms of** regarding; concerning

ter'mi·nal a. 1 of or at the end 2 final —n. 1 end (part) 2 main station, as for buses 3 keyboard and video screen connected to a computer

ter'mi·nate' v. 1 stop; end 2 form the end of —**ter'mi·na'tion** n.

ter'mi·nol'o·gy n., pl. -**gies** special words or phrases

ter'mi·nus n., pl. -**nus·es** or -**ni'** (-nī') an end, limit, etc.

ter'mite' n. antlike insect that eats wood

tern n. gull-like seabird

ter'race (-əs) n. 1 patio 2 flat mound with sloping side 3 row of houses on this —v. make a terrace of

ter'ra cot'ta n. brownish-red earthenware or its color

ter'ra fir'ma n. solid ground

ter'rain' n. area of land with regard to its fitness for use

ter'ra·pin n. freshwater turtle

ter·rar'i·um (-rer'-) n., pl. -**i·ums** or -**i·a** glass enclosure for small plants, etc.

ter·raz'zo (-rät'sō, -raz'ō) n. polished flooring of small marble chips in cement

ter·res'tri·al a. 1 worldly 2 of the earth 3 of, or living on, land

ter'ri·ble a. 1 causing terror 2 extreme 3 [Col.] very bad —**ter'**

ri·bly adv.

ter'ri·er n. breed of small, lively dog

ter·rif'ic a. 1 terrifying 2 [Col.] very great, etc.

ter'ri·fy' v. -**fied'**, -**fy'ing** fill with terror

ter'ri·to'ry n., pl. -**ries** 1 land ruled by a nation 2 national region not yet a State 3 region —**ter'ri·to'ri·al** a.

ter'ror n. great fear, or cause of this

ter'ror·ism' n. use of force and threats to intimidate —**ter'ror·ist** n., a.

ter'ror·ize' v. 1 terrify 2 coerce by terrorism

ter'ry (cloth) n. cloth having a pile of uncut loops

terse a. concise; to the point —**terse'ly** adv.

ter'ti·ar'y (-shē-) a. third

test n. examination or trial to determine a thing's value, a person's knowledge, etc. —v. subject to a test

tes'ta·ment n. 1 [T-] either part of the Bible 2 legal will

tes'ti·cle n. either of the two male sex glands

tes'ti·fy' v. -**fied'**, -**fy'ing** 1 give evidence in court 2 indicate

tes'ti·mo'ni·al n. 1 statement of recommendation 2 thing given as a tribute

tes'ti·mo'ny n., pl. -**nies** 1 statement of one who testifies in court 2 indication

tes'tis n., pl. -**tes** (-tēz') testicle

tes·tos'ter·one' (-ōn') n. male sex hormone

test tube n. tubelike glass container

tes'ty a. -**ti·er**, -**ti·est** irritable; touchy

tet'a·nus n. acute infectious disease

tête-à-tête (tāt'ə tāt') a., n. (of) a private talk between two people

teth'er (teth'-) n. rope or chain to animal to confine it —v. tie as with this

text n. 1 author's words 2 main part of a printed page 3 textbook 4 Biblical passage 5 topic —**tex'tu·al** (-chōō-) a.

text'book' n. book used in teaching a subject

tex'tile (-til', təl) n. woven fabric —a. 1 of weaving 2 woven

tex'ture n. 1 look and feel of a fabric 2 structure —**tex'tur·al** a.

than *con.* compared to

thank *v.* give thanks to —**thank you** I thank you

thank'ful *a.* showing thanks —**thank'ful·ly** *adv.*

thank'less *a.* ungrateful or unappreciated

thanks *n.pl.* expression of gratitude —*int.* I thank you —**thanks to 1** thanks be given to **2** because of

thanks'giv'ing *n.* **1** thanks to God [T-] U.S. holiday: fourth Thursday in November

that *pron., pl.* **those 1** the one mentioned **2** the farther one or other one **3** whom, whom, or which **4** when —*a., pl.* **those** being that one —*con.* That is used to introduce certain dependent clauses —*adv.* to that extent —**all that** [Col.] so very —**that is 1** to be specific **2** in other words

thatch *v., n.* (cover with) a roof of straw, etc.

thaw *v.* melt or become so warm that ice melts —*n.* period of thawing weather

the *a., definite article* that or this one in particular or of a certain kind —*adv.* that much or by that much

the'a·ter, the'a·tre *n.* **1** place where plays, movies, etc. are shown **2** scene of events **3** dramatic art —**the·at'ri·cal** *a.*

thee *pron.* objective case of THOU

theft *n.* act of stealing

their *a.* of them

theirs *pron.* that or those belonging to them

the'ism' *n.* belief in god(s) —**the'ist** *n., a.*

them *pron.* objective case of THEY

theme *n.* **1** topic **2** short essay **3** main melody

them·selves' *pron.* intensive or reflexive form of THEY

then *adv.* **1** at that time **2** next **3** in that case **4** besides —*n.* that time

thence *adv.* from that place

thence'forth' *adv.* from that time on: also **thence'for'ward**

the·oc'ra·cy *n., pl.* **-cies** (a) government by a church

the·ol'o·gy *n.* study of God and of religious beliefs —**the·o·lo'gi·an** (-lō'jən) *n.* —**the'o·log'i·cal** *a.*

the'o·rem *n.* Math. statement (to be) proved

the'o·ret'i·cal *a.* based on theory,

not on practice

the'o·ry *n., pl.* **-ries 1** explanation based on scientific study and reasoning **2** principles of an art or science **3** guess, conjecture, etc. —**the'o·rize** *v.*

ther'a·peu'tic (-pyōō'-) *a.* serving to cure or heal

ther'a·py *n., pl.* **-pies** method of treating disease or disorders —**ther'a·pist** *n.*

there *adv.* **1** at, in, or to that place **2** at that point **3** in that respect —*n.* that place

there'a·bouts' *adv.* near that place, time, amount, etc.: also **there'a·bout'**

there·af'ter *adv.* after that

there·by' *adv.* by that

there'fore' *adv., con.* for this or that reason

there·in' *adv.* in that place, matter, writing, etc.

there·of' *adv.* **1** of that **2** from that as a cause

there·on' *adv.* **1** on that **2** thereupon

there·to' *adv.* to that place, thing, etc.

there'to·fore' *adv.* up to that time

there·up·on' *adv.* **1** just after that **2** because of that

there·with' *adv.* **1** with that or this **2** just after that

ther'mal *a.* of heat

ther'mo·dy·nam'ics *n.* science of changing heat into other forms of energy

ther·mom'e·ter *n.* device for measuring temperature

ther'mo·nu'cle·ar *a.* of or using the heat energy released in nuclear fission

ther'mos (bottle) *n.* container for keeping liquids at the same temperature

ther'mo·stat' *n.* device for regulating temperature

the·sau'rus (-sôr'əs) *n.* book containing lists of synonyms or related words

these *pron., a.* pl. of THIS

the'sis *n., pl.* **-ses'** (-sēz') **1** statement to be defended **2** essay written to obtain an academic degree

Thes'pi·an *n.* [often t-] actor

thews *n.pl.* muscles or sinews

they *pron.* **1** the ones mentioned **2** people

they'd 1 they had **2** they would

they'll 1 they will **2** they shall

they're they are

they've they have

thi·a·mine (thī′ə min) *n.* vitamin B₁, found in liver, etc.

thick *a.* 1 great in extent from side to side 2 as measured from side to side 3 dense 4 not clear —*n.* the most active part —**thick′en** *v.* —**thick′ly** *adv.* —**thick′ness** *n.*

thick′et *n.* thick growth of shrubs or small trees

thick′set′ *a.* thick in body

thick′-skinned′ *a.* unfeeling

thief *n.*, *pl.* **thieves** one who steals

thieve *v.* —**thiev′er·y** *n.*, *pl.* **-ies** —**thiev′ish** *a.*

thigh *n.* the leg between the knee and the hip

thim′ble *n.* protective cap worn on the finger in sewing

thin *a.* **thin′ner, thin′nest** 1 small in extent from side to side 2 lean; slender 3 sparse 4 watery 5 weak 6 transparent; flimsy —*v.* **thinned, thin′ning** make or become thin —**thin′ness** *n.*

thine [Ar.] *pron.* yours —*a.* [Ar.] your

thing *n.* 1 real object or substance 2 a happening, act, event, etc. 3 matter or affair 4 *pl.* belongings

think *v.* **thought, think′ing** 1 form in or use the mind 2 consider 3 believe 4 remember: with *of* or *about* 5 have an opinion of: with *of* or *about* 6 consider: with *about* 7 conceive (*of*) —**think better of** reconsider —**think up** invent, plan, etc.

thin′ner *n.* substance added to paint, etc. for thinning

thin′-skinned′ *a.* sensitive

third *a.* preceded by two others —*n.* 1 third one 2 one of three equal parts

third′-rate′ *a.* very inferior

thirst *n.* 1 need or craving for water 2 strong desire —*v.* feel thirst —**thirst′y** *a.*

thir′teen′ *a.*, *n.* three more than ten —**thir′teenth′** *a.*, *n.*

thir′ty *a.*, *n.*, *pl.* **-ties** three times ten —**thir′ti·eth** *a.*, *n.*

this *a.*, *pron.*, *pl.* **these** (being) the one mentioned or nearer —*adv.* to this extent

this′tle (-əl) *n.* prickly plant

thith′er (thith′-) *adv.* there

tho, tho′ *con.*, *adv.* though

thong *n.* strip of leather used as a lace, strap, etc.

tho′rax′ *n.* 1 CHEST (*n.* 3) 2 middle segment of an insect

thorn *n.* short, sharp point on a plant stem —**thorn′y** *a.*

thor·ough (thur′ō) *a.* 1 complete 2 very exact

thor′ough·bred′ *n.*, *a.* (an animal) of pure breed

thor′ough·fare′ *n.* main highway

thor′ough·go′ing *a.* very thorough

those *a.*, *pron.* *pl.* of THAT

thou *pron.* [Ar.] you (sing. subject of *v.*)

though (thō) *con.* 1 although 2 yet 3 even if —*adv.* however

thought *v.* pt. & pp. of THINK —*n.* 1 act or way of thinking 2 idea, plan, etc.

thought′ful *a.* 1 full of thought 2 considerate

thought′less *a.* 1 careless 2 inconsiderate

thou′sand *a.*, *n.* ten hundred —**thou′sandth** *a.*, *n.*

thrash *v.* 1 thresh 2 beat 3 toss about violently

thread *n.* 1 fine cord of spun cotton, silk, etc. 2 spiral ridge of a screw, etc. —*v.* 1 put a thread through a needle 2 make one's way

thread′bare′ *a.* shabby

threat *n.* 1 warning of plan to harm 2 sign of danger

threat′en *v.* make or be a threat

three *a.*, *n.* one more than two

three′-di·men′sion·al *a.* having depth or thickness

three′score′ *a.* sixty

thresh *v.* beat out (grain) from its husk —**thresh′er** *n.*

thresh′old′ *n.* 1 sill of a door 2 beginning point

threw *v.* pt. of THROW

thrice *adv.* three times

thrift *n.* careful managing of money, etc. —**thrift′i·ly** *adv.* —**thrift′less** *a.* —**thrift′y** *a.*, **-i·er, -i·est**

thrill *v.*, *n.* (feel or make feel) great excitement

thrill′er *n.* suspenseful novel, film, etc.

thrive *v.* **throve** or **thrived, thrived** or **thriv′en, thriv′ing** 1 be successful 2 grow luxuriantly

throat *n.* 1 front of the neck 2 upper passage from mouth to stomach or lungs

throb *v.* **throbbed, throb′bing** beat or vibrate strongly —*n.* a throbbing

throe (thrō) *n.* pang of pain: used in *pl.*

throm·bo′sis *n.* a clotting in the circulatory system

throne n. 1 official chair, as of a king 2 his power

throng n., v. crowd

throt'tle n. valve to control fuel mixture —v. 1 choke

through (thrōō) prep. 1 from end to end of 2 by way of 3 to places in 4 throughout 5 by means of 6 because of —adv. 1 in and out of 2 all the way 3 entirely —a. 1 open; free 2 to the end without stops 3 finished

through-out' adv., prep. in every part (of)

through'way' n. expressway

throw v. threw, thrown, throw'ing 1 send through the air from the hand 2 make fall 3 put suddenly 4 move, as a switch 5 direct, cast, etc. —n. 1 a throwing 2 distance thrown —throw off get rid of, expel, etc. —throw together make hastily —throw up 1 give up 2 vomit

throw'a·way' a. designed to be discarded after use

throw'back' n. (a) return to an earlier type

thru prep., adv., a. [Col.] through

thrush n. any of a large group of songbirds

thrust v. thrust, thrust'ing push with sudden force —n. 1 sudden push 2 stab 3 forward force

thru'way n. expressway

thud v., n. thud'ded, thud'ding (hit with) a dull sound

thug n. rough criminal

thumb n. short, thick finger nearest the wrist

thumb'nail' n. nail of the thumb —a. brief

thumb'tack' n. tack with wide, flat head

thump n. 1 a blow with a heavy, blunt thing 2 its dull sound —v. hit or pound with a thump

thun'der n. loud noise after lightning —v. 1 cause thunder 2 shout loudly —thun'der·ous a.

thun'der·bolt' n. flash of lightning and its thunder

thun'der·struck' a. amazed

Thurs'day n. fifth day of the week

thus adv. 1 in this way 2 to this or that degree 3 therefore

thwack v., n. whack

thwart v. block; hinder

thy (thī) a. [Ar.] your

thyme (tīm) n. plant of the mint family

thy'mus (thī'-) n. small gland in the throat

thy'roid a., n. (of) a gland secreting a growth hormone

thy·self' pron. [Ar.] yourself

ti·ar·a (tē er'ə, ·är'-) n. woman's crownlike headdress

tib'i·a n. thicker bone of the lower leg

tic n. muscle spasm

tick n. 1 light clicking sound 2 blood-sucking insect —v. make a ticking sound

tick'er n. 1 one that ticks 2 telegraphic device recording stock prices on paper tape

tick'et n. 1 printed card entitling one to a theater seat, etc. 2 tag, label, etc. 3 list of a party's candidates —v. put a ticket on

tick'ing n. cloth holding a pillow's contents

tick'le v. 1 stroke lightly and make twitch or laugh 2 feel tickled 3 amuse; delight —n. a tickling

tick'lish a. 1 sensitive to tickling 2 touchy

tid'al a. of, having, or caused by a tide

tidal wave n. very large, destructive wave caused by an earthquake or strong wind

tid'bit' n. choice morsel

tide n. 1 rise and fall of the ocean twice a day 2 trend —v. chiefly in **tide over** help through a difficulty

tide'land' n. land covered by tide

tide'wa'ter n. 1 water affected by tide 2 seaboard

ti'dings n.pl. news

ti'dy a. ·di·er, ·di·est 1 neat; orderly 2 [Col.] quite large —v. ·died, ·dy·ing make tidy

tie v. tied, ty'ing 1 fasten with string, rope, etc. 2 make (a knot) 3 bind in any way 4 to equal, as in a score —n. 1 thing that ties or joins 2 necktie 3 contest with equal scores

tie'-dye' n. dyeing method affecting only exposed areas —v. dye in this way

tie'-in' n. connection

tier (tir) n. any of a series of rows, one above another

tie'-up' n. 1 temporary stoppage, as of traffic 2 connection

tiff n. slight quarrel

ti'ger n. large, striped jungle cat —ti'gress n.fem.

tight a. 1 made to keep water, air, etc. out or in 2 fitting

closely or too closely 3 taut 4 difficult 5 [Col.] stingy —*adv.*
closely —**tight'en** v. —**tight'ly** adv.
tight'fist'ed a. stingy
tight'-lipped' a. secretive
tight'rope' n. taut rope on which acrobats perform
tights n.pl. tight garment from the waist to the feet
tight'wad' n. [Sl.] miser
til'de (-da) n. diacritical mark (˜)
tile n. thin piece of baked clay, stone, plastic, etc. for roofing, flooring, etc. —v. cover with tiles
till prep., con. until —v. cultivate land for crops —n. drawer for money
till'er n. bar or handle to turn a boat's rudder
tilt v., n. 1 slope; tip 2 joust —**at full tilt** at full speed
tim'ber n. 1 wood for building houses, etc. 2 wooden beam 3 trees
tim'bre (tam'bər) n. the distinctive sound of a voice or musical instrument
time n. 1 period; duration 2 the right instant, hour, etc. 3 the passing hours, day, etc.; or, system of measuring them 4 an occasion 5 set period of work, or pay for this 6 tempo or rhythm —v. 1 choose a right time for 2 measure the speed of —a. 1 of time 2 set to work at a give time —**at times** sometimes —**in time** 1 eventually 2 before it is too late —**on time** 1 not late 2 by installment payments —**tim'er** n.
time'keep'er n. one who records time played, as in games, or hours worked
time'less a. eternal
time'ly a. -li·er, -li·est at the right time
time'out' n. temporary suspension of play in sports
time'piece' n. clock; watch
times prep. multiplied by
time'ta'ble n. schedule of arrivals and departures
time'worn' a. 1 worn out 2 trite
tim'id a. shy; easily frightened —**ti·mid'i·ty** n.
tim'ing n. regulation of speed, etc. to improve performance
tim'or·ous a. timid
tim'o·thy n. a tall grass used for fodder
tim'pa·ni n.pl. kettledrums
tin n. soft, silvery metal, a

chemical element —**tin'ny** a., -ni·er, -ni·est
tinc'ture n. solution of medicine in alcohol —v. tinge
tin'der n. any dry, easily ignited material
tin'der·box' n. 1 flammable object, etc. 2 place, etc. likely to have trouble or war
tine n. prong, as of a fork
tin'foil' n. 1 thin sheet of tin 2 [Col.] tin sheet of aluminum
tinge n. 1 tint 2 slight trace —v. give a tinge to
tin'gle v. sting slightly; prickle —n. a tingling
tin'ker n. mender of pots and pans —v. 1 mend clumsily 2 to putter
tin'kle n. ring of a small bell —v. make a tinkle
tin'sel n. 1 thin strips of metal foil, for decorating 2 showy, cheap thing
tin'smith' n. one who works with tin: also **tin'ner**
tint n. 1 light color 2 a shading of a color —v. give a tint to
ti'ny a. -ni·er, -ni·est very small
-tion suf. 1 act of 2 condition of being 3 thing that is
tip n. 1 a point or end 2 thing fitted to an end 3 light blow; tap 4 secret information 5 a warning 6 gratuity 7 slant —v. 1 make or put a tip on 2 give a tip 3 overturn 4 slant —**tip one's hand** [Sl.] reveal a secret, etc.
tip'-off' n. a TIP (n. 4 & 5)
tip'ple v. drink liquor
tip'sy a. -si·er, -si·est 1 unsteady 2 drunk
tip'toe' n. tip of the toes —v. -toed', -toe'ing walk stealthily on one's toes
tip'top' a., adv., n. (at) the highest point
ti'rade' n. long, angry speech
tire v. make or become weary, bored, etc. —n. hoop or rubber tube around a wheel —**tire'less** a.
tired a. weary; exhausted
tire'some a. tiring
tis·sue (tish'ōō) n. 1 tissue paper 2 cellular material of organisms 3 thin cloth
tissue paper n. thin, soft paper
ti'tan n. giant —**ti·tan'ic** a.
tit for tat this for that
tithe (tith) v., n. (pay) a tenth part of one's income
ti·tian (tish'ən) n., a. reddish yellow

tit'il·late v. excite pleasurably —**tit·il·la'tion** n.

ti'tle n. 1 name of a book, picture, etc. 2 word showing rank or occupation 3 legal right 4 championship —v. name

ti'tlist n. champion in some sport or competition

tit'mouse n., pl. **-mice** small, dull-colored bird

tit'ter v., n. giggle

tit'u·lar (tich'-) a. 1 in name only 2 of or having a title

tiz'zy n., pl. **-zies** [Col.] frenzied excitement

TNT n. an explosive

to prep. 1 toward 2 as far as 3 on, onto, or against 4 until 5 causing 6 with 7 in each *To* may indicate an infinitive or a receiver of action —adv. 1 forward 2 shut

toad n. froglike land animal

toad'stool' n. poisonous mushroom

toad'y n., pl. **-ies** servile flatterer —v. **-ied**, **-y·ing** be a toady (to)

toast v. 1 brown by heating, as bread 2 warm 3 drink in honor of —n. 1 toasted bread 2 a toasting

toast'mas'ter n. one who presides at a banquet

to·bac'co n., pl. **-cos** plant with leaves dried for smoking, chewing, etc.

to·bog'gan v., n. (coast on) a flat, runnerless sled

toc'sin n. alarm bell

to·day' adv. 1 during this day 2 nowadays —n. this day or time

tod'dle v. walk unsteadily, as a child —**tod'dler** n.

tod'dy n., pl. **-dies** whiskey, etc. mixed with hot water, sugar, etc.

to-do' n. [Col.] a fuss

toe n. any of five end parts of the foot —v. **toed**, **toe'ing** touch with the toes —**on one's toes** alert —**toe the line** (or **mark**) follow orders, etc. strictly —**toe'nail'** n.

tof'fee, tof'fy n. taffy

to'fu n. Japanese cheeselike food made from soybeans

to'ga n. loose garment worn in ancient Rome

to·geth'er adv. 1 in one group or place 2 at the same time 3 so as to meet, agree, etc. —**to·geth'er·ness** n.

togs n.pl. [Col.] clothes

toil v. 1 work hard 2 go with effort —n. hard work

toi'let n. 1 fixture to receive body waste 2 bathroom 3 one's grooming: also **toi·lette'** (twä-, toi-)

toi'let·ry n., pl. **-ries** soap, cosmetics, etc.

toilet water n. cologne

to'ken n. 1 sign or symbol 2 keepsake 3 metal disk, as for fare —a. pretended

told v. pt. & pp. of TELL

tol'er·a·ble a. 1 endurable 2 fairly good —**tol'er·a·bly** adv.

tol'er·ance n. 1 a tolerating, as of another's ways 2 power to resist a drug's effect 3 deviation allowed —**tol'er·ant** a.

tol'er·ate' v. 1 to put up with; endure 2 permit

toll n. 1 charge on a turnpike, for a long-distance phone call, etc. 2 the number lost, etc. —v. ring with slow, regular strokes, as a bell

tom'a·hawk' n. light ax used by North American Indians

to·ma'to n., pl. **-toes** red, round, juicy vegetable

tomb (tōōm) n. vault or grave for the dead

tom'boy' n. girl who behaves like an active boy

tomb'stone' n. stone marking a tomb or grave

tom'cat' n. male cat

tome n. large book

tom'fool'er·y n., pl. **-ies** foolish behavior; silliness

to·mor'row adv., n. (on) the day after today

tom'-tom' n. primitive drum

ton n. 2,000 pounds

to·nal'i·ty n. 1 KEY (n. 7) 2 tonal character

tone n. 1 vocal or musical sound; spec., a full interval of a diatonic scale 2 style, character, feeling, etc. 3 shade or tint 4 healthy condition, as of muscles —**tone down** give a less intense tone to —**ton'al** a.

tongs n.pl. device for seizing, lifting, etc., made of two long, hinged arms

tongue (tuŋ) n. 1 movable muscle in the mouth, used in eating and speaking 2 act or manner of speaking 3 language 4 tonguelike part

tongue'-lash'ing n. [Col.] harsh scolding

tongue'-tied' a. speechless

ton'ic n. medicine, etc. that invigorates

to-night' adv., n. (on) this night

ton'nage (-ij) *n.* **1** amount in tons of shipping, etc. **2** carrying capacity of a ship

ton'sil *n.* either of two oval masses of tissue at the back of the mouth

ton'sil·lec'to·my *n., pl.* **-mies** surgical removal of the tonsils

ton'sil·li'tis (-lit'is) *n.* inflammation of the tonsils

ton'sure *n.* shaven crown of a priest's or monk's head

too *adv.* **1** also **2** more than enough **3** very

took *v.* pt. of TAKE

tool *n.* **1** instrument, implement, etc. used for some work **2** stooge —*v.* shape or work with a tool

toot *v., n.* (make) a short blast on a horn, etc.

tooth *n., pl.* **teeth 1** any of a set of bony structures in the jaws, used for biting and chewing **2** toothlike part, as of a saw, gear, etc. —**tooth and nail** with all one's strength —**tooth'ache'** *n.* —**tooth'brush'** *n.*

tooth'paste' *n.* paste for brushing the teeth

tooth'pick' *n.* pointed stick for picking food from between the teeth

tooth'some *a.* tasty

tooth'y *a.* **-i·er, -i·est** having prominent teeth

top *n.* **1** highest point or surface **2** uppermost part or covering **3** highest degree or rank **4** toy that spins round —*a.* of, at, or being the top —*v.* **topped, top'ping 1** provide with a top **2** be at the top of **3** surpass; exceed —**on top of 1** resting upon **2** besides —**top complete**

to'paz' *n.* yellow gem

top'coat' *n.* light overcoat

top'-draw·er *a.* of first importance

top'-flight' *a.* [Col.] first-rate

top hat *n.* man's tall, black hat

top'-heav'y *a.* too heavy at the top and, thus, unstable

top'ic *n.* subject of an essay, speech, etc.

top'i·cal *a.* of current or local interest

top'mast' *n.* second mast above the deck of a ship

top'most' *a.* uppermost

top'-notch' *a.* [Col.] first-rate

to·pog'ra·phy *n.* **1** surface features of a region **2** science of showing these, as on maps —**top'o·graph'i·cal, top'o-**

graph'ic *a.*

top'ple *v.* (make) fall over

top'sail' *n.* sail next above the lowest sail on a mast

top'soil' *n.* upper layer of soil, usually richer

top'sy-tur'vy *adv., a.* **1** upside down **2** in disorder

to'rah (-rə) *n.* Jewish scriptures; spec. [T-] first five books of the Bible

torch *n.* **1** portable flaming light **2** device that makes a very hot flame, as in welding —**torch'light'** *n.*

tore *v.* pt. of TEAR (pull apart)

tor'e·a·dor' (-ē·ə-) *n.* bullfighter

tor'ment (*v.:* tôr·ment') *n.* great pain —*v.* make suffer —**tor·men'tor** *n.*

torn *v.* pp. of TEAR (pull apart)

tor·na'do *n., pl.* **-does** violent wind with a whirling, funnel-shaped cloud

tor·pe'do *n., pl.* **-does** large, cigar-shaped, underwater projectile —*v.* **-doed, -do·ing** to destroy or ruin

tor'pid *a.* dull; sluggish —**tor'por** *n.*

torque (tôrk) *n.* force that gives a twisting motion

tor'rent *n.* swift, violent stream —**tor·ren'tial** (-shəl) *a.*

tor'rid *a.* very hot

tor'sion *n.* a twisting or being twisted

tor'so *n., pl.* **-sos** human body minus head and limbs

tort *n. Law* wrongful act, injury, etc.

torte *n.* rich cake

tor·tel·li'ni *n.* tiny, ring-shaped pasta

tor·til'la (-tē'ə) *n.* flat, unleavened corn cake

tor'toise (-təs) *n.* turtle, esp. one living on land

tor'toise-shell' *a.* made of a mottled, yellow-and-brown substance

tor'tu·ous (-chōō-) *a.* full of twists and turns

tor'ture *n.* **1** inflicting of great pain **2** great pain —*v.* **1** subject to torture **2** twist

To·ry (tôr'ē) *n., pl.* **-ries 1** Br. loyalist in American Revolution **2** [often t-] a conservative

toss *v.* **tossed, toss'ing 1** throw lightly from the hand **2** fling or be flung about **3** jerk upward —*n.* a tossing

toss'up' *n.* **1** flipping of a coin to decide **2** even chance

tot n. young child

to'tal n. 1 the whole amount; sum —a. 1 entire; whole 2 complete —v. add (up to) —**to·tal'i·ty** n. —**to'tal·ly** adv.

to·tal·i·tar'i·an a. of a dictatorship

tote v. [Col.] carry; haul

to'tem pole n. pole with animal symbol(s), made by Indians of NW North America

tot'ter v. 1 rock as if about to fall 2 stagger

tou'can' (tōō'-) n. tropical bird with a large beak

touch v. 1 put the hand, etc. on so as to feel 2 bring or come into contact 3 tap lightly 4 handle; use 5 concern 6 arouse pity, etc. in 7 treat in passing: with on or upon —n. 1 a touching 2 way things feel 3 sense of this 4 small bit 5 contact —**in touch** in contact —**touch on** mention —**touch up** improve by additions

touch'-and-go' a. uncertain, risky, etc.

touch'down' n. 1 goal scored in football, for six points 2 moment when an aircraft lands

touch'stone' n. criterion

touch'y a. -i·er, -i·est 1 irritable 2 difficult

tough a. 1 hard to chew, cut, break, etc. 2 strong or rough 3 very difficult —n. ruffian —**tough'en** v.

tou·pee (tōō pā') n. small wig for a bald spot

tour n. long trip, as to see sights, put on plays, etc. —v. go on a tour (through) —**tour'ist** n., a.

tour'na·ment n. 1 series of contests for a championship 2 knights' jousting contest

tour'ney n., pl. -neys tournament

tour'ni·quet (-kət) n. device for compressing a blood vessel to stop bleeding

tou·sle (tou'zəl) v. muss

tout (tout) [Col.] v. 1 praise highly 2 sell tips on (race horses) —n. one who touts

tow v. pull by a rope or chain —n. a towing

toward (tôrd, twôrd) prep. 1 in the direction of 2 concerning 3 near 4 for Also **towards**

tow'el n. piece of cloth or paper to wipe things dry

tow'er n. high structure, often part of another building —v. rise high

tow'head' (tō'-) n. person with light yellow hair

town n. 1 small city 2 business center —**towns'peo'ple, towns' folk'** n.pl.

town'ship n. 1 part of a county 2 U.S. land unit 6 miles square

tox·e'mi·a a. condition of toxins or poisons spread throughout the blood

tox'ic a. 1 of or caused by a toxin 2 poisonous

tox·i·col'o·gy n. science of poisons and their effects —**tox'i·col'o·gist** n.

tox'in n. poison, esp. from bacteria, viruses, etc.

toy n. thing to play with —a. small —v. play (with)

trace n. 1 mark or track left 2 small bit 3 harness strap connecting to vehicle —v. 1 follow (the trial or course of) 2 draw, outline, etc. —**trac'er** n.

trac'er·y n., pl. -ies design of interlacing lines

tra·che·a (-kē-) n. air passage from the larynx to the bronchial tubes

tra·che·ot·o·my n., pl. -mies emergency incision of the trachea, as to allow breathing

track n. 1 footprint, wheel rut, etc. 2 path, trail, or course 3 running sports, etc. 4 pair of rails a train runs on —v. 1 follow the track of 2 leave footprints on —**keep** (or **lose**) **track of** keep (or fail to keep) informed about

tract n. 1 large stretch of land 2 system of bodily organs 3 booklet

trac'ta·ble a. manageable

trac'tion n. 1 power to grip a surface 2 a pulling

trac'tor n. 1 motor vehicle to pull farm machines, etc. 2 truck to haul a trailer

trac·tor-trail'er n. coupled TRACTOR (n. 2) and trailer or semitrailer

trade n. 1 skilled work 2 buying and selling 3 an exchange —v. 1 buy and sell 2 exchange

trade'-in' n. thing used as part payment

trade'mark' n. special mark or name (**trade name**) put on a product

trades'man n., pl. -men [Chiefly Br.] storekeeper

trade union n. labor union

trade wind n. wind that blows toward the equator

tra·di'tion n. 1 custom, etc. handed down from the past 2 such handing down —**tra·di'tion·al** a.

tra·duce' v. to slander

traf'fic n. 1 vehicles moving along streets, etc. 2 amount of business done 3 TRADE (n. 2) —v. -ficked, -fick·ing do business, esp. illegally

tra·ge'di·an (trə jē'-) n. actor of tragedy —**tra·ge'di·enne'** n.fem.

trag'e·dy n., pl. -dies 1 serious play with a sad ending 2 tragic event

trag'ic a. 1 of or like tragedy 2 very sad —**trag'i·cal·ly** adv.

trail v. 1 drag or lag behind 2 follow or drift behind 3 dwindle —n. 1 thing trailing behind 2 beaten path

trail'blaz'er n. 1 one who blazes a trail 2 pioneer in any field

trail'er n. wagon or van pulled by a car or truck, sometimes used as a home

train n. 1 a thing that drags behind 2 procession 3 connected series 4 locomotive with cars —v. 1 guide the development of 2 instruct or prepare 3 aim —**train·ee'** n.

traipse v. [Col. or Dial.] to walk, tramp, etc.

trait n. characteristic

trai'tor n. disloyal person —**trai'tor·ous** a.

tra·jec'to·ry n., pl. -ries curved path of a missile

tram'mel n., v. (thing) to hinder or restrain

tramp v. 1 walk, or step, heavily 2 roam about —n. 1 vagrant 2 a tramping

tram'ple v. step hard on or crush underfoot

tram'po·line' (-lēn') n. apparatus with springs and taut canvas, used for acrobatic tumbling

trance n. state of shock, hypnosis, or deep thought

tran'quil a. calm; quiet —**tran'quil'li·ty, tran·quil'i·ty** n.

tran'quil·ize', tran'quil·lize' v. make tranquil —**tran'quil·iz'er, tran'quil·liz'er** n.

trans- pref. over, across, beyond

trans·act' v. do; complete —**trans·ac'tion** n.

trans·cend' (-send') v. exceed —**tran·scend'ent** a.

tran·scen·den'tal a. 1 transcendent 2 supernatural

tran·scribe' v. 1 write or type out 2 record for rebroadcast

tran·scrip'tion n.

tran'script' n. written or typewritten copy

tran'sept' n. shorter part of a cross-shaped church

trans·fer' v. -ferred', -fer'ring move or change from one person, place, etc. to another —n. 1 a transferring 2 ticket letting one change to another bus, etc. —**trans·fer'a·ble** a. —**trans·fer'ence** n.

trans·fig'ure v. 1 transform 2 make seem glorious —**trans·fig·u·ra'tion** n.

trans·fix' v. pierce through

trans·form' v. change the form or condition of —**trans'for·ma'tion** n.

trans·form'er n. device that changes voltage

trans·fuse' v. 1 imbue; fill 2 transfer blood to another —**trans·fu'sion** n.

trans·gress' v. 1 break a law; do wrong 2 go beyond —**trans·gres'sion** n. —**trans·gres'sor** n.

tran'si·ent (-shənt, -sē ənt) a. temporary —n. one who stays only a short time

tran·sis'tor n. small electronic device that controls current flow

trans'it n. 1 passage across 2 conveying

tran·si'tion n. a passing from one condition, place, etc. to another

tran'si·tive a. taking a direct object, as some verbs

tran'si·to·ry a. temporary

trans·late' v. put into another language, form, etc. —**trans·la'tion** n. —**trans·la'tor** n.

trans·lu'cent a. letting light pass through but not transparent

trans·mis'sion n. 1 a transmitting 2 car part sending power to wheels

trans·mit' v. -mit'ted, -mit'ting 1 transfer 2 pass or convey 3 send out radio or TV signals —**trans·mit'ter** n.

tran'som n. small window above a door or window

trans·par'ent a. that can be seen through; clear —**trans·par'en·cy** n., pl. -cies

tran·spire' v. 1 become known 2 happen

trans·plant' (n.: trans'plant') v. 1 dig up and plant in another place 2 to transfer (tissue or organ) from one to another; graft —n. something transplanted

tran·spon'der n. radio transmitter and receiver that automatically transmits signals

trans·port' (n.: trans'pôrt') v. 1 carry from one place to another 2 carry away with emotion —n. thing for transporting —**trans' por·ta'tion** n.

trans·pose' v. 1 to interchange 2 Mus. change the key of

trans·sex'u·al n. one who identifies with the opposite sex, sometimes so strongly as to undergo sex-change surgery

trans·verse' a. situated, placed, etc. across

trans·ves'tite' n. one who gets sexual pleasure from wearing clothes of the opposite sex

trap n. 1 device for catching animals 2 tricky ruse 3 bend in a drainpipe —v. **trapped', trap'ping** 1 catch in a trap 2 set traps for animals —**trap'per** n.

trap'door' n. hinged or sliding door in a roof or floor

tra·peze' n. swinglike bar for acrobats

trap·e·zoid' n. figure with two of four sides parallel

trap'pings n.pl. adornments

trap'shoot'ing n. sport of shooting clay disks sprung into the air from throwing devices (traps)

trash n. rubbish —**trash'y** a., -i·er, -i·est

trau'ma n. emotional shock with lasting psychic effects —**trau·mat'ic** a.

tra·vail' (tra vāl') n. 1 labor 2 agony

trav'el v. 1 make a journey (through) 2 move or pass —n. 1 a traveling 2 pl. journeys —**trav'el·er** n.

trav'e·logue', trav'e·log' n. illustrated lecture or movie of travels

tra·verse' (a.: trav'ərs) v. to cross —a. of drapes drawn by pulling cords

trav'es·ty n., pl. -ties farcical imitation —v. -tied, -ty·ing to make a travesty of

trawl v., n. (fish with) a large dragnet —**trawl'er** n.

tray n. flat, low-sided server to carry things

treach'er·ous (trech'-) a. 1 disloyal 2 not safe or reliable —**treach'er·y** n.

tread (tred) v. **trod, trod'den** or **trod, tread'ing** 1 walk on, along, over, etc. 2 trample —n. 1 way or sound of treading 2 part for treading or moving on

trea·dle (tred'l) n. foot pedal to operate a wheel, etc.

tread'mill' n. device worked by treading an endless belt

trea·son (trē'zən) n. betrayal of one's country —**trea'son·a·ble, trea'son·ous** a.

treas'ure n. 1 accumulated money, jewels, etc. 2 valued person or thing —v. 1 save up 2 cherish

treas'ure-trove' n. 1 treasure found hidden 2 valuable discovery

treas'ur·y n., pl. -ies 1 place where money is kept 2 funds of a state, corporation, etc. —**treas'ur·er** n.

treat v. 1 deal with or act toward 2 pay for the food, etc. of 3 subject to a process, medical care, etc. —n. 1 food, etc. paid for by another 2 thing giving pleasure —**treat'ment** n.

trea·tise (trēt'is) n. a formal writing on a subject

trea'ty n., pl. -ties agreement between nations

tre·ble (treb'əl) a. 1 triple 2 of or for the treble —n. 1 Mus. highest part 2 high-pitched voice or sound —v. to triple

tree n. large, woody plant with one main trunk and many branches —v. **treed, tree'ing** to chase up a tree

tre'foil' n. 1 plant with three-part leaves 2 design like such a leaf

trek v., n. **trekked, trek'king** (make) a slow, hard journey

trel'lis n. lattice on which vines, etc. are grown

trem'ble v. 1 shake from cold, fear, etc. 2 quiver or vibrate —n. act or fit of trembling

tre·men'dous a. 1 very large 2 [Col.] wonderful

trem'or n. a trembling, shaking, etc.

trem'u·lous (-yōō-) a. trembling

trench n. ditch, esp. one dug for cover in battle

trench'ant a. incisive

trench coat n. belted raincoat in a military style

trend v., n. (have) a general direction or tendency

trend'y a. -i·er, -i·est [Col.] of or in the latest style

trep'i·da'tion n. fearful uncertainty

tres'pass v. 1 enter another's property unlawfully 2 sin —n. a trespassing —**tres'pass·er** n.

tress *n.* lock of hair

tres'tle (-əl) *n.* **1** framework support, as for a bridge **2** sawhorse

trey (trā) *n.* playing card with three spots

tri- *pref.* three

tri'ad' *n.* group of three

tri'al *n.* **1** hearing and deciding of a case in a law court **2** attempt **3** test **4** pain, trouble, etc.

tri'an'gle *n.* three-sided figure with three angles —**tri·an'gu·lar** *a.*

tribe *n.* **1** group of people living together under a chief **2** group or class —**trib'al** *a.* —**tribes'man** *n.*, *pl.* -**men**

trib·u·la'tion (-yoo-) *n.* great misery or distress

tri·bu'nal *n.* law court

trib·une' *n.* public defender

trib'u·tar'y (-ter'-) *n.*, *pl.* -**ies** river that flows into a larger one

trib'ute *n.* **1** forced payment, as by a weak nation to a stronger **2** gift, speech, etc. showing respect

trich'i·no'sis (trik'i-) *n.* disease caused by worms in the intestines and muscles

trick *n.* **1** something done to fool, cheat, etc. **2** prank **3** clever act or skillful way **4** turn at work **5** personal habit **6** cards played in one round —*v.* fool or cheat —**trick'er·y** *n.*

trick'le *v.* **1** flow in drops or a thin stream **2** move slowly —*n.* slow flow

trick'y *a.* -**i·er**, -**i·est** **1** deceitful **2** difficult

tri'col'or *n.* flag having three colors

tri'cy·cle (-si-) *n.* three-wheeled vehicle

tri'dent *n.* three-pronged spear

tried *v.* pt. & pp. of TRY —*a.* tested or trustworthy

tri'fle *n.* **1** thing of little value **2** small amount —*v.* **1** act jokingly **2** play

tri'fling *a.* unimportant

trig'ger *n.* lever pressed in firing a gun

trig·o·nom'e·try *n.* mathematics dealing with relations between sides and angles of triangles — **trig'o·no·met'ric** *a.*

trill *v.*, *n.* (sing or play with) a rapid alternation of two close notes

tril'lion *n.* thousand billions — **tril'lionth** *a.*, *n.*

tril'o·gy *n.*, *pl.* -**gies** set of three

novels, plays, etc.

trim *v.* **1** trimmed, trim'ming **1** clip, lop, etc. **2** decorate **3** put (sails) in order —*n.* **1** good condition **2** decoration —*a.* trim'mer, trim'mest **1** orderly; neat **2** in good condition —**trim'mer** *n.*

trim'ming *n.* **1** decoration **2** *pl.* parts trimmed off

Trin'i·ty Father, Son, and Holy Ghost as one God

trin'ket *n.* small ornament

tri·o (trē'ō) *n.*, *pl.* -**os** musical composition for three performers

trip *v.* **1** tripped, trip'ping **1** move with light, rapid steps **2** stumble or make stumble **3** err or cause to err —*n.* a journey

tri·par'tite' *a.* **1** having three parts **2** between three parties, as a treaty

tripe *n.* stomach of a cow, etc. used as food

tri·ple (trip'əl) *a.* **1** of or for three **2** three times as much or as many —*n.* Baseball hit putting the batter on third —*v.* to make or become triple —**tri'ply** *adv.*

trip'let *n.* any of three children born at one birth

trip'li·cate (-kət) *a.* triple —*n.* one of three exact copies

tri'pod' *n.* three-legged stool, support, etc.

trite *a.* worn-out; stale

tri'umph *n.* victory; success —*v.* gain victory or success —**tri·um'phal**, **tri·um'phant** *a.*

tri·um'vi·rate (-rət) *n.* government by three persons

triv'et *n.* three-legged stand for holding pots

triv'i·a *n.pl.* trifles

triv'i·al *a.* unimportant —**triv'i·al'i·ty** *n.*, *pl.* -**ties**

trod *v.* pt. & alt. pp. of TREAD

trod'den *v.* alt. pp. of TREAD

trog'lo·dyte' (-dīt) *n.* **1** cave dweller **2** hermit

troll (trōl) *v.* **1** fish with a moving line **2** sing loudly —*n.* Folklore cave-dwelling giant

trol'ley *n.*, *pl.* -**leys** **1** overhead device that sends electric current to a streetcar **2** electric streetcar: also **trolley car**

trol'lop *n.* prostitute

trom'bone' *n.* brass-wind instrument with a sliding tube

troop *n.* **1** group of persons **2** *pl.* soldiers **3** cavalry unit —*v.* move in a group

troop'er n. 1 cavalryman 2 mounted policeman

tro'phy n., pl. **-phies** souvenir of victory, etc.

trop'ic n. 1 either of two parallels of latitude (**Tropic of Cancer** and **Tropic of Capricorn**) N and S of the equator 2 [also T-] pl. hot region between these latitudes —**trop'i·cal** a.

trot v. **trot'ted, trot'ting** go at a trot —n. 1 running gait of a horse 2 slow, jogging ruin —**trot'ter** n.

troth (trôth, trōth) n. 1 promise, esp. to marry 2 truth

trou·ba·dour (trōo'bə dôr') n. medieval lyric poet

trou'ble n. 1 worry, distress, bother, etc. 2 disturbance 3 difficulty —v. be or give trouble to —**trou'ble·some** a.

trou'ble-shoot'er n. one who finds and fixes what is out of order

trough (trôf) n. 1 long, narrow, open container, as for feeding animals 2 long, narrow hollow

trounce v. beat; flog

troupe (troop) n. troop of actors, etc. —**troup'er** n.

trou'sers n.pl. man's two-legged outer garment

trous·seau (trōo sō') n., pl. **-seaus'** or **-seaux'** (-sōz') bride's outfit of clothes, linen, etc.

trout n. freshwater food fish related to the salmon

trow'el (trou'-) n. 1 flat tool for smoothing 2 scooplike tool for digging

troy (**weight**) n. system of weights for gold, silver, etc. in which 12 oz. = 1 lb.

tru'ant n. 1 pupil who stays away from school without leave 2 one who shirks his or her duties —**tru'an·cy** n.

truce n. cessation of fighting by mutual agreement

truck n. 1 large motor vehicle for carrying loads 2 wheeled frame 3 vegetables raised for market 4 [Col.] dealings —v. carry on a truck —**truck'er** n.

truck'le v. be servile

truc·u·lent (-yōo-) a. fierce —**truc'u·lence** n.

trudge v. walk wearily

true a. 1 loyal 2 not false 3 accurate 4 lawful 5 real; genuine —adv. exactly —n. that which is true —**tru'ly** adv.

tru'ism n. an obvious truth

trump n. (playing card of) a suit ranked highest —v. take with a trump —**trump up** devise deceitfully

trump'er·y n., pl. **-ies** showy but worthless thing

trum'pet n. brass instrument with a flared end —v. proclaim loudly

trun'cate' v. cut off a part —**trun·ca'tion** n.

trun'cheon (-chan) n. short, thick club

trun'dle v. roll along

trundle bed n. low bed on small wheels

trunk n. 1 main stem of a tree 2 body, not including the head and limbs 3 long snout of an elephant 4 large box for clothes, etc. 5 main line 6 pl. very short pants worn for sports

truss v. tie, fasten, or tighten —n. supporting framework or device

trust n. 1 belief in the honesty, reliability, etc. of another 2 one trusted 3 responsibility 4 custody 5 CREDIT (n. 4) 6 property managed for another 7 a monopolistic group of corporations —v. 1 have trust in 2 put in the care of 3 believe 4 hope 5 let buy on credit —**trust'ful** a. —**trust'wor'thy** a.

trust·ee' n. 1 one put in charge of another's property 2 member of a controlling board —**trust·ee'ship** n.

trust fund n. money, stock, etc. held in trust

trust'y a. **-i·er, -i·est** dependable —n., pl. **-ies** a convict with privileges

truth n. 1 being true, honest, etc. 2 that which is true 3 established fact —**truth'ful** a.

try v. **tried, try'ing** 1 conduct the trial of 2 test 3 afflict 4 attempt —n., pl. **tries** attempt; effort

try'ing a. hard to bear

try'out' n. test of fitness

tryst (trist) n. 1 appointment to meet made by lovers

T'-shirt' n. short-sleeved, pullover undershirt

T square n. T-shaped ruler

tub n. 1 large, open container 2 bathtub

tu'ba n. large, deep-toned brass instrument

tube n. 1 slender pipe for fluids 2 tubelike, sealed container 3 electron tube —**tu'bu·lar** a.

tu'ber n. thickened part of an

underground stem —**tu′ber·ous** a.

tu′ber·cle n. 1 small, round projection 2 hard growth

tu·ber·cu·lo′sis n. wasting disease, esp. of the lungs —**tu·ber′cu·lous, tu·ber′cu·lar** a.

tube′rose′ n. flower with a bulblike root

tuck v. 1 gather up in folds 2 push the edges of something under 3 cover snugly 4 press into a small space —n. sewn fold

tuck′er v. [Col.] tire (out)

-tude suf. quality; state

Tues′day n. third day of the week

tuft n. bunch of hairs, grass, etc. growing or tied together —v. form in tufts

tug v. **tugged, tug′ging** pull; drag —n. 1 hard pull 2 tugboat

tug′boat′ n. small boat for towing or pushing ships

tug of war n. contest with two teams pulling at a rope

tu·i′tion (-ish′ən) n. charge for instruction

tu′lip n. bulb plant with cupshaped flower

tulle (tōōl) n. fine netting for veils, etc., made of silk, etc.

tum′ble v. 1 fall or move suddenly or clumsily 2 toss about 3 do acrobatics —n. 1 a fall 2 disorder

tum′ble-down′ a. dilapidated

tum′bler n. 1 drinking glass 2 acrobat 3 part of a lock moved by a key

tum′ble·weed′ n. plant that breaks off and is blown about

tu′mid a. 1 swollen; bulging 2 inflated; pompous

tum′my n., pl. **-mies** stomach: child's word

tu′mor n. abnormal growth in or on the body

tu′mult′ n. 1 uproar 2 confusion —**tu·mul′tu·ous** (-chōō əs) a.

tu′na (fish) n. large ocean fish with oily flesh

tun′dra n. large arctic plain without trees

tune n. 1 melody 2 Mus. right pitch 3 agreement —v. 1 put in TUNE (n. 2) 2 adjust to proper performance —**tune** in adjust radio or TV set to receive (a station, program, etc.) —**tun′er** n.

tune′ful a. full of melody

tune′up′, tune′-up′ n. an adjusting, as of an engine, to proper condition

tung′sten n. hard metal in alloys,

a chemical element

tu′nic n. 1 loose gown worn in ancient Greece and Rome 2 long, belted blouse

tun′nel n. underground passageway —v. make a tunnel

tun′ny n., pl. **-nies** tuna

tur′ban n. scarf wound round the head, as in the Middle East

tur′bid a. 1 muddy or cloudy 2 confused

tur′bine (-bin, -bīn′) n. engine driven by the pressure of air, steam, or water on the vanes of a wheel

tur′bo·jet′ n. airplane engine with a jet-driven turbine to work the air compressor

tur′bo·prop′ n. airplane engine with a jet-driven turbine to drive the propeller

tur′bu·lent a. 1 disorderly 2 agitated —**tur′bu·lence** n.

tu·reen′ n. large, deep dish with a lid, for soup, etc.

turf n. top layer of earth with grass —**the turf** (track) for horse racing

tur′gid (-jid) a. 1 swollen 2 pompous —**tur·gid′i·ty** n.

Turk n. native of Turkey

tur′key n. 1 large bird with a spreading tail 2 its flesh, used as food

Turk′ish n., a. (language) of Turkey

tur′moil′ n. noisy, excited condition

turn v. 1 revolve or rotate 2 change in position or direction 3 make or perform 4 reverse 5 change in feelings, etc. 6 change in form, etc. 7 drive, set, etc. 8 to wrench or twist 9 divert; deflect 10 upset 11 depend 12 reach or pass 13 become 14 become sour —n. 1 a turning around 2 change in position or direction 3 short walk, ride, etc. 4 bend; twist 5 chance; try 6 deed 7 turning point 8 style; form 9 sudden shock —**in** (or **out of**) **turn** in (or not in) proper order —**turn down** to reject —**turn in** 1 hand in 2 [Col.] go to bed —**turn off** 1 shut off 2 [Sl.] cause to be bored, etc. —**turn on** 1 make go on 2 [Sl.] make or become elated, etc. —**turn out** 1 shut off 2 come 3 make 4 result —**turn to** rely on —**turn up** happen, appear, etc.

turn′a·bout′ n. reversal

turn′a·round′ n. 1 wide area for

turning a vehicle around **2** time taken by a business to complete a job

turn'buck'le *n.* metal loop used as a coupling

turn'coat' *n.* traitor

tur'nip *n.* plant with an edible, round root

turn'off' *n.* place to turn off a highway, etc.

turn'out' *n.* gathering of people

turn'o'ver *n.* **1** small pie with crust folded over **2** rate of replacement of workers, goods, etc.

turn'pike' *n.* highway, esp. one on which a toll is paid

turn'stile' *n.* gate admitting one at a time

turn'ta'ble *n.* round, revolving platform

tur'pen·tine' *n.* oil from trees, used in paints, etc.

tur'pi·tude' *n.* vileness

tur'quoise' (-kwoiz', -koiz') *n.* greenish-blue gem

tur'ret *n.* **1** small tower on a building **2** armored dome, as on a tank **3** lathe part holding cutting tools

tur'tle *n.* hard-shelled land and water reptile

tur'tle-dove' *n.* wild dove

tur'tle-neck' *n.* a high, snug, turned-down collar

tusk *n.* long, projecting tooth, as of an elephant

tus'sle *n., v.* struggle

tu·te·lage (tōōt''l ij) *n.* **1** instruction **2** protection

tu'tor *n.* private teacher —*v.* teach —**tu·to'ri·al** (-tôr'ē-) *a.*

tut·ti-frut·ti (tōōt'ē frōōt'ē) *n., a.* (ice cream, etc.) made with mixed fruits

tux·e'do *n., pl.* **-dos** man's semiformal suit

TV *n.* **1** television **2** *pl.* **TVs** or **TV's** television set

twad'dle (twäd''l) *n.* nonsense

twain *a., n.* [Poet.] two

twang *n.* **1** sharp, vibrating sounds **2** nasal sound —*v.* to make, or utter with, a twang

'twas it was

tweak *v., n.* (give) a sudden, twisting pinch

tweed *n.* **1** rough wool fabric **2** *pl.* clothes of tweed

tweet *v., n.* chirp

tweet'er *n.* small speaker for high-frequency sounds

tweez'ers *n.pl.* small pincers for plucking hairs

twelve *a., n.* two more than ten

—**twelfth** *a., n.*

twen'ty *a., n., pl.* **-ties** two times ten —**twen'ti·eth** *a., n.*

twerp *n.* [Sl.] insignificant or contemptible person

twice *adv.* **1** two times **2** two times as much

twid'dle *v.* twirl idly

twig *n.* small branch

twi'light' *n.* **1** dim light after sunset **2** gradual decline

twill *n.* cloth woven with parallel diagonal lines

twin *n.* **1** either of two born at the same birth **2** either of two very much alike —*a.* being a twin or twins

twine *n.* strong cord made of twisted strands —*v.* **1** interweave **2** wind around

twinge *v., n.* (have) a sudden pain or a qualm

twin'kle *v.* **1** sparkle **2** light up —*n.* a twinkling

twirl *v., n.* spin; twist

twist *v.* **1** to wind together or around something **2** force out of shape **3** pervert meaning of **4** sprain **5** rotate **6** curve —*n.* **1** something twisted **2** a twisting

twist'er *n.* [Col.] tornado or cyclone

twitch *v.* pull or move with a sudden jerk —*n.* sudden, spasmodic motion

twit'ter *v.* **1** chirp rapidly **2** tremble excitedly —*n.* a twittering

two *a., n.* one more than one —**in two** in two parts

two'-bit' *a.* [Sl.] cheap, inferior, etc.

two'-faced' *a.* deceitful

two'fold' *a.* **1** having two parts **2** having twice as much or as many —*adv.* twice as much or as many

two'some *n.* couple

two'-time' *v.* [Sl.] be unfaithful to

two'-way' *a.* allowing passage in two directions

-ty *suf.* quality or condition of

ty·coon' (ti-) *n.* powerful industrialist

ty'ing *v.* ppr. of TIE

tyke (tik) *n.* [Col.] small child

tym·pan'ic membrane (tim-) *n.* eardrum

tym'pa·num *n.* **1** cavity beyond eardrum **2** eardrum

type (tip) *n.* **1** kind or sort **2** model; example **3** metal piece or pieces for printing **4** printed letters, etc. —v. 1 classify 2 typewrite

type′cast′ v. to cast (an actor) repeatedly in similar role

type′write′ v. write with a typewriter

type′writ′er n. a keyboard machine for making printed letters on paper

ty′phoid′ n. infectious disease with fever, intestinal disorders, etc.: also **typhoid fever**

ty·phoon′ n. cyclonic storm, esp. in the W Pacific

ty′phus n. infectious disease with fever, skin rash, etc.: also **typhus fever**

typ′i·cal (tip′-) a. 1 being a true example of its kind 2 characteristic —**typ′i·cal·ly** adv.

typ′i·fy′ (tip′-) v. -fied′, -fy′ing be typical of; exemplify

typ′ist (tīp′-) n. one who operates a typewriter

ty′po n., pl. -pos [Col.] typographical error; mistake in typing

ty·pog′ra·phy n. 1 setting of, and printing with, type 2 style, design, etc. of matter printed from type —**ty·pog′ra·pher** n. —**ty′po·graph′i·cal** a.

ty·ran′no·saur (-ə sôr′) n. huge, two-footed dinosaur

tyr·an·ny (tir′-) n. 1 government of a tyrant 2 cruel and unjust use of power —**ty·ran′ni·cal** a. —**tyr′an·nize′** v.

ty′rant (tī′-) n. 1 absolute ruler 2 cruel, unjust ruler

U

u·biq·ui·tous (yōō bik′wə təs) a. everywhere at the same time —**u·biq′ui·ty** n.

ud′der n. large, milk-secreting gland of cows, etc.

UFO n., pl. **UFOs** or **UFO′s** unidentified flying object

ugh int. exclamation of disgust, horror, etc.

ug′ly a. -li·er, -li·est 1 unpleasant to see 2 bad 3 dangerous —**ug′li·ness** n.

u′kase (yōō′-) n. official decree

u·ku·le·le (yōō′kə lā′lē) n. small, four-stringed guitar

ul′cer n. open sore, as on the skin —**ul′cer·ate′** v. —**ul′cer·ous** a.

ul·te′ri·or (-tir′ē-) a. beyond what is expressed

ul′ti·mate (-mət) a. 1 farthest 2

final 3 basic —n. final point or result —**ul′ti·mate·ly** adv.

ul·ti·ma′tum n. final offer or demand

ultra- pref. 1 beyond 2 extremely

ul′tra·ma·rine′ a. deep-blue

ul′tra·son′ic a. above the range of humanly audible sound

ul′tra·sound′ n. ultrasonic waves used in medical diagnosis, therapy, etc.

ul′tra·vi′o·let a. of the invisible rays just beyond the violet end of the spectrum

um′ber n. reddish brown

um·bil′i·cal cord n. cord connecting a fetus with the placenta

um′brage (-brij) n. resentment and displeasure

um·brel′la n. cloth screen on a folding frame, carried for protection against rain

um′pire n. 1 one who judges a dispute 2 an official in certain sports —v. act as umpire

un- pref. 1 not, lack of 2 back; reversal of action   See list below

un·a′ble
un·a·fraid′
un·aid′ed
un·a·shamed′
un·au·thor·ized′
un·a·void′a·ble
un·bear′a·ble
un·be·liev′a·ble
un·bi′ased
un·bro′ken
un·but′ton
un·changed′
un·com′fort·a·ble
un·con·trol′la·ble
un·con·ven′tion·al
un·de·served′
un·de·sir′a·ble
un·de·vel′oped
un·dis·cov′ered
un·earned′
un·em·ployed′
un·em·ploy′ment
un·e′ven
un·ex·plained′
un·ex·plored′
un·fair′
un·fas′ten
un·fa′vor·a·ble
un·fit′
un·fore·seen′
un·for′tu·nate
un·gra′cious
un·harmed′
un·heed′ed
un·hurt′
un·i·den′ti·fied′

un'im·por'tant
un'in·hab'it·ed
un'in·jured'
un'in·ter·est·ing
un'in·vit'ed
un·just'
un·lace'
un·man'ly
un·mar'ried
un·named'
un·nec'es·sar·y
un·no'ticed
un'of·fi'cial
un·o'pened
un·or'gan·ized
un·paid'
un·pop'u·lar
un·pre·pared'
un'pro·fes'sion·al
un'pro·tect'ed
un·qual'i·fied
un're·li'a·ble
un·ripe'
un·sat'is·fac'to·ry
un·scram'ble
un·self'ish
un·sight'ly
un·skilled'
un·skill'ful
un·sound'
un·spoiled'
un·suit'a·ble
un·ti'dy
un·tir'ing
un·tried'
un·trou'bled
un·true'
un·want'ed
un·war'rant·ed
un·war'y
un·whole'some
un·will'ing
un·wise'
un·wor'thy
un·wrap'

un·yield'ing

un'a·bridged' a. not abridged; complete

un'ac·count'a·ble a. 1 inexplicable 2 not responsible

un'ac·cus'tomed a. 1 not accustomed (to) 2 unusual

u·nan'i·mous (yōō-) a. without dissent —u'na·nim'i·ty n. —u·nan'i·mous·ly adv.

un'ap·proach'a·ble a. 1 aloof 2 without equal

un·armed' a. having no weapon

un'as·sum'ing a. modest

un'at·tached' a. 1 not attached 2 not engaged or married

un'a·vail'ing a. useless

un'a·ware' a. not aware —adv. unawares

un'a·wares' adv. 1 unintentionally 2 by surprise

un·bal'anced a. 1 not in balance 2 mentally ill

un'be·com'ing a. 1 not suited 2 not proper

un'be·lief' n. lack of belief, esp. in religion —un'be·liev'er n.

un·bend' v. -bent' or -bend'ed, -bend'ing 1 relax 2 straighten

un·bend'ing a. 1 rigid; stiff 2 firm; unyielding

un·blush'ing a. shameless

un·bolt' v. withdraw the bolt of (a door, etc.); open

un·born' a. 1 not born 2 not yet born; future

un·bos'om (-booz'-) v. to tell (secrets)

un·bound'ed a. not restrained

un·bri'dled a. 1 with no bridle on 2 uncontrolled

un·bur'den v. relieve by disclosing (guilt, etc.)

un·called'-for' a. unnecessary and out of place

un·can'ny a. 1 weird 2 unusually good, acute, etc.

un'cer·e·mo'ni·ous a. rudely abrupt

un·cer'tain a. 1 not sure or certain 2 vague 3 not steady or constant —un·cer'tain·ty n., pl. -ties

un·char'i·ta·ble a. severe or harsh

un'cle n. 1 brother of one's father or mother 2 husband of one's aunt

un·com'mon a. 1 not usual 2 extraordinary

un'com·pro·mis'ing a. unyielding; firm

un'con·cern' n. lack of interest or worry; indifference —un'con·cerned' a.

un'con·di'tion·al a. without conditions or limits

un'con·scion·a·ble (-shən-) a. 1 unscrupulous 2 unreasonable

un·con'scious (-shəs) a. 1 not conscious 2 not aware (of) 3 unintentional —the unconscious part of the mind storing feelings, desires, etc. of which one is unaware

un·count'ed a. 1 not counted 2 innumerable

un·couth' (-kōōth') a. rude; crude

un·cov'er v. 1 to disclose 2 remove the cover from

unc'tion n. 1 an anointing 2 anything soothing

unc'tu·ous (-chōō-) a. 1 oily 2

insincerely earnest

un·cut' *a.* 1 not shaped: said of a gem 2 not abridged

un·daunt'ed *a.* not hesitating because of fear

un·de·cid'ed *a.* not (having) decided

un·de·ni'a·ble *a.* that cannot be denied

un'der *prep.* 1 lower than; below; beneath 2 covered by 3 less than 4 below and across 5 subject to 6 undergoing —*adv.* 1 in or to a lower position 2 so as to be covered —*a.* lower

under– *pref.* 1 below than usual or proper

un·der·a·chieve' *v.* fail to do as well as expected

un'der·age' *a.* below the legal age

un'der·brush' *n.* small trees, bushes, etc. in a forest

un'der·car'riage *n.* supporting frame

un'der·clothes' *n.pl.* underwear: also **un'der·cloth'ing**

un'der·cov'er *a.* secret

un'der·cur'rent *n.* underlying tendency, opinion, etc.

un'der·de·vel'oped *a.* inadequately developed, esp. economically

un'der·dog' *n.* one that is expected to lose

un'der·es'ti·mate' *v.* make too low an estimate

un'der·foot' *adv., a.* 1 under the feet 2 in the way

un'der·gar'ment *n.* piece of underwear

un'der·go' *v.* –went', –gone', –go'ing experience; endure

un'der·grad'u·ate (-ət) *n.* college student who does not yet have a degree

un'der·ground' *a., adv.* 1 beneath the earth's surface 2 secret 3 unconventional, radical, etc. —*n.* secret revolutionary movement

un'der·growth' *n.* underbrush

un'der·hand' *a.* 1 with the hand held below the elbow 2 underhanded; sly —*adv.* 1 with an underhand motion 2 in an underhanded way

un'der·hand'ed *a.* sly, deceitful, etc.

un'der·lie' *v.* 1 lie beneath 2 support

un'der·line' *v.* 1 to draw a line under 2 to stress

un'der·ling *n.* subordinate

un'der·ly'ing *a.* basic

un'der·mine' *v.* 1 dig beneath 2 weaken gradually

un'der·neath' *adv., prep.* under; below

un'der·pants' *n.pl.* undergarment of short pants

un'der·pass' *n.* road under a railway or highway

un'der·pin'ning *n.* prop or foundation

un'der·priv'i·leged *a.* needy; poor

un'der·rate' *v.* rate too low

un'der·score' *v.* underline

un'der·sec're·tar'y *n., pl.* –ies assistant secretary

un'der·sell' *v.* sell for less than

un'der·shirt' *n.* undergarment worn under a shirt

un'der·shorts' *n.pl.* men's or boys' short underpants

un'der·stand' *v.* –stood', –stand'ing 1 get the meaning (of) 2 take as a fact 3 know or perceive the nature, etc. of 4 sympathize with —**un'der·stand'a·ble** *a.*

un'der·stand'ing *n.* 1 comprehension 2 intelligence 3 mutual agreement

un'der·state' *v.* say with little or no emphasis

un'der·stud'y *v.* –ied, –y·ing; *n., pl.* –ies (be ready to) substitute for an actor

un'der·take' *v.* –took', –tak'en, –tak'ing 1 begin (a task, etc.) 2 promise —**un'der·tak'ing** *n.*

un'der·tak'er *n.* funeral director

un'der·things' *n.pl.* women's or girls' underwear

un'der·tone' *n.* subdued tone

un'der·tow' (-tō') *n.* strong flow of water back under breaking waves

un'der·wa'ter *a., adv.* beneath the surface of the water

un'der·wear' *n.* clothes worn next to the skin

un'der·weight' *a.* weighing too little

un'der·world' *n.* 1 the world of criminals 2 Hades

un'der·write' *v.* –wrote', –writ'ten, –writ'ing 1 agree to finance 2 write insurance for —**un'der·writ'er** *n.*

un·do' *v.* –did', –done', –do'ing 1 open, untie, etc. 2 cancel or destroy

un·do'ing *n.* 1 a bringing to ruin 2 cause of ruin

un·done' *a.* 1 not done 2 ruined

un·doubt'ed *a.* certain

un·dress' *v.* take the clothes off

un·due' *a.* more than is proper

—**un·du′ly** adv.

un′du·late′ (-joo-, -dyoo-) v. 1 move in waves 2 have or give a wavy form —**un′du·la′tion** n.

un·dy′ing a. eternal

un·earth′ v. 1 dig up from the earth 2 find

un·earth′ly a. 1 supernatural 2 weird

un·eas′y a. **-i·er, -i·est** uncomfortable —**un·eas′i·ness** n.

un·e′qual a. 1 not equal in size, value, etc. 2 not adequate (to)

un·e′qualed a. without equal

un·e·quiv′o·cal a. straightforward; clear

un·ex·pect′ed a. not expected; sudden —**un·ex·pect′ed·ly** adv.

un·fail′ing a. always dependable

un·faith′ful a. 1 not faithful 2 adulterous

un·fa·mil′iar a. 1 not well-known 2 not acquainted (with)

un·feel′ing a. 1 insensible 2 hardhearted; cruel

un·feigned′ (-fānd′) a. real; genuine

un·fin′ished a. 1 incomplete 2 not painted, etc.

un·flap′pa·ble a. [Col.] not easily excited

un·flinch′ing a. steadfast

un·fold′ v. 1 spread out 2 make or become known

un·found′ed a. not based on fact or reason

un·friend′ly a. not friendly, kind, or favorable

un·furl′ v. unfold

un·gain′ly a. awkward

un·gov′ern·a·ble a. unruly

un·guard′ed a. 1 unprotected 2 frank; candid 3 careless

un′guent (-gwent) n. salve

un′gu·late (-gyoo lət, -lāt′) a. having hoofs —n. ungulate mammal

un·hand′ v. let go of

un·hap′py a. **-pi·er, -pi·est** 1 unlucky 2 sad; wretched

un·health′y a. **-i·er, -i·est** 1 not well 2 harmful to health

un·heard′ a. not heard or listened to

un·heard′-of′ a. never known or done before

un·hinge′ v. 1 remove from the hinges 2 unbalance (the mind)

un·ho′ly a. **-li·er, -li·est** 1 not sacred 2 wicked; sinful

un·horse′ v. make fall from a horse

uni- pref. having only one

u′ni·corn′ (yōōn′ə-) n. mythical horse with a horn in its forehead

u′ni·form′ a. 1 never changing 2 all alike —n. special clothes for some group —v. dress in a uniform —**u′ni·form′i·ty** n.

u′ni·fy′ v. **-fied′, -fy′ing** make into one —**u′ni·fi·ca′tion** n.

u′ni·lat′er·al a. 1 of one side only 2 involving only one of several parties

un′im·peach′a·ble a. without fault

un·ion (yōōn′yən) n. 1 a uniting 2 group of nations or states united 3 marriage 4 a labor union

un′ion·ize′ v. organize into a labor union

u·nique (yōō nēk′) a. 1 one and only 2 without equal 3 unusual

un′i·sex′ a. not differentiated for the sexes

u′ni·son n. 1 Mus. sameness of pitch 2 agreement

u′nit n. 1 single part of a whole 2 a special part 3 a standard measure 4 one

u·nite′ v. 1 put together as one; combine 2 join together (in)

u′ni·ty n., pl. **-ties** 1 a being united 2 harmony; agreement

u′ni·ver′sal a. 1 of or for all 2 present everywhere —**u′ni·ver′sal·i·ty** n.

u′ni·ver′sal·ly adv. 1 in every case 2 everywhere

u′ni·verse′ n. 1 space and all things in it 2 the world

u′ni·ver′si·ty n., pl. **-ties** school made up of college and, often, graduate schools

un·kempt′ a. untidy; messy

un·known′ a., n. unfamiliar or unidentified (person or thing)

un·law′ful a. against the law —**un·law′ful·ly** adv.

un·lead′ed a. not containing lead compounds, as gasoline

un·learn′ed a. not educated

un′leash′ v. release as from a leash

un·less′ con. except if

un·like′ a. not alike —prep. not like

un·like′ly a. not likely to happen, be true, succeed, etc.

un·lim′it·ed a. without limits or bounds

un·load′ v. 1 remove (a load) 2 take a load from 3 get rid of

un·lock′ v. open by undoing a lock

un·luck′y a. **-i·er, -i·est** having or bringing bad luck

un·manned' *a.* without people aboard and operated remotely

un·mask' *v.* **1** remove a mask (from) **2** expose

un·mis·tak'a·ble *a.* that cannot be mistaken; clear —**un'mis·tak'a·bly** *adv.*

un·mit'i·gat'ed *a.* **1** not lessened **2** absolute

un·nat'u·ral *a.* **1** abnormal **2** artificial

un·nerve' *v.* to make (someone) lose nerve, courage, etc.

un·num'bered *a.* **1** countless **2** not numbered

un·pack' *v.* take things out of a trunk, box, etc.

un·par'al·leled' *a.* that has no equal or counterpart

un·pleas'ant *a.* offensive; disagreeable

un·prec'e·dent'ed *a.* having no precedent; unique

un·prin'ci·pled *a.* without good principles

un·print'a·ble *a.* not fit to be printed

un·ques'tion·a·ble *a.* certain —**un·ques'tion·a·bly** *adv.*

un'quote' *int.* that ends the quotation

un·rav'el *v.* **1** undo the threads of **2** make clear

un·read' (-red') *a.* **1** not having been read **2** having read little

un·re'al *a.* fantastic

un·re'al·ized' *a.* not having been achieved

un·rea'son·a·ble *a.* **1** not reasonable **2** excessive

un·re·lent'ing *a.* **1** refusing to relent **2** cruel

un·rest' *n.* **1** restlessness **2** angry discontent

un·ri'valed, un·ri'valled *a.* having no rival or equal

un·roll' *v.* to open (something rolled up)

un·ruf'fled *a.* calm; smooth

un·rul'y (-rōōl'ē) *a.* **-i·er, -i·est** not obedient or orderly

un·sa'vor·y *a.* **1** tasting or smelling bad **2** disgusting

un·scathed' (-skāthd') *a.* uninjured

un·screw' *v.* detach or loosen by removing screws

un·scru'pu·lous *a.* without scruples; dishonest

un·seal' *v.* to open

un·sea'son·a·ble *a.* not usual for the season

un·seat' *v.* **1** throw from a seat **2** remove from office

un·seem'ly *a.* improper

un·set'tle *v.* disturb, displace, or disorder

un'so·phis'ti·cat'ed *a.* simple, naive, etc.

un·speak'a·ble *a.* so bad, evil, etc. that description is impossible

un·sta'ble *a.* **1** not fixed, firm, etc. **2** changeable **3** emotionally unsettled

un·stead'y *a.* unstable

un·struc'tured *a.* not strictly organized; loose, free, open, etc.

un·strung' *a.* nervous; upset

un'sub·stan'tial *a.* not solid, firm, real, etc.

un·sung' *a.* not honored

un·tan'gle *v.* free from tangles; straighten out

un·taught' *a.* **1** uneducated **2** got without teaching

un·think'a·ble *a.* that cannot be considered

un·think'ing *a.* thoughtless

un·tie' *v.* unfasten (something tied or knotted)

un·til' *prep.* **1** up to the time of **2** before —*con.* **1** to the point, degree, etc. that **2** before

un·time'ly *a.* **1** premature **2** at the wrong time —*adv.* too soon —**un·time'li·ness** *n.*

un'to *prep.* [Poet.] to

un·told' *a.* **1** not told or revealed **2** very great

un·to'ward (-tō'ərd) *a.* **1** unfortunate **2** hard to control

un·truth' *n.* lie; falsehood —**un·truth'ful** *a.*

un·tu'tored *a.* uneducated

un·used' *a.* **1** not in use **2** unaccustomed (*to*) **3** never used before

un·u'su·al *a.* not usual; rare —**un·u'su·al·ly** *adv.*

un·ut'ter·a·ble *a.* that cannot be spoken or described —**un·ut'ter·a·bly** *adv.*

un·var'nished *a.* **1** plain; simple **2** not varnished

un·veil' *v.* remove a veil from; disclose

un·well' *a.* not well; sick

un·wield'y *a.* **-i·er, -i·est 1** hard to handle because of size, etc. **2** clumsy —**un·wield'i·ness** *n.*

un·wind' *v.* **1** make or become undone or uncoiled **2** relax

un·wit'ting *a.* **1** not knowing **2** not intentional —**un·wit'ting·ly** *adv.*

un·wont'ed *a.* unusual; rare

un·writ'ten *a.* **1** not in writing **2** observed through custom, as some rules

up *adv.* 1 to, in, or on a higher place, level, etc. 2 to a later time 3 upright 4 into action, discussion, etc. 5 aside; away 6 so as to be even 7 completely 8 apiece —*prep.* up along, on, in, etc. —*a.* 1 put, brought, going, or gone up 2 at an end —*v.* **upped, up'ping** [Col.] increase —**ups and downs** changes in fortune —**up to** 1 doing or scheming 2 capable of 3 as many as 4 as far as 5 dependent upon

up'-and-com'ing *a.* 1 promising 2 gaining prominence

up'beat' *a.* [Col.] cheerful or optimistic

up·braid' *v.* scold

up·bring'ing *n.* training received as a child

up'com'ing *a.* coming soon

up·date' (*n.*: up'dāt') *v.* make conform to most recent facts, etc. —*n.* updated information

up·end' *v.* set on end

up'front' *a.* [Col.] 1 forthright 2 in advance

up'grade' *n.* upward slope —*v.* raise in grade or rank

up·heav'al *n.* 1 a heaving up 2 quick, violent change

up·hill' *a., adv.* 1 upward 2 with difficulty

up·hold' *v.* 1 support 2 confirm; sustain

up·hol'ster *v.* fit out (furniture) with coverings, etc. —**up·hol'ster·y** *n.*

up'keep' *n.* 1 maintenance 2 cost of maintenance

up·lift' (*n.*: up'lift') *v.* 1 lift up 2 raise to a better level —*n.* a lifting up

up·on' *prep., adv.* on, or up and on

up'per *a.* higher in place, rank, etc. —*n.* part of a shoe above the sole

up'per·case' *a., n.* (of or in) capital letters

upper hand a position of advantage or control

up'per·most' *a.* highest in place, power, etc. —*adv.* in the highest place; first

up'right' *a.* 1 standing up; erect 2 honest; just —*adv.* in an upright position —*n.* upright pole, beam, etc.

up·ris'ing *n.* a revolt

up'roar' *n.* loud, confused noise or condition

up·roar'i·ous *a.* 1 making an uproar 2 boisterous

up·root' *v.* 1 pull up by the roots 2 remove entirely

up'scale' *a.* for affluent or stylish people

up·set' (*n.*: up'set') *v.* **-set', -set'ting** 1 overturn 2 disturb or distress 3 defeat unexpectedly —*n.* an upsetting —*a.* 1 overturned 2 disturbed

up'shot' *n.* result; outcome

up'side' down *adv.* 1 with the top part underneath 2 in disorder —**up'side'-down'** *a.*

up'stage' *v.* draw attention away from

up'stairs' *adv., a.* to or on an upper floor —*n.* upper floor or floors

up'stand'ing *a.* honorable

up'start' *n.* presumptuous newcomer

up'stream' *adv., a.* against the current of a stream

up'swing' *n.* upward trend

up'take' *n.* a taking up —**quick (or slow) on the uptake** [Col.] quick (or slow) to understand

up'tight' *a.* [Sl.] very tense, nervous, etc.: also **up'-tight'**

up'-to-date' *a.* 1 having the latest facts, ideas, etc. 2 of the newest or latest kind

up'town' *n.* part of city away from the business district

up'turn' *n.* upward trend

up'ward *adv., a.* toward a higher place, position, etc.: also **up'wards** *adv.* —**upward(s) of** more than

u·ra'ni·um *n.* radioactive metallic chemical element

ur'ban *a.* of or in a city —**ur'ban·ize'** *v.*

ur·bane' *a.* suave; refined —**ur·ban'i·ty** *n.*

ur'chin *n.* small mischievous child, esp. a boy

-ure *suf.* 1 act, result, or means of 2 state of being

u·re'a *n.* substance found in urine

u·re'mi·a *n.* toxic condition caused by kidney failure —**u·re'mic** *a.*

u·re'ter *n.* tube from a kidney to the bladder

u·re'thra *n.* duct for discharge of urine from bladder

urge *v.* 1 insist on 2 to force onward 3 plead with 4 incite —*n.* impulse

ur'gent *a.* 1 needing quick action 2 insistent —**ur'gen·cy** *n.*

u·ric (yoor'ik) *a.* of or from urine

u·ri·nal (yoor'ə-) n. fixture in which to urinate

u'ri·nar'y a. of the organs that secrete or discharge urine

u'ri·nate' v. discharge urine from the body

u·rine (yoor'in) n. waste fluid from the kidneys, which passes through the bladder

urn n. 1 footed vase 2 container with a faucet

us pron. the objective case of WE

us'a·ble, use'a·ble a. that can be used

us'age n. 1 treatment 2 custom; habit

use (yōōz; n.: yōōs) v. 1 put into action 2 treat 3 consume —n. 1 a using or being used 2 power or right to use 3 need to use 4 utility or function —used to 1 did once 2 familiar with

used a. not new; secondhand

use'ful a. that can be used; helpful —**use'ful·ness** n.

use'less a. worthless

us'er n. one that uses something; spec., a) drug addict b) computer operator

us'er-friend'ly a. easy to use or understand, as a computer program

ush'er v. show the way to or bring in —n. one who ushers

u'su·al a. in common use; ordinary —**u'su·al·ly** adv.

u·surp' v. take by force and without right —**u'sur·pa'tion** n. —**u·surp'er** n.

u·su·ry (yōō'zhər ē) n. lending of money at an excessive interest rate —**u'su·rer** n. —**u·su'ri·ous** a.

u·ten'sil n. container or tool for a special purpose

u'ter·ine (-in) a. of the uterus

u'ter·us n. hollow female organ in which a fetus grows

u·til'i·tar'i·an (-ter'-) a. useful or practical

u·til'i·ty n., pl. -ties 1 usefulness 2 water, gas, etc. for public use 3 company providing this

u'ti·lize' v. put to use —**u'ti·li·za'tion** n.

ut'most' a. 1 most distant 2 greatest or highest —n. the most possible

U·to'pi·a, u·to'pi·a n. any imaginary place where all things are perfect —**U·to'pi·an, u·to'pi·an** a., n.

ut'ter a. complete; absolute —v. express with the common voice —**ut'ter·ly** adv.

ut'ter·ance n. 1 an uttering 2 something said

ut'ter·most' a., n. utmost

u'vu·la (yōō'vyoo-) n., pl. -las or -lae' (-lē') small part hanging down above the back of the tongue

V

va'cant a. 1 empty; unoccupied 2 free from work 3 stupid —**va'can·cy** n., pl. -cies

va'cate' v. 1 make a place empty 2 annul

va·ca'tion v., n. rest from work, study, etc. —**va·ca'tion·er, va·ca'tion·ist** n.

vac'cine' (-sēn') n. preparation injected for immunity to a disease —**vac'ci·nate'** v. —**vac'ci·na'tion** n.

vac'il·late' (vas'-) v. 1 waver 2 show indecision —**vac'il·la'tion** n.

vac'u·ous a. 1 empty 2 stupid; senseless —**va·cu'i·ty** n., pl. -ties

vac'u·um (-yōō əm, -yōōm') n. 1 completely empty space 2 space with most of the air or gas taken out —a. of, having, or working by a vacuum —v. use a vacuum cleaner

vacuum cleaner n. machine that cleans by means of suction

vacuum tube n. electron tube

vag'a·bond' a., n. vagrant

va·ga·ry (or vā'gər ē) n., pl. -ies odd action or idea

va·gi'na (-jī'-) n. canal leading to the uterus —**vag'i·nal** a.

va'grant n. homeless wanderer; tramp —a. 1 nomadic 2 wayward —**va'gran·cy** n.

vague (vāg) a. indefinite; unclear —**vague'ly** adv. —**vague'ness** n.

vain a. 1 conceited 2 futile 3 worthless —**in vain** 1 without success 2 profanely

vain'glo'ry n. boastful pride —**vain'glo'ri·ous** a.

val'ance (val'-) n. short drapery forming a border

vale n. [Poet.] valley

val'e·dic'to·ry n. farewell speech, as at graduation —**val'e·dic·to'ri·an** n.

va'lence (vā'-) n. Chem. combining capacity of an element

val'en·tine' n. sweetheart or card for St. Valentine's Day

val·et (val'ət, va lā') n. male

servant to another man

val'iant (-yənt) *a.* brave

val'id *a.* 1 true or sound 2 having legal force —**val'i·date'** *v.* —**va·lid'i·ty** *n.*

va·lise' (-lēs') *n.* suitcase

val'ley *n., pl.* **-leys** 1 low land between hills 2 land drained by a river system

val'or *n.* courage; bravery —**val'or·ous** *a.*

val'u·a·ble *a.* 1 having value 2 worth much money —*n.* valuable thing: *usually used in pl.*

val·u·a'tion *n.* 1 the fixing of a thing's value 2 value set on a thing

val'ue *n.* 1 importance, desirability, utility, etc. 2 worth in money 3 buying power 4 *pl.* standards —*v.* 1 set the value of 2 think highly of —**val'ue·less** *a.*

valve *n.* 1 device in a pipe, etc. to control the flow of a gas or liquid 2 body membrane like this

vamp *n.* part of a shoe over the instep

vam'pire *n.* 1 one who preys on others 2 bat that lives on other animals' blood: also **vampire bat**

van *n.* 1 vanguard 2 large closed truck

van'dal *n.* one who destroys another's property on purpose

van'dal·ize' *v.* destroy maliciously —**van'dal·ism'** *n.*

Van·dyke' (beard) (-dīk') *n.* short, pointed beard

vane *n.* 1 device that swings to show wind direction 2 blade of a windmill, etc.

van'guard' *n.* 1 front part of an army 2 leading group or position in a movement

va·nil'la *n.* flavoring made from the pods of an orchid

van'ish *v.* disappear

van'i·ty *n., pl.* **-ties** 1 a being vain, or conceited 2 futility 3 low table with mirror

van'quish *v.* conquer

van'tage *n.* 1 advantage 2 position allowing a clear view, etc.: also **vantage point**

vap'id *a.* tasteless; dull

va'por *n.* 1 thick mist, as fog or steam 2 gas formed by heating a liquid or solid —**va'por·ous** *a.*

va'por·ize' *v.* change into vapor —**va'por·i·za'tion** *n.* —**va'por·iz'er** *n.*

var'i·a·ble *a.* that varies or can be varied —*n.* variable thing

var'i·ance *n.* a varying —**at variance** disagreeing

var'i·ant *a.* slightly different —*n.* variant form

var'i·a'tion *n.* 1 change in form, etc. 2 amount of change

var'i·col'ored *a.* of several or many colors

var'i·cose' *a.* swollen, as veins

var'ied *a.* 1 of different kinds 2 changed

var'i·e·gat'ed *a.* 1 marked with different colors 2 varied

va·ri'e·ty *n., pl.* **-ties** 1 change 2 kind; sort 3 number of different kinds

var'i·ous *a.* 1 of several kinds 2 several or many

var'mint *n.* [Col. or Dial.] vermin; vile creature

var'nish *n.* resinous liquid forming a hard, glossy surface —*v.* cover with this

var'si·ty *n., pl.* **-ties** school's main team in contests, esp. in athletic events

var'y *v.* **-ied, -y·ing** 1 make or become different; change 2 differ

vas'cu·lar *a.* of vessels carrying blood, etc.

vase *n.* open container for flowers, etc.

vas·ec'to·my *n., pl.* **-mies** removal or tying of sperm ducts

Vas·e·line' (-lēn') *trademark* petrolatum —*n.* [v-] petrolatum

vas'sal *n.* 1 feudal tenant 2 subject, servant, etc.

vast *a.* very great in size, degree, etc. —**vast'ly** *adv.* —**vast'ness** *n.*

vat *n.* large tank or cask

vaude'ville (vôd'vil) *n.* stage show with song and dance acts, skits, etc.

vault *n.* 1 arched roof or ceiling 2 arched room 3 burial chamber 4 room for keeping money, etc. as in a bank 5 a vaulting or leap —*v.* 1 provide with a vault 2 leap over, balancing on a pole or the hands —**vault'er** *n.*

vaunt *v., n.* boast

VCR *n.* videocassette recorder

VDT *n.* video display terminal

veal *n.* meat from a calf

veer *v., n.* shift; turn

veg'e·ta·ble (vej'tə-) *n.* 1 plant eaten raw or cooked 2 any plant

veg'e·tar'i·an *n.* one who eats no meat —*a.* 1 of vegetarians 2 of vegetables only

veg'e·tate' *v.* live or grow like a plant

veg'e·ta'tion n. plant life

ve'he·ment (-ə-) a. 1 showing strong feeling 2 violent —**ve'he·mence** n.

ve'hi·cle (-ə-) n. means of conveying; esp. a device on wheels —**ve·hic'u·lar** a.

veil (vāl) n. 1 piece of thin fabric worn by women over the face or head 2 thing that conceals —v. 1 cover with a veil 2 conceal

vein (vān) n. 1 blood vessel going to the heart 2 line in a leaf or an insect's wing 3 body of minerals in a fissure or zone of rock 4 colored streak 5 trace or quality —v. mark as with veins

Vel'cro trademark nylon material for fastenings, with opposing strips of tiny hooks and clinging pile —n. [v-] this material

veld, veldt (velt) n. South African grassy land

vel'lum n. fine parchment

ve·loc'i·ty n. speed

ve·lour', ve·lours' (-loor') n., pl. -lours (-loorz', loor') fabric with a velvety nap

vel'vet n. fabric of silk, rayon, etc. with a soft, thick pile —**vel'vet·y** a.

vel'vet·een' n. cotton cloth with a nap like velvet

ve'nal a. open to bribery —**ve·nal'i·ty** n.

vend v. sell —**ven'dor, vend'er** n.

ven·det'ta n. feud, esp. vengeful one between families

ve·neer' n. thin, covering layer, as of fine wood —v. cover with a veneer

ven'er·a·ble a. worthy of respect because of age, etc. —**ven'er·a·bil'i·ty** n.

ven'er·ate' v. show deep respect for —**ven'er·a'tion** n.

ve·ne're·al (-nir'ē-) a. of or passed on by sexual intercourse

Ve·ne'tian blind (-shən) n. [also v- b-] window blind of thin, adjustable slats

venge'ance n. revenge —**with a vengeance** 1 with great force 2 very much

venge'ful a. seeking revenge

ve'ni·al a. pardonable

ven'i·son n. flesh of deer

ven'om n. 1 poison of some snakes, spiders, etc. 2 malice —**ven'om·ous** a.

vent n. 1 outlet 2 opening to let gas, etc. out —v. let out

ven'ti·late' v. circulate fresh air in —**ven'ti·la'tion** n. —**ven'ti·la'tor** n.

ven'tral a. of, near, or on the belly

ven'tri·cle n. either lower chamber of the heart

ven·tril'o·quism' n. art of making one's voice seem to come from another point —**ven·tril'o·quist** n.

ven'ture n. risky undertaking —v. 1 place in danger 2 dare to do, say, etc.

ven'ture·some a. 1 daring; bold 2 risky

ven'tur·ous a. venturesome

ven'ue' (-yōō') n. 1 locality of a crime, trial, etc. 2 locale of a large gathering

ve·ra'cious (-shəs) a. truthful or true —**ve·rac'i·ty** (-ras'-) n.

ve·ran'da, ve·ran'dah n. open, roofed porch

verb n. word expressing action or being

ver'bal a. 1 of or in words 2 in speech 3 like or derived from a verb —n. verbal derivative, as a gerund —**ver'bal·ly** adv.

ver·ba'tim adv., a. word for word

ver·bi·age' (-bē it') n. wordiness

ver·bose' a. wordy —**ver·bos'i·ty** (-bäs'-) n.

ver'dant a. covered with green vegetation

ver'dict n. decision, as of a jury in a law case

ver'di·gris' (-grēs') n. greenish coating on brass, copper, or bronze

ver'dure (-jər) n. 1 green vegetation 2 color of this

verge v., n. (be on) the edge or border

ver'i·fy' v. -fied', -fy'ing 1 prove to be true 2 test the accuracy of —**ver'i·fi'a·ble** a. —**ver'i·fi·ca'tion** n.

ver'i·ly adv. [Ar.] really

ver'i·ta·ble a. true; real

ver'i·ty n., pl. -ties (a) truth

ver·mil'ion n. bright yellowish red

ver'min n., pl. -min small, destructive animal, as a fly or rat

ver·mouth' (-mōōth') n. a white wine

ver·nac'u·lar a., n. (of) the everyday speech of a country or place

ver'nal a. 1 of or in the spring 2 springlike

ver'sa·tile (-təl) a. able to do many things well —**ver'sa·til'i·ty**

verse *n.* 1 poetry 2 stanza 3 short division of a Bible chapter

versed *a.* skilled

ver'si·fy' *v.* **-fied'**, **-fy'ing** 1 write poetry 2 tell in verse —**ver'si·fi·ca'tion** *n.* —**ver'si·fi'er** *n.*

ver'sion *n.* 1 translation 2 an account; report

ver'sus *prep.* against

ver'te·bra *n.*, *pl.* **-brae** (-brē', -brā') or **-bras** any single bone of the spinal column

ver'te·brate (-brət) *n.*, *a.* (animal) having a spinal column

ver'tex *n.*, *pl.* **-tex'es** or **-ti·ces'** (-tə sēz') highest or farthest point

ver'ti·cal *n.*, *a.* (line, plane, etc.) that is straight up and down

ver'ti·go' *n.* dizzy feeling

verve *n.* vigor; enthusiasm

ver'y *a.* 1 complete; absolute 2 same; identical 3 actual —*adv.* 1 extremely 2 truly

ves'i·cle *n.* small, membranous cavity, sac, etc. —**ve·sic'u·lar** *a.*

ves'pers *n.* [also **V-**] evening prayer or service

ves'sel *n.* 1 container 2 ship or boat 3 tube of the body, as a vein

vest *n.* 1 man's sleeveless garment 2 undershirt —*v.* 1 to clothe 2 give power over or right to

ves'ti·bule' (-byool') *n.* 1 small entrance hall 2 enclosed passage

ves'tige (-tij) *n.* a trace or mark, esp. of something gone —**ves·tig'i·al** *a.*

vest'ment *n.* garment, esp. one for a clergyman

ves'try *n.*, *pl.* **-tries** 1 church meeting room 2 lay church group with certain powers

vet *n.* 1 veteran 2 veterinarian 3 veterinary

vetch *n.* plant grown for fodder

vet'er·an *a.* experienced —*n.* 1 former member of the armed forces 2 long-time employee, etc.

vet'er·i·nar'i·an *n.* doctor for animals

vet'er·i·nar'y *a.* of the medical care of animals —*n.* veterinarian

ve'to *n.*, *pl.* **-toes** 1 power, or right, to prohibit or reject 2 use of this —*v.* **-toed**, **-to·ing** use a veto on

vex *v.* annoy; disturb —**vex·a'tion** *n.* —**vex·a'tious** *a.*

VHS *trademark* electronic system for recording videocassettes

vi·a (vī'ə, vē'ə) *prep.* by way of

vi'a·ble *a.* able to exist

vi'a·duct' *n.* bridge held up by a series of towers

vi'al *n.* small bottle

vi'and *n.* 1 article of food 2 *pl.* fine food

vibes *n.* [Col.] vibraphone —*n.pl.* [Sl.] qualities producing emotional reaction

vi'brant *a.* 1 quivering 2 resonant 3 energetic

vi'bra·phone' *n.* musical instrument like a xylophone, with electrically enhanced sound

vi'brate' *v.* 1 move rapidly back and forth; quiver 2 thrill —**vi·bra'tion** *n.* —**vi'bra'tor** *n.*

vi·bur'num *n.* shrub or small tree with white flowers

vic'ar *n.* 1 Church of England priest 2 *R.C.Ch.* deputy of a bishop, etc.

vic'ar·age *n.* vicar's residence

vi·car'i·ous (-ker'-) *a.* 1 felt by imagined participation 2 taking another's place —**vi·car'i·ous·ly** *adv.*

vice *n.* 1 bad or evil conduct 2 bad or evil habit

vice- *pref.* substitute or subordinate

vice'-pres'i·dent *n.* officer next in rank to a president

vice'roy' *n.* deputy ruler for a sovereign

vi'ce ver'sa (vī'sə, vis'-) *adv.* the other way around

vi·cin'i·ty *n.*, *pl.* **-ties** 1 nearness 2 nearby area

vi'cious (vish'əs) *a.* 1 evil 2 unruly 3 malicious —**vi'cious·ly** *adv.* —**vi'cious·ness** *n.*

vi·cis'si·tude' (-sis'ə-) *n.* any of one's ups and downs; change

vic'tim *n.* 1 one killed, hurt, etc. 2 one cheated, tricked, etc. —**vic'tim·ize'** *v.*

vic'tor *n.* winner

vic·to'ri·ous *a.* having won a victory; conquering

vic'to·ry *n.*, *pl.* **-ries** success in war or any struggle

vict'uals (vit'lz) *n.pl.* [Dial. or Col.] food

vid'e·o' *a.*, *n.* 1 (of) television 2 (of) performance on videocassette, etc.

vid'e·o·cas·sette' *n.* cassette containing videotape, recorded on and played back esp. by using a videocassette recorder

vid'e·o·tape' *n.* magnetic tape

for recording and playing back images and sounds —v. to record on a videotape

vie v. **vied, vy'ing** to compete as in a contest

view n. 1 a looking 2 range of vision 3 idea or thought 4 scene 5 opinion 6 aim; goal —v. 1 look at or see 2 consider —**in view** of because of

view'point' n. 1 place of observation 2 attitude

vig'il n. 1 watchful staying awake 2 watch kept 3 eve of a religious festival

vig'i·lant a. watchful —**vig'i·lance** n.

vig'i·lan·te (-tē) n. one of a group illegally organized to punish crime

vi·gnette (vin yet') n. 1 short literary sketch 2 picture that shades off at the edges

vig'or n. active force; strength and energy —**vig'or·ous** a. —**vig'or·ous·ly** adv.

vik'ing n. [also V-] Scandinavian pirate of the Middle Ages

vile a. 1 evil; wicked 2 disgusting 3 lowly and bad

vil'i·fy v. **-fied, -fy'ing** defame or slander

vil'la n. showy country house

village n. small town

vil'lain (-ən) n. evil or wicked person —**vil'lain·ous** a. —**vil'lain·y** n.

vim n. energy; vigor

vin'ai·grette' (-ə-) n. dressing of vinegar, oil, herbs, etc.

vin'di·cate v. 1 clear from criticism, blame, etc. 2 justify —**vin'di·ca'tion** n.

vin·dic'tive a. 1 revengeful in spirit 2 done in revenge

vine n. plant with a stem that grows along the ground or climbs a support

vin'e·gar n. sour liquid made by fermenting cider, wine, etc. —**vin'e·gar·y** a.

vine'yard (vin'yərd) n. land where grapevines are grown

vin'tage (-tij) n. wine of a certain region and year

vint'ner n. 1 wine merchant 2 one who makes wine

vi'nyl (-nəl) a. of a group of chemical compounds used in making plastics

vi·o'la (vē-) n. instrument like, but larger than, the violin —**vi·ol'ist** n.

vi'o·late' v. 1 break (a law, etc.) 2 rape 3 desecrate 4 disturb —

vi'o·la'tion n. —**vi'o·la'tor** n.

vi'o·lent a. 1 showing or acting with wild force or feeling 2 intense —**vi'o·lence** n.

vi'o·let n. delicate spring flower, usually bluish-purple

vi'o·lin' n. four-stringed instrument played with a bow —**vi'o·lin'ist** n.

vi'o·lon·cel'lo (vē'-) n., pl. **-los** cello

VIP (vē'ī pē') n. very important person

vi'per n. 1 venomous snake 2 treacherous person

vi·ra'go (vi rä'-) n., pl. **-goes** or **-gos** shrewish woman

vir'gin n. person, esp. a woman, who has not had sexual intercourse —a. chaste, untouched, pure, etc. —**vir·gin'i·ty** n.

Vir'go sixth sign of the zodiac; Virgin

vir'ile (-əl) a. 1 masculine 2 strong, vigorous, etc. —**vi·ril'i·ty** n.

vir'tu·al (-chōō-) a. being so in effect if not in fact —**vir'tu·al·ly** adv.

vir'tue n. 1 moral excellence 2 good quality, esp. a moral one 3 chastity —**by** (or **in**) **virtue of** because of —**vir'tu·ous** a.

vir·tu·o'so n., pl. **-sos** musician, etc. having great skill —**vir·tu·os'i·ty** n.

vir'u·lent (-yŏō-) a. 1 deadly 2 full of hate —**vir'u·lence** n.

vi'rus n. 1 infective agent that causes disease 2 harmful influence 3 unauthorized computer program instructions added as a joke or to sabotage —**vi'ral** a.

vi·sa (vē'zə) n. endorsement on a passport, granting entry into a country

vis·age (viz'ij) n. the face

vis-à-vis (vēz'ə vē') prep. in relation to

vis'cer·a (-ər ə) n.pl. internal organs of the body —**vis'cer·al** a.

vis'cid (-id) a. viscous

vis'count' (vī'-) n. nobleman above a baron

vis'cous (-kəs) a. thick, syrupy, and sticky —**vis·cos'i·ty** n.

vise n. device with adjustable jaws for holding an object firmly

vis·i·bil'i·ty n. distance within which things can be seen

vis'i·ble a. that can be seen; evident —**vis'i·bly** adv.

vi'sion n. 1 power of seeing 2 something seen in a dream, trance, etc. **3** mental image **4** foresight

vi'sion·ar·y a., n., pl. **-ies** idealistic and impractical (person)

vis'it v. **1** go or come to see **2** stay with as a guest **3** afflict — n. a visiting —**vis'i·tor** n.

vis·it·a'tion n. **1** visit to inspect **2** punishment sent by God

vi'sor n. **1** movable part of a helmet, covering the face **2** brim on a cap for shading the eyes

vis'ta n. view; scene

vis'u·al (vizh'-) a. **1** of or used in seeing **2** visible

vis'u·al·ize' v. form a mental image of

vi'tal a. **1** of life **2** essential to life **3** very important **4** full of life —**vi'tal·ly** adv.

vi·tal'i·ty n. **1** energy; vigor **2** power to survive

vi'tal·ize' v. give life or vigor to

vi'ta·min n. any of certain substances vital to good health: vitamins A and D are found in fish-liver oil, eggs, etc.; vitamin B (complex), in liver, yeast, etc.; vitamin C, in citrus fruits

vi'ti·ate' (vish'ē-) v. make bad; spoil —**vi'ti·a'tion** n.

vit're·ous a. of or like glass

vit'ri·fy' v. **-fied'**, **-fy'ing** change into glass by heating

vit'ri·ol (-ōl) n. caustic remarks —**vit'ri·ol'ic** (-äl'-) a.

vi·tu'per·ate' v. berate

vi·va'cious (-shəs) a. spirited; lively —**vi·vac'i·ty** n.

viv'id a. **1** full of life **2** bright; intense **3** strong; active —**viv'id·ly** adv.

viv'i·fy' v. **-fied'**, **-fy'ing** give life to

vi·vip'a·rous a. bearing living young, as most mammals

viv'i·sec'tion n. surgery on living animals for medical research

vix'en n. **1** female fox **2** shrewish woman

vo·cab'u·lar·y n., pl. **-ies** all the words used by a person, group, etc. or listed in a dictionary, etc.

vo'cal a. **1** of or by the voice **2** speaking freely —**vo'cal·ly** adv.

vocal cords n. membranes in the larynx that vibrate to make voice sounds

vo'cal·ist n. singer

vo'cal·ize' v. speak or sing

vo·ca'tion n. one's profession, trade, or career —**vo·ca'tion·al** a.

vod'ka n. Russian alcoholic liquor made from grain

vogue (vōg) n. **1** current fashion **2** popularity

voice n. **1** sound made through the mouth **2** ability to make such sound **3** sound like this **4** right to express one's opinion, etc. **5** expression —v. utter or express

voice box n. larynx

voice mail n. electronic storage and delivery of telephone messages

voice'-o'ver n. voice of an unseen speaker, as on TV

void a. **1** empty; vacant **2** lacking **3** of no legal force —n. empty space —v. **1** to empty **2** cancel

voile (voil) n. thin fabric

vol'a·tile (-təl) a. **1** quickly evaporating **2** changeable —**vol'a·til'i·ty** n.

vol·ca'no n., pl. **-noes** or **-nos** mountain formed by erupting molten rock —**vol·can'ic** a.

vo·li'tion n. WILL (n. 3)

vol'ley n., v., pl. **-leys 1** discharge (of) a number of weapons together **2** return (of) a tennis ball before it hits the ground

vol'ley·ball' n. game between teams hitting a large, light ball back and forth over a net

volt n. unit of electromotive force

volt'age n. electromotive force, shown in volts

volt'me'ter n. instrument for measuring voltage

vol'u·ble a. talkative

vol'ume n. **1** a book **2** cubic measure **3** amount **4** loudness of sound

vo·lu'mi·nous a. **1** filling or producing volumes **2** large; full

vol'un·tar'y a. **1** by choice; of one's own free will **2** controlled by the will —**vol'un·tar'i·ly** adv.

vol'un·teer' n. offer, give, etc. of one's own free will —n. one who volunteers

vo·lup'tu·ous (-chōō əs) a. sensual

vom'it v., n. (have) matter from the stomach ejected through the mouth

voo'doo' n. religion of the West Indies, based on magic, charms, etc.

vo·ra'cious (-shəs) a. **1** greedy or ravenous **2** very eager

vor'tex n., pl. **-tex'es** or **-ti·ces'**

(-tə sēz´) 1 whirlpool 2 whirlwind

vo´ta·ry n., pl. **-ries** worshiper; devotee

vote n. 1 a decision or choice shown on a ballot, etc. 2 all the votes 3 the right to vote —v. 1 cast a vote 2 decide by vote — **vot´er** n.

vo´tive a. given or done to fulfill a vow or promise

vouch v. give or be a guarantee (for)

vouch´er n. a paper serving as proof of payment, etc.

vouch·safe´ v. be kind enough to grant

vow v., n. (make) a solemn promise or statement —**take vows** enter a religious order

vow´el n. speech sound of the letters a, e, i, o, u

voy´age n., v. journey by ship

voy·eur´ (vwä yur´) n. one having very strong interest in viewing sexual activities, etc.

vul´can·ize´ v. treat rubber to make it stronger and more elastic

vul´gar a. 1 popular 2 lacking culture; crude —**vul´gar·ly** adv.

vul´gar·ism´ n. coarse word or phrase that is considered improper

vul·gar´i·ty (-ger´-) n. 1 vulgar state or quality 2 pl. **-ties** vulgar act, etc.

vul´ner·a·ble a. 1 that can be hurt, attacked, etc. 2 easily hurt; sensitive —**vul´ner·a·bil´i·ty** n.

vul´ture n. 1 large bird of prey 2 greedy, ruthless person

vul´va n. external female sex organs

W

wack´y a. **-i·er, -i·est** [Sl.] erratic, eccentric, or irrational

wad n. 1 small, soft mass 2 small lump —v. **wad´ded, wad´ding** 1 roll into a wad 2 stuff as with padding

wad´dle v., n. walk with short steps, swaying from side to side

wade v. 1 walk through water, mud, etc. 2 proceed with difficulty 3 cross by wading

wa´fer n. 1 thin, crisp cracker 2 disklike thing

waf´fle n. crisp cake baked between two flat, studded plates (**waffle iron**)

waft v. carry or move lightly over water or through the air —n. 1 odor, sound, etc. carried through the air 2 wafting motion

wag v. **wagged, wag´ging** move rapidly back and forth or up and down —n. 1 a wagging 2 a wit; comic

wage v. take part in —n. pl. money paid for work done

wa´ger n., v. bet

wag´gish a. 1 roguishly merry 2 said, done, etc. in jest

wag´gle v. wag abruptly

wag´on n. four-wheeled vehicle, esp. for hauling

waif n. homeless child

wail v., n. 1 (make a) loud, sad cry 2 lament

wain´scot n. wall paneling of wood —v. panel with wood

waist n. 1 body part between the ribs and the hips 2 waistline

waist´band´ n. band fitting around the waist on slacks, a skirt, etc.

waist´coat´ (or wes´kət) n. [Br.] man's vest

waist´line´ n. middle or narrow part of the waist

wait v. 1 remain until something occurs 2 remain undone 3 serve food at 4 await —n. act or time of waiting —**wait on** (or **upon**) 1 be a servant to 2 serve food to

wait´er n. man who serves food at table —**wait´ress** n.fem.

waiting list n. list of applicants, as for a vacancy

waiting room n. room where people wait, as in a doctor's office

waive v. 1 give up, as a right 2 postpone

waiv´er n. Law waiving of a right, claim, etc.

wake v. **woke** or **waked, waked** or **wok´en, wak´ing** 1 come or bring out of a sleep 2 become alert (to) 3 stir up —n. 1 all-night vigil over a corpse 2 track or trail left behind

wake´ful a. 1 watchful 2 unable to sleep

wak´en v. to wake

wale n. 1 welt 2 ridge, as on corduroy

walk v. 1 go on foot at moderate speed 2 walk along, over, with, etc. 3 Baseball advance to first base by a walk —n. 1 way of walking 2 stroll; hike 3 path for walking 4 Baseball advancement by batter to first base on four pitches not strikes —**walk**

of life way of living

walk'ie·talk'ie n. portable radio for sending and receiving

walk'out' n. **1** labor strike **2** abrupt departure in protest

walk'-up' n. apartment house without an elevator

wall n. upright structure that encloses, divides, etc. —v. to divide, or close up, with a wall

wal'la·by (wäl'-) n., pl. **-bies** or **-by** small kangaroo

wal'let n. flat case for carrying money, cards, etc.

wall'eye' n. North American freshwater food fish

wall'flow'er n. [Col.] shy or unpopular person

wal'lop [Col.] v. **1** hit hard **2** defeat completely —n. a hard blow

wal'low v. **1** roll around in mud or filth, as pigs do **2** live selfishly

wall'pa'per v., n. (apply) paper for covering walls or ceilings

wall'-to-wall' a. covering a floor completely

wal'nut' n. **1** tree bearing an edible nut in a hard shell **2** its nut **3** its wood

wal'rus n. large seallike animal with two tusks

waltz n. ballroom dance in 3/4 time —v. dance a waltz

wam'pum (wäm'-) n. beads used as money by North American Indians

wan (wän) a. sickly pale

wand n. slender rod, as one of supposed magic power

wan'der v. **1** roam idly about **2** go astray; stray —**wan'der·er** n.

wan'der·lust' n. strong urge to wander or travel

wane v. **1** get smaller, weaker, etc. **2** approach the end —n. a waning

wan'gle v. [Col.] get by sly or tricky means

want v. **1** wish for; desire **2** need **3** lack —n. **1** lack; need **2** poverty **3** desire

want'ing a. **1** lacking **2** inadequate —prep. minus

wan'ton a. **1** senseless and cruel **2** irresponsible **3** immoral —n. wanton person

wap·i·ti (wäp'ət ē) n. North American elk

war n. **1** armed conflict, as between nations **2** any fight —v. **warred, war'ring** carry on war —**war'like'** a.

war'ble v. sing with trills, runs,

etc. —n. a warbling —**war'bler** n.

ward n. **1** one under the care of a guardian **2** division of a hospital **3** voting district of a city —**ward off** turn aside

-ward suf. in a (specified) direction: also **-wards**

war'den n. **1** one who takes care of something **2** head official of a prison

ward'er n. watchman; guard

ward'robe' n. **1** a closet for clothes **2** all one's clothes

ware n. **1** thing for sale: usually used in pl. **2** pottery

ware'house' n. building where goods are stored

war'fare' n. war or any conflict

war'head' n. front part of a bomb, etc., with the explosive

war'lock' n. wizard; male witch

warm a. **1** moderately hot **2** enthusiastic **3** kind and loving —v. make or become warm —**warm'ly** adv.

warmed'-o'ver a. **1** reheated **2** presented again, without significant change

warm'heart'ed a. kind; loving

war'mon·ger (-muŋ'-, -mäŋ'-) n. one who tries to cause war

warmth n. **1** a being warm **2** strong feeling

warn v. **1** tell of danger; advise to be careful **2** inform; let know —**warn'ing** n., a.

warp v. **1** bend or twist out of shape **2** distort —n. **1** a warping or twist **2** long threads in a loom

war'rant n. **1** justification **2** legal writ authorizing an arrest, search, etc. —v. **1** authorize **2** justify

warrant officer n. officer just above enlisted man

war'ran·ty n., pl. **-ties** GUARANTEE (n. 1)

war'ren n. (limited) area in which rabbits are raised

war'ri·or n. soldier

war'ship' n. ship for combat use

wart n. small, hard growth on the skin —**wart'y** a.

war·y (wer'ē) a. **-i·er, -i·est** on guard; cautious —**wary of** careful of —**war'i·ly** adv.

was v. pt. of BE: used with he, she, or it

wash v. **1** clean with water **2** wash clothes **3** flow over or against **4** remove by washing **5** coat thinly —n. **1** a washing **2** clothes (to be) washed **3** rush of water 4 eddy from propeller, oars, etc. —**wash'a·ble** a.

wash'board' n. ridged board to scrub clothes on

wash'bowl' n. bowl for washing the hands and face: also **wash'ba·sin**

wash'cloth' n. small cloth to wash the face or body

washed'-out' a. [Col.] 1 tired 2 pale

washed'-up' a. 1 [Col.] tired 2 [Sl.] having failed

wash'er n. 1 machine for washing 2 flat ring used to make a bolt, nut, etc. fit tight 3 one who washes

wash'out' n. 1 washing away of soil, etc. 2 [Sl.] a failure

wash'room' n. restroom

wash'stand' n. plumbing fixture with a washbowl

was'n't was not

wasp n. flying insect: some have a sharp sting

wasp'ish a. bad-tempered

was·sail (wäs'əl) n. toast (drink)

waste v. 1 use needlessly 2 fail to take advantage of 3 wear away 4 lose strength or weaken 5 destroy —a. 1 barren or wild, as land 2 left over —n. 1 a wasting 2 wasted matter; refuse; etc. 3 wasteland —**go to waste** be wasted —**lay waste (to)** devastate —**waste'ful** a.

waste'bas'ket n. container for discarded paper, etc.

was·trel (wās'trəl) n. profligate person

watch n. 1 act of guarding or observing 2 guard(s), or period of guard duty 3 small clock for wrist or pocket 4 Naut. period of duty, or crew on duty —v. 1 keep vigil 2 observe 3 guard or tend 4 be alert (for) —**watch out** be alert or careful —**watch'ful** a.

watch'dog' n. 1 dog kept to guard property 2 one that watches to prevent waste, etc.

watch'man n., pl. **-men** person hired to guard

watch'word' n. slogan

wa'ter n. 1 colorless liquid of rivers, lakes, etc. 2 water solution 3 body secretion, as urine —v. 1 to supply with water 2 dilute with water 3 fill with tears 4 secrete saliva —a. of, for, in, or by water

water buffalo n. oxlike work animal of Asia and Africa

wa'ter·col'or n. 1 paint made by mixing pigment and water 2 picture painted with such paints

wa'ter·course' n. river, brook, canal, etc.

wa'ter·craft' n., pl. **-craft'** boat, ship, or other water vehicle

wa'ter·cress' n. water plant with leaves used in salads

wa'ter·fall' n. steep fall of water, as from a cliff

wa'ter·fowl' n. swimming bird

wa'ter·front' n. land or docks at the edge of a river, harbor, etc.

wa'ter·lil'y n., pl. **-ies** water plant with large, showy flowers

wa'ter·logged' a. soaked or filled with water

wa'ter·mark' n. 1 mark showing how high water has risen 2 design pressed into paper —v. to mark (paper) with a watermark

wa'ter·mel'on n. large melon with juicy, red pulp

water moccasin n. large, poisonous snake of southern U.S.

wa'ter·proof' v., a. (to make) impervious to water

wa'ter·shed' n. 1 area a river systems drains 2 ridge between two such areas

wa'ter·ski' v. be towed over water on a kind of ski

wa'ter·spout' n. whirling water funnel rising from sea

water table n. level below which the ground is saturated with water

wa'ter·tight' a. so tight no water can get through

wa'ter·way' n. navigable river, lake, canal, etc.

wa'ter·works' n.pl. system of reservoirs, pumps, etc. supplying water to a city

wa'ter·y a. 1 of, like, or full of water 2 diluted

watt n. unit of electric power —**watt'age** n.

wat'tle (wät'l) n. 1 sticks woven with twigs 2 flap of skin hanging at the throat of a chicken, etc.

wave v. 1 move to and fro 2 wave the hand, etc., or signal thus 3 arrange in curves —n. 1 curving swell moving along on the ocean, etc. 2 wavelike vibration 3 curve(s), as in the hair 4 a waving, as of the hand —**wav'y** a., **-i·er**, **-i·est**

wa'ver v. 1 flutter, falter, flicker, etc. 2 show indecision —n. a wavering

wax n. 1 plastic substance secreted by bees 2 substance like this, as paraffin —v. 1 put polish or wax on 2 get larger, stronger, etc. 3 to become —**wax'y** a., **-i·er, -i·est** —**wax'en** a.

wax bean n. bean with long, edible yellow pods

wax museum n. exhibit of wax figures of famous people: also **wax'works'**

wax paper n. paper made moisture-proof by a wax coating: also **waxed paper**

way n. 1 road or route 2 movement forward 3 method, manner, etc. 4 distance 5 direction 6 particular 7 wish; will 8 pl. framework on which a ship is built —adv. [Col.] far —**by the way** incidentally —**by way of** passing through 2 as a means of —**give way** 1 yield 2 break down —**under way** moving ahead

way'far'er (-fer'-) n. traveler, esp. on foot —**way'far·ing** a., n.

way·lay' v. **-laid', -lay'ing** to ambush

way'-out' a. [Col.] very unusual or unconventional

way'side' a., n. (at or along) the edge of a road

way'ward a. 1 willful; disobedient 2 irregular —**way'ward·ness** n.

we pron. persons speaking or writing

weak a. lacking strength, power, etc.; not strong effective, etc. —**weak'en** v.

weak'-kneed' a. timid; cowardly

weak'ling n. weak person

weak'ly a. **-li·er, -li·est** sickly —adv. in a weak way

weak'ness n. 1 a being weak 2 fault 3 special liking

weal n. skin welt

wealth (welth) n. 1 riches 2 large amount —**wealth'y** a., **-i·er, -i·est**

wean v. 1 stop suckling 2 withdraw from a certain habit, etc.

weap'on (wep'-) n. 1 thing used for fighting 2 means of attack or defense

weap'on·ry n. weapons

wear v. **wore, worn, wear'ing** 1 have on the body as clothes 2 make or become damaged by use 3 endure in use 4 to tire or exhaust —n. 1 clothing 2 impairment

wea·ry (wir'ē) a. **-ri·er, -ri·est** 1 tired 2 bored —v. **-ried, -ry·ing** make or become weary —**wea'ri·ness** n. —**wea'ri·some** a.

wea·sel (wē'zəl) n. small, flesh-eating mammal —v. [Col.] avoid or evade a commitment: with out

weath·er (weth'-) n. condition outside as to temperature, humidity, etc. —v. 1 to pass through safely 2 wear, discolor, etc. by exposure to sun, rain, etc.

weath'er-beat'en n. roughened, etc. by the weather

weath'er·ize' v. insulate (a building) to conserve heat

weath'er·man' n., pl. **-men'** weather forecaster

weath'er·proof' v., a. (make) able to withstand exposure to the weather

weath'er·strip' n. strip of metal, felt, etc. for covering joints to keep out drafts, etc.: also **weath'er·strip'ping** —v. provide with weatherstrips

weather vane n. VANE (n. 1)

weave v. **wove, wo'ven, weav'ing** 1 make cloth by interlacing threads, as on a loom 2 twist or move from side to side or in and out —n. pattern of weaving

web n. 1 network, esp. one spun by a spider 2 skin joining the toes of a duck, frog, etc.

web'bing n. strong fabric woven in strips

web'foot' n., pl. **-feet'** foot with a WEB (n. 2) —**web'-foot'ed** a.

wed v. **wed'ded, wed'ded** or **wed, wed'ding** 1 marry 2 unite

we'd 1 we had 2 we should 3 we would

wed'ding n. ceremony of marrying

wedge n. piece of wood, etc. tapering to a thin edge —v. 1 fix in place with a wedge 2 pack tightly

wed'lock' n. matrimony

Wednes'day (wenz'-) n. fourth day of the week

wee a. very small; tiny

weed n. unwanted plant, as in a lawn —v. 1 remove weeds 2 take (out) as useless; etc.

weeds n.pl. black clothes for mourning

week n. 1 period of seven days, esp. Sunday through Saturday 2 the hours or days one works each week

week'day' n. any day of the week except Sunday and, often,

Saturday

week'end', week'-end n. Saturday and Sunday —v. spend the weekend

week'ly a. 1 lasting a week 2 done, etc. once a week —adv. once a week —n., pl. **-lies** periodical coming out weekly

weep v. **wept, weep'ing** 1 shed tears 2 mourn (for)

wee'vil n. beetle larva that destroys cotton, grain, etc.

weft n. threads woven across the warp in a loom

weigh (wā) v. 1 determine the heaviness of, as on a scale 2 have a certain weight 3 consider with down 4 burden: with down 5 hoist (an anchor)

weight n. 1 (amount of) heaviness 2 unit of heaviness 3 solid mass 4 burden 5 importance or influence —v. to burden —**weight'y** a., **-i-er, -i-est**

weight'less a. having little or no apparent weight

weir (wir) n. 1 low dam in a river, etc. 2 fencelike barrier in a stream, etc. for catching fish

weird (wird) a. 1 mysterious 2 bizarre

weird'o n., pl. **-os** [Sl.] bizarre person or thing

wel'come a. 1 gladly received 2 freely permitted 3 under no obligation —v. a welcoming —v. greet with pleasure

weld v. unite by melting together —n. welded joint

wel'fare' n. health, happiness, and comfort —**on welfare** receiving government aid because of poverty, etc.

well n. 1 natural spring 2 hole dug in the earth to get water, oil, etc. 3 hollow shaft 4 source —v. gush or flow —adv. **bet'ter, best** 1 in a pleasing, good, or right way 2 prosperously 3 much 4 thoroughly —a. in good health —int. exclamation of surprise —**as well (as)** 1 in addition to 2 equally (with)

we'll 1 we shall 2 we will

well'-ap-point'ed a. excellently furnished

well'-be'ing n. welfare

well'-bred' a. showing good manners; courteous

well'-dis-posed' a. friendly or receptive

well'-done' a. 1 done with skill 2 thoroughly cooked

well'-found'ed a. based on facts or good judgment

well'-ground'ed a. having good basic knowledge of a subject

well'-heeled' a. [Sl.] rich; prosperous

well'-known' a. famous or familiar

well'-man'nered a. polite

well'-mean'ing a. with good intentions —**well'-meant'** a.

well'-nigh' adv. almost

well'-off' a. 1 fortunate 2 prosperous

well'-read' (-red') a. having read much

well'spring' n. source of a stream, continual supply, etc.

well'-to-do' a. wealthy

well'-worn' a. much worn or used

Welsh a., n. (of) the people or language of Wales

Welsh rabbit (or **rarebit**) n. melted cheese on toast

welt n. 1 leather strip in the seam between shoe sole and upper 2 ridge raised on the skin by a blow

wel'ter v. wallow —n. confusion

wen n. skin cyst

wench n. young woman: derogatory or humorous

wend v. proceed or go on (one's way)

went v. pt. of GO

wept v. pt. & pp. of WEEP

were v. pt. of BE: used with you, we, or they

we're we are

weren't were not

were'wolf' (wir'-, wer'-) n., pl. **-wolves'** Folklore a person changed into a wolf

west n. 1 direction in which sunset occurs 2 region in this direction 3 [W-] Europe and North and South America —a., adv. in, toward, or from the west —**west'er-ly** a., adv. —**west'ern** a. —**west'ern-er** n. —**west'-ward** a., adv. —**west'wards** adv.

wet a. **wet'ter, wet'test** 1 covered or soaked with water 2 rainy 3 not dry yet —n. water, rain, etc. —v. **wet** or **wet'ted, wet'ting** make or become wet

wet suit n. closefitting rubber suit worn by divers

we've we have

whack v., n. hit or slap with a sharp sound

whack'y a. **-i-er, -i-est** wacky

whale n. huge, fishlike sea mammal —v. 1 hunt for whales 2 [Col.] beat

whale'bone n. horny substance

whal'er n. a person or ship engaged in hunting whales

wham int. sound imitating a heavy blow —n. heavy blow

wharf (hwôrf) n., pl. **wharves** or **wharfs** platform at which ships dock to load, etc.

what pron. 1 which thing, event, etc.? 2 that which —a. 1 which or which kind of 2 as much or as many as 3 how great! —adv. 1 how 2 partly —int. exclamation of surprise, etc. —**what for?** why? —**what if** suppose

what-ev'er pron. 1 anything that 2 no matter what 3 what —a. 1 of any kind 2 no matter what

what'so-ev'er pron., a. whatever

wheat n. cereal grass with seed ground for flour, etc.

whee'dle v. coax

wheel n. round disk turning on an axle —v. 1 move on wheels 2 turn, revolve, etc.

wheel'bar'row n. single-wheeled cart with handles

wheel'base' n. distance from front to rear axle

wheeze v., n. (make) a whistling, breathy sound

whelk n. large sea snail with a spiral shell

whelp n. puppy or cub —v. give birth to whelps

when adv. at what time? —con. 1 at what time 2 at which 3 at the time that 4 if —pron. what or which time

whence adv. from where

when-ev'er adv. [Col.] when —con. at whatever time

where adv. 1 in or to what place? 2 in what way? 3 from what source? —con. 1 in or at what place 2 in or at which place 3 to the place that —pron. 1 what place? 2 the place at which

where'a-bouts' adv. at what place? —n. location

where-as' con. 1 because 2 while on the contrary

where'by' adv. by which

where'fore' adv. why? —con. therefore —n. the reason

where-in' con. in which

where-of' adv. of what, which, or whom

where'up-on' con. at or after which —adv. on what

wher-ev'er adv. [Col.] where? —con. in or to whatever place

where'with-al' n. necessary

means, esp. money

whet v. **whet'ted, whet'ting** 1 sharpen, as by grinding 2 to stimulate

wheth'er con. 1 if it is true or likely that 2 in either case that

whet'stone' n. abrasive stone for sharpening knives

whew int. exclamation of relief, surprise, etc.

whey (hwā) n. watery part of curdled milk

which pron. 1 what one or ones of several 2 the one or ones that 3 that —a. 1 what one or ones 2 whatever

which-ev'er pron., a. any one that; no matter which

whiff n. 1 light puff of air 2 slight odor

while n. period of time —con. 1 during the time that 2 although —v. to spend (time) pleasantly: often with away

whim n. sudden notion

whim'per v., n. (make) a low, broken cry

whim'sy (-zē) n., pl. **-sies** 1 whim 2 fanciful humor — **whim'si-cal** a.

whine v., n. (make) a long, high cry, as in complaining

whin'ny v., n. **-nied, -ny-ing** (make) a low, neighing sound

whip v. **whipped, whip'ping** 1 move suddenly 2 strike, as with a strap 3 beat (cream, etc.) into a froth 4 [Col.] defeat —n. 1 rod with a lash at one end 2 dessert of whipped cream, fruit, etc. —**whip up** 1 rouse (interest, etc.) 2 [Col.] to prepare quickly

whip'lash' n. severe jolting of the neck back and forth

whip'pet n. small, swift dog

whip'poor-will' n. North American bird active at night

whir v. **whirred, whir'ring** fly or revolve with a buzzing sound — n. this sound

whirl v. 1 move or spin rapidly 2 seem to spin —n. 1 a whirling 2 confused condition

whirl'pool' n. water in violent, whirling motion

whirl'wind' n. air whirling violently and moving forward

whisk v. move, pull, etc. with a quick, sweeping motion —n. this motion

whisk broom n. small broom

whisk'er n. 1 pl. the hair on a man's face 2 a long hair, as on a cat's upper lip

whis′key n., pl. **-keys** or **-kies** strong liquor made from grain: also sp. **whis′ky,** pl. **-kies**

whis′per v. 1 say very softly 2 tell as a secret —n. a whispering

whist n. card game like bridge

whis′tle (-əl) v. 1 make, or move with, a high, shrill sound 2 blow a whistle —n. 1 device for making whistling sounds 2 a whistling

whit n. least bit; jot

white a. 1 of the color of snow 2 pale 3 pure; innocent 4 having light skin —n. 1 color of pure snow 2 a white thing, as egg albumen —**white′ness** n.

white ant n. termite

white′cap′ n. wave with its crest broken into foam

white′-col′lar a. of clerical or professional workers

white elephant n. useless thing expensive to maintain

white′fish′ n. white, freshwater fish in cool Northern lakes

whit′en v. make or become white

white′wall′ n. tire with a white band on the side

white′wash′ n. mixture of lime, water, etc. as for whitening walls —v. 1 cover with whitewash 2 conceal the faults of

whith′er (hwith′-) adv. where

whit′ing (hwit′-) n. any of various edible sea fishes

whit′ish a. somewhat white

whit′tle v. 1 cut shavings from wood with a knife 2 reduce gradually

whiz, whizz v., n. **whizzed, whiz′zing** (make) the hissing sound of a thing rushing through air

who pron. 1 what person? 2 which person 3 that

whoa int. stop!: command to a horse

who·ev′er pron. 1 any person that 2 no matter who

whole a. 1 not broken, damaged, etc. 2 complete 3 not divided up 4 healthy —n. 1 entire amount 2 thing complete in itself —**on the whole** in general —**whole′ness** n.

whole milk n. milk from which no butterfat has been removed

whole′sale′ n. sale of goods in large amounts, as to retailers —a. 1 of such sale 2 extensive —v. to sell at wholesale —**whole′sal′er** n.

whole′some a. 1 healthful 2

improving one's morals 3 healthy —**whole′some·ness** n.

whol′ly adv. completely

whom pron. objective case of WHO

whoop v., n. (to utter) a loud shout, cry, etc.

whoop′ing cough n. infectious disease, esp. of children

whop′per n. [Col.] 1 any large thing 2 big lie

whore (hôr) n. prostitute

whorl (hwôrl, hwurl) n. design of circular ridges

whose pron. that or those belonging to whom —a. of whom or of which

who·so·ev′er pron. whoever

why adv. 1 for what reason 2 because of which 3 reason for which —n., pl. **whys** the reason —int. exclamation of surprise, etc.

wick n. piece of cord, etc. for burning, as in a candle

wick′ed a. 1 evil 2 unpleasant 3 naughty

wick′er n. 1 long, thin twigs or strips 2 wickerwork —a. made of wicker

wick′er·work′ n. baskets, etc. made of wicker

wick′et n. 1 small door, gate, or window 2 wire arch used in croquet

wide a. 1 great in width, amount, degree, etc. 2 of a specified width 3 far from the goal —adv. 1 over or to a large extent 2 so as to be wide —**wide′ly** adv. —**wid′en** v.

wide′-a·wake′ a. 1 completely awake 2 alert

wide′-eyed′ a. surprised, fearful, or naive

wide′spread′ a. occurring over a wide area

wid′ow n. woman whose husband has died —v. make a widow of —**wid′ow·hood′** n.

wid′ow·er n. man whose wife has died

width n. 1 distance side to side 2 a piece so wide

wield (wēld) v. 1 handle with skill 2 use (power, etc.)

wie′ner n. frankfurter

wife n., pl. **wives** married woman —**wife′ly** a.

wig n. false covering of hair for the head

wig′gle v., n. twist and turn from side to side —**wig′gly** a., **-gli·er, -gli·est**

wig′wag′ v. **-wagged′, -wag·ging**

1 wag 2 send messages by visible code

wig'wam' n. cone-shaped tent of North American Indians

wild a. 1 in its natural state 2 not civilized 3 unruly 4 stormy 5 enthusiastic 6 reckless 7 missing the target —adv. in a wild way —n. pl. wilderness

wild'cat' n. fierce cat of medium size, as the bobcat —a. 1 risky 2 unauthorized

wil'der-ness n. wild region

wild'-eyed' a. 1 staring wildly 2 very foolish

wild'fire' n. rapidly spreading fire, hard to put out

wild'life' n. wild animals

wile v., n. trick; lure

will n. 1 wish; desire 2 strong purpose 3 power of choice 4 attitude 5 legal document disposing of one's property after death —v. 1 decide 2 control by the will 3 bequeath —**at will** when one wishes

will v. pt. **would** auxiliary verb showing: 1 future time 2 determination or obligation 3 ability or capacity

will'ful a. 1 done deliberately 2 stubborn Also sp. **wil'ful** —**will'ful-ly** adv. —**will'ful-ness** n.

will'ing a. 1 consenting 2 doing or done gladly —**will'ing-ly** adv. —**will'ing-ness** n.

will'-o'-the-wisp' n. anything elusive

wil'low n. a tree with narrow leaves

wil'low-y a. slender

will'pow'er n. self-control

wil'ly-nil'ly a., adv. (happening) whether one wishes it or not

wilt v. 1 make or become limp 2 make or become weak

wil'y a. **-i-er, -i-est** crafty; sly —**wil'i-ness** n.

wimp n. [Sl.] weak, dull person —**wimp'y, wimp'ish** a.

win v. **won, win'ning** 1 gain a victory 2 get by work, effort, etc. 3 persuade —n. [Col.] victory

wince v. draw back; flinch

winch n. machine for hoisting by a cable, etc. wound on a drum

wind (wind) v. **wound, wind'ing** 1 turn, coil, or twine around 2 cover, or tighten, by winding 3 move or go indirectly —n. a turn —**wind up** finish

wind (wind) n. 1 air in motion 2 gales 3 breath 4 smell —v.

put out of breath

wind'break' n. fence, trees, etc. protecting a place from the wind

wind'ed a. out of breath

wind'fall' n. unexpected gain, as of money

wind instrument n. Mus. instrument played by blowing air, esp. breath, through it

wind'lass (-ləs) n. winch

wind'mill' n. machine operated by the wind's rotation of a wheel of vanes

win'dow n. 1 opening for light and air in a building, car, etc. 2 glass in a frame set in this

win'dow-pane' n. pane of glass in a window

wind'pipe' n. trachea

wind'shield' n. in cars, etc. glass shield in the front

wind'up' (wind'-) n. end

wind'ward a., adv., n. (in or toward) the direction from which the wind blows

wind'y a. **-i-er, -i-est** 1 with much wind; breezy 2 long-winded, pompous, etc.

wine n. fermented juice of grapes or of other fruits —v. entertain with wine

wing n. 1 organ used by a bird, insect, etc. in flying 2 thing like a wing in use or position 3 political faction —v. 1 to fly 2 send swiftly 3 wound in the wing or arm 4 extension of a building —**on the wing** in flight —**take wing** fly away —**under one's wing** under one's protection, etc. —**winged** a. —**wing'less** a.

wink v. 1 close and open the eyelids quickly 2 do this with one eye, as a signal 3 twinkle —n. 1 a winking 2 an instant

win'ner n. one that wins

win'ning a. 1 victorious 2 charming —n. 1 a victory 2 pl. something won

win'now (-ō) v. 1 blow the chaff from grain 2 sort out

win'some (-səm) a. charming

win'ter n. coldest season of the year —a. of or for winter —v. spend the winter

win'ter-green' n. oil from the leaves of an evergreen plant, used for flavoring

win'ter-ize' v. put into condition for winter

win'try a. **-tri-er, -tri-est** of or like winter

wipe v. 1 clean or dry by rubbing 2 rub (a cloth, etc.) over something —n. a wiping —**wipe out** 1 remove 2 kill —**wip′er** n.

wire n. 1 metal drawn into a long thread 2 telegraph 3 telegram —a. made of wire —v. 1 furnish or fasten with wire(s) 2 telegraph

wire′less a. operating by electric waves, not with conducting wire —n. 1 wireless telegraph or telephone 2 [Chiefly Br.] radio

wire′tap′ v. tap (telephone wire) to get information secretly —n. 1 act of wiretapping 2 device for wiretapping

wir′ing n. system of wires, as for carrying electricity

wir′y a., -i·er, -i·est 1 like wire; stiff 2 lean and strong —**wir′i·ness** n.

wis′dom n. 1 a being wise; good judgment 2 knowledge

wisdom tooth n. back tooth on each side of each jaw

wise a. 1 having good judgment 2 informed or learned —n. manner —**wise′ly** adv.

-wise suf. 1 in a certain direction, position, or manner 2 with regard to

wise′a·cre n. one annoyingly conceited in claiming knowledge

wise′crack′ v., n. [Sl.] (make) a flippant remark

wish v. 1 to want; desire 2 express a desire concerning 3 request —n. 1 a wishing 2 something wished for 3 request

wish′ful a. showing a wish

wish′y-wash′y a. weak

wisp n. slight thing or bit —**wisp′y** a., -i·er, -i·est

wis·te′ri·a (-tir′ē-) n. twining shrub with clusters of flowers

wist′ful a. yearning —**wist′ful·ly** adv.

wit n. 1 (one with) the ability to make clever remarks 2 pl. powers of thinking —**to wit** namely

witch n. woman supposed to have evil, magic power

witch′craft′ n. power or practices of witches

witch doctor n. one thought to have magical power in curing disease, etc.

witch hazel n. lotion made from a plant extract

with prep. 1 against 2 near to; in the care or company of 3 into 4 as a member of 5 concerning 6 compared to 7 as well as 8 in the opinion of 9 as a result of 10 by means of 11 having or showing 12 to; onto 13 from 14 after

with·draw′ v. -drew′, -drawn′, -draw′ing 1 take back 2 move back 3 leave —**with·draw′al** n.

with·drawn′ a. shy, reserved, etc.

with′er (with′-) v. wilt

with′ers (with′-) n.pl. highest part of a horse's back

with·hold′ v. -held′, -hold′ing 1 keep back; restrain 2 refrain from granting

with·in′ adv. in or to the inside —prep. 1 inside 2 not beyond

with·out′ adv. on the outside —prep. 1 outside 2 lacking 3 avoiding

with·stand′ v. -stood′, -stand′ing resist; endure

wit′less a. stupid

wit′ness n. 1 one who saw and can testify to a thing 2 testimony; evidence 3 an attesting signer —v. 1 see 2 act as a witness of 3 be proof of —**bear witness** testify

wit′ti·cism′ v. witty remark

wit′ty a. -ti·er, -ti·est cleverly amusing

wives n. pl. of WIFE

wiz′ard n. magician

wiz′ard·ry n. magic

wiz′ened (-and) a. dried up and wrinkled

wob′ble v. move unsteadily from side to side —n. a wobbling —**wob′bly** a.

woe n. grief or trouble —**woe′ful** a. —**woe′ful·ly** adv.

woe′be·gone′ a. showing woe

wok n. bowl-shaped frying pan

woke v. pt. of WAKE

wolf n., pl. **wolves** 1 wild, doglike animal 2 cruel or greedy person —v. eat greedily —**cry wolf** give a false alarm —**wolf′ish** a.

wol·ver·ine′ (-ēn′) n. strong animal like a small bear

wom′an n., pl. **wom′en** adult female person —**wom′an·hood′** n. —**wom′an·ly** a.

womb (wōōm) n. uterus

won v. pt. of WIN

won′der n. 1 amazing thing; marvel 2 feeling caused by this —v. 1 feel wonder 2 be curious about

won′der·ful a. 1 causing wonder 2 [Col.] excellent

won′der·land′ n. place of wonders, great beauty, etc.

won′der·ment n. amazement

won′drous a., adv. [Poet.] amazing(ly)

wont (wônt, wänt) a. accus-

tomed —*n.* habit —**wont'ed** *a.*
won't will not
woo *v.* seek to win, esp. as one's spouse
wood *n.* **1** hard substance under a tree's bark **2** lumber **3** *pl.* forest —*a.* **1** of wood **2** of the woods —**wood'ed** *a.*
wood alcohol *n.* poisonous alcohol used as fuel, etc.
wood'bine' *n.* climbing plant
wood'chuck' *n.* North American burrowing animal
wood'cut' *n.* print made from a wood engraving
wood'en *a.* **1** made of wood **2** lifeless, dull, etc.
wood'land' *n., a.* forest
wood'peck'er *n.* bird that pecks holes in bark
wood'wind' *a., n.* (of) any of the wind instruments, esp. of wood, as the clarinet, oboe, flute, etc.
wood'work' *n.* wooden doors, frames, moldings, etc.
wood'work'ing *n.* art or work of making wooden items
wood'y *a.* **-i·er, -i·est** **1** tree-covered **2** of or like wood
woof *n.* weft
woof'er *n.* large loudspeaker for low sounds
wool *n.* **1** soft curly hair of sheep, goats, etc. **2** yarn or cloth made of this
wool'en *a.* of wool —*n. pl.* woolen goods
wool'gath'er·ing *n.* daydreaming
wool'ly *a.* **-li·er, -li·est** of, like, or covered with wool: also sp. **wool'y**
wooz'y *a.* **-i·er, -i·est** [Col.] dizzy or dazed, as from drink
word *n.* **1** a sound or sounds as a speech unit **2** letter or letters standing for this **3** brief remark **4** news **5** promise **6** *pl.* quarrel —*v.* put into words
word'ing *n.* choice and arrangement of words
word'y *a.* **-i·er, -i·est** using too many words —**word'i·ness** *n.*
wore *v.* pt. of WEAR
work *n.* **1** effort of doing or making; labor **2** occupation, trade, etc. **3** task; duty **4** thing made, done, etc. **5** *pl.* factory **6** *pl.* engineering structures, as bridges **7** workmanship —*v.* worked or wrought, work'ing **1** do work; toil **2** to function **3** cause to work **4** be employed **5** bring about **6** come or bring to some condition **7** solve (a problem) —**at work** working —**the**

works **1** working parts (of) **2** everything: also **the whole works** —**work off** get rid of
work on **1** influence **2** try to persuade —**work out 1** develop or result **2** to exercise —**work up 1** advance **2** develop **3** excite; arouse —**work'a·ble** *a.* —**work'er** *n.* —**work'man** *n., pl.* **-men**
work'a·day' *a.* ordinary
work'a·hol'ic *n.* person having an uncontrollable need to work
work'book' *n.* book of exercises, etc. for students
work'horse' *n.* reliable worker
work'house' *n.* jail where prisoners are put to work
work'ing·man' *n., pl.* **-men** worker, esp. in industry
work'man·like' *a.* done well
work'man·ship' *n.* worker's skill or product
work'out' *n.* strenuous exercise, practice, etc.
work'shop' *n.* room or building where work is done
work'sta'tion *n.* person's work area, esp. including a computer terminal
world *n.* **1** the earth **2** the universe **3** all people **4** any sphere or domain **5** secular life **6** *often pl.* great deal
world'ly *a.* **-li·er, -li·est** **1** of the world; secular **2** sophisticated
worm *n.* **1** long, slender creeping animal **2** thing like a worm **3** *pl.* disease caused by worms —*v.* **1** move like a worm **2** get in a sneaky way —**worm'y** *a.*
worm'wood' *n.* bitter herb
worn *v.* pp. of WEAR
worn'-out' *a.* **1** no longer usable **2** very tired
wor'ry *v.* **-ried, -ry·ing 1** make, or be, troubled or uneasy **2** annoy **3** shake with the teeth —*n., pl.* **-ries 1** troubled feeling **2** cause of this —**wor'ri·er** *n.*
wor'ri·some *a.*
wor'ry·wart' *n.* [Col.] one who worries too much
worse *a.* **1** more evil, bad, etc. **2** more ill —*adv.* in a worse way —*n.* that which is worse
wor'sen *v.* make or become worse
wor'ship *n.* **1** prayer, service, etc. in reverence to a deity **2** intense love or admiration —*v.* **1** show reverence for **2** take part in worship service
worst *a.* most evil, bad, etc. —*adv.* in the worst way —*n.* that

which is worst

wor·sted (woos'tid, wur'stid) *n.* smooth wool fabric

worth *a.* 1 value or merit 2 equivalent in money —*a.* 1 deserving 2 equal in value to — **worth'less** *a.*

worth'while' *a.* worth the time or effort spent

wor·thy *a.* **-thi·er, -thi·est** having worth or value 2 deserving —*n.* worthy person —**wor'thi·ness** *n.*

would *v.* pt. of WILL: would is used to express a condition, a wish, a request, etc.

would'-be' *a.* wishing, pretending, or meant to be

wound (wōōnd) *n.* 1 injury to the body tissue 2 scar 3 injury to the feelings, etc.—*v.* injure; hurt

wound (wound) *v.* pt. & pp. of WIND (turn)

wove *v.* pt. of WEAVE

wo'ven *v.* pp. of WEAVE

wow *int.* expression of surprise, pleasure, etc.

wrack *n.* destruction

wraith *n.* ghost

wran·gle *v., n.* quarrel; dispute

wrap *v.* **wrapped** or **wrapt, wrap'ping** 1 wind or fold (a covering) around 2 enclose in paper, etc. —*n.* outer garment —**wrap'per** *n.*

wrath *n.* great anger; rage — **wrath'ful** *a.*

wreak (rēk) *v.* 1 inflict (vengeance, etc.) 2 give vent to (anger, etc.)

wreath (rēth) *n., pl.* **wreaths** twisted ring of leaves, etc.

wreathe (rēth) *v.* 1 encircle 2 decorate with wreaths

wreck *n.* 1 remains of a thing destroyed 2 rundown person 3 a wrecking —*v.* 1 destroy or ruin 2 tear down —**wreck'age** (-ij) *n.* —**wreck'er** *n.*

wren *n.* small songbird

wrench *n.* 1 sudden, sharp twist 2 injury caused by a twist 3 tool for turning nuts, bolts, etc. —*v.* 1 twist or jerk sharply 2 injure with a twist

wrest *v.* take by force

wres·tle (-əl) *v.* 1 struggle with (an opponent) trying to throw him 2 contend (*with*) —*n.* a struggle —**wres'tler** *n.* —**wres'tling** *n.*

wretch *n.* 1 very unhappy person 2 person despised

wretch·ed *a.* 1 very unhappy 2

distressing 3 unsatisfactory — **wretch'ed·ness** *n.*

wrig·gle *v.* twist and turn, or move along thus —*n.* a wriggling —**wrig'gler** *n.*

wring *v.* **wrung, wring'ing** 1 squeeze and twist 2 force out by this means 3 get by force — **wring'er** *n.*

wrin·kle *n.* 1 small crease or fold 2 [Col.] clever idea, etc. — *v.* form wrinkles (in)

wrist *n.* joint between the hand and forearm

writ *n.* formal court order

write *v.* **wrote, writ'ten, writ'ing** 1 form (words, letters, etc.) 2 produce (writing or music) 3 write a letter —**write off** cancel, as a debt —**writ'er** *n.*

writhe (rīth) *v.* twist and turn, as in pain

wrong *a.* 1 not right or just 2 not true or correct 3 not suitable 4 mistaken 5 out of order 6 not meant to be seen —*adv.* incorrectly —*n.* something wrong —*v.* treat unjustly

wrong'do'ing *n.* unlawful or bad behavior —**wrong'do'er** *n.*

wrong'ful *a.* unjust, unlawful, etc. —**wrong'ful·ly** *adv.*

wrong'head'ed *a.* stubbornly holding to false ideas, etc.

wrought (rôt) *a.* 1 made 2 shaped by hammering

wrought iron *n.* tough, malleable iron used for fences, etc. — **wrought'-i'ron** *a.*

wrought'-up' *a.* very disturbed or excited

wrung *v.* pt. & pp. of WRING

wry (rī) *a.* **wri'er, wri'est** twisted or distorted —**wry'ly** *adv.* — **wry'ness** *n.*

X

Xe·rox (zir'äks') *trademark* device for copying printed material electrically —*v.* [x-] to copy using this device —*n.* [x-] a copy made with this device

X'mas *n.* [Col.] Christmas

X'-ray' *n.* 1 ray that can penetrate solid matter 2 photograph made with X-rays —*a.* of or by X-rays —*v.* photograph, treat, or examine with X-rays Also X ray, x-ray, or x ray

xy'lem (zī'-) *n.* woody plant tissue

xy'lo·phone' (zī'-) *n.* musical instrument of a row of wooden bars struck with hammers

Y

-y *suf.* 1 full of or like 2 rather 3 apt to 4 state of being 5 act of

yacht (yät) *n.* small ship —*v.* sail in a yacht —**yachts'man** *n.*, *pl.* **-men**

yak [Sl.] *v.* **yakked, yak'king** talk much or idly —*n.* a yakking

yak *n.* wild ox of Asia

yam *n.* 1 starchy, edible root of a tropical plant 2 [Dial.] sweet potato

yam'mer *v.* [Col.] whine or complain

yank *v.*, *n.* [Col.] jerk

Yan'kee *n.* 1 U.S. citizen 2 native of a northern State

yap *v.*, *n.* **yapped, yap'ping** (make) a sharp, shrill bark

yard *n.* 1 measure of length, three feet 2 ground around a building 3 enclosed place 4 slender spar

yard'age (-ij) *n.* distance or length in yards

yard'stick' *n.* 1 measuring stick one yard long 2 standard for judging

yarn *n.* 1 spun strand of wool, cotton, etc. 2 [Col.] tale or story

yaw *v.*, *n.* turn from the course, as of a ship

yawl *n.* kind of sailboat

yawn *v.* open the mouth widely, as when one is sleepy —*n.* a yawning

yaws *n.* tropical, infectious skin disease

ye (yē; *a.:* thə) [Ar.] *pron.* you —*a.* the

yea (yā) *adv.* 1 yes 2 truly —*n.* vote of "yes"

yeah (ya) *adv.* [Col.] yes

year *n.* 1 period of 365 days (366 in leap year) or 12 months 2 *pl.* age 3 *pl.* a long time

year'book' *n.* book with data of the preceding year

year'ling *n.* animal in its second year

year'ly *a.* 1 every year 2 of a year —*adv.* every year

yearn (yurn) *v.* feel longing —**yearn'ing** *n.*, *a.*

year'-round' *a.* open, in use, etc. throughout the year

yeast *n.* 1 frothy substance causing fermentation 2 yeast mixed with flour or meal

yell *v.*, *n.* scream; shout

yel'low *a.* 1 of the color of ripe lemons 2 [Col.] cowardly —*n.* yellow color —*v.* to make or become yellow —**yel'low-ish** *a.*

yellow fever *n.* tropical disease carried by a mosquito

yellow jacket *n.* bright-yellow wasp or hornet

yelp *v.*, *n.* (utter) a short, sharp cry or bark

yen *n.* [Col.] deep longing

yeo'man (yō'-) *n.*, *pl.* **-men** U.S. Navy clerk

yes *adv.* 1 it is so 2 not only that, but more —*n.*, *pl.* **yes'es** 1 consent 2 affirmative vote

yes'ter-day' *n.* 1 day before today 2 recent time —*adv.* on the day before today

yet *adv.* 1 up to now 2 now 3 still; even now 4 nevertheless —*con.* nevertheless

yew *n.* evergreen tree

Yid'dish *n.* German dialect using the Hebrew alphabet

yield *v.* 1 produce; give 2 surrender 3 concede; grant 4 give way to force —*n.* amount produced

yip *v.*, *n.* **yipped, yip'ping** *n.* [Col.] yelp or bark

yo'del *v.* sing with abrupt, alternating changes to the falsetto —*n.* a yodeling

yo'ga *n.* Hindu discipline for uniting self with supreme spirit through various exercises

yo'gurt, yo'ghurt *n.* thick, semi-solid food made from fermented milk

yoke *n.* 1 frame for harnessing together a pair of oxen, etc. 2 thing that binds or unites 3 servitude 4 part of a garment at the shoulders —*v.* 1 harness to 2 join together

yo'kel *n.* person living in rural area; contemptuous term

yolk (yōk) *n.* yellow part of an egg

yon *a.*, *adv.* [Dial.] yonder

yon'der *a.*, *adv.* over there

yore *n.* [Obs.] long ago

you *pron.* [*sing.* or *pl. v.*] 1 the person(s) spoken to 2 person(s) generally

you'd 1 you had 2 you would

you'll 1 you will 2 you shall

young *a.* 1 in an early stage of life or growth 2 fresh —*n.* young offspring —**with young** pregnant —**young'ish** *a.*

young'ster *n.* child

your *a.* of you

you're you are

yours *pron.* that or those belonging to you

your·self *pron.*, *pl.* **-selves'** intensive or reflexive form of YOU

youth *n.* **1** state or quality of being young **2** adolescence **3** young people **4** young man —**youth'ful** *a.*

you've you have

yowl *v., n.* howl; wail

yo'-yo' *n., pl.* **-yos'** spool-like toy on a string on which it is made to spin up and down

yuc'ca *n.* lilylike plant

yuck [Sl.] *n.* something disgusting, etc. —*int.* an expression of disgust —**yuck'y** *a.*, **-i-er, -i-est**

yule *n.* [*often* Y-] Christmas

yule'tide' *n.* [*often* Y-] Christmas time

yum'my *a.* **-mi-er, -mi-est** [Col.] very tasty; delicious

yup'pie *n.* [Col.] affluent, ambitious, young professional

Z

za'ny *a.* **-ni-er, -ni-est** of or like a foolish or comical person —*n.*, *pl.* **-nies** such a person —**za'ni-ness** *n.*

zap *v.* **zapped, zap'ping** [Sl.] move, kill, etc. suddenly and with great speed —*int.* exclamation used to express such action

zeal *n.* eager endeavor or devotion

zeal'ot (zel'-) *n.* one showing zeal, esp. fanatic zeal

zeal'ous (zel'-) *a.* full of zeal —**zeal'ous·ly** *adv.*

ze'bra *n.* striped African animal similar to the horse

ze'bu' *n.* oxlike animal with a hump

Zen *n.* form of Buddhism seeking intuitive knowledge through meditation

ze'nith *n.* **1** point in the sky directly overhead **2** the highest point

zeph'yr (zef'ər) *n.* breeze

zep'pe·lin *n.* dirigible

ze'ro *n., pl.* **-ros** or **-roes** **1** the symbol 0 **2** point marked 0 in scale **3** nothing —*a.* of or at

zero

zest *n.* **1** stimulating quality **2** keen enjoyment —**zest'ful** *a.*

zig'zag' *n.* line with sharp turns back and forth —*a.*, *adv.* in a zigzag —*v.* **-zagged', -zag'ging** to move or form in a zigzag

zilch *n.* [Sl.] nothing; zero

zinc *n.* bluish-white metal, a chemical element

zing *n.* [Sl.] shrill, whizzing sound

zin'ni·a *n.* daisylike flower thick with petals

zip *v.* **zipped, zip'ping** **1** make a short, sharp hissing sound **2** [Col.] move fast **3** fasten with a zipper —*n.* **1** a zipping sound **2** [Col.] energy; vigor —**zip'py** *a.*, **-pi-er, -pi-est**

zip'per *n.* fastener with interlocking tabs worked by a sliding part

zir'con' *n.* transparent gem

zit *n.* [Sl.] pimple, esp. on face

zith'er *n.* stringed instrument, played by plucking

zo'di·ac' *n.* imaginary belt along the sun's apparent path divided into 12 parts named for constellations

zom'bie *n.* **1** animated corpse in folklore **2** [Sl.] one listless, machine-like, etc.

zone *n.* **1** any of the five areas into which the earth is divided according to climate **2** area set apart in some way —*v.* mark off into zones —**zoned** *a.*

zonked *a.* [Sl.] **1** drunk or under drug influence **2** exhausted

zoo *n.* place with wild animals on exhibition

zo'o·log'i·cal garden (zō'-) *n.* zoo

zo·ol'o·gy (zō-) *n.* science of animal life —**zo'o·log'i·cal** *a.* —**zo·ol'o·gist** *n.*

zoom *v.* **1** make a loud, buzzing sound **2** speed upward or forward —*n.* a zooming

zuc·chi·ni (zoō kē'nē) *n.* cucumberlike squash

zwie·back (swē'bäk, swī'-) *n.* dried, toasted slices of a kind of bread

zy'gote' *n.* fertilized egg cell before it divides

PUNCTUATION

The **Period** (.) is used: 1) at the end of a sentence; 2) after many abbreviations; 3) in a decimal fraction; 4) as one of a series (usually three spaced periods) to indicate an omission, an interruption, or a break in continuity.

The **Comma** (,) is used: 1) between short independent clauses in parallel construction and between clauses joined by conjunctions such as *and, but, or, nor, yet,* and *for;* 2) after a fairly long dependent clause that precedes an independent one; 3) before and after a dependent clause that comes in the middle of a sentence; 4) to set off a nonrestrictive word, phrase, or clause; 5) to set off transitional words and phrases; 6) to separate words, phrases, or clauses in series; 7) to set off the word indicating the one spoken to in direct address; 8) to set off a direct quotation; 9) to set off a title, an address, a place name, a date, etc. 10) after the salutation of an informal letter; 11) after the complimentary close of any letter.

The **Semicolon** (;) is used: 1) in a compound sentence between independent clauses that are not joined by connectives, or between such clauses joined by a conjunctive adverb (such as *thus*); 2) between phrases or clauses that contain internal punctuation.

The **Colon** (:) is used: 1) before a long series; 2) before a lengthy quotation; 3) between chapter and verse, volume and page, hour and minute, etc.; 4) after the salutation of a business letter.

The **Question Mark** (?) is used: 1) after a direct question; 2) as an indication of uncertainty or doubt.

The **Exclamation Point** (!) is used after a word, phrase, or sentence to indicate strong emotion, surprise, etc.

The **Hyphen** (-) is used: 1) to separate the parts of a compound word or numeral; 2) to indicate syllabification.

The **Dash** (—) is used: 1) between sentence parts, to show a break in continuity; 2) between numbers, dates, times, places, etc. that mark limits.

Quotation Marks: *Double* (" ") are used: 1) to enclose a direct quotation; 2) to enclose the titles of articles, short stories, short poems, etc., or the divisions or chapters of books, periodicals, long poems, etc. *Single* (' ') are used to enclose a quotation within a quotation.

Italic Type is used: 1) to set off the titles of books, periodicals, newspapers, etc. 2) to indicate foreign words or phrases 3) to emphasize a word within a sentence.

The **Apostrophe** (') is used: 1) in place of an omitted letter or letters in a word or contraction; 2) with an added *s* to form the possessive case of all nouns that do not end in an *s* or *z* sound; 3) with an added *s* to form the possessive of monosyllabic singular nouns that end in an *s* or *z* sound; 4) without an added *s* to form the possessive of all nouns that end in an *s* or *z* sound except monosyllabic singular nouns and nouns ending in -*ce*; 5) with a letter, a number, etc., to form its plural.

Parentheses, ( ), are used: 1) to enclose nonessential material in a sentence; 2) to enclose letters or numbers of reference, as in an outline.

Brackets, [ ], are used to indicate an insertion, a comment, a correction, etc. made by a person other than the original author of the material.

A **Capital Letter** is used: 1) to begin a sentence, or a quotation or direct question within a sentence; 2) to begin every word, except conjunctions, articles, and short prepositions that are not the first word, in the name of a book, magazine, work of music or art, business, agency, religion, holiday, etc.; 3) to begin every main word in a proper noun; 4) to begin every main word in the name of a day, month, era, etc.; 5) to begin many abbreviations; 6) to begin a noun or a pronoun referring to the Deity; 7) to begin the salutation and the complimentary close of a letter.

ABBREVIATIONS

Many abbreviations can be written in various ways (p.m., P.M., pm, PM). The most commonly used forms are listed here.

a. adjective
A *Sports* assist(s)
AA, A.A. Associate in Arts
AB, A.B. Bachelor of Arts
abbr., abbrev. abbreviated; abbreviation
AC air conditioning; alternating current
acct. account
A.D. in the year of our Lord
adj. adjective
Adm. Admiral
admn. administration
adv. adverb
AFDC Aid to Families with Dependent Children
agcy. agency
Ala. Alabama
Alas. Alaska
alt. alternate; altitude
a.m., A.M. before noon
AM, A.M. Master of Arts
Am. America(n)
anon. anonymous
Apr. April
apt. apartment
Ariz. Arizona
Ark. Arkansas
assn. association
assoc. associate
asst. assistant
Attn. attention
atty. attorney
Aug. August
av. average (also **avg.**); avoirdupois
Av(e). Avenue
b. born
BA, B.A. Bachelor of Arts
bbl. barrel(s)
B.C. before Christ
biol. biology
bldg. building
Blvd. Boulevard
Br., Brit. Britain; British
Bros. Brothers
BS, B.S. Bachelor of Science
Btu British thermal unit(s)
bu. bushel(s)
bur. bureau
c centimeter; copyright
c. century
C Celsius (or centigrade)
C. cup(s)
c(a). circa (about)
Cal., Calif. California
cal. calorie(s)
Can. Canada; Canadian (also **Cdn.**)
cap. capacity; capital(ize)
Capt. Captain
cc carbon copy; cubic centimeter(s)
cent. century; centuries

cert. certificate; certified
cf. compare
cg centigram(s)
Ch. Church
ch., chap. chapter(s)
chem. chemistry
chg(d). charge(d)
CIA Central Intelligence Agency
cm centimeter(s)
Cmdr. Commander
CO Commanding Officer
C/O, c/o care of
Co. Company; County
COD collect on delivery
Col. Colonel
Colo. Colorado
Cong. Congress
Conn. Connecticut
cont. continued
Corp. Corporal; Corporation
CPA Certified Public Accountant
CST Central Standard Time
cu. cubic
d. degree(s); diameter; died
DA, D.A. District Attorney
dba doing business as
D.C. District of Columbia
DC direct current
DD, D.D. Doctor of Divinity
DDS, D.D.S. Doctor of Dental Surgery
dec. deceased
Dec. December
Del. Delaware
Dem. Democrat(ic)
dept. department; deputy
dir. director
dist. district
div. division
d(o)z. dozen(s)
Dr. Doctor; Drive
DST Daylight Saving Time
DWI driving while intoxicated
E *Baseball* error(s)
E, E. east(ern)
ea. each
econ. economics
ed. edited (by); edition; editor; education
e.g. for example
EKG electrocardiogram
elem. elementary
enc(l). enclosure
Eng. England; English
EPA Environmental Protection Agency
ERA earned run average; Equal Rights Amendment
ESP extrasensory perception
esp. especially
Esq. Esquire
EST Eastern Standard Time
est. established (also **estab.**); estimate(d)

ABBREVIATIONS

ETA estimated time of arrival
et al. and (the) others
et seq. and the following
ex. example; exchange
exec. executive; executor
ext. extension
f. folio
F Fahrenheit; female
FBI Federal Bureau of Investigation
FCC Federal Communications Commission
FDA Food and Drug Administration
Feb. February
Fed. Federal; Federation
fem. feminine
ff. folios; following (pages, etc.)
FG *Sports* field goal(s)
FICA Federal Insurance Contributions Act
fig. figuratively; figure(s)
fl. flourished; fluid
Fla. Florida
Fr. Father; French
Fri. Friday
FT *Basketball* free throw(s)
ft. foot; feet
Ft. Fort
FTC Federal Trade Commission
g *Sports* goal(s); gram(s)
Ga. Georgia
gal. gallon(s)
Gen. General
gen., genl. general
Ger. German(y)
GM General Manager
GOP Grand Old (Republican) Party
Gov. Governor
gov., govt. government
GP, G.P. general practitioner
Gr. Greece; Greek
grad. graduate(d)
Gr. Brit. Great Britain
gram. grammar
guar. guaranteed
H *Baseball* hit(s)
hdqrs. headquarters
hist. history
H.J. here lies
HMO health maintenance organization
HP horsepower
HQ headquarters
HR *Baseball* home run(s)
HR, H.R. House of Representatives
hr. hour
HS, H.S. high school
ht. height
hwy. highway
Hz, hz hertz
Ia. Iowa
ib., ibid. in the same place
ICC Interstate Commerce Commission

id. the same
Ida. Idaho
i.e. that is (to say)
Ill. Illinois
illus. illustrated; illustration; illustrator
in. inch(es)
Inc., inc. incorporated
incl. including; inclusive
Ind. Indiana
ins. insurance
Inst. Institute; Institution
int. interest; interjection; international (also **intl.**)
IRA Independent Retirement Account
IRS Internal Revenue Service
It., Ital. Italian; Italy
ital. italic type
IV intravenous
Jan. January
JD, J.D. Doctor of Laws
JP, J.P. Justice of the Peace
Jpn. Japan(ese)
Jr. Junior
Jul. July
Jun. June
k karat(s); kilogram(s); kilometer(s)
K karat(s); kilobyte(s); kilometer(s); *Baseball* strikeout(s)
Kans. Kansas
KB kilobyte(s)
kc kilocycle(s)
kg kilogram(s)
kHz, khz kilohertz
km kilometer(s)
KO *Boxing* knockout
Ky. Kentucky
l. line
L *Sports* loss(es)
L, l liter(s)
L. Lake; Latin
LA, L.A. Los Angeles
La. Louisiana
Lat. Latin
lat. latitude
lb. pound(s)
l.c. in the place cited; lowercase
Lieut. Lieutenant
lit. literal(ly); literature
ll. lines
LLB, LL.B. Bachelor of Laws
LLD, LL.D. Doctor of Laws
loc. cit. in the place cited
long. longitude
LPN, L.P.N. Licensed Practical Nurse
Lt. Lieutenant
Ltd., ltd. limited
m meter(s); mile(s) (also **m.**)
M male
M. Monsieur
MA, M.A. Master of Arts
Maj. Major
Mar. March
masc. masculine
Mass. Massachusetts

ABBREVIATIONS

math. mathematics
max. maximum
MB megabyte(s)
MC Master of Ceremonies
MD, M.D. Doctor of Medicine
Md. Maryland
mdse. merchandise
Me. Maine
med. medical; medicine; medium
met. metropolitan
Mex. Mexican; Mexico
mfg. manufacturing
mfr. manufacture(r)
mg milligram(s)
mgr. manager
MHz, Mhz megahertz
mi. mile(s)
Mich. Michigan
mil. military
min. minimum; minute(s)
Minn. Minnesota
misc. miscellaneous
Miss. Mississippi
mkt. market
ml milliliter(s)
Mlle. Mademoiselle
mm millimeter(s)
Mme. Madame
MO mode of operation; money
    order
Mo. Missouri
mo. month
Mon. Monday
Mont. Montana
MP Member of Parliament
    (also M.P.); Military Police
mpg miles per gallon
mph miles per hour
MS, M.S. Master of Science
MS manuscript; multiple
    sclerosis
MST Mountain Standard Time
Mt., mt. mount; mountain
mtg. meeting; mortgage
mun. municipal
mus. museum; music
myth. mythology
n. noun
N, N. north(ern)
N.A. North America
NASA National Aeronautics and
    Space Administration
NATO North Atlantic Treaty
    Organization
naut. nautical
n.b. note well
N.C. North Carolina
NCO noncommissioned officer
N.D., N.Dak. North Dakota
NE, N.E. northeast(ern)
Neb., Nebr. Nebraska
neg. negative
Nev. Nevada
N.H. New Hampshire
N.J. New Jersey
N.M., N.Mex. New Mexico
no. number

non seq. it does not follow
Nov. November
nt. wt. net weight
NW, N.W. northwest(ern)
N.Y. New York
NYC, N.Y.C. New York City
O *Baseball* out(s)
O. Ohio
Oct. October
off. office; officer; official
Okla. Oklahoma
op. cit. in the work cited
Oreg. Oregon
orig. origin(al)(ly)
OT overtime
oz. ounce(s)
p. page; participle; past
PA public address (system)
Pa. Pennsylvania
PAC political action committee
pat. patent(ed)
pc. piece
pct. percent
pd. paid
Penn., Penna. Pennsylvania
pg. page
PhD, Ph.D. Doctor of Philosophy
phys. physical; physician; physics
pk. pack; park; peck
pkg. package(s)
pl. place; plate; plural
PM, P.M. Postmaster; Prime
    Minister
p.m., P.M. after noon
PO, P.O. Post Office (box)
pop. popularly; population
pos. positive
POW prisoner of war
PP parcel post
pp. pages; past participle
ppd. postpaid
ppr. present participle
P.R. public relations (also PR);
    Puerto Rico
pr. pair(s); price
prec. preceding
pref. preferred; prefix
prelim. preliminary
prep. preparatory; preposition
Pres. President
pres. present
prim. primary
prob. probably; problem
Prof. Professor
pron. pronoun; pronunciation
prop. proper(ly); property;
    proprietor
P.S. postscript
PST Pacific Standard Time
pt. part; past tense; pint; point
pub. public; published; publisher
Pvt. Private
Q question
qb *Football* quarterback
Q.E.D. which was to be
    demonstrated
qt. quart(s)

340

ABBREVIATIONS

qty. quantity
quot. quotation
q.v. which see
R *Baseball* run(s)
rbi, RBI *Baseball* runs batted in
R.C. Roman Catholic
Rd. Road
recd., rec'd. received
ref. referee; reference; reformed; refund
reg. registered; regular; regulation
rel. relative(ly); religion
Rep. Representative; Republic(an)
rep. report(ed)
rept. report
res. reserve; residence; resigned
ret. retired; return(ed)
Rev. Reverend
rev. revenue; revise(d); revolution
R.I. Rhode Island
R.I.P., RIP may he (she) rest in peace
RN, R.N. Registered Nurse
Rom. Roman
ROTC Reserve Officers Training Corps
rpm revolutions per minute
RR railroad; rural route
R.S.V.P. please reply
Rte. Route
S, S. south(ern)
Sat. Saturday
S.C. South Carolina
ScD, Sc.D. Doctor of Science
S.D., S.Dak. South Dakota
SE, S.E. southeast(ern)
sec. second(s); secondary; secretary (also secy.); section(s) (also sect.)
Sen. Senate; Senator
Sept. September
seq(q). the following (ones)
Sgt. Sergeant
shpt. shipment
sing. singular
soc. social; society
Sp. Spain; Spanish
sp. special; spelling
spec. special; specifically (also specif.); specification
sq. square
Sr. Senior; Sister
SST supersonic transport
St. Saint; Strait; Street
STD sexually transmitted disease
suf. suffix
Sun. Sunday
Supt. Superintendent
SW, S.W. southwest(ern)
t. teaspoon(s); tense; ton(s)
T. tablespoon(s)
TB tuberculosis
tbs. tablespoon(s)

TD *Football* touchdown
tech. technical; technology
tel. telegram; telephone
temp. temperature; temporary
Tenn. Tennessee
Tex. Texas
theol. theology
Thur., Thurs. Thursday
TKO *Boxing* technical knockout
TM trademark
tr. translated (by); translation; translator; transpose
trans. translated (by); translation; translator; transportation
treas. treasurer; treasury
tsp. teaspoon(s)
Tue., Tues. Tuesday
U. Union; United; University
u.c. uppercase
UHF ultrahigh frequency
UK, U.K. United Kingdom
UN United Nations
Univ. University
U.S., US United States of America
USA United States of America (also U.S.A.); United States Army
USAF United States Air Force
USDA United States Department of Agriculture
USMC United States Marine Corps
USN United States Navy
U.S.S.R., USSR Union of Soviet Socialist Republics
Ut. Utah
v. verb; verse; versus; very
V, v volt(s)
VA Veterans Administration
Va. Virginia
VD venereal disease
vet. veteran; veterinary
VHF very high frequency
viz. namely
vol. volume
vs. versus
VP, V.P. Vice President
Vt. Vermont
W watt(s) (also w); west(ern) (also W.); *Sports* win(s)
Wash. Washington
Wed. Wednesday
Wis., Wisc. Wisconsin
wk. week
wt. weight
W.Va. West Virginia
Wyo. Wyoming
yd. yard(s)
YMCA Young Men's Christian Association
yr. year
YWCA Young Women's Christian Association

341

WEIGHTS AND MEASURES

Linear

12 inches = 1 foot
3 feet = 1 yard
5½ yards = 1 rod
40 rods = 1 furlong
8 furlongs = 1 mile

Liquid

4 gills = 1 pint
2 pints = 1 quart
4 quarts = 1 gallon
31½ gals. = 1 barrel
2 barrels = 1 hogshead

Metric Equivalents

1 inch	=	2.5400 centimeters
1 foot	=	0.3048 meter
1 yard	=	0.9144 meter
1 mile	=	1.6093 kilometers
1 centimeter	=	0.3937 inch
1 decimeter	=	3.9370 inches
1 meter	=	39.3701 inches
1 kilometer	=	0.6214 mile
1 quart (dry)	=	1.1012 liters
1 quart (liq.)	=	0.9464 liter
1 gallon	=	3.7854 liters
1 liter	=	0.9081 dry quart
1 liter	=	1.0567 liquid quarts

Square

144 sq. inches = 1 sq. foot
9 sq. feet = 1 sq. yard
30¼ sq. yards = 1 sq. rod
160 sq. rods = 1 acre
640 acres = 1 sq. mile

Circular

60 sec. = 1 min.
60 min. = 1 degree
90 deg. = 1 quadrant
180 deg. = 1 semicircle
360 deg. = 1 circle

Metric Equivalents

1 sq. inch	=	6.452 sq. centimeters
1 sq. foot	=	929.030 sq. centimeters
1 sq. mile	=	2.590 sq. kilometers
1 sq. centimeter	=	0.155 sq. inch
1 sq. meter	=	1.196 sq. yards
1 sq. kilometer	=	0.386 sq. mile

Cubic

1,728 cu. inches = 1 cu. foot
27 cu. feet = 1 cu. yard
128 cu. feet = 1 cord (wood)

Dry

2 pints = 1 quart
8 quarts = 1 peck
4 pecks = 1 bushel

Metric Equivalents

1 cu. inch	=	16.3872 cu. centimeters
	=	0.0164 liter
1 cu. foot	=	0.0283 cu. meter
	=	28.3170 liters
1 cu. meter	=	35.3145 cu. feet
1 ounce (avdp.)	=	28.3495 grams
1 pound	=	0.4536 kilogram
1 gram	=	0.0353 ounce
1 kilogram	=	2.2046 lbs.
1 ton (2000 lbs.)	=	907.1848 kilograms

Longitude and Time

1 second	of longitude	=	⅟₁₅ sec. of time
1 minute	" "	=	4 sec. of time
1 degree	" "	=	4 min. of time
15 degrees	" "	=	1 hour
360 degrees	" "	=	24 hours

Nation	Capital	Monetary Unit
Afghanistan	Kabul	afghani
Albania	Tirana	lek
Algeria	Algiers	dinar
Andorra	Andorra la Vella	franc (Fr.)
		peseta (Sp.)
Angola	Luanda	kwanza
Antigua and Barbuda	St. John's	dollar
Argentina	Buenos Aires	peso
Armenia	Yerevan	ruble
Australia	Canberra	dollar
Austria	Vienna	schilling
Azerbaijan	Baku	ruble
Bahamas	Nassau	dollar
Bahrain	Manama	dinar
Bangladesh	Dhaka	taka
Barbados	Bridgetown	dollar
Belarus	Minsk	ruble
Belgium	Brussels	franc
Belize	Belmopan	dollar
Benin	Porto Novo	franc
Bhutan	Thimphu	ngultrum
Bolivia	La Paz; Sucre	boliviano
Bosnia and Herzegovina	Sarajevo	dinar
Botswana	Gaborone	pula
Brazil	Brasília	cruzeiro
Brunei	Bandar Seri Begawan	dollar
Bulgaria	Sofia	lev
Burkina Faso	Ouagadougou	franc
Burundi	Bujumbura	franc
Cambodia	Phnom Penh	riel
Cameroon	Yaoundé	franc
Canada	Ottawa	dollar
Cape Verde	Praia	escudo
Central African Republic	Bangui	franc
Chad	N'Djamena	franc
Chile	Santiago	peso
China	Beijing	yuan
Colombia	Bogotá	peso
Comoros	Moroni	franc
Congo	Brazzaville	franc
Costa Rica	San José	colon
Croatia	Zagreb	Croatian dinar
Cuba	Havana	peso
Cyprus	Nicosia	pound
Czech Republic	Prague	koruna
Denmark	Copenhagen	krone
Djibouti	Djibouti	franc
Dominica	Roseau	dollar
Dominican Republic	Santo Domingo	peso
Ecuador	Quito	sucre
Egypt	Cairo	pound
El Salvador	San Salvador	colon
Equatorial Guinea	Malabo	franc
Estonia	Tallinn	ruble
Ethiopia	Addis Ababa	birr
Fiji	Suva	dollar
Finland	Helsinki	markka
France	Paris	franc
Gabon	Libreville	franc
Gambia	Banjul	dalasi
Georgia	Tbilisi	ruble
Germany	Berlin	deutsche mark
Ghana	Accra	cedi

NATIONS OF THE WORLD

Nation	Capital	Monetary Unit
Greece	Athens	drachma
Grenada	St. George's	dollar
Guatemala	Guatemala City	quetzal
Guinea	Conakry	franc
Guinea-Bissau	Bissau	peso
Guyana	Georgetown	dollar
Haiti	Port-au-Prince	gourde
Honduras	Tegucigalpa	lempira
Hungary	Budapest	forint
Iceland	Reykjavik	króna
India	New Delhi	rupee
Indonesia	Jakarta	rupiah
Iran	Tehran	rial
Iraq	Baghdad	dinar
Ireland	Dublin	pound
Israel	Jerusalem	shekel
Italy	Rome	lira
Ivory Coast	Yamoussoukro	franc
Jamaica	Kingston	dollar
Japan	Tokyo	yen
Jordan	Amman	dinar
Kazakhstan	Alma-Ata	ruble
Kenya	Nairobi	shilling
Kiribati	Tarawa	dollar (Austral.)
Korea, North	Pyongyang	won
Korea, South	Seoul	won
Kuwait	Kuwait	dinar
Kyrgyzstan	Bishkek	ruble
Laos	Vientiane	kip
Latvia	Riga	ruble
Lebanon	Beirut	pound
Lesotho	Maseru	loti
Liberia	Monrovia	dollar
Libya	Tripoli	dinar
Liechtenstein	Vaduz	franc (Swiss)
Lithuania	Vilnius	ruble
Luxembourg	Luxembourg	franc
Macedonia	Skopje	dinar
Madagascar	Antananarivo	franc
Malawi	Lilongwe	kwacha
Malaysia	Kuala Lumpur	ringgit
Maldives	Malé	rufiyaa
Mali	Bamako	franc
Malta	Valletta	lira
Mauritania	Nouakchott	ouguiya
Mauritius	Port Louis	rupee
Mexico	Mexico City	peso
Moldova	Kishinev	ruble
Monaco	Monaco	franc (Fr.)
Mongolia	Ulan Bator	tugrik
Morocco	Rabat	dirham
Mozambique	Maputo	metical
Myanmar	Yangon	kyat
Namibia	Windhoek	rand
Nauru	—	dollar (Austral.)
Nepal	Katmandu	rupee
Netherlands	Amsterdam	guilder
New Zealand	Wellington	dollar
Nicaragua	Managua	cordoba
Niger	Niamey	franc
Nigeria	Abuja	naira
Norway	Oslo	krone
Oman	Muscat	rial
Pakistan	Islamabad	rupee
Panama	Panama City	balboa

NATIONS OF THE WORLD

Nation	Capital	Monetary Unit
Papua New Guinea	Port Moresby	kina
Paraguay	Asunción	guaraní
Peru	Lima	sol
Philippines	Manila	peso
Poland	Warsaw	złoty
Portugal	Lisbon	escudo
Qatar	Doha	riyal
Romania	Bucharest	leu
Russia	Moscow	ruble
Rwanda	Kigali	franc
San Marino	San Marino	lira (It.)
São Tomé and Príncipe	São Tomé	dobra
Saudi Arabia	Riyadh	riyal
Senegal	Dakar	franc
Seychelles	Victoria	rupee
Sierra Leone	Freetown	leone
Singapore	Singapore	dollar
Slovakia	Bratislava	koruna
Slovenia	Ljubljana	tolar
Solomon Islands	Honiara	dollar
Somalia	Mogadishu	shilling
South Africa	Pretoria (administrative)	rand
Spain	Madrid	peseta
Sri Lanka	Colombo	rupee
St. Kitts-Nevis	Basseterre	dollar
St. Lucia	Castries	dollar
St. Vincent and the Grenadines	Kingstown	dollar
Sudan	Khartoum	pound
Suriname	Paramaribo	guilder
Swaziland	Mbabane	lilangeni
Sweden	Stockholm	krona
Switzerland	Bern	franc
Syria	Damascus	pound
Taiwan	Taipei	dollar
Tajikistan	Dushanbe	ruble
Tanzania	Dodoma	shilling
Thailand	Bangkok	baht
Togo	Lomé	franc
Tonga	Nukualofa	pa'anga
Trinidad and Tobago	Port-of-Spain	dollar
Tunisia	Tunis	dinar
Turkey	Ankara	lira
Turkmenistan	Ashkhabad	ruble
Tuvalu	Fongafale	dollar (Austral.)
Uganda	Kampala	shilling
Ukraine	Kiev	hryvnia
United Arab Emirates	Abu Dhabi	dirham
United Kingdom	London	pound
United States	Washington, D.C.	dollar
Uruguay	Montevideo	peso
Uzbekistan	Tashkent	ruble
Vanuatu	Vila	vatu
Vatican City	—	lira (It.)
Venezuela	Caracas	bolívar
Vietnam	Hanoi	dong
Western Samoa	Apia	tala
Yemen	Sana	riyal
Yugoslavia	Belgrade	dinar
Zaire	Kinshasa	zaire
Zambia	Lusaka	kwacha
Zimbabwe	Harare	dollar

UNITED STATES AND CANADA

State	Capital	Postal Code
Alabama	Montgomery	AL
Alaska	Juneau	AK
Arizona	Phoenix	AZ
Arkansas	Little Rock	AR
California	Sacramento	CA
Colorado	Denver	CO
Connecticut	Hartford	CT
Delaware	Dover	DE
[District of Columbia]	—	DC
Florida	Tallahassee	FL
Georgia	Atlanta	GA
Hawaii	Honolulu	HI
Idaho	Boise	ID
Illinois	Springfield	IL
Indiana	Indianapolis	IN
Iowa	Des Moines	IA
Kansas	Topeka	KS
Kentucky	Frankfort	KY
Louisiana	Baton Rouge	LA
Maine	Augusta	ME
Maryland	Annapolis	MD
Massachusetts	Boston	MA
Michigan	Lansing	MI
Minnesota	St. Paul	MN
Mississippi	Jackson	MS
Missouri	Jefferson City	MO
Montana	Helena	MT
Nebraska	Lincoln	NE
Nevada	Carson City	NV
New Hampshire	Concord	NH
New Jersey	Trenton	NJ
New Mexico	Santa Fe	NM
New York	Albany	NY
North Carolina	Raleigh	NC
North Dakota	Bismarck	ND
Ohio	Columbus	OH
Oklahoma	Oklahoma City	OK
Oregon	Salem	OR
Pennsylvania	Harrisburg	PA
Rhode Island	Providence	RI
South Carolina	Columbia	SC
South Dakota	Pierre	SD
Tennessee	Nashville	TN
Texas	Austin	TX
Utah	Salt Lake City	UT
Vermont	Montpelier	VT
Virginia	Richmond	VA
Washington	Olympia	WA
West Virginia	Charleston	WV
Wisconsin	Madison	WI
Wyoming	Cheyenne	WY

UNITED STATES AND CANADA

U.S. Territories

American Samoa	Pago Pago	AS
Belau	Koror	PW
Guam	Agana	GU
Northern Marianas	Saipan	MP
Puerto Rico	San Juan	PR
Virgin Islands	Charlotte Amalie	VI

Canadian Provinces and Territories

Provinces

Alberta	Edmonton	AB
British Columbia	Victoria	BC
Manitoba	Winnipeg	MB
New Brunswick	Fredericton	NB
Newfoundland	St. John's	NF
Nova Scotia	Halifax	NS
Ontario	Toronto	ON
Prince Edward Island	Charlottetown	PE
Quebec	Quebec	PQ
Saskatchewan	Regina	SK

Territories

Northwest Territories	Yellowknife	NT
Yukon Territory	Whitehorse	YT

U.S. CITIES

City, State	1990 Pop.	City, State	1990 Pop.
New York, NY	7,322,564	Wichita, KS	304,011
Los Angeles, CA	3,485,398	Santa Ana, CA	293,742
Chicago, IL	2,783,726	Mesa, AZ	288,091
Houston, TX	1,630,553	Colorado Springs, CO	281,140
Philadelphia, PA	1,585,577	Tampa, FL	280,015
San Diego, CA	1,110,549	Newark, NJ	275,221
Detroit, MI	1,027,974	St. Paul, MN	272,235
Dallas, TX	1,006,877	Louisville, KY	269,063
Phoenix, AZ	983,403	Anaheim, CA	266,406
San Antonio, TX	935,933	Birmingham, AL	265,968
San Jose, CA	782,248	Arlington, TX	261,721
Indianapolis, IN	741,952	Norfolk, VA	261,229
Baltimore, MD	736,014	Las Vegas, NV	258,295
San Francisco, CA	723,959	Corpus Christi, TX	257,453
Jacksonville, FL	672,971	St. Petersburg, FL	238,629
Columbus, OH	632,910	Rochester, NY	231,636
Milwaukee, WI	628,088	Jersey City, NJ	228,537
Memphis, TN	610,337	Riverside, CA	226,505
Washington, DC	606,900	Anchorage, AK	226,338
Boston, MA	574,283	Lexington-Fayette, KY	225,366
Seattle, WA	516,259	Akron, OH	223,019
El Paso, TX	515,342	Aurora, CO	222,103
Nashville-Davidson, TN	510,784	Baton Rouge, LA	219,531
Cleveland, OH	505,616	Stockton, CA	210,943
New Orleans, LA	496,938	Raleigh, NC	207,951
Denver, CO	467,610	Richmond, VA	203,056
Austin, TX	465,622	Shreveport, LA	198,525
Fort Worth, TX	447,619	Jackson, MS	196,637
Oklahoma City, OK	444,719	Mobile, AL	196,278
Portland, OR	437,319	Des Moines, IA	193,187
Kansas City, MO	435,146	Lincoln, NE	191,972
Long Beach, CA	429,433	Madison, WI	191,262
Tucson, AR	405,390	Grand Rapids, MI	189,126
St. Louis, MO	396,685	Yonkers, NY	188,082
Charlotte, NC	395,934	Hialeah, FL	188,004
Atlanta, GA	394,017	Montgomery, AL	187,106
Virginia Beach, VA	393,069	Lubbock, TX	186,206
Albuquerque, NM	384,736	Greensboro, NC	183,521
Oakland, CA	372,242	Dayton, OH	182,044
Pittsburgh, PA	369,879	Huntington Beach, CA	181,519
Sacramento, CA	369,365	Garland, TX	180,650
Minneapolis, MN	368,383	Glendale, CA	180,038
Tulsa, OK	367,302	Columbus, GA	179,278
Honolulu, HI	365,272	Spokane, WA	177,196
Cincinnati, OH	364,040	Tacoma, WA	176,664
Miami, FL	358,548	Little Rock, AR	175,795
Fresno, CA	354,202	Bakersfield, CA	174,820
Omaha, NE	335,795	Fremont, CA	173,339
Toledo, OH	332,943	Fort Wayne, IN	173,072
Buffalo, NY	328,123	Newport News, VA	170,045